CHURCH DOG

For further resources, including the forewords to the original 14-volume edition of the *Church Dogmatics*, log on to our website and sign up for the resources webpage: http://www.continuumbooks.com/dogmatics/

KARL BARTH
CHURCH DOGMATICS

VOLUME IV

THE DOCTRINE
OF RECONCILIATION

§ 57–59

THE SUBJECT MATTER AND PROBLEMS
OF THE DOCTRINE OF RECONCILIATION
JESUS CHRIST, THE LORD AS SERVANT I

EDITED BY
G. W. BROMILEY
T. F. TORRANCE

t&t clark

Published by T&T Clark

A Continuum Imprint

The Tower Building, 11 York Road, London, SE1 7NX

80 Maiden Lane, Suite 704, New York, NY 10038

www.continuumbooks.com

Translated by G. W. Bromiley

Copyright © T&T Clark, 2010

Authorised translation of Karl Barth, *Die Kirchliche Dogmatik IV*
Copyright © Theologischer Verlag Zürich, 1953–1967

British Library Cataloguing-in-Publication Data
A catalogue record for this book is available from the British Library

ISBN13: 978-0-567-58710-7

Typeset by Interactive Sciences Ltd, Gloucester, and Newgen Imaging Systems Pvt Ltd, Chennai
Printed and bound in Great Britain by CPI Antony Rowe, Chippenham, Wiltshire

PUBLISHER'S PREFACE TO THE STUDY EDITION

Since the publication of the first English translation of *Church Dogmatics I.1* by Professor Thomson in 1936, T&T Clark has been closely linked with Karl Barth. An authorised translation of the whole of the *Kirchliche Dogmatik* was begun in the 1950s under the editorship of G. W. Bromiley and T. F. Torrance, a work which eventually replaced Professor Thomson's initial translation of *CD I.1*.

T&T Clark is now happy to present to the academic community this new *Study Edition* of the *Church Dogmatics*. Its aim is mainly to make this major work available to a generation of students and scholars with less familiarity with Latin, Greek, and French. For the first time this edition therefore presents the classic text of the translation edited by G. W. Bromiley and T. F. Torrance incorporating translations of the foreign language passages in Editorial Notes on each page.

The main body of the text remains unchanged. Only minor corrections with regard to grammar or spelling have been introduced. The text is presented in a new reader friendly format. We hope that the breakdown of the *Church Dogmatics* into 31 shorter fascicles will make this edition easier to use than its predecessors.

Completely new indexes of names, subjects and scriptural indexes have been created for the individual volumes of the *Study Edition*.

The publishers would like to thank the Center for Barth Studies at Princeton Theological Seminary for supplying a digital edition of the text of the *Church Dogmatics* and translations of the Greek and Latin quotations in the original T&T Clark edition made by Simon Gathercole and Ian McFarland.

London, April 2010

HOW TO USE THIS
STUDY EDITION

The *Study Edition* follows Barth's original volume structure. Individual paragraphs and sections should be easy to locate. A synopsis of the old and new edition can be found on the back cover of each fascicle.

All secondary literature on the *Church Dogmatics* currently refers to the classic 14-volume set (e.g. II.2 p. 520). In order to avoid confusion, we recommend that this practice should be kept for references to this *Study Edition*. The page numbers of the old edition can be found in the margins of this edition.

CONTENTS

§ 57–59

THE WORK OF GOD THE RECONCILER

The subject-matter, origin and content of the message received and proclaimed by the Christian community is at its heart the free act of the faithfulness of God in which He takes the lost cause of man, who has denied Him as Creator and in so doing ruined himself as creature, and makes it His own in Jesus Christ, carrying it through to its goal and in that way maintaining and manifesting His own glory in the world.

1. GOD WITH US

We enter that sphere of Christian knowledge in which we have to do with the heart of the message received by and laid upon the Christian community and therefore with the heart of the Church's dogmatics: that is to say, with the heart of its subject-matter, origin and content. It has a circumference, the doctrine of creation and the doctrine of the last things, the redemption and consummation. But the covenant fulfilled in the atonement is its centre. From this point we can and must see a circumference. But we can see it only from this point. A mistaken or deficient perception here would mean error or deficiency everywhere: the weakening or obscuring of the message, the confession and dogmatics as such. From this point either everything is clear and true and helpful, or it is not so anywhere. This involves a high responsibility in the task which now confronts us.

It would be possible and quite correct to describe the covenant fulfilled in the work of reconciliation as the heart of the subject-matter of Christian faith, of the origin of Christian love, of the content of Christian hope. But the faith and love and hope of the Christian community and the Christians assembled in it live by the message received by and laid upon them, not the reverse. And even if we tried to put them in the forefront, we should have to lay the emphasis upon their subject-matter, origin and content, which are not immanent to them, and which do not exhaust themselves in them. For Christian faith is faith *in*, Christian love is love *through*, and Christian hope is hope *in* God the Father, Son and Holy Spirit. There is something prior, outside, differ- [004] ent from them which encounters them. It is God whom they encounter, from whom they have their being, whom they can lay hold of but not apprehend or exhaust. Not even the message by which faith and love and hope live, not even the confession with which the community responds to the message, not even the dogmatics in which it gives an account of the message and its own response, and finally of its faith and love and hope as such, can take the place of God. If we tried to start with faith and love and hope, we would still have to go back to that free and higher other in which they have their basis. And in the face of it we should have to say even of them that at their heart they have to do with the covenant fulfilled in the work of atonement, and that it is in their relation to this covenant that they are secure or insecure, effective or impotent, genuine or false.

Our first task will be to describe this Christian centre in a first and most general approximation. The title "God with Us" is meant as a most general description of the whole complex of Christian understanding and doctrine which here confronts us.

At its heart the Christian message is a common statement on the part of certain men, i.e., those who are assembled in the Christian community. It includes a statement about themselves, about the individual existence of these men in their own time and situation. And it is essential to it that this should be so. But it only includes it. For primarily it is a statement about God: that it is He who is with them as God. *Only* with those who dare to make this statement, who as the recipients and bearers of the Christian message, as members of the Christian community, must dare to make it? With them, to the extent that they know that it is actually the case: God with us. They dare to make this statement because they were able to become and can constantly become again the recipients of this message. God with you, God with thee and thee, was its first form, and they are what they are to the extent that they hear this again and again. But as recipients they are also bearers of the message. And to this extent it is not only to them. They dare to make the statement, that God is the One who is with them as God, amongst men who do not yet know this. And it is to such that they address the statement. They do not specifically include them in that "us." Their aim is to show them what they do not yet know but what they can and should know. What? About themselves, and their individual existence in their own time and situation? That is certainly included. Much depends upon their coming to see that it applies to *them.* But everything depends upon their coming to see that it all has to do with God; that it is God who is with them as God. For it is this that applies to them. "God with us" as the core of the Christian message, the decisive general statement of the Christian community, can indeed be interpreted as "God with us men," but with the clear distinction, [005] with us men who know it but are always learning it afresh—and as the word of our declaration to all others, and therefore with "us" other men who have always to learn it afresh because we do not yet know it, although we can know it. In this movement from a narrower to a wider usage the statement "God with us" is the centre of the Christian message—and always in such a way that it is primarily a statement about God and only then and for that reason a statement about us men.

That is the roughest outline of the matter. We must now look at this outline rather more closely in order that we may understand it correctly even in this basic form.

To this end it is perhaps instructive to recall that this "God with us" is the translation of the remarkable name Emmanuel which is mentioned three times in Is. 7[14], 8[8], [10], and according to Mt. 1[21f.] finds its fulfilment in the name of Jesus.

The three passages in Isaiah seem to belong to three independently transmitted oracles. In the redaction of the book of Isaiah they were all related to that remarkable period (cf. Martin Noth, *Geschichte Israels*, 1950, 218 f.) when Assyria began to emerge as a world-power and to encroach upon Syria and Palestine. This process was explained by the prophets, and primarily Isaiah, as something which ran quite contrary to the political and religious tradition of Israel, a change in the relationship between God and His people, not a breach between them, but the irruption of His judgment upon their unfaithfulness, the transition from the Yes of His grace to the No. The final form of that unfaithfulness is the refusal of Ahaz, King of Judah, to trust in *Yahweh* and therefore to be bold enough to offer resistance to the two kings Rezin of Damascus and Pekah of Samaria who, themselves a prey to illusions, try to force him into an alliance against Assyria. In face of this situation Isaiah announces (7[14f.]) the divine sign which is at once a promise and a warning, a sign of grace and a sign of judgment: a child will now be conceived and born. The old controversy whether his mother is called a young wife or a virgin does not in any way affect the real sense. What is important in the text is that when the child is born, that is in less than a year, he will be given the name Emmanuel, because God will have saved His people from the threat of Rezin and Pekah and they will again be rejoicing in His goodness. That is the one side of the sign. But the other is that before the child can distinguish between good and evil, a few years later, he will have to eat milk and honey, the food of the nomad. The true evil, that of the Assyrians, will then have supervened. Emmanuel will be present, but only in the wilderness, under the wrath of God. We are told the same (according to this other aspect of the sign) in Is. 8[6]: "Forasmuch as this people refuseth the waters of Shiloah that go softly, and rejoice in Rezin and Remaliah's son, now therefore behold, the Lord bringeth upon them the waters of the river (Euphrates), strong and many, and he shall come up over all his channels, and go over all his banks: and he shall pass through Judah; he shall overflow and go over, he shall reach even to the neck; and the stretching out of his wings shall fill the breadth of thy land, O Emmanuel." In contrast, Is. 8[9f.] looks again in the opposite direction, evidently beyond the momentarily irresistibly triumphant Assyria (though this is not perhaps a compelling reason why we should not ascribe it to Isaiah): "Rage furiously, ye people, and be afraid. Give ear, ye of far countries. Gird yourselves and be afraid, yes gird yourselves and be afraid. Take counsel together, and it shall come to nought. Resolve, and it shall not stand. For—Emmanuel."

Who is "Emmanuel?" Hardly a historical figure of the period. Perhaps a traditional name, [006] or one selected by the prophet, to describe the expected Redemptor-King of the last day, to whom a kind of pre-existence is here ascribed. Perhaps the personification of what the remnant-Israel of Judah understood its God to be, and therefore itself, or according to the prophets ought to have done so. Perhaps both? Certainly a special key to the continual mystery of the history of this people in days of prosperity and in days of adversity, under the hand of God in blessing and in cursing. "God with us" is true when the people is at rest. It is also true when the enemy invades and devastates its land. It is always true, in spite of and in the most irresistible movements of history. It is so because and to the extent that in all these things there is revealed the gracious action of God to His people. No matter who or what is concretely envisaged in these passages, they obviously mean this: Emmanuel is the content of the recognition in which the God of Israel reveals Himself in all His acts and dispositions;

He is the God who does not work and act without His people, but who is with His people as their God and therefore as their hope.

We are reminded of this remarkable name in Mt. 1²¹ᶠ. The reference here is to a single, final and exclusive act of the God of Israel as the goal and recapitulation of all His acts. But this act, the birth and naming of Jesus, is similar to the events in the days of King Ahaz in that once again we have come to a change in the relationship between God and His people. As the Evangelist sees it, it is this time the great change compared with which what took place before was only from his point of view a prelude. And now it is the equally unexpected change from perdition to salvation, from an age-long judgment to a new and final blessing. And the Emmanuel-sign has it in common with the name of Jesus that the latter, too, although this time in the reverse direction, is a sign for both: a sign "for the fall and rising again of many in Israel" (Lk. 2³⁴), a sign both of the deepest extremity imposed by God (as in Is. 8⁶ᶠ·) and also of the uttermost preservation and salvation ordained by God (as in Is. 8⁹ᶠ·). Over and in both it is Emmanuel, "God with us," and now therefore (ἵνα πληρωθῇ τὸ ῥηθὲν ὑπὸ κυρίου διὰ τοῦ προφήτου λέγοντος ᴱᴺ¹) Jesus, Jehoshuah, "God helps."

1. Our starting-point is that this "God with us" at the heart of the Christian message is the description of an act of God, or better, of God Himself in this act of His. It is a report, not therefore a statement of fact on the basis of general observation or consideration. God with us, or what is meant by these three words, is not an object of investigation or speculation. It is not a state, but an event. God *is*, of course, and that in the strictest sense originally and properly, so that everything else which is, in a way which cannot be compared at all with His being, can be so only through Him, only in relation to Him, only from Him and to Him. Now even when He is "with us," He is what He is, and in the way that He is; and all the power and truth of His being "with us" is the power and truth of His incomparable being which is proper to Him and to Him alone, His being as God. He is both in His life in eternity in Himself, and also in His life as Creator in the time of the world created by Him; by and in Himself, and also above and in this world, and therefore according to the heart of the Christian message with us men. And He is who He is, and lives as what He is, in that He does what He does. How can we know God if His being is unknown or obscure or indifferent? But how can we know God if we do not find the truth and power of His being in His life, and of His life in His act? We [007] know about God only if we are witnesses—however distantly and modestly—of His act. And we speak about God only as we can do so—however deficiently— as those who proclaim His act. "God with us" as it occurs at the heart of the Christian message is the attestation and report of the life and act of God as the One who is.

But if it means that God is with us—and the message of the Christian community certainly implies that it does really apply to us men—then that presupposes that we men, in our own very different way, which cannot be compared with the being of God, but which on the basis of the divine being and life and act is a very real way, that we also *are*, and that we are in that we live in our time,

---

ᴱᴺ¹ in order that what was said by the Lord through the prophet as he spoke

and that we live in that we ourselves act in our own act. If the fact that God is with us is a report about the being and life and act of God, then from the very outset it stands in a relationship to our own being and life and acts. A report about ourselves is included in that report about God. We cannot therefore take cognisance of it, be more or less impressed by it, and then leave it as the report of something which has taken place in a quite different sphere in which we ourselves have no place. It tells us that we ourselves are in the sphere of God. It applies to us by telling us of a history which God wills to share with us and therefore of an invasion of our history—indeed, of the real truth about our history as a history which is by Him and from Him and to Him. The divine being and life and act takes place with ours, and it is only as the divine takes place that ours takes place. To put it in the simplest way, what unites God and us men is that He does not will to be God without us, that He creates us rather to share with us and therefore with our being and life and act His own incomparable being and life and act, that He does not allow His history to be His and ours ours, but causes them to take place as a common history. That is the special truth which the Christian message has to proclaim at its very heart.

2. We have just said, and this is what is meant in the Christian message, that we have to do with an event, with an act of God. The whole being and life of God is an activity, both in eternity and in worldly time, both in Himself as Father, Son and Holy Spirit, and in His relation to man and all creation. But what God does in Himself and as the Creator and Governor of man is all aimed at the particular act in which it has its centre and meaning. And everything that He wills has its ground and origin in what is revealed as His will in this one act. Thus it is not merely one amongst others of His works as Creator and Governor. Of course, it can and must be understood in this way, in accordance with the general will and work of God. But within this outer circle it forms an inner. The one God wills and works all things, but here He wills and works a particular thing: not one with others, but one for the sake of which He wills and works all others. As one with others this act is also the *telos* of all the acts of God; of the eternal activity in which He is both in Himself and in the history of His acts in the world created by Him. It is of this that the "God with us" speaks. [008]

Therefore even from the standpoint of us men the "God with us" does not refer to the existence of man generally as the creaturely object of the will and work of His Lord. It does refer to it. It includes it. The being, life and act of man is always quite simply his history in relation to the being, life and act of his Creator. We can say the same of all creatures. But it is far more than this. For within and beyond this general activity, God Himself in His being, life and act as Creator wills and works a special act. All His activity has its heart and end in a single act. Within and out of the general history, which with all creatures man can have in common with God in His being, life and act, there arises this act of God and that which corresponds to it in the being, life and activity of man, as a qualified history, his true history. And if the "God with us" at the heart of the

5

Christian message speaks of the unifying factor between God and man, it speaks of a specific conjoining of the two, not always and everywhere but in a single and particular event which has a definite importance for all time and space but which takes place once and for all in a definite *hic et nunc*[EN2].

3. From the standpoint of its meaning the particularity of this event consists in the fact that it has to do with the salvation of man, that in it the general history which is common to God and man, to God and all creation, becomes at its very heart and end a redemptive history. Salvation is more than being. Salvation is fulfilment, the supreme, sufficient, definitive and indestructible fulfilment of being. Salvation is the perfect being which is not proper to created being as such but is still future. Created being as such needs salvation, but does not have it: it can only look forward to it. To that extent salvation is its *eschaton*. Salvation, fulfilment, perfect being means—and this is what created being does not have in itself—being which has a part in the being of God, from which and to which it is: not a divinised being but a being which is hidden in God, and in that sense (distinct from God and secondary) eternal being. Since salvation is not proper to created being as such, it can only come to it, and since it consists in participation in the being of God it can come only from God. The coming of this salvation is the grace of God—using the word in its narrower and most proper sense. In the wider sense the creation, preservation and over-ruling of the world and man are already grace. For if this is not proper to created being as such, it can only come to it. Only from God as the One who is originally and properly can it come about that it also has being, that it is, and not that it is not. And by that very fact there is always held out to it the opportunity of salvation: the expectation of being in perfection in partici-

[009] pation in the divine being. But the "God with us" at the heart of the Christian message does not mean this general grace. It means the redemptive grace of God. It is this which constitutes, factually, the singularity of the event. It is this which marks out the event within the whole history of the togetherness of God and man. Not merely the creating, preserving and over-ruling of created being, not merely the creating of an opportunity for salvation, but the fact that it actually comes, that God gives it. God gives to created being what can only be given to it and what can be given only by Him. And He does really give it: Take what is mine—this final, supreme, insurpassable gift; take it, it is meant for you. It is because it has to do with this that the activity of God indicated by the "God with us" is singular and unique. And so, too, is the invasion of the history of our own human being, life and activity described by this "God with us." And so, too, is the whole circle of God in which we find ourselves according to this centre of the Christian message. The general grace of God in creation, preservation and over-ruling still remains. That is already grace. We recognise it distinctly as such only when we see God and ourselves in the inner and special circle of His will and work, in the light of this one, particular, redemptive act of

---

[EN2] here and now

God. It is only from this standpoint that the general grace of being and the opportunity which it offers can and do become a subject for genuine gratitude and a source of serious dedication. For here it is provided that that opportunity is not offered in vain, that it is actually taken, taken by God Himself. What concerns us here is the redemptive grace of God, and to that extent something that is more and greater.

4. In the light of this we must now try to outline this particular event with rather greater precision. According to the Christian message "God with us" means God with the man for whom salvation is intended and ordained as such, as the one who is created, preserved and over-ruled by God as man. It is not as though the expectation belonged to his created being. It is not as though he had any kind of claim to it. God cannot be forced to give us a part in His divine being. The matter might have ended quite well with that general grace of being—which even in itself is great enough. But where God is not bound and man has no claim, even more compelling is the will and plan and promise of God. It goes beyond, or rather it precedes His will and work as Creator. Therefore it has to be distinguished from it, as something prior, which precedes it. The ordaining of salvation for man and of man for salvation is the original and basic will of God, the ground and purpose of His will as Creator. It is not that He first wills and works the being of the world and man, and then ordains it to salvation. But God creates, preserves and over-rules man for this prior end and with this prior purpose, that there may be a being distinct from Himself ordained for salvation, for perfect being, for participation in His own being, because as the One who loves in freedom He has determined to exercise redemptive grace—and that there may be an object of this His redemptive [010] grace, a partner to receive it. A further point which we must now make in describing the event indicated by the "God with us" is this. The "God with us" has nothing to do with chance. As a redemptive happening it means the revelation and confirmation of the most primitive relationship between God and man, that which was freely determined in eternity by God Himself before there was any created being. In the very fact that man is, and that he is man, he is as such chosen by God for salvation; that *eschaton* is given him by God. Not because God owes it to him. Not in virtue of any quality or capacity of his own being. Completely without claim. What takes place between God and man in that particular redemptive history is fulfilment to this extent too, that in it God—the eternal will of God with man—is justified, the eternal righteousness of His grace is active and revealed, in and with the divine right, and so too the right which He has freely given and ascribed to man by determining this concerning him. It belongs to the character of this event and its particularity that with the end it reveals the basis and beginning of all things—the glory of God, which is that of His free love, and with it—well below, but eternally grounded upon it—the dignity of man, that dignity with which He willed to invest man although it is not proper to him.

7

5. But again we must go further. "God with us" in the sense of the Christian message means God with us men who have forfeited the predetermined salvation, forfeited it with a supreme and final jeopardising even of our creaturely existence. As the way from that beginning in God to the end of man with God is revealed in this particular event, its line is not a straight one, but one which is radically and—if God Himself were not there as hope—hopelessly broken. The situation of man in this event is this. He occupies a position quite different from that which he ought to occupy according to the divine intention. He does not conduct himself as the partner God has given Himself to receive His redemptive grace. He has opposed his ordination to salvation. He has turned his back on the salvation which actually comes to him. He does not find the fulfilment of his being in participation in the being of God by the gift of God. Instead, he aims at another salvation which is to be found in the sphere of his creaturely being and attained by his own effort. His belief is that he can and should find self-fulfilment. He has himself become an *eschaton*. This is the man with whom God is dealing in this particular redemptive history: the man who has made himself quite impossible in relation to the redemptive grace of God; and in so doing, the man who has made himself quite impossible in his created being as man, who has cut the ground from under his feet, who has lost his whole *raison d'être*[EN3]. What place has he before God when he has shown himself to be so utterly unworthy of that for which he was created by God, so utterly inept, so utterly unsuitable? when he has eliminated himself? What place is there for his being, his being as man, when he has denied his goal, and therefore his beginning and meaning, and when he confronts God in this negation? Despising the dignity with which God invested him, he has obviously forfeited the right which God gave and ascribed to him as the creature of God. But it is with this lost son in a far country, with man as he has fallen and now exists in this sorry plight, that God has to do in this redeeming event. And this is what reveals the gulf. This is what shows us how it stands between God and man. This is where we see the inadequacy of the partner, the point where the relationship breaks down. At a pinch this can be overlooked if we do not think of the redeeming event as the heart and end of their interconnexion, if we conceive it abstractly as the interconnexion of Creator and creature. We may take this antithesis very seriously, but we shall always have good grounds to think of it as an antithesis which can be bridged. As such it does not contain any breach, any gulf, any enmity, either on the one side or on the other, any judgment and punishment on the part of God or suffering on the part of man. But this cannot possibly be overlooked in the redeeming event referred to in the "God with us." On the contrary, what constitutes the particularity of this event is that as a redeeming event, as the fulfilment of the gracious will of God, as the reaffirmation of His right and ours, it can be conceived only in the form of a Yet and a Nevertheless, which means that it cannot be conceived at all. If

[011]

[EN3] reason for existence

8

man has forfeited his salvation, what do we have to grasp in this event but the inconceivable fact that all the same it is given to him? If in so doing man has lost his creaturely being, what do we have to grasp but again the inconceivable fact that all the same he will not be lost? Is it not the case that only here, in the light of the antithesis which is here revealed and overcome, is grace really known as grace, that is, as free grace, as mercy pure and simple, as *factum purum*[EN4], having its basis only in itself, in the fact that it is posited by God? For who really knows what grace is until he has seen it at work here: as the grace which is *for* man when, because man is wholly and utterly a sinner before God, it can only be against him, and when in fact, even while it is for him, it is also a plaintiff and judge against him, showing him to be incapable of satisfying either God or himself? And looking back once again, it is the grace of God as mercy pure and simple, as a sheer Yet and Nevertheless, which reveals, and by which we have to measure, how it stands with the man to whom it is granted. It is not independent reflection on the part of man, or an abstract law, but grace which shows incontrovertibly that man has forfeited his salvation and in so doing fatally jeopardised his creaturely being—which reveals his sin and the misery which is its consequence. From the redemption which takes place here we can gather from what it is that man is redeemed; from the *factum purum*[EN5] of the salvation which comes to man without and in spite of his own deserts we may know the *factum brutum*[EN6] which he for his part dares to set against God. [012] Because the "God with us" at the heart of the Christian message has to do with that *factum purum*[EN7] of the divine mercy, we must not fail to recognise but acknowledge without reserve that we, and those for whom God is according to this message, are those who have nothing to bring Him but a confession of this *factum brutum*[EN8]: "Father, I have sinned."

6. But if the Christian "God with us" does nevertheless speak, not of a renunciation, but of the fulfilment of the redemptive will of God in that event, then no matter how inconceivable may be that which we have to grasp in this connexion, it refers to something quite different from the blind paradox of an arbitrary act of the divine omnipotence of grace. We are confronted here by the determination of that event which reveals unequivocally its uniqueness amongst the acts of God, that it declares an absolutely unique being and attitude and activity on the part of God. "God with us" means more than God over or side by side with us, before or behind us. It means more than His divine being in even the most intimate active connexion with our human being otherwise peculiar to Him. At this point, at the heart of the Christian message and in relation to the event of which it speaks, it means that God has made Himself the One who fulfils His redemptive will. It means that He Himself in

---

[EN4] pure fact
[EN5] pure fact
[EN6] brute fact
[EN7] pure fact
[EN8] brute fact

His own person—at His own cost but also on His own initiative—has become the inconceivable Yet and Nevertheless of this event, and so its clear and well-founded and legitimate, its true and holy and righteous Therefore. It means that God has become man in order as such, but in divine sovereignty, to take up our case. What takes place in this work of inconceivable mercy is, therefore, the free over-ruling of God, but it is not an arbitrary overlooking and ignoring, not an artificial bridging, covering-over or hiding, but a real closing of the breach, gulf and abyss between God and us for which we are responsible. At the very point where we refuse and fail, offending and provoking God, making ourselves impossible before Him and in that way missing our destiny, treading under foot our dignity, forfeiting our right, losing our salvation and hopelessly compromising our creaturely being—at that very point God Himself intervenes as man. Because He is God He is able not only to be God but also to be this man. Because He is God it is necessary that He should be man in quite a different way from all other men; that He should do what we do not do and not do what we do. Because He is God He puts forth His omnipotence to be this other man, to be man quite differently, in our place and for our sake. Because He is God He has and exercises the power as this man to suffer for us the consequence of our transgression, the wrath and penalty which necessarily fall on us, and in that way to satisfy Himself in our regard. And again because He is God, He has and exercises the power as this man to be His own partner in our [013] place, the One who in free obedience accepts the ordination of man to salvation which we resist, and in that way satisfies us, i.e., achieves that which can positively satisfy us. That is the absolutely unique being, attitude and activity of God to which the "God with us" at the heart of the Christian message refers. It speaks of the peace which God Himself in this man has made between Himself and us.

We see the seriousness and force of the divine redemptive will in the fact that it is not too little and not too much for Him to make peace between Himself and us. To that end He gives Himself. He, the Creator, does not scorn to become a creature, a man like us, in order that as such He may bear and do what must be borne and done for our salvation. On the contrary, He finds and defends and vindicates His glory in doing it. Again, we see our own perversion and corruption, we see what is our offence and plight, in the fact that God (who never does anything unnecessary) can obviously be satisfied only by this supreme act, that only His own coming as man is sufficient to make good the evil which has been done. So dark is our situation that God Himself must enter and occupy it in order that it may be light. We cannot fully understand the Christian "God with us" without the greatest astonishment at the glory of the divine grace and the greatest horror at our own plight.

But even when we understand the entry of God for us in becoming man as the making of peace between Himself and us, we have still not said the decisive thing about this action. What He effects and does and reveals by becoming

man—for us—is much more than the restoration of the *status quo ante*[EN9]—
the obviating of the loss caused by our own transgression and our restoration
to the place of promise and expectation of the salvation ordained for us. God
makes Himself the means of His own redemptive will, but He is obviously more
than this means. And in making peace by Himself He obviously gives us more
than this peace, i.e., more than a *restitutio ad integrum,*[EN10] more than the preserving and assuring to us of our creaturely being and this as our opportunity
for salvation. For when God makes Himself the means of His redemptive will
to us, this will and we ourselves attain our goal. What is at first only God's
gracious answer to our failure, God's gracious help in our plight, and even as
such great and wonderful enough, is—when God Himself is the help and
answer—His participation in our being, life and activity and therefore obviously our participation in His; and therefore it is nothing more nor less than
the coming of salvation itself, the presence of the *eschaton* in all its fulness. The
man in whom God Himself intervenes for us, suffers and acts for us, closes the
gap between Himself and us as our representative, in our name and on our
behalf, this man is not merely the confirmation and guarantee of our salvation, but because He is God He is salvation, our salvation. He is not merely the
redeemer of our being but as such the giver and Himself the gift of its fulfilment and therefore the goal and end of the way of God—and all that as the   [014]
peacemaker and saviour. It is when this great thing takes place that there takes
place the even greater. This great thing is included in the "God with us" of the
Christian message in so far as this speaks of God's intervening and becoming
man, but in this great thing there is also included the even greater, indeed the
greatest of all.

7. From all this it is surely obvious that the "God with us" carries with it in all
seriousness a "We with God": the fact that we ourselves are there in our being,
life and activity.

This does not seem to be apparent at a first glance. For who are we? We have
seen already that we are (1) those whose history is absorbed into the history of
the acts of God, and (2) made to participate in that event which is the centre
and end of all the divine acts, and (3) given a share in the grace with which
God actually brings salvation to man, and (4) that we are such as those whom
God has thereto ordained from all eternity, but unfortunately (5) we are those
who have refused His salvation and in that way denied their own destiny and
perverted and wasted and hopelessly compromised their own being, life and
activity, who inevitably therefore find themselves disqualified and set aside as
participants in that event, and cannot be considered in relation to it. Yet
beyond that and in a sense conclusively (6) we are those whose place has been
taken by another, who lives and suffers and acts for them, who for them makes
good that which they have spoiled, who—for them, but also without them and

---

[EN 9] situation as it had previously been
[EN10] restoration to wholeness

11

even against them—is their salvation. That is what we are. And what is left to us? What place is there for us when we are like that? In what sense is the history of the acts of God at this centre and end our history? Are we not without history? Have we not become mere objects? Have we not lost all responsibility? Are we not reduced to mere spectators? Is not our being deprived of all life or activity? Or does it not lack all significance as our life and activity? "God with us"—that is something which we can easily understand even in these circumstances. But how is it to include within it a "We with God"? And if it does not, how can it really be understood as a "God with us"?

The answer is that we ourselves are directly summoned, that we are lifted up, that we are awakened to our own truest being as life and act, that we are set in motion by the fact that in that one man God has made Himself our peacemaker and the giver and gift of our salvation. By it we are made free for Him. By it we are put in the place which comes to us where our salvation (really ours) can come to us from Him (really from Him). This actualisation of His redemptive will by Himself opens up to us the one true possibility of our own being. Indeed, what remains to us of life and activity in the face of this actualisation of His redemptive will by Himself can only be one thing. This one thing [015] does not mean the extinguishing of our humanity, but its establishment. It is not a small thing, but the greatest of all. It is not for us a passive presence as spectators, but our true and highest activation—the magnifying of His grace which has its highest and most profound greatness in the fact that God has made Himself man with us, to make our cause His own, and as His own to save it from disaster and to carry it through to success. The genuine being of man as life and activity, the "We with God," is to affirm this, to admit that God is right, to be thankful for it, to accept the promise and the command which it contains, to exist as the community, and responsibly in the community, of those who know that this is all that remains to us, but that it does remain to us and that for all men everything depends upon its coming to pass. And it is this "We with God" that is meant by the Christian message in its central "God with us," when it proclaims that God Himself has taken our place, that He Himself has made peace between Himself and us, that by Himself He has accomplished our salvation, i.e., our participation in His being.

This "We with God" enclosed in the "God with us" is Christian faith, Christian love and Christian hope. These are the magnifying of the grace of God which still remain to us—and remain to us as something specifically human, as the greatest thing of all, as action in the truest sense of the word. We do not forget that it is a matter of magnifying God out of the deeps, *e profundis*[EN11]. Our magnifying of God can only be that of the transgressors and rebels that we are, those who have missed their destiny, and perverted and wasted their being, life and activity. Therefore our magnifying of God cannot seek and find and have its truth and power in itself, but only in God, and therefore in that

---

[EN11] out of the depths

one Man in whom God is for us, who is our peace and salvation. Our faith, therefore, can only be faith in Him, and cannot live except from Him as its object. Our love can only be by Him, and can only be strong from Him as its basis. Our hope can only be hope directed upon Him, and can only be certain hope in Him as its content. Our faith, love and hope and we ourselves—however strong may be our faith, love and hope—live only by that which we cannot create, posit, awaken or deserve. And although our believing, loving and hoping themselves and as such are in us, they are not of us, but of their object, basis and content, of God, who in that one man not only answers for us with Him but answers for Himself with us, who gives it to us in freedom that we may believe, love and hope: open eyes, ears and hearts for Himself and His work, knowledge to the foolish, obedience to the wayward, freedom to the bound, life to the victims of death; and all in such a way that the glory of our own being, life and activity is still His, and can be valued, and exalted and respected by us only as His; but all in such a way that in and with His glory we too are really exalted, because in the depths where we can only give Him the glory, we find our true and proper place. It is in this way and in this sense that the [016] Christian community proclaims "We with God" when it proclaims "God with us."

In these seven points we have said in rough outline—many things need to be amplified, explained and made more precise—almost everything that has to be said about the "God with us" as the covenant between God and us men fulfilled in the work of atonement. But we have not yet said it with the concreteness with which it is said at the heart of the Christian message, or at the heart (in the second article) of the Creed, and with which it must also be said at the heart of dogmatics, even in the briefest survey, if we are not to speak mistakenly or falsely.

For where does the community which has to deliver the message learn to know and say this "God with us"? And to what does it point those to whom the message is addressed? How far can and must this "God with us," the report of the event which constitutes its meaning and content, be declared and received in truth? How can men come to stand where they obviously have to stand—in that inner circle of the relationship between God and man—to dare to make this report as a declaration of reality? And how do other men come to hear this report in such a way that it is to them a report of reality, and they find themselves challenged and empowered to pass it on to others still? How do they come to stand in the same place as the first men, as the Christian community? In other words: How does it come about amongst men that there is a communication of this "God with us," of this report, or rather, of that which is reported? That is the question which we can answer only as we say everything once again in the concrete way in which it is said at the heart of the Christian message. Everything depends upon its concrete expression: the whole truth and reality of the report, and the whole secret of the communication of the matter.

13

We must realise that the Christian message does not at its heart express a concept or an idea, nor does it recount an anonymous history to be taken as truth and reality only in concepts and ideas. Certainly the history is inclusive, i.e., it is one which includes in itself the whole event of the "God with us" and to that extent the history of all those to whom the "God with us" applies. But it recounts this history and speaks of its inclusive power and significance in such a way that it declares a name, binding the history strictly and indissolubly to this name and presenting it as the story of the bearer of this name. This means that all the concepts and ideas used in this report (God, man, world, eternity, time, even salvation, grace, transgression, atonement and any others) can derive their significance only from the bearer of this name and from His history, and not the reverse. They cannot have any independent importance or role based on a quite different prior interpretation. They cannot say what has to be said with some meaning of their own or in some context of their own [017] abstracted from this name. They can serve only to describe this name—the name of Jesus Christ.

This name is the answer to our earlier question. In the Christian "God with us" there is no question of any other source and object than that indicated by this name. Other than in this name—as on the basis of the necessity and power of its conceptual context—it cannot be truth, either on the lips of those who speak it or in the ears and hearts of those who receive it. Without this name it is left insecure and unprotected. It is exposed to the suspicion that it might be only a postulate, a pure speculation, a myth. It is truth as it derives from this name and as it points to it, and only so. Where is it that the men stand who declare this message? The answer is that they stand in the sphere of the lordship of the One who bears this name, in the light and under the impelling power of His Spirit, in the community assembled and maintained and overruled by Him. They have not placed themselves there but He has placed them there, and it is as they stand there by Him that their report is a report of actuality. Again, where will those others stand to whom they address their report and witness, who both receive it and then, on their own responsibility, spread it further? The answer is that they too stand in the sphere of the lordship, which has now claimed them, of the One who bears this name, of His Spirit, of the call to His community which has now come to them. They too have not placed themselves there. And those who said to them "God with us" have not brought it about. But, again, it is He Himself who bears this name that has called and led and drawn them, and it is as that happens that it is given to them, too, to pass on to others their report of actuality as such. Therefore the One who shows and persuades and convinces and reveals and communicates from man to man that it is so, "God with us," is the One who bears this name, Jesus Christ, no other, and nothing else. That is what the message of the Christian community intends when at its heart it declares this name. If it were a principle and not a name indicating a person, we should have to describe it as the epistemological principle of the message. Where between man and man there is real communication of the report of what took place in Him and through Him, He Himself is there and at work, He Himself makes Himself to be recognised and acknowledged. The Christian message about Him—and without this it is not the Christian message—is established on the certainty that He is responsible for it, that He as the truth speaks through it and is received in it, that as it serves Him He Himself is present as actuality, as His own witness. He Himself by His Spirit is its guarantor. He Himself is the one who establishes and maintains and directs the community which has received it and upon which it is laid. He Himself is the strength of its defence and its offensive. He Himself is the hope of freedom and enlightenment for the many who have not yet received and accepted it. He Himself above all is the comfort, and the restless- [018] ness, and yet also the uplifting power in the weakness of its service. In a word, the Christian message lives as such by and to the One who at its heart bears the name of Jesus Christ. It becomes weak and obscure to the extent that it thinks it ought to live on other resources. And it becomes strong and clear when it is established solely in confidence in His controlling work exercised by His Spirit; to the extent that it abandons every other conceivable support or impulse, and is content to rest on His command and commission as its strength and pledge. He, Jesus Christ, is Emmanuel, "God with us." How else can He be proclaimed except as the One who proclaims Himself? And how else can human activity and speech and hearing be effective in His service except in the prayer and expectation that He will constantly do it?

The name of Jesus Christ covers the whole power of the Christian message because it indicates the whole of its content, because at its heart, which is normative for the whole, it is a message about Him, and therefore a message about the event of that "God with us."

It means Jesus Christ when (1) with this "God with us" it describes an act of God, or rather the being of God in His life and activity. If as a statement about God it is the report of an event (not a statement of fact), the report of a history in which we have a part with our being, life and activity, which God has in common with us, which inaugurated by Him is our own history, then it is so because and in so far as it is a report about Jesus Christ as the One who actually unites the divine being, life and activity with ours.

It means Jesus Christ again when (2) it describes the "God with us" as an act of God, a particular, once and for all and unique event in the midst of events in general. It is a report of this one event and of this event alone, of its meaning and importance for all of us, for men of all times and places, because and to the extent that it is a report about Him as the person who in His existence and work is absolutely unique and therefore universal in effectiveness and significance. It means the event which unites God and man and which has been accomplished in Him and in Him alone, the event of which He alone is the subject and in which we can have a part only by Him.

It means Jesus Christ again when it describes the event of "God with us" (3) as a redemptive event; as the fulfilment of man's being by participation in the divine being which comes to him by the grace of God. It is a message of redemption, and therefore a message of the last and greatest and unsurpassable thing which man can experience from God and has in fact experienced, of the gift of eternal life which has been made to him, because and in so far as it is the message of Jesus Christ—that He is the One who, Himself God, is also man, that He therefore was and is and will be the salvation of God for us other [019] men, that in one person He is the God who gives salvation and the man to whom it is given and who allows it to be given by Him, that as such He is the power and witness of the *eschaton* in the human present—a human present which is itself in the *eschaton*.

But the Christian message again means Jesus Christ when (4) it looks through the redemptive event of the "God with us" as through glass to the basis and beginning of all things, of the world and of man, in God, to the original ordination of man to salvation and of salvation for man as the meaning and basis even of the divine creative will. It has the particular emphasis and the specific weight of an original Word which underlies and embraces all other words so that no other word has any independent significance, as one historical report with others, it has none of the contingence of the record of one historical fact with many others, because and in so far as it is a message about Jesus Christ: that He is the One who according to the free and gracious will of God is Himself eternal salvation, the last and also the first; our eternal yesterday in God who is the same to-day and for ever.

But it means Jesus Christ again when (5) it sees and presupposes that we men with whom God is are those who have forfeited the salvation destined for us from all eternity, letting slip the opportunity for it, and in that way fatally jeopardising their creaturely being and indeed perishing were it not that God is God and therefore their hope. It is not out of mere pessimism that it sees and understands man in this way. As a message about Jesus Christ it cannot do otherwise. This name is the real Emmanuel-sign and therefore—although in the reverse direction from Is. 7^{14}—the twofold sign which speaks of both the judgment of God and the grace of God in His dealings with His people. Also and first of all the sign of judgment. The well-deserved and incontestable sentence on man, His wrath and punishment, is first introduced and revealed in Jesus Christ. And it is the utterly free and unmerited nature of the grace of God introduced by Him as *factum purum*[EN12] which first reveals the true relationship with God of the man to whom it is granted in Him, the *factum brutum*[EN13] with which we have to do on the part of man.

And now it is absolutely clear that the Christian message means Jesus Christ, and has to name His name and does not know of any other, when (6) it says that God has made Himself the One who fulfils His redemptive will, that He has become man for us, that in the power of His Godhead He might take up

---

[EN12] pure fact
[EN13] brute fact

our cause in our place. Jesus Christ is the man in whom God satisfies Himself in face of our transgression and us in face of our plight. It says Jesus Christ when it speaks of this absolutely unique being, attitude and activity of God, of the peace which has been made by Him between Himself and us. And it does so because in speaking of this peace made in this way by God as a man amongst men, in speaking of this great thing, it at once goes on to speak of a greater [020] and of the greatest thing of all, of salvation itself, which has already come to us in and with the opportunity for salvation restored in Jesus Christ, which has already been given to us, which has already become our salvation.

To conclude: How can (7) the reverse side be possible or legitimate, how can a "We with God" be really included and enclosed in the "God with us," how can it be true or actual, if it does not have reference to Jesus Christ? It is with reference to Him that in spite of all appearances to the contrary the Christian message dares to address man too as an active subject in the event of redemption, and to its content there belong the praise which we offer to the grace of God *e profundis*[EN14], man's own faith and love and hope. We have already seen in what sense this by no means self-evident fact is true, to what extent we others who are not that One belong to the redemptive act, that is, to the extent that our human being, life and activity, in the form of the praise of God, of faith and love and hope, live by their object, basis and content, to the extent that it is given to us in that way to be able to praise and believe and love and hope. But in that way means in Jesus Christ, in the fellowship between Him and us created by His Spirit, in virtue of our being, life and activity in His, and His in ours. We other men are Christians—or prospective Christians—and therefore partakers of His being, life and activity, in so far as Jesus Christ makes us such and wills to maintain and rule us as such. There is a Christian community with its special distinction and service to the extent that Jesus Christ assembles it and is present with it by His Spirit. Therefore this final part of the content of the Christian message stands or falls with Him—its characterisation and description with the naming of His name.

A note by way of final delimitation and confirmation. Our formulation is again and again that the Christian message (in all its content) means Jesus Christ. In the declaration and development of its whole content it always has reference to Him. His name, therefore, is not incidental to it. It is not a name which has to be pronounced for the sake of completeness or adornment. It is there at the very heart of it as the central and decisive Word, the Word which is always present with every other word and to which it must always return. For in uttering His name it says that it refers to Him, and therefore to its true object. It is not trying to say something in general, a mere this or that, but it is trying to speak of Him, to show Him, to proclaim Him, to teach Him. To do this it can and must say many things. But these many things are all His things. They can be rightly said only as they look back or look away to Him. As they are said they can only be referred to Him. The Christian message is service, and the one whom it serves is at all points Jesus Christ Himself. What it says at its heart as the doctrine of the atonement is that He Himself is and lives and rules and acts, very God and very man,

---

[EN14] out of the deeps

and that He is peace and salvation. He Himself is the whole. And in every individual part He is the One of whom it speaks, the truth of all that it attests and proclaims as true, the actuality of all that it attests and proclaims as actual. It cannot be silent when it remembers His name and utters it. It can and must at once declare it. In and with His name it can and must at once declare His cause, but only in and with His name and therefore only as His cause. This cause of His has no existence or life or validity of its own apart from or side by side with Him. It cannot be distinguished, let alone separated from Him. Everything that is said about it is measured by whether it faithfully reflects Him, whether indirectly but distinctly it refers to Him, declares Him, portrays Him, magnifies and exalts Him. It is not, therefore, the case that properly and basically the Christian message is concerned about its own affair and introduces His name only as the One who is responsible for it. To avoid this impression we have chosen the way of climax, showing the concrete form of the Christian "God with us" to be the message of Jesus Christ, not at the outset, but at the very end. Everything moves towards and everything stands and falls by the fact that it is the message about Jesus Christ.

It is no mere battle of words whether we understand it merely as the Gospel of Jesus Christ or also—and as such—the Gospel about Jesus Christ. Obviously it is the Gospel of Jesus Christ. We have laid on this every possible emphasis. He Himself is the "epistemological principle." But we must be careful not to understand Him only in this way, for, if we do, the Christian message will at once degenerate into the self-declaration of an ecclesiastical form of redemption instituted indeed by Him but now self-resting and self-motivated, or into a devotional and ethical system taught indeed by Him but self-justified and self-sufficient, or into an illumination of existence strikingly fulfilled by Him in history but living by its own light. And when this happens, the Christian message as such will no longer have anything individual or new or substantial to say to man. What it will have to say to him will not be worth saying because in the last resort and basically he can say the same thing to himself. In one form or another it has simply become the recitation of a myth. But the Christian message does say something individual, new and substantial because it speaks concretely, not mythically, because it does not know and proclaim anything side by side with or apart from Jesus Christ, because it knows and proclaims all things only as His things. It does not know and proclaim Him, therefore, merely as the representative and exponent of something other. For it, there is no something other side by side with or apart from Him. For it, there is nothing worthy of mention that is not as such His. Everything that it knows and proclaims as worthy of mention, it does so as His.

It is not, therefore, doing Him a mere courtesy when it names the name of Jesus Christ. It does not use this name as a symbol or sign which has a certain necessity on historical grounds, and a certain purpose on psychological and pedagogic grounds, to which that which it really means and has to say may be attached, which it is desirable to expound for the sake of clarity. For it, this name is not merely a cipher, under which that which it really means and has to say leads its own life and has its own truth and actuality and would be worth proclaiming for its own sake, a cipher which can at any time be omitted without affecting that which is really meant and said, or which in other ages or climes or circumstances can be replaced by some other cipher. When it speaks concretely, when it names the name of Jesus Christ, the Christian message is not referring simply to the specific form of something general, a form which as such is interchangeable in the phrase of Lessing, a "contingent fact of history" which is the "vehicle" of an "eternal truth of reason." The peace between God and man and the salvation which comes to us men is not something general, but the specific thing itself: that concrete thing which is indicated by the name of Jesus Christ and not by any other name. For He who bears this name is Himself the peace and salvation. The peace and salvation can be known, therefore, only in Him, and proclaimed only in His name.

So much concerning the "God with us" as the most general description of our theme.

2. THE COVENANT AS THE PRESUPPOSITION OF RECONCILIATION [022]

Jesus Christ is God, God as man, and therefore "God with us" men, God in the work of reconciliation. But reconciliation is the fulfilment of the covenant between God and man.

"Reconciliation" is the restitution, the resumption of a fellowship which once existed but was then threatened by dissolution. It is the maintaining, restoring and upholding of that fellowship in face of an element which disturbs and disrupts and breaks it. It is the realisation of the original purpose which underlay and controlled it in defiance and by the removal of this obstruction. The fellowship which originally existed between God and man, which was then disturbed and jeopardised, the purpose of which is now fulfilled in Jesus Christ and in the work of reconciliation, we describe as the covenant.

Covenant, *berith*, διαθήκη, is the Old Testament term for the basic relationship between the God of Israel and His people. The etymology of the word (cf. W. Eichrodt, *Theologie des Alten Testaments*, Vol. I. 1933, 7, n. 5; G. Quell, *Theologisches Wörterbuch zum Neuen Test.* II, 106 f.) seems to be uncertain. Does it mean "circumcision" as a sacrificial ceremony, or "binding" as a binding of the will of the covenant-partner, or a "meal" as the ratification of the ceremony? Or does it come from the same root as *barah* and mean "choice?" Either way it denotes an element in a legal ritual in which two partners together accept a mutual obligation. We refer at this point to the historical reality with which the Old Testament is concerned whether it actually uses the word or not: "I will be your God, and ye shall be my people" (Jer. 7^{23}, 11^4, 30^{22}, 31^{33}, 32^{38}; Ezek. 36^{28}).

"Your God" is the almighty and gracious and holy One who reveals Himself under the name of *Yahweh*. He is the One according to whose will and commandment and with whose powerful assistance a group of blood-related nomadic tribes of Semitic descent consciously set out to capture and did indeed capture the land of Canaan against the unforgettable background of an act of deliverance on the border of Egypt. He is the One in whose worship they found themselves united in that land, and to whose sole recognition as God and to the honouring of whose decrees they knew themselves to be pledged.

"My people" (the people "Israel") is not simply the concept of those tribes in their interconnexion as a nation, let alone the state or one of the states in which this nation took on an external political form. It is rather the sacral federation (the Amphiktyonic league) of those tribes (only indirectly identical with the nation or state of Israel) gathered together as the twelve; the Israelitish congregation or community of tribes which as such recognised in that God their unseen founder, overlord, protector and law-giver, and which had their visible cultic centre in the ark, which perhaps represented the empty throne of *Yahweh* and which was preserved first in Shechem, then in Bethel, then in Shiloh, being finally brought to Jerusalem in the time of David (cf. M. Noth, *Das Gesetz im Pentateuch*, 1940, 63 f., 70 f.; *Geschichte Israels*, 1950, 74 f.). According to the formulation of G. Quell (*op. cit.*, p. 111) the "covenant" between the two is the answer to that problem of man before God which is presupposed by Old Testament religion in all its forms and at all its stages. It is the relationship with God as such which is everywhere presumed in the Old Testament cultus, in the law-

[023] giving, the prophecy, the historical and poetical writings. It is "a kind of common denominator" of Israelitish religion. There is relatively little direct mention of it. It is an "eternal covenant." It embraces everything that takes place between the two partners. The basic fact indicated by the word *berith* is presupposed even where on the ground and in the sphere of the covenant there are serious, even the most serious crises: movement of disloyalty, disobedience and apostasy on the part of portions or even the whole of that "community of tribes;" and to meet them divine threatenings which seem ultimately to compromise the whole status of Israel, and indeed the almost (but not more than almost) unceasing execution of these threatenings. We can hardly agree with W. Eichrodt (*op. cit.*, p. 11) that the covenant may be dissolved, that at its climax the judgment which breaks on Israel means the "setting aside" of the covenant (p. 250 f.). Does it not belong to the very nature of a *berith* even between man and man that it is "unalterable, lasting and inviolable" (G. Quell, *op. cit.*, p. 116)? Can this be less, is it not much more, the case with the *berith* between God and man? Does not the saying of Deutero-Isaiah about the covenant of peace which will not be removed (Is. 54^{10}) stand over everything that takes place in the relations between *Yahweh* and Israel?

What is true at all events is that the Old Testament covenant is a covenant of grace. It is instituted by God Himself in the fulness of sovereignty and in the freest determination and decree. And then and for that reason it is a matter of free choice and decision on the part of "Israel." God chooses for Himself this His people: this people, the community of tribes, chooses for itself this their God. This mutual choice, which takes place in this order and sequence, we have described as the basic fact, the presupposition of Old Testament religion, the standing of man before God which is always found in it. But the Old Testament understanding and the Old Testament representation of the early history of Israel make it clear that we can speak of a fact only with the greatest caution, for what is meant shows itself to be the occurrence of a basic act, something which happened there and then, and which as such can be placed alongside earlier—and also later—events. Obviously as an act which took place it cannot lose its actuality, but bears the character of an in itself inexhaustible occurrence. The Old Testament covenant, against the background and on the presupposition of which the events between God and Israel endorsed in the Old Testament take place, is not therefore a truth which is, as it were, inherent to this God or to the existence of this people or to their relationship one with another from a certain period in time, from an event which took place there and then. It is not a truth which as such has ceased to be event, the act of God and of Israel. It can, of course, be thought of as a historical fact. And it can be represented and worked out in institutions. But it is not itself an institution. It does not cease to be actual. It cannot be something given apart from the act of God and man. When the *berith* came to be understood as a given fact and an institution, in connexion with the ultimate location of a central worship in Jerusalem, but obviously even with the earlier cultus, especially in Shiloh, then at once it came under the fire of the severest prophetic criticism. The covenant remains—and it is in this way and only in this way that it does remain—the event of a divine and human choice, just as God Himself *exists* to the very depths of His being, and is therefore a (personally) living, active, acting and speaking God, and just as His human partner, His Israel, is actual only in its history, in the doing of its good and evil deeds, in the acting and suffering of the men who compose it.

For this reason there is no single and definitive narration of the original conclusion of this covenant—as there would have to be on that other view. According to the opinion advanced by many to-day, it is in the account in Josh. 24 of the action taken by Joshua in Shechem on the completion of the conquest that we have a representation which approximates most closely to an event of this kind. The conclusion of the covenant is portrayed in a very striking and solemn manner in this passage, so that if we did not know to the contrary, we might

conclude that it was necessarily the only occurrence of this nature. But according to Deut.   [024]
26–30, already at the end of Moses' life and under his leadership—not this time in Canaan
but in the land of Moab—it had been preceded by a conclusion of the covenant which is
described as equally unique and definitive. And both these accounts stand under the shadow
of the account in Ex. 24 of a covenant mediated by the same Moses at Sinai, which became so
important in tradition right up to the time of the Christian Church. And even the priority of
this covenant is apparently shaken by the covenant between God and Abraham which is
narrated in two versions in Gen. 15 and 17, and later recalled with particular emphasis. But
according to 2 K. 13^{23} this could be understood as a covenant "with Abraham, Isaac and
Jacob," and in any case it was preceded by the covenant with Noah in Gen. 8 and 9. And in
Neh. 8–9, at the opposite end of the historical period covered by the Old Testament narratives, we have a description of the action taken in Jerusalem under Ezra after the return from
exile, which can hardly be otherwise understood than as a further conclusion of the covenant, under whose strong impress—it might be supposed—the earlier narratives could easily
have lost their force for that generation. And in the light of 2 Sam. 7$^{5-29}$ are we not forced to
speak of a particular covenant with David, which also represents the whole? And we ought at
least to ask whether there are not many conversations reported in the Old Testament
between God and various individuals who in their different ways represent the whole community of Israel, in which the word *berith* is not actually used as a description, but which in
substance do belong to the same series: especially the calling and commissioning of the
prophets, but also of Moses, Aaron, the Judges, Saul and David? In these encounters
between God and those who had special gifts in Israel, is it not possible that we have to do
with the original view of the covenant between God and His people as such? And when on
festivals (like that of the enthronement) the people remembered the conclusion of the covenant, it was surely not understood as a "jubilee" of that event, but realistically as a contemporary happening. Certainly the conclusion of the covenant in the Old Testament
represents a series of many such events, and we should not be thinking in Old Testament
categories if we tried to understand one of them as the original, i.e., as the basic form of all
the others which is simply repeated, renewed and varied in the others, and therefore as the
basic act which constitutes Old Testament history and religion. The autonomy and importance which the Old Testament literature gives to each of these many events, quite irrespective of their mutual relationship, seems to make it impossible to try to find some pragmatic,
historical connexion. We have to hold together Deut. 5^2: "The Lord our God made a covenant with us in Horeb ... not with our fathers, but with us, even us, who are all of us here alive
this day"—and Deut. 29^{14}: "Neither with you only do I make this covenant and this oath, but
with him that standeth here with us this day before the Lord our God, and also with him that
is not here with us this day." It is enough that all the accounts are at one in this, and that even
in their puzzling variety they make it clear, that the presupposition of all the Old Testament
happenings has itself always to be understood as an event, the event of the mutual electing of
the God of Israel and His people.

But the concept of mutuality must now be elucidated. The saying of Jeremiah: "I will be
your God and you will be my people" certainly speaks of a mutuality. But it also speaks (even
in those passages in which the order of the two parts of the saying is reversed) of a willing on
the part of God and of a subordinate obligation, or becoming and being on the part of
Israel. And it is uttered as a statement made by God and not by a human writer. We have here
a negation of "the compulsory union of God with His people" (W. Eichrodt, *op. cit.* p. 11)
which is found in the other religious systems of the ancient East. Further, we have a decisive
proof that in this context the word "covenant" does not denote a two-sided contract between
two equal partners, but a more or less one-sided decree (M. Noth, *Geschichte Israels*, 111, n.   [025]
1). The covenant can (and must) be thought of as a "dictation on the part of an active to a

passive person" (G. Quell, *op. cit.*, p. 120). In the words of Jacques Ellul (*Die theologische Begründung des Rechts*, 1948, 37 f.) it is a contract of adherence (*contract d'adhésion*), i.e., a contract in which one of the parties makes the arrangements and the other simply agrees. The sense in which the LXX and the New Testament speak about the διαθήκη brings out exactly the meaning of the Old Testament *berith*. It is "in every respect the arrangement of God, the mighty declaration of the sovereign will of God in history, by which He creates the relationship between Himself and the human race in accordance with His redemptive purpose, the authoritative ordinance (institution) which brings about the order of things" (J. Behm, *Theol. Wörterbuch zum N. Test.* II, 137). For that reason it was rightly described by the Reformed federal theologians of the 17th century as a *foedus* μονόπλευρον EN15. This is clear in contexts like Deut. 27[16-19], where the conclusion of the covenant is represented as an act of law, in which both partners clarify their position and engage in a mutual contract. Certainly *Yahweh*, too, accepts an obligation. But He does so on His own free initiative. He does not have to make a contract with Israel. And the obligation which He accepts consists only in the fact that He wills to be who He is as the God of Israel: "salvation" (*Yahweh shalom*, Jud. 6[24]) and therefore—as "our" God—"our righteousness" (*Yahweh zidqenu*, Jer. 23[6], 33[16]). *Yahweh* does not stand above the covenant, but in it, yet He is also not under it. It is always "my covenant." Certainly there is a parallel obligation on the part of Israel. Certainly Israel declares that it will be *Yahweh's* "peculiar people" (*am segullah* EN16) and that as such it will keep His commandments. But it does not do so on its own judgment, but because it has been told by God that it is so. And its keeping of the commandments consists only in the fulfilment of its being as the people which God Has made it (Ps. 100[3]). Certainly between the two obligations there is a correspondence which is brought out particularly by Deuteronomy. That *Yahweh* is the salvation and righteousness of Israel is something which is known and experienced by His people only when as such it keeps His commandments. Conversely, when this does take place on the part of Israel, it cannot fail to enjoy this knowledge and experience. But if it does not happen, if there is done in Israel what ought not to be done (Gen. 34[7]; 2 Sam. 13[12]), then the salvation of its God necessarily becomes loss and His righteousness judgment. But this correspondence, too, rests on the free ordering of God, and its fulfilment is on both sides a matter of His righteousness, judgment and control. He alone is King and Judge. The correspondence, therefore, is in no sense a relationship of *do ut des* EN17 between two equal partners, a limitation which can be imposed on the activity of God by the attitude of Israel, and the acceptance of such a condition by God. The obligation which rests on God is always one which He wills to lay upon Himself. If ever Israel takes up the attitude to God that its relationship with Him is one of *do ut des* EN18, if ever it thinks that it can control God in the light of its own attitude, if ever it tries to assert a claim in relation to God, then it is unfaithful to its own election as His peculiar people and to its own electing of God. It has already fallen away to the worship of false gods and the transgression of all His commandments. It has already rushed headlong into the judgment of God and its own destruction. And when Israel does keep the commandments of its God, when it is faithful to His election and to its own electing of Him, it will necessarily appreciate that the knowledge and experience that He is its salvation and righteousness, and the blessing in which it stands, are God's free grace, the fulfilment of an obligation which God does not owe, but which He has Himself taken upon Himself, making the execution of it His own affair.

Now in the Old Testament the whole occurrence in and with and concerning the com-

---

EN15 unilateral treaty
EN16 peculiar people
EN17 I give so that you give
EN18 I give so that you give

munity of tribes which is "Israel," from its formation in the earliest period to the return of the captives from exile, is regarded as the fulfilment of this covenant, as the series of positive, critical and negative deductions which God draws from it and which this community comes to know and experience in the covenant in which it exists. Of these we cannot speak in the present context. They are the great example, the great commentary on the fulfilment of that covenant which now concerns us. But necessarily we shall be reminded of this example and commentary in our whole consideration of the doctrine of the atonement.

[026]

What we have still to consider is whether the Old Testament gives us any right or title to take over that concept of the covenant which is there shown to be the presupposition of the history of Israel and to use it as a description of the presupposition of the relationship and occurrence between God and all men—"the Jew first, but also the Greek" (Rom. 1^{16})—of that free connexion between God and man, based on the free grace of God, which we always have before us when we consider the universal atonement which is an event in Jesus Christ. Does the Old Testament allow or does it even perhaps command us to give to the concept of covenant the wider sense which obviously it will have to have in this context? So far there are three aspects of the meaning of the covenant in the Old Testament which we have not brought into consideration.

1. The first is at least touched on in the mention of the Noachic covenant. The detailed account offered in Gen. 9$^{1-17}$ belongs to the priestly writing. But this is making use of an older tradition, as is proved from the immediately preceding J passage in Gen. 8$^{20-22}$. For although this does not mention the word covenant, and is only a soliloquy of *Yahweh* as He smells the sweet savour of the sacrifice offered up by Noah, there is in content a decisive connexion between what *Yahweh* says to Himself in this passage and what He says to "Noah and his sons" in Gen. 9$^{1\ 8}$. Both passages speak of an obligation which God imposes upon Himself. In both passages we can see a corresponding obligation on the part of man. But "man" here is not the community of tribes which is Israel but the whole of humanity after Noah. If, then, as accounts of a covenant—which they are—they stand in the same series as all the other accounts from Sinai to the covenant under Ezra, they differ from all the others in that they speak of a covenant of God with the whole of humanity before and outside Abraham, and indeed, in 9$^{10\ 12\ 15f.}$, with all the living creatures which with Noah escaped the Flood. If we compare this with Gen. 12 f. we find that in relation to the "covenant" there are indeed (cf. W. Eichrodt, *op. cit.*, p. 19) "two concentric circles" (Proksch) in which the relationship of God to man is actualised: in the Noachic covenant it is with the human race as a whole, in the covenant with Abraham only with Israel. But in its own way, according to the tradition enshrined in the texts in Gen. 8 and 9, the covenant in the outer circle is no less real and unforgettable than the other. There, too, in the general occurrence in the relationship "between me and all flesh" (Gen. 9^{17}) we not only have to reckon with a living and active relation between the ruling and providing Creator and His creature, but we have also a covenant: a particular act of God in which He for His part pledges Himself to the man who is under pledge to Him. Nowadays the Noachic covenant is often referred to as a covenant of preservation in contrast to the covenant with Abraham as a covenant of grace and salvation. Certainly the Noachic covenant has to do with the "preservation " of the race. But we must not forget that even in the later covenant or covenants with Israel it is still a question of preservation. And again, in Gen. 8 and 9 it is not simply and abstractly a matter of "preservation," of the continuance of this relation between the Creator and the creature. What is attested here is not simply what we call the general control of divine providence. The very fact that the reference is only to man and to creatures subordinate to him ought in itself to warn us. What the texts say is not simply that the relation will in fact continue, but—and this is not quite so self-evident—that it will continue in face and in spite of the apostasy of man. "I

23

[027] will not again curse the ground any more for man's sake; for the imagination of man's heart is evil from his youth; neither will I again smite any more every living thing, as I have done"— is what *Yahweh* says in Gen. 8^{21}. And "neither shall all flesh be cut off any more by the waters of a flood; neither shall there any more be a flood to destroy the earth" is what He pledges to Noah and his sons in 9^{11}. He has once carried out the threat of destruction evoked by the sin of man, in the Flood, although even then a remnant was preserved. But He will not do it again: "He lets go displeasure, and he does not ask concerning our guilt." Certainly it means preservation when He says: "While the earth remaineth, seedtime and harvest, and cold and heat, and summer and winter, and day and night shall not cease" (8^{22}). And for that reason: "Be ye fruitful and multiply; bring forth abundantly in the earth, and multiply therein" (9^7). But in view of the wickedness of the heart of man even after the Flood, which God knows well enough, this preservation of the race is by a special activity of God, that is to say, by the exercise of His longsuffering, in which He wills that men as they are—having been shown once and for all under what threat they stand—should go forward to meet One who (as yet completely unseen) has still to come, and therefore that they should not be allowed to perish, but preserved. Therefore the Noachic covenant—in a way which remarkably is much more perceptible than in the case of the covenant or covenants with Israel—is already a covenant of grace in the twofold sense of the concept grace: the free and utterly unmerited self-obligation of God to the human race which had completely fallen away from Him, but which as such is still pledged to Him (as is shown by the sacrifice of Noah in Gen. 8^{20} and the divine direction in Gen. $9^{1f.}$); and as the sign of the longsuffering of God obviously also the promise of the future divine coming which will far transcend the mere preserving of the race.

It is astonishing and yet it is a fact that the Old Testament should have considered the race prior to and outside Abraham in this way, on the presupposition not merely of the general relation of Creator and creature, but of a concrete activity of God in relation to it, which is not positively His redemptive activity—the same can be said of the covenant concluded with Israel—but an activity on the basis of which the nations preserved by God cannot be excluded from His redemptive work. In this sense the race, as a whole, is in covenant. It is the outer circle of which the inner is revealed from Gen. 12 onwards as Israel. It is in covenant, not by nature, not as humanity, to whom the Creator as such is obliged to show longsuffering, but on the basis of the free divine initiative and act. And genuinely so on this basis. In the light of Israel elected and called out from them, the nations can and must be regarded under this sign: under this correspondence to the sign under which Israel itself found itself placed, and therefore as itself to some extent a great community of tribes. From this point we can well understand how the Old Testament necessarily dared to present the history of creation—without using the word *berith* in the text, but factually—in an indissoluble relation to the divine covenant. The history of creation is a great cosmic prelude and example of that history of Israel which is the proper theme of the Old Testament. Creation is the outward basis of the covenant (Gen. 1) and the covenant the inward basis of creation (Gen. 2). Cf. *C.D.* III 1, § 41. Finally, the story of the fall and its consequences (Gen. 3) is a happening which, for all its fearfulness, like the later resistance of Israel and the divine judgments which came upon it in consequence, does not take place outside but within a special relationship of the affirmation of man by God, of God's faithfulness to man, which is self-evidently presupposed to be unshakable. We can also understand how it is that, for all the exclusiveness with which the Old Testament speaks of the election and call of Israel, it never has any hesitation in allowing figures from outside, from the nations, time and again and sometimes with the very highest authority and function to enter the inner circle: Melchizedek, King of

[028] Salem, who in Gen. 14^{18} is called "a priest of the Most High God," Jethro the Midianite, the father-in-law of Moses (Ex. $18^{1f.}$), Balaam, the prophet of Moab (Num. 22–24) who is forced

to bless Israel against his will, the harlot Rahab of Canaan (Josh. 2) who saves the spies, Ruth the Moabitess who is the ancestress of David, the Philistine Ittai (2 Sam. 15[19]) who is one of the loyal few who pass over Kedron with David, the Syrian general Naaman (2 K. 5[1f.]), to mention only a few out of a list which is remarkably continued in the New Testament. We can also understand the respect, the sympathy, even the granting of equality, which is so often enjoined upon Israel in the Law in relation to the "stranger," and the petition in which the stranger is expressly accepted in Solomon's prayer of dedication in 1 K. 8[41f.] (seeing that strangers could sometimes be found in the temple at Jerusalem). Those who come from outside do not come from a vacuum, but from the sphere of a relationship of God to man which is also in its own way effective—not generally and naturally, but historically, in virtue of a particular divine act.

2. A second important qualification of the Old Testament concept of the covenant arises from the conception of the final mission of Israel to the nations which we find particularly in the latter part but also in the earlier portions of the book of Isaiah. Why did God separate and take to Himself and address this people? In the older tradition this question was left unanswered. But now in the light of the future an answer is given. It is given in the form of a prophecy which arises out of the situation of Israel at the end of its historical independence, but which absolutely transcends every historical consideration, possibility or probability. In the last days it will be wonderfully shown that the covenant of *Yahweh* with Israel was not an end in itself, but that it had a provisional and a provisionally representative significance. Israel had and has a mission—that is the meaning of the covenant with it. In Israel—this is what will be revealed in the last days—there is to be set up a sign and a witness to all peoples. The redemptive will of God is to be declared to all humanity. That is what we are told in the particularly important saying to the Ebed *Yahweh* in Is. 49[6]: "It is a light thing that thou shouldest be my servant to raise up the tribes of Jacob, and to restore the preserved of Israel: I will also give thee for a light to the Gentiles, that thou mayest be my salvation unto the end of the earth." The prophetic portrayal of this future event is not unitary. In Is. 2[2–4]—which is ascribed to Isaiah, the son of Amoz, although it is found word for word in Mic. 4[1–4]—we are told: "And it shall come to pass in the last days, that the mountain of the Lord's house shall be established in the top of the mountains, and shall be exalted above the hills; and all nations shall flow unto it. And many people shall go and say. Come ye, and let us go up to the mountain of the Lord, to the house of the God of Jacob; and he will teach us of his ways, and we will walk in his paths for out of Zion shall go forth the law, and the word of the Lord from Jerusalem. And he shall judge among the nations, and shall rebuke many people: and they shall beat their swords into ploughshares, and their spears into pruninghooks: nation shall not lift up sword against nation, neither shall they learn war any more." Zion is also referred to in Is. 25[6–8], but this time in relation to a redemptive happening of universal significance which does not go and, as it were, spread out from it, but which takes place within it: "And in this mountain shall the Lord of hosts make unto all people a feast of fat things, a feast of wines on the lees, of fat things full of marrow, of wines on the lees well refined. And he will destroy in this mountain the face of the covering cast over all people, and the vail that is spread over all nations. He will swallow up death in victory; and the Lord God will wipe away tears from off all faces; and the rebuke of his people shall be taken away from off all the earth: for the Lord hath spoken it." Different again is the picture unfolded in Is. 19[18–25]. In the most concrete possible way the presentation of a historical situation—which seems to be very like that of the time of Isaiah himself—is merged into a vision of events in the last days: "In that day shall five cities in the land of Egypt speak the language of Canaan and swear to the Lord of hosts. ... In that day there shall be an altar to the Lord in the midst of the land of Egypt, and a pillar at the border thereof to the Lord. And it shall be for a sign and for a witness to the Lord of hosts in the land of Egypt. ... And the Lord shall be known to Egypt,

25

and the Egyptians shall know the Lord in that day, and shall do sacrifice and oblation; yea, they shall vow a vow unto the Lord, and perform it. ... In that day shall there be a highway out of Egypt to Assyria, and the Assyrian shall come into Egypt, and the Egyptian into Assyria, and the Egyptians shall serve with the Assyrians. In that day shall Israel be the third with Egypt and with Assyria, even a blessing in the midst of the land: whom the Lord of hosts shall bless, saying, Blessed be Egypt my people, and Assyria the work of my hands, and Israel mine inheritance."

In the texts so far quoted we may wonder whether the eschatological event described is not conceived too much as the one-sided arrangement and miraculous operation of *Yahweh*. But in the Ebed-*Yahweh* songs of Deutero-Isaiah the emphasis is unmistakably on the active co-operation of the human partner of *Yahweh*. The question whether this partner, the servant of the Lord, is meant as collective Israel or as a single person—and if so, which? a historical? or an eschatological?—can never be settled, because probably it does not have to be answered either the one way or the other. This figure may well be both an individual and also the people, and both of them in a historical and also an eschatological form. What is certain is that in and with this servant of the Lord Israel as such is at any rate introduced also as the partner of *Yahweh*. And in a whole series of passages it is introduced as the partner of *Yahweh* in an eschatological encounter with the nations, the powerful witness of *Yahweh* in the midst of the heathen. It is, therefore, in the light of a service which Israel has to perform that the actualisation of the prophecy of salvation is now understood. Is. 42¹⁻⁴: "Behold my servant, whom I uphold; mine elect, in whom my soul delighteth; I have put my spirit upon him; he shall bring forth judgment (*mishpat*) to the Gentiles. He shall not cry, nor lift up, nor cause his voice to be heard in the street. A bruised reed shall he not break, and the smoking flax shall he not quench: he shall bring forth judgment unto truth. He shall not fail nor be discouraged, till he have set judgment in the earth; and the isles shall wait for his law." And Is. 42⁵⁻⁸: "Thus saith God the Lord, he that created the heavens, and stretched them out; he that spread forth the earth, and that which cometh out of it; he that giveth breath unto the people upon it, and spirit to them that walk therein: I the Lord have called thee in righteousness (*b'zedeq*), and will hold thine hand, and will keep thee, and give thee for a *berith am* (this remarkable expression recurs in Is. 49⁸: the Zurich Bible paraphrases: "a mediator of the covenant on behalf of the race"), for a light of the Gentiles; to open the blind eyes, to bring out the prisoners from the prison, and them that sit in darkness out of the prisonhouse. I am the Lord, that is my name: and my glory will I not give to another, neither my praise to graven images."

The saying in Is. 49⁶ has already been mentioned. But above all there is what is rightly the best known of all the Servant Songs, Is. 52¹²–53¹², which, however we understand the one of whom it speaks, definitely belongs to this context. It is now the nations themselves—once again we have the eschatological event—who acknowledge that they have at last understood the meaning of the existence of Israel amongst them—its historical role as a mediator and the message which it has addressed to them: "Behold, my servant shall prosper, he shall be exalted and extolled, and be very high. As many were astonished at thee; his visage was so marred more than any man, and his form more than the sons of men: So shall he astonish many nations; the kings shall shut their mouths at him: for that which had not been told them shall they see; and that which they had not heard shall they consider" (Is. 52¹³⁻¹⁵). The

[030]

historical background and outlook of the song is a time and situation of the last and deepest and most hopeless abasement of the people of the covenant, or of its (kingly? or prophetic?) representative. But according to this song, in the last days the nations will recognise and acknowledge that his mission, and the universally valid word and universally effective work of God, is present even in this utter hiddenness of the historical form of His witness: "Who hath believed our report? and to whom is the arm of the Lord revealed? For he shall grow up before him as a tender plant, and as a root out of a dry ground: he hath no form nor comeliness; and when we shall see him, there is no beauty that we should desire him. He is despised and rejected of men; a man of sorrows, and acquainted with grief: and we hid, as it were, our faces from him; he was despised, and we esteemed him not" (53^{1-3}). "He was cut off out of the land of the living" (v. 8). "He made his grave with the wicked, and with the rich in his death" (v. 9). "Who shall declare his generation?" (v. 8). And then the great confession of the nations at the end of the age, which does not deny but confirms and even lights up this appearance: "Surely he hath borne our griefs, and carried our sorrows" (v. 4). "But he was wounded for our transgressions, he was bruised for our iniquities: the chastisement of our peace was upon him; and with his stripes we are healed. All we like sheep have gone astray; we have turned every one to his own way; and the Lord hath laid on him the iniquity of us all" (vv. 5–6). And all this means: "He shall see his seed, he shall prolong his days, and the cause of the Lord shall prosper in his hand," because he made himself "an offering for sin" (v. 10). Just as the passage begins with a soliloquy of *Yahweh*, so it also ends, accepting and confirming this confession of the Gentiles: "He shall see of the travail of his soul, and shall be satisfied: by his knowledge shall my righteous servant justify many; for he shall bear their iniquities. Therefore will I divide him a portion with the great, and he shall divide the spoil with the strong; because he hath poured out his soul unto death: and he was numbered with the transgressors; and he bare the sin of many, and made intercession for the transgressors" (vv. 11–12).

Seen and understood eschatologically, this is the meaning and function of the particular covenant of God with Israel. The word *berith* occurs only once in the passages quoted, in the obscure *berith am*[EN19] of Is. 42^8. But, in fact, it forces itself upon us, for it is the covenant people which lives and cries and suffers here, which is hemmed in and oppressed and threatened, which is more than threatened, actually overthrown and given up to destruction (and all according to the will and disposing of its God). The relatively short time of its modest existence in the sphere of world-history or of contemporary middle-eastern politics draws quickly to its close—in pain and grief and shame. What is it that the covenant-God is saying in all this? What is it that He wills by this work of His—He who has from the first and again and again shown and attested Himself as the One who is in covenant with His people? The prophets evidently associated the happenings primarily with the message that Israel had to see in it that judgment for its unfaithfulness to the Lord of the covenant which had been held before it from the very first. When that judgment began to fall—first on Samaria, then on Jerusalem—at every stage they warned and admonished and pleaded and threatened, like swimmers struggling against the twofold stream of human disobedience and the consequent wrath of God, which they tried to arrest with their call to repentance, but which by reason of its ineffectiveness they could not arrest, and therefore did not try to do so any longer but could only affirm it to be holy and just and necessary. But quite apart from the vain and empty confidence held out by the false prophets, even the true and authentic spokesmen for the covenant-God spoke always of His unchangeable faithfulness in contrast to the unfaithfulness of Israel, of the inflexibility of His purpose for His people, and therefore of the positive meaning of its history including its end. It is in this context that there [031] arises the prophecy of the redemptive future of Israel in the last days. It presupposes the dark state of things at the present. It views it with pitiless clarity. And it does not overlay this view with the mere promise of better times to come. It does not offer by way of comfort the prospect of later historical developments. Its nerve and centre is the reference to an event which will terminate all history and all times, a history of the end. It is in this—and from this point of view the necessary destruction of Israel is only "a moment of wrath" (Is. $54^{7f.}$; Ps.

[EN19] convenant people

27

30⁵)—that the Yes which *Yahweh* has spoken to His people in and with the conclusion of the covenant will be revealed and expressed as a Yes. The last time, the day of *Yahweh*, will indeed be the day of final judgment—the prophets of a false confidence must make no mistake about that. But as such it will also be the day of Israel's redemption—the day when the covenant which *Yahweh* has made with it finds its positive fulfilment.

And it is particularly the teaching of the book of Isaiah which makes it clear that as such the last day which is the day of redemption for Israel will also be the day of redemption for the nations—the day of judgment, too, but, as the day of the last judgment, the day of redemption. It will then be revealed to the nations that it is not in vain and not for its own sake that Israel was and is, that its divine election and calling and all the history which followed in its brighter or darker aspects was no mere episode but an epoch, was not accidental but necessary, that its purpose was not a particular one, but the universal purpose of its mission, that its existence was the existence of a light for all men, a light which was once overlooked, but which then shone out unmistakably in the gross darkness which covered the earth (Is. 60¹ᶠ—we may also recall the four rivers of Paradise in Gen. 2¹⁰ᶠ, and the river which flows out of the temple in Ezek. 47¹⁻¹²). It will then be the case actually and visibly that "salvation is of the Jews" (Jn. 4²²). All the texts quoted speak of this in their varied eschatological imagery. They make it plain that the race as a whole is not forgotten in the importance of those shattering events between *Yahweh* and Israel which are the main subject of the Old Testament testimony. They do not speak only of the judgments which necessarily fall on the nations in relation to that which overtakes Israel. They also connect the salvation which is the final goal of the history of Israel with the salvation of the Assyrians and the Egyptians and all nations, and in such a way that the special existence of Israel is an instrument by which God finally manifests and accomplishes salvation for the nations. They speak, in fact, of a concrete presupposition which underlies the dealings of God as Lord of the world and the nations, and which for all its dissimilarity is similar to that of the history of Israel, and indeed identical with it, in that it has as its aim the grace which is to come upon them. The line which reveals this eschatological aspect of the Old Testament is not a broad one. It is only a kind of border to the true narrative and message of the Old Testament. But it belongs to it quite unmistakably. It is like the reference to that corresponding event in the earlier history, the covenant of God with the human race before Abraham, which is also a narrow line marking the earlier border of the true narrative and message of the Old Testament. But that narrative and message do have their beginning at the one point and their end at the other, the one in primal history, and the other in the corresponding eschatological history. They have this aspect even as the narrative and message of the happenings which take place on the basis of the covenant. And how could they be understood as a unity unless they had this aspect? By these strangely complementary aspects on the borders of the Old Testament we are not merely enabled but summoned to take even the most exclusive thing of which it speaks, the covenant relationship between *Yahweh* and Israel, which is the presupposition of everything that takes place in the relations between these two partners, and, without denying its exclusiveness, to understand it inclusively, as that which points to a covenant which was there at the beginning and which will be there at the end, the covenant of God with all men.

[032]

3. We come finally to a third strand which we cannot overlook in an intensive amplification of the Old Testament covenant concept. Even in itself and as such the covenant with Israel is capable of a radical change in structure which it will actually undergo in the last days, as we learn from Jer. 31³¹ᶠ and 32³⁸ᶠ. "Behold, the days come, saith the Lord, that I will make a new covenant with the house of Israel, and with the house of Judah" (31³¹). "I will make an everlasting covenant with them" (32⁴⁰). The elements are exactly the same as in that covenant with Abraham, Moses and Joshua which is normative for the Old Testament as

2. The Covenant as the Presupposition of Reconciliation

a whole. The formula "I will be your God, and ye shall be my people" is emphatically endorsed in both these passages and in the parallel passage in Ezek. 11²⁰. We cannot therefore speak of a "replacement" of the first covenant by this "new" and "eternal" covenant of the last days except in a positive sense. Even in the verses Jer. 31³⁵⁻³⁷ which immediately follow the main passage 31³¹⁻³⁴, there is a most definite stress on the imperishable nature of the covenant with Israel: neither here nor elsewhere can there be any question of its interruption or cessation. What happens to this covenant with the conclusion of a new and eternal covenant is rather—and the wider context of the passage points generally in this direction—that it is upheld, that is, lifted up to its true level, that it is given its proper form, and that far from being destroyed it is maintained and confirmed. There is no question of a dissolution but rather of a revelation of the real purpose and nature of that first covenant. The relationship of God with Israel, which is the substance of the covenant, is not held up,* that is to say, arrested, and set aside and destroyed, even on the New Testament understanding of the passage. What is done away (Calvin) is only its "economy," the form in which it is revealed and active in the events of the Old Testament this side of the last days. In accordance with the completely changed conditions of the last time this form will certainly be altered, and so radically that it will no longer be recognisable in that form, and to that extent a new covenant will actually have been concluded: The form in which it was revealed and active in all the events from the exodus from Egypt to the destruction of Israel and Judah was such that in it the faithfulness and power of *Yahweh* seemed always to be matched and limited by the perpetually virulent and active disobedience and apostasy of the covenanted people. The prophecy says that this will end in the last days. The new and eternal covenant will not be "according to the covenant that I made with their fathers when I took them by the hand to bring them out of the land of Egypt; which my covenant they brake, although I was a Lord unto them" (31³²). It is this that God will no longer tolerate in the last days, but will repeal and remove: "But this shall be the covenant that I shall make with the house of Israel; After those days, saith the Lord, I will put my law in their inward parts, and write it in their hearts; and will be their God, and they shall be my people" (31³³). "And I will give them one heart, and one way, that they may fear me for ever, for the good of them, and of their children after them" (32³⁹ᶠ·). Ezek. 11¹⁹ᶠ· (cf. 36²⁶ᶠ·) is even clearer: "And I will ... put a new spirit within you; and I will take the stony heart out of their flesh, and will give them an heart of flesh; that they may walk in my statutes, and keep mine ordinances, and do them: and they shall be my people, and I will be their God." Similarly in Deut. 30⁶ we are told about a circumcision of the heart of the people which God Himself will accomplish: "to love the Lord thy God with all thine heart, and with all thy soul, that thou mayest live." All this clearly means that the circle of the covenant which in its earlier form is open on man's side will in its new form be closed: not because men will be better, but because God will deal with the same men in a completely different way, laying His hand, as it were, upon them from behind, because He Himself will turn them to Himself. To His faithfulness—He himself will see to it—there will then correspond the complementary faithfulness of His people. The covenant—God Himself will make it so—will then be one which is mutually kept, and to that extent a *foedus* δίπλευρον. ᴱᴺ²⁰

[033]

The strange but necessary consequence will then be: "And they shall teach no more every man his neighbour, and every man his brother, saying. Know the Lord: for they shall all know me, from the least of them unto the greatest of them, saith the Lord" (31³⁴). But if the new and eternal form of the covenant means the ending of the fatal controversy between God

---

* Note: There is a play here on the German word *aufheben*, which positively means to "raise up," but negatively means to "repeal" or "set aside."—Trans.
ᴱᴺ²⁰ bilateral covenant

29

and man it also means the ending of the corresponding necessity (the redemptive necessity) for that human antithesis or opposition between wise and foolish, prophets and people, teachers and scholars, the *ecclesia docens* and the *ecclesia audiens*[EN21], which even at its very best indicates a lack and encloses a judgment. It is at this point that Paul comes in (2 Cor. 3[6f.]) with his doctrine of the old and the new διαθήκη[EN22], the one of the prescriptive letter, the other of the liberating spirit which leads to obedience. In the light of this he expounds the covering on the face of Moses (Ex. 34[35f.]) as that of the temporal nature of his ministry, and he finds the same covering on the hearts of the Jews who hear Moses read without perceiving that his ministry (i.e., the ministry of the prescriptive letter) does in fact belong to the past (2 Cor. 3[15f.]). He then goes on to proclaim: "Now the Lord is that Spirit: and where the Spirit of the Lord is, there is liberty" (2 Cor. 3[17]). He then contrasts the Jew who is one only outwardly with the Jew who is one inwardly and in truth: "by the circumcision that is of the heart, in the spirit, and not in the letter" (Rom. 2[29])—that is to say, the Gentiles who have come to faith in Jesus Christ, who apart from the Law do by nature the works of the Law, who are a law to themselves in that they reveal that the Law is written in their hearts (Rom. 2[14f.]). He then can and must say with reference to the Christian community (cf. also Rom. 15[14]; Phil. 1[9f.]) that although prophecy, tongues and knowledge will fade away, love can never fail (1 Cor. 13[8]).

And now we come to the most remarkable thing of all: What is the basis and possibility of this complete change in the form of the covenant which is to take place in the last days and therefore beyond the history of Israel considered in the Old Testament? A conclusive answer is given in Jer. 31[34b]: "For I will forgive their iniquity, and I will remember their sin no more." I would not say with G. Quell (*op. cit.*, p. 126) that a covenant which has this basis is obviously no longer a covenant. I would say rather that in this way and on this basis it becomes a perfect covenant. For in this way and on this basis God will break the opposition of His people, creating and giving a new heart to the men of His people, putting His Spirit in their inward parts, making the observance of His commandments self-evident to them (Paul in Rom. 2[14] uses the word φύσις[EN23] in relation to Gentile Christians), and in that way completing the circle of the covenant. In this way and on this basis the Israelitish history in the old form of the covenant—in so far as it stood under the sign of the sin of Israel and the divine reaction against it—will come to an end, together with that earlier form, to give way to the new and proper form. This ending and new beginning will be posited in the fact that God not only exercises patience as in the Noachic covenant, but that He remits guilt, that He does not remember sin, and that in this way and on this basis He not only allows an unmerited continuation of life, again as in the Noachic covenant, but reduces to order, and in a sense compulsorily places in the freedom of obedience which we owe Him as His covenant partners. This sovereign act of God which fulfils His will and plan and in which He vindicates at one and the same time His own right and that of man, is the subject of the prophecy in Jeremiah: the new basis of the new covenant. This covenant will be the covenant of the free but effective grace of God.

[034]   We must remember, however, that this conclusion of the covenant in the last days, like the Noachic covenant of the first days, is in the same series as those which were made first with Abraham and finally with Ezra. As we have seen, the prophecy of it does not mean to discredit or invalidate these others, or the covenant with Israel as such. It denies what had so far taken place on the basis of the presupposition to which those conclusions of the covenant point: the breaking of the covenant on the part of the people, and ensuing judgments on the

---

EN21 teaching church ... hearing church
EN22 covenant
EN23 nature

part of God. But it does not deny the presupposition as such. It negates—or rather according to this prophecy God Himself negates—the unfaithfulness of Israel, but not the faithfulness of God Himself, nor His covenant will in relation to His people. What God will do in accordance with this prophecy will be a revelation and confirmation of what He had always willed and indeed done in the covenant with Israel. And for all the antithesis between the faithfulness of God and unfaithfulness of man, and the divine judgments which follow this antithesis, in everything that takes place in the Old Testament do we not find something of the forgiveness of the guilt and the gracious forgetting of the sin of His people, which belong to the last days, and which in fact obviously answer to the deepest being of the covenant, however out of place they may seem to be outwardly? And on this basis were there not always in this people new and fleshly and circumcised hearts, and the Spirit and freedom, and even a simple and genuine keeping of the commandments? How could there ever have been prophets, how could there have been that remnant in Israel, how could there have been penitence and prayer and also the bright and joyful worship of God in the Psalms, if not on the basis which Jer. 31 describes as the new basis of the new covenant? This basis was not simply absent in the "old" covenant—or in the one covenant in its old form (as though this had had some other basis!). It was only hidden: hidden under the form of a relationship in which, viewed as a whole, the human lack of grace was bound to be revealed side by side with the divine grace, in which therefore even grace itself, viewed as a whole, was bound to have the form of judgment. Jer. 31 is the final word in matters of the divine covenant with Israel. In the light of the last days it describes it as the covenant of the free but effective grace of God. But at the same time it is also the first word in these matters. And this description is an indication of what the divine covenant with Israel had been in substance from the very first.

What, then, we gather from the Noachic covenant, and everything that belongs to this strand, is that according to the Old Testament conception itself the special divine covenant made with Israel does not exclude the human race as a whole from the gracious will of God towards it. What we find in Isaiah's view of the status of Israel as a representative and messenger to the nations is that the covenant made with Israel has a meaning and purpose which reaches out beyond the existence of Israel. And now, from the prophecy in Jeremiah of a new covenant of forgiveness and of the Spirit and of free obedience on the part of man, we learn that the Old Testament looks beyond the past and present to a form of the relationship between God and Israel in which the covenant broken by Israel will again be set up, that the Israelite, for whom ultimately God has nothing but forgiveness, but does have it actually and effectively, must now take his place directly alongside his Gentile fellows, and that if at all he can hope for the grace and salvation of God only on this presupposition. In the light of this passage in Jer. 31 we are indeed enabled and summoned to give to the concept of the covenant the universal meaning which it acquired in the form which it manifestly assumed in Jesus Christ.

Jesus Christ is the atonement. But that means that He is the maintaining and accomplishing and fulfilling of the divine covenant as executed by God Himself. He is the eschatological realisation of the will of God for Israel and therefore for the whole race. And as such He is also the revelation of this divine will [035] and therefore of the covenant. He is the One for whose sake and towards whom all men from the very beginning are preserved from their youth up by the longsuffering of God, notwithstanding their evil heart. And in this capacity He reveals that the particular covenant with Israel was concluded for their sake too, that in that wider circle it also encloses them. He is the servant of God who stands before God as the representative of all nations and stands amongst the nations as the representative of God, bearing the judgments of God, living and testifying by the grace of God—Himself the Israel elected and called to the covenant and to be the mediator of the covenant. And in that capacity He reveals that this covenant with Israel is made and avails for the whole race. In His own person He is the eschatological sovereign act of God who renews men and summons them to obedience by forgiving their sins. And in that capacity He reveals that the meaning and power of the covenant with Israel for the whole race is that it is a covenant of free and therefore effective grace.

The work of God in Jesus Christ is also the Word of God—the Word in which He makes known His will even as it is done to those who can hear it. And this will of God which is done begins with the institution and establishment of His covenant with man. It is done in acts of grace and mercy, of judgment and punishment, and in His Word as Gospel and Law, as comfort, admonishment and counsel. It is done primarily and basically as His will to be the God of man, to let man be His man. The whole actualisation of the will of God has its source there, in the "kindness of God toward man" (Tit. 3^4). This is the presupposition of all the works and words of God. The whole plan and law and meaning of them derives from this source, that God the Creator wanted to make and did in fact make Himself the covenant partner of man and man the covenant partner of God. The whole doing of the will of God is the doing of His covenant will. As this covenant will it strives and conquers against the sin of man and its consequences in the atonement accomplished in Jesus Christ. But primarily, in face of the sin of man, and God's striving with it and conquering of it and of its consequences, it is His covenant will. It remains His covenant will in this antithesis, conflict and victory. It is through those that it finds its fulfilment. And the antithesis, conflict and fulfilment reveal it for what it is. They also show its origin—that it was first of all His covenant will.

It is in Jesus Christ that that antithesis is met and overcome. It is Jesus Christ who accomplishes and fulfils the will of God in face of human sin and its consequences. It is not something provisional but final that takes place in the atonement accomplished by Him. In Him God Himself enters in, and becomes man, a man amongst men, in order that He Himself in this man may carry out His will. God Himself lives and acts and speaks and suffers and triumphs for all men as this one man. When this takes place, atonement takes place. But the final thing which takes place here—just as it cannot be something provisional —cannot be a second or later thing. It can only reveal the first thing. What takes place here is the accomplishment and therefore the revelation of the original and basic will of God, as a result of which all the other works and words of God take place. What breaks out at this point is the source of all that God wills and does.

This, then, is the actualisation of the will of God in this matter, in the overcoming of this antithesis. The will of God is done in Jesus Christ, in God's own

[036]

being and acting and speaking as man. But if this is so, then this actualisation, the overcoming of this antithesis, is characterised as an act of faithfulness, of constancy, of self-affirmation on the part of God, as the consequence of a pre-supposition already laid down by Him, as the fulfilment of a decision which underlies and therefore precedes that actualisation, an "earlier" divine decis-ion, as the successful continuation of an act which God had already begun, from the very beginning. He becomes and is man in Jesus Christ, and as such He acts and speaks to reconcile the world to Himself, because He has bound Himself to man by the creation of heaven and earth and all things, because He cannot tolerate that this covenant should be broken, because He wills to uphold and fulfil it even though it is broken. The work of atonement in Jesus Christ is the fulfilment of the communion of Himself with man and of man with Himself which He willed and created at the very first. Even in face of man's transgression He cannot allow it to be destroyed. He does not permit that that which He willed as Creator—the inner meaning and purpose and basis of the creation—should be perverted or arrested by the transgression of man. He honours it and finally fulfils it in this conflict with the transgression and overcoming of it. The transgression can and must be understood as an episode and its overcoming in Jesus Christ as the contingent reaction of God in face of this episode. But the reaction as such takes place along the line of that action determined from the very first in the will of God and already initi-ated. It is only the particular form of that action in face of this episode. And in this particular form, in the fact that God becomes man for our sake, to set aside our sin and its consequences, we see both the fact and also the manner in which it is determined from the very first and already initiated. It is not only a reaction, but a work of the faithfulness of God. And the faithfulness of God has reference to the covenant between Himself and men. Even in this particular form it is the accomplishment of His covenant will. Even more, it is the affirm-ation and consummation of the institution of the covenant between Himself and man which took place in and with the creation. It is this covenant will which is carried out in Jesus Christ. It is this institution of the covenant which is fulfilled in Him. He does it in face of human sin, as the One who overcomes it, [037] as the Mediator between God and man. He does it, therefore, in fulfilment of the divine reaction in face of that episode. But primarily it is the action of God, disturbed but not broken by that episode, which is now consummated. He therefore fulfils and reveals the original and basic will of God, the first act of God, His original covenant with man. It is of this, the presupposition of the atonement, that we must first speak.

What is revealed in the work of atonement in Jesus Christ, as its presuppos-ition, is that God does not at first occupy a position of neutrality in relation to man. He is not simply distant from him and high above him. He is not merely God in His own divine sphere allowing man to be man in his sphere. He does not merely know about him and view him as a spectator. This is excluded from the outset by the fact that He is the living Creator and Lord of man, and therefore the One who actively guarantees and accompanies and controls his existence. This might, of course, imply a certain neutrality, for He is the Creator and Lord of heaven and earth and all creatures, the living One who preserves and accompanies and controls them all, so that He is for man only what He is for all other things. But in becoming man for the sake of man in the work of atonement, He reveals an attitude and purpose in respect of man which goes beyond His attitude and purpose as Creator and Lord in respect of all things. He is disposed towards man in a special way which could not be said of any other creature, and which is not only that of the Creator and Lord of man. He remains his Creator and Lord. With all other creatures, and in a special way amongst other creatures, He lavishes upon him all the riches of His goodness as Creator—why should we not say, of His grace as Creator? He gives and preserves to this human creature his human life in all the plenitude and with all the limitations of its particular possibilities. He is to him a faithful and watchful Father. He does not leave him without counsel and commandment. But that is not all. And all that, His general acting and working and speaking as Creator, has in relation to man a particular meaning and purpose: not only because it has to do with the particular creature which is man, but because from the very first His relationship with this creature is of itself a particular one and has a particular goal. The fatherly faithfulness and provision shown to him by God has a different meaning and purpose from that which is undoubtedly exercised in respect of other creatures. And so, too, the counsels and commandments which are given him by the Creator have a different meaning and purpose from the ordinances under which all other creatures undoubtedly have their being according to His will.

What God does to man and for man even as Creator has its origin in the fact that among all the creatures. He has linked and bound and pledged Himself originally to man, choosing and determining and making Himself the God of [038] man. The distinguishing mark of Israel is the fact that there is said to Israel and heard by Israel that which at the end of the history of Israel becomes an event in Jesus Christ: "I will be your God and ye shall be my people." And this is a revelation of the divine choice and decision, the divine word and the divine act, in which, in and with creation, it became truth and actuality that God made Himself the God of man: that in willing man God willed to be God for him, with him, in relation to him, acting for him, concerned with him, for his sake. God: and therefore nothing other than what He was and is and always will be in Himself as Father, Son and Holy Spirit; and all that, not for Himself alone, but for man, in his favour, in a true and actual interest in his existence, with a view to what he is to become, and therefore in a participation in what he is and lives and does and experiences; just that, nothing more but also nothing less, in fellowship with man. "I will be your God": that is the original emergence of God from any neutrality, but also His emergence from what is certainly a gracious being and working as Creator and Lord in relation to man.

That is more than the creation, more than the preservation, accompaniment and over-ruling of His creatures. That is the covenant of God with man, from which He has bound and pledged Himself always to begin, and in virtue of which He has constituted Himself his God.

And that is the presupposition of the atonement as revealed in its actualisation in Jesus Christ: the presupposition whose consequences are deduced in the atonement; the presupposition which in the atonement is fulfilled in spite of the opposition of man. We do not postulate it. We do not grope for it in the void. We find it in that which has actually taken place in Jesus Christ. But we cannot refuse to find it in that which has actually taken place in Jesus Christ. If the final thing is true, that in Him God has become man for us men, then we cannot escape the first thing, that it is the original will of God active already in and with creation that He should be God for us men. If for us men God Himself has become man, we can, we must look into the heart of God—He Himself has opened His heart to us—to accept His saying as a first as well as a final saying: "I will be your God." We cannot, therefore, think of Him except as the One who has concluded and set up this covenant with us. We would be mistaking Him, we would obviously be making ourselves guilty of transgression, of sin, if we were to try to think of Him otherwise, if we were to try to reckon with another God, if we were to try to know and fear and love any other God but Him—the One who from the very first, from the creation of heaven and earth, has made Himself the covenant God of man, our covenant God. For according to the Word which He Himself has spoken in His supreme and final work, there is no other God.

All other gods, all gods which are hostile to man, are false gods. Even though we bring the deepest reverence or the highest love, even though we bring the greatest zeal or sincerity, if they are offered to other gods. to gods that are [039] hostile to man, we are simply beating the air, where there is no God, where God is not God. "I will be your God": not only for Israel, but, according to the revelation accomplished in Jesus Christ at the end of the history of Israel, for all men of all times and places, this was and is the critical point of all faith in God and knowledge of God and service of God. This God, or none at all. Faith in this God, the knowledge and service of this God, or godlessness. He Himself has decided this in revealing Himself as the One who was and is and is to come—God for us, our God, the God who has concluded and set up the covenant.

It is simply a matter of analysis when we go on to say that the covenant is a covenant of grace. This concept implies three things.

The first is the freedom in which it is determined and established by God, and therefore the undeservedness with which man can receive and respond to the fact that God has chosen and determined and made Himself his God. In the atonement in which the presupposition is revealed, "I will be your God," this is clear beyond any possible doubt. By his transgression man has prevented God from affirming it and holding any further fellowship with him. Man is not

35

in a position to atone for his transgression, to reconcile himself with God. Man cannot bring forward a Jesus Christ in which his atonement with God can take place. If it is to take place, it must be from God, in the freedom of God and not of man, in the freedom of the grace of God, to which we have no claim, which would necessarily judge and condemn us, because we have sinned against it and always will sin against it, because we have shown ourselves unworthy of it. Atonement is free grace. Even the fact that God wills to be our God and to act and speak with us as such is free grace on God's side and something entirely undeserved on ours. We have only to think—God for us men, God in His majesty, God the Father, Son and Holy Spirit, God in all the fulness of His divine being, God in His holiness, power, wisdom, eternity and glory, God, who is completely self-sufficient, who does not need a fellow in order to be love, or a companion in order to be complete: God for us men. If that is what He is, if that is what He is as the true and real and living and only God—as the One who Himself willed to become man, and in so doing proved and revealed that He cares for man, and that He does so originally and properly and intensely, if He is this God, the *Deus pro nobis*[EN24], the covenant-God, then He is so, not as limited and conditioned by our freedom, but in the exalted freedom of His grace. That is what free grace, the overflowing of His love, was and is, that He willed to be our Creator and Lord, and how much more the One who says: "I will be your God." Why among all creatures does He will to be our God? Why the God of man? Because of the peculiarities and qualities of human creatureliness? But other creatures have theirs too, and how are we to say that

[040]   those of men are greater? And even if they were, it would by no means follow that man would have a claim that God must be God for man, that He should enter into covenant with us, that there should be this divine Yes originally addressed only to us. The covenant of God with man is a fact which, since it is a fact according to His revelation in Jesus Christ, we cannot deny as such. But according to the prophetic warnings God entered into covenant with other peoples as well as Israel. Why then (if He willed to contract such a relationship with creatures at all) should He not also have done so with some quite different creature as well? Why not to His greater honour with some creature which is supposed to be or actually is lower or more lowly? The fact of the covenant of God with man is obviously a fact of His free choice, the choice of His grace. There is no complementary claim of man to such a distinction. We can only accept and affirm this choice as true and actual. We can only cling to it as a fact which He has chosen and posited. We can only recognise and honour it as completely undeserved. That is the first sense in which we have to say that the covenant as the presupposition of all God does and says in relation to us men is a covenant of grace.

The second thing implied in the concept is the beneficent character proper to this presupposition of the atonement. Positively, grace means the giving of

---

[EN24] God for us

something good and redemptive and helpful. Grace is a powerful Yes spoken to the one to whom it is addressed. This, too, can be perceived at once in the atonement in which it is revealed. Atonement means the redemption of man, the fact that he is prevented from falling into the abyss into which he ought to fall as a transgressor, as the one who has interrupted the divine purpose, as the enemy of grace. And consisting as it does in the fellowship of temporal man with Jesus Christ and therefore with God, it means further that he is placed in the certain expectation of eternal salvation, which has become a temporal present and a living promise in Jesus Christ. But in this sense, too, it is simply a matter of grace to grace. For the divine benefit is simply the first thing in consequence of which the second took place. We think again—God for us men. God who in His triune being, in the fulness of His Godhead, is Himself the essence of all favour, the source and stream and sea of everything that is good, of all light and life and joy. To say God is to say eternal benefit. Now the work of His creation, and His control as the One who preserves and accompanies and rules the creature and therefore man, is certainly a favour out of His fulness. But in the covenant with man, as his God, He does not merely give out of His fulness. In His fulness He gives Himself to be with man and for man. As the benefit which He is in Himself, He makes Himself the companion of man. He does not merely give him something, however great. He gives Himself, and in so doing gives him all things. It is only of God that what man comes to experience in covenant with Him is favour. It is not always so, not by a long [041] way in all the supposed or actual experience of man. Even in his experience of what comes to him from God, man can be blind or half-blind, and can therefore make mistakes, and can find terror and destruction in what God has allotted and given as a supreme benefit. And necessarily the benefit offered him by God can in fact and objectively become terror and destruction if he flees from God and opposes Him. Even the divine favour will then take on the aspect of wrath. God's Yes will then become a No and His grace judgment. The light itself will blind him and plunge him in darkness. Life will be to him death. But this does not mean that God will not keep His covenant, or that this will cease to be the covenant of grace, or that its meaning and purpose will cease to be the favour shown to man. How can Yahweh cease to be salvation? What it does mean is that in certain situations of its execution and history the true character must be hidden under another form—which may later be put off and (whether it is recognised by man or not, or properly recognised or not) give place again to its true form. In this form, in itself, by virtue of its meaning and purpose, and just as surely as that God is always sovereign in it, the covenant is always a relationship in which there is the conferring and receiving of a benefit, not the opposite, not a relationship of wrath and perdition, not even when it does (necessarily) appear to men like that (as it did to Job), not even when the merciful but just and holy God Himself can and will maintain and execute it in that other form (as He did so often in the history of Israel). In this positive sense, too, in its proper form and by virtue of its origin it is always the covenant of grace.

The third thing which we maintain when we describe the covenant as the covenant of grace is that the covenant engages man as the partner of God only, but actually and necessarily, to gratitude. On the side of God it is only a matter of free grace and this in the form of benefit. For the other partner in the covenant to whom God turns in this grace, the only proper thing, but the thing which is unconditionally and inescapably demanded, is that he should be thankful. How can anything more or different be asked of man? The only answer to χάρις EN25 is εὐχαριστία EN26. But how can it be doubted for a moment that this is in fact asked of him? χάρις EN27 always demands the answer of εὐχαριστία EN28. Grace and gratitude belong together like heaven and earth. Grace evokes gratitude like the voice an echo. Gratitude follows grace like thunder lightning. Not by virtue of any necessity of the concepts as such. But we are speaking of the grace of the God who is God for man, and of the gratitude of man as his response to this grace. Here, at any rate, the two belong together, so that only gratitude can correspond to grace, and this correspondence cannot fail. Its failure, ingratitude, is sin, transgression. Radically and basically all sin is simply ingratitude—man's refusal of the one but necessary thing which is proper to and is required of him with whom God has graciously entered into covenant. As far as man is concerned there can be no question of anything but gratitude; but gratitude is the complement which man must necessarily fulfil.

[042]

This leads us to a further point which is revealed in the atoning work accomplished in Jesus Christ, and as the presupposition of that work, that man cannot first be neutral towards God. Man is not simply distant from God and far beneath Him. He cannot let Him be God in His sphere in order in his own sphere to try to be man *in abstracto* and on his own account. He cannot simply know about God, or believe "in a God." We may say that such neutrality is excluded already by the fact that man is the living creature of God, and that as such in all his movements—whether he knows it or not—he is thrown back entirely upon God, he is dependent upon Him and bound up with Him. But there is more to it than that, for he is bound to all other creatures in that way, and all other creatures are similarly bound. When God Himself becomes man for men in the work of atonement, then quite apart from the general and in a sense external being of men under and with God this means that as creatures preserved, accompanied and over-ruled by God men have a character, we can call it a *character indelibilis* EN29, which transcends their creatureliness as such. When God reveals in Jesus Christ that from the very first He willed to be God

EN25 grace
EN26 gratitude
EN27 grace
EN28 gratitude
EN29 ineradicable character

for man, the God of man, He also reveals that from the very first man is His man, man belongs to Him, is bound and pledged to Him. The man for whose sake God Himself became man cannot be basically neutral. He can only be a partner in His activity. For as in Jesus Christ there breaks out as truth the original thing about God: "I will be your God," so in Jesus Christ there breaks out as truth the original thing about man, "Ye shall be my people." That was and is the distinctive mark of Israel, which at the end of the history of Israel became event in Jesus Christ and in that event is revelation, the divine revelation of the destiny of man, of all men, as their determination for Him. According to this revelation, from the very first God was and is God for man, inclined to him, caring for him, his God. But so, too, according to this revelation of God from the very first man was and is man for God, subordinated and referred to Him. "Ye shall be my people" means that it is proper to you and required of you in your being, life and activity to correspond to the fact that in My being, life and activity for you I am your God.

And if the essence of God as the God of man is His grace, then the essence of men as His people, that which is proper to and demanded of them in covenant with God, is simply their thanks. But this is actually and necessarily proper to and demanded of them. Thanks is the one all-embracing, but as such valid and inescapable, content of the law of the covenant imposed upon man. It is the one and necessary thing which has to take place on the part of man. All the laws of Israel and all the concrete demands addressed by God to individual [043] men in Israel are simply developments and specific forms of this one law, demands not to withhold from the God of the covenant the thanks which is His due, but to render it with a whole heart. The grace of God calls for this modest but active return. It is for this reason and on this basis that in the Old Testament even the detailed commands are always urged so forcefully and earnestly and emphatically, that which God wills of man being unconditionally pressed irrespective of the apparent greatness or littleness of the thing which is demanded. What is divinely required in the Old Testament has this irresistible force, the force of an either-or, which is a matter of life and death, because the thanks is demanded which cannot possibly fail to follow grace. Obedience to the commands of other gods, false gods, is usually a matter of the free inclination and judgment of man. But where the One who commands is the *Deus pro nobis*[EN30], obedience is not something which is in our hands, but the self-evident human complement and response. It is only here in the existence of man in the covenant which as such is the covenant of grace that we see the true horror of disobedience, of sin. That he should be thankful is the righteousness which is demanded of him before God. And if he is not thankful, that is his unrighteousness.

This is the basic determination of the relationship between God and man which is revealed as applicable to all men from the very first in the atonement

---

[EN30] God for us

which took place in Jesus Christ and in which the history of Israel attained its goal. This is the last thing which is revealed as the first thing for man too. When (in Jesus Christ) we look into the heart of God—for in Him He has revealed to us: "I will be your God"—we are permitted, indeed we are constrained, to look at ourselves, that what is proper to and is required of us is: "Ye shall be my people." As God is gracious to us, we may—and this "may" is the seriousness and force of every "ought"—on that account be thankful. By deciding for us God has decided concerning us. We are therefore prevented from thinking otherwise about ourselves, from seeing or understanding or explaining man in any other way, than as the being engaged and covenanted to God, and therefore simply but strictly engaged and covenanted to thanks. Just as there is no God but the God of the covenant, there is no man but the man of the covenant: the man who as such is destined and called to give thanks. And it is again transgression, sin, if even for a moment we ignore this man who is true man, trying to imagine and construct a man in himself, and to regard his destiny to give thanks to God as something which is in his own power, a matter of his own freedom of choice. The real freedom of man is decided by the fact that God is his God. In freedom he can only choose to be the man of God, i.e., to be thankful to God. With any other choice he would simply be groping in the void, betraying and destroying his true humanity. Instead of choosing in freedom, he would be choosing enslavement. By revealing Himself in Jesus Christ as from the very first the gracious God, God has decided that man can only be grateful man, the man who takes up and maintains his place in the covenant with Him, the gracious God.

[044]

It can only be by way of analysis and emphasis that we maintain that grace is not only the basis and essence, the ontological substance of the original relationship between God and man which we have described as the covenant between them willed and instituted and controlled by God. The recognition of this original covenant is also grace and therefore a free divine favour. We have described the covenant as from every point of view the presupposition of the atonement which is revealed and therefore can be recognised only in the atonement. We now need to emphasise: only in the atonement, and therefore only in Jesus Christ. Concerning the covenant fulfilled as God became man in Jesus Christ, concerning the covenant will of God executed and accomplished in Jesus Christ, concerning God's institution of the covenant as the first and basic divine act continued and completed in the action fulfilled in Jesus Christ—concerning all these things we have no other source of knowledge than through the One who is the one Word of God "whom we must hear, and trust and obey in life and in death." In all that we have said about the original place and status of God and man in their relationship one with another, we have tried never to look past Jesus Christ, but always to consider it as seen through Him and with a steadfast regard fixed on Him, "as it was in the beginning."

2. *The Covenant as the Presupposition of Reconciliation*

We have tried to make the movement to which we are summoned by the fact that in the New Testament we are told both directly (e.g., Jn. 1³ ¹⁰; Col. 1¹⁶; Heb. 1³) and also indirectly that the creation of God took place in Him, i.e., that it was willed and planned and completed with a view to Him as the *telos* of all things and all events, and that He is "the first-born of all creation" (Col. 1¹⁵). We have tried to paraphrase and give the sense of Eph. 1⁴⁻⁶: "According as he hath chosen us in him before the foundation of the world (πρὸ καταβολῆς κόσμου), that we should be holy and without blame before him in love: having predestinated us (προορίσας ἡμᾶς) unto the adoption of children by Jesus Christ to himself, according to the good pleasure of his will, to the praise of the glory of his grace." We have understood the atonement as "predestinated according to the purpose (κατὰ πρόθεσιν) of him who worketh all things according to the counsel of his own will" (Eph. 1¹¹), as accomplished "according to the eternal purpose (κατὰ πρόθεσιν τῶν αἰώνων) which he purposed (or: already fulfilled as such? ἣν ἐποίησεν EN31) in Christ Jesus our Lord" (Eph. 3¹¹).

From that which in Jesus Christ took place in time according to the will of God we have tried to gather what was and is and will be the will of God at the beginning of all time, and in relation to the whole content of time. By the perception of grace at the end of the ways of God we have been led to the perception of grace at their beginning, as the presupposition of all His ways, We are certainly not in any position, nor are we constrained, to recognise this [045] presupposition of all the ways of God, and finally of the atonement accomplished in Jesus Christ, as the covenant of grace, if we look to any other source, if we follow any other supposed Word of God than that which is spoken in Jesus Christ and in His work. When we spoke of the original and basic will of God, of His "first act" fulfilled in and with creation but transcending creation, we did not speak of an "original revelation" which we must differentiate from Jesus Christ because it is in fact different from Him. We did not speak in the light of the results of any self-knowledge or self-estimate of human reason or existence. We did not speak with reference to any observations and conclusions in respect of the laws and ordinances which rule in nature and human history. We certainly did not speak in relation to any religious disposition which is supposed to be or actually is proper to man. There is only one revelation. That revelation is the revelation of the covenant, of the original and basic will of God. How else could this be revealed to us? The concept of an "original revelation" which must be differentiated from the revelation in Jesus Christ because it is actually different from it is a purely empty concept, or one that can be filled only by illusions.

In a word, the covenant of grace which is from the beginning, the presupposition of the atonement, is not a discovery and conclusion of "natural theology." Apart from and without Jesus Christ we can say nothing at all about God and man and their relationship one with another. Least of all can we say that their relationship can be presupposed as that of a covenant of grace. Just because it is a covenant of grace, it cannot be discovered by man, nor can it be demonstrated by man. As the covenant of grace it is not amenable to any kind

---

EN31 which he made

41

of human reflection or to any questions asked by man concerning the meaning and basis of the cosmos or history. Grace is inaccessible to us: how else can it be grace? Grace can only make itself accessible. Grace can never be recalled. To remember grace is itself the work of grace. The perception of grace is itself grace. Therefore if the covenant of grace is the first thing which we have to recognise and say about God and man in their relationship one with another, it is something which we can see only as it makes itself to be seen, only as it fulfils itself—which is what happened in Jesus Christ—and therefore reveals itself as true and actual. From all eternity God elected and determined that He Himself would become man for us men. From all eternity He determined that men would be those for whom He is God: His fellow-men. In willing this, in willing Jesus Christ, He wills to be our God and He wills that we should be His people. Ontologically, therefore, the covenant of grace is already included and grounded in Jesus Christ, in the human form and human content which God willed to give His Word from all eternity. The order of cognition cannot be [046] disobedient to, but must follow, the actual order of things. If we are to know God and man and their basic and unalterable relationship one with the other, we have to hear the Word of God only in the form and with the content which God Himself has given to it, and by which He willed to lay down His own place and status, and ours, from the very first. It is only by this Word, which is Jesus Christ, and which is itself in this form and with this content the basis and meaning of the covenant, that we can learn about the covenant. This Word is not only the basis and meaning of the covenant. As a revealed Word it is also the instruction concerning it which we have to receive.

What is involved in this knowledge of the covenant, the covenant of grace which is the presupposition of the atonement fulfilled and revealed in the atonement? It is important that we should be clear about this point. For we are not in fact dealing with a theologoumenon which is no doubt permissible and may be introduced in passing, but which is in any event dispensable and may in the last resort be regarded as superfluous.

In this knowledge or recognition we make the right distinction between the atonement accomplished in Jesus Christ, which is the centre and the proper subject of the Christian message and the Christian faith, and all events which are purely contingent, which have only a relative significance, which concern certain men but not all men, which may not even be necessary *rebus aliter stantibus*[EN32]. Or, to put it positively, in this recognition we make a proper acknowledgment of the unconditional, eternal and divine validity and scope of the atonement accomplished in Jesus Christ, of the general and inescapable and definitive claim of that which took place in it. It is in this recognition that we are committed to a genuine regard for this centre of the Christian message and the Christian faith. Without it we cannot attain to the joy or certainty or freedom to which we are summoned by this event.

[EN32] under different circumstances

The atonement accomplished in Jesus Christ is God's retort to the sin of man and its consequences. And the sin of man is an episode. It is the original of all episodes, the essence of everything that is unnecessary, disorderly, contrary to plan and purpose. It has not escaped the knowledge and control of God. But it is not a work of His creation and not a disposition of His providence. It really comes about and is only as that which God did not will and does not will and never will will. It has its being only in the fact that it is non-being, that which from the point of view of God is unintelligible and intolerable. It takes place only as the powerful but, of course, before God absolutely powerless irruption of that which is not into the fulfilment of His will. It takes place, therefore, only under the original, radical, definitive and therefore finally triumphant No of God. It is not a limitation of His positive will. Rather it exists as it is completely conditioned by His non-will. It is alive and active in all its fearfulness only on the left hand of God.

But the atonement accomplished in Jesus Christ, like creation and the provi- [047] dential rule of God, is a work on the right hand of God, a work of His positive will. It is so in the highest possible sense, in a way which gives it priority and precedence over creation and providence. In Jesus Christ God comes to grips with that episode. Jesus Christ is in fact God's retort to the sin of man. This does not mean even remotely that it, too, is only an episode. Even from the point of view of God's antithesis to the sin of man, what took place in it is rather the execution, that is, the sealing and revelation, the original fact of the positive will of God in His relationship with man, and therefore of His whole will in creation and preservation. It is not simply to combat the interruption of that will, it is not merely to assert and purify polemically and yet also irenically His relationship with man, and therefore with the whole world as it was created by Him, in face of the breaking out and in of human sin, that God willed to become man and did in fact do so. He willed to do it and did it first and foremost for this positive end, to give concrete reality and actuality to the promise "I will be your God" and the command "Ye shall be my people" within the human race which could not say this of itself, but was to hear it as His Word and to live by this Word to His glory. He willed to do it and did it in order to fulfil both the promise and the command in divine truth and power, in order not only to make it possible for us men to receive them, but actually to make them heard by us (in an act which is at once one of utter condescension and supreme majesty), in order to set them amongst us and therefore to make them effective for us. What takes place in Jesus Christ, in the historical event of the atonement accomplished by Him in time, is not simply one history amongst others and not simply the reaction of God against human sin. It stands at the heart of the Christian message and the Christian faith because here God maintains and fulfils His Word as it was spoken at the very first. He affirms to us and sets among us His original promise and His original command in the concrete reality and actuality of His own being as man. He maintains and fulfils it in His conflict with our sin, vindicating His own glory and accomplishing our salvation. But He maintains and fulfils it first and foremost in affirmation and execution of the original purpose of His relationship with us men: *propter nos homines*[EN33] and therefore *propter nostram salutem*[EN34] (*Nic. Const.*). The atonement in Jesus Christ takes place as a wrestling with and an overcoming of human sin. But at the same time and primarily it is the great act of God's faithfulness to Himself and therefore to us—His faithfulness in the execution of the plan and purpose which He had from the very first as the Creator of all things and the Lord of all events, and which He wills to accomplish in all circumstances. For this reason in Jesus Christ we are not merely dealing with one of many beings in the sphere of the created world and the world of men. He is this, too. Because He is this, because He is a being like us and with us, He enables us actually to hear the Word of God and the promise and commandment of God, and the execution of the divine purpose is fulfilled for us and as such revealed to us. As such He is born in time, at His own time. But in Jesus Christ we are not merely dealing with the author of our justification and sanctification as the sinners that we are. We are not merely dealing with the One who has saved us from death, with the Lord and Head of His Church. As such, as the One who fulfils this divine work in the world, which would be lost without Him, He is born in time, at His own time. But at the same time and beyond all that—and the power of His saving work as the Mediator is rooted and grounded in this—He is "the first-born of all creation" (Col. 1^{16})—the first and eternal Word of God delivered and fulfilled in time. As very God and very man He is the concrete reality and actuality of the divine command and the divine promise, the content of the will of God which exists prior to its fulfilment, the basis of the whole project and actualisation of creation and the whole process of divine providence from which all created being and becoming derives. Certainly the sin of man contradicts this first and eternal Word of God. But in the first and eternal Word of God the sin of man is already met, refuted and removed from all eternity. And in delivering and fulfilling this first and eternal Word in spite of human sin and its consequences, as He would in fact have delivered and fulfilled it quite apart from human sin, sin is also met, refuted and removed in time.

In this sense the atonement accomplished in Jesus Christ is a necessary happening. This is its unconditional validity and scope and binding force. This is why it commands the reverence due to it as the heart of the Christian message (a reverence which is the basis of all the joy and certainty and freedom of faith). For in Jesus Christ we do not have to do with a second, and subsequent, but with the first and original content of the will of God, before and above which there is no other will—either hidden or revealed in some other way—in the light of which we might have to understand and fear and love God and interpret man very differently from how they are both represented in Jesus

[048]

[EN33] for us men
[EN34] for our salvation

Christ. We do not need to look beyond Jesus Christ. We do not need to consider whether it may be obligatory or legitimate to look beyond Him. When we look at Him we have all conceivable clarity and certainty. We only need to look at Him. We only need to hear the word of His historical existence and we shall hear the Word of God and look into the basis and essence of God and man and all things. The covenant between God and man, the promise and command of God, which Jesus Christ announces to us as their unity, is therefore the final thing to which we can and should and must cling, because Jesus Christ as their unity is also the first thing, because the covenant is by promise and command- ment eternally grounded in Him, in the unity of God and man accomplished in Him. The recognition that this covenant is the presupposition of the atone-   [049] ment is therefore nothing more or less than a recognition of the sure basis of the Christian message and the Christian faith. Quite apart from the fact that it is true and necessary in itself, it would be quite out of place to ignore it.

In this recognition it is a matter of the basis of a right distinction, a right acknowledgment and a right regard for the act of atonement. Therefore once again—and from two angles—we must be quite clear with what we have to do in the presupposition which it confirms and reveals. It consists in this, that Jesus Christ, very God and very man, born and living and acting and suffering and conquering in time, is as such the one eternal Word of God at the begin- ning of all things.

This means at once that as the beginning of all things the presupposition of the atonement is a single, self-sufficient, independent free work of God in itself, which is not identical with the divine work in creation or with the divine creative will realised in this work. The achievement of atonement and there- fore the historical actuality of Jesus Christ is not the highest evolutionary con- tinuation, the crown and completion of the positing which God has willed and accomplished of a reality of the world and man which is distinct from Himself. It is not the immanent *telos* of such a reality.

Here again we part company with Schleiermacher. To do him justice, he was in his own way concerned about the eternal basis and necessity of the appearance of Jesus Christ and therefore of the atonement as the overcoming of human sin. But this was how he conceived of the connexion and made the required reference and regress to the beginning of all things. The fulfilling of time in Jesus Christ meant for him that at the end of their historical development man, and in man finite being as such, attained in Jesus Christ that form to which they had always been potentially inclined and endowed in the relationship of com- plete dependence on God as infinite being. God's eternal will is done in Jesus Christ in such a way that in Him—in the undisturbed unity of His man-consciousness with His God- consciousness—man attains to the perfection ordained and necessary to him as man.

In this conception (as so often in Schleiermacher) there is a strange mixture of truth and error. Truth, because the New Testament itself indicates quite clearly, in the light of what is revealed in Jesus Christ, that we cannot understand too intimately or emphasise too strongly the relationship of the being of man and the world in their creatureliness with the being of Jesus Christ. Error, because everything is plainly topsy-turvy if we picture this relationship in such a way that the being of Jesus Christ is deduced and interpreted from the being of man

45

and the world instead of the other way round, if we derive the atonement from creation instead of creation from the atonement, if we describe as the first and eternal Word of God that which we think we can recognise, i.e., postulate and maintain as the final word on the evolutionary process of finite being and development. No ideas or pronouncements on a supposedly attainable or attained *telos* of the immanent development of creaturely being can do justice to the *telos*, and therefore the beginning, revealed in Jesus Christ. We cannot overlook the fact that in relation to Jesus Christ the New Testament speaks of a new creation (Gal. 6[15]; 2 Cor. 5[17]), of a new man created by God (Eph. 4[24]), not of a continuation of man but of a "new birth" (Jn. 3[3]), and indeed of a new heaven and a new earth (Rev. 21[1]; 2 Pet. 3[13]). And Jesus Christ is not regarded as the fulfilment and highest form of the first Adam, but in sharp antithesis He is described as the last Adam ("The first man is of the earth, earthy, the second man is the Lord from heaven," 1 Cor. 15[44f.]).

[050]

The right distinction of the atonement from every purely contingent event, the right acknowledgment of its validity and scope, the right regard for that which God has said and done in it, and therefore the right recognition of the covenant which is its presupposition and which is revealed in it, the right recognition, then, of the sure basis of the Christian message and Christian faith— all these things depend on the insight that in Jesus Christ we really have to do with the first and eternal Word of God at the beginning of all things. With the beginning of all things in God, in His will and purpose and resolve, which does not follow or derive from but underlies and precedes all that reality which is distinct from Himself, the existence and history of the world and man, and therefore creation. Jesus Christ is in truth the first, i.e., the content and subject of that first divine will and purpose and resolve which underlies the beginning of the creaturely world and is therefore superior to it. This is what makes Him so new in relation to all that precedes Him in the creaturely world. He is the other, the second and last Adam as opposed to the first, just because He was before him. This is what marks Him out and distinguishes Him from Adam and from everything else that is, happens, becomes, comes and goes before and after and beside Him. He cannot, therefore, be deduced from that which is other than Himself, from that which was before Him. He is not a product— not even the most perfect—of the created world as such. He is in it. He belongs to it. He exists and works and reveals Himself in its history. But He does not derive from it: it derives from Him. He is in it but He is also quite different from it. He stands over against it as the One who was from the beginning—its beginning—with God. He is the content and form of the divine thought of grace, will of grace and decree of grace in relation to the created world, before the created world was. He is the One for whose sake God willed it and created it. He is the meaning and purpose which it has because God willed to give it to it and did in fact give it to it. The creation, too, and the preservation and direction of the world and man, must be described as pure acts of divine grace. But even here we must think strictly of Jesus Christ in whom these acts had and have their meaning and purpose. The existence and work of Jesus Christ do not follow from the gracious act of creation or the gracious act of divine providence. It is for the sake of Jesus Christ that creation takes place and

46

God rules as the preserver and controller of world-events. These things are all acts of divine grace only because they take place for His sake.

For in Jesus Christ we have to do with something that is new and special in relation to creation as such—the fact that God has elected and determined Himself as the fellow and friend of man, and elected and determined man as His own friend and fellow. This is the divine thought of grace and will of grace and decree of grace in relation to the world before the world was. This is the meaning and purpose which He had in creating it. How can this derive from the world itself? How can it be its product or *telos*? How can it be deduced from it or explained by it? Man has his real being in the fact that his existence was willed and is actual in this meaning and purpose. Man is—and he is what he is as the creature of God and by divine providence—only as and because, before he himself was, there was in the will and purpose and decree of God this grace towards him. He is in virtue of this eternal Word of God, which is free in relation to himself and the whole world, which has already made disposition concerning himself and the whole world. He is in virtue of the covenant already concluded with God. This is the presupposition of the atonement revealed in it and fulfilled in history by the fact that God became man. But this covenant of God with man is grace. It is not given in and with the nature of the creature. It is not the product or goal of that nature, although that nature itself is from God. God did not and does not owe it to the creature, not even to man, to elect and determine Himself for him, and him for Himself, to will and posit his existence and essence according to this meaning and purpose. Man has no right or claim as man—because he is created man for this purpose—to stand in covenant with God. The fact that he is created for it is something beyond the grace of his created nature. It is the free covenant grace of God which is especially for him. He can perceive and accept it only in the first eternal Word of God as spoken to him in the atonement accomplished in time, in Jesus Christ. It is not in an act of spontaneous self-knowledge, but in the hearing of this first and eternal Word of God, that he can know that he does actually stand on this ground, that he is actually placed in this sphere and atmosphere, in the sphere of the covenant as the being with whom God has associated Himself and whom God has associated with Himself. But that this grace is truth, the first and final truth behind which there is concealed no other or different truth, that he can be and live absolutely by this truth, is something which he can and must perceive and accept in the first and eternal Word of God as it is spoken to him in time. This is the presupposition of the atonement revealed in the atonement. And in the recognition of this presupposition he comes to a right distinction, acknowledgment and regard.

But we must now add, or emphasise and underline a second point. The first and eternal Word of God, which underlies and precedes the creative will and work as the beginning of all things in God, means in fact Jesus Christ. It is identical with the One who, very God and very man, born and living and acting and suffering and conquering in time, accomplishes the atonement. It is

[051]

He alone who is the content and form of the gracious thought and will and resolve of God in relation to the world and man before ever these were and as God willed and created them.

[052]

In this context we must not refer to the second "person" of the Trinity as such, to the eternal Son or the eternal Word of God *in abstracto*, and therefore to the so-called λόγος ἄσαρκος EN35. What is the point of a regress to Him as the supposed basis of the being and knowledge of all things? In any case, how can we make such a regress? The second "person" of the Godhead in Himself and as such is not God the Reconciler. In Himself and as such He is not revealed to us. In Himself and as such He is not *Deus pro nobis* EN36, either ontologically or epistemologically. He is the content of a necessary and important concept in trinitarian doctrine when we have to understand the revelation and dealings of God in the light of their free basis in the inner being and essence of God. But since we are now concerned with the revelation and dealings of God, and particularly with the atonement, with the person and work of the Mediator, it is pointless, as it is impermissible, to return to the inner being and essence of God and especially to the second person of the Trinity as such, in such a way that we ascribe to this person another form than that which God Himself has given in willing to reveal Himself and to act outwards. If it is true that God became man, then in this we have to recognise and respect His eternal will and purpose and resolve—His free and gracious will which He did not owe it either to Himself or to the world to have, by which He did not need to come to the decision to which He has in fact come, and behind which, in these circumstances, we cannot go, behind which we do not have to reckon with any Son of God in Himself, with any λόγος ἄσαρκος EN37, with any other Word of God than that which was made flesh. According to the free and gracious will of God the eternal Son of God is Jesus Christ as He lived and died and rose again in time, and none other. He is the decision of God in time, and yet according to what took place in time the decision which was made from all eternity. This decision was made freely and graciously and undeservedly in an overflowing of the divine goodness. Yet—for us to whom it refers and for whose sake it was taken—it was also made bindingly, inescapably and irrevocably. We cannot, therefore, go back on it. We must not ignore it and imagine a "Logos in itself" which does not have this content and form, which is the eternal Word of God without this form and content. We could only imagine such a Logos. Like Godhead abstracted from its revelation and acts, it would necessarily be an empty concept which we would then, of course, feel obliged to fill with all kinds of contents of our own arbitrary invention. Under the title of a λόγος ἄσαρκος EN38 we pay homage to a *Deus absconditus* EN39 and therefore to some image of God which we have made for ourselves. And if we were to deal with a figure of this kind, we should be dangerously susceptible to the temptation, indeed we could hardly escape it, of asking whether the revelation and activity of this "Logos in itself" can altogether and always be confined to this phenomenon, the incarnation in Jesus Christ. If this is not as such the content of the eternal will of God, if Jesus Christ is not the one Word of God from all eternity, why are we not free, or even perhaps obliged, to reckon with other manifestations of the eternal Word of God, and to look at Him in the light of such manifestations? But how can we really, as it were, bracket that which God has actually done and therefore willed in Jesus Christ, not taking it seriously as His eternal will, not holding to it as the beginning of all things which in His free grace God willed to posit and has in fact posited, to which therefore we must hold? How can

---

EN35 discarnate Word
EN36 God for us
EN37 discarnate Word
EN38 discarnate Word
EN39 hidden God

we look away past and beyond Him? Is it real faith and obedience which concerns itself with this regress to a pre-temporal being of the Word of God which is not His incarnate being, the being of the *Deus pro nobis*[EN40]? Is it real faith and obedience which tries to set itself on the throne of God and there to construct the content and form of His will and Word which He Himself has not chosen, although He might perhaps have chosen it? We are told that it is inconceivable that all men, "even those who lived thousands of years before Jesus," should have their being in the history of Jesus, that the history of human existence should derive from that of the man Jesus (Brunner, *ZThK*, 1951, 98). But is it so inconceivable, does it need such a great imagination to realise, is it not the simplest thing in the world, that if the history of Jesus is the event of atonement, if the atonement is real and effective because God Himself became man to be the subject of this event, if this is not concealed but revealed, if it is the factor which calls us irresistibly to faith and obedience, then how can it be otherwise than that in this factor, and therefore in the history of Jesus, we have to do with the reality which underlies and precedes all other reality as the first and eternal Word of God, that in this history we have actually to do with the ground and sphere, the atmosphere of the being of every man, whether they lived thousands of years before or after Jesus? Does not this question, this protest against the incarnate Word as the content of the eternal will of God, involve a retrogression even behind Schleiermacher, who with his doctrine of the fulfilment of creation accomplished in Jesus Christ could at least in his own way do justice to the necessary connexion between the totality of the human race and the particular history of Jesus? What is there to protest against if we simply accept that act of the greatest divine condescension and supreme divine majesty, the incarnation of His Word in Jesus Christ in the work of atonement, thus taking it in all earnest and not merely half in earnest. [053]

But if Jesus Christ is the content and form of the first and eternal Word of God, then that means further that the beginning of all things, of the being of all men and of the whole world, even the divine willing of creation, is preceded by God's covenant with man as its basis and purpose: His promise, in which He binds and pledges Himself to man, and His command by which He pledges and binds man to Himself. At the beginning of all things in God there is the Gospel and the Law, the gracious address of God and the gracious claim of God, both directed to man, both the one Word of the *Deus pro nobis*[EN41] who is the one God and beside whom there is no other. For Jesus Christ—not an empty *Logos*, but Jesus Christ the incarnate Word, the baby born in Bethlehem, the man put to death at Golgotha and raised again in the garden of Joseph of Arimathea, the man whose history this is—is the unity of the two. He is both at one and the same time. He is the promise and the command, the Gospel and the Law, the address of God to man and the claim of God upon man. That He is both as the Word of God spoken in His work, as the Word of God which has become work, is something which belongs to Himself as the eternal Son of God for Himself and prior to us. In this He is the pre-existent *Deus pro nobis*[EN42]. He alone is at once and altogether very God and very man. To that extent He alone is there at the beginning of all things. As the basis and purpose of the covenant He and He alone is the content of the eternal will of God

---

[EN40] God for us
[EN41] God for us
[EN42] God for us

which precedes the whole being of man and of the world. But that which He is for Himself and prior to us. He is with a view to us. He is, therefore, the concrete reality and actuality of the promise and command of God, the fulfilment of both, very God and very man, in one person amongst us, as a fellow-man.

[054] This first and eternal Word of God is not spoken in the void, but addressed to us. Therefore the event of the atonement is clearly His being for our sake, for our salvation, for the restoration of our relationship with God interrupted by sin. It is, therefore, this relationship with God, grounded on God's relationship with us, which in His person, that is so different and yet directed to us and in its humanity so near to us because perfectly identical with us, is revealed as the basis of the atonement and made effective for us—the pre-existent *Deus pro nobis*[EN43].

He and He alone is very God and very man in a temporal fulfilment of God's eternal will to be the true God of man and to let the man who belongs to Him become and be true man. Ultimately, therefore, Jesus Christ alone is the content of the eternal will of God, the eternal covenant between God and man. He is this as the Word of God to us and the work of God for us, and therefore in a way quite different from and not to be compared with anything we may become as hearers of this Word and those for whose sake this work is done. Yet in this difference, in the majesty with which He confronts us, but does confront us, He is the Word and work of the eternal covenant. In the truth and power of this eternal Word and work He speaks the Word and accomplishes the work of atonement in its temporal occurrence. And as we look at this Word and work, and trust in it and build upon it, we can be assured of the atonement which in it has been made in time. And since Jesus Christ is not only the subject but also the eternal and primary basis of this act of atonement, this act is definitively distinguished from all others. It demands our unconditional recognition. It lays claim to our regard. And we can have the certainty and the joy and the freedom of the faith that in spite of our sin and to take away our sin and all its consequences it has taken place once and for all. All this depends on a right recognition of the presupposition of the atonement in the counsel of God, and especially on the fact that we perceive and maintain the content and form of the eternal divine counsel exactly as it is fulfilled and revealed in time.

It is now time, and it will serve as an illustration of what we have just said, to consider a development in the history of theology to which we have so far only alluded. In the older Reformed Church there was a theology in which the concept of the covenant played so decisive a role that it came to be known as the Federal theology. It is usually connected with the name of John Coccejus (1603–1669, and Prof. in Bremen, Franeker and Leiden) in whose *Summa doctrinae de foedere et testamento Dei* (1648) it did indeed find classical and systematic form. But even before Coccejus the concept *foedus*[EN44] had with varying emphasis been given prominence in a variety of conceptions, expositions and applications by quite a

---

[EN43] God for us
[EN44] covenant

number of writers of whom only the best known will be mentioned. The immediate predecessors of Coccejus were his own teachers, the theologians of the Herborn school (with whom we must also reckon the then Count John the Elder of Nassau-Dillenburg): Matthias Martini, Ludwig Crocius, W. Amesius, J. Cloppenburg. But these in turn were preceded by the Basel writers Polanus and Wolleb and the Dutch Gomarus, and we can then work back to Z. Ursinus (who was not uninfluenced by Melanchthon) and K. Olevian in Heidelberg, Andreas Hyperius in Marburg, Wolfgang Musculus in Berne, P. Boquin in France, Stephan [055] Szegedin in Hungary, and ultimately the Reformers themselves, Zwingli, Bullinger and Calvin. And the Federal theology continued to develop even after Coccejus, making headway in spite of the opposition of the older aristotelian-scholastic schools. In Holland it made alliance with Cartesian philosophy and found well-equipped and independent champions in Abraham Heidan and Franz Burmann, also Heinrich Heidegger in Zurich. We can say indeed that in the second half of the 17th century it was the ruling orthodoxy of the Reformed Church. Certainly what H. Heppe in the 19th century represented as the theology of the Reformed Evangelical Church corresponds to it. It even had an influence on political and juridical theory in the person of J. Althusius, a jurist of the Herborn school which preceded Coccejus. The Bremen theologian, F. A. Lampe, then secured its acceptance amongst the Pietists, who developed and applied it in many different ways. At the beginning of the 18th century it also had an occasional influence amongst Lutherans, and if the Lutheran historian G. Schrenk is right (*Gottesreich und Bund im älteren Protestantismus*, 1923) the earlier form of the "redemption-history" school of Erlangen and especially J. C. K. von Hofmann would have been quite unthinkable without it, and indirectly it had a certain exemplary significance for the philosophy of history of German Idealism, and in this way even for the Marxist view of history. This is not the place for a historical or systematic exposition and estimate of a development which was certainly remarkable in its own way. But from the standpoint which we have ourselves reached we must make certain distinctions in relation to what was and was not said in the course of this doctrinal tradition of the older Reformed Church.

1. The Federal theology was an advance on mediaeval Scholasticism, and the Protestant Scholasticism which preceded and surrounded it, in that (true to the century of the *baroque*) it tried to understand the work and Word of God attested in Holy Scripture dynamically and not statically, as an event and not as a system of objective and self-contained truths. When we read Coccejus—even as compared with Polan, Wolleb and the Leidner Synopsis—we cannot escape the impression that the traditional dogmatics had started to move like a frozen stream of lava. The "Loci" are no longer "Loci," common places, to which this and that must be related either not at all or on the basis of a presupposed concept, as abstract doctrine and truth revealed in and for itself. They are now different stages in a series of events, the individual moments in a movement. This movement is now understood as such to be Christian truth, and Christian doctrine is the description of this movement. This theology is concerned with the bold review of a history of God and man which unfolds itself from creation to the day of judgment. In relation to the two partners it is concerned with the history of the covenant (a history which is naturally initiated and controlled and guided to its proper end by God)—or what in the 19th century came to be called the history of redemption. We find something of the living dynamic of this history in the famous chapters in which Calvin himself (*Instit.* II, 9–11) had tried to apprehend the relationship between the Old and the New Testament under the concept of the one covenant.

But the more embracing and central and exact this apprehension becomes in the main period of the Federal theology, the more insistently the question imposes itself from what standpoint this occurrence is really regarded and represented as such. What happens when the work, the Word of God, is first isolated and then reconnected, according to the teaching of pragmatic theology, with a whole series of events which are purposefully strung out but which belong together? Does this really correspond to the state of affairs as it is prescribed for theology in Scripture? Can we historicise the activity and revelation of God? The Federal theologians were the first really to try to do this in principle, just as they were the first to read [056] the Bible as a divinely inspired source-book by the study of which the attentive and faithful reader can gain an insight and perspective into the whole drama of the relationship between God and man, act by act, as by the help of some other source-book he might do in any other historical field. They saw excellently that the Bible tells us about an event. But they did not see that in all its forms this narrative has the character of testimony, proclamation, evangel, and that it has as its content and subject only a single event, which in every form of the attestation, although they all relate to a whole, is the single and complete decision on the part of God which as such calls for a single and complete decision on the part of man. They overlooked the fact that in all the forms of its attestation this single and complete event is a special event which has to be understood in a special way. Because of the difference of the attestation it cannot be broken up into a series of different covenant acts, or acts of redemption, which follow one another step by step, and then reassembled into a single whole. The Federal theologians did not notice that for all the exclusiveness with which they read the Scriptures, in this analysis and synthesis of the occurrence between God and man they were going beyond Scripture and missing its real content. If we think that we can handle the work and Word of God in this manner, then in our dynamic way we go beyond or fall short of Scripture and its content no less than did the older orthodoxy with its predominantly static terminology. As becomes increasingly plain in the sketches of the Federal theologians, the atonement accomplished in Jesus Christ ceases to be the history of the covenant, to which (in all the different forms of expectation and recollection) the whole Bible bears witness and in face of which theology must take up and maintain its standpoint, and it becomes a biblical history, a stage in the greater context of world-history, before which, and after which, there are other similar stages. In the case of the Federal theologians the standpoint directly in face of the witness to this one event changed its character and became a higher vantage-point from which they could see it together with all the other stages, from which they thought that they could and should make it their business to portray these stages in their variety and inter-relationship. They brought the whole under the concept of the covenant, but they did not read the concept out of this one event. Instead, they imported the concept into this one event like all the others, as the supposed essence of the varied occurrence at every stage. The Federal theology was a theological historicism to the extent that it did not allow itself to be bound to Scripture and confined to the event attested in Scripture in accordance with its reformation inheritance. And with its analysis and synthesis was it not more autonomous in relation to Scripture than it would admit to itself and gave impression to others—for it was here that what is still called "biblicism" had its origin? Could it be long before there would be a necessary demand for a wider outlook from that vantage-point, and a transition to a philosophy of general religious history, the perception and portrayal of a gradual "education of the human race"? It is clear that we cannot follow this theology even in its first and formal statement.

2. We will now look in a different direction. There was a very remarkable reason for the first introduction of the covenant concept by Zwingli (cf. G. Schrenk, *op. cit.* p. 36 f.). He used it purely and simply for the defence of infant baptism. The Anabaptists in Switzerland and elsewhere liked to describe themselves as "covenant-members," and their believers' baptism as a covenant, the sign of the true covenant, the covenant of grace, in contrast to the Abrahamic covenant of circumcision—the covenant which in a wild misunderstanding of

the name Pontius* in the Apostles' Creed they described as the covenant of Pilate under which Christ suffered. In his writings *De peccato originali* (1526) and *In catabaptistarum strophas elenchus* (1527)—his practical concern was to defend the national Church—Zwingli used against them the following argument. God first made a covenant with Adam, then with Noah, for the whole human race. He then made a covenant with Abraham for the people of Israel. But it was always the one covenant valid from the foundation of the world to its end, providing for human sin with the determination of Jesus as Mediator and Redeemer. Therefore we heathen who believe in Jesus are one in faith with Abraham, and therefore one people, one Church, with the people of Israel, heirs of the one testament, the only difference being that now that Christ has appeared in accordance with the original determination it is proclaimed and delivered to all nations, the ceremonies of the covenant with Israel are done away, and the light which lightened the fathers has shone out all the more brightly on us. The drift of the argument is this. If the children of Israel were as such, before they believed, included in the Abrahamic covenant, why should the same not be true of our children? If they received the covenant sign of circumcision, are ours not placed at an intolerable disadvantage if they do not receive baptism? But—apart from the christological content—the real point of interest in Zwingli's conception is the universal meaning and purpose which he tried to give to the covenant concept, his insistence on the covenant with Noah and even a covenant with Adam, in relation to which, and in the light of its limitations done away at the appearance of Christ, the Abrahamic covenant would almost appear to be an episode were it not that by virtue of its aiming at Christ it is already so complete that everything *post Christum natum*[EN45] is seen to be only the carrying out of it and is measured by it as its standard. For Bullinger, too—who had the same practical concern about infant baptism—the new covenant is the fulfilment of the covenant with Abraham, and as such it is also the ratification of the *foedus Dei æternum*[EN46] with the whole human race, which did not cease to be a covenant of grace, or to apply to all men, because of the intervention of the law of the covenant with Israel. If it can be said that these two Zurich reformers already had a Federal theology, this universalism is its most remarkable feature. As they see it, the covenant consists in the primitive institution and revelation of a promise and of the command of faith in that promise, and of the corresponding obedience. The people or Church of the covenant is not identical with the whole race. But from the very first the covenant is open to the whole race. It is not a private concern either of Israel or of pious Christians. If the covenant is understood as the presupposition of the atonement accomplished in Jesus Christ as it is revealed in that event, then necessarily the concept does have this universal orientation: not in the sense that all men are members as such and without further ado—if that were the case it would no longer be a covenant of the free grace of God—but in the sense that as the promise and command of God it does seriously apply to all men and is made for all men, that it is the destiny of all men to become and to be members of this covenant. In this way it is the living work and Word of God in contrast to a truth concerning the being of all men as such, a metaphysical concept necessarily implicated in the being of man—or in contrast to a truth concerning the being of some men but not of others. The scheme was not altogether satisfactory as a basis for infant baptism, but in its actual content it stood for something which cannot be surrendered, the character of the covenant as the true light which lighteth every man (Jn. 1⁹) and for which, therefore, every man is claimed.

[057]

---

* The misunderstanding derives from the superficial resemblance between the Swiss-German "*puntnus*" (covenant) and Pontius.—Trans.

[EN45] after the birth of Christ
[EN46] eternal covenant

Unfortunately in the later development of the Federal theology this universalism in the thought of the covenant was quickly obscured if not obliterated, as we can see from its classical form in Coccejus. The reason was that these "modern" theologians, and it is remarkable that it was the "moderns," tried to maintain the grim doctrine (which does logically follow from Calvin's conception of predestination) that Christ did not die for all men but only for the elect. It was deduced that the covenant, at any rate the covenant of grace (beside which they now believed they could discern another covenant) is from all eternity and in its temporal fulfilment a kind of separate arrangement between God and these particular men, the *electi*, which means in practice the true adherents of the true Israelitish-Christian religion. A theology of biblical history was now replaced by a theology of biblical histories. In the recognition of the covenant the atonement made in Jesus Christ was no longer accepted as the revelation of it. Scripture was not understood as the witness to this one event. It was not read as a witness at all, but as a historical record of a pragmatico-theological character. In these circumstances the outcome was inevitable. The most significant thing in these histories and the *telos* of all of them was that they offered examples in which certain men as distinct from others emerged as genuine hearers of the Word of God and partners in His work. They, and others like them, must obviously be regarded as the covenant-partners of God, and only they. In this way the conception of the covenant led into a blind alley in which it could not embrace and apply to all but only to some: those who could be regarded as the elect in virtue of their personal relationship with God as determined one way or another—as though this is not necessarily contradicted by the calling and attitude of all genuine hearers of the Word of God and partners in His work; as though in relation to the God active and revealed in Jesus Christ we cannot, and must not, see that all other men are under the sign of the covenant set up by Him, so that far from any particularism we have to look on them with hope. But if we do not look exclusively to Jesus Christ and therefore to God we lose the capacity on this basis to think inclusively. Historicism in theology always involves psychologism, and with those who try to be serious Christians in spite of their historicism it will be of a gloomy and pessimistic and unfriendly type; although at any moment, and this is what happened in the 18th century, it can transform itself without difficulty into its very opposite, a cheap universalism. Clearly we cannot follow the Federal theology when it takes this path, in opposition to its own earlier, from a historical standpoint, very remarkable form.

3. What is the meaning and character of the covenant according to this theology? We have seen that Zwingli and Bullinger regarded it quite unequivocally as a covenant of grace. So, too, does Calvin in those two chapters of the *Institutes*, II, 9–11, which the shadow of his doctrine of an eternal double predestination has hardly touched. As he sees it, the covenant made with the fathers was already the *foedus evangelii*[EN47], of which Christ was not only the fulfilment but the eternal basis. The distinctions between the fathers and us do not any of them relate to the substance of the covenant, which was and is the same, but only to the *modus administrationis*[EN48]. It is only its *accidentia, annexa accessoria*[EN49] which have been abrogated and made obsolete by the appearance of Christ. We live with them, and they lived with us, by the same promises, under the same command, by the same grace. The only difference is that for us they are incomparably more sure and certain, and that whereas for them the covenant meant servitude for us it means freedom. Similarly—and here Calvin was writing against the Anabaptists and in favour of the national Church—the sacraments of the Old Testament have changed only in form, but in substance they are identical with those of the New. In Calvin there can be no question of the Law destroying the character of the covenant

---

[EN47] covenant of the Gospel
[EN48] means of its administration
[EN49] accidence, the additional essentials

as a covenant of grace, nor can we find any combination of the covenant concept with a primitive *lex naturae*[EN50]. This idea came in as a result of the influence which Melanchthon came to exercise on Reformed theology—in his old age he for his part was accused of a leaning to Calvinism. In this respect we first find it in W. Musculus and S. Szegedin. Here, in contrast to Zwingli, Bullinger and Calvin, the concept of the *foedus*[EN51] is suddenly divided into that of a *foedus generale*[EN52], the temporal covenant of God with the universe, the earth and man as part of creation, and the eternal *foedus speciale*[EN53], which embraces all the elect from the beginning of the world as the true seed of Abraham, and which is split up into three periods, *ante legem, sub lege, post legem*[EN54]. Notice the part allotted already to the Law as a principle of order. Notice, too, that here the *foedus speciale*[EN55] is the eternal covenant while the *foedus generale*[EN56] is only a temporal. The introduction of what later became the dominant twofold concept must be attributed to Ursinus (*S. Theol*, 1584, *qu*. 36, cf. 10 and 30 f.). There is a *foedus naturae*[EN57] which was contracted with man at creation and is therefore known to man by nature. It promises eternal life to those who obey, but threatens eternal punishment to those who disobey. In contrast there is a *foedus gratiae*[EN58] which is not known to man by nature. This is the fulfilling of the Law accomplished by Christ, our restoration by His Spirit, the free promise of the gift of eternal life to those who believe in Him. Nature and grace are both on the same historical level, and confront one another as the principles of individual covenants. We hear the voice of Calvin again and find traces of a different spirit in Olevian's work, *De substantia foederis gratuiti* (1585), in which, following Jer. 31, the covenant is again described uniformly, unequivocally and exclusively as the covenant of grace. But although Coccejus thought of Olevian with particular gratitude as his predecessor, in this important respect the later development followed the lead of Ursinus. In Franz Gomarus (*Oratio de foedere Dei*, 1594), who was clearly inclined to a certain unity of outlook—he was a strict Supralapsarian—we find the peculiar doctrine of two covenants which are founded at the same time and run concurrently and everywhere merge into each other. The first is a *foedus naturale*[EN59], which demands perfect obedience, concluded with the first parents and in them with the whole of the human race after creation, and repeated by Moses the Lawgiver. The second is a *foedus supernaturale*[EN60], in which Christ is made over to those who believe in Him and repent, not by the power of nature, but by grace. But the rivalry of the two principles cannot be overcome. Polan (in whom the covenant played only an incidental role) seems to have rendered the doubtful service of replacing the concept *foedus naturale*[EN61] by what was regarded as a better description *foedus operum*[EN62], and occasionally at any rate Wolleb followed his example.

[059]

We can ignore the variations of the Herborn school in their presentation of what had now become an established dualism (given confessional status for the first time in Art. 7 of the *Westminster Confession*). Instead we will turn at once to Coccejus himself. He begins with the covenant of works, which is for him the ruling principle. This covenant is based on the Law

---

[EN50] law of nature
[EN51] covenant
[EN52] general covenant
[EN53] special covenant
[EN54] before the law, under the law, after the law
[EN55] special covenant
[EN56] general covenant
[EN57] covenant of nature
[EN58] covenant of grace
[EN59] natural covenant
[EN60] supernatural covenant
[EN61] natural covenant
[EN62] covenant of works

with its promise and threats. The Law was written on the heart of Adam and is still attested by conscience. It was pronounced as the Word of God in the prohibition concerning the tree of knowledge of good and evil in Paradise, and in content it agrees with the Mosaic decalogue. The tree of life is the symbol and sacrament of the eternal life promised to the perfectly obedient man and accruing to him as a reward. The divine likeness of Adam, which is taken to mean the wisdom of his understanding, the right disposition of his will and the innocence of his spirit and affections, meant that he was fully equipped (and with him the human race covenanted with God in his person) to keep the command and therefore to participate in the promise. But his will was not unalterable and it had not yet become established in obedience. According to Coccejus everything else follows as a series of abrogations (*abrogationes, antiquationes*EN63) of this covenant of works.

The first abrogation is by sin. Consciously and voluntarily, and with God's permission, Adam does that which is forbidden. In so doing, he and all his descendants forfeit their friendship with God, their divine likeness and the status of promise, falling under the divine curse and judgment.

The second is related to the first and consists in the institution of the covenant of grace. Man as mercifully preserved by God is bound to Him by the law of nature and the mercy of God, but He is incapable of fulfilling his obligation. Therefore God creates an effective instrument to restore man, an instrument which answers at once both to His goodness and also to His righteousness. He adopts man into a new agreement by which He wills to give man a Mediator and therefore in this just person new fellowship and peace with Himself and the promised eternal life—not now as a reward which has been earned but as a free gift. The only response demanded of sinful man is that of faith. This third step, and therefore the second abrogation of the covenant of works—we will return to this later—is understood by Coccejus as the unfolding of a pre-temporal occurrence, an eternal and free contract (*pactum*) made between God the Father and God the Son, in which the Father represents the righteousness and the Son the mercy of God, the latter adopting the function of a Mediator and pledge in the place of men.

[060]

In the third abrogation of the covenant of works as Coccejus sees it, we return to the earth and history. It is the announcing of the covenant of grace in the economy of the Old Testament prefigured in the proto-Gospel of Gen. 3^15f. This is a form of the relationship between God and man which has the covenant of grace as its hidden basis, but a basis which is occasionally revealed. In this form as we are told in Rom. 3, there is a πάρεσις EN64, an overlooking and ignoring of human sin, but not its ἄφεσις EN65, its real forgiveness, and therefore the justification of sinners. It is all still a matter of type and instruction. The righteous are still intermingled with the wicked. Bondage still rules, and with it the fear of death. But all the same the Law, with its demand for righteousness and its types and shadows, is a witness to the promise. Circumcision and the passover already point to the atoning death of Christ. Everything is still a matter of expectation. It is only the Old Testament. But it is a sure expectation of the covenant of grace and therefore of the New Testament. And to that extent it is an abrogation of the first, of the covenant of works. This is revealed in the benefits of the New Testament: in the demonstration of our perfect righteousness in the obedience of the Son of God fulfilling the whole Law; in the revelation of the name of God; in the writing of the Law on our human hearts by the Spirit; in the freeing of consciences by that ἄφεσις τῶν

EN63 abrogations, antiquations
EN64 passing over
EN65 forgiveness

ἁμαρτιῶν EN66 which now replaces the mere πάρεσις EN67; in the liberation from the fear of death and the planting of the Church among the Gentiles.

The fourth abrogation of the covenant of works Coccejus calls the death of the body, i.e., the sanctification which in the work of Christ goes hand in hand with justification, sanctification as purification, as the destruction of the works of the devil and the darkness of the intellect and the badness of the human will. The Law is now a weapon in the warfare of the spirit against the flesh. The tribulations which still remain, including death, are instruments for the testing of faith and the taming of sin, opportunities for the exercise of love. That this conflict takes place distinguishes the regenerate from the unregenerate. The regenerate will not commit wilful sin, and from those that remain he will always seek refuge in the grace of God, earnest self-examination, and prayer for a pure heart.

The fifth and final abrogation of the covenant of works is what Coccejus calls the reawakening of the body. He is thinking here of the eschatological redemption and consummation. With this the validity of the covenant of works ceases altogether—that is, for the righteous. Nothing remains but the operation of the mediatorship of the guarantor of the covenant of grace and its obedience, and this operation is eternal life and salvation by the resurrection from the dead in virtue of His merit, in which the souls of the pious participate directly at death.

We relate our question concerning the essence and character of the covenant to this sketch of Coccejus because for all his individuality in relation to his predecessors and successors Coccejus represents the Federal theology in a form which is not only the most perfect, but also the ripest and strongest and most impressive.

There was one point in which the successors of Coccejus at once departed from his scheme, and it has been the subject of most of the objections against him right up to the [061] presentations given in the dogmatic history of our own day. This is his at first sight exclusively negative estimate and presentation of the whole history of the covenant in relation to its beginning, as a gradual abrogation of the covenant of works. And in this respect two discordant features have to be noted. First, the second and obviously decisive abrogation as distinct from all the others is not a temporal event, but—like a scene in heaven in the religious plays of the Middle Ages—an eternal happening between the Father and the Son. And second, the New Testament economy has no autonomous place among these temporal events, but is mentioned only in contrast with that of the Old. In my estimation the main strength of the thinking of Coccejus is at the very point where formally the main objection is made against him, and at the point where these two discordant features are to be found within the order selected by him. Certainly, he took over from his predecessors that idea of a covenant of nature or works which was alien to the Reformers. But—and it was because of this that he felt so strong an affinity with Olevian—he had such a strong sense of the uniqueness of the divine covenant as a covenant of grace that, although he could begin his narration with the covenant of works, he could understand everything that followed only in antithesis to it, as its increasing abrogation. The doctrine of the covenant of grace was developed in relation, but only in this negative relation, to a covenant of works. The fact that he did try to bring the two together, but could do so only in the antithetical form of the abrogation of the one by the other, was obviously even to himself a disquieting reminder that his attitude to the second—if it really was the second—would have to be quite different from his attitude to the first. That is how we have to judge the scene in heaven which so singularly interrupts the series of temporal events to form the second stage. Coccejus could find no similar eternal pact between God the Father and God the Son to correspond to the covenant

---

EN66 forgiveness of sins
EN67 passing over

57

of nature or works. In presenting the institution of the covenant of grace in this way, did he not contradict his own historicism and say that in this covenant we have to do with a *Prius*[EN68] and not a *Posterius*[EN69] in relation to that which he and his predecessors had sought to characterise and describe as a special and supposedly first *foedus naturale* or *legale* or *operum*[EN70]? In spite of the inconsistency in his own scheme, was he not faithful here to what he saw very well to be the real logic of the matter? And is not the same true of his other architectonic failure—that he did not try to understand and explain the particular subject of the New Testament witness, the historical incarnation of the Son of God, and the atonement made in Him, as a particular stage in this series of events, but "only" as the fulfilling or replacing of the Old Testament economy? How is it that he could and necessarily did look at it in that way? For one thing, because obviously—and this must be said in his favour—he did not want to give to the historical difference between the two economies, which he perceived and emphasised very strongly (much more strongly than Calvin), the character of a theological antithesis, but aimed rather to present the Old Testament as the witness to the promise of Jesus Christ and the New as the witness to its fulfilment. And then most of all because everything that can be said of the New Testament economy as such is already included and stated in and with what has been said in relation to that abrogation of the covenant of works which has already taken place in the bosom of the Godhead. For him the new thing in the New Testament is the oldest thing of all, that which goes back to the very beginning. And this original thing he found revealed and active as the first thing (not as a second economy following that of the Old Testament) in the New Testament economy which dissolved that of the Old Testament.

The questions which we can answer only with difficulty if at all in respect of Coccejus do not begin until we have done him justice in these matters. The meaning and character of the covenant as a covenant of grace impressed itself upon him forcefully in this way. And in his

[062]

outline (even in the very things which might formally be objected against him) he has emphasised this in a remarkable manner. How was it, then, that he came to put first the covenant of nature or works or Law, negatively at least taking his direction from it, as though the covenant of grace were a covenant of grace only in antithesis to it, and ultimately therefore only in its fulfilment and confirmation? The same question may be asked of his predecessors from Ursinus onwards. Granted that we can seriously speak of a *lex naturae*[EN71], how does it come to be connected with the divine likeness of man, his status before the fall, the Word of God to Adam, the tree of life in Paradise, and the decalogue? And in this connexion, within the series of main theological concepts, how does it attain to the dignity of a first and special divine covenant, which then becomes the schema within which (antithetically in Coccejus) the covenant of grace is set up and its history gradually fulfilled? The more so as men who knew the Scripture as Coccejus and his fellows undoubtedly did could never speak of any institution of this second covenant in God Himself (as Coccejus did in relation to the covenant of grace)! But it is still this covenant which becomes the first and is as such the framework and standard of reference for the covenant of grace. There is only one historical explanation for this innovation, the introduction of this first stage in the history for which the Federal theology thought that it had biblical reference. This is that biblical exegesis had been invaded by a mode of thought in which this history, however extraordinary the course it took, could only unfold itself and therefore only begin as the history of man and his works, man who is good by nature and who is therefore in covenant with God—a

---

[EN68] before
[EN69] after
[EN70] covenant of nature or law or works
[EN71] law of nature

God who is pledged to him by virtue of his goodness. To this mode of thinking it became more and more foreign to think of the history as conversely the history of God and His works, the God who originally turns to man in grace, and therefore as from the very first the history of the covenant of grace. We have seen that Coccejus did try (with Calvin and Olevian and all the older tradition) to think this second thought which was becoming so foreign to his generation. But in face of the increasing pressure to a mode of thought which started exclusively with man (for his contemporaries had come to terms with the Cartesians), he no longer had sufficient freedom to make the leap which he really ought to have made in accordance with the biblical control of his thinking. Formally, at any rate, the thought which was becoming so foreign to the new thinking of his generation, but to which he wanted to do justice, and in his own way did do justice, could have only a secondary authority even in his writings. The first place is taken by the strange spectacle of man in Paradise to whom eternal life is promised as a reward which he has earned, whose works can perfectly fulfil the command of God (even if his obedience is not yet secure), to whom God is just as much bound by this fulfilment as he is to God, between whom and God the relationship is clearly that of a *do ut des*[EN72]. And this relationship is supposed to be the original form of the covenant. In this original form it breaks down in that series of abrogations. And it does not break down first by reason of the divine covenant of grace, but by reason of human sin. Characteristically, and necessarily in view of that pressure, the second most pressing problem is not that of God's grace but that of man's sin. Through all the abrogations of the covenant of nature and works, what sin is—even as it will finally disappear—is measured by the Law of this first covenant. And it will be the decisive gift of the covenant of grace, and the function of the Mediator as the second Adam, to fulfil in our place the Law of the covenant of nature and works which was transgressed by Adam and all of us, and in that way to become our guarantor with God. And far from the first covenant being really superseded by the intervention of the Mediator, the gifted righteousness of Law (which is promised and certain to faith in Him) is necessarily followed by that further abrogation of the Law, distinguished under the concept of sanctification, which Coccejus calls the "death of the body," the battle of spirit against the flesh in the regenerate, in which the decisive weapon is once again the Law, while [063] grace is the place to which the regenerate must always flee in view of the imperfection of his fulfilment of the Law. The first covenant and its Law loses its relevance only in that *eschaton* which is the fifth and final stage of the whole development. In spite of all assurances to the contrary, this side of the *eschaton*, in time, there is no effective abrogation of the covenant of nature and works, either in the Old Testament economy or consequently in the New. For the New Testament freedom is only freedom from the Law of the Old Testament—impressively maintained by Coccejus, e.g., in relation to the Sabbath—but the validity of the Law of that first covenant is the guiding thread which runs through the whole development, indeed it controls that development. Grace itself, whether as justification or sanctification, is always the fulfilling of that Law (perfect in Christ, imperfect in us). There is no escape from the relationship of *do ut des*[EN73], no liberation from the insecurity of the whole connexion between man and God, the fear of punishment and the expectation of reward, no radical cessation of the unfortunate preoccupation of man with himself and his works and of the even more unfortunate control of God to which this inevitably gives rise. This is impossible even in the covenant of grace connected with the covenant of works and orientated by it. This covenant of grace could not be clearly and convincingly portrayed as such. Where it was portrayed as such in the proclamation of the older Reformed Church, this was not because but in spite of its starting-point, in virtue of those elements which were foreign and ran

---

[EN72] tit-for-tat
[EN73] tit-for-tat

contrary to it, and made it innocuous. Unfortunately they did not always make it innocuous.

4. We have seen that Coccejus solemnly distinguished the covenant of grace, his second abrogation of the covenant of works, by describing it as a pretemporal and intertrinitarian happening, a pact between God the Father and God the Son. It is grounded, not in the proclamation of the proto-Gospel, or in the Noachic or Abrahamic covenants, not between God and man at all, but in eternity before all worlds, in the bosom of the Godhead itself. We can ignore the rather difficult juristic details of the conception in Coccejus and his predecessors and successors. What is essential is that: God forgives sinful man and gives him a new righteousness on the one condition of faith and repentance. Ultimately this rests on the free disposing of God the Father, by virtue of which He has once and for all ascribed to a chosen portion of sinful humanity righteousness and eternal life in His Son. There is a corresponding disposing of the Son of God in virtue of which He for His part has undertaken once and for all the cause of those sinful men who are elected to sonship. The two together result in the covenant: the *pactum mutuum inter Patrem et Filium, quo Pater Filium dat ut* λυτρώτην *et caput populi praecogniti et Filius vicissim se sistit ad* ἀπολύτρωσιν *hanc peragendam*[EN74] (F. Burmann, *Syn. Theol.*, 1671, II, 15, 2). The whole christologico-soteriological happening of the atonement is simply the historical execution of the engagements freely accepted by, but strictly binding on, the two divine partners, i.e., God with God. The older Reformed theology had spoken more simply of an eternal divine "decree," as an *opus Dei internum ad extra*[EN75], and its temporal fulfilment. And in content this decree could only be the eternal divine election of grace. Coccejus and those who shared his view could also understand that which they described as the *testamentum aeternum*[EN76] or the *sponsio aeterna*[EN77] between the Father and the Son as an aspect of the decree of predestination (in so far as this has positive reference to election to salvation in Christ). We will have to return to this in a fifth and final point. The question we must now ask as it arises from the third point is as follows. When this supreme basis was ascribed to the covenant of grace, how was it thought possible that another covenant, the *foedus naturae* or *operum*[EN78], could be placed alongside it and even given precedence over it?—a covenant which had already been superseded and rendered superfluous by this eternal basis of the covenant of grace? which could at once be broken by

[064] the sin of man? which could then be destroyed and abrogated and made obsolete by the historical promise and fulfilment of the covenant of grace? which would completely disappear in the *eschaton*? but which, as we have seen, still constitutes the guiding thread which actually runs through the whole occurrence of salvation and by which it is measured right up to the very end? Although this covenant and its Law are plainly opposed to the covenant of grace! Although it is not possible to try to explain it by a divine decree, an eternal and intertrinitarian decision and agreement! If the covenant of grace alone was seen to be grounded in God, did not this mean that any dualism in the concept of the covenant was at once negated? Even where it was thought necessary to speak of a first covenant of nature or works, was it really possible to see anything but the one covenant of grace, which had been instituted in eternity, which had come into force, therefore, in and with the beginning of human history, which at once embraced man and claimed him, which man had, of course, broken, but which God in faithfulness to Himself and His partner had not abrogated but

---

[EN74] mutual contract between the Father and the Son, in which the Father grants to the Son that the Son in turn might establish himself as the redeemer and head of his foreknown people that this redemption be accomplished

[EN75] internal work of God for outside of himself

[EN76] eternal covenant

[EN77] eternal promise

[EN78] covenant of nature or of works

maintained and ratified? Why was it thought necessary to see man in any other light than that of the pledge which God Himself had made for him in His Son even before he ever existed? Why was it thought necessary to see him in any other way than the one who in the eternal will of God was predestinated to be the brother of this Son and therefore to divine sonship? Why is there ascribed to him a status in which he did not need the Mediator and which, if it had lasted, would have made superfluous the appearance of the Mediator and therefore the fulfilment of the eternal (!) covenant of grace? Why was sin robbed of its true and frightful seriousness as a transgression of the law given to man as the predestinated brother of the Son and child of the Father, as a falling away from the special grace which the Creator had shown him from all eternity? Why instead was the grace of God made a second or a third thing, a wretched expedient of God in face of the obvious failure of a plan in relation to man which had originally had quite a different intention and form? Why, again, was it not possible completely to banish all thought of this other plan in relation to the historical promise and fulfilment, the Old and New Testament economy? Why had the history of the covenant of grace to be presented as though it had to do only with the execution of that original plan?—of that plan concerning whose divine meaning and basis there was nothing that could be said because nothing was or could be known of it from the Gospel they were trying to expound? Why on this side of the *eschaton* is everything always measured by a form of the relationship between God and man which had been maintained as the beginning of all things only with a *sic volo sic iubeo*[EN79]? How was that even possible? How was it possible to know of the eternal basis of the covenant of grace and then not to think exclusively in the light of it, to understand and present it as the one covenant of God, as though there were some other eternity in God or elsewhere, an eternity of human nature and its connexion with God and its law and the works of this law?

5. The riddle posed by the older Federal theology at this its strongest point appears to be insoluble. But perhaps we shall find the solution if we examine rather more closely how it understood that eternal basis of the covenant of grace. As we have seen, it was taken to consist in an intertrinitarian decision, in a freely accepted but legally binding mutual obligation between God the Father and God the Son. Now there are three doubtful features in this conception.

For God to be gracious to sinful man, was there any need of a special decree to establish the unity of the righteousness and mercy of God in relation to man, of a special intertrinitarian arrangement and contract which can be distinguished from the being of God? If there was need of such a decree, then the question arises at once of a form of the will of God in which this arrangement has not yet been made and is not yet valid. We have to reckon with the existence of a God who is righteous *in abstracto*[EN80] and not free to be gracious from the very first, who has to bind to the fulfilment of His promise the fulfilment of certain conditions by man, and punish their non-fulfilment. It is only with the conclusion of this contract with Himself that He ceases to be a righteous God *in abstracto*[EN81] and becomes the God who in His righteousness is also merciful and therefore able to exercise grace. In this case it is not impossible or illegitimate to believe that properly, in some inner depth of His being behind the covenant of grace, He might not be able to do this. It is only on the historical level that the theologoumenon of the *foedus naturae* or *operum*[EN82] can be explained by the compact of the Federal theology with contemporary humanism. In fact it derives from anxiety lest there might be an essence in God in which, in spite of that contract,

[065]

EN79 an 'I command as I will
EN80 in the abstract
EN81 in the abstract
EN82 covenant of nature or of works

His righteousness and His mercy are secretly and at bottom two separate things. And this anxiety derives from the fact that the thought of that intertrinitarian contract obviously cannot have any binding and therefore consoling and assuring force. This anxiety and therefore this proposition of a covenant of works could obviously never have arisen if there had been a loyal hearing of the Gospel and a strict looking to Jesus Christ as the full and final revelation of the being of God. In the eternal decree of God revealed in Jesus Christ the being of God would have been seen as righteous mercy and merciful righteousness from the very first. It would have been quite impossible therefore to conceive of any special plan of a God who is righteous *in abstracto*[EN83], and the whole idea of an original covenant of works would have fallen to the ground.

The conception of this intertrinitarian pact as a contract between the persons of the Father and the Son is also open to criticism. Can we really think of the first and second persons of the triune Godhead as two divine subjects and therefore as two legal subjects who can have dealings and enter into obligations one with another? This is mythology, for which there is no place in a right understanding of the doctrine of the Trinity as the doctrine of the three modes of being of the one God, which is how it was understood and presented in Reformed orthodoxy itself. God is one God. If He is thought of as the supreme and finally the only subject, He is the one subject. And if, in relation to that which He obviously does amongst us, we speak of His eternal resolves or decrees, even if we describe them as a contract, then we do not regard the divine persons of the Father and the Son as partners in this contract, but the one God—Father, Son and Holy Spirit—as the one partner, and the reality of man as distinct from God as the other. When the covenant of grace was based on a pact between two divine persons, a wider dualism was introduced into the Godhead—again in defiance of the Gospel as the revelation of the Father by the Son and of the Son by the Father, which took place in Jesus Christ. The result was an uncertainty which necessarily relativised the unconditional validity of the covenant of grace, making it doubtful whether in the revelation of this covenant we really had to do with the one will of the one God. If in God there are not merely different and fundamentally contradictory qualities, but also different subjects, who are indeed united in this matter, but had first of all to come to an agreement, how can the will of God seen in the history of the covenant of grace be known to be binding and unequivocal, the first and final Word of God? The way is then opened up on this side too for considering the possibility of some other form of His will. The question is necessarily and seriously raised of a will of God the Father which originally and basically is different from the will of God the Son. And this naturally carried with it the hypothesis of a covenant of quite a different structure and purpose preceding and underlying the covenant of grace, the hypothesis of a law in the relationship of God to man which is not the Law of His grace and which in default of a special revelation of the Father can be pictured at once according to the analogy of human ordinances. And how is the will of the eternal Son or Word of God in Himself and as such, in His pure Godhead, to become so clear and certain that we can and must cling to it alone as the revealed eternal and therefore unequivocal and binding will of God as the basis of the covenant of grace? Even the thought of the eternal divine Logos is not in itself and as such necessarily a defence against the thought of a law which is different from the Law of grace.

[066]

And this leads us to the third and decisive point. The thought of a purely intertrinitarian decision as the eternal basis of the covenant of grace may be found both sublime and uplifting. But it is definitely much too uplifting and sublime to be a Christian thought. What we

---

[EN83] in the abstract

have to do with it is not a relationship of God with Himself but the basis of a relationship between God and man. How can even the most perfect decision in the bosom of the God-head, if the Godhead remains alone, be the origin of the covenant, if it is made in the absence of the one who must be present as the second partner at the institution of the covenant to make it a real covenant, that is, man? To unite God in His attitude to man—whether in respect of His properties, or as Father, Son and Holy Spirit—there is no need of any particular pact or decree. God would not be God if He were not God in this unity. And a covenant with man is not grounded merely in this unity of God in and with Himself. It is not self-evident but a new thing that in His unity with Himself from all eternity God wills to be the God of man and to make and have man as His man. This is the content of a particular act of will which has its basis neither in the essence of God nor in that of man, and which God does not owe either to Himself or to any other being, and least of all to man. This is what we can call a decree, an *opus Dei internum ad extra*[EN84], and therefore a pact: God's free election of grace, in which even in His eternity before all time and the foundation of the world, He is no longer alone by Himself, He does not rest content with Himself, He will not restrict Himself to the wealth of His perfections and His own inner life as Father, Son and Holy Spirit. In this free act of the election of grace there is already present, and presumed, and assumed into unity with His own existence as God, the existence of the man whom He intends and loves from the very first and in whom He intends and loves all other men, of the man in whom He wills to bind Himself with all other men and all other man with Himself. In this free act of the election of grace the Son of the Father is no longer just the eternal Logos, but as such, as very God from all eternity He is also the very God and very man He will become in time. In the divine act of predestination there pre-exists the Jesus Christ who as the Son of the eternal Father and the child of the Virgin Mary will become and be the Mediator of the covenant between God and man, the One who accomplishes the act of atonement. He in whom the covenant of grace is fulfilled and revealed in history is also its eternal basis. He who in Scripture is attested to be very God and very man is also the eternal *testamentum*[EN85], the eternal *sponsio*[EN86], the eternal *pactum*[EN87], between God and man. This is the point which Coccejus and the Federal theology before and after Coccejus missed. Their doctrine of a purely intertrinitarian pact did not enable them to give an unequivocal or binding answer to the question of the form of the eternal divine decree as the beginning of all things. The result was that for all their loyalty to Scripture they inherited the notion that the covenant of grace fulfilled and revealed in history in Jesus Christ was perhaps only a secondary and subsequent divine arrangement (the foundation and history of a religion?) and not the beginning of all the ways of God. Their view of the covenant became dualistic. The idea of a basic and always determinative and concurrent covenant of nature or works was superimposed on their conception of the covenant of grace. Yet this could have been avoided—even though as children of their time they were exposed to the temptation of humanism—if they could have determined to know the eternal and therefore the only basis of the divine work in the work itself, in its temporal occurrence, to know the eternal divine Logos in His incarnation. And on this basis they might well have overcome the other weak-nesses in their doctrine: the abandonment of an original universalism in the conception of the covenant; and finally the radical historicism of their understanding of Scripture.

[EN84] internal work of God for outside of himself
[EN85] covenant
[EN86] promise
[EN87] contract

3. THE FULFILMENT OF THE BROKEN COVENANT

From the concept of the covenant as the presupposition of the reconciliation which took place in Jesus Christ we will now turn to the reconciliation itself and therefore to the fulfilment of the covenant. It consists in the fact that God realises His eternal will with man, that He makes the covenant true and actual within human history. It consists in the historical proclamation attested in the Old Testament, and the historical existence attested in the New, of the Mediator, that is, of the eternal Word of God and therefore of God Himself in His historical identity with the man Jesus of Nazareth: in the coming of His kingdom on earth, that is, in the coming and being and living and speaking and acting of this man, in the establishing and maintaining and revealing in Him of the sole supremacy of His grace in the world of men, and of the subordination of that world to this supremacy. It consists in the fact that He causes the promise and command of the covenant: "I will be your God and ye shall be my people," to become historical event in the person of Jesus Christ. It consists, therefore, in the fact that God keeps faith in time with Himself and with man, with all men in this one man.

But this fulfilment of the covenant has the character of atonement. The concept speaks of the confirmation or restoration of a fellowship which did exist but had been threatened with disruption and dissolution. Atonement does have its eternal and unshakable basis in the covenant between God and man which God willed and set up before the foundation of the world. But the covenant is successfully fulfilled by the overcoming of an obstruction which if the basis had not been unshakable would inevitably have made that fulfilment doubtful or impossible. In face of that obstruction the fulfilment can be regarded only as a divine protest effectively and redemptively made with the power of that eternal basis. And in relation to man it can be regarded only as an inconceivable overflowing of the grace of God to him.

This history of man from the very first—and the same is true of the history of every individual man—consisted, not in the keeping but the breaking of the covenant, not in the receiving but the rejecting of the promise, not in the fulfilling but the transgressing of the command, not in the gratitude which corresponds to the grace of God but in a senseless and purposeless rebellion against it, a rebellion which at bottom is quite negative, but terribly real even in this negativity. It was revealed from the very first, and it is revealed daily in small things as well as big, in the disposition as well as the acts of man, that the eternal grace of God is not merely undeserved by man, but was and is given to [068] him as one who does not deserve it. He does not recognise it. He does not want it. At bottom he hates it. He does not see that this and this alone is life in freedom. He chafes for another freedom which can only be bondage. He does not accept the fact that he can be a member of the people of God. Therefore he does not accept the fact that God is the Lord of His people. He finds and chooses other lords and gods, and lives as though he belonged to their people.

And so the grace of God to him seems to be in the void. The man to whom it comes fails to receive it. As far as he is concerned he is without grace, and therefore he fails even as a creature. Therefore it seems that although God elected man to a covenant with Himself, and created heaven and earth and man himself for the sake of this covenant, He will finally be left by Himself: God above, but not God—which is surely impossible—in these dark depths; God in heaven, but not God on an earth which is the scene of this nonsensical history; God in His own inner glory, but without that attestation of the creature for which He designed and made it and which is not merely the capacity but the destiny of its nature as He made it; God with His covenant will, but without the execution of that will, the execution of it hindered by the one whom He honoured and singled out and exalted in this will from all eternity.

This is the enormous incident of sin which openly opposes the fulfilment of the covenant and in face of which that fulfilment, if it is to come about at all, can have only the character of an atonement. And this atonement can come only from God. In face of human ingratitude, it can consist only in an overflowing of His grace and therefore in the overcoming and removing of that obstruction. There is nothing that man can contribute to it as the one who has denied his relationship with God and failed as God's partner. He cannot accomplish or expect or explain and comprehend it for himself. If it takes place, he can only accept it as a fact, whose validity and effectiveness, as the enemy of God that he is and must recognise and acknowledge himself to be, he can believe only because God does in fact show Himself and make Himself known as the one who is the master of man and his sin.

God's faithfulness cannot be mistaken, nor can it be mocked. What is the unfaithfulness of man in relation to it, and what can it accomplish ? The grace of God triumphs over man and his sin—that is the fulfilment of the covenant which takes place in Jesus Christ. But it assumes and has the character of a "Yet" and a "Notwithstanding." It triumphs now—in face of human opposition—miraculously, unilaterally and autocratically—to its own self-glory.

Can we say: all the more gloriously? Is it only now that it acts and reveals itself as free grace? Is it only now that there is disclosed and operative the sovereign divine resolve which is its basis? We can and must say: "Where sin abounded, grace did much more abound" (Rom. 5^{20}). It is true that the nature and power of the grace of God is finally and unmistakably revealed only [069] where it shows itself and acts as His free grace to the undeserving, as grace for lost sinners.

But, all the same, when the early Church dared to sing: *O felix culpa quae tantum et talem meruit habere salvatorem*[EN88], it went too far with the *meruit habere*[EN89]. For there can be no more question of man "deserving" and achieving and winning that overflowing of the grace

---

[EN88] O happy fault, that merited having such and so great a salvation
[EN89] 'merited having'

of God by his sin than there can in any other way. It can only be recognised and acknowledged and reverenced as a fact that this depth of the love of God is revealed and active in relation to human sin in a way which is so inconceivably profound, in all the power and mystery of eternity. How can we ever ascribe this fact to ourselves? The recognition of this fact carries within it the deepest and most comforting but also the most terrifying abasement of man: that as the transgressor he is he can live only by that which he does not do himself, which it is impossible even to ask of him, which, in fact, he denies and resists; by the atonement which God has made—and all because the grace of God makes against him and the opposition he has stirred up that triumphant, effective and redemptive protest. Even the association of the words *felix*[EN90] and *culpa*[EN91] cannot really stand. This divine protest is effective and redemptive, but it is in bitter earnest. The grace of God does not abandon us, but only because it makes good what we have spoiled, and therefore only in that humiliation of us which brings us help and comfort, but which is inescapable in this wealth of help and comfort. Therefore—unless we do not recognise and accept this humiliation as such—we cannot possibly speak of a "happy fault." To be at fault before God is unhappiness even where the grace of God overflows in answer to and in favour of the guilty, even where the faithfulness of God is first active and revealed as such in face of man's unfaithfulness. If we cannot boast of any happy sufficiency of our being and work, we certainly cannot do so of our "happy fault," which is far more than an insufficiency, which stands indeed in opposition to and conflict with the gracious will of God.

No praise can be too high for the mighty and triumphant grace of God in the atonement as the fulfilment of the covenant. But this praise must not be spoiled by any undertone which directly or indirectly minimises or even approves the incident in virtue of which the fulfilment of the covenant necessarily has the character of an atonement. It must not be made misleading or harmful to those who hear it, or unacceptable to God. The wisdom of God which allows this episode in order to make, not the episode itself, but the overcoming of it an occasion to magnify His grace and to reveal and actualise it— we have to say for the first time—as free grace in it, in accordance with His eternal will and purpose: that wisdom is one thing. But quite a different thing is the human pseudo-wisdom which tries to pretend that this episode is in some sense necessary, and in that way to excuse or exculpate the man who is responsible for it, or even to hide from him the full danger and fatality of his action. The sin which abounds is indeed sin. As the opposition of man to the God who is in covenant with Him it is inexcusable. As the self-opposition of the man who is in covenant with God it is fatal. And the fact that grace much more abounds does not alter or limit or weaken this fact. It is a fact which must be included in our praise of the grace of God. Our praise cannot be genuine [070] except as the praise of faith. But faith flees and clings and reclines and trusts on the God who in His free grace leads us to judgment. Faith finds its comfort and praise in His grace. But it knows that this grace is "dear" and not "cheap" (Dietrich Bonhoeffer). Therefore it does not lessen our accusation and sentence. If we live, we do not live because the confession of our sin and guilt laid

---

[EN90] happy
[EN91] fault

on our hearts and lips by the grace of God has been weakened or embellished, but because the forgiveness of our sin has been accomplished by God in the event of the atonement. Therefore the praise of faith cannot be a denial of the truth but rather a confirmation of it: first and primarily in respect of the inconceivable glory of that which is said and given to man; but then and consequently in respect of the unutterable unworthiness of man as the recipient. Where this is not clear, with all that it entails, there is no faith. What are thought to be believing thought and speech do not revolve around the more abundant free grace of God present in the atonement made in Jesus Christ. They are in fact speculation about a myth current under the name of Jesus Christ. There is no knowledge and proclamation of what has actually been done by God under this name. We must pay attention to the warning which there is here. There is no doctrine more dangerous than the Christian doctrine of the atonement, it does indeed make "wild and careless folk" (*Heid. Cat.*, qu. 64), if we do not consider it with this warning in view. The fact that it speaks of God making good what we have spoiled does not mean that we can call evil good (unless we would also call good evil). All our thinking and all that we say on this matter must be disciplined by an observance of this limit, and a refusal to transgress it in any circumstances, sense or direction.

We will now give a very general outline of what is meant by reconciliation as the fulfilment of the covenant. For this purpose we will take and expound two of the New Testament sayings which in a classic way encompass the whole of this field.

Precedence must be given to Jn. 3[16]: "For God so loved the world, that he gave his only begotten Son, that whosoever believeth on him should not perish, but have everlasting life."

ἠγάπησεν [EN92] tells a definite story, gives news of a unique event: the event of God's loving. This event did not take place in heaven but on earth. It did not take place in secret, but it can be known (i.e., not as a purely spiritual process, but as something which, according to 1 Jn. 1[1], can be heard and seen with our eyes and touched, yes, handled with our hands). This being the case, it became, it made itself the content of the message proclaimed by the Christian community. Now the object of the divine loving was the κόσμος [EN93], which means (for what follows, cf. R. Bultmann, *Das Evangelium Johannes*, 1950) the human world as a single subject in hostile antithesis to God. Not from the very first. Not because it is bad in itself. For the world was made by God (Jn. 1[10]). Not because it is posited against God in itself. Not because it is authorised or empowered to stand in this position of hostility to God. It is His possession (Jn. 1[11]). Not because God has left it to itself. Not because He has given it cause for this hostility. The true light, the light of the covenant promising life, was and is present: and bright enough for every man (Jn. 1[9]). But the world knew it not (Jn. 1[10]). In contrast to it the world is σκοτία [EN94], darkness (Jn. 1[5]). It does not understand God—either in itself as His creature or as illuminated by that light. But with all these characteristics it is the object of the divine loving. For with all these characteristics it is the cosmos. Created by God and illuminated by Him from the beginning, not recognising Him and therefore dark, it is still the object of His loving. This event takes place absolutely. It has this in common with

[071]

[EN92] 'loved'
[EN93] 'world'
[EN94] darkness

the creation of the world, and the illumination which comes to it from God by creation (the covenant with God from which man always derives as from his creation), that God does not owe it to the world to love it. The world is not, as Philo and others imagined, the son of God. It is not begotten by Him. It does not share His nature, so that He is bound to it by nature, essentially. It is the free will and the free act of God that He willed to be the basis of its existence and its light. The meaning of this event is from the very first a free loving. And in its relation to that loving and in every other respect the cosmos is darkness. It has disqualified itself. Even as the world created and illuminated by Him it has ceased to be worthy of His love. But God did not in fact cease to love it. Only now did He begin genuinely and supremely to love it. Only now did this event take place and irresistibly as the event of His own pure free love, a love grounded in Himself and not in the object, a love turned toward the object only for His own sake. There can be no question of any claim of the cosmos to be loved, or consequently of any mitigation of its character as darkness, which is only revealed in all its impossibility in this event, and for which it will now be plainly accused and judged and sentenced. But this does not take place because God rejects it, but because He loves it. And His love is not merely a disposition but an act, an active measure in relation to it. Jn. 3¹⁶ describes the fulfilment and scope of this measure.

The οὕτως EN95 in relation with the later ὥστε EN96 means more than "in such a way," *hoc modo*EN97. It does not refer only to the divine *procedere*EN98 as such, although I have often expounded it in this narrower sense in the *C.D.* It implies this *hoc modo*EN99, but it has the force of "so much." It indicates (as Luther intended when he translated it *also*) the extraordinary nature of this loving. It is not self-evident that there should be a divine loving of the cosmos in any case. It is even less so that the divine act of love should take this form. God loves the cosmos so much, with such inconceivable strength and depth, "that (ὥστε) He gave his only begotten son." God has a Son. This Son is not the cosmos but the One whom He gave in loving the cosmos. Can we interpret the "Son" here as the "Revealer"? He is that (although not only that) when God gives Him. The fact that He is—that He declares the grace and truth of God which no man has seen (Jn. 1¹⁸)—presupposes that He was πρὸς τὸν θεόν EN100 and that He Himself was θεός EN101 (Jn. 1¹), that He was "in the bosom of the Father" (Jn. 1¹⁸), the beloved Other in relation to whom God is called and is love in Himself, in His inward life (1 Jn. 4⁸), the One who knows God as Himself and Himself as God, who does the will of God as His own will and His own will as the will of God, the One without whom—and we cannot say this of the cosmos—God would not only not be revealed but would not be God, whose existence πρὸς τὸν θεόν EN102 and as θεός EN103 is a constituent part of the existence of God. Therefore, υἱὸς μονογενής EN104, the only one of His kind? or the only-begotten, and therefore the One beside whom God has no other son, no one who is His equal, or who corresponds to Him, no other who is in Himself the object of His love, a constituent part of His divine being? In both senses: as this eternally Other in God Himself the only One who as such is able to fulfil all that God wills and does.

EN 95 so
EN 96 such that
EN 97 in this manner
EN 98 process
EN 99 in this manner
EN100 with God
EN101 God
EN102 with God
EN103 God
EN104 only-begotten Son

But it is not self-evident that in loving the world God should "give" this one. ἔδωκεν EN105 in the first instance means "gifted" Him. He did not merely gift a highest and best, a power of life and light which would help the cosmos, perhaps an endowment of the creation, perhaps a strengthening of the light of His covenant. No: He gifted to the cosmos His only Son and therefore nothing more or less than Himself. And in this context ἔδωκεν EN106 has the same [072] force as παρέδωκεν EN107: He surrendered Him, He gave Him up, He offered Him. He sends Him into the cosmos which is actually darkness as the light (Jn. 1⁵) which is to shine in the darkness but which will not be apprehended or grasped, which cannot be apprehended or grasped by the darkness. In giving Him—and giving Himself—He exposes Him—and Himself—to the greatest danger. He sets at stake His own existence as God. "He came unto His own, and His own (that is, those who are His possession) received him not" (Jn. 1¹¹). He did it. But what result is possible when in relation to Him the world is irremediable darkness? What will it mean for God? Well, in this act God loved the world so much, so profoundly, that it did in fact consist in the venture of His own self-offering, in this hazarding of His own existence as God. It is His self-revelation and self-realisation (in and for the world) as a gift, and *rebus sic stantibus* EN108 that can mean only as the offering of that without which He cannot be God, and therefore of the greatest possible danger for Himself. "God so loved the world." The Christian message is the message of this act of God, of the atonement which was made in this way, of God's pledging of Himself for His creature, for His partner in the covenant, for the man who has opposed Him as an enemy. It consists in the fact that God has given Himself up into the hands of this enemy. It is in this radical sense that according to the Christian message God has loved first (πρῶτος EN109, 1 Jn. 4¹⁹), not merely before we loved Him, but while we were yet sinners, while we were yet enemies (Rom. 5⁸ ¹⁰).

And now the clause introduced by ἵνα EN110 (an ἵνα which is both *finale* EN111 and *consecutivum* EN112) speaks of the effect, the result of this offering of the Son and self-offering of God, and therefore of the purpose and the actual scope of this so perfect act of love. Those who believe in Him will not perish but have everlasting life. To understand this we do well to remember the opening and controlling part of the sentence: "For God so loved the world." What happens to those who believe on the Son is the effect of the love with which in that event God has loved not only them but the world. In the person of believers, therefore, it happens indirectly, with a view, and as a witness, to the world. We also do well to follow the hint in the commentary of E. Hoskyns (*The Fourth Gospel*, 1947, 218), and especially to notice what it is that is here described as happening to believers: "the divine purpose in the sending of Jesus Christ is redemption and not judgment, eternal life and not destruction and perdition." It is a matter primarily of salvation from perishing. This is the reverse side of the darkness in which the world opposes God, ranging itself against God, contradicting and withstanding Him. It has fallen a victim to destruction and perdition. In so doing it has forfeited its right to exist as the creature of God. It cannot continue but can only be delivered up to the nothingness to which it has itself turned. The divine loving in the form of the sending of the Son is the will of God not to allow the destruction and perdition of the world. This will is His redemptive will in relation to the creature—His will not to let it perish, to maintain His creation and not to cause it to perish, not even because of the opposition of the

---

EN105 he gave
EN106 gave
EN107 handed over
EN108 as things stand
EN109 first
EN110 so that
EN111 final
EN112 consecutive

creature, especially not because of it. But that is not all. Eternal life as the continuance of man in fellowship with God Himself, in the *consortium divinitatis*[EN113], is not in any way assured to man simply because he is the creature of God. It is rather the particular promise of that light which lighteth every man from the beginning, the light of the covenant which God has made with man. When he denies this light, when he is therefore darkness, when he does not know God, he excludes himself from the sphere of this promise. When he is lost as a creature, how can he participate in eternal life? If he breaks the covenant, he is lost as a creature, and if he is lost as a creature, the promise of the covenant cannot hold good for him. But the divine loving in the form of the sending of the Son is the confirmation of the will of God not to acquiesce in this but to cause man to have the eternal life which he has [073] forfeited with his right to exist as a creature. It is His will not merely to rescue, but to save. He not only wills the creature to continue, but to continue in eternal fellowship with Himself. And He does not allow Himself to be foiled even in this far-reaching purpose for man by the opposition of man.

This loving Yet and Notwithstanding of God (proclaimed in the sending and therefore in the offering of the Son, in the divine self-offering) is what actually happens within this world to those who believe on the Son. Those who believe on the Son are the members of the cosmos who, while they necessarily participate as such in its opposition, and are therefore subject to perishing and have forfeited eternal life, in the sending of the Son and therefore in the self-offering of God can and must recognise God as God, and His will as a will of love, a will to rescue and to save, being ready to accept its validity and application against themselves and therefore for themselves. Those who believe on the Son are those in the cosmos who in face of the work and revelation of God, because in the giving of the Son it includes within itself God's own presence, are free but also constrained to justify God (even against themselves as members of the cosmos, and therefore against the whole cosmos). They are those who without being in any way different from others are under the forceful permission and command to affirm God and the will of God as it has been revealed to them. This is not because, as distinct from others, they are disposed and able of themselves, but because God is too strong for them. Their freedom and constraint cannot be explained by the men themselves. It can be explained only by the presence of God, His glory in the flesh (Jn. 1^{14}). Only then is it genuine and strong and lasting. That is why the New Testament describes it as discipleship, the result of an act of majesty on the part of Jesus. And it is this that constitutes faith. And just as the Son on whom they believe is not of this world ($\dot{\epsilon}\kappa\ \tau o\hat{v}\ \kappa\acute{o}\sigma\mu o\upsilon$), so it is with believers (Jn. $17^{14\ 16}$), although they are undoubtedly in the world (Jn. 17^{11}). They are not of the world, or, to put it positively—in believing in the Son, in seeing His glory in the flesh—they are "born from above" (Jn. 3^3). It is in this way that there takes place in them what is the purpose of the divine loving of the cosmos and therefore of the giving of the Son. As those who believe on the Son they do not perish with the world but they are rescued; they do not lose eternal life but have it. That this is the case with believers is the scope of that event and its promise for the whole world. What happens to them, and as such is only theirs, applies to the whole world, as we see from the verse which immediately follows, and is connected to v. 16 by a $\gamma\acute{a}\rho$ [EN114]: "For God sent not his Son into the world to condemn the world, but that the world through him might be saved" (v. 17). Within the world, and therefore as a witness directed and appointed to it, there are men who belong to it, yet who do not perish but have everlasting life. In the setting up of this witness within the world the atonement is shown to be an atonement which is made for the world.

We will now turn to the parallel saying of Paul in 2 Cor. 5^{19}: "God was in Christ reconciling

---

EN113 fellowship with divinity
EN114 for

70

the world unto himself, not imputing their trespasses unto them; and hath committed unto us the word of reconciliation."

We are taking this sentence out of its context, and even out of its (in any case loose) syntactical connexion with the preceding verse. It is the main verse in the passage, enclosing and bringing together in a pregnant way all the decisive elements in the surrounding verses. It, too, speaks of that fulfilling of the covenant which is our concern here—its execution and its scope—and in doing so it makes express use of the concept of atonement (cf. for what follows the article καταλλάσσειν EN115, etc., by F. Büchsel, in *THWB* 3 *N.T.*, 1, 254 f.).

Again in the main part of the sentence a story is recounted. And it is obviously the same as that which we found in Jn. 3¹⁶. θεός EN116 is again the acting subject and κόσμος EN117 the object of His activity. The narrative serves as a basis for the preceding verse where Paul had said that his being as καινὴ κτίσις EN118, a man for whom old things have passed away and all things have become new (v. 17), is the work of God. (ἐκ τοῦ θεοῦ EN119) who has reconciled [074] him to Himself in Christ and committed to him the ministry of reconciliation. In verse 19 this is repeated with a wider reference, the particular being made universal and basic. Instead of the apostle being reconciled by God to Himself in Christ, it is now the world which is reconciled by God to Himself in Christ. The apostolic ἡμεῖς EN120 in v. 18 and the κόσμος EN121 in v. 19 are not contrasted, but in a remarkable way the apostolic "we" is a kind of particle of the world (almost the world *in nuce* EN122, a microcosm) and the "world" is only the supreme form, the widest reference of the apostolic "we." In this way the saying about God's reconciling of the world can in fact be the basis of the preceding saying about His reconciling of the apostle. Naturally, this does not exclude the fact that for the apostle the knowledge of the reconciling of the world is grounded in the knowledge of his own reconciliation. The context makes it quite certain that the two cannot be separated.

We must insist at once that the initiative and the decisive action in the happening described as atonement are both with God (as in Jn. 3¹⁶). This is not to say that man's part is only passive; we will see later that there is a proper place for his activity, and what this activity is. But atonement is not "mutual in the sense of both parties becoming friends instead of enemies. Rather, in every respect the transcendence of God over man is safeguarded in the atonement" (Büchsel). We must put this even more strongly. Atonement is altogether the work of God and not of man; καταλλάσσειν EN123 is said only of God, and καταλλαγῆναι EN124 only of man. Compared with Jn. 3¹⁶, the statement of this divine reconciling is striking in its compactness. It does not say that God loved the world in what He did, but it simply describes the act itself. And nothing is said about the "giving of the Son" or the sending of Christ. All the more impressive, therefore, is the way in which the decisive point of Jn. 3¹⁶ is made in the participle construction, "God was in Christ reconciling … ": it is God Himself who intervened to act and work and reveal. The apostle and the world came to have dealings with God Himself. In Paul the concept "world" is not so all-embracing but in most passages it has the same negative force as in John, and certainly in this context. Atonement

---

EN115 (reconciliation)
EN116 God
EN117 world
EN118 new creation
EN119 from God
EN120 we
EN121 world
EN122 a nutshell
EN123 reconciling
EN124 being reconciled

takes place only where there has been strife. According to Rom. 5^6f, those who are reconciled with God are such as were formerly weak and godless, sinners and enemies. That is how Paul judged his own case, and it is in the light of this that he usually understands and uses the concept $\kappa \acute{o} \sigma \mu o s$ EN125. Neither here nor in Rom. 5 does he speak of an enmity of God against man which is removed by the atonement. According to Rom. 5^1, the peace established by the atonement is our peace, $\pi \rho \grave{o} s \ \tau \grave{o} \nu \ \theta \epsilon \acute{o} \nu$ EN126, not the reverse. And his subject here is the reconciling of Paul and the world made by God with Himself, not the reconciling of God with Paul and the world. The hurt which has to be made good is on our side. Notice that in Rom 1^18 the presentation of the $\acute{o} \rho \gamma \grave{\eta} \ \theta \epsilon o \hat{v}$ EN127 consists solely in a description of the corruption of man to which God has given him up. God does not need reconciliation with men, but men need reconciliation with Him, and this verse tells us that God has made this reconciliation, and how He has made it. We are clearly taught the aim of His reconciling activity in Rom. 5^5: "The love of God is shed abroad in our hearts by the Holy Ghost which is given unto us." It is remarkable enough that if that is the goal there has to be a reconciling of the world, and this has already taken place. But that there is a reconciling activity of God in relation to the world may be read in Rom. 11^15 and Col. 1^20. And the goal is undoubtedly this complete conversion of the world to Him. That is how Paul had clearly experienced and known it as God's activity in his own life. But he sees this activity in his own life in the context of God's activity in the world—according to the common denominator of the event of God's intervening in Christ to reconcile the world, and His actual reconciling of the world to Himself. We cannot overlook the scope of this thought in this verse any more (and even less) than we can in Jn. 3^16.

[075] But what does "reconciling" mean? How does God accomplish this conversion of the world to Himself? Here Paul agrees with John: By His own active presence in Jesus Christ, by His special presence and activity under this name and in this form, as distinct from His being in Himself as God and within His activity as Creator and Lord of the world. With his $\mathring{\eta} \nu$ $\kappa \alpha \tau \alpha \lambda \lambda \acute{a} \sigma \sigma \omega \nu$ EN128 he, too, recounts the concrete and unique story of Christ. What took place in this story? I do not see how in this context we can avoid going back to the basic meaning of $\kappa \alpha \tau \alpha \lambda \lambda \acute{a} \sigma \sigma \epsilon \iota \nu$ EN129. The conversion of the world to Himself took place in the form of an exchange, a substitution, which God has proposed between the world and Himself present and active in the person of Jesus Christ. That is what is expressly stated in the verse (21) with which the passage closes.

On the one side, the exchange: "He hath made him to be sin for us (in our place and for our sake), who knew no sin (God Himself being present and active in Him)." Here we have it in the simplest possible form. He has set Him there and revealed Him and caused Him to act and Himself acted as one who was weak and godless, a sinner and an enemy like ourselves. Here we see what is involved in that sending, that offering of the Son, that self-offering and self-hazarding of God for the sake of the world, of which we read in Jn. 3^16. It means that in being present and active in the world in Christ, God takes part in its history. He does not affirm or participate in its culpable nature, its enmity against Himself, but He does take it upon Himself, making His own the situation into which it has fallen. Present and active in Christ, He enters into it. Indeed, it is His divine will—naturally without sinning Himself—to accept a complete solidarity with sinners, to be one with us.

And on the other side, the exchange: He does it. He takes our place in Christ, "that we

---

EN125 world
EN126 towards God
EN127 wrath of God
EN128 'was reconciling'
EN129 reconciling

(again in the simplest possible form) might be made the righteousness of God ($\delta\iota\kappa\alpha\iota\sigma\sigma\acute{\nu}\nu\eta$ $\theta\epsilon\sigma\hat{\nu}$) in Him." It does not say simply that He was made sin and we the righteousness of God. The first is obviously the means or the way to the second. But here, too, the $\ddot{\iota}\nu\alpha$ EN130 is both final and consecutive. God willed the second with the first, and brought it about by means of it. There is an exchange on this side, too. In Christ we are made the righteousness of God as Christ was made sin for us. To be made the righteousness of God means (as the positive complement to Christ's being made sin) being put in a place or status in which we are right with God, in which we are pleasing and acceptable to Him, in which we have already been received by Him, in which we are no more and no less right than God Himself is right. And all this in utter contrast to our place and status as the enemies of God, in which we cannot possibly be right with Him, in which we break His covenant with us as far as in us lies. To be made the righteousness of God means to become covenant-partners with God who keep the covenant just as faithfully as He Himself does. To make us that, God made Christ sin. And because He made Christ sin, we have in fact become that. For because He in whom God was present and active, He who knew no sin took our place and status, caused our situation to be His, accepted solidarity with us sinners, in so doing He made our place and status as sinners quite impossible. For in so doing He has finally judged sin in our place and status ($\dot{\epsilon}\nu$ $\sigma\alpha\rho\kappa\acute{\iota}$, Rom. 8³), i.e., He has done away with it as our human possibility. Where are we as sinners when our sin has been done away in Him? Where can we stand when our former place and status has been made impossible as such? There is obviously no other place or status than that of the One who expatriated us by becoming ours: the place and status of the faithful covenant-partner who is pleasing and acceptable to God and who has been accepted by Him; the place and status of Christ Himself, yes, of the God present and active in Him. In that He took our place, and was made sin for us, we are made the righteousness of God in Him, because we are put in His place.

This exchange is what happened in Christ, according to v. 21. And of the happening in Christ understood in this way Paul says in v. 19 that it is the atonement, or reconciliation— [076] we can now return to the more obvious meaning of the concept—of the world with God which has taken place in Him. The conversion of the world to God has therefore taken place in Christ with the making of this exchange. There, then, in Christ, the weakness and godlessness and sin and enmity of the world are shown to be a lie and objectively removed once and for all. And there, too, in Christ, the peace of the world with God, the turning of man to Him, his friendship with Him, is shown to be the truth and objectively confirmed once and for all. That is the history which Paul has to narrate. As such it is the history of God with Himself, as he has already said in v. 18. But now it is also the history of God with the world, as we are told in v. 19. And notice that in this respect too (and the two cannot be separated) it has taken place once and for all, the history of a decision which has been taken and which cannot be reversed or superseded. That is how He was in Christ—we might say with Jn. 3¹⁶ that is how He loved the world—and it is so, it is in force, and must and will be, whether there are few or many who know the fact, and whatever attitude the world may take to it. The world is God's. Whatever else we may have to say about it (e.g., that it perishes) we must also remember that it is God's—not merely because it is His creature, not merely because God has sworn to be faithful to man, but because God has kept His oath, because He has taken the world from a false position in relation to Himself, because He has put it in that place which belongs to it in relationship with Himself. The reconciliation of the world with God has taken place in Christ. And because it has taken place, and taken place in Christ, we cannot go back on it. The sphere behind it has, in a sense, become hollow and empty, a sphere which we cannot enter. The old has passed away, everything has become new. The

---

EN130 so that

73

new is conversion to God. In v. 18 Paul said that this had happened to him personally in Christ. In v. 19, and as the basis of the former verse, he says that it has happened to the world in Christ. It was a definitive and self-contained event.

Against this understanding of the statement we cannot appeal to v. 20 of the same passage, in which Paul singles out as the content of his activity in the "ministry of reconciliation" the entreaty: "Be ye reconciled to God." This does not refer to an extension of the atonement in the form of something which man himself can decide. We recall that in Jn. 3^{16} there is a corresponding mention of faith in the Son gifted, or offered up by God. The Pauline concept of faith is perhaps too narrow to permit us to equate the "Be ye reconciled to God" with a call for faith. But it does point in this direction. We can put it generally in this way. It is a request for the openness, the attention and the obedience which are needed to acknowledge that what has happened in Christ has really happened, to enter the only sphere which is now left to man, that of the new, that of the conversion to God which has taken place in Christ. The ministry of reconciliation which consists in this entreaty is not of itself self-contained, but it begins only with this self-contained and completed event. This ministry is its first concrete result. The world (the Jew first but also the Gentile) needs this ministry. The community in the world also needs it in order to be and to remain and continually to become a community. But reconciliation in itself and as such is not a process which has to be kept in motion towards some goal which is still far distant. It does not need to be repeated or extended or perfected. It is a unique history, but as such—because God in Christ was its subject—it is present in all its fulness in every age. It is also the immediate future in every age. And finally, it is the future which brings every age to an end. It rules and controls all the dimensions of time in whose limits the world and the human race exist. It is that turning from the lie to the truth, i.e., from the unfaithfulness of man to his faithfulness, and therefore from death to life, which is the basis of all world occurrence, and in a hidden but supremely true sense the purpose and measure of all contemporary occurrence, and also its

[077] goal, enclosing it on every side in order to direct it and set it right. As this completed and perfectly completed turning, reconciliation makes necessary the ministry of reconciliation, giving to it a weight and a power to arouse and edify which no other ministry and indeed no other human activity can ever emulate.

The second participle-clause in v. 19 is as follows: "not imputing their trespasses unto them" (i.e., to men in the world). It indicates the presupposition of this ministry. God took the trespasses of men quite seriously. But He did it, as we are told in v. 21, by accepting solidarity, oneness, with those who committed them. And by taking them seriously in this way. He did something total and definitive against human trespasses. He took them out of the world by removing in that exchange their very root, the man who commits them. They cannot continue, just as a plant or tree cannot live on without its root. They can still be committed, but they can no longer count, they can no longer be entered up—like items in a well-kept statement or account. What counts now, what is reckoned to men, is the righteousness of God which they are made in Jesus Christ. That and that alone is their true yesterday and to-day and tomorrow. It is on this basis that Paul takes himself and the world seriously. And it is on this basis that the world must take itself seriously, not on the basis of its trespasses which are written off in Jesus Christ, but on the basis of the righteousness of God which is reckoned to it in Jesus Christ. To call the world to the very different accounting which is only possible in Jesus Christ, that is the task and goal of the ministry of reconciliation, in which Paul finds himself placed as one who has experienced and known it.

This is what we are told in the third participle-clause in v. 19: "and hath committed unto us (the person of the apostle) the word of reconciliation." Between the apostle and the rest of the world there is the decisive difference that he has eyes and ears for the atonement which has been made, and therefore for the conversion of the world to God, for the new thing which has come and therefore for the passing away of the old, whereas the world is still blind and deaf to it. The world still lives as though the old had not yet passed away and the new come. Not recognising the truth, it still regards the lie as the truth. It still believes that it can and must maintain itself in that sphere which is hollow and empty and in which we cannot live. It is still self-deceived. And Paul sees it dreadfully held by this deception and doomed to its consequences. But it is not this difference, and the tension of it, and the dynamic of this tension, which makes him an apostle. What moves him in this difference, what prevents him from evading the tension as a kind of private person reconciled with God, what forces him to make it his own, to bear it in his own person, is the fact that what has come about for him in Christ as his reconciliation with God has come about for him for the sake of the world. His conversion as such was his calling to be an apostle, his placing in this ministry of reconciliation, or, as it is expressed here, the committing of the "word of reconciliation" to the existence of his person. The "word of reconciliation" is the indicating and making known of reconciliation in the world to which it is still unknown and which is still in the grip of the most profound and tragic self-deception. As Paul is given by Christ eyes and ears for Christ, as the atonement made in Christ becomes his, the God to whom he owes this makes him a mouthpiece to speak of this atonement to those who are still blind and deaf, who are not yet aware of the valid and effective atonement which has been made for them, who therefore lived in opposition to this fact as those who are still unreconciled, as strangers to Christ and therefore to God, and for that reason in the most painful sense of the word, strangers also to the world and to themselves. As one who has been made to see and hear, Paul cannot be silent. Called to this office by God, he has to be the mouthpiece of reconciliation. And that is what makes him an apostle. That is what constrains him. And it is the concrete reach of the turning made in Christ that where it is experienced and known it evokes this movement, underlying the community and its ministry of attestation in the world and against the world [078] and yet also for the world.

We concluded our consideration of Jn. 3[16] with a reference to the ministry of those who, believing on the Son of God, do not perish but have everlasting life. It is not there explicitly in the text. We can only say that the verse can be logically understood only when we find in it this reference. But in 2 Cor. 5[19] both the context and the wording make it the point of the whole verse. Where the atonement made in Jesus Christ is experienced and known, it necessarily evokes this witness. In this case, therefore, we have even better justification for concluding with the judgment that reconciliation manifests itself in the establishment and the actual bearing of a witness to it as the reconciliation of the world.

§ 58

THE DOCTRINE OF RECONCILIATION (SURVEY)

The content of the doctrine of reconciliation is the knowledge of Jesus Christ who is (1) very God, that is, the God who humbles Himself, and therefore the reconciling God, (2) very man, that is, man exalted and therefore reconciled by God, and (3) in the unity of the two the guarantor and witness of our atonement.

This threefold knowledge of Jesus Christ includes the knowledge of the sin of man: (1) his pride, (2) his sloth and (3) his falsehood—the knowledge of the event in which reconciliation is made: (1) his justification, (2) his sanctification and (3) his calling—and the knowledge of the work of the Holy Spirit in (1) the gathering, (2) the upbuilding and (3) the sending of the community, and of the being of Christians in Jesus Christ (1) in faith, (2) in love and (3) in hope.

1. THE GRACE OF GOD IN JESUS CHRIST

In order to be able to survey the whole, we will first select from the many things that we have to consider and explain in greater detail one primary thing, that in reconciliation as the fulfilment of the covenant of grace, as in the covenant of grace itself, we have to do with a free act of the grace of God. God re-establishes the covenant, or, rather, He maintains and continues it, in order to lead to his goal the man whom He has brought into covenant with Him. Whatever connexions there may be before or behind, they do not alter the fact that in so doing God makes a completely new start as the freest possible subject. No one who really knows Him in this activity will ever be able to think of Him as bound by these connexions or committed to this activity.

He acts to maintain and defend His own glory. But no one and nothing outside Himself could ordain for Him that this should be a matter of His glory. He acts with a view to the goal to which He wills to bring man, but there is not really any necessity which constrains Him to do this. He acts as a Creator to a creature, but sin is the self-surrender of the creature to nothingness. If this is what man wanted, God might easily have allowed man to fall and perish. He had and has plenty of other creatures in whose presence man would not necessarily be missed. He acts with the faithfulness of a covenant-Lord, but He would not have been unfaithful to Himself if He had regarded the covenant [080] which man had broken as invalidated and destroyed. He loved the world of men, but He did not need to continue to love the sinful world of men. We can

76

yet does everything in order, who could not be more powerfully holy and right-eous than when by His Word and in His Son He calls us who are His enemies His children, when He causes us to be His children, because in His freedom to do that He is truly the Lord. Reconciliation is God's crossing the frontier to man: supremely legitimate and yet supremely inconceivable—or conceivable only in the fact of His act of power and love.

We are reminded of the remarkable verbs used by Paul to indicate the reality of grace when he came to speak of it *expressis verbis*[EN2]: $\pi\lambda\epsilon o\nu\acute{a}\zeta\epsilon\iota\nu$ (to grow, to increase, Rom. $6^{1\ 2}$, 2 Cor. 4^{15}), $\dot{\upsilon}\pi\epsilon\rho\pi\lambda\epsilon o\nu\acute{a}\zeta\epsilon\iota\nu$ (to be present in fulness, 1 Tim. 1^{14}), $\dot{\upsilon}\pi\epsilon\rho\beta\acute{a}\lambda\lambda\epsilon\iota\nu$ (to surpass, to exceed, to excel, 2 Cor. 9^{14}), $\dot{\upsilon}\pi\epsilon\rho\pi\epsilon\rho\iota\sigma\sigma\epsilon\acute{u}\epsilon\iota\nu$ (to overflow, to superabound, Rom. 5^{20}). We find a kind of boundless astonishment on the part of the apostle at the divine intervention acknowledged in the concept grace (or love).

The frontier is a real one. On the one side there is God in His glory as Creator and Lord, and also in the majesty of His holiness and righteousness. And on the other side there is man, not merely the creature, but the sinner, the one who exists in the flesh and who in the flesh is in opposition to Him. It is not merely a frontier, but a yawning abyss. Yet this abyss is crossed, not by man, not by both God and man, but only by God. It happens that God the Creator and the Lord, the Holy and the Righteous, the One who can only hide His face from what man is and does, emerges from the impenetrable mystery of His Godhead, which has become so dreadful to the sin of man, and gives Himself to man and to be known by man, to the one who has the faculties to receive and know Him, but has no will or capacity to use these faculties. He gives Himself to him as his God, as the One who did not and will not cease to be his God, the God of sinful and wholly carnal man. This man does not even know how it comes about or happens to him ("Depart from me, for I am a sinful man, O Lord," Lk. 5^8). Even afterwards he cannot explain what has happened by any point of contact which God has found in him. But it does in fact happen that by God's intervention this man finds himself accused and humbled and judged by his God, but also and primarily received by Him and reclaimed as His possession and hidden in Him and sustained by Him and addressed and treated as His friend and indeed His child.

So, then, man can have "peace with God" (Rom. 5^1). But how and on what [083] basis? We can only answer: by the Word of God, in Jesus Christ, by faith in Him, by the Holy Spirit who awakens faith. But all that (and especially the naming of the name of Jesus Christ) simply points us to a riddle which confronts every human How? or On what basis?, because it is the grace of God, the coming of God to man which is grounded only in itself and can be known only by itself, the taking place of the atonement willed and accomplished by Him, the sover-eign act which God did not owe to Himself or the world or any man, on which no one could bank, yet which has in fact taken place and been made manifest. It is only as willed and accomplished by God that it can be true and known to

---

[EN2] expressed in words

be true that that peace is given to man, that he can have it, because the covenant broken by us has been kept and fulfilled by God and is therefore in being, that in spite of ourselves, and therefore in a way which at bottom is inconceivable to us, we who are gainsayers and rebels are genuinely converted to God and are His people in the same sense that He is our God. That is the insoluble mystery of the grace of God enclosed in the name of Jesus Christ before which we stand at this point.

As His act, it is the most actual thing in heaven or earth. Effective by Him, it is effective as nothing else is effective. Revealed in Him, as His revelation it is brighter and clearer and more certain than the light of the sun or the light of any other knowledge. Already in this preliminary survey we can and must state that the righteousness with which man finds himself in some sense clothed is His righteousness and therefore new and strange, the holiness is His holiness and therefore new and strange, the truth His truth and therefore new and strange: "crowned with mercy and lovingkindness" (Ps. 103⁴, cf. Ps. 5¹²). Because of this everything depends absolutely on His blessing, everything on His Word which is itself the reconciling act, everything on God Himself in the uniqueness of His action in Jesus Christ for each and every man, which as such is also the mystery of the present and future of each and every man. Everything depends on Him who is above, and therefore on what comes to man from Him and therefore from above. It does not depend at all on what man had or has or will have to contribute from below. When man is asked concerning his righteousness or holiness or truth, he can only point to his utter lack of all these things and then at once point away from himself to his clothing or crowning with all these things, that is, to Jesus Christ. The event of atonement and the actuality of man reconciled with God can be described by those who know it only in the words of Lk. 15²: "This man receiveth sinners, and eateth with them." It is the Holy Spirit who lays this self-knowledge upon their hearts and this confession upon their lips. It is faith and love and hope which know and speak in this way. Christian obedience consists in this, and its joy and certainty rest and renew themselves on this: that by the grace of God this is the relationship of God with man. For what the Christian community can have specially as knowledge and experience of the atonement made in Jesus Christ, for the power, therefore, of its witness to the world, everything depends on the simplicity of heart which is ready to let the grace of God be exclusively His grace, His sovereign act, His free turning to man as new and strange every morning, so that it does not know anything higher or better or more intimate or real than the fact that quite apart from anything that he can contribute to God or become and be in contrast to Him, unreservedly therefore and undeservedly, man can hold fast to God and live by and in this holding fast to Him.

[084]

In this introductory survey we must also state that unfortunately the paths of Evangelical and Roman Catholic understanding have diverged widely at this point. In the light of the latest doctrine in relation to the Virgin Mary (1950), the proclamation of which has shed a new and garish light on the situation, we can only say that, humanly speaking, they have diverged hopelessly. The heart and guiding principle of the Romanist doctrine of grace is the negation of the unity of grace as always God's grace to man, as His sovereign act which is everywhere new and strange and free. It is the negation of the unity of grace as His grace in Jesus Christ. It is the division of grace by which it is first of all His, but then—and this is where the emphasis falls—effected and empowered by His grace, it is also our grace. Against this view we must at once and quite definitely set our face (for what follows, cf. the survey given in B. Bartmann, *Dogm. Handb.* 2, 1929, 113).

In the Romanist teaching a distinction is made between *gratia increata*[EN3], which is God Himself, who is the divine will of love and therefore the ground of all grace, and *gratia creata*[EN4], which is the "finite product" of the former, "but which is essentially different from God Himself, a created good." We ask: What is this created good when it is a matter of peace between man and the Creator who has been offended by him? How and in what sense can he rely on this "finite product"? How can it be essentially different from God and yet be His grace which reconciles us with Himself?

In the Romanist teaching there is a *gratia externa*[EN5] which works on us only from without in the form of teaching and example. "We have to do here with the life and death of Christ, His Gospel, His miracles, providence, personal experiences, the effectiveness of the Church, the exemplary conversation of the saints. This influence is moral." For the most part it is, of course, connected with the *gratia interna*[EN6]. It aims ultimately at inward effects. But it does not produce them of itself. It simply prepares the way. It makes the soul receptive. In contrast, the inward grace "effects the soul and its basic faculties, raising it to a new order of being. Its influence is physical." It adheres to the soul as a new form. We ask: How can the life and death of Christ and the Gospel (mentioned in the same breath as the effectiveness of the Church and the exemplary conversation of the saints and other good things) be described as "only" an external grace and as such obviously impotent and defective? What is this "physical" influence compared with which that of the Gospel is "only" moral?—as though the outward moral grace were not the most inward and physical. And what is this form of the soul in a higher order of being in which we are not referred absolutely and exclusively to that *gratia externa*[EN7] which has only moral significance but can find comfort and be reconciled with God physically, in and by ourselves?

Within the decisive *gratia interna*[EN8] there is a personal grace of sanctification (*gratia gratiam faciens*[EN9]) and a grace of office (*gratia gratis data*[EN10]), the charismatic endowment "which is for the most part firmly linked with the priestly *ordo*[EN11]" and which reveals itself in the official power of the priesthood. We ask: Is there a personal sanctification, or a charismatic, or shall we say a priestly endowment which can be wrested even for a moment from the hand of the God who shows His grace to sinful man, and made a possession of the man who receives it, so that it does not have to be sought and received every morning afresh from God? If either the one or the other or both are really effective, how can they be so except from the very first in the event of their giving and receiving? [085]

EN 3 uncreated grace
EN 4 created grace
EN 5 external grace
EN 6 internal grace
EN 7 external grace
EN 8 internal grace
EN 9 grace creating grace
EN10 grace given freely
EN11 order

A further distinction is then made between *gratia actualis*[EN12] and *gratia habitualis*[EN13]. Both of these are subdivisions of the grace of sanctification. The first is a *motio divina*[EN14] "which is given only for a time to do one or more acts." It serves to prepare the way for the reception of habitual grace, and to maintain it when it has been received, increasing it and enabling it to bring forth fruit. Habitual grace itself is constant, creating in man a kind of state of grace. We ask: Can a *motio divina*[EN15] really be only a preparation for something higher and better, a means only to maintain and prosper it? Not an awakening of faith and obedience, but the *conditio sine qua non*[EN16] of a real grace which consists in a human competence? And what kind of a competence is this? And what place is there for it in face of the actuality—not of human acts, but of the being and action of the gracious God? Is there a human *habitus*[EN17] which deserves to be called a *habitus*[EN18] of grace in itself, and as such is opposed to the actual grace of God?

There is a further distinction between *gratia medicinalis*[EN19] and *gratia elevans*[EN20]. Once again, the first is simply a preparation for the second, the capacitating of men for acts of the supernatural life, by the healing of his nature from the wounds of original sin and the removal of human ignorance and concupiscence. As against this, *gratia elevans*[EN21], which is the substance of *gratia interna*[EN22], as its very name indicates, accomplishes the lifting up of the faculties of the soul to another order of being, making men capable of purely supernatural activities. We ask: Is then the work of Christ as a Healer only preparatory? Does He not in this way lift us up to the supernatural life? Does He only prepare us in this way for a true being in grace, in which we will no longer need Him as a Healer, in which we are no longer the sick folk that He came to heal?

Again, there is a distinction between *gratia praeveniens*[EN23] and *gratia concomitans*[EN24]. The first precedes our free decision, stirring up the will to do good. The other accompanies and supports and gives stability to the activity of man as he is already free. We ask: In relation to the free will of sinful man, is grace only a stirring up of that will to do good, and then the accompanying and supporting and continual strengthening of its activity? Is there then no new creation? No awakening from the dead? Of what two partners are we really speaking then? If we are speaking of the gracious God and sinful man, how can we ever cease at any point to understand the grace which comes from God to man wholly and utterly and exclusively as *gratia praeveniens*[EN25]? Can it really be understood, will it be understood, except as the grace which heals us and for that very reason lifts us up?

A further distinction is made between *gratia operans*[EN26] and *gratia cooperans*[EN27]. The first is active in us alone and without any co-operation on our part (*in nobis sine nobis*[EN28]). Again,

---

[EN12] actual grace
[EN13] habitual grace
[EN14] divine movement
[EN15] divine movement
[EN16] necessary condition
[EN17] disposition
[EN18] disposition
[EN19] restorative grace
[EN20] elevating grace
[EN21] elevating grace
[EN22] internal grace
[EN23] prevenient grace
[EN24] concomitant grace
[EN25] prevenient grace
[EN26] operative grace
[EN27] co-operative grace
[EN28] in us, without us

this is thought of as only preparatory to our own good actions: "It sets in motion those pious thoughts and stimulations of the will which always precede the free decision." As against that, *gratia cooperans*EN29 always works together with the free will (*in nobis cum nobis*EN30). We ask: On what basis is there ever a *cooperari*EN31 in the relationship between the gracious God and sinful man which is not also and as such a pure *operari*EN32? How do the work of God and the work of man ever come to stand on the same level, so that they can mutually limit and condition each other? How can the "above" of God which renews, and the "below" of man which stands in need of renewal, ever be placed side by side? How can the "below" of man,   [086] even when it has in fact been renewed, ever come to imagine that its renewal is a result of co-operation between the renewing "above" of God and itself?

Again, there is a distinction between *gratia sufficiens*EN33 and *gratia efficax*EN34. The one is a grace which merely reaches out and is sufficient, but is not in itself and as such accompanied by any result. It is a grace which has to be completed by the free decision of the human will or by *gratia efficax*EN35 (a grace maintained by the Thomists in their controversy with the Molinists). This latter grace is added to the former and lends it the necessary force. We ask: Is grace as such ever *sufficiens* without being *efficax*? EN36 Is it ever effective objectively without being effective subjectively? Is grace ever a precondition for something else, a precondition which can come into force only by the free will of man or the addition of a further grace? Does the fact that man believes he can evade or resist it mean that we can speak of a grace which is not effective? Is not the really dreadful thing about human resistance to it the fact that in itself and as such, as an act of divine sovereignty, it is not merely a condition proposed to man but the absolutely binding and effective determination of his existence, which he contradicts by his resistance?

Finally, there is a distinction (the most remarkable of all) between *gratia Christi*EN37 and *gratia Dei*EN38, or *gratia supernaturalis*EN39 and *gratia naturalis*EN40. Since all the graces so far mentioned are extended in virtue of the merits of Christ, "they are all called the grace of Christ." Over against, or rather preceding them, there is a special "grace of God," *gratia sanitatis*EN41, granted to man in Paradise when he was at any rate not positively unworthy of it. This grace became his own, and it is evident that it was not simply removed even from sinful man, but still remains as *gratia naturalis*EN42. We ask: Is the concept "grace of Christ" only a kind of generic name for all the other graces? Are they merely called the grace of Christ, or are they all really His one grace? And if they are called this because they really are, is it enough to say that they are because the merits of Christ constitute the possibility and condition of their distribution? Does not this mean that at bottom the grace of Christ is restricted to those graces which are distinguished by the special concepts of *gratia externa, praeveniens, operans, sufficiens*EN43, whereas the true graces, *gratia interna, habitualis, cooperans,*

EN29 co-operative grace
EN30 in us, and with us
EN31 co-operation
EN32 operation
EN33 sufficient grace
EN34 effectual grace
EN35 effectual grace
EN36 sufficient ... effectual
EN37 the grace of Christ
EN38 the grace of God
EN39 supernatural grace
EN40 natural grace
EN41 grace of health
EN42 natural grace
EN43 external, prevenient, operative and sufficient grace

efficax[EN44], being only prepared and made possible by it, will necessarily bear another name because they derive from another source? Can we say "the grace of Christ" and mean less than the whole reality of the grace of God, the grace which cannot be exceeded by any other or higher grace, which cannot precede a true grace because it is itself the only true grace and all that grace? "The Catholic conception understands the essence of grace to be that which mediates between the will of God and the will of man" (Bartmann, p. 17). If we accept this as our "conception," how then in this mediatorial capacity can it be anything other than the grace of Christ and therefore the one grace of God—as though there were other mediators or mediations which we have to distinguish from the one Mediator? But if it is the one grace of God, how does it come about that before or alongside it there is a special *gratia Dei*[EN45], a *gratia sanitatis*[EN46] or *naturalis*[EN47] extended to our first parents or to man in his creaturely nature? At what point in his history or in what depth of his creaturely nature can the grace of God come to man except as the grace of Christ? Is it that we are dealing with another God than the One who is Father, Son and Holy Spirit, and who has elected from all eternity to be the God of man in Jesus Christ—so that naturally we are dealing with the other grace of this other God? But what other God can be the God of man, and what other grace can there be as a *gratia sanitatis*[EN48]? But again, if the grace of Christ is the one grace of God, what place is there for these distinctions, which all have the one result, of distinguishing and indeed separating a grace in itself from a grace for us, a grace which is objectively indispensable from a grace which is subjectively effective, a grace which is merely stimulative and [087] preparatory from a grace which co-operates with us, e.g., a *gratia operans*[EN49] which, as a pure act of God, is enclosed in itself as in a glass-case from a *gratia cooperans*[EN50] which lays claim upon us, or a grace which merely cleanses us from a grace which lifts us up, in short a grace which is manifestly incomplete from a grace which is perfect and complete? How dare we split up the grace of Christ and the grace of God in this way? Is it not the case that as outward grace, for example (that which is described as the grace of the life and death of Christ, of the Gospel, etc.), it is wholly inward and proper to man, and conversely, that as inward grace which is proper to us it is altogether outward, the grace of the life and death of Christ and the grace of the Gospel? Similarly, is it not the case that actual grace is habitual, and habitual actual? That *gratia praeveniens*[EN51] is *concomitans*[EN52], and *sufficiens efficax*[EN53], and *vice versa*? How can that which is described as the second and perfect be perfect except in the power of the first, which is regarded as so meagre and impotent as a purely enabling and preparatory grace? How can the first not have already in itself the perfection of the second? If there is one God, and one Mediator between God and man, and therefore one grace—what place is there for all these abstractions? These are the questions which crowd in upon us as we face the final Roman Catholic distinction.

But the Romanist doctrine of grace insists on these abstractions. Naturally it also maintains—rather more emphatically on the Thomist side and rather less emphatically on the Jesuit—that in the last resort there is only one grace. But it merely says this: it does not make any use of it. It simply commemorates the fact. It says it as a precaution, e.g., to ward off the

---

[EN44] internal, habitual, co-operative and effectual grace
[EN45] grace of God
[EN46] grace of health
[EN47] nature
[EN48] grace of health
[EN49] operative grace
[EN50] co-operative grace
[EN51] prevenient grace
[EN52] concomitant
[EN53] sufficient, effectual

84

kind of questions that we have been putting. When left to itself and following its own inclination it says something very different; it talks about the division of grace. It says the first thing as a bracket in which to say the second: but it does not abolish the parenthesis in order to say it.

For, if it did, the fact would be revealed which is plainly enough proclaimed by all these characterisations and emphases, that it is definitely much more interested in the *gratia interna*EN54 than the *gratia externa*EN55, in habitual grace than actual, in the grace which uplifts than the grace which heals, in *gratia cooperans*EN56 than *gratia operans*EN57, in other words in the state and life and activity of grace in man than in Christ as the One who accomplishes the sovereign act of God and what man is in and by Him, in Mary than the Son of Mary, in the sacraments as the supposed means of grace than the Word and Spirit of God who reveals and attests and in that way really mediates it, in the Church as the form of grace, in the priesthood and its authority than the Lord of the community which lives by the Word and Spirit of God and therefore in His service. This is the system of fatal preferences which would be revealed if the theology of Rome were to speak of the unity of grace instead of its division, and it is to be feared that the unity which it would choose would necessarily be that of man in grace, of Mary, of the sacraments, of the Church ruled and directed by the priesthood.

Alternatively, the revelation of this strange preference might cause it to take fright and to abandon it. It would then have to decide to become a real doctrine of the grace of Christ. It would have to notice that the subjective side to which it has everywhere addressed itself in the sphere of those twofold concepts is utterly dependent upon and can be known and determined only by the objective, which it has commemorated but then abandoned it as though it were only a *conditio sine qua non*EN58. It would have to learn to trust that the genuinely subjective is already included in the true objective, and will be found in it and not elsewhere. But in this case the Romanist theology would have to become Evangelical. And in view of its authoritative pronouncements it seems less likely to happen to-day than at any time.

What is certain is that we have to take warning at this point. If it is a matter of the grace of the one God and the one Christ, there can be only one grace. We cannot, therefore, split it up into an objective grace which is not as such strong and effective for man but simply comes [088] before him as a possibility, and a subjective grace which, occasioned and prepared by the former, is the corresponding reality as it actually comes to man. But the grace of the one God and the one Christ, and therefore the objective grace which never comes to man except from God, must always be understood as the one complete grace, which is subjectively strong and effective in its divine objectivity, the grace which does actually reconcile man with God. And the test of this understanding of grace must be that the state of man in relation to it—apart from what we can positively say concerning him in the light of it—is clearly and unequivocally described as one of absolute need: a state in which—with all that this involves—he is and remains always a recipient, a state in which he not only does not cease but can never do more than begin (and he will always be a beginner) to beg and to reach out for it in his poverty, in order that in that poverty he may be rich. The Romanist doctrine of grace cannot survive this test. It ascribes to man in grace an *exousia*EN59 in which he can look back to the grace of Christ as such as to an indispensable but preliminary stage which he has already passed. It furnishes him with a wealth in which he is no longer poor and needy and

---

EN54 internal grace
EN55 external grace
EN56 co-operative grace
EN57 operative grace
EN58 necessary condition
EN59 authority

hungry and sick, in which, therefore, he cannot be the recipient of the one complete grace of God and of Christ. At the point where its true interest emerges, it definitely does not describe him as the being which has known and experienced and acknowledged the atonement as the sovereign act of God. As reflected in its description of man in grace, God has ceased to be the free subject of the atonement, the grace of the atonement has ceased to be His grace. And since this is so, there can be no peace between this and the Evangelical doctrine of grace.

But we must not omit an irenical and ecumenical word at the conclusion of this confessional polemic. There is a very deep peace (beyond any understanding) between us Evangelical Christians and our Catholic fellow-Christians who are badly instructed in this doctrine. We cannot believe that they do in fact live by the grace which is so dreadfully divided in their dogmatics. Rather, we have to believe, and it is comforting to believe, that they as well as we—if only we did it better—do live by the one undivided grace of Jesus Christ. We have badly misunderstood what we have had to say in clear opposition to their teaching if we do not believe and therefore confess this. We wish that they would abandon both their teaching and many—very many—things in their practice which correspond so closely to it. We wish that they would give God the glory which their dogmatics (and not only their dogmatics) obviously does not give, so that we could then stand with them in a genuine *communio in sacris*[EN60]. But we trust in that *communio in sacris*[EN61] which—not made with hands—has already been achieved by the sovereign act of the God who reconciles us men with Himself and therefore with one another: on the far side of the Church's doctrine and practice, which even at its best (whether Evangelical or Catholic) can only be a witness made with the best of human understanding and conscience to the God who is greater than us all.

It is fitting that at this point we ourselves should now look very carefully in this other direction—at the man to whom this sovereign act applies, the man who is reconciled with God on the basis of this sovereign act. God has acted in His grace (which is always His). He has acted, therefore, without us and against us and for us, as a free subject in Jesus Christ. He has by Himself posited a new beginning. But He has really acted. What He has done is not just something which applies to us and is intended for us, a proffered opportunity and possibility. In it He has actually taken us, embraced us, as it were surrounded us, [089] seized us from behind and turned us back again to Himself. We are dealing with the fulfilment of the covenant. God has always kept it but man has broken it. It is this breach which is healed in the sovereign act of reconciliation. God was not ready to acquiesce in the fact that while He was for us we were against Him. That had to be altered, and in Jesus Christ it has in fact been altered once and for all. That is the original and unilateral and sovereign triumph of God. That is the meaning of the crossing of the frontier or abyss from God's side as it took place in the existence of the man Jesus. The offence offered to God by the unfaithfulness of His covenant-partner, and the misery of that partner, are both removed in Him. In Him man keeps and maintains the same faithfulness to God that God had never ceased to maintain and keep to him. God keeps and maintains His faithfulness by looking and going away past the transgression of man and Himself entering in and providing for the faithfulness of man

---

[EN60] communion in the sacraments
[EN61] communion in the sacraments

and therefore for the fulfilment of the covenant, even on the side of man. In this way God takes care for His own glory. And He does it by bringing man to glory. That is His sovereign act in the atonement. That is the grace of Jesus Christ.

It is apparent at once that the formula "God everything and man nothing" as a description of grace is not merely a "shocking simplification" but complete nonsense. Man is nothing, i.e., he has fallen a prey to nothingness, without the grace of God, as the transgressor who has delivered himself up to death, as the covenant breaker he has shown himself to be in relation to God. In the giving of His Son, however, in reconciling the world to Himself in Christ, God is indeed everything but only in order that man may not be nothing, in order that he may be His man, in order that as such he, too, may be everything in his own place, on his own level and within his own limits. The meaning and purpose of the atonement made in Jesus Christ is that man should not cease to be a subject in relation to God but that he should be maintained as such, or rather—seeing that he has himself surrendered himself as such—that he should be newly created and grounded as such, from above. This creating and grounding of a human subject which is new in relation to God and therefore in itself is, in fact, the event of the atonement made in Jesus Christ. This is what was altered in Him. This is what was accomplished by the grace of God effective and revealed in Him. In Him a new human subject was introduced, the true man beside and outside whom God does not know any other, beside and outside whom there is no other, beside and outside whom the other being of man, that old being which still continues to break the covenant, can only be a lie, an absurd self-deception, a shadow moving on the wall—the being of that man who has been long since superseded and replaced and who can only imagine that he is man, while in reality he is absolutely nothing. Yes, the atonement is the filling of this abyss of nothing, of human perdition. And it is by the abyss of the divine mercy that that other abyss is filled. It is this pure divine mercy [090] which fills the abyss, the mercy which we have to recognise and adore in this act of God, the mercy which we have to seek afresh every morning, the mercy for which we can only ask and reach out as beggars, the mercy in relation to which we can only be recipients. By the grace of God, therefore, man is not nothing. He is God's man. He is accepted by God. He is recognised as himself a free subject, a subject who has been made free once and for all by his restoration as the faithful covenant partner of God. This is something which we must not conceal. It is something which we must definitely proclaim in our Evangelical understanding of grace. We cannot say and demand and expect too much or too great things of man when we see him as He really is in virtue of the giving of the Son of God, of the fact that God has reconciled the world to Himself in Christ.

We underline the fact that it is a matter of a being of man. We can and must experience and know this—that is what makes a Christian a Christian. But first of all, and in itself, and as the object of this experience and knowledge it is a being. Being reconciled is not a matter of the mere hoping or thinking or feeling or experience or even conviction of man. It cannot in any sense be interpreted as a matter of hypothesis (with all the "uncertainty" to which this necessarily gives rise). Its force does not depend upon the intensity with which it is hazarded, while all the time its truth is in the last resort a matter for doubt. No, the old has indeed passed away, all things are become new, God was in Christ reconciling the world to Himself, and those who believe in Him do not perish but have everlasting life. The new man who keeps the covenant has been born and is alive and revealed. Therefore we have peace with God—without any uncertainty. This alteration in the human situation has already taken place. This being is self-contained. It does not have to be reached or created. It has already come and cannot be removed. It is indestructible, it can never be superseded, it is in force, it is directly present. This is the mystery of the man reconciled to God in Jesus Christ. This is what is experienced and known in Christian knowledge and experience. And if in describing this knowledge and experience as such we have to mention all kinds of human hopes and thoughts and feelings and experiences and convictions and hypotheses and "uncertainties"—and why should not this be the case, why is it not necessarily the case in this connexion?—it is always clear that if we are really dealing with Christian knowledge and experience all these things are only comparable with the foam of a waterfall plunging down from the highest mountain tops. They derive necessarily from that being. Any truth and power that they have can come only from that in itself enduring being. Human experience and knowledge cannot of themselves attain to the being of reconciled man. They have no power to rise from appearance to being. The being is there first, and

[091]   in the power of it it is then followed by everything which may happen as a more or less clear and certain acknowledgment on the part of man. Notice that we are not talking *in abstracto*[EN62] of the being of God or the reality and power of the divine act of sovereignty. We are now looking at man. We are speaking of the being of man reconciled to God in Jesus Christ. For it is the meaning and reach of the atonement made in Jesus Christ, the power of the divine act of sovereignty in grace, that God willed not to keep to Himself His own true being, but to make it as such our human being and in that way to turn us back to Himself, to create the new man, to provide for the keeping of the covenant by us, to give us peace with Himself. In the atonement it is a matter of God and His being and activity for us and to us. And that means an alteration of the human situation, the result of which is an altered being of man, a being of man divinely altered. It is on this basis that as Christians we cannot think or demand or expect too much or too high things of man. He is reconciled to God in Jesus Christ. If he is to be understood aright, he can and should be understood in the light of this fact. This is the denominator by which we have to view everything that he is and does and everything that we can think and say concerning

---

[EN62] in the abstract

him. He can still rebel and lie and fear, but only in conflict, in impotent conflict, with his own most proper being. He can and necessarily will be judged, but his own most proper being will be his judge. All his mistakes and confusions and sins are only like waves beating against the immovable rock of his own most proper being and to his sorrow necessarily breaking and dashing themselves to pieces against this rock. But human obedience, too, human constancy and virtue, useful human knowledge, human faith and love and hope, all these are only a standing and walking on the rock which bears him up, the rock of the new being given to him as his own. An Evangelical doctrine of the grace of God—if it is not to give offence and to lay itself open to the objections of its Romanist opponents—will not be guilty of a nominalism which compromises or even negates this being of the man reconciled to God in Jesus Christ. This being is the first and basic thing which we must seriously and definitively ascribe to the man reconciled to God in Jesus Christ. It is something that we have to expound and understand. We cannot go back a single step behind this being of the reconciled man. Whatever we have to think and say of man, and not only of the Christian but of man in general, at every point we have to think and say it of his being as man reconciled in Jesus Christ.

We speak of man reconciled in Jesus Christ and therefore of the being which is that of man in Him. In so doing we will characterise and describe it in its concrete reality, its individuality and power. The grace of God in which it comes and is made over to us is the grace of Jesus Christ, that is, the grace in which God from all eternity has chosen man (all men) in this One, in which He has bound Himself to man—before man even existed—in this One. He, Jesus Christ, is the One who accomplishes the sovereign act in which God has [092] made true and actual in time the decree of His election by making atonement, in which He has introduced the new being of all men. Notice that it is those that know this new being as their own who can openly and confidently and joyfully hail it as such. It is Christians therefore who, when they have spoken of it relevantly, seriously and authoritatively, have always characterised and described it as the being which has met them as their own in Jesus Christ, which they sought and found, and found again in Him, on which they cannot pride themselves, and by which they can live only because they found it exclusively in Him.

Those who believe in Jesus Christ will never forget for a single moment that the true and actual being of reconciled man has its place in that Other who is strange and different from them, and that that is why they can participate in it with a fulness and clarity the knowledge of which would only be broken if they were to look aside to any other place. They will know that they can speak about the being of the new man only in the light of this One, and that they can never speak about it definitely enough in the light of this One. It is the being of the new man reconciled with God which in Him has truly and actually been appropriated to them and to all men.

2. THE BEING OF MAN IN JESUS CHRIST

We cannot speak of the being of man except from the standpoint of the Christian and in the light of the particular being of man in Jesus Christ. To the Christian it is a matter of experience and knowledge. He knows about Jesus Christ, and the reconciliation of the world to God made in Him, and therefore the new being of man in Him. He can give an account and testify to himself and others how this new being originates. God has given it to all men in Jesus Christ. But we cannot expect that all men will be in a position to know and to give an account of Him and therefore of their true and actual being as it is hidden and enclosed and laid up for them in Him. Yet we must remember that what we can say primarily only of the Christian has a general application in the sense that we could at once say it of all men if they came to know of Jesus Christ and of what they are in Him. Christians exist in Him. In practice this is the only thing that we can call their peculiar being. But they do so only as examples, as the representatives and predecessors of all other men, of whom so long as their ears and eyes and hearts are not opened we can only say definitely that the same being in Jesus Christ is granted to them and belongs to them in Him. But Christians know and can declare what it is that belongs to them and all other men in Jesus Christ. And by the existence of the Christian we can make this clear. The being of man reconciled with God in Jesus Christ is reflected in [093] the existence of the Christian. That is something we cannot say of others. It is not that they lack Jesus Christ and in Him the being of man reconciled to God. What they lack is obedience to His Holy Spirit, eyes and ears and hearts which are open to Him, experience and knowledge of the conversion of man to God which took place in Him, the new direction which must correspond to the new being given to them in Him, life in and with His community, a part in its ministry, the confession of Him and witness to Him as its Lord and as the Head of all men. For that reason the being of man reconciled to God in Jesus Christ is not—yet—reflected in them. To understand and describe it, therefore, we must confine ourselves to Christians and the Christian community. The being of man reconciled to God in Jesus Christ has three aspects which are clearly different. We will first of all describe these under the three concepts of faith and love and hope. We will then see how the being of the new man described in this way has its root and basis in Jesus Christ Himself, His person and mission and work, how it is in fact hidden and enclosed and laid up in Him. But in the faith and love and hope of the Christian that which is hidden in Jesus Christ is known, that which is enclosed is opened, that which is laid up is distributed and shared. Yet they know, and they keep to this strictly, that it is known to them only as that which is hidden in Him, it is opened only as that which is enclosed in Him, it is shared only as that which is laid up in Him. They are put in this relationship to Him by the presence and operation of the Holy

Spirit. It is this relationship which is described by the concepts of faith and love and hope. We will now try to follow the lines indicated by these three concepts.

The conversion of man to God in Jesus Christ takes place (1) in the fulfilment and revelation of a verdict of God on man. The being of the new man in the form of faith is man's recognition, acknowledgment and acceptance of this verdict, the making of his own subjection to this verdict. That man does accept and bow to this verdict is the work of the Holy Spirit which makes him a Christian. The verdict of God to which faith subjects itself is two-sided. It has both a negative and also a positive meaning and content.

On the one side it is a verdict which disowns and renounces. With all the truth and validity and force of a sentence which has not only been pronounced but executed, and therefore pronounced once and for all, it declares that man is no longer the transgressor, the sinner, the covenant-breaker that God has found him and he must confess himself to be, that as such he has died and perished from the earth, that he cannot be dealt with as such, that as such he has no future. Jesus Christ has taken his place as a malefactor. In his place Jesus Christ has suffered the death of a malefactor. The sentence on him as a sinner has been carried out. It cannot be reversed. It does not need to be repeated. It has fallen instead on Jesus Christ. In and with the man who was taken down dead on Golgotha man the covenant-breaker is buried and des- [094] troyed. He has ceased to be. The wrath of God which is the fire of His love has taken him away and all his transgressions and offences and errors and follies and lies and faults and crimes against God and his fellowmen and himself, just as a whole burnt offering is consumed on the altar with the flesh and skin and bones and hoofs and horns, rising up as fire to heaven and disappearing. That is how God has dealt with the man who broke covenant with Himself, God has vindicated Himself in relation to this man, as He did as Creator in relation to chaos. He could not, and would not, use this man. He could not, and would not, tolerate and have him any longer. He could and would only do away with him. He could and would only disown and renounce his existence. And that is what He has done, not merely in the form of a protest and contradiction, which would clarify but not alter the situation between them, but in the form of his destruction. This event is the divine verdict, the Word in which Christian faith believes. In virtue of this Word, i.e., in the power of this event, the existence of man as a sinner and all his transgressions are now behind him. Whatever else he may be, he will no longer be this man, the transgressor. Most definitely not, as the man who is placed under this Word. The word "forgiveness" speaks of a judicial act in which God has maintained His glory in relation to man. But it does not speak of a new purpose or disposition or attitude on the part of God. And least of all does it speak of any mitigation of the severity with which sinful man is rejected by God. Rather it speaks of the fulfilment of that rejection. The being of the new man reconciled with God in Jesus Christ is one in which man has no more future as sinful man. And in the form of Christian faith it is a being in subjection to this verdict, and in that way and to that extent a being in "the forgiveness of sins."

But the verdict of God on man in which the conversion of man to God is fulfilled has also a positive meaning and content. It is a verdict which recognises and accepts. With all the truth and validity and force of a sentence which has not only been pronounced but executed and therefore pronounced once and for all, it declares that God receives man, and that man in accordance with his election and institution as a covenant-partner—can confess himself a faithful servant of God, His recognised friend and well-loved child. In that event and verdict and Word God willed to snuff out and kill and destroy. He has done so. But He did it to secure freedom for the man in whom He delights, the man who is not merely innocent but positively righteous, the man who fulfils His will. This man alone is man's future. For it was as such that Jesus Christ took his place. And in his place Jesus Christ rendered that obedience which is required of the covenant partner of God, and in that way found His good-pleasure. He did it by taking to Himself the sins of all men, by suffering as His death the death to which they had fallen a prey, by freely offering Himself as [095] the sacrifice which had to be made when God vindicated Himself in relation to man, by choosing to suffer the wrath of God in His own body and the fire of His love in His own soul. It was in that way that He was obedient. It was in that way that He was the righteous One. It was in that way that He was recognised by God—and since He took the place of all, all men in Him. Even on this side, as the positive justification of man, the judgment of God was executed, and can never be reversed and does not need to be repeated. The resurrection of Jesus Christ from the dead is at once the fulfilment and the proclamation of this positive sentence of God. Man is a suitable human partner for the divine partner. He is the one in whom God delights. He is a faithful servant and a friend and a dear child of God. This man was brought in with the resurrection of Jesus Christ from the grave, and with just the same energy with which the old man of contradiction and opposition was done away in the death of Jesus Christ. With the creation of the new man God has vindicated Himself to us, pronouncing His verdict upon us. He willed this man. And what He willed took place. This man came, the man who is righteous for us all, who is our righteousness before God. There is no room for any fears that in the justification of man we are dealing only with a verbal action, with a kind of bracketed "as if," as though what is pronounced were not the whole truth about man. Certainly we have to do with a declaring righteous, but it is a declaration about man which is fulfilled and therefore effective in this event, which corresponds to actuality because it creates and therefore reveals the actuality. It is a declaring righteous which without any reserve can be called a making righteous. Christian faith does not believe in a sentence which is ineffective, or only partly effective. As faith in Jesus Christ who is risen from the dead it believes in a sentence which is absolutely effective, so that man is not merely called righteous before God, but is righteous before God. He believes that God has vindicated Himself in relation to man, not partly but wholly, not negatively only but positively, replacing the old man by a new and obedient man. He believes that by calling that One His own dear Son in whom He is well pleased, God has set up not a provisional but a definitive order in the relationship between Himself and man. He believes in the freedom of the children of God which is not merely demonstrated but given and made over in the resurrection of Jesus Christ from the dead. He believes in the fulfilment of the divine election actualised in this event, and therefore in the revelation and demonstration of it given in this event. As faith it lives by the divine Word of power spoken in this event. The being of the new man reconciled with God in Jesus Christ is one in which man has a future only as the righteous one that he is before God in Jesus Christ. In Christian faith man subjects himself to the judgment by which eternal life is already—effectively—ascribed and promised to him, a judgment beside which he is not able to see before him any other.

We have been speaking of what is usually comprised under the concept of   [096] justification. Justification definitely means the sentence executed and revealed in Jesus Christ and His death and resurrection, the No and the Yes with which God vindicates Himself in relation to covenant-breaking man, with which He converts him to Himself and therefore reconciles him with Himself. He does it by the destruction of the old and the creation of a new man.

But we can understand the concept justification (the justification of the sinner) in all its truth and individual force only when we see that basically and inclusively it stands for God's acting and speaking in His own cause, in fulfilment of His eternal will with man. Only then and on that basis does it stand for the grace and goodness and mercy of God as they come to man. These inconceivable benefits do, of course, come to man. It is the eternal will of God to let them do so. But Christian faith finds all its comfort and joy in the fact, and it clings to it, that this gracious and good and merciful judgment of God on man is primarily God's own cause, that in this judgment the cause of man is safeguarded—and with a sovereign assurance—by the fact that God has made it His own cause, and that as such, quite apart from anything that we can do about it, He carried it through to a successful conclusion. In the light of this Christian faith itself, as man's subjection to this verdict, can be understood as a form of the being of the new man. It is in faith that man can find and know that he is justified with an ultimate confidence and assurance. For His own honour and glory, acting solely in His own cause, God has denied and renounced his being in unrighteousness. That is the force of this verdict on the negative side. That is the meaning of it in all circumstances. That is why the believer will not perish. That is why his sins are forgiven. Again, for His own honour and glory, acting solely in His own cause, God has recognised and accepted a being in righteousness. That is the force of the verdict on the positive side. And in all circumstances man can and should hold to the fact that this verdict is in force and that he is the servant and friend and child of God. In virtue of this verdict he has eternal life. The truth and power of faith depend on the fact that it is not a work of human arbitrariness, not even the arbitrariness of a supreme need and longing for redemption, but man's subjection to the divine verdict in which it is a matter of God's own honour and glory—and as such a subjection an act of pure obedience. As this act of obedience faith is a work of the Holy Spirit, and as true faith, and only as such, it is justifying faith.

Why is it so necessary to be clear about this? There are other forms of the new man besides faith and therefore subjection to God's sentence of negative and positive pardon. But in the conversion of man to God we have to do with this basic thing. The being of the new man is a being in the truth and force of this twofold pardon. To that extent faith is the only form of this new being.

[097] Before God, i.e., in relationship to God, we are not unrighteous and rejected but righteous and accepted only by faith, not by love and hope. And we are this by faith in so far as faith is that act of obedience, that subjection to the will of God acting and speaking in His own cause and therefore in sovereign power, that acknowledgment of the honour and glory of God in relation to man. It cannot, therefore, be an arbitrary human act. Even if it is a knowledge and acceptance of what has taken place negatively and positively for all men in Jesus Christ, it is not enough—if it is really to be justifying faith and the form of the new being of man—that it should simply know this and accept it. Even if it is the heart's confidence of this or that man that what took place for all men in Jesus Christ took place and is true and actual and applies in his case, too, it is still not enough—however great may be the depth and sincerity of this confidence—if faith is to justify him and in faith he is to be a new man. It is not enough because that twofold divine pardon was pronounced in Jesus Christ, that destruction of the unrighteous and creation of the righteous being took place—and this is why it is true and actual—in Him. It was for man, but it was for man in Him, in the One who is another, a stranger, confronting even man with his sincere acceptance and heart's confidence, in the One to whom man can only cling as to the high-priest who officiates and speaks and acts for him, that is to say, in faith in Him. Not in faith in himself.

To put it even more clearly and pointedly—only with a lack of faith in himself. The great gulf between the believer and the One in whom he believes carries with it the fact that he cannot receive that pardon and experience his liberation from unrighteousness and to righteousness without having to become aware and recognise and confess that in himself he is altogether unworthy of it, that although he is liberated in very truth by Jesus Christ, yet in himself, in his daily and even hourly thoughts and words and works, he is not liberated at all. His own being contradicts his being in Jesus Christ. Confronted with that being, in the clear light of that being, he finds that in his own being the old man is not yet dead or the new created. In his own being—contrary to the divine judgment—he will again and again find that he is a covenant-breaker, a sinner, a transgressor. In his own being—contrary to the

94

divine verdict—he will never find the faithful servant and friend and dear child of God. In his own being he will never with his own eyes see himself as in any respect justified, but always in supreme need of justification by God. And all this in faith itself and as such. How then is he going to find himself sinless, and even positively righteous? Certainly not by the sincerity and depth of his faith, or the fineness of it as a theological virtue. For where would be the virtue of this faith if as a believer he saw himself in the light and under the judgment of the One in whom he believes? As a being and work liberated from the unrighteousness of the old man and filled with the righteousness of the new [098] he cannot plead before Him his faith—let alone anything else. And remark- ably enough, the more sincere and deep our faith actually is, the less we will find in our faith as in all our other being and activity, the more strange and impossible will be the thought that we can please God with this one work of faith, the more we will try to cling to the fact that we have died as the old man in Jesus Christ, and that we are created and alive as a new man in Jesus Christ, and that we have not to produce our own confirmation of this righteousness before God in our life and being, not our own Christian righteousness, not our own righteousness of faith as a product and achievement and state of our own heart and mind in which we can lay hold of the truth and power of the divine verdict. In faith the Christian will find himself justified because believing in this divine sentence fulfilled and revealed in Jesus Christ he dashes himself against the rock of that work of God which God has willed and done, certainly on behalf of man, but primarily for His own sake, to assert His honour and to maintain His glory against him. Believing in Jesus Christ he will encounter the divine decision which is basically the self-affirmation of God against the crea- ture and therefore the decision of grace in his favour, thus making quite impossible and irrelevant any counter-question concerning that which might correspond to it in the way of human work or life or faith. Because seriously and ultimately the justifying sentence of God is the self-affirmation of God worked out and revealed in this way, it will have incontrovertible truth and an unconditional force against everything that man either is of himself or does of himself, the truth and force of the divinity with which God intervened against man and therefore for him, and which cannot be limited by anything that may or may not correspond on the part of man. Christian faith will cling to and find its confidence and support in this divinity of the justifying sentence, with- out concerning itself about anything—indeed in face and spite of anything— that the believer may find and will necessarily bewail as his own being and essence. This divine judgment will demand a subjection and sheer obedience (and find them in faith) in which man must resolutely turn his back on his own being, in which he finds the old man still there and the new man not yet pres- ent, and sets his face equally resolutely to his being in Jesus Christ in which the former is dead and the latter lives. In faith there will be no place for looking back to our own righteousness or unrighteousness; for conclusions as to the freedom reached or not reached by us, for reflections concerning the worthiness or unworthiness of our response to the divine verdict. Faith can and must be faith only in the truth and actuality of the work of God done and revealed in Jesus Christ, faith in the transcendent and victorious nature of this work, based upon the honour and glory of God which are so clearly asserted in face of all human opposition that however dark and malicious this may be it can never be more than a shadow dispersing before the light, and can be regarded and treated only as such. Both before and behind man will dare to live only by his faith. When faith is like this, it is the faith which justifies a man in spite of his sin. For then it is his genuine conversion from himself as a covenant-breaker and transgressor to the gracious and mighty God—a conversion in which he ceases to be unrighteous and begins to be the righteous man he is, pleasing to God and God's dear child. Faith of this kind is the work of the Holy Spirit which makes man a Christian.

[099]

But this is not the only form of the conversion of man to God accomplished in Jesus Christ. It is the first form: negative and positive justification by the true and mighty sentence of God, and therefore the form of faith. But there is also another form, (2) the placing of man under the divine direction. We might also speak of the law, commandment, ordinance, demand or claim of God. The being of man in the form of Christian love consists in the fact that he accepts the divine direction. That he does this is another form of the work of the Holy Spirit which makes him a Christian.

God's justifying sentence is His all-powerful decision what man really is and is not. In Jesus Christ he is not a rebel but a servant, not an enemy but a friend, not lost to God but a child in the Father's house. God's direction is also an all-powerful decision, His own divine act of lordship. By this means, too, God vindicates His honour and maintains His glory. By this means, too, He exercises authority. But in God's direction it is plain how He exercises authority, how His divine authority is constituted as opposed to all other authorities, what it means radically and finally to stand under the divine lordship. God's direction is the directing of man into the freedom of His children. It is this which has taken place in Jesus Christ no less uniquely than the once-for-all fulfilment of the divine sentence on man. In suffering in our stead the death of the old man, and bringing in by His resurrection the life of the new, He has made room for the being of all men at peace with God. On the basis of what man is and is not by virtue of the divine sentence passed and revealed in Jesus Christ, in face of that twofold pardon, he has no other place but this—the kingdom in which God can be at peace with him and he at peace with God. Jesus Christ—and this is the second element in His work and ministry as the Reconciler between God and us—is the all-powerful direction of God to us to occupy this place, to live in this kingdom. If we are told in Him who we are and are not, we are also told in Him where we belong, where we have to be and live. Only told? Only directed? Only informed? Is it only an invitation or a demand to enter? All that and more. Jesus Christ is God's mighty command to open our eyes and to realise that this place is all around us, that we are already in this kingdom, that we have no alternative but to adjust ourselves to it, that we have our being and continuance here and nowhere else. In Him we are already there, we already belong to it. To enter at His command is to realise that in Him we are already inside. To follow His invitation and demand is to find ourselves in the situation already created in Him and in Him already our own situation. That is man's reconciliation with God in the form of the issuing and receiving of the divine direction.   [100]

Words like law, commandment, ordinance, etc., although they are quite possible and relevant, do not quite suffice to indicate what is meant, because they so easily give the impression of something which has not been already done, which has still to be done by the decision and act which are demanded of man himself. The decision and act of man are, of course, required by the direction given and revealed in Jesus Christ. But the requirement of the divine direction is based on the fact that in Jesus Christ man has already been put in the place and kingdom of peace with God. His decision and act, therefore, can consist only in obedience to the fact that he begins and does not cease to breathe in this place and kingdom, that he follows the decision already made and the act already accomplished by God, confirming them in his own human decision and act; that he, for his part, chooses what has already been chosen and actualised for him. That is why we use the word direction—we might almost say the advice or hint. It is not a loud and stern and foreign thing, but the quiet and gentle and intimate awakening of children in the Father's house to life in that house. That is how God exercises authority. All divine authority has ultimately and basically this character. At its heart all God's ruling and ordering and demanding is like this. But it is in the direction given and revealed in Jesus Christ that the character of divine authority and lordship is unmistakably perceived.

What is it, then, that we are dealing with? What is this place and kingdom in which God's direction summons man to awaken and remain and act? We have already mentioned the decisive concept: it is a matter of man's direction into the freedom for which he is made free in Jesus Christ (in that twofold pardon), in peace with God. It is the place and kingdom which already surrounds him, in which he is already placed, in which he has only to find himself. God's direction is the direction to do this, to make use of his freedom. He has not won his freedom himself. He has not come to this place in his own power or worth, by reason of his own virtue or skill. He does not control it. The kingdom of freedom is not one in which he can act as lord. It is not for him to try to act in it according to his own judgment. If he did, he would certainly not be free, he would secretly have left that place. It is the house of his Father, and he needs the Father's guidance to act in it and therefore to be free. But he receives and has this. And it is the essence of the freedom for which he is freed in Jesus Christ that he is not alone, that he is not left to himself, that he is not directed to his own judgment, that he must not be his own lord and master, or

[101]   exist in himself imprisoned in his own arbitrariness and self-sufficiency. In every form this would be bondage—the unfreedom of the lost rebel and enemy from which he has been loosed. Freedom means being in a spontaneous and therefore willing agreement with the sovereign freedom of God. This freedom is the being of man, not in himself but in Jesus Christ, in the place and kingdom which have been opened up to us in Him and which already surround us in Him. Because it is not in ourselves but in Jesus Christ that we are free, that we are the covenant-partners and children of God, we need His direction and lordship and therefore the direction and lordship that come to us in Him. And because it is in Him that we are really free, He is Himself our direction, our guiding into freedom, our awakening to life in that freedom, our guidance to make use of it, our Lord and King, and therefore in this sense too our reconciliation with God, the One who fulfils our conversion to Him.

As distinct from justification, and as its necessary consequence, this subjection of man to the divine direction is usually called sanctification. It is nothing other than the basic presupposition of all Christian ethics. Sanctification is the claiming of all human life and being and activity by the will of God for the active fulfilment of that will.

We must note first that this subjection of man under God's direction and therefore his sanctification is a form of the atonement, of the conversion of man to God accomplished and revealed in Jesus Christ. It is an element in His activity as man's reconciliation with God. Sanctification cannot then be separated from justification, as though it has to do with man's contribution to his reconciliation with God. Sanctification does not mean our self-sanctifying as the filling out of the justification which comes to man by God. It is sanctification by and in Jesus Christ, who, according to 1 Cor. 1[30], is made unto us both justification and sanctification. Certainly we have to do with the work of man, what he does and what he leaves undone. But it is his work in a peace with God which he himself has not made, and in which he cannot of himself take a single step that is a work in which he really shows himself a faithful and adequate covenant-partner of God and God's dear child. The fact that he does take these steps, that he does good works, is something which takes place only in the truth and power of the divine direction. It is just as much a matter of God's free grace as is the decision who and what he is and is not before God. In Christian ethics, therefore, the atonement made in Jesus Christ cannot simply be a presupposition which has been left far behind. Ethics, too, must testify directly to the atonement which man himself does not make, but which God has made in him as His own work, by giving him direction in Jesus Christ.

And equally clearly we must then say that sanctification consists in the fact that in and through Jesus Christ man is called by God into freedom; summoned to use the freedom in which he has already been put in Jesus Christ.

[102]   God's direction and man's subjection to it has no other meaning and purpose than this. Everything that it means concretely, all the individual directions which have to be unfolded in Christian ethics, can only be concretions of the

one necessary direction to the freedom given to man. The placing of man under this direction must not be understood as his subjection to any other law. On the contrary, all the legislation and commanding of God that we meet with in the Old and New Testaments has to be understood as a call to the awakening to that freedom, as a direction to make use of that freedom which is given us once and for all in Jesus Christ, and which we can never abandon on any pretext if our action is obedience. It is a matter of learning to breathe and to live in that freedom, of taking it with all seriousness.

As Christian faith is the human response to God's justifying sentence, so Christian love is the human response to His direction. The reconciliation of the world with God, i.e., man's conversion to God in Jesus Christ, his being as liberated both negatively and positively—this is something which is experienced and known and acknowledged in Him. And when this is the case, then in the truth and power of the one Holy Spirit God's direction or guidance or hint is also received: in Jesus Christ man is directed by God to awakening and life in the freedom for which He has made him free. If it is given to us to know Jesus Christ as the priestly Representative of all men, that is, as the One in whom in the name of all, and therefore for us, the human covenant-breaker was put to death and the faithful servant and intimate friend and dear child of God is brought into being, then it is ordained and given that we should accept Him as the King and Lord of all men and therefore as our Lord. The obedience of faith is followed by the obedience of love—in practice, of course, it may sometimes precede, but it always accompanies it as a second form of the particular being of the Christian in Jesus Christ, which cannot be separated from the first but is quite distinct from it. Sanctification is the second aspect of the reconciliation of man with God willed and accomplished and revealed by God. It comes after and together with the redemption of man from the power of darkness. It consists in his placing into "the kingdom of the son of his love" (Col. 1^{13}). God Himself is love and revealed Himself as such by sending His only Son into the world in order that we might live through Him (1 Jn. 4$^{8f.}$). In Jesus Christ God has created a final and indestructible fellowship between Himself and all men, between all men and Himself, a fellowship which is final and indestructible because it is based upon His own interposition and guaranteed by it. That is the actualisation and revelation of His love which is as such the direction to which man is subjected and the Christian love which receives it responds. It consists simply in the affirmation of the existence of this fellowship as such, just as faith consists in the affirmation of its foundation. In Jesus Christ God has demonstrated, He has made it visible and audible and perceptible, that He loved the world, that He did not will to be God without it, without all men, without each individual man in particular. And in the same Jesus Christ He has demonstrated, He has made it visible and audible and perceptible, that the world and all men and each individual man in particular cannot be without Him. The demonstration that He belongs to the world and the world to Him is the choice and work of His love in Jesus Christ, "the kingdom

[103]

99

of the son of his love." In general terms Christian love is the active human recognition of this proof of the love of God. It recognises it by following it, imitating it, modelling itself upon it. It is the attitude in which man gives himself to reflect the divine attitude. That he can do this, that he can love, is his sanctification, his breathing and living in the place and atmosphere of freedom, his keeping of the covenant as a faithful partner. That he can love is the work of the Holy Spirit which makes man a Christian. And now we must distinguish two separate elements, or, better, dimensions, in Christian love.

The love of God in Jesus Christ is decisively, fundamentally and comprehensively His coming together with all men and their coming together with Him. This coming together is not deserved by man, but forfeited. Yet it has been accomplished by God in His free grace, defying and overcoming the sin of man. As this coming together the love of God active and revealed in Jesus Christ is the fulfilling of the covenant by Him. It embraces *realiter*[EN63] both the world and the community, non-Christians and Christians. But the knowledge and proclamation of it is a matter only for the Christian community. Those who know it are marked off from all other men as Christians. But this coming together of God and man cannot be known to be fulfilled except as it is actively worked out. God has conjoined Himself with man, existing in his own activity, and He has conjoined man existing in his own activity with Himself. God is not idle but active. For good or evil, therefore, man must be active too. Therefore the recognition of this coming together as such is not merely a conscious but an active being of man in God. And this active being consists in the fact that man for his part in answer to that divine activity not merely knows himself to be brought together but does actively come together with God in thought and word and work: within the limits, of course, of his human capacity, and humbly seeking the One who has already found him in His own free grace, but within those limits with all his heart and soul and mind and strength (Mk. 12[29f.]). This active coming together of man with God will be the realising of all the possibilities of his active being beside which, in the knowledge of the communion achieved by God and therefore of the love of God, he cannot see any other possibilities. In this way it will be an activity which is at bottom voluntary, which excludes the fear of any other forces but God, which claims him wholly and utterly. It will be accomplished as an act of pure gratitude, which does not make any claim and which is therefore complete. And in all this it will be a kind of silhouette of the elective, free and total activity of God Himself to whom he makes a human response. To that extent it will be a following and imitation of that activity, the love to God which is the response to the love of God. In accordance with what He did and revealed in Jesus Christ, God willed from all eternity not to be without man. And now, recognising this will of God, man wills not to be without God. His activity is therefore characterised by the will to seek God and to find Him, that is, to enquire concerning His command-

[104]

[EN63] in a real sense

ment, to be guided by His decisions and attitudes, and to follow His direction. Existence without love has now been left behind as an error and a lie. Therefore he no longer needs to have any fear. He no longer takes pleasure in being self-sufficient and self-responsible, his own lord and master because his own owner. That is the delusion which he has left behind in the knowledge of his coming together with God as God willed and accomplished it. He cannot live in it any longer. He still knows it. It still presses in upon him. But because of that knowledge it has no more power over him. He now lives by suppressing it wherever it arises. He now lives as one who seeks God in his activity. Poetically and rhetorically we might describe the Christian life in much stronger terms. But we will be careful to remember that the substance of anything we might say will always be this, that we are dealing with a fact which is not at all self-evident—that man for his part will seek the God who in Jesus Christ has already sought and found him that was lost, corresponding to the divine action, realising on his side the fellowship which has been set up by God. And above all we will be careful not to separate the concept of this love for God and therefore of this seeking of God from the human activity conditioned by it. We need not be fanatically anti-mystical. As one element in the activity which puts the love to God into effect, there may be a place for a feeling of enjoyable contemplation of God. But it cannot take the place of that activity. Man's being reconciled with God, his conversion to God, is from this second standpoint of sanctification his active being. It is in this being as such that God is either loved or not loved.

But this carries with it the fact that there can be no question of a justification of man by his love to God—perhaps as a continuation or actualisation of his justification by faith. Certainly the divine direction, the direction into love to God, can never be lacking in the man who has subjected himself to the divine sentence in the knowledge of it. But it is the pardoning sentence of God alone which is the basis of fellowship between God and man, and which therefore justifies man. And the fact that he is justified is something which he finds to be true and actual only in faith. That he can love, i.e., seek God is his freedom to live in that fellowship on the basis which has been laid down by God and God alone. But because we are here dealing with human activity, with the sum of [105] the Christian *ethos* and its always doubtful fulfilment, it can as little contribute to the setting up of that fellowship and therefore to justification as can faith itself as the human recognition that it has been set up.

It amounts to this, that in love man is occupied with something else, and he ought always to be so. It would completely destroy the essential character of Christian love as the freedom given to man and to be kept by man if we tried to burden it with the, in itself, impossible and superfluous task of accomplishing or actualising or even completing the justification of man. No one can and will love God who does not believe. No one can and will love God except in the grounding of his being in the fellowship with God realised in that divine judgment. If we are to be justified by faith, in faith we will not look either at our works or our sins. Similarly in love—in the works of our love to God—we will not consider the possibility of trying subsequently to fulfil or to complete of ourselves that grounding of our being. Christian love does not will anything from God. It starts from the point that there is nothing to will which has not already been given. It does not will anything from the One who is everything to it. It wills only God Himself because He is God, because He is this God. It wills simply to love Him, as the man who is reconciled with Him on the basis of His sentence fulfilled and revealed in Jesus Christ can love Him immediately and unquestioningly and unreservedly, but as also he must love Him. The love in which man thinks that he can justify himself before God is not as such a love which derives from faith. It is not a free and pure love which loves God for His own sake, because He is God. It is rather a work of the old mercenary spirit, of the man who at bottom hates the grace of God instead of praising and honouring it. It is therefore a return to the state of sin, of covenant-breaking. Christian love to God is a free and pure love which honours and praises unreservedly the grace of God. For Christian ethics everything depends on the fact that it should be understood as an independent form of the conversion of man to God (and therefore of His reconciliation with Him) and not otherwise. The erroneous teaching of the Council of Trent involves a false understanding both of justification by faith and also of sanctification in love.

But Christian love has a second dimension inseparably connected with the first. The love of God in Jesus Christ brings together Himself with all men and all men with Himself. But at the same time it is obviously the coming together of all men one with another. And as that communion is known it is at once and necessarily evident that there is a solidarity of all men in the fellowship with God in which they have all been placed in Jesus Christ, and a special solidarity of those who are aware of the fact, the fellowship of those who believe in Him, the Christian community. In this horizontal dimension Christian love is love to [106] the neighbour or the brother. This must be distinguished from love to God which is Christian love in the vertical dimension It will not take place without love to God. And there would be no love to God if it did not take place. But while it can only follow, and must follow, this prior love, it is an autonomous loving, for God in heaven and the neighbour on earth are two and not one. Love to others cannot exhaust itself in love to God, nor can love to God exhaust itself in love to others. The one cannot be replaced and made unnecessary by the other. But love to God—to the God who reconciles the world to Himself in Jesus Christ—evokes love to the neighbour and the brother. And love to the man who is made a neighbour and a brother in Jesus Christ follows love to God. The following of the divine loving in Christian love would be incomplete, indeed it would fail altogether—and we must remember the very sharp warnings on this point in the First Epistle of John—if it did not take this twofold form, the one having priority as the great commandment of Mk. 12$^{29f.}$ and the other being subordinate to it as the second commandment. Within the great reflection of the love of God in Christian love as such and generally, love to the neighbour and the brother must again reflect the Christian love to God. Jesus Christ alone is made unto us sanctification. He is the King who is appointed the ruler and law-giver and judge of every man. But with His known people this King has also a much larger unknown people, which, according to Heb. 2^{11}, He, the only Son of the Father, is not ashamed to call His brethren even down to the most lowly members. And according to Mt. $25^{31f.}$ the criterion at His judgment will be the question what we have done or not done to Him in the person of the least of His brethren. They are not identical with Him, but they are witnesses which we must not overlook or ignore, witnesses of the poverty which He accepted to establish that fellowship between God and man which is given to the world and gives light to the Christian community, witnesses of the wealth which in Him is given secretly to the world and openly to the Christian community in that fellowship. In their person they represent Him as the neighbour, as the one who fell among thieves, and as the Good Samaritan who took him and poured oil into his wounds and brought him to the inn at his own expense. They are not identical with Him. But He cannot be had without them. And that means that God cannot be had without them, nor can reconciliation with Him nor conversion to Him. He cannot be had without gratitude for their witness and a willingness to be witnesses to them, without love to them, without their indispensability to each one whom God loves, without that one seriously setting out and never ceasing to seek and to find them, both in the community and therefore in the world as well, Christian and also non-Christian neighbours. Christian love is at one and the same time love to God and love to the neighbour—and it is love to the neighbour because it is love to God. This is the test whether it is the response to God's own love, whether it is the work of the Holy Spirit. If it stands this test, [107] then *mutatis mutandis*EN64 but substantially everything that can be said of love to God can be said of love to the neighbour. It is a coming together on the horizontal level, of man and man. As such it is not merely conscious, but ready and indeed voluntary. It is a total coming together which excludes all other possible relationships to the neighbour and claims a man wholly and utterly. To that extent it is a perfect counterpart to the vertical coming together of man with God. And it cannot be exhausted by mere feelings, or a mere outlook, let alone mere words. It is an active being.

But it does not on that account contribute anything at all to the justification of man. And it is the glory of it that it cannot even think of trying to do so, because it derives from the justification of man, from the divine sentence of pardon, and therefore it lives by the faith in which we cannot look away to anything else—either our good works or bad—but must be content to be what we are by God's sentence fulfilled and revealed in Jesus Christ without any co-operation on our part. Even neighbourly love cannot look away to anything that might be won or attained from God by means of it. Just as love to God can

---

EN64 allowing for differences

envisage and seek and love only God, and for His own sake, so love to the neighbour can envisage and seek and love only the neighbour, and for his own sake. As in the vertical, so in the horizontal dimension, it is free and pure love. There is no question of any gain accruing to the one who loves, either in time or in eternity. There is no ulterior thought of another end, even if this were the highest and most necessary end for man. The neighbour will notice the fact, and he will not find himself loved even in the most fervent and zealous works of Christian charity, if this love is one which looks away, and not a pure act of obedience—as faith also is in its own way. Christian love as the complement of love to God is real neighbourly and brotherly love to the extent that it is exercised without any ulterior thought or question, being shown freely and purely to the neighbour as a neighbour and the brother as a brother, being shown only because in his Christian and also in his non-Christian form he is a member of the people of which Jesus Christ is the King, because this King wills that those who recognise Him should recognise Him again in the members of His people in the narrower and wider sense, because the coming together of God and man accomplished in Him carries with it unconditionally and without reserve and therefore with genuine force the work of bringing together man and man.

Where love exists in both dimensions without any ulterior motive, where it is grounded in itself and does not try to be anything but a necessary response to the love of God, it is that "fulfilling of the law" of which we read in Mk. 12²⁹ᶠ· and Rom. 13¹⁰. It is obedience to God's direction, the keeping of covenant faithfulness by man, the meaning of the whole *ethos* of the man reconciled and converted to God in Jesus Christ.

[108]   The conversion of man to God which took place in Jesus Christ has another form as well as these two, and it will now be our task to characterise and briefly to describe this final form. It consists (3) in the positing and equipping of man as the bearer of the divine promise. In the fact that he participates in this promise and lives in the light of it the being of man consists in Christian hope. And in this third form the work of the Holy Spirit which makes man a Christian is that man—for this is hope—is obedient to the promise as Abraham was, that he is ready to participate in it and to live in the light of it.

God's judgment and direction, and therefore man's justification and sanctification, and therefore faith and love do not embrace the whole of that act of atonement accomplished and revealed in Jesus Christ which reconstitutes the being of man, and therefore they do not embrace the whole of the specifically Christian being established and formed by the knowledge of Jesus Christ. In our presentation so far there is lacking any consideration of what we might call the teleological determination of the being of man and of the Christian in Jesus Christ.

In that section of dogmatics which is specifically known as soteriology, i.e., the doctrine of the salvation which comes to man in Jesus Christ, it has been customary since the Reformation to think in the main only in the two categories so far mentioned. The doctrine of Luther centred upon the contrast and complementarity or faith and works, that is, love, or, conversely, the Law and the Gospel. And Calvin returned constantly to the dialectic of justification and sanctification. These were the two concepts which dominated the Reformed theology which succeeded Calvin. But they are also the iron basis and core of what the Lutheran orthodox thought it possible to describe as the *ordo salutis*[EN65]. And in line with the general Protestant tradition Schleiermacher in this context treated first of regeneration (conversion and justification) and then of sanctification. Our consideration of the two spheres described in this or some similar way has certainly convinced us of the correctness and importance—an importance which cannot be over-estimated—of these two aspects, and their indispensability as the basic description of the man reconciled in Jesus Christ and especially of the Christian who knows Jesus Christ. The Reformers did well to concentrate on them as they wrestled with the problems of their own day. In the controversy with Roman Catholicism their exact treatment will always play a decisive part. Even in relation to the subject-matter as presented for our consideration by the biblical witness, there can be no question that here in justification and sanctification, or faith and love, or at an even higher level God's verdict and direction, we find ourselves at what is from this standpoint, the being of man reconciled to God in Jesus Christ, the very heart and centre of the Christian message. There can be no escaping the questions: How can I lay hold of a gracious God? and, How can I live in accordance with the fact that I have a gracious God? And these questions must always be rightly answered with all the actuality which they can never lose. But we must not overlook the fact that as we take note of the witness of the New Testament at this very heart and centre of the matter there is a third moment which we have to treat independently and as true in and for itself. It is of this that we must now speak, the moment of the promise given to man in Jesus Christ, and therefore Christian hope, and therefore the calling of man side by side with his justification and sanctification.

It was not enough—that is, it did not correspond to the fulness of the New Testament witness and a comprehensive investigation of the point at issue—when under the title *De vocatione*[EN66] the Protestant tradition tried to speak only in an introductory and comprehensive way about the subjective *applicatio salutis*[EN67], i.e., man's entry into the sphere of justification and sanctification, of faith and love, his regeneration and conversion as his entry into a state of grace, the basic activity of the Holy Spirit in general and the rise of faith in particular. In a treatment of this kind it necessarily seems that the sphere of justification and sanctification, of faith and love, is marked off from behind as that which is properly sacred—although not without some reference to its limitation by what has to be said separately in the doctrine of the last things. We must admit that Calvin did see very clearly the problem of the teleological determination and direction of the whole being and status of man as changed in Christ and shaped for conversion to God. He felt the problem, and he treated it in a lasting and impressive way in his conception of the *promissio*[EN68] as the basis of faith and his presentation of the *vita christiana*[EN69] as directed to the *vita futura*[EN70]. But for him the *spes*[EN71] seems to be only an essential and indeed the properly compulsive element in *fides*[EN72]. It is this in the New Testament. But in the New Testament it is more than this. And in the New Testament the calling of God is never simply as it was described in Protestant orthodoxy, the

[109]

[EN65] order of salvation
[EN66] On Calling
[EN67] application of salvation
[EN68] promise
[EN69] Christian life
[EN70] future life
[EN71] hope
[EN72] faith

basis of the entry into the specific state of grace, or Christianity. This state never has the character of a being which is included and exhausted in the form of faith and love, a being which will then be superseded by and merged into the, as it were, quite different being in eternal glory to which it moves. In the New Testament the being of man in Jesus Christ is rather a being under and with the promise, as it is also a being under the verdict and direction, of God. It is a being which in its totality is teleologically directed, an eschatological being. Calling speaks of more than calling into a state of justification and sanctification. As such and with independent truth and power calling is man's forward direction to God as his future, his new creation as a being which not only derives from the sentence of God in faith and is placed under His present direction in love but beyond that receives and embraces His promise in hope, looking forward therefore and moving forward to Him. The Protestant tradition was, of course, helped and corrected by the fact that it never neglected to consider the last things. Inevitably, too, something of this had to be brought out indirectly in the discussion of justification and sanctification, of faith and love. But it is still only too true that in that tradition the being of man in Jesus Christ has as such a very this-worldly, immanentist, even middle-class appearance. The older Protestant soteriology with its classical and in its way magnificent pre-occupation with the two first points did not make it sufficiently clear that this being as such is a being under the promise, that the reality of the salvation given to man is as such the gift of this promise, that the Christian affirmation and appropriation of the divine gift is as such hope based upon and directed to this promise. In Evangelical dogmatics we must not neglect the two first points. But we must bring out no less emphatically the prophetic element of the being of man reconciled with God in Jesus Christ.

The restoration, renewal and fulfilment of the covenant between God and man in the atonement made and revealed in Jesus Christ is complete as man's justification as a covenant-partner and his sanctification to be a covenant-partner, as the establishment and formation of the fellowship between himself and God, just as God's creation was perfect as the beginning of all His ways with the created order. But, like creation, it is not an end but a beginning—complete in itself and as such, but still a beginning. It is not, therefore, an end in itself. Nor is it simply conditioned by what might happen further between God and man on quite different presuppositions, just as the (in itself) perfect [110] creation of God was not simply conditioned by the subsequent history of the covenant, but took place for the sake of the covenant and to that extent was itself the beginning of the covenant. So, too, reconciliation, the being of man converted to God in Jesus Christ, is as such a beginning. It is not merely a *restitutio ad integrum*[EN73]. It is not merely the creation of a final and stable relationship in which the disturbance of the balance between God and the world has been corrected, and, with the re-establishment of the normal order of superiority demanded by their conjunction, God and the world can co-exist quietly and contentedly: God having pronounced His verdict and giving His direction, man in faith in Him and in love to Him and his neighbour. It is not the restoration of a parallelism and equipoise in which God and the world, God and man, will now continue to live together happily. This is—slightly caricatured—the this-worldly, immanentist and middle-class understanding of the

---

[EN73] restoration to wholeness

being in Jesus Christ given by God to the world and known and experienced by Christians. In contrast to all such ideas, this being in all its completeness is only a beginning—a being in which man looks eagerly forward to the activity of God and his own fellowship with Him, just as in faith he looks back to it and in love he sees it as present. It is a being which is still open for God, open for that which has not yet happened in the restoration of the covenant as such, for that which has yet to happen on the basis of that restoration. It is not only under the verdict and direction of God but also under the promise of God, in which we have to do with this future event, with this still expected being of God for man, with yet another form of the fellowship between God and man. The justification and sanctification of man have a purpose and goal.

It is not self-evident that they should have, that apart from what he may be under God's verdict and direction man as reconciled with God should also be given by this same God a future, a *telos*. Those limited ideas might well correspond to the reality. For what man may be under God's verdict and direction, in faith and love, is certainly complete enough in itself. But, in fact, they do not correspond to the reality. In fact the perfection of the being in Jesus Christ (without anything lacking in the first two forms) has a further extension. The justification and sanctification of man do in fact include a purpose and goal. This is not self-evident. It is only as a further proof of the overflowing goodness of God that it is in fact the case that the being of man in Jesus Christ is a being not merely in possession and action but also in expectation. And for this reason the calling of man is obviously a thing apart and additional to his justification and sanctification, as is also Christian hope in relation to Christian faith and Christian love. For it is a thing apart, it is the grace of God in a new and particular form, that He not only wills to make man His servant and friend and child, His faithful covenant-partner, to have him as such and to cause him to walk before Him as such, but also that beyond and in all this (as is shown in a [111] type in the figure of Abraham) He wills to make something of him, He has for him a purpose, an end. According to the promise given him in Jesus Christ, God has in fact a purpose for man in all this. And in the knowledge of the promise given in Jesus Christ man is, in fact, called to give to God not merely the response of the obedience of faith and the obedience of love, but also the response of the obedience of hope. We must therefore regard the calling of man as the third aspect of the reconciliation of man with God which God Himself has willed and accomplished and revealed.

What does the promise of God mean? It means that the being of man acquires a direction, because it acquires a destiny and a perspective. This is something which the verdict and direction of God do not mean taken and understood by themselves, even though they are as such the perfect Word of God. The end of man's justified and sanctified being, of Christian faith and Christian love, belongs to the conversion of man to God. Man cannot take this to himself. But God gives it to him in reconciling him to Himself in Jesus Christ. He gives him His pledge—already redeemed and operative in Jesus

Christ—that is the strong sense of the word promise. And now he can and must live as the one who has this pledge, and therefore with the forward direction and destiny given by it and perspective opened up by it: forward to what he will be according to this pledge. In the fulfilment of the covenant he receives this pledge and accepts this call to advance.

But to what does it point him? In a very general way, to the actualisation and preservation of the fellowship between God and himself established in the fulfilment of the covenant. God's promise shows him that this fellowship is not simply a—two-dimensional—connexion, not simply a relationship, but that it has a depth in which at first it is alien and unknown to man, yet in which it is to be confided and made known to him, that there is something common to both God and man upon which man cannot lay his hand but which God promises to lay in his hand.

For a proper understanding everything depends upon our giving the right name to what is shown and pledged to man by the divine promise. In the New Testament it is briefly and very well described as "eternal life" (cf. Jn. 3^{16}). This brings out with a clarity which can hardly be excelled the fact that it is a being in a depth of fellowship with God which has yet to be disclosed. Only God lives an "eternal life." If man is to have it, it can only be on the ground that God wills to live in fellowship with him. But if God wills that, it can be said and promised by Him to man living in his present only as a thing which is new to him in his present. It is, then, to his actual future with God that he moves forward in the possession of this promise. But what is meant by "eternal life" if it is promised
[112] to man as his future with God, if, therefore, in eternal life he is not to cease to be a man, a creature and as such identical with himself, the one he now is? if in that depth of fellowship with God he is not to be merged into God or changed into some quite different being?—which would necessarily mean that it was not really a matter of his future, that the promise did not concern and apply to him, man, as such, that it had nothing whatever to do with his present.

How can eternal life be promised to him, man? How can it be his future with God in this present? In this connexion we usually speak of man's future resting in God or his future supreme bliss before God, or of a contemplation and adoration of God which in its permanence constitutes his future beatitude. And, rightly understood, all this must not be rejected. But if we describe the content of the promise in this way, we must be careful not to form pagan conceptions of God and the eternal life that He lives and the eternal life that He promises to man, as though at bottom God was a supreme being with neither life, nor activity, nor history, in a neutrality which can never be moved or affected by anything, a being with which man can ultimately be united only in rest or in some kind of passive enjoyment or adoring contemplation. The God who is Father, Son and Holy Spirit, active and revealed to us as the eternally living God in Jesus Christ, is not in any sense this supposedly "supreme" being. And unless we say something very much more, rest and enjoyment and contemplation are not the right words to describe a being in the depth of fellowship with Him. According to the witness of Holy Scripture—in correspondence with His triune being, and as indicated by the biblical concept of eternity—God is historical even in Himself, and much more so in His relationship to the reality which is distinct from Himself. He is the Lord of His kingdom, deciding, acting, ruling, doing good, creating peace, judging, giving joy, living in His will and acts. And that kingdom is not merely a kingdom which He possesses in the cosmos created by Him. It is the kingdom which He sets up in the course of a historical movement which has a beginning, a middle and an end. It is the kingdom which comes from heaven to earth. And that is how He encounters us and reveals Himself to us in Jesus Christ, for He is still the active ruler when He combats the sin and misery of the world, when in the work of atonement He converts it to Himself in this One. If it is the case that man is given a promise for his own future in this as yet unrevealed depth of fellowship with God, it cannot be otherwise than that the content of the promise should correspond to the being of God. The fellowship of man with God is completed and completes itself as it enters this depth. And this complete fellowship, the "eternal" life of man, must consist in a future being of man with God as this active ruler. And it is hard to see how we can better describe it in summary form than by calling it a being which is in the words of Lk. 20^{36} like that of the angels in that it is a being in the service of God. Luther showed a perception amounting to genius—for in some way he transcended himself— [113] when in his exposition of the second article in the *Shorter Catechism* he described the end of the redemption of man accomplished in Jesus Christ in the following way: "in order that I may be His, and live under Him in His kingdom, and serve Him in eternal righteousness and virtue and blessedness, as He is risen from the dead and lives and reigns in eternity." To live under Him in His kingdom and to serve Him: it is here that all rest and joy and contemplation and adoration in the eternal life promised to man have their meaning and basis. It is the calling to this which is the *telos* of justification and sanctification. The future of man in covenant with God (in the position and function which he will have in relation to that of God) is to be the partner of God and to live as such. We are, in fact, dealing with what synergism of every age and type has tried to ascribe to man at a place where it does not yet belong to him, and has confused and falsified everything by trying to ascribe it to him at that place, that is, in his status under the verdict and direction of God. The fact that he is subjected to the divine verdict and can believe in the knowledge of it, the fact that he is placed under the divine direction and can love in the knowledge of it, does not in any sense include within itself a co-operation of man with God, but in faith and love man responds, he corresponds, to what is simply the work of God for him and to him, the Word of God spoken to him and concerning him. Of course, the same is true in hope. As a recipient and bearer of the divine promise he stands in relation to God as one who can only respond or correspond.

But here we are speaking of the content of the promise, not of his status in hope, but of what he hopes for as he receives the promise and knows it as such. And of this, of the future of man as indicated and pledged in the divine promise, we have to say that it is a being in a co-operation of service with God. This being is in His kingdom, and therefore under Him. But its form now is not simply one of response and correspondence. It is not simply in the distinctness and antithesis which even in the status of hope must be our attitude. To be sure, the creatureliness and identity of man will certainly not be destroyed. Therefore the distinctness and antithesis in relation to God will also remain. But this being will be a being by the side of God, the participation of man in the being and life of God, a willing of what He wills and a doing of what He does. It will be a being not only as object, but as an active subject in the fellowship of God with the created world and man, a being in a partnership with God which is actively undertaken and maintained, a being in man's own free responsibility with God for the cause of God. That is the inconceivable height which is promised to man when he is reconciled with God, converted to God, justified and sanctified. That is the honour, the dignity, the glory of eternal life [114] which God has pledged. That is how man will come to eternal rest and enter into eternal joy and really contemplate God and adore Him. He will serve God, for that is what God has ordained for him and for the race, that is what He has appointed ultimately for the whole non-human cosmos. God does not regard man as too lowly or incapable or unworthy to consider him for this or to promise that this is what he will be. And He does not regard Himself as too exalted to will to set him beside Him and to make use of his service like that of the angels. It is obviously because everything depends on man being set there and used in that way, on his being called to service at His side, it is obviously for that reason—and we can only wonder afresh when we consider the fact—that He let it cost Him the offering of His Son and therefore His own interposition to convert man to Himself.

And the men of the Christian community are those who hear the promise given to the world of men, just as they are those who hear the verdict pronounced on it and the direction given to it. They are those who see the light as it shines before man, as it has already shone most definitely into and for the present being of man. They are those who can therefore walk with open eyes in this light given to the world. They are those who know that everything and all things—including themselves, and they are the ones who grasp it—are appointed and set up for this purpose. They are those who have the perspective that they will "live under Him in His kingdom, and serve Him." Christians, therefore, are those who are able not only to believe and love but also to hope—to hope for the future of the world with God and therefore for their own future with Him. Christians are those who are able to accept and consciously to apprehend not only the justification and sanctification of man, but also his calling in Jesus Christ to eternal life.

This calling took place in what was done for man and the world in the atonement made in Jesus Christ. The atonement accomplished in Him is not only the fulfilment of the sentence and the disclosure of the direction but also the effective proclamation of the promise or pledge of God. It is the divine call to advance under which man is placed by the fulfilment of the covenant and his conversion to God. It alone! We have to do here again only with the grace of God. How can man—even the man who believes and loves—ever come to the point of calling himself to advance, of promising himself the inconceivable height of eternal life with God in His service? As the content of his hope he could perhaps imagine either "immortality" in another life decked out with various characteristics, or all kinds of significant possibilities in this life. Let him beware lest he be deluded and disillusioned in the one respect no less than the other. But no man can imagine of himself his future with God, his service of God as his future being (in this life as in that which is to come). No man can take and ascribe it to himself, anticipating it as his eternal or even his temporal future, that he will render to God a service which he himself offers and God accepts, a service which is complete and real both objectively and subjectively. Not even the pious Christian can do this, any more than he can take and ascribe to himself his justification and sanctification. He can and should live under the promise. He is so placed and equipped that he can have this future and move towards it in the present. But only because the promise and the pledge of it are given him by God, just as he can only accept the verdict and direction of God and therefore his justification and sanctification. The more clearly we see that in the content of this pledge we have to do with nothing less than the acceptance of what synergism falsely believes can be ascribed to man, the more clearly we will see that the pledge that he will serve God can only be given to man and can never be the arrogant postulate of man. Here, as everywhere in the event of atonement, such a postulate is quite superfluous. For in Jesus Christ the promise or pledge of God—which cannot be compared with anything we might promise ourselves—is already given to us. It is actually made to the world. So then (without having to create illusions about itself) the world is no longer a world without hope. As it stands under the verdict and direction of God, so too it stands under the promise of God. It is the world set in the light of its future with God. Hence man is the being which exists in this direction, under this determination, with this perspective. And the Christian is the man who for himself and others can know this and therefore hope. His hope derives from Jesus Christ, for Jesus Christ is Himself the divine pledge as such. And He hopes in Jesus Christ, for Jesus Christ is also the content of the divine pledge. That is what we have now briefly to explain.

Jesus Christ is the divine pledge as such—its effective and authentic proclamation. In Him that to which it refers has already taken place. It is already present. He is the man who lives not only under the verdict and direction of God but also in the truth of His promise. He is not merely righteous and well pleasing to God and the object of His love, but beyond that He is taken and

[115]

used by Him, standing in His service and at His side, working with Him, living eternal life, clothed with His honour and dignity and glory. He Himself as the eternally living God is also the eternally living man. The world is reconciled and converted to God in Him in the fact that He is this man, not merely in distinctness and antithesis in relation to God, but also in participation in His being and work, not merely in responsibility to Him, but with a responsibility for His cause, not merely as His servant and friend and child, but as a ruler in His kingdom. No one beside Him is man in this way, just as no one, beside Him is as man the same divine Son of the Father. For that reason He (alone) is for all of us (only) the pledge of what we ourselves will be, we who are and will be only men and not God. For that reason in His present (alone) we have to do (only) with our future with God. For that reason the future allotted to us in [116] Him cannot be that of rulers, but only of servants of the one God who alone is King. Our present emphasis, however, must not be upon the qualifications but upon the positive truth that the reconciliation of the world with God consists in the fact that a promise is given it by God Himself and therefore absolutely, that in Him its own future is already present, that in Him even in its present life it is already seized and determined by its future being. Because God has made Himself one with it in Jesus Christ, because He Himself was and is present in it, it has the divine pledge of its future life. Therefore whether it knows it or not, it is not a world without hope, just as on the same ground it cannot be simply a lost world or a completely loveless and unsanctified world. In Him it has become a world in which the divine call to advance has been heard once and for all and is now regulative. In Him it has been constituted in the fact and appointed to it, it exists in the perspective, that it belongs to God, and that while it will not be divinised in some way and made identical with Him, it will find the essence of all creaturely glory in serving Him, actively siding with Him and helping Him and in this way—for all its unlikeness like Jesus Christ— being clothed with all the honour and also with all the joy and peace of eternal life. When the Christian knows Jesus Christ as the One in whom this has taken place for the world, he not only believes and loves, but also hopes. And his hope derives from Jesus Christ, i.e., as he hears and understands the pledge which God has given in Him, making it his own, letting his life be shaped by this promise and opened up for the future.

But Jesus Christ is also the content of the divine pledge, the One in whom the Christian is summoned to hope. It is a terrible thing if at this point, at the last moment, we ignore Him as though He were only a means or instrument or channel, and look to something different from Him, some general gift mediated by Him, regarding this as the object of Christian hope, the future posited for the world and man. The question of the future of the being of man and its direction to that future is such an important and burning question that everything hinges upon whether we answer it rightly or wrongly. If we look aside here, trying to understand the awaited and expected being of man and all creation in the service of God only as the manifestation of a general idea of man or of being, we shall betray the fact that for all our recalling and appealing to the name of Jesus Christ earlier—indeed from the very first in our discussion of the being of reconciled man—we have not really been thinking or answering in relation to Him, but have been developing an anthropological concept which we have found elsewhere and to which we have simply given a christological superscription. In its own way this might or might not have value. But it does not belong to the Christian message or to the heart of that message. The great truth which is proper to what we have to see at this point does not shine out from a concept like that, nor can we expect from it that comfort in living and dying which we need to find at this point. This can be [117] expected, and the divine promise can be understood in its kerygmatic and pneumatic force, only when it is continually seen and understood that, like the divine verdict and the divine direction, the divine promise of the future of the being of man is not only revealed but is actual, an event, only in Jesus Christ, that it is therefore in every way, not only noetically but ontically, enclosed in Him and indeed identical with Him. If we abide by the witness of the New Testament, it will keep us at this point from the mistake of separating the promise itself from that which is promised, and therefore from a new uncertainty. By that witness we are compellingly summoned to regard Jesus Christ not only as the revelation and form of the divine promise but also as its fulfilment and content. The future promised to the world and man, and awaited by the uplifted head of the Christian, is in the New Testament concentrated and comprehended in the one event of the coming of Jesus Christ Himself. He is the eternally living man who as such is the future of the world and of every man, and the hope of the Christian. By His coming to His disciples after His resurrection in the revelation of the forty days He pointed to Himself as their hope and future. In so doing He showed them and the whole community that their own hope and future and that of the world are to be found in His own coming as revealed in a way which none will fail to see and recognise. His own coming is the end to which in its supreme consummation, in its form as God's promise, the covenant fulfilled by Him, the reconciliation of the world with God accomplished by Him, can only move and point as to something beyond itself. As He is the meaning and basis of creation, so He is the bearer and substance of the redemption and consummation which closes the time of the creature, human time. Therefore the calling to expect and hasten towards this end and goal and new beginning, the divine call to advance which opens up the way for man, is the summons to look and to move forward to the One who not only was—before all time and in His own time—who not only is, as the centre of all time, but who also comes as the end of all time, as the Judge of all things which have lived and will live at any time, and therefore as the beginning of the being of the world and man the beginning of their eternal being on the right hand or the left. The calling of man is related to Him no less totally than his justification and sanctification. In hope no less than faith and love we have to do with Him, with the revelation and operation of the grace of God shown to the world and man in Him. And according to what we have already said, this means that in Him man is taken up into that dimension of depth of his being in fellowship with God which is still concealed, which is still only indicated to him. The fact that man can serve God, like the fact that he is justified and sanctified before God, is His affair. It is true for us in Him. The eternal life of man will be found in Him. In Him it will be true, and it will

[118] remain true and always be true afresh in eternity as the time of God, that man "may live under Him in His kingdom, and serve Him." In Him he will show himself accepted by God, worthy and capable and usable, able to be with Him to will what He wills, to do what He does, to support His cause. In Him all this will be his rest and joy in God, his eternal contemplation and adoration of God. In Him he will be clothed with the glory of his own eternal life with God. In eternal life, in the glory of the service of God promised to man, it is not a question of a future which is peculiar to man as such and in general. It is a question of His future, the future of Jesus Christ, and of the future of humanity and each individual man in Him.

In Him alone! The exclusiveness of the promise as of the sentence and direction of God, of the calling as of the justification and sanctification of man—the fact that everything is enclosed in Jesus Christ alone—inevitably carries with it the judgment of the world to which each individual moves. For if everything is in Him alone, there is nothing outside of Him. Who does not have to fear this "outside of Him," since none of us can take and ascribe it to himself that he will be found in Him and that he will therefore live under Him and serve Him in His kingdom? But how can our fear be anxious, how can it be anything but a joyful awe even in respect of all men, when the exclusiveness of this future is known as His, when He is known as the Judge who will come to judge the quick and the dead? And when He is not known? Then He must be believed and loved and hoped for as the eternally living One, and the future of the whole world, by those who do know Him. The last word in the matter, both in theory and in practice, is that it is their concern, their task, their responsibility to shine as light in the darkness, to proclaim Him to others as the eternally living One, even to those who do not seem to know Him as such. It is one thing to be unreservedly in earnest to-day about the possibility of eternal damnation for some, and to rejoice equally unreservedly to-morrow at that of eternal reconciliation for all. But it is quite another (and this is the task of the Christian community) to know that one is responsible for attesting with the Christian word and the Christian existence (and the existence no less clearly than the word) Jesus Christ not only as the Lord but also as the Saviour of the world and therefore its future. Christians will never find that they are called to anything other than hope—for themselves and the world. If they were, they would find that they were called to look and to move forward to someone or something other than their Saviour. But then *eo ipso*[EN74] they would no longer be Christians.

We have still to say a few words about the hope of Christians as such. Let us say first that in their own case they hope for the eternal life in the service of God which comes to them in Jesus Christ. The fact that they can be obedient to the divine calling, recognising and understanding the divine promise as such, includes the fact that as these men amongst others they are themselves [119] reached and approached by that promise, that they can relate themselves to it in person. Jesus Christ and their future in Him is their own personal hope, the hope of their own personal redemption and consummation. They await their own personal being at the end to which they are pointed by the covenant fulfilled in Jesus Christ. But if this is their affair it is not their private affair. Called by God, they are called with their hope of their own future, without asking what will be the outcome, to be the first representatives of all those who so far do not have this hope either for themselves or at all, just as faith and love are so far alien to them, because Jesus Christ Himself is not known to them, because they do not yet know of the atonement made in Him. The relation of Christians to others is that they can hope for them. The one thing is the measure of the other. The more earnestly they hope for themselves, the more earnestly they will do so as (scattered and isolated) witnesses to the promise given to the whole world in their by no means easy status as representatives of others. And the more serious they are in their hoping for others—however isolated and scattered—the more seriously they will be able to hope for themselves, the more compellingly they will have to ask themselves whether they really do hope for themselves.

But what does it mean to hope? We have said concerning the divine promise that, like the divine verdict and the divine direction in the atonement made in Jesus Christ, it has come down, as it were, from above, from God into the world of men loved by God, that it has in a sense been incorporated or implanted into their status and being and non-being, so that objectively they cannot be without it, objectively they have their goal and future in Jesus Christ and therefore in the service of God. In the light of this we can and must understand Christian hope as the coming alive of the promise incorporated in the world of men, or as the taking root of the promise implanted in it. From this standpoint the coming alive or taking root of the promise in the world of men is the work of the Holy Spirit which makes man a Christian. And that means that in the act of Christian hope the objective becomes subjective. It is affirmed. In the person of the Christian the world of men strives after and seizes the goal and future given to it in Jesus Christ. It waits for it, it hastens towards it, it reaches out for it. In the act of Christian hope that which is promised (as promised and

---

[EN74] by definition

therefore future) is already present. Jesus Christ as the (promised and coming) eternally living One is already present. Not merely virtually and effectively, but actually and actively in the person of the Christian. In the act of Christian hope man lives not merely in the factuality of the decision made by God concerning his whole being, but also in the factuality of his own corresponding thoughts and words and works in relation to the service of God, conditioned for and directed towards that service, and in the perspective of that goal. This particular factuality constitutes the particularity of Christian being in hope which is revealed only in the particularity of Christian perception. Christians do not merely see things differently from others. From God's point of view they are different from others, just as they are different from others in relation to the divine verdict and direction when the Holy Spirit awakens them to faith and love. They do not merely live under the promise, which could be said of all men. They live in and with and by the promise. They seize it. They apprehend it. They conform themselves to it. And therefore in their present life they live as those who belong to the future. That which is promised and He who is promised are seen and heard by them in all their futurity. Here and now in their hearts and minds and senses He unsettles and consoles them, moves and compels them, carries and upholds them (judging and establishing and directing). Within their present life and that of the world they are arrested by this future One and pledged and committed to Him. This particularity of their present being distinguishes Christians from other men, and it is in this very particularity that they are the representatives of other men. And to hope means to be different from other men and to act for them in this particularity.

But at this point we must take note of an important distinction. Christian hope is a present being in and with and by the promise of the future. But in the one hope there will always be inseparably the great hope and also a small hope. All through temporal life there will be the expectation of eternal life. But there will also be its expectation in this temporal life. There will be confidence in the One who comes as the end and new beginning of all things. There will also be confidence in His appearing within the ordinary course of things as they still move towards that end and new beginning. There is a joy in anticipation of the perfect service of God which awaits man when God is all in all. But in this joy there is also a joy and zest for the service which to-day or to-morrow can be our transitory future. The promise and therefore our calling are in two dimensions. They refer to the last and ultimate things, but also to the penultimate and provisional. They refer to the whole, but also concretely to the details, to the one in all, but also to the all in one. The promised future is not only that of the day of the Lord at the end of all days, but because it is the end and goal of all days it is also to-day and to-morrow. In Christian hope there is no division in this respect, but again the one is the measure of the other.

Hope seizes, or rather is seized by, the promise of the future. To that extent it is the great hope, the expectation of the eternal life which has still to be

[120]

manifested and given to us, confidence in the coming Jesus Christ as the end
and new beginning of all things, the joy in anticipation of the perfect being of
man and all creatures in the service of God which is pledged because it is
already actualised in Him. As it seizes the promise of the future it is in every
respect—not only hope which derives from Him but also hope in Him as the
eternally living One. He, the content of the promise and the object of hope,
cannot be replaced by any other. If there is also a small hope for to-day and
to-morrow, if there are also temporal, penultimate, provisional and detailed
hopes for the immediate future, it is only because He is the future One who
shows Himself in every future; it is only in the framework and setting, in the
power and the patience of the great and comprehensive hope which is present
to man in Him. It is He alone in His futurity, and to that extent as the One who
is beyond, who gives hope to the present, the life of man in this world, where
otherwise there is no hope. The small hopes are only for the sake of the great
hope from which they derive. The provisional promise is only in the light and
power of the final promise. If the latter is weak, the former cannot possibly be
strong. If the latter perishes, the former will perish with it. If man does not
seriously wait for Jesus Christ, at bottom he will not wait for anything else. Daily
hope can persist only where in basis and essence it is itself eternal hope.

[121]

But the converse must also be perceived and stated. Christian hope is a present being in and with and by the promise of the future, a being which is seized
by the promise of God and called. If a man does not seize this hope, apprehend it, conform himself to it here and now as a man who belongs to the
future, he is not one who has Christian hope. Rather, it will be revealed that he
does not genuinely hope for the perfection and wholeness of His being in the
service of God, for eternal life in its futurity, that he does not wait for Jesus
Christ as the coming One. If he waits for Him here and now, then the here and
now cease to be futureless. He looks for Him, the coming One, to-day and
to-morrow, that is, in the decisions in which he has to live to-day and
to-morrow as long as time and space are given him. He does not make them
without direction or into a future which is empty, but in obedience to his calling, towards that future promised him by God by which the future of to-day
and to-morrow is surrounded and lit up, in the light of which every temporal,
provisional, penultimate, detailed future necessarily becomes a sign and summons, a detailed and therefore a concrete call to advance which he can only
observe and obey. Where there is the great hope, necessarily there are small
hopes for the immediate future. These hopes have their basis and strength
only in the great hope. They are small, relative and conditioned. In their
detailed content they may be mistaken and open to correction. But within
these limits they are genuine hopes. And it is certainly in these many little
hopes that the Christian lives from day to day if he really lives in the great
hope. And perhaps he is most clearly distinguished from the non-Christian by
the fact that, directed to the great hope, and without any illusions, he does not

[122] fail and is never weary to live daily in these little hopes. But this necessarily means that he is daily willing and ready for the small and provisional and imperfect service of God which the immediate future will demand of him because a great and final and perfect being in the service of God is the future of the world and all men, and therefore his future also.

3. JESUS CHRIST THE MEDIATOR

To get a complete view of the event of the reconciliation of man with God as the fulfilment of the covenant we have so far looked in two directions: first upwards, to God who loves the world, and then downwards, to the world which is loved by God; first to the divine and sovereign act of reconciling grace, then to the being of man reconciled with God in this act. We must now look at a third aspect, between the reconciling God above and reconciled man below. Even when we looked in those two first directions we had continually to bear in mind that there is a middle point between them. And more than a middle point, there is one thing which both differentiates and comprehends the reconciling God above and reconciled man below, one thing in which there is actualised and revealed both in themselves and in their inseparable connexion, indeed identity, the reconciling God as such in the sovereign act of His grace, and reconciled man as such in his being grounded in that divine act, the turning of God to man, and based upon it the conversion of man to God. The atonement as the fulfilment of the covenant is neither grace in itself as the being of the gracious God, nor is it the work of grace in itself and as such, the being of the man to whom God is gracious. Nor is it the sum of the two nor their mutual relationship. It is rather the middle point, the one thing from which neither the God who turns to man nor man converted to God can be abstracted, in which and by which both are what they are, in which and to which they stand in that mutual relationship. It is only from this middle point that we have been able to look upwards and downwards, and as we tried always to find and name something concrete we had all the more necessarily to come back to it again and again. But that one thing in the middle is one person, Jesus Christ. He is the atonement as the fulfilment of the covenant. In Him that turning of God to man and conversion of man to God is actuality in the appointed order of the mutual inter-relationship, and therefore in such a way that the former aims at the latter and the latter is grounded in the former. In Him both are in this order the one whole of the event of reconciliation. Our third task—in our present order of thinking—is obviously to understand Him as this one whole.

[123] We have already been on our guard against the possibility of regarding and treating the name of Jesus Christ in a purely "nominalistic" way, as a formal historical or symbolical sign of the event of atonement. This event is not merely outward but inward. It corresponds not only to cognition but to being.

It is not in any sense accidentally but necessarily enclosed in Him, as it also took place in Him. It looks both to the reconciling God and reconciled man, and it is found in its unity and completeness in His existence. For that reason He who bears this name, and His existence, must really be regarded as the middle point which embraces the whole and includes it within itself, the middle point in which the sovereign act of the reconciling God and the being of reconciled man are one.

We spoke about a third task, but this third task is simply to show the basis and aim of the answers we gave to the first two, to name and describe the truth in all answers to the question of the gracious God and the man who participates in His grace. Jesus Christ cannot be a third theme which we can separate from the two first. He is the one theme expounded in the two first. If we could speak of the reconciling God and reconciled man only by looking upwards and downwards from Jesus Christ, and constantly looking back to Him, we can speak of Jesus Christ only as we consistently keep before us the one whole of the covenant between God and man fulfilled by Him, and therefore of both the above and the below. He exists as the Mediator between God and man in the sense that in Him God's reconciling of man and man's reconciliation with God are event. He exists in the sense that in this event God encounters and is revealed to all men as the gracious God and in this event again all men are placed under the consequence and outworking of this encounter and revelation. He exists in this action of God for and with all men and in that which happens to all men in the course of it. He exists in the totality of his being and work as the Mediator—He alone as the Mediator, but living and active in His mediatorial office. When we come to speak of Jesus Christ, therefore, it is necessary that what we have to say about Him particularly should for all its particularity be shown to be that which gathers together all that we said in relation to both the above and the below.

But at this point we have to make an important decision in relation to the form and method of the Christian doctrine of the atonement.

It was and is customary to have a single complete and self-contained chapter on Jesus Christ, the so-called "Christology," as the climax in the whole presentation. This includes (1) a special doctrine of the "person" of Christ, i.e., the incarnation of the Word of God, and also His Godhead and manhood in their relationship the one to the other, (2) a special doctrine of His work (following the *munus triplex*[EN75] arrangement of the Reformation period), and usually (3) a special doctrine of the two "states" of Christ, His humiliation and exaltation. It is then customary to leave the Christology and to develop a special doctrine of the subjective application and appropriation of the salvation objectively accomplished by Jesus Christ, and finally a doctrine of the Church and the means of grace as the mediation between Christ and the Christian. It is also part of the traditional form of the doctrine, just to mention it in passing, that this whole complex is preceded by a doctrine of sin as its negative presupposition and the *terminus a quo*[EN76] for the whole. [124]

[EN75] threefold office
[EN76] starting point

For the moment our question is simply this, whether it is actually the case that what we have to say concerning Jesus Christ can be gathered together in the one section on Christology, over against which there is a completely different section which includes what we have to say concerning man and the Church. This schematism seems logically very illuminating, and didactically useful. At a first glance it may even seem unavoidable from this standpoint. Yet it is not really calculated to enable us to expound the actual subject-matter. In the New Testament there are many christological statements both direct and indirect. But where do we find a special Christology?—a Christ in Himself, abstracted from what He is amongst the men of Israel and His disciples and the world, from what He is on their behalf? Does He ever exist except in this relationship? Certainly He is the absolutely dominating figure, the absolutely unique One in this environment. Certainly He is the determinative and creative subject of everything that takes place in it. But how and in what sense can He be separated from it and considered apart? Where and how else can He be seen and heard and grasped except as their revelation and grace and judgment and liberation and calling and promise, as the One who is absolutely with and for these men? And at what point do the New Testament writers leave their Christology behind? At what point does it not constantly advance in the form of new insights concerning both God and man?

We have said that Jesus Christ exists in the totality of His work as the Mediator. He alone is the One who fulfils it, but He does completely fulfil it, so that in and with what we have to say about Him in particular we necessarily speak about that comprehensive whole which constitutes its particularity.

But we shall do this either obscurely or not at all if we think that we can crystallise the necessary statements concerning Jesus Christ Himself and as such into a self-contained Christology, in which what He is and means and does and accomplishes for man is not yet revealed or revealed only in the far distance, which must be completed by a special presentation of the relevance of His existence for us, by a related but relatively autonomous soteriology and ecclesiology. The necessary result which this separation has always had is twofold. On the one hand Christology takes on the appearance of an ontology and dramatics arbitrarily constructed from Scripture and tradition. The bearing of it may or may not be seen, but in any case it can never emerge from the half-light of the contingency or non-necessity of a purely historical record or even the recitation of a myth. On the other hand, soteriology and ecclesiology either as a doctrine of the grace and justification and sanctification which comes to us or simply as a doctrine of Christian piety can never escape the tendency to commend itself in relation to Christology, and ultimately to free itself from it, as that which is true and essential, as that which is of practical importance and necessity, as that which is "existentially relevant." And at a pinch can we not omit and dispense with Christology altogether as a doctrine of the being and work of Christ as such? In the last resort, even if we do away with the christological preliminaries, can we not still succeed in working out either a doctrine of grace, of sanctification or justification, or a practical individual or congregational life as such—especially in relation to the non-Christian world? Is not the Christology ultimately only so much ballast which can be jettisoned without loss?—especially when this appears to be desirable on historico-critical and philosophical grounds? On two sides the traditional order has given too much occasion for this kind of division and abstraction for us not to have to ask seriously whether we ought still to follow it. What is said about Jesus Christ Himself, the christological propositions as such, are constitutive, essential, necessary and central in the Christian doctrine of reconciliation. In them we have to do with that one whole. They cannot, therefore, bear that respectful isolation with which they have been and are so often treated. They cannot and will not stand alone and be true alone, with all the

[125]

120

other statements about God and man and sin and grace and justification and the Church true alongside them. Rather they must be represented and thought of as the statement from which all truth derives, which control the whole nexus, which themselves constitute and reveal this nexus. Self-evidently they have to be made, they cannot simply disappear, their own content must not be dissolved, they cannot be transposed into purely interpretative subordinate statements descriptive of the grace actual and active in Jesus Christ. Otherwise we would be well on the way to asserting the autonomy of the event of atonement in relation to the One who must be regarded and understood as the subject, executor and Lord.

To all appearances Franz Hermann Reinhold Frank has not escaped this tendency, although of all modern dogmaticians he is of special interest in that he felt strongly, as I see it, the problematical nature of the traditional order and made the most determined efforts to overcome it. The whole doctrine of the atonement (which he calls "regeneration") is brought by him (*Syst. der Chr. Wahrheit*, 2, 2, 1886) under the one concept of the "evolving humanity of God with its centre in the divine-human redeemer." He then describes how this "humanity of God" evolved in fallen humanity and especially in Israel for the sake of the God-man, how it was posited in the person of the God-man in order to grow out of the God-man: objectively by the Holy Spirit and the means of grace in word and sacrament; subjectively in the *ordo salutis*[EN77] of justifying and renewing faith; objectively-subjectively in the existence of the Church. Here we have a powerful concern—in its own way it amounts to what we can only call a genius—to see together what traditional dogmatics had always separated, the God-man and the humanity of God. And in its own way it is very impressive. But we have to ask whether in spite of his fine "for the sake of" and "in" and "out of" Frank has not (in an excess of good intention) slipped speculatively into a view which alters ever so slightly the Christian message. His main theme is the regenerate "humanity of God." The God-man is rightly described as the centre, but He is pictured only in this function, being made subservient to the evolving and positing and growing of the humanity of God. But while it is true that He does serve this end, does this exhaust what He is for it and in relation to it? Ontologically is it not a matter of Him first, and only then and in Him of the "humanity of God"?

On the one side, then, our task is so to present the doctrine of reconciliation that it is always clear that it has to do wholly and utterly with Jesus Christ, that He is the active subject (and not simply, a means or predicate of its happening). This means that we have to develop and present the doctrine of reconciliation in the light of definite christological perceptions and propositions, focussing attention upon Jesus Christ as the beginning and the middle and the end. And it is clear that to do this we must introduce what we have to say particularly about Jesus Christ in all its particularity into the basis of every individual thought-sequence. For in its particularity it includes within itself the whole. But, on the other hand, it is our task not to separate what we have to say particularly about Jesus Christ but to bring it into immediate connexion with what He is not for Himself but for us, what He is as the One who makes recon- [126] ciliation, as the One who fulfils the covenant, as the One in whom the world and man have been and are converted to God. This means that we have to indicate the fact and the extent to which He does in fact establish and control this happening, to which He is its beginning and middle and end. It is clear,

---

[EN77] order of salvation

then, that what we have to say particularly about Jesus Christ can only be the culminating sentence in every thought-sequence, the sentence which controls the whole, and in the light of which we can apply ourselves seriously to the problems of soteriology and ecclesiology, of the application and appropriation of the salvation which appeared in Him and was given to man, the problem, therefore, of the existence of the community.

But who is He, the One who is the middle point, the Mediator between the reconciling action of God and the reconciled being of man, in whom both at once are actual and revealed? If we have rightly grasped and described the event of reconciliation in these two main points, then we shall not be mistaken if in relation to the Mediator Jesus Christ we start with the fact that in Him—we will make a general statement and then explain it later—we have to do wholly with God and wholly with man, and with both in their complete and utter unity. Not with any god, but with the God who in all the divine freedom of His love, in all His omnipotence and holiness and eternity, is gracious and merciful and long-suffering, who is this not as the One who is self-existent, self-reposing and self-motivated, but in His movement to man. And not with any man, but with the man who in all his creaturely and earthly humanity is converted to God and willing and ready in relation to Him, who is only as he is thankful and therefore obedient. And not with any relationship between them, not with a mere encounter and mutual correspondence, not with a mere being together, but with their unity, with the being of God in and with the human being of man, with the being of man in and with the divine being of God. This is Jesus Christ. We cannot avoid the old formula: very God, very man, very God-man. It is as this One that He is the middle point, and the being of God in His sovereign action of grace and the being of reconciled man are both in Him and are both one in Him. As this One He is the subject of the act of reconciliation between God and all men. As this One He is known in the Christian community: its Lord, the Messiah of Israel, the Saviour of the world, the object of its faith, the basis of its love, the content of its hope.

We hasten to explain that the being of Jesus Christ, the unity of being of the living God and this living man, takes place in the event of the concrete existence of this man. It is a being, but a being in a history. The gracious God is in this history, so is reconciled man, so are both in their unity. And what takes place in this history, and therefore in the being of Jesus Christ as such, is atonement. Jesus Christ is not what He is—very God, very man, very God-man—in order as such to mean and do and accomplish something else which is atonement. But His being as God and man and God-man consists in the completed act of the reconciliation of man with God.

[127]

We are again faced with a critical decision in relation to the form of the doctrine of reconciliation.

We have seen that a distinction was and is made between a doctrine of the "person" and a

3. *Jesus Christ the Mediator*

doctrine of the "work" of Christ: *De persona Christi*[EN78] θεανθρώπου and *De officio Christi mediatorio*[EN79]. Of the conceptual perspicacity of the two titles and the convenience of the division there can be no question. But, again, we have to consider whether it corresponds to the facts, i.e., whether Jesus Christ is rightly seen if first of all (to follow especially the thinking of the Eastern Church) He is seen in a being which does, of course, rest on an act, the incarnation, but which—introduced and established in this way—is as a *unio*[EN80] of the person of the Logos and therefore of the divine nature with the human only a static and idle being, not an act or a work—and only then (here we come to the special interest of the Western Church) seen in a work, which does, of course, have its presupposition in that being, but only a formal presupposition, not being identical with it. We have to ask again whether there is in the New Testament any precedent for this division of approach and concept. In the Fourth Gospel does the Son of God exist in any other way than in the doing of the work given Him by the Father? Does the Jesus of the Synoptics exist in any other way than in His addresses and conversations and miracles, and finally His going up to Jerusalem? Does the Christ of Paul exist in any other way than as the Crucified and Risen? Does the New Testament *kyrios* generally ever exist except in the accomplishment and revelation of His ministry and lordship as such? Certainly it is always a matter of His divine and human being and of both in their unity, not yet described in the formulae of the 4th and 5th centuries, but with no other meaning and intention in relation to the presupposed content. The only thing is that we have to seek the presupposition, the answer to the question "Whom say men that I am?" (Mk. 8^{27}), not behind but directly within the speech and action and living and suffering and dying (Mt. 11$^{4f.}$) of the New Testament Jesus or Christ or Jesus Christ. The consequences of abstraction at this point can never be good. We must not forget that if in the doctrinal decisions of Nicaea and Constantinople and Ephesus and Chalcedon it was a matter of the being of Jesus Christ as such, these decisions had a polemical and critical character, their purpose being to delimit and clarify at a specific point. They are to be regarded as guiding lines for an understanding of His existence and action, not to be used, as they have been used, as stones for the construction of an abstract doctrine of His "person." In Himself and as such the Christ of Nicaea and Chalcedon naturally was and is a being which even if we could consistently and helpfully explain His unique structure conceptually could not possibly be proclaimed and believed as One who acts historically because of the timelessness and historical remoteness of the concepts (person, nature, Godhead, manhood, etc.). He could not possibly be proclaimed and believed as the One whom in actual fact the Christian Church has always and everywhere proclaimed and believed under the name of Jesus Christ. An abstract doctrine of the person of Christ may have its own apparent importance, but it is always an empty form, in which what we have to say concerning Jesus Christ can never be said. Again, it is almost inevitable that a doctrine of the work of Christ separated from that of His person will sooner or later give rise to the question, and perhaps even impose it, whether this work cannot be understood as that of someone other than that divine-human person. Can we not make use of the concept of a created *tertium quid*[EN81] (as in certain gnostic speculations concerning angels), or more simply of a man specially endowed with divine grace, to help us to understand the subject of this action? Is not such a concept more service- [128] able than the *vere Deus vere homo*[EN82] of a doctrine of the person which is merely presupposed? If this is the way of it, an abstract doctrine of the work of Christ will always tend

---

[EN78] On the person of Christ, the God-man
[EN79] On the office of Christ, the mediator
[EN80] union
[EN81] third nature
[EN82] truly God, truly man

secretly in a direction where some kind of Arianism or Pelagianism lies in wait. What is needed in this matter is nothing more or less than the removal of the distinction between the two basic sections of classical Christology, or positively, the restoration of the hyphen which always connects them and makes them one in the New Testament. Not to the detriment of either the one or the other. Not to sacrifice the Eastern interest to the Western. Not to cause the doctrine of the person of Christ to be absorbed and dissolved in that of His work, or *vice versa*[EN83]. But to give a proper place to them both, and to establish them both securely in that place.

It is in the particular fact and the particular way that Jesus Christ is very God, very man, and very God-man that He works, and He works in the fact and only in the fact that He is this One and not another. His being as this One is His history, and His history is this His being. This is the truth which must light up the doctrine of reconciliation as Christology. When this is done, it will naturally follow that, as a whole, as a doctrine of the justifying and sanctifying and calling grace of God, as a doctrine of thankfulness, of faith and love and hope, as a doctrine of the community, its human and divine reality, its existence and task, it will be completely dominated and determined by Christology. It will also follow that Christology will not be idle or come under the suspicion that it may be dispensed with. It will take its place without diminution or alteration as the necessary beginning. And it will work itself out in the whole.

4. THE THREE FORMS OF THE DOCTRINE OF RECONCILIATION

If in this sense and with this understanding we return to the being of Jesus Christ as we have briefly defined it, we find at once that there are three "christological" aspects in the narrower sense—aspects of His active person or His personal work which as such broaden into three perspectives for an understanding of the whole event of the atonement.

The first is that in Jesus Christ we have to do with very God. The reconciliation of man with God takes place as God Himself actively intervenes, Himself taking in hand His cause with and against and for man, the cause of the covenant, and in such a way (this is what distinguishes the event of reconciliation from the general sway of the providence and universal rule of God) that He Himself becomes man. God became man. That is what is, i.e., what has taken place, in Jesus Christ. He is very God acting for us men, God Himself become man. He is the authentic Revealer of God as Himself God. Again, He is the effective proof of the power of God as Himself God. Yet again, He is the fulfiller of the covenant as Himself God. He is nothing less or other than God Himself, but God as man. When we say God we say honour and glory and eternity and power, in short, a regnant freedom as it is proper to Him who is distinct from and superior to everything else that is. When we say God we say the Creator and Lord of all things. And we can say all that without reservation

[129]

[EN83] the other way around

or diminution of Jesus Christ—but in a way in which it can be said in relation to Him, i.e., in which it corresponds to the Godhead of God active and revealed in Him. No general idea of "Godhead" developed abstractly from such concepts must be allowed to intrude at this point. How the freedom of God is constituted, in what character He is the Creator and Lord of all things, distinct from and superior to them, in short, what is to be understood by "Godhead," is something which—watchful against all imported ideas, ready to correct them and perhaps to let them be reversed and renewed in the most astonishing way—we must always learn from Jesus Christ. He defines those concepts : they do not define Him. When we start with the fact that He is very God we are forced to keep strictly to Him in relation to what we mean by true "Godhead."

This means primarily that it is a matter of the Godhead, the honour and glory and eternity and omnipotence and freedom, the being as Creator and Lord, of the Father, Son and Holy Spirit. Jesus Christ is Himself God as the Son of God the Father and with God the Father the source of the Holy Spirit, united in one essence with the Father by the Holy Spirit. That is how He is God. He is God as He takes part in the event which constitutes the divine being.

We must add at once that as this One who takes part in the divine being and event He became and is man. This means that we have to understand the very Godhead, that divine being and event and therefore Himself as the One who takes part in it, in the light of the fact that it pleased God—and this is what corresponds outwardly to and reveals the inward divine being and event— Himself to become man. In this way, in this condescension, He is the eternal Son of the eternal Father. This is the will of this Father, of this Son, and of the Holy Spirit who is the Spirit of the Father and the Son. This is how God is God, this is His freedom, this is His distinctness from and superiority to all other reality. It is with this meaning and purpose that He is the Creator and Lord of all things. It is as the eternal and almighty love, which He is actually and visibly in this action of condescension. This One, the One who loves in this way, is the true God. But this means that He is the One who as the Creator and Lord of all things is able and willing to make Himself equal with the creature, Himself to become a creature; the One whose eternity does not prevent but rather permits and commands Him to be in time and Himself to be temporal, whose omnipotence is so great that He can be weak and indeed impotent, as a man is weak and impotent. He is the One who in His freedom can and does in fact [130] bind Himself, in the same way as we all are bound. And we must go further: He, the true God, is the One whose Godhead is demonstrated and plainly consists in essence in the fact that, seeing He is free in His love, He is capable of and wills this condescension for the very reason that in man of all His creatures He has to do with the one that has fallen away from Him, that has been unfaithful and hostile and antagonistic to Him. He is God in that He takes this creature to Himself, and that in such a way that He sets Himself alongside this creature, making His own its penalty and loss and condemnation to nothing-ness. He is God in the fact that He can give Himself up and does give Himself up not merely to the creaturely limitation but to the suffering of the human creature, becoming one of these men, Himself bearing the judgment under which they stand, willing to die and, in fact, dying the death which they have deserved. That is the nature and essence of the true God as He has intervened actively and manifestly in Jesus Christ. When we speak of Jesus Christ we mean the true God—He who seeks His divine glory and finds that glory, He whose glory obviously consists, in the fact that because He is free in His love He can be and actually is lowly as well as exalted; He, the Lord, who is for us a servant, the servant of all servants. It is in the light of the fact of His humiliation that on this first aspect all the predicates of His Godhead, which is the true Godhead, must be filled out and interpreted. Their positive meaning is lit up only by this determination and limitation, only by the fact that in this act He is this God and therefore the true God, distinguished from all false gods by the fact that they are not capable of this act, that they have not in fact accomplished it, that their supposed glory and honour and eternity and omnipotence not only do not include but exclude their self-humiliation. False gods are all reflections of a false and all too human self-exaltation. They are all lords who cannot and will not be servants, who are therefore no true lords, whose being is not a truly divine being.

The second christological aspect is that in Jesus Christ we have to do with a true man. The reconciliation of the world with God takes place in the person of a man in whom, because He is also true God, the conversion of all men to God is an actual event. It is the person of a true man, like all other men in every respect, subjected without exception to all the limitations of the human situation. The conditions in which other men exist and their suffering are also His conditions and His suffering. That He is very God does not mean that He is partly God and only partly man. He is altogether man just as He is altogether God—altogether man in virtue of His true Godhead whose glory consists in His humiliation. That is how He is the reconciler between God and man. That is how God accomplishes in Him the conversion of all men to Himself. He is true man, and altogether man, for in Him we have to do with the manifest-[131] ation of the glory of the One who is true God and altogether God, and with the conversion to God of the One who is true man and altogether man. Here, too, there is no reservation and no diminution, which would be an immediate denial of the act of atonement made in Him. Jesus Christ is man in a different way from what we are. That is why He is our Mediator with God. But He is so in a complete equality of His manhood with ours. To say man is to say creature and sin, and this means limitation and suffering. Both these have to be said of Jesus Christ. Not, however, according to the standard of general concepts, but only with reference to Him, only in correspondence with His true manhood. As in relation to His Godhead, so also in relation to His manhood, we must not allow any necessary idea of the human situation and its need to intervene.

What His manhood is, and therefore true manhood, we cannot read into Him from elsewhere, but must be told by Him. But then we find that it is a matter of the manhood of the eternal Son of God. It is a matter of the real limitation and suffering of the man with whom the high God has ordained and elected and determined to be one, and has therefore humbled Himself. In His limitation and suffering, this is the true man. And that means at once that He is the man exalted by God, lifted above His need and limitation and suffering in and out of His need and limitation and suffering. In virtue of the fact that He is one with God He is free man. He is a creature, but superior to His creatureliness. He is bound by sin, but quite free in relation to it because He is not bound to commit it. He is mortal, and has actually died as we must all die. But in dying He is superior to death, and at once and altogether rescued from it, so that (even as a man like us) He is triumphant and finally alive. As the true God, i.e., the God who humbles Himself, Jesus Christ is this true man, i.e., the man who in all His creatureliness is exalted above His creatureliness. In this He is also exalted above us, because He is different from us, and is given the precedence in the ranks of our common humanity. But He does precede us. As God He was humbled to take our place, and as man He is exalted on our behalf. He is set at the side of God in the humanity which is ours. He is above us and opposed to us, but He is also for us. What has happened in Him as the one true man is the conversion of all of us to God, the realisation of true humanity. It is anticipated in Him, but it is in fact accomplished and revealed. As in Him God became like man, so too in Him man has become like God. As in Him God was bound, so too in Him man is made free. As in Him the Lord became a servant, so too in Him the servant has become a Lord. That is the atonement made in Jesus Christ in its second aspect. In Him humanity is exalted humanity, just as God-head is humiliated Godhead. And humanity is exalted in Him by the humili-ation of Godhead. We cannot regard the human being of Jesus Christ, we cannot—without denying or weakening them—interpret His predicates of liability to sin and suffering and death, in any other way than in the light of the liberation and exaltation accomplished in His unity with God. It is in its impo-tence that His being as man is omnipotent, in its temporality that it is eternal, in its shame that it is glorious, in its corruptibility that it is incorruptible, in its servitude that it is that of the Lord. In this way, therefore, it is His true being as man—true humanity.

[132]

The Evangelists clung to this in their representation of the human being of Jesus Christ. They left no doubt that it was a human being like others, but even less so that as such it was the human being of the true God, and therefore in spite of its likeness to all others dis-tinguished from all others in its freedom in face of limitation and suffering. From the very first they describe it in the light and clear reference of the final thing they have to report concerning Him: His resurrection from the dead as the event in which His exaltation cannot merely be discerned but is openly manifested—lighting up both that which precedes and that which follows. Therefore they describe the man Jesus as the One who, being tempted and suffering and dying as King, overcomes as King, and therefore passes through the midst of all others as King. That is how we must see Him.

In so far as He was and is and will be very man, the conversion of man to God took place in Him, the turning and therefore the reconciliation of all men, the fulfilment of the covenant. And in the light of Jesus Christ the man who is still not free in relation to limitation and suffering, who is still not exalted, who is still lowly (lowly, as it were, *in abstracto*[EN84]), can be understood only as false man—just as in the light of Jesus Christ the empty loveless gods which are incapable of condescension and self-humiliation can be understood only as false gods.

Before we pass on to the third christological aspect, we may at this point interpose another discussion concerning the method of treating the doctrine of reconciliation. In considering the first two aspects we brought together in rather an unusual way two elements in traditional Christology: the doctrine of the two "natures" of Christ, His deity and humanity, and the doctrine of the two "states" of Christ, His humiliation (*status exinanitionis*[EN85]) and His exaltation (*status exaltationis*[EN86]). We must now consider to what extent this presentation involves a change in traditional Christology and soteriology, and how far that change is right and necessary.

In comparison with older dogmatics, our presentation has undoubtedly the advantage that it does far greater justice to the particular doctrine of the two states.

In the older Lutherans this doctrine forms a great excursus in the doctrine of the human nature of Christ, which as they understood it was not merely exalted in the incarnation but actually divinised, i.e., according to their particular doctrine of the communication of the attributes furnished with all the attributes of Godhead. For them the only significance of the doctrine of the two states was that it answered what was for them the very difficult question how far Jesus Christ could have lived and suffered and died as a real man in time and space and under all the other restrictions of human life. For them *exinanitio*[EN87] meant that for a time, for the period of His life up to and including death, the God-man denies Himself that divinisation of His humanity (either by concealment or by genuine renunciation), but then reassumes it with the *exaltatio*[EN88] which begins with His triumphant descent into hell.

[133]   The older Reformed writers described the two states rather obscurely as the humiliation and exaltation of the divine Logos, and with them the doctrine is simply left in the air, following that of the work of Christ but not organically related to it. It was brought in for the sake of completeness, but on their presuppositions it had only an incidental application. If our presentation is right, then at least the doctrine of the humiliation and exaltation of Christ does acquire a place and function in line with its scriptural and factual importance. But this necessitates certain decisive innovations in relation to the older dogmatics which we must openly admit and for which we must give our reasons.

Now (1) we have not spoken of two "states" (*status*) of Jesus Christ which succeed one another, but of two sides or directions or forms of that which took place in Jesus Christ for the reconciliation of man with God. We used the concepts humiliation and exaltation, and we thought of Jesus Christ as the servant who became Lord and the Lord who became ser-

---

[EN84] in the abstract
[EN85] state of humiliation
[EN86] state of exaltation
[EN87] humiliation
[EN88] exaltation

vant. But in so doing we were not describing a being in the particular form of a state, but the twofold action of Jesus Christ, the actuality of His work: His one work, which cannot be divided into different stages or periods of His existence, but which fills out and constitutes His existence in this twofold form. Our question is whether this does not better correspond to the witness of the New Testament concerning Jesus Christ. Where and when is He not both humiliated and exalted, already exalted in His humiliation, and humiliated in His exaltation? Where in Paul, for example, is He the Crucified who has not yet risen, or the Risen who has not been crucified? Would He be the One whom the New Testament attests as the Mediator between God and man if He were only the one and not the other? And if He is the Mediator, which of the two can He be alone and without the other? Both aspects force themselves upon us. We have to do with the being of the one and entire Jesus Christ whose humiliation detracts nothing and whose exaltation adds nothing. And in this His being we have to do with His action, the work and event of atonement. That is the first reason for this alteration of the traditional dogmatic form.

But even more penetrating (2) is the fact that understanding the doctrine of the two states in this way we have tried to interpret it in the light of the doctrine of the two natures, and *vice versa*[EN89].

Notice that there can be no question of abandoning the *vere Deus vere homo*[EN90]. If it is a matter of the reconciliation of man with God in Jesus Christ, i.e., the reconciliation of man with God and by God, then obviously we have to do truly and wholly with God and truly and wholly with man. And the more exact determination of the relationship between God and man in the famous Chalcedonian definition, which has become normative for all subsequent development in this dogma and dogmatics, is one which in our understanding has shown itself to be factually right and necessary. But according to our understanding there can be no question of a doctrine of the two natures which is autonomous, a doctrine of Jesus Christ as God and man which is no longer or not yet related to the divine action which has taken place in Him, which does not have this action and man as its subject-matter. There is no such doctrine in the New Testament, although we cannot say that the New Testament envisages the being and relationship of God and man in Jesus Christ in any other way than it became conceptually fixed in the doctrine of the two natures.

Similarly, there can be no autonomous doctrine of the humiliation and exaltation which took place in Jesus Christ, especially without a reference to what took place in Jesus Christ between God as God and man as man. There is a humiliation and exaltation—it hardly needs to be demonstrated that in Phil. 2[6f.] and indeed all the New Testament Jesus Christ is regarded in the light of these two aspects and concepts. But if there is, it is not something incidental to His being. It is the actuality of the being of Jesus Christ as very God and very man. We cannot, therefore, ascribe to Jesus Christ two natures and then quite independently two states. But we have to explain in mutual relationship to one another what Jesus Christ is as very God and very man and what takes place as the divine work of atonement in His humiliation and exaltation.   [134]

But this brings us (3) to what is perhaps the greatest objection which might be brought against our presentation from the standpoint of the older dogmatics. To explain in the light of each other the deity and humanity of Jesus Christ on the one hand and His humiliation and exaltation on the other means that in Jesus Christ God—we do not say casts off His Godhead but (as the One who loves in His sovereign freedom) activates and proves it by the fact that He gives Himself to the limitation and suffering of the human creature, that He, the Lord, becomes a servant, that as distinct from all false gods He humbles Himself—and

---

[EN89] the other way around
[EN90] truly God, truly man

again, that in Jesus Christ man, without any forfeiture or restriction of His humanity, in the power of His deity and therefore in the power of and thanks to the humiliation of God, is the man who is freed from His limitation and suffering, not divinised man, but man sovereign and set at the side of God, in short, man exalted by God. The humiliation, therefore, is the humiliation of God, the exaltation the exaltation of man: the humiliation of God to supreme glory, as the activation and demonstration of His divine being; and the exaltation of man as the work of God's grace which consists in the restoration of his true humanity. Can we really put it in this way? We have to put it in this way if we are really speaking of the deity and humanity of Jesus Christ, of *His* humiliation and exaltation, of *His* being and *His* work.

For who is the God who is present and active in Him? He is the One who, concretely in His being as man, activates and reveals Himself as divinely free, as the One who loves in His freedom, as the One who is capable of and willing for this inconceivable condescension, and the One who can be and wills to be true God not only in the height but also in the depth—in the depth of human creatureliness, sinfulness and mortality.

And who is the man Jesus Christ? He is the One in whom God is man, who is completely bound by the human situation, but who is not crushed by it, who since it is His situation is free in relation to it, who overcomes it, who is its Lord and not its servant.

Conversely, what is the humiliation of Jesus Christ? To say that He is lowly as a man is tautology which does not help us in the least to explain His humiliation. It merely contains the general truth that He exists as a man in the bondage and suffering of the human situation, and is to that extent actually lowly—a general truth which is in fact very forcibly called in question by the humanity of Jesus Christ. But the peculiar thing about the humiliation of Jesus Christ, the significant thing, the effective thing, the redemptive thing, is that it is the work of atonement in its first form. In Him it took place that while maintaining His true deity God became man, in Him to make His own the cause of man. In Him God Himself humiliated Himself—not in any disloyalty but in a supreme loyalty to His divine being (revealing it in a way which marks it off from all other gods). That is the secret of Christmas and Good Friday and the way which leads from the one to the other. Jesus Christ is the Reconciler of all men of all times and places by the fact that in Him God is active and revealed as the One who in His freedom, in His divine majesty, so loves that in Him the Lord became a servant, a servant like all of us, but more than that, the servant of us all, the man who did for us what we ourselves would not and could not do.

Again, what is the exaltation of Jesus Christ? To say that as God He is transcendent, free, sovereign, above the world, and therefore above the limitation and suffering of the human situation is again tautology which does not help us to understand His exaltation. God is always free in His love, transcendent God. He does not cease to be God transcendent when He makes it His glory to be in the depths, in order to make peace on earth to the men of His good will. In His Godhead, as the eternal Son of the Father, as the eternal Word, Jesus Christ never ceased to be transcendent, free, and sovereign. He did not stand in need of exaltation, nor was He capable of it. But He did as man—it is here again that we come up against that which is not self-evident in Jesus Christ. The special thing, the new thing about the exaltation of Jesus Christ is that One who is bound as we are is free, who is tempted as we are is without sin, who is a sufferer as we are is able to minister to Himself and others, who is a victim to death is alive even though He was dead, who is a servant (the servant of all servants) is the Lord. This is the secret of His humanity which is revealed in His resurrection and ascension and therefore shown retrospectively by the Evangelists to be the secret of His whole life and death. It is not simply that He is the Son of God at the right hand of the Father, the *kyrios*, the Lord of His community and the Lord of the cosmos, the bearer and executor of divine authority in the Church and the world, but that He is all this as a man—as

[135]

a man like we are, but a man exalted in the power of His deity. This is what makes Him the Mediator between God and man, and the One who fulfils the covenant.

If we have correctly related these four considerations concerning the deity, the humanity, the humiliation and the exaltation of Jesus Christ, we not only can but must speak as we have done on this matter. The doctrine of reconciliation in its first two forms will then necessarily begin with a discussion of the God who humbles Himself in Jesus Christ and of the man who in Jesus Christ is exalted.

In the light of this we shall have to consider the whole event of atonement twice over, examining it in detail. The correct titles for these first two sections will be "Jesus Christ, the Lord as Servant" and "Jesus Christ, the Servant as Lord." We shall still follow the traditional path to the extent that in content and meaning this division corresponds exactly to what earlier dogmatics worked out as the doctrine of the high-priestly and kingly office of Christ (in the framework of that doctrine of the threefold office of Christ in which they used to picture His work). I prefer the first two titles as more precise and also more comprehensive (since they also include the earlier doctrine of the person of Christ).

The third christological aspect to which we must now turn is at once the simplest and the highest. It is the source of the two first, and it comprehends them both. As the God who humbles Himself and therefore reconciles man with Himself, and as the man exalted by God and therefore reconciled with Him, as the One who is very God and very man in this concrete sense, Jesus Christ Himself is one. He is the "God-man," that is, the Son of God who as such is this man, this man who as such is the Son of God.

The New Testament obviously speaks of Jesus Christ in both these ways: the one looking and moving, as it were, from above downwards, the other from below upwards. It would be idle to try to conclude which of the two is the more original, authentic and important. Both are necessary. Neither can stand or be understood without the other. A Christ who did not come in the flesh, who was not identical with the Jesus of Nazareth who suffered and died under Pontius Pilate, would not be the Christ Jesus—and a Jesus who was not the eternal Word of God, and who as man was not raised again from the dead, would not be the Jesus Christ—of the New Testament. The New Testament, it is true, knows nothing of the formulae of later ecclesiastical Christology, which tried to formulate the two aspects with conceptual strictness. But it knows even less of the docetic and ebionite abstractions, the attempts to make absolute either the Godhead or the manhood, which it was the concern of the later Christology to rebut. In fact the one aspect is given the greater prominence at this point, the other at that. But it knows only the one person, Jesus Christ Himself, who without division or distinction is both God and man. We remember: both, not in a general and arbitrarily determined sense of the concepts, but in that sense which has been specifically filled out and made concrete. We must never lose sight of Him in the (often very abstract) content given to the concepts in the fathers and later development. The One who is both in this concrete sense is the Jesus Christ of the New Testament. To understand, we must emphasise the phrase: the One who is both—both, and not a third between God and man or a mixture of the two. The Judaic and Hellenistic environment of the New Testament did know such mixtures. The New Testament speaks the language of this environment, but it does not speak of this kind of third. The concrete views of God and man which it has before it in Jesus

[136]

131

Christ cannot be mixed but can only be seen together as the forms of a history: the reconciling God and the man reconciled by Him. In face of the history which took place in Jesus Christ the New Testament says that these two elements of the one grace, the divine and the human, are one in Him, not in one form but in two. For that reason its statements concerning Him always move in either the one direction or the other, from above downwards or from below upwards. The only statement in the New Testament which brings together both in one is properly the name of Jesus Christ, which forbids and makes quite impossible any separation of the one from the other or any fusion of both in a third. When, therefore, the later Christology safeguarded against any confusion or transmutation of the two natures the one into the other and therefore into a third, the innovation was not one of substance but only of theology, and one which the substance itself demanded.

There can be no question of our trying to see a third thing in what we have called the third christological aspect. Everything that can be said materially concerning Jesus Christ and the atonement made in Him has been said exhaustively in the twofold fact—which cannot be further reduced conceptually but only brought together historically—that He is very God and very man, i.e., the Lord who became a servant and the servant who became Lord, the reconciling God and reconciled man. The third aspect can be only the viewing of this history in its unity and completeness, the viewing of Jesus Christ Himself, in whom the two lines cross—in the sense that He Himself is the subject of what takes place on these two lines. To that extent the reconciliation of the world with God and the conversion of the world to God took place in Him. To that extent He Himself, His existence, is this reconciliation. He Himself is the Mediator and pledge of the covenant. He is the Mediator of it in that He fulfils it—from God to man and from man to God. He is the pledge of it in that in His existence He confirms and maintains and reveals it as an authentic witness—attesting Himself, in that its fulfilment is present and shines out and avails and is effective in Him. This is the new thing in the third christological aspect. Jesus Christ is the actuality of the atonement, and as such the truth of it which speaks for itself. If we hear Jesus Christ, then whether we realise it or not we

[137] hear this truth. If we say Jesus Christ, then whether we realise it or not we express and repeat this truth: the truth of the grace in which God has turned to the world in Him and which has come to the world in Him; the truth of the living brackets which bring and hold together heaven and earth, God and all men, in Him; the truth that God has bound Himself to man and that man is bound to God. The One who bears this name is Himself this truth in that He is Himself this actuality. He attests what He is. He alone is the pledge of it because He alone is the Mediator of it. He alone is the truth of it. But He is that truth, and therefore it speaks for itself in Him. It is not in us. We cannot produce it of ourselves. We cannot of ourselves attest it to ourselves or to others. But it encounters us majestically in Him—the promise of the truth which avails for us as the atonement—of which it is the truth—took place for us and as ours, the truth which for that reason can and should be heard and accepted and appropriated by us, which we can and should accept as the truth which applies to us. It encounters us in Him as the promise of our own future. It is

He, and therefore the actuality of our atonement, who stands before us. It is to Him, and therefore to the revelation of this actuality, that we move. He is the Word of God to men which speaks of God and man and therefore expresses and discloses and reveals God and ourselves—God in His actual relationship to us and us in our actual relationship to God. He is the Word of God by which He calls us in this relationship and therefore calls us to Him and therefore calls us also to ourselves. He was and is the will of God to speak this Word—this Word of His act. And it is our destiny to hear this Word, to live under and with and by this Word. That is the third christological aspect.

Of the doctrine of reconciliation as such we must now say that in the light of this aspect a third and concluding section will be necessary in our presentation: concluding, but at the same time opening up and forming a transition to the doctrine of the redemption or consummation, the "eschatology" in which all dogmatics culminate. It is easy to find a title for this third section: "Jesus Christ the Guarantor." "Jesus Christ the Witness" would also be possible and impressive, but it might be understood too formally, whereas the neutral concept "guarantor" expresses more clearly what we are trying to say—that He who is Himself the material content of the atonement, the Mediator of it, stands security with man as well as God that it is our atonement—He Himself being the form of it as well as the content.

In this section we shall be dealing substantially with what the older dogmatics used to present as the doctrine of the "prophetic" office of Christ. We can only say that as compared with the doctrines of the *munus sacerdotale*[EN91] and the *munus regium*[EN92]—which it normally preceded as a kind of unaccented syllable—this doctrine played a rather difficult part and one which did not seem to shed any very great light of its own. It was hardly related, if at all, to the first two offices, and for that reason it had a largely formal character and could be left out altogether by some of the later writers. And it was because its proper role could not be found in the orthodox period that at the time of the *Aufklärung*[EN93] it emerged from its decline in a form which was fatal. For it now pushed to the forefront as the supposed truth behind all Christology, but in the form of the representation of Jesus as the supreme teacher and example of perfect divine and human love—a representation which has practically nothing in common with the biblical concept of prophecy. The result was that the doctrines of the priestly and kingly office of Christ were now pushed back into the same obscurity of the less important in which this doctrine itself had laboured for so long. The atonement as a work of divine grace for man and to man, which means, the whole actuality of Jesus Christ, was necessarily concealed apart from a few confused and tedious and not very profitable relics. That this may not happen again, we must give due weight to the *munus propheticum*[EN94] in its proper content and its peculiar significance.

[138]

It is not a matter of the content of truth but of the character of truth, of the identity of the divine work of grace with the divine Word of grace, of Jesus Christ who not only is what He is and does what He does but in so doing

---

[EN91] priestly office
[EN92] royal office
[EN93] Enlightenment
[EN94] prophetic office

encounters us, testifying to us, addressing us, promising to us, pledging Himself to us, in all His majesty summoning us—in the right sense as a teacher and example—to come to Him, and in that way His own prophet, the prophet of His future as ours and ours as His.

We have to develop the whole doctrine of reconciliation in accordance with our Christology and the three basic christological aspects. We shall do so in three sections which correspond to the three aspects. The Christology is the key to the whole. From each of the three aspects suggested it will be our starting point and will necessarily control all the detailed developments. But in the light of the Christology there have to be these developments: the three great expositions of the fact and the extent to which the reconciliation of the world with God is actual in Him—in His servitude for us, in the humiliation of God for man which took place in Him, in His lordship over us, in the exaltation of man to God's glory which took place in Him, and all this as truth which He Himself has guaranteed and pledged.

But the christological bases of the doctrine of reconciliation bring us face to face at once and directly with a problem which has met us everywhere in this survey. This problem seems to form, as it were, a second and obscure centre side by side with Jesus Christ. The whole event of atonement seems to be strangely related to it on its negative side just as on its positive side it is grounded and enclosed in Jesus Christ. But so far we have not given it any independent consideration. It is the problem of the sin which has come into the world, or of man as the responsible author but also the poor victim of sin, the one who is blinded by it and closed to the truth. Atonement is the fulfilment by God of the covenant broken by man. Because he sins, and because the world is the world of sin and its consequences, man has need of conversion to God if he is not to perish. And it is in face of this, striving against and overcoming the sin of man, that God in His mercy does what He does, and there happens to man what does happen to him in the divine mercy when Jesus Christ intervenes as the Mediator of the covenant. It is clear that at this heart of its message Christian proclamation must speak very definitely of this hostile element, that therefore there has to be a very clear doctrine of sin in the Church's dogmatics.

[139]

But it must not be a doctrine of sin which is autonomous, which considers the matter and investigates and presents it in a vacuum, and therefore again abstractly.

That is what we find in the older theology and, of course, in most modern theology as well. Between the doctrine of creation and that of the atonement it was and is customary (and logically it is very instructive and didactically most illuminating) to interpose a special section *De peccato*[EN95]: a doctrine of the fall, of original sin and its consequences, of the state and constitution of sinful man, of individual or actual sins.

It cannot be disputed that this whole sphere—this dark prelude or counter-

---

EN95 On Sin

part to the divine covenant and work of grace—has to be taken very seriously. If there is to be any understanding of the Christian message, we have to investigate it closely and take it into account. There is in fact no page in the Bible in which it does not figure, and many pages in which it seems to do so almost alone. But all the same, we cannot with a good conscience follow the procedure which would give it a treatment which is independent, self-originating and self-contained.

For what is the ontological place of sin in the Bible? Surely not in a realm of its own where it has its own being and can exist in and for itself? In the sphere of Christian thinking at any rate, we cannot seriously and responsibly maintain that it was created by God and belongs, therefore, to the constitution of the world as He willed it. There is no support for any such view in what the Bible itself says. In the Bible sin in all its fearful reality is at a disadvantage compared with even the most modest creature in that it has only "entered into" the world, as we are told in Rom. 5^{12}. It does not belong to the creation of God. It can be present and active within it only as an alien. It has no appointed place, no place which belongs to it. If it has its place, it is that of an usurpation against the creative will of God, the place of an interloper. It is there where it has no business at all to be as that which God has not willed. It is there where it has nothing either to seek or to tell. And only there can it be sought out and found. And even there, in its nothingness, it does not exist in any way on the basis of its own independent right, or even in its dreadful reality by its own independent power. How could it ever have any such right or power? It has its right, but it is the stolen right of wrong. It has its power, but it is the stealthy power of impotence. It exists and is only in opposition to the will of God and therefore in opposition to the being and destiny of His creature. It can only say No where God says Yes, and where in its own very different fashion the creature of God can also say Yes. When and where has the word and work of sin ever been a solemn Yes? It can only negate, deny, destroy, break down, dissolve. Even where God uses it in His service—and there is no doubt that it is under His lordship and must serve Him, as the Bible makes perfectly plain—it can serve only to fulfil His judgment, which is to shame and oppose and punish itself, or contrary to its own nature to accomplish some positive good in unwilling subservience to His higher control. It is neither a creature nor itself a creator. It is not only incapable of creation, but, being without root or soil in the creaturely world into which it has pushed its alien being, it is quite unproductive. In all its forms it exists and is only as that which negates and therefore as that which is itself negated, on the left hand of God, where God in saying Yes has already said No, where in electing He has rejected, where in willing He has not willed.

[140]

But the divine Yes which sin negates and by which it is negated is the Yes of God's covenant with man which is the mystery of creation—the covenant of grace concluded in Jesus Christ from all eternity and fulfilled and revealed in time. What God has determined and done as the Lord of this covenant is His will. The sin of man, being his doing and accomplishing of what God does not will, negates and withstands and rejects it. Sin is therefore not merely an evil, but a breach of the covenant which as such contradicts God and stands under His contradiction. Sin is man's denial of himself in face of the grace of His Creator. It is not directed against a so-called law of nature. There is no law of nature which is both recognisable as such and yet also has divine character and authority. There is no law and commandment of God inherent in the creatureliness of man as such, or written and revealed in the stars as a law of the cosmos, so that the transgression of it makes man a sinner. It is characteristic of the sin of man—and one of its results—that man should think he can know such a law of nature and direct and measure himself and others in accordance with it. But in his creatureliness, in his nature—which is the sum of his possibilities and destiny and nothing more—man is called to hold to the grace of His Creator, to be thankful for it, to bow to it and adapt himself to it, to honour it as the truth. And the essence of sin is that he does not do this. He denies and despises and hates grace and breaks its commandment, the law of the covenant. It is in this opposition that sin takes place, that it has its place and reality: as man's turning aside from God, and therefore as the perversion of his own nature; as the abuse and disturbance and destruction of the possibilities of his creaturely being and the radical compromising of his destiny.

This being the case, sin cannot be recognised and understood and defined and judged as sin in accordance with any general idea of man, or any law which is different from the grace of God and its commandment, the law of the coven-[141] ant. If it takes place as a breach of the covenant, and not in any other way, it can be known only in the light of the covenant. But since man has broken the covenant, that can mean only in the light of the covenant fulfilled and restored in Jesus Christ and therefore in the light of the atonement made in Him. The Old Testament dispensation with its Law consists in the proclamation of it. But what in the Old Testament Law was meant to be the Law of the covenant of grace moving to its fulfilment has now been revealed by the actual fulfilment of the covenant, by the accomplishment in Jesus Christ of that which was proclaimed in the covenant of God with Israel. God wills what He has done in Jesus Christ. And in so doing He has brought in the Law given to man, the Law against which man as a covenant-breaker has sinned from the very first, the Law in whose transgression all human sin has consisted and does consist and will consist. In the light of Jesus Christ the darkness is revealed as such. It is made plain that man is a sinner. It is shown in what his sin consists. It is that being and acting and thinking and speaking and bearing of man which in Jesus Christ God has met, which in Him He has opposed and overcome and judged, which in Him He has passed over, in spite of which He has converted man to Himself in Him. God is the Lord of the covenant of grace and none else. As such He is revealed in the fulfilment of it and therefore in Jesus Christ, and not otherwise. What He has done in Him is His will with man and therefore that and nothing else is His commandment. But if this is the case, sin is simply that in which man contradicts this will of God, and because of which he for his part is decisively contradicted and opposed by this will of God. The knowledge of sin can relate only to what we are told concerning our being and activity by Jesus Christ as the Mediator and Guarantor of the atonement, to what we have to say after Him, if that knowledge is to be serious. And the confession of sin ("Against thee only have I sinned," Ps. 51⁶) can be accomplished only in the turning to Him and therefore in the knowledge of the conversion of man to God which has taken place in Him. Only in this way is it an actual confessing of real sin as opposed to outbreaks of remorse or depression or bemoaning or despair.

But this means that there can be no place in dogmatics for an autonomous section *De peccato*EN96 constructed in a vacuum between the doctrine of creation and that of reconciliation. Who can summon us to keep a law of God which is supposed to be known to man by nature? Who can try to measure the sin of man by such a law? To do that—even in the form of a "doctrine of sin"— is surely to do precisely what we are forbidden to do by the real Law of God revealed by God Himself. To do that is surely to pass by the grace of God, to evolve our own thoughts in relation to the will of God instead of those which He Himself has given us in the commandment held out before us in His grace. And is not this necessarily to sin again—theologically! Or, again, who can summon us in this matter of sin to follow the abstractly considered Law of the [142] covenant of the Old Testament dispensation which is only moving to its fulfilment?—as though we had not yet heard or taken to heart the warnings of Paul against the *nomos*EN97 abstractly understood in this way; as though there were even one unconverted Jew who had come to a knowledge of his real sin by following this law; as though it were a good thing to advise Christians first to become such unconverted Jews and to follow this law, in order to push them forward from that point to what will certainly never be a knowledge of their real sin.

If we are not to be guilty of these two errors, we have no option but to consider and answer the question of sin in the light of the Gospel and therefore within the doctrine of reconciliation, to take it up into that doctrine instead of giving it precedence over it as though it were an autonomous question. In this context we shall find the natural place for it immediately after the Christology. It is in the knowledge of Jesus Christ as the revelation of the grace of God that we shall necessarily perceive step by step both the fact that man is a transgressor, and the nature of the transgression in which he contradicts the grace of God and for the sake of which he is decisively contradicted by that grace. Step by step, for if the content of the doctrine of sin—man's active opposition to the God who actively encounters him—is really to be brought out, the complex of the doctrine, like that of the Christology, demands a definite structure

EN96 On Sin
EN97 Law

in which we will be safest to follow that of the Christology. Necessarily, therefore, it will appear not simply at one point, but at three points corresponding to the three christological bases of the three main sections of the doctrine of reconciliation, and at every point in a corresponding form.

Sin is obviously (1) the negation, the opposite of what God does for us in Jesus Christ in condescending to us, in humbling Himself, in becoming a servant to take to Himself and away from us our guilt and sickness. This is the grace of God in its first form: God gives Himself to us, He makes Himself responsible for our cause, He takes it into His own hand. And the commandment is clear—it is necessarily a matter of our basing our being and activity on the fact that God is ours, that we are the recipients of this gift which is so inconceivably great. Sin in its first form is pride. When God condescends to man, when He makes Himself one with Him in order to be truly his God, man cannot fall away from the work of this mercy of God to him. But what Adam did, what Israel did at all stages in its history, what the world does so long as it does not see itself as the world reconciled in Jesus Christ, what even the Christian does when he forgets that he is a Christian, is the very thing which is forbidden by this first form of grace, the very thing which is made impossible, which is excluded, which is negated because it is itself a negation. It is the fall in the form of presumption, acting as though God had not humbled Himself

[143] to man, as though He had not encountered man as the unfathomably merciful One, as though He had not taken to Himself the cause of man. Sin is man's act of defiance. In this first part of the doctrine of reconciliation the doctrine of sin will have to be described and portrayed in the closest connexion with the consideration of Jesus Christ as the Lord who became an obedient servant for us (and therefore with His high-priestly office). It will be characterised, therefore, as the act of pride.

But further, sin is (2) the negation, the opposite of what God did in Jesus Christ, the servant who became Lord, to exalt man—not to deity but to His own right hand in a fellowship of life with Himself. This is the grace of God in its second form: He wills and seeks us as we are, in our creatureliness, as men, that we may be raised to the status of children. That is why He humbled Himself. That is the meaning and force of His mercy. And again the commandment is clear—it is a matter of our being and activity as men in accordance with the exaltation which has come to us. As against that, sin in its second form is sloth. God Himself has not merely shown man the way, but made it for him. God Himself has already exalted him. Therefore man must not wilfully fall. He must not set against the grace of God which is addressed to him, and leads him, and orders his going, his own dark ways of frivolity or melancholy or despair which he seeks and chooses and follows. Adam at the very first fell into this sin too. Israel did it again and again. The world lives and thinks and speaks and seeks and finds on this downward way. Even forgetful Christians are on this way. This is man's disorder—corresponding to the order established by the grace of God. The doctrine of sin will have to treat of this sloth of man in the second part of the doctrine of reconciliation, and therefore in connexion with the consideration of Jesus Christ as the servant who became Lord (the doctrine of His kingly office).

Finally, sin is (3) the negation, the opposite of the fact that God in Jesus Christ has made Himself the Guarantor of the reality of that which has been done by Him as servant and Lord in that movement from above downwards and below upwards, of the fact that in Jesus Christ God has made Himself the witness of the truth of the atonement. This is the grace of God in its third form: God does not act above our heads, He does not ignore us, but He addresses us and calls us. He tells us what He does and He tells us as He does it. His action for us and with us is itself and as such His Word to us. Again the commandment of His grace is clear—it is a matter of hearing and obeying the truth which is told us, a matter of active joy in it. We have to see that that which is told us is true for us: that Jesus Christ is the Lord who became a servant for us, and the servant who became Lord for us, our Lord. As against this, sin in its third form is falsehood. When God Himself is the pledge that He has done all this, man cannot pretend that he knows better. When the truth speaks for itself, man's knowing better is only falsehood, a lie. And, again, this is the sin of [144] Adam, and repeated in many forms it is the sin of Israel, and of the world and of all forgetful Christians. We are all at times, incorrigibly, those who know better—and, therefore, because grace is the truth revealed and known to us, we are all incorrigible liars. The consequences follow. Falsehood is self-destruction. Because man and the world live under the dominion of sin, lying to God and deceiving themselves, they live in self-destruction. At this point it is plain that sin cannot say Yes but only No, that it cannot build up but only pull down, that it can create only suffering and death. Sinful man is as such man without hope. This conflict of sin against the promise and hope given to man in the Word of God will have to be presented in the third part of the doctrine of reconciliation in connexion with the consideration of Jesus Christ as the Guarantor, the doctrine of His prophetic office.

And now we must try to go further. Sin is a reality—as the antithesis to God it is so almost as God Himself is, *sui generis*[EN98]. But it is not an autonomous reality. As the No which opposes the divine Yes, it is only a reality related to and contradicting that Yes. Therefore it can be known—and all the horror of it can be known—only in the light of that Yes. In all its reality and horror it can never be a first word, nor can it ever be a final word. The atonement made in Jesus Christ teaches us (as nothing else can) to know it and to take it seriously, but we also have to perceive and state that the gracious will and act of God in Jesus Christ are superior to it and overcome it. We ourselves do not look down on it or master it or conquer it or set it aside. We ourselves are not superior to it. But Jesus Christ, against whom sin properly and finally rears itself, is superior to it. In all the forms of the grace of God revealed and active in Him He is superior

---

[EN98] in a category of its own

139

to sin in all its forms. He looks back on it. He looks down on it. And when we look at Him, for good or evil we, too, can and must look back on it and down on it. He has already effectively contradicted its contradicting. He has already banished the alien and defeated the usurper. In Him, in opposition to this enemy, the kingdom of God has already been victoriously inaugurated, and is present and revealed in power. We should be questioning everything that He is and has done, we should be making ourselves guilty of sin in its last mentioned form of falsehood (and therefore in its other forms as ingratitude and disorder), if we were to try to have it otherwise, if we were to try to think and speak less confidently in relation to Him, with reservations and limitations, and probably at bottom with doubts and denials. The reality of sin cannot be known or described except in relation to the One who has vanquished it. In His light it is darkness, but a darkness which yields. That He is the victor is therefore a Christian axiom which is not only not shaken but actually confirmed by sin. It is He who has the final word.

[145]   The fact that He does have the final word, and the extent to which He does, is something which we will have to show in the further development of the doctrine of reconciliation. It will be a matter of perceiving that the atonement made in Him is God's triumphant and effective decision in relation to sin as the great episode. And it will be a matter of understanding this decision concretely and in its context, which is obviously in the light of the Christology and the three christological bases. Therefore we shall have to adduce three propositions, all of which have the same content—that the sinful No of man has been matched and opposed and destroyed by the divine Yes spoken by Jesus Christ even in the sphere of man and the world which we have just considered in the doctrine of sin. Or positively, we shall have to show what is the divine Yes spoken by God in answer to the human No, in what form it is maintained and fulfilled in the sphere of sinful man and the sinful world, how it is vindicated as the first and final word.

To explain at this point the one and threefold being and work of Jesus Christ in its relevance for the world we shall have to speak first of the three forms of the grace of God which comes to man in Him. We are here dealing with the objective material presented in older dogmatics under the title *De applicatione salutis*[EN99] (soteriology). On the basis of our presuppositions this complex will work out as follows.

1. In relation to the doctrine of God's self-humiliation for us men accomplished in Jesus Christ, and in direct answer to the doctrine of sin as the human act of pride, the first part of the doctrine of reconciliation will necessarily continue with the doctrine of the divine verdict in Jesus Christ by which man is justified. This justifying sentence of God is His decision in which man's being as the subject of that act is repudiated, his responsibility for that act, his guilt, is pardoned, cancelled and removed, and there is ascribed to him

---

EN99 On the Application of Salvation

instead a being as the subject of pure acts of thankfulness for this liberation. At this point we have to make it plain that the Gospel is an effective because a well-founded word of consolation resting on the righteousness of God. This is the positive content of the Reformation insight into salvation in the form particularly affected by Luther. And we must weigh it in relation to the Roman (Tridentine) doctrine and also mark it off and confirm it against Protestant misunderstandings and misrepresentations. But all this must be done with the reservation that in spite of the great importance of this insight we are dealing here with only one form of the grace of Jesus Christ. Only Jesus Christ Himself can be the principle of the doctrine of reconciliation, not justification or any other of the true but secondary forms of His grace.

2. In relation to the doctrine of the exaltation of man by God in Jesus Christ, and in direct answer to the doctrine of sin as the sloth of man, the second part of the doctrine of reconciliation will necessarily emphasise the direction given in Jesus Christ in which the sanctification of man is accomplished. This sanctifying direction of man is His decision by which sinful man is addressed and treated as a new subject, so that instead of causing himself to fall he can stand [146] and proceed along the way which God has appointed for him as the way of true freedom, in this way rendering obedience. At this point we have to make it plain that the Gospel is a saving committal and an uplifting obligation, the Reformation insight into salvation as particularly understood and represented by Calvin. We must do this primarily in its positive content, but also in antithesis especially to the Roman conception of the Christian life and to every form of secular humanism. In some respects we will have to set it even against Lutheranism, marking it off from all kinds of false developments both internal and external, old and new. But, of course, in spite of the rightness and importance of the matter, we shall never do so as though sanctification could or should replace Jesus Christ as the principle, the One and All, of the doctrine of reconciliation.

3. In relation to the doctrine of the unity of God and man introduced in Jesus Christ, and in direct answer to the doctrine of sin as the falsehood of man, the third part of the doctrine of reconciliation will have to set out the promise of God proclaimed in and with His verdict and direction, in which the calling of man takes place. This promise of God, which as the truth overcomes the lie, is God's decision in which He has given to man, quite contrary to the destruction of his existence, an eternal future in fellowship with Himself, that is, in His service, and therefore a teleological direction of his life in time, so that even this life in time acquires a perspective and therefore (small, relative and provisional) ends. In this respect we have to speak of the Gospel as a clarifying directive. And it is here that historically we have to look beyond the circle of vision of the 16th century Reformation, or, rather, to bring to light certain insights into Christian salvation which were then dismissed too summarily or suppressed altogether: life in the present, in expectation of the kingdom of God, in the rest and unrest which this causes, in the discipleship of Jesus

Christ, in its eschatological orientation, in its dynamic in this-worldly criticism and construction. In short, this is the place where on the one hand we must find a place for what, since the Reformation, we have surely added to our understanding of the New Testament in respect of its teleological elements, and where, on the other, we may seek agreement between what to-day is felt to be and is, in fact, an antithesis between continental Protestantism and Anglo-Saxon, which was more influenced by the humanistic and enthusiastic movements of the Reformation period. In the light of the particular christological starting-point—and here the doctrine of the prophetic office of Christ will be normative—it will now be a question of bringing together the first two soteriological aspects. All the more carefully, then, we must avoid all appearance of claiming that from this standpoint of calling we are dealing with more than a part of what is the One and All in this matter. It is clear that this, too, can only be one form of the grace of Jesus Christ.

[147]   In all three developments we must ensure that Jesus Christ is constantly known and revealed as the One and All that is expounded. He is the One who justifies, sanctifies and calls. He is the High-Priest, King and Prophet. In the measure that He is shown to be the subject of the whole occurrence, the *autor*[EN100] and *applicator salutis*[EN101], the doctrine of His grace, of the mercy of God directed in Him to man, will not in any way obscure by the necessary systematising and sub-dividing of its presentation the unity in which that grace is His grace.

In the whole event of atonement, justification, sanctification and calling, as grounded in the divine verdict, direction and promise, have as it were a central function. In them, in the understanding of grace under these concepts, it is still a matter of expounding the being and work of Jesus Christ as the Reconciler of the sinful world and therefore of sinful man with God. It is still a matter, then, of what took place in Him for the conversion of the world to God. That is how it must be to the very end. When we say justification, sanctification and calling, on the one side we are already expounding the relevance of what was done in Jesus Christ, but, on the other, we are expounding only the objective relevance of it and not its subjective apprehension and acceptance in the world and by us men. We might say, we are dealing with the ascription but not the appropriation of the grace of Jesus Christ, or with what has taken place in Him for the world as such but not for the Christian in particular. In the Christian there is an appropriation of the grace of God ascribed to all men in Jesus Christ, a subjective apprehension of what has been done for the whole world in the happening of atonement. It is absolutely and exclusively in the being and work of Jesus Christ Himself and not in men that this specific form of grace has its basis and power, that it is true and actual that there are amongst other men those who are reconciled with God in Jesus Christ, who recognise

---

[EN100] author
[EN101] executor of salvation

and affirm their being as such, who can confess from the heart, with word and deed, that God makes Himself known to the world in the work of atonement, that He faithfully maintains and fulfils His covenant with man in opposition to the fall and sin of man, that He activates and reveals Himself in Jesus Christ as the God of man, that in so doing He has claimed man in all His omnipotence as His man. The doctrine of justification, sanctification and calling must obviously be followed by a discussion of this particular form of grace.

In this connexion the specific point that we have to make is that the being and work of Jesus Christ—for even here we cannot abandon the christological basis—must now be understood as the being and work of His Holy Spirit, or His own spiritual being and work. The appropriation of the grace of Jesus Christ ascribed to us, the subjective apprehension of the reconciliation of the world with God made in Him, the existence of Christians, presupposes and includes within itself the presence, the gift and the reception, the work and accomplishment of His Holy Spirit. The Holy Spirit is the one eternal God in [148] His particular power and will so to be present to the creature in His being and activity, so to give Himself to it, that it can recognise and embrace and experience Himself and His work and therefore the actuality and truth of its own situation, that its eyes and ears and senses and reason and heart are open to Him and willing and ready for Him. The particular existence of the Son of God as man, and again the particular existence of this man as the Son of God, the existence of Jesus Christ as the Lord who becomes a servant and the servant who becomes Lord, His existence as the Guarantor of truth is itself ultimately grounded in the being and work of the Holy Spirit. He is *conceptus de Spiritu sancto*[EN102]. And this is the distinctive mark of the existence of the men who perceive and accept and receive Him as the Reconciler of the world and therefore as their Reconciler, who—vicariously for the whole world reconciled by Him—discover that they are His because He is theirs, who on the basis of this discovery and therefore in this special sense exist "in Him," who can be with Him and for Him as He is with them and for them (with and for the whole world). It is the Holy Spirit, the being and work of the one eternal God in this special form, that is still lacking in the world at large. That God did not owe His Son, and in that Son Himself, to the world, is revealed by the fact that He gives His Spirit to whom He will. The hand of God the Reconciler is over all men. Jesus Christ was born and died and rose again for all. The work of atonement, the conversion of man to God, was done for all. The Word of God is spoken to all. God's verdict and direction and promise have been pronounced over all. To that extent, objectively, all are justified, sanctified and called. But the hand of God has not touched all in such a way that they can see and hear, perceive and accept and receive all that God is for all and therefore for them, how therefore they can exist and think and live. To those who have not been touched in this way by the hand of God the axiom that Jesus Christ is the Victor

---

EN102 conceived by the Holy Spirit

is as such unknown. It is a Christian and not a general axiom; valid generally, but not generally observed and acknowledged. Similarly, they do not know their sin or even what sin is, since it can be known only in the light of that axiom. And naturally they do not know their justification, sanctification and calling as they have already taken place in Jesus Christ. But the hand of God has touched and seized Christians in this way—which means the presence and activity of the Holy Spirit. In this special sense Christians and only Christians are converted to Him. This is without any merit or co-operation on their part, just as the reconciliation of the whole world in Jesus Christ is without its merit or co-operation. But they are really converted to God in this special sense. The free grace of the sovereign God has in relation to them the special form that they themselves can reach after it. They can understand it as the grace directed [149] to the world and therefore to them. They can live in the light and power of it— under its judgment, but all in all, under the Word, and readily and willingly under the Word, under the divine sentence and direction and promise. There-fore the being and work of Jesus Christ, the One and All of His achievement and the relevance of it has also this—shall we call it for the sake of clarity subjective?—dimension, in which the same One and All is now in the eyes and ears and hearts, in the existence of these men, Christians, who are specially taken and determined by His Holy Spirit. They have over the rest of the world the one inestimable advantage that God the Reconciler and the event of rec-onciliation can be to them a matter of recognition and confession, until the day when He and it will be the subject of His revelation to all eyes and ears and hearts, and therefore of the recognition and confession of all men. The being and work of Jesus Christ in the form of the being and work of His Holy Spirit is therefore the original and prefigurative existence of Christianity and Chris-tians.

It is of this that we shall have to speak in the two concluding sections of all the three parts of the doctrine of reconciliation. And two things will have to be borne in mind. It is a matter of Christendom and of Christians, of the com-munity ("Church") of Jesus Christ and of its members (individual Christians in their personal relationship to Jesus Christ). There cannot be the one without the other. The Holy Spirit is not a private spirit, but the power by which the Son of God (*Heid. Cat. Qu.* 54) "has from the beginning of the world to the end assembled out of the whole race of man, and preserves and maintains, an elect congregation." But He assembles and preserves and maintains it, not as a pile of grains of sand or as an aggregate of cells, but as a community of those of whom each one can individually recognise and confess by His power "that I am a living member of the same, and will be so for ever." Within this particular group of problems it is clearly a matter of a correspondence, a reflection and a repetition of the relationship between the objective ascription and the subject-ive appropriation of salvation. Salvation is ascribed to the individual in the existence of the community, and it is appropriated by the community in the existence of the individuals of which it is composed.

4. *The Three Forms of the Doctrine of Reconciliation*

In the light of this correspondence it is more fitting to take the question of Christendom before that of the individual Christian.

Traditional dogmatics went to work differently. Logically, and again most instructively from the didactic standpoint, it proceeded at once from the objective demonstration of divine grace to its subjective apprehension in the life of man, i.e., the individual Christian. Or it treated both in the one context, speaking of personal Christian faith, for example, in the same breath as justification, and personal Christian obedience in the same breath as sanctification. We, too, must speak of them in the same breath, so that it is clear that the work of the Holy Spirit is in fact only a particular form of the being and work of Jesus Christ Himself. But we should be making it private in a way which is quite illegitimate if we were to relate it directly to the personal appropriation of salvation by the individual Christian. It was [150] an intolerable truncation of the Christian message when the older Protestantism steered the whole doctrine of the atonement—and with it, ultimately, the whole of theology—into the *cul de sac*[EN103] of the question of the individual experience of grace, which is always an anxious one when taken in isolation, the question of individual conversion by it and to it, and of its presuppositions and consequences. The almost inevitable result was that the great concepts of justification and sanctification came more and more to be understood and filled out psychologically and biographically, and the doctrine of the Church seemed to be of value only as a description of the means of salvation and grace indispensable to this individual and personal process of salvation. We will only ask in passing whether and to what extent Luther's well-known question in the cloister—which was and will always be useful at its own time and place—contributed if only by way of temptation to this truncation, or whether it is simply an aberration first of orthodoxy and then of the Pietism which began in it and followed it. What is more to the point is to remember (and this, too, is something we can only mention) that we will do well not to allow ourselves to be crowded again into the same *cul de sac*[EN104] on the detour via Kierkegaard.

Certainly the question of the subjective apprehension of atonement by the individual man is absolutely indispensable. And it belongs properly to the concluding section of the doctrine of reconciliation—yet not in the first place, but in the second, and therefore at the close of this concluding section.

Our theme is the reconciliation of the world with God in Jesus Christ, and only in this greater context the reconciliation of the individual man. This is what was completely overlooked in that truncation. And if it is to be brought to light again, the prior place which the Christian individual has for so long—we might almost say unashamedly—claimed for himself in the dogmatics of the Christian community must be vacated again. We must not cease to stress the individual. We must not throw doubt on the importance of his problem. But!

Only in the proper place. The "pillar and ground of truth" (1 Tim. 3^{15}), the salt of the earth, the light of the world, the city set on a hill, is the community of God and not the individual Christian as such, although the latter has within it his assured place, his indispensable function, and his unshakable personal promise. It is not he but the *ecclesia una sancta catholica et apostolica*[EN105] that stands (in close connexion with the Holy Spirit) in the third article of the

---

[EN103] dead end
[EN104] dead end
[EN105] one holy catholic and apostolic Church

Creed. It is the Church which with its perception and experience of the grace of God stands vicariously for the rest of the world which has not yet partaken of the witness of the Holy Spirit. It is the Church which in this particularity is ordained to the ministry of reconciliation and the witness of the grace of God in relation to the rest of the world. It is in its existence, therefore—and only in the sphere of its existence in that of individual Christians—that the salvation ascribed to the world is appropriated by man. It is primarily in it that there is fulfilled in the sphere of sinful man and his world, as the work of the Holy Spirit of Jesus Christ, the subjective apprehension of the atonement objectively [151] made in Him. It is of the Church, then, that in the light of the three christological origins we shall have to speak first in all three parts of the doctrine of reconciliation.

1. The Holy Spirit as the Spirit of Jesus Christ is the awakening power of the Word spoken by the Lord who became a servant and therefore of the divine sentence which judges and justifies sinful man. The work of the Holy Spirit as this awakening power is the historical reality of the community. When that verdict—that verdict of God which, we recall, repudiates and accepts, kills and makes alive—is heard by men, there is in their inner fellowship and there arises in their outward assembly a new humanity within the old. A new history begins within world-history. A new form of fellowship is quietly founded amongst other sociological forms: the apostolate, the disciples, the community, the Church. Its members are those who can believe and understand that sentence, and therefore regard as accomplished the justification of man in Jesus Christ. It is not the faith and understanding of its members which constitute the community, but the Word and verdict of God believed and understood, Jesus Christ Himself in whose death on the cross that verdict is pronounced. It is not that they know God, but that they are known of God. But these men can know and believe and understand God in that verdict. In the midst of others they are one and conjoined by the fact that they must accept His saying. It is only by that, but actually, visibly and perceptibly by that—and irrevocably—that they are constituted the community. At this point we shall have to speak of the origin and being of the Church in its humanity—of that being which since it is always conditioned by the Holy Spirit as the awakening power of that divine verdict must again and again be an insignificant origin: a continual awaiting of the Holy Spirit as pictured in its constant gatherings, its ever renewed proclamation of the Word, its repeated prayer, its celebration of baptism; but an awaiting in the certainty of receiving, and therefore of its own life in His presence. The community exists in this fruitful expectation which can never cease and never be unrealised. In its humanity it is one historically feeble organism with others, but it is the redeemed community justified by the divine sentence and honoured with the knowledge of the justification of the world.

2. The Holy Spirit of Jesus Christ is the life-giving power of the Word spoken by the servant who became Lord, and therefore of the divine direction which

sanctifies sinful man. The work of the Holy Spirit as this life-giving power is the inner upbuilding of the community. When that direction is heard by men, these men are united in a common action, in a common action orientated by a commonly imposed obedience, and, we can and must also say, by a commonly given freedom. The community grows in rendering this obedience, or in this freedom. In it it gains consistency, it acquires order and form, it becomes capable of action. Its members are men who not only regard that direction as [152] given and normative, but who love it for the sake of the One who has given it, who accept it because they see in it the love in which God loved the world and themselves in this special way. The direction of God willingly followed in the power of the Holy Spirit is the life-principle of the Christian Church. Again, it is not by the obedience, the freedom, or even the love of these men that the Church is built up and lives. It lives wholly in the power of its Lord and His Spirit. In His power: the power of its Lord exalted as man to the right hand of God, who summons and draws it onwards and upwards as the community of His brethren, who transforms it into His image (2 Cor. 3^{18}), by whom it is given to it to seek and to find that which is above, in whom it has already here and now a part in His resurrection and therefore in the future life of eternity. Because and to the extent that He is mighty in the community by His Spirit, that which it does can and must be done with joy; its worship, its order, the fellowship of Christians, its mutual service, the celebration of the Lord's Supper, even its teaching and theology can and must take on the character of a festival; and in it all God can and must be thanked and worshipped. What we have to show is the fact and way in which the Church has never to look after itself, to build up itself, to rule and maintain and defend itself, but simply to live according to the direction of its Lord and His Spirit and in that way to be vigorous and active and truly alive.

3. The Holy Spirit as the Spirit of Jesus Christ is the enlightening power of Him who as very God and very man is the Guarantor of the truth of the atonement made in Him—and therefore the summoning power of the promise given in Him to sinful man. When the promise is heard by men, inwardly and outwardly these men are together ordained to be the community sent out as a witness in the world and to the world. The historical reality and inward upbuilding of this community are not ends in themselves. It is now actually the case that in its particular existence it stands vicariously for the whole world. The Holy Spirit is the enlightening, and as the enlightening the summoning power of the divine promise, which points the community beyond itself, which calls it to transcend itself and in that way to be in truth the community of God—in truth, i.e., as it bears witness to the truth known within it, as it knows itself to be charged with this witness and sent out to establish it. Its members are men who can hope on the basis of the promise. But if they hope seriously, they hope in God, and in God for the world—for themselves, too, but for themselves as those who belong to the world which God has reconciled with Himself in Jesus Christ. They hope to see this the case, i.e., to see the world—

and themselves with it—fulfilling its being in the service of God. But, again, it is not the sincerity or drive of this Christian hope which constitutes the light of the community sent out to witness. Only the Holy Spirit of Jesus Christ active [153] within it is this light. But He is the light of the Christian community which shines here in the darkness on earth and in time. And since He is this light, and the community lives by God's promise, necessarily the community itself is bright in the world: a community which proclaims the coming kingdom of God as the substance of the whole future of man; but for that reason a missionary community; a community which is responsible and looks and points forward in face of every development in state or society; an element of prophecy in relation to the world, of greater and smaller rest and unrest, of soberness and daring confidence in relation to the ultimate, and also and for that reason to penultimate horizons. It is of the community in this ministry of witness that we must speak in the third ecclesiological section of the doctrine of reconciliation.

And then, to conclude, we have to speak in all three parts of the life of individual Christians as such, of their being in Jesus Christ, of their personal knowledge and experience of the atonement, i.e., of the work and witness of the Holy Spirit, by whom in the community, by the service and for the service of the community, but as individuals, they are (1) awakened to faith, (2) quickened in love and (3) enlightened in hope.

It is not necessary to develop this here, since it has already been anticipated under the second heading of this section. We will simply make a general observation on this final theme. In the theology of Schleiermacher and his more or less loyal and consistent followers, this last theme was the first, and it also became the last because on their presupposition there could not be any other. Theology in general and with it the doctrine of the atonement could only be the self-interpretation of the pious Christian self-consciousness as such, of the *homo religiosus incurvatus in se*[EN106]. In this way Schleiermacher's genius was to bring to its logical conclusion the truncating tendency in the older Protestantism to which we have already alluded. From the very first the present sketch of the doctrine of reconciliation has stood implicitly in the most decided opposition to this conception. We do not intend to avoid the problem of the *homo religiosus*[EN107] or *christianus*[EN108]. In the final development of the doctrine of reconciliation we shall have to treat very seriously of this special question of the *homo christianus*[EN109], of the Christian and what makes him a Christian, of his understanding of himself. It is, in fact, "self-understood" that he must occupy a special place in dogmatics, and undoubtedly in the analysis of the concepts faith, love and hope we have to do with a *conditio sine qua non*[EN110] of

---

[EN106] religious man turned in on himself
[EN107] religious
[EN108] Christian man
[EN109] Christian man
[EN110] necessary condition

the whole. Apart from the faith and love and hope of the individual Christian and his understanding of himself as such we cannot see the Christian community, nor can we see the justifying verdict, the sanctifying direction and the summoning promise of God. But faith and love and hope are relative concepts. The being of the Christian indicated by them is a being in relation. Faith lives by its object, love by its basis, hope by its surety. Jesus Christ by the Holy Spirit is this object and basis and surety. And faith and love and hope in this relation to Jesus Christ are all primarily His work, and His work first in the community of God, and only then His work in individual Christians. We must not confuse the *conditio sine qua non*[EN111] of the knowledge of the atonement with its *ratio essendi*[EN112]. The doctrine of reconciliation must end where it began. We shall speak correctly of the faith and love and hope of the individual Christian only when it remains clear and constantly becomes clear that, although we are dealing with our existence, we are dealing with our existence in Jesus Christ as our true existence, that we are therefore dealing with Him and not with us, and with us only in so far as absolutely and exclusively with Him.

[154]

[EN111] necessary condition
[EN112] ground of being

§ 59

THE OBEDIENCE OF THE SON OF GOD

That Jesus Christ is very God is shown in His way into the far country in which He the Lord became a servant. For in the majesty of the true God it happened that the eternal Son of the eternal Father became obedient by offering and humbling Himself to be the brother of man, to take His place with the transgressor, to judge him by judging Himself and dying in his place. But God the Father raised Him from the dead, and in so doing recognised and gave effect to His death and passion as a satisfaction made for us, as our conversion to God, and therefore as our redemption from death to life.

1. THE WAY OF THE SON OF GOD INTO THE FAR COUNTRY

The atonement is history. To know it, we must know it as such. To think of it, we must think of it as such. To speak of it, we must tell it as history. To try to grasp it as supra-historical or non-historical truth is not to grasp it at all. It is indeed truth, but truth actualised in a history and revealed in this history as such—revealed, therefore, as history.

But the atonement is the very special history of God with man, the very special history of man with God. As such it has a particular character and demands particular attention. As such it underlies and includes, not only in principle and virtually but also actually, the most basic history of every man. It is the first and most inward presupposition of his existence, and it reveals itself as such. First of all, there took place and does take place the history of God with man and man with God, and then and for that reason and definitely on that basis man exists, and he can be called to knowledge and his own fully responsible decision and in that way have an actual part in that happening. The atonement takes precedence of all other history. It proves itself in fully responsible attitudes. It cannot be revealed and grasped and known without this proof. But when it is revealed and grasped and known, it is so in its priority, [158] its precedence, its superiority to all other histories, to the existence of all the men who take part in it. In this sense everyone who knows it as truth knows in it the truth of his own existence.

The atonement is, noetically, the history about Jesus Christ, and ontically, Jesus Christ's own history. To say atonement is to say Jesus Christ. To speak of it is to speak of His history. If we do not simply speak of it, but know it as we speak of it, if we take part in it as we know it, if we decide with full responsibility as a result of it, we decide in relation to Jesus Christ. For He is the history of God with man and the history of man with God. What takes place in this history— the accusation and conviction of man as a lost sinner, his restoration, the founding and maintaining and sending of the community of God in the world, the new obedience of man—is all decided and ordained by Him as the One who primarily acts and speaks in it. It is His work which is done. He Himself accomplishes and guarantees it, for in Him it comes to pass that God is the reconciling God and man is reconciled man. He is Himself this God and this man, and therefore the presupposition, the author, in whom all human existence has its first and basic truth in relation to that of God. It is in His self-offering to death that God has again found man and man God. It is in His resurrection from the dead that this twofold rediscovery is applied and proclaimed to us. It is in His Holy Spirit that it is present and an event for us. In all its different aspects the doctrine of reconciliation must always begin by looking at Him, not in order to leave Him behind in its later developments, but to fix the point from which there can and must be these later developments.

The first aspect under which we shall try to consider the doctrine of reconciliation in this chapter is that of the condescension active and known in it, that condescension in which God interests Himself in man in Jesus Christ. We might put it in this way: the aspect of the grace of God in Jesus Christ in which it comes to man as the (sinful) creature of God freely, without any merit or deserving, and therefore from outside, from above—which is to say, from God's standpoint, the aspect of His grace in which He does something unnecessary and extravagant, binding and limiting and compromising and offering Himself in relation to man by having dealings with him and making Himself his God. In the fact that God is gracious to man, all the limitations of man are God's limitations, all his weaknesses, and more, all his perversities are His. In being gracious to man in Jesus Christ, God acknowledges man; He accepts responsibility for his being and nature. He remains Himself. He does not cease to be God. But He does not hold aloof. In being gracious to man in Jesus Christ, He also goes into the far country, into the evil society of this being which is not God and against God. He does not shrink from him. He does not pass him by as did the priest and the Levite the man who had fallen among thieves. He does not leave him to his own devices. He makes his situation His own. He does not forfeit anything by doing this. In being neighbour to man, in order to deal with him and act towards him as such, He does not need to fear for His Godhead. On the contrary. We will mention at once the thought which will be decisive and basic in this section, that God shows Himself to be the great and true God in the fact that He can and will let His grace bear this cost, that He is capable and willing and ready for this condescension, this act of extravagance, this far journey. What marks out God above all false gods is that they are not capable and ready for this. In their otherworldliness and supernaturalness and otherness, etc., the gods are a reflection of the human pride which will not unbend, which will not stoop to that which is beneath it. God is not proud. In His high majesty He is humble. It is in this high humility that He

[159]

speaks and acts as the God who reconciles the world to Himself. It is under this aspect first that we must consider the history of the atonement.

That is why the title of this chapter is "Jesus Christ, the Lord as Servant." At every point we shall be dealing with the action and work of the Lord God. This is true in relation to the eternal decree, and the execution of the atonement once and for all. It is also true of the fruit of it brought forth by the Holy Spirit, and the existence of the Christian community and the human decision of faith. But because we are dealing with the true Lord God, because it is a matter of the atonement which was made and is made in His action and work, we have to do with Him in that form of a servant which as the true Lord He was capable and willing and ready to assume in order to exist in it, and in which He is the true Lord God and as such the true Reconciler of man with God.

That is why the title of our first section is "The Obedience of the Son of God." Our theme in it is Christology in the narrower sense of the word, a first aspect of the person of Jesus Christ acting for the world and us and of the work of Jesus Christ done for the world and us: how He was and is and will be very God in the fact that as the Son He willed to be obedient to the Father, and to become the servant of all and therefore man and therefore the One who fulfilled in His death the reconciling will of God; and how in the power of His resurrection He is all this for us by the Holy Spirit. In relation neither to His person nor to His work can we under this aspect say everything that has to be said about Him, or everything that makes the history of the atonement this particular history. It is a matter of the whole Christ and the whole atonement from this one standpoint. And obviously here—in dealing with the person and work of the true Son of the true God—we have to do with the indispensable basis and substance of all that follows.

To come to the point. The New Testament tradition—in this respect most clearly documented in the so-called Synoptic Gospels—is self-consistent in one [160] great truth. There can be no doubt about the full and genuine and individual humanity of the man Jesus of Nazareth, but in that man there has entered in and there must be recognised and respected One who is qualitatively different from all other men. He is not simply a better man, a more gifted, a more wise or noble or pious, in short a greater man. But as against all other men and their differences we have in the person of this man One who is their Lord and Law-giver and Judge. He has full power to condemn them or to pardon. He has full power to call them and bind them to Himself. He has full power, as against their cosmic limitation, to pronounce in His existence a final Word concerning them and all human history. He is the Saviour before whom there was none other, neither shall be after. This is the "act of God," the "eschato-logical event of salvation," to use our modern jargon. In attestation of this understanding of the man Jesus the New Testament tradition calls Him the Messiah of Israel, the *Kyrios*, the second Adam come down from heaven, and, in a final approximation to what is meant by all this, the Son or the Word of God. It lifts Him right out of the list of other men, and as against this list (including Moses and the prophets, not to mention all the rest) it places Him at the side of God.

The New Testament community does not merely think, but lives and acts in the knowledge and on the presupposition that in this man "dwells all the fulness of the Godhead bodily" (Col. 2⁹). In seeing Him, it sees the Father (Jn. 14⁹). In honouring Him, it honours the Father (Jn. 5²³). It calls on His name (1 Cor. 1², Rom. 10¹², Ac. 9¹⁴ ²¹, 22¹⁶), and in so doing, according to Jn. 20²⁸, it addresses Him: "My Lord and my God." Stephen prays to Him (Ac. 7⁵⁹), as does also Paul (2 Cor. 12⁸), and the whole community expects that requests made to God in His name will be heard (Jn. 14¹³ᶠ⁻).

The post-apostolic community was based on this knowledge of Jesus Christ and the corresponding confession.

In this respect we have to note what is said and expounded with great theological naivete but for that reason all the more clearly in the first Christian sermon known to us, the so-called 2 Clement: "Brethren, we must think of Jesus Christ as of God ($\dot{\omega}s$ $\pi\epsilon\rho\dot{\iota}$ $\theta\epsilon o\hat{v}$), as of the judge of the quick and the dead. For we ought not to think meanly of our redemption. If we think meanly of Him ($\pi\epsilon\rho\dot{\iota}$ $a\dot{v}\tau o\hat{v}$), that means that we expect only mean things ... that we do not know whence and by whom and to whom we are called." And although the accounts are uncertain and primitive, it is noteworthy that what the governor Pliny had heard from lapsed Christians and reported to the emperor Trajan about 113 was this: They had confessed that the sum (*summa*) of their error or fault was that they used to meet before sunrise *carmenque Christo quasi Deo dicere secum in vicem*[EN1], and to pledge themselves—not to break the law, but to refrain from theft, murder and adultery, and not to break faith or loyalty, etc. It may be that these songs were like those which have come down to us in Phil. 2⁵ᶠ⁻, Rev. 5⁹ᶠ⁻ or 1 Tim. 3¹⁶. Pliny seems to have in mind this peculiar practice and theory in relation to Christ when he summed up his own judgment of the matter in the view that they were dealing with a *superstitio prava, immodica*[EN2]. On his orders the lapsed had to show their true repentance by paying respect to images of the emperor and the gods and cursing Christ. In the same connexion we might mention the caricature found in the Palatine at Rome, although it belongs to a later date. It depicts an ass fastened to a cross, and the form of a man worshipping it, with the inscription: "Alexamenos (obviously a Christian who is meant to be ridiculed) honours God ($\sigma\dot{\epsilon}\beta\epsilon\tau a\iota$ $\theta\epsilon\dot{o}v$)." It is quite clear from the impressions and reactions of these outsiders in what category the primitive Christians placed Christ, quite apart from more exact doctrinal definitions.

[161]

The dogma of the 4th and 5th centuries tried to formulate this same insight in the face of several obscurities and ambiguities which still obtained in the first centuries and also in face of the conceptual denials which constantly arose. The primitive insight presupposed and confirmed in the dogma—not the dogma itself—was the decisive point at which the different spirits in the Church (or rather that which was the Church and not the Church) always divided. And to this day there is hardly a point of Christian knowledge and confession which is not positively or negatively, directly or indirectly, related to this one point, to this primitive Christian insight.

EN1 chant hymns alternately amongst themselves to Christ as if to a God
EN2 wicked, unruly superstition

It has been described as a "religious valuation" (F. Loofs) or estimation or judgment added later to the man Jesus by the disciples or the early Palestinian or especially the Hellenistic Church. This valuation rests, we are told, on the impression which the Christians had of the person and word and work of Jesus, and it was filled out intellectually in the form offered by the ideology of the later Jewish and Hellenistic world in which they lived. It is obviously true that in Jesus the disciples and the first communities were confronted with a riddle which they had to solve, a question which they had to answer on the basis of what they had seen and heard, a phenomenon which they had to estimate at its meaning and judge accordingly. It is also true that they gave their judgment in the language of the intellectual world to which they belonged. It is from them that there derive the titles of value "attached" to the man Jesus in the New Testament. But the following considerations have to be kept clearly in mind.

There is no discernible stratum of the New Testament in which—always presupposing His genuine humanity—Jesus is in practice seen in any other way or—whatever terms may be used—judged in any other way than as the One who is qualitatively different and stands in an indissoluble antithesis to His disciples and all other men, indeed to the whole cosmos. There is no discernible stratum which does not in some way witness that it was felt that there should be given to this man, not merely a human confidence, but that trust, that respect, that obedience, that faith which can properly be offered only to God. Allowing for every difference in viewpoint and concept, the heavenly Father, His kingdom which has come on earth, and the person of Jesus of Nazareth are not quantities which can be placed side by side, or which cut across each other, or which can be opposed to each other, but they are practically and in effect identical. This would still be true even if it could be proved [162] and not merely suspected that Jesus Himself did not expressly speak of His majesty, His Messiahship, His divine Sonship. In the context of what we know of the disciples and the community in the New Testament there is no ground for even suspecting the existence of disciples or a community which could be practically related to Him except on the presupposition of His majesty.

So, then, we can speak of this and that title being "conferred" on Jesus only with the reservation that this conferring is not represented as something arbitrary which we might omit or handle otherwise. This conferring, and the valuation and estimation and judgment which underlies it, has nothing whatever to do with the free apotheosis of a man. In spite of all the mitigations of later Judaism this would have been an unprecedented thing in the original Palestinian community, in the direct sphere of the Old Testament concept of God. And since there has never been a Christian community without the Old Testament, it could not possibly have been carried through in Hellenistic Christianity (or only *per nefas*[EN3]). The exaltation of a man as a cult-god, or his investiture with the dignity of a gnostic hypostasis, was not at all easy on this

---

[EN3] wrongly

presupposition. We do not understand either the practical attitude to Jesus discernible on all levels of the New Testament tradition, or the titles of majesty conferred upon Him, if we do not at least hazard the hypothesis that the peculiar place and function of the man Jesus for New Testament Christians was not a hypothesis, that the practice and theory of their relationship to Him was not a religious experiment—however earnest and sincere—against the background of an "as though" which secretly left the question open. Their estimation and judgment of Jesus is as such something secondary, a necessary consequence. It is not itself their theme, the subject-matter of their preaching. They are occupied with Jesus Himself. They aim to be His witnesses. They answer His question. They give an account of His existence. He has placed them in this attitude. He has put these titles of majesty on their lips. They do not try to crown Him in this way, but they recognise Him as the One who is already crowned, to whom these titles belong.

And so they do not try to win others for their own sure christological conviction, but they aim to "bring into captivity every thought to the obedience of Christ" (2 Cor. 10⁵). If possible, this fact is brought out even more clearly if we are ready to accept that when they spoke about Christ they often used directly or indirectly sayings of Jesus about Himself, repeating them as coming from His mouth. It is not they who represented Him, but He who represented Himself to them, in this majesty.

He is to them the Christ, the *Kyrios*ᴱᴺ⁴, the Son of Man and the Son of God, the One who is absolutely different and exalted, even before they describe Him in this way. And when they do describe Him in this way, they appeal in some sense to Himself—that He Himself continually attests Himself as such. And in relation to others they count on it happening that they too may accept—not their own representation and appraisal of a man honoured by them—but the Word of Jesus, His self-attestation of His majesty, of His unity with God.   [163]

It is clear that we can reject this New Testament witness concerning the man Jesus. It has been rejected again and again—even within the community. But there can be no disputing the fact that, in the sense of those who gave it, this witness is to the simple effect that, prior to any attitudes of others to Him or statements of others about Him, the man Jesus did in fact occupy this place and function, that, prior to any knowledge of His being or temporally conditioned confession of it, He actually was and is and will be what He is represented in the reflection of this witness, the Son of the Heavenly Father, the King of His kingdom, and therefore "by nature God." We have to let go the whole New Testament witness step by step and turn it into its opposite if we read it as a documentation of "religious valuations," if we do not see and admit that step by step it relates to the being and revelation of this man in the unprecedented and quite unique determination of His existence. It is not a Christian conception of Him, and to that extent not the Christian *kerygma*, but He

---

ᴱᴺ⁴ Lord

Himself in His revelation and being, who according to the New Testament builds His community and calls the world to decision: He Himself in the power of His resurrection, the Lord who is the Spirit. Only when this is seen and admitted do we know what we are doing when we either accept or reject the New Testament witness.

But now we must be more precise. Assuming that the witness of the New Testament is true because it is grounded in its object and corresponds to it and is confirmed by it, it is to the man Jesus that according to the New Testament this majesty belongs. It is as this man that He is the Messiah, the *Kyrios*[EN5], or—in a final approximation to the mystery of His existence—the Son, or as the prologue to the Gospel of St. John has it, the Word of God. But the fact that He is this has to be called the mystery of His existence—on this point the New Testament is quite clear. The fact that He is this can be known only as He Himself reveals it, only by His Holy Spirit. When the New Testament attests Him to be such, it speaks of His resurrection from the dead. Only secondarily, and in this way, does it speak of the records of it. And in relation to others His witnesses expect that the same Holy Spirit who has revealed this to them will not be silent to others. The witness concerns the self-revelation of the Son of God who is identical with this man, not an existing acquaintance with His being and work as such. All such acquaintance with Jesus the Son of God is repudiated. His form as a man is regarded and described rather as the concealing of His true being, and therefore this true being as the Son or Word of God is a hidden being.

The New Testament does not speak of the One whom it calls "Lord" in the way we might expect, as a human lord furnished with sovereignty and authority and the plenitude of power, maintaining and executing his own will. According to this presentation what distinguishes the man Jesus as the Son of God is that which apparently stands in the greatest possible contradiction to the being of God: the fact that in relation to God—and therefore to the world as well—this man wills only to be obedient—obedient to the will of the Father, which is to be done on earth for the redemption of man as it is done in heaven.

[164]

At the river Jordan (Mk. 1[11]) the voice of God proclaims this man the beloved Son at the very time when He allows Himself to be baptised by John, thus subjecting Himself to God with the same publicity and obligation as those who were baptised with Him. He shows that He is the Son of God (Mt. 4[1f.]) by resisting the temptation—expressly described as the temptation of the devil—to prove it in the way that a human lord endowed with divinity would have had to do, as the wonder-workers of the time, who also called themselves "sons of God", tried to do. In direct distinction from and opposition to this, His prayer in Gethsemane (Mt. 26[39]) was: "Not as I will, but as thou wilt." Because He is the servant of God, He is the servant of all men, of the whole world, not come to be ministered unto but to minister (Mk. 10[45]). He is the man in the parable who when invited to a wedding did not take the chief place but the lower (Lk. 14[10]), or even more pointedly (Lk. 22[27]) the One who serves His disciples as

---

[EN5] Lord

they sit at meat, or even more pointedly (Jn. 13$^{1-11}$) the One who washes their feet before they sit down to meat. This is obviously the concrete will of God to which He is obedient. Nowhere is the recognition of the divine Sonship more explicit than in the Gospel of John, yet it is this Gospel which causes Jesus to say expressly: "The Father is greater than I" (Jn. 14^{28}). And in line with this it is this Gospel which cannot emphasise too much that Jesus does not seek His own glory (8^{50}), that He does only that which He has been commissioned to do by the Father (14^{31}, cf. 10^{18}), that He keeps His Father's commandments (15^{10}, cf. 8^{29}), that it is His meat to do the will of Him that sent Him and to finish His work (4^{34}, cf. 5^{36}, 17^{4}).

The true God—if the man Jesus is the true God—is obedient. We have to keep before us the difficulty of this equation if we are to be clear what we have to understand and to accept or reject as the content of the New Testament witness to Christ. Obedience—even obedience which serves—does not of itself exclude a way of outstanding human greatness and power and glory, a being as man which is fulfilled in the best sense, and effective and successful in the world, and in its own way satisfying and triumphant. But according to the New Testament it is not the being of the man Jesus which has this character. On the contrary, the New Testament describes the Son of God as the servant, indeed as the suffering servant of God. Not accidentally and incidentally. Not merely to prove and show His mind and disposition. Not merely to win through by conflict to a concrete goal. Not merely as a foil to emphasise His glory. But necessarily and, as it were, essentially, and so far as can be seen without meaning or purpose. He is a suffering servant who wills this profoundly unsatisfactory being, who cannot will anything other in the obedience in which He shows Himself the Son of God.

In this respect the decisive expressions are in what is now accepted as a hymn quoted by Paul in Phil. 2 from some earlier source. They are as follows: "He emptied (ἐκένωσεν) Him- [165] self (that is, of His divine form: He renounced it) and took the form of a servant" (v. 7); and again, "He humbled (ἐταπείνωσεν) Himself, and became obedient unto death, even the death of the cross" (v. 8). In the words of Paul Himself: "He who was rich became poor" (2 Cor. 8^{9}). In Heb. 5^{8}: "He who is the Son learned obedience in what He had to suffer." The Lucan narrative of the childhood of Jesus mentions no less than three times that the first resting place of Jesus was a crib, because His parents could find no room in the inn (2^{7}). The narrative in Matthew tells of the shadow of death which immediately fell on Him: of Herod, who sought His life; of the flight into Egypt and the slaughter of the innocents in Bethlehem (Mt. 2$^{13f.}$). The later saying fits in with this: "The foxes have holes, and the birds of the air have nests, but the Son of man hath not where to lay his head" (Lk. 9^{58}). In Jn. 17^{5} we also hear of a glory which the Son had with the Father before the world was, but which He prays that He may be clothed with again, which He has therefore obviously renounced. He has taken "flesh and blood" (Heb. 2^{14}). He has suffered and been tempted (2^{18}), being made like His brethren in everything (2^{17}), "feeling for our infirmities" and "in all points like as we are" (κατὰ πάντα καθ᾽ ὁμοιότητα, 4^{15}). The community confesses (1 Jn. 4$^{2f.}$, 2 Jn. 7) that Jesus Christ "is come in the flesh." "God sent his Son in the likeness of sinful flesh to condemn sin in the flesh" (Rom. 8^{3}). In the pregnant words of Jn. 1^{14}, the Word became flesh. "Flesh" in the language of the New (and earlier the Old) Testament means man standing under the divine verdict and judgment, man who is a sinner and whose existence therefore must perish before God, whose existence has already become nothing, and hastens to nothingness and is a victim to death. "Flesh" is the concrete form of human nature and the being of man in his world under the sign of the fall of Adam—the being of man as corrupted and therefore destroyed, as unreconciled with God and therefore lost. In 2 Cor. 5^{21} we have it in a way which is almost unbearably severe: "He (God) hath made him to be sin who knew no sin". He has caused Him to be regarded and treated as a sinner. He has Himself regarded Him and treated Him as a sinner. He was made a curse for us, as Paul unhesitatingly concluded from Deut. 21^{23} (Gal. 3^{13}). What this means is reflected in all the dreadful things which the Evangelists report were said of Jesus: "He is beside Himself" (Mk. 3^{21}), "He hath Beelzebub" (Mk. 3^{22}), He is a "gluttonous man and a wine-bibber, a friend of publicans and sinners" (Mt. 11^{19}), "He deceiveth the people" (Jn. 7^{12}), "He blasphemeth God" (Mt. 9^3, 26^{65}). There is unmistakable reference to the suspicion which surrounded His birth (Mt. 1^{19}). His first public appearance is that of a penitent in unreserved solidarity with other penitents who confess themselves to be such in the baptism of John, and can look only for the remission of their sins in the coming judgment (Mt. 3^{15})—a clear anticipation of the story of the passion, towards which the narrative in all the Evangelists hastens with a momentum recognisable from the very first, and at the climax of which Jesus is crucified between two thieves (Mt. 27^{38}). The prophecy which occurs three times in all the Synoptics, that the Son of Man must and will be delivered up to men, to the high-priests and the scribes, and finally the Gentiles, explicitly reveals the character of the whole story of the man Jesus as a story of suffering—whatever we may think of the place of these passages in the history of the tradition. To the same context belongs also the fact, which is constantly emphasised, that among the twelve—that is to say, in the original form of the new people of God of the last days—and himself a disciple and apostle, there is the "traitor" Judas. In short, according to the New Testament the *Heidelberg Catechism* is quite right when in *Qu.* 37 it says that "during the whole time of His life on earth Jesus ... bore the wrath of God against the sin of the whole human race." And in the same sense the ancient creeds were also right when under the concepts *passus, crucifixus, mortuus, sepultus*[EN6], they believed that they were saying every-

[166] thing that is decisive about the man Jesus. In the dreadfully paradoxical language of Jn. 3^{14}, 8^{28}, 12^{32}, this humiliation, this raising up as the One nailed to the cross, is His "lifting up from the earth" (His ὑψωθῆναι[EN7]). And this humiliation, this human existence of Jesus in the flesh and therefore under the wrath and judgment of God, is not an accident or fate, but His own free and in that way genuinely obedient will. The story of Gethsemane (like the story of the temptation at the beginning of the Gospels) shows two things: first, that we have to do with His genuine human decision; and second, that it is a decision of obedience. He chooses, but He chooses that apart from which, being who He is, He could not choose anything else. As the Lamb whose blood is shed He "is foreordained before the foundation of the world" (1 Pet. $1^{19f.}$). God did not spare Him, but delivered Him up (Rom. 8^{32}). It is written of the Son of Man that "He will suffer many things and be set at nought" (Mk. 9^{12}). And in accordance with the divine determination He emptied Himself, He humbled Himself (Phil. $2^{7f.\ 8}$), He gave Himself up (Gal. 2^{20}, Eph. 5^2) even before Judas did. He came in order to give His life. "No man taketh it from me, but I lay it down of myself. I have power to lay it down, and I have power to take it again. This commandment have I received of my Father" (Jn. 10^{18}). Peter with his "Be it far from thee" does not think in divine terms but human, and he has to be resisted as a satanic tempter (Mt. $16^{22f.}$). Jesus would not be Jesus if His way could be different or bear a different character.

Exegetes old and new have been right in their references and comments when they have seen all this and tried to consider the deity of Jesus Christ in the light of it. On the other hand, it has always led and always does lead to confusion where this more precise under-

---

[EN6] suffered, crucified, died, was buried
[EN7] exaltation

standing of the human being of God and the divine being of the man Jesus is disregarded or weakened or not taken as the starting-point for all further discussion.

But there is one thing which we must emphasise especially. It is often over-looked in this context. It is not taken seriously or seriously enough. Yet from this one thing everything else, and particularly what we have just stressed, acquires its contour and colour, its definiteness and necessity. The Word did not simply become any "flesh," any man humbled and suffering. It became Jewish flesh. The Church's whole doctrine of the incarnation and the atone-ment becomes abstract and valueless and meaningless to the extent that this comes to be regarded as something accidental and incidental. The New Testa-ment witness to Jesus the Christ, the Son of God, stands on the soil of the Old Testament and cannot be separated from it. The pronouncements of New Tes-tament Christology may have been shaped by a very non-Jewish environment. But they relate always to a man who is seen to be not a man in general, a neutral man, but the conclusion and sum of the history of God with the people of Israel, the One who fulfils the covenant made by God with this people. And it is as such that He is the obedient Son and servant of God, and therefore the One who essentially and necessarily suffers.

It may be maintained, and it may actually be the case, that the philosophical and concep-tual world of the New Testament was influenced by Gnosticism and the mystery religions. But this does not alter in the least the fact that the New Testament message as such does not find its subject-matter, which is also its origin, in the empty sphere of abstract principles and relations, or in the sphere of myth. On the contrary, in its decisive factual statement con-cerning what took place between God and man it definitely resists translation into a state-ment about an event which did not take place at a specific time and place, and therefore takes place at all times and in all places. Nor does it accidentally concern a man of a particu-lar type and descent which might just as well have been different. Necessarily and emphatic-ally it concerns an event which was prophesied in the testimonies of the dealings of God with the people Israel and fulfilled within the sphere of this people. It concerns, therefore, the existence of a man of Israel, an Israelite. The Christian message is at its heart a message about Jesus the Son of God. But when it is addressed to men and groups of men who are of non-Israelitish type and descent, it not only presupposes this original connexion, but it has always to be accepted and understood with this original connexion. The Christian *kerygma*[EN8] as it is addressed to the world has this statement about an Israelite at its very heart. This means nothing more or less than the bringing of the world into the sphere of the divine dealings with the people Israel. It does not speak generally of the existence of a Son of Man who became man for many (with many in view), but of the fact that the Jesus who has come as the Messiah of Israel has come into the world as the Saviour of the world. It relates to Jesus as such. It describes Him as the One who proclaims Himself in the history of Israel, as the aim and end of that history. It describes Him as the One who has in that very way appeared to all peoples. His universality is revealed in this particularity, which is plain even in a writing so obviously directed to the Gentiles as the Gospel of Luke. It was so plain that at first it could appear to the Gentile world to be simply a particular form or corruption of Jewish propaganda—rather strangely repudiated by official Judaism. It was only in the 2nd

[167]

[EN8] proclamation

century (and, theoretically, first of all in the well-meant efforts of the so-called Apologists) that Christian universalism began to lose its particularist character, to the great detriment of the understanding of this very heart of the Christian message. It was Marcion who tried to do away with it in principle, taking the Old Testament to be the document which attests the work and revelation of another and evil god, the demiurge, from whose lordship we have been freed by Christ. Marcion wanted to see the Old Testament completely eliminated as the source and norm of Christian proclamation. The Church was now preponderately a Gentile Church, but it instinctively kept itself from this dangerous temptation. It did the same later in relation to the Socinians, to Schleiermacher and to Harnack. In spite of all the allegorising and generalising interpretation which it has not escaped to soften the offence, the Old Testament still remains from generation to generation to ensure that the particularist aspect of the Christian message directed to the world, the simple truth that Jesus Christ was a born Jew, is never lost sight of, but constantly survives the irruption of all too generalised views of the man Jesus.

This is the meaning and purpose of the complete linking of the New Testament witness with that of the Old which the New Testament itself never overlooks. It prevents the rounding off of the picture of Jesus into a kind of ideal-picture of human existence, which would necessarily degenerate into a free sketch of the man who was and is the Son of God, i.e., a sketch which is quite independent of the Israelitish components of the New Testament. It keeps before the attention of the reader and hearer the fact that the end and point of the Gospel of Jesus Christ, His self-proclamation documented in the Gospel, the nerve of the history between God and man which took place in it, the history of redemption, is essentially the history of the passion. The fact [168] that it is this essentially and necessarily, the fact that it is a history of victory only with this orientation, is something which we always miss, in plain contradiction to the New Testament itself, if we are not ready to listen to the Old Testament as an authentic commentary whenever we listen to the New.

In its bracketing with the Old Testament the New closes the door against every kind of Docetism, however crude or subtle, by positing the man who was and is the Son of God in His singularity and at the same time in the relevance of His existence for every man of every place, by setting the happening of the redemption history between God and man in world-history, at a cosmic place, a place on earth. Docetism is the old enemy, an enemy which is constantly reappearing, of the concrete truth of the history of redemption as the history of the passion. When Docetism threatens, this truth is threatened. And when the authenticity of the Old Testament is disputed in its unity with the New, Docetism threatens. When it names Israel as that place, the New Testament says that it is a definite and limited place, this place and no other. When it recognises and addresses and proclaims Israel as the people of God from which the man who was and is the Son of God came forth at the time appointed by God, when it refers back to the covenant made between God and Israel, when it describes this man as the Christ promised to this people, or as the Son of Man from heaven whose future (according to Dan. 7) will destroy and overcome the beast-kingdoms of the great world-powers, when it lets Him be born in Bethlehem as the Son of Mary and therefore as the Son of David, it says that this place is not such by chance, but is elected and ordained by God from the very first, indeed from all eternity. "The Word was made flesh" means that the Son of God does not take any place as man, but this place. As God's Son in His unity with the Father He stands necessarily—with a divine necessity—at this place. The act of God which takes place in this man for us takes place contingently on earth and in time, as the creeds have emphasised with their mention of Mary and Pilate. The particularity of the man Jesus in proceeding from the one elect people of Israel, as the confirmation of its election, means decisively that the reconciliation of sinful and lost man has, above all, the character of a divine condescension, that it takes place as God goes into the far country. The Father who is one with the man Jesus His Son (Jn. 10^{30}) is the God who years before was not too good, and did not count it too small a thing, to bind and engage Himself to Abraham and his seed, and to be God in this particularity and limitation—"I will be your God." From the horizontal point of view, and in terms of human history, He attested and revealed Himself as a national numen like so many others, to be precise, the common numen of that coalition of tribes in which the people of Israel emerged as a unit. He is the one true God who is respected and worshipped as the only God by this people, and neither theoretically nor practically will He be compared or exchanged with other [169] gods. He is the same high God who in supreme humility elected Himself the God of this one small people.

Under the name of Son of God Jesus took the very place which in the Old Testament had often enough been allotted to the "children" of Israel in their relation with God. According to Ex. 4^{22} it is the task of Moses to tell Pharaoh: "Israel is my firstborn, and I command thee: Let my son go, that he may serve me." Similarly in Hosea (11^1) God says: "Out of Egypt have I called my son." And Jeremiah (31^{20}): "Is Ephraim my dear son? Is he a pleasant child? for since I spake against him, I do earnestly remember him still: therefore my bowels are troubled for him; I will surely have mercy upon him." This is affirmed by the voice of God Himself at the time of the exile: "Bring my sons from far, and my daughters from the ends of the earth; even every one that is called by my name, for I have created him for my glory, I have formed him" (Is. 43$^{6f.}$). The same answer is given in the last book of the Old Testament: "I will spare them, as a man spareth his own son that serveth him" (Mal. 3^{17}). And in the same way a later prophet cries in the name of the people to their God: "Doubtless thou art our father, though Abraham be ignorant of us, and Israel acknowledge us not: thou, O Lord, art our father. … Why hast thou made us to err from thy ways, and hardened our heart from thy fear?" (Is. 63^{16}). *Yahweh* can be called the Father of Israel and Israel His son because He has created and made and prepared this people as such (Deut. 32^6), and that to His own glory (Is. 43^7); because it is the "work of his hand" (Is. 45^{11}). Because the Israelites are His sons in this sense, He does not allow Himself to be questioned or commanded by anyone concerning them, but it is also presupposed that they for their part are bound to obey and serve Him, as is specifically emphasised in Ex. 4^{23} and Mal. 3^{18}. The most direct saying in this respect is in Deut. 14^1: "Ye are the children of the Lord your God," and its purpose is simply to initiate a series of particular prohibitions in relation to participation in heathen mourning customs and the eating of unclean foods. We will see later how important it is to emphasise this ethical moment in the concept.

Mal. 1⁶ perhaps presupposes that occasionally the priests were also called "sons of God": "A son honoureth his father, and a servant his master: if then I be a father, where is mine honour? and if I be a master, where is my fear? saith the Lord of hosts unto you, O priests, that despise my name." There is no doubt—and here the connexion with general Eastern mythology and phraseology can hardly be questioned—that although the Old Testament monarchy is a rather problematic institution the king is also given this name on occasion. "I will be to him a father, and he shall be to me a son" is promised to David (2 Sam. 7¹⁴) in relation to his son and successor. The verse continues: "If he commit iniquity, I will chasten him with the rod of men, and with the stripes of the children of men, But my mercy shall not depart away from him." And in Ps. 89 (which is closely related with the whole context of 2 Sam. 7) we are told in v. 26 f.: "He shall cry unto me, Thou art my father, my God, and the rock of my salvation. Also I will make him my firstborn, higher than the kings of the earth." Here again, in v. 30 f., there is not lacking a warning of divine punishment in case the king's descendants forsake the Law of God. But here again it is, of course, capped by the promise that the grace of God will not depart from them. Finally there is the well-known passage in Ps. 2⁷, where the king himself declares: "I will declare the decree: the Lord hath said unto me, Thou art my Son; this day have I begotten thee." If in spite of the extra-biblical analogies these verses are not to be torn completely out of the setting of Old Testament thought, we must accept the fact that in them the king is envisaged as the *membrum praecipuum*EN9 of the people elected to divine sonship, and that he is so in the form of the eschatological future. And there can be little doubt that all these statements—and in the last resort the saying [170] about the priests in Malachi—do conform in sense with what must be said about the people as the son of God. It is God who creates the king and priests as such, making and preparing them for their office. By the grace of God they stand under the promise of His faithfulness, but also under the obligation to be obedient to Him. They are what they are as a particular form of that which makes Israel as such the chosen people of God. It is to be noted that in the Old Testament this father–son relationship is undoubtedly only the relationship between God and Israel, this people, and in particular its king and priests. In the Old Testament God has defined and limited it in that way from the very first. It is in that way, therefore, that He has condescended in His grace. It was and is electing grace, but the grace which elects Israel.

But where in the Old Testament we find Israel, or the king of Israel, in the New Testament we find the one Israelite Jesus. He is the object of the same electing will of the Creator, the same merciful divine faithfulness. He is bound to the same obedience and service of God. He is the Son of the Father with the same singularity and exclusiveness. Of course, what is and takes place between Him and the Father is relatively much greater, and as the self-humiliation of God much more singular, than anything indicated by the father–son relationships of the Old Testament. For this one man—it is as if the framework is now filled out and burst through—is the Son of God who is one with God the Father and is Himself God. God is now not only the electing Creator, but the elect creature. He is not only the giver, but also the recipient of grace. He is not only the One who commands, but the One who is called and pledged to obedience. He does not merely go into lowliness, into the far country, to be Himself there, as He did in His turning to Israel. But now He Himself becomes lowly.

EN9 advance member

He Himself is the man who is His Son. He Himself has become a stranger in Him. And Israel and its kings and priests were only the provisional representatives of this incomparable Son. The mystery of Israel was merely the proclamation, which had still to be unriddled, of the real mystery which unriddles itself from within. In the Old Testament we cannot find anything more than these representatives. But we must not overlook these representatives. The Old Testament, and also the New Testament in its constant implicit and explicit connexion with the Old, makes it quite clear that for all its originality and uniqueness what took place in Christ is not an accident, not a historical *novum*EN10, not the arbitrary action of a *Deus ex machina*, but that it was and is the fulfilment—the superabundant fulfilment—of the will revealed in the Old Testament of the God who even there was the One who manifested Himself in this one man Jesus of Nazareth—the gracious God who as such is able and willing and ready to condescend to the lowly and to undertake their case at His own cost.

But we must go further. The grace and work and revelation of God has the particular character of election. To that extent it includes a self-limitation and a self-humiliation on the part of God. But that is only the general fact which makes the Old Testament a provisional witness to Christ and distinguishes the   [171] New as its fulfilment. The next thing that we are unequivocally and indispensably told by the Old Testament is the particular fact that the man elected by God, the object of the divine grace, is not in any way worthy of it. From what we hear of the people of Israel and its kings, he shows by his action that he is a transgressor of the commandment imposed on him with his election, an enemy of the will of God directed and revealed to him. The God of the Old Testament rules amongst His enemies. He is already on the way into the far country to the extent that it is an unfaithful people to whom He gives and maintains His faithfulness.

We have seen that according to the Old Testament Israel is the son who is pledged to obedience and service to God as its Father and Creator, and that according to the New Jesus accepted this obligation in its place. But what is the normal answer of Israel to the question put to it in its election? The information given by the Old Testament in connexion with the thought of Israel's sonship is unequivocal: The "children" of Israel are "corrupted children; they have forsaken the Lord, they have provoked the Holy One of Israel unto anger, they are gone away backward" (Is. 1⁴). "I have nourished and brought up children, and they have rebelled against me" (Is. 1²). They are "rebellious children, that take counsel but not of me" (Is. 30¹). They are "lying children, children that will not hear the law of the Lord" (Is. 30⁹). They are "backsliding children" who have "perverted their way, and forgotten the Lord their God" (Jer. 3²¹ᶠ·). In the verse that tells us of the Son called out of Egypt, the continuation is: "The more I called them, the more they went from me" (Hos. 11²). We have seen that in Mal. 1⁶ the same complaint was lodged against the priests as the sons of God. And we hardly need to develop in detail the way in which the history of the kings in Samaria and Jerusalem—who are the special bearers of this title—is, as a whole—there are exceptions which only confirm

---

EN10 novelty

163

the rule—a history of defiance of the promises of 2 Sam. 7 and Ps. 89—bringing out the gracious character of these promises. It is a history of the most outrageous and fatal insubordination to *Yahweh* as the "Father" of these kings. The place taken by the one Israelite Jesus according to the New Testament is, according to the Old Testament, the place of this disobedient son, this faithless people and its faithless priests and kings.

This involves an obvious sharpening of the idea and concept of the humiliation of the Son of God, of the alien life in which He identifies Himself with the man Jesus, of the revelation of the grace in which God compromises Himself. "The Word was made flesh." The Old Testament testifies pitilessly what is meant by "flesh." The Old Testament was needed to testify this because the Old Testament alone attests the election of God, and it is only in the light of God's election that we see who and what is man—his unfaithfulness, his disobedience, his fall, his sin, his enmity against God. Without anything to excuse or cover it, without any appearance of the accidental or merely external, the being and nature of man are radically and fundamentally revealed in the human people of Israel as chosen and loved by God, in the history of that people, in Jewish flesh. From the negative standpoint that is the mystery of the Jews and their representative existence. That is what anti-Semitism old and [172] new has constantly thundered, but without understanding that we have here a mirror held up to the men of all peoples. The Son of God in His unity with the Israelite Jesus exists in direct and unlimited solidarity with the representatively and manifestly sinful humanity of Israel. Everything which can be said against it, everything which is said against it, not by men, but by God speaking through His prophets—He allows to be said against Him. He accepts personal responsibility for all the unfaithfulness, the deceit, the rebellion of this people and its priests and kings. And that is infinitely more than when Israel itself (and in Israel more or less expressly every individual Israelite) comes under this accusation. It is infinitely more than could and did take place when the perception and confession of communal sin and guilt came together in an individual Israelite in such a way that, among others incapable of this perception and unprepared for this confession, they became to him a question of personal life in relation to God. Naturally, Moses, David, Jeremiah, the authors of many of the Psalms, and, above all, the significant figure of the Servant of the Lord in Isa. 53, do seem, as it were, to be projected shadows of the one Lamb of God which taketh away the sin of the world. And naturally they are that. But there takes place here infinitely more than can be shadowed in the figures of these men who representatively perceive and confess the sin of the whole people; and infinitely more, of course, than could be represented by the institution of sacrificial worship, in which an innocent beast was regarded and dealt with as the object of the accusation made by God against the people, against man. Infinitely more—for in the one Israelite Jesus it was God Himself who as the Son of the Father made Himself the object of this accusation and willed to confess Himself a sinner, and to be regarded and dealt with as such. What is all our human repentance either in our own name or in that of others compared with this perfect repentance? In this respect, too, we cannot expect to find in the Old Testament more than a prophecy which is supremely inadequate in relation to this fulfilment. The radical and fundamental admission of human incapacity, unwillingness and unworthiness manifest in the human people of Israel as chosen and loved by God is not their own work. Or rather, it takes place as their own work only in the person of the one Israelite in whom God Himself has come amongst sinners in the form of a sinner. It is He who reveals how it is with man in his relation to God. But, again, He does not do it abruptly, abstractly, as a *Deus ex machina*, but in continuity with His grace as already demonstrated and revealed. It was always grace for sinners—grace shown to His enemies—grace in the light of which man can only stand and acknowledge himself a transgressor, and therefore unworthy of it. The Son of Man from heaven had to be the friend of publicans and sinners, and die between two thieves. He had to, because God was already the God who loved His enemies, who "endured such contradiction of sinners against himself" (Heb. 12³). For a   [173] knowledge of this continuity of the being and activity of God, of His condescension, the Old Testament is indispensable as the presupposition of the New.

And now we must make a final step, in which we are directed no less decisively to the Old Testament. Because he negates God, the man elected by God, the object of the divine grace, is himself necessarily, and logically, and with all that it involves, the man negated by God. It is also true that God has sworn to be, and actually is, faithful, that God's grace does not fail but persists towards him. But within these limits it is unconditionally the case that as a sinner he is rejected by God, that he not only stands under the wrath and accusation of God, but because this wrath is well-founded and this accusation is true, he stands under His sentence and judgment. The grace of God is concealed under His sentence and judgment, His Yes under His No. The man elected by God is the man who with his contradiction is broken and destroyed by the greater contradiction of God. He cannot stand before Him, and therefore he cannot stand at all. He chooses a freedom which is no freedom. He is therefore a prisoner of the world-process, of chance, of all-powerful natural and historical forces, above all of himself. He tries to be his own master, and to control his relations with God and the world and his fellow-men. And as he does so, the onslaught of nothingness prevails against him, controlling him in death in an irresistible and senseless way and to his own loss. This is the *circulus vitiosus*EN11 of the human plight presupposed and revealed in and with the grace of God. And there is no man who, whether he experiences it or not, is not in this plight. But the man elected by God not only suffers and experiences it. He knows it. He knows that he must perish. He considers that he must die. The connexion between his guilt and the righteous judgment of God is constantly before him. Occasionally and for the moment he may forget it, he may

---

EN11 vicious circle

deceive himself about it, he may fall asleep to it. But he would not be the elect of God if the dreadful fact did not awaken him again, and pursue him even in his dreams, that everything is as it is and will come to pass as it will come to pass, that there is no escape from it. He is not merely in the jaws of death, but out of the depth of his election, from God whose elect he is, he must constantly hear the voice which tells him and charges him and forces him to live in the knowledge that he is in the jaws of death, that he is lost. "It is a fearful thing to fall into the hands of the living God" (Heb. 10^{31}).

[174] This is the situation of Old Testament man. He may, of course, eat and drink and sleep in this plight. He may distract himself in his care and sorrow. He may console himself like others with all kinds of illusions of self-help. But—because Israel is the chosen people of God—the voice of the prophets brings before him again and again the sentence and judgment under which he lives, writing it in the heart where he cannot escape it, in spite of all his pride or levity or complacency. He does not merely perish, but he must constantly be told, and tell himself that he has to perish. The writings of the prophets and the Psalms are full of passages which confirm this. Of several individual texts, I will quote only from one, the so-called Song of Moses in Deut. 32, in which the thought of sonship again plays a particular part: "For the Lord's portion is his people; Jacob is the lot of his inheritance. He found him in a desert land, and in the waste howling wilderness; he led him about, he instructed him, he kept him as the apple of his eye. As an eagle stirreth up her nest, fluttereth over her young, spreadeth abroad her wings, taketh them, beareth them on her wings; so the Lord alone did lead him, and there was no strange god with him. He made him ride on the high places of the earth, that he might eat the increase of the fields" (v. 9 f.). But what happened? "They have corrupted themselves, they are not his children, that is their blot: they are a perverse and crooked generation. Do ye thus requite the Lord, O foolish people and unwise? is not he thy father that hath bought thee? hath he not made thee and established thee?" (v. 5 f.). "But Jacob ate and was satisfied; Jeshurun waxed fat, and kicked; thou art waxen fat, thou art grown thick ... then he forsook God which made him, and lightly esteemed the rock of his salvation. ... Of the rock that begat thee thou art unmindful, and hast forgotten God that formed thee" (v. 15 f.). And then the answer: "The Lord saw it, and he abhorred them, because of the provoking of his sons, and of his daughters" (v. 19). "For a fire is kindled in mine anger, and shall burn unto the lowest hell, and shall consume the earth with her increase, and set on fire the foundations of the mountains. I will heap mischiefs upon them; I will spend mine arrows upon them. They shall be burnt with hunger, and devoured with burning heat, and with bitter destruction: I will also send the teeth of beasts upon them, with the poison of serpents of the dust. The sword without, and terror within, shall destroy both the young man and the virgin, the suckling also with the man of gray hairs" (v. 22 f.). "How should one chase a thousand, and two put ten thousand to flight, except their Rock had sold them, and the Lord had shut them up?" (v. 30 f.). The clear commentary on this and many similar passages is the history of Israel in its broad outlines and in its outcome and result. In the light of its great beginning and of the opportunities and assistances and redemptions and hopes continually given to this people that history is the history of a great humiliation and disillusionment, a history of suffering. Necessarily it evoked again and again the question: "Where is now thy God?", the desire to reckon with God, to complain about His hiddenness, to remind Him of His covenant and promises. But it had to be a history of suffering and it had to be fulfilled as such—not in spite of the fact but because of the fact that it was the history of the chosen people of God, because it was inevitable that there should be revealed in the people chosen and loved and blessed by God

not only the fall and disobedience of man, but the scorching fire of the love of God, and the breaking and destruction of man on God. Hence the necessary silence of man suffering before Him, not able to plead any right, not able to confront Him with any well-grounded "Why?", able only as Job finally did to submit under His mighty hand—because as the God who has turned in grace to a sinful and therefore a lost people He is always in the right. In the sphere of the Old Testament there is no legitimate human complaint against God—not even in face of the most bitter thing which man might experience at His hand. Man knows that it comes to him in a righteousness which is supremely necessary and therefore in confirmation of the faithfulness and grace of God. He knows that his history is necessarily what the history of Job was, a history of suffering.

We now have a complete outline of what it means that according to the New Testament the Word, or Son of God, was made flesh. To be flesh means to exist with the "children" of Israel under the wrath and judgment of the electing and loving God. To be flesh is to be in a state of perishing before this God. This is [175] what the Old Testament says, and we can hardly maintain that the mythologies and tragedies and philosophies of the rest of antiquity have said the same thing in different words. The Old Testament says this of man. But the New Testament says that the Son of God was a man, and therefore it says it of Him, too. *He* stands under the wrath and judgment of God, *He* is broken and destroyed on God. It cannot be otherwise. It has to be like this. His history must be a history of suffering. For God is in the right against Him. He concedes that the Father is right in the will and action which leads Him to the cross. At this point we can and must think of the history of the Jews right up to our own day. Whether the Jews and those around them understand it or not, it has been a part of the living Old Testament that in its great outlines this history, too, is an individual history of humiliations and disillusionments, a history of suffering. If the Old Testament history was the type, this history has been an additional attestation of its fulfilment in the one Israelite Jesus. The Son of God in His unity with this man exists in solidarity with the humanity of Israel suffering under the mighty hand of God. He exists as one of these Old Testament men. He does not suffer any suffering, but their suffering; the suffering of children chastised by their Father. He does not suffer any death, but the death to which the history of Israel moves relentlessly forward. He is silent where Job too had to be silent before God. But, again, there takes place here something quite different from what took place there. In Him God has entered in, breaking into that *circulus vitiosus*[EN12] of the human plight, making His own not only the guilt of man but also his rejection and condemnation, giving Himself to bear the divinely righteous consequences of human sin, not merely affirming the divine sentence on man, but allowing it to be fulfilled on Himself. He, the electing eternal God, willed Himself to be rejected and therefore perishing man. That is something which never happened in all the dreadful things attested in the Old Testament concerning the wrath of God and the plight of man. In the Old Testament there is always the antithesis between the righteous

---

[EN12] vicious circle

God and the bitter things which man has to accept from Him without murmuring. In the passion story of the New Testament this antithesis is done away. It is God Himself who takes the place of the former sufferers and allows the bitterness of their suffering to fall upon Himself. In this respect, too, the prophecy is quite inadequate in relation to the fulfilment. There is suffering and death in the Old Testament, but it is only in the New that we see what suffering and death really means, as it becomes the work of God Himself, as God gives Himself to this most dreadful of all foreign spheres. But, again, it is the indispensable function of the Old Testament to show that the grace of God in the form of His judgment on man and man's perishing before Him in suf-

[176] fering and death is an element in the previously existing order. What took place on the cross of Golgotha is the last word of an old history and the first word of a new. God was always the One whose condescension showed itself to be unlimited in the suffering and death of the man Jesus. He is the same God who was truly gracious to Israel in the hiddenness of His love in the form of His righteous wrath.

According to the unanimous testimony of the New Testament, in the man Jesus of Nazareth described by those titles of majesty we have to do with the One who is qualitatively different, transcendent and uplifted in relation to all other men and the whole cosmos. His friends and enemies, and those to whom He means nothing, and all men of all times and countries have to do in Him with God. And again according to the unanimous testimony of the New Testament, this is the mystery of His existence. In other words, it is true, but in hiddenness, in a way which is unexpected, which is new in relation to all general concepts of God and those concretely delivered in other places, in a way which contradicts them, and to that extent in a way which is not perceived or known. The Almighty exists and acts and speaks here in the form of One who is weak and impotent, the eternal as One who is temporal and perishing, the Most High in the deepest humility. The Holy One stands in the place and under the accusation of a sinner with other sinners. The glorious One is covered with shame. The One who lives for ever has fallen a prey to death. The Creator is subjected to and overcome by the onslaught of that which is not. In short, the Lord is a servant, a slave. And it is not accidental. It could not be otherwise. For on the presupposition of the Old Testament witness and in the closest connexion with it, the New Testament tells us that it is essential and necessary for the one true God whom it finds in the man Jesus to act and to reveal Himself in this way, to take this form in the coming of His kingdom and the accomplishment of the reconciliation of the world with Himself, in this way to be in the world and for the world the Almighty, the Eternal, the Most High, the Holy One, the Living One, the Creator, the Lord. Prophecy shows (and in this respect it is indissolubly connected with its fulfilment) that God was always the One who worked and was indirectly revealed as He now reveals Himself directly in the secret of the existence of the man Jesus of Nazareth, having set Himself as a man among men for men.

The secret of God's making Himself present in this way was already known to Christian theology even in the 2nd century—especially that which derived from the tradition of Asia Minor. In Ignatius of Antioch (*ad Eph.* 19³) Jesus Christ is called θεὸς ἀνθρωπίνως φανερούμενος[EN13], or, in clear reminiscence of the passages adduced from John, ἐν σαρκὶ γενόμενος θεός[EN14] (*ad Eph.* 7²), or simply ὁ θεὸς ἡμῶν[EN15] (*ad Rom. prooem.*), so that in relation to Him He could speak of an αἷμα θεοῦ[EN16] (*ad Eph.* 1¹) and a πάθος θεοῦ[EN17] (*ad Rom.* 6³). Similarly in Irenaeus (*C.o.h.* III, 16, 6) we read: *Invisibilis visibilis factus et incomprehensibilis comprehensibilis et impassibilis passibilis*[EN18]. And in Melito of Sardis (*fragm.* 13): *Horruit creatura stupescens ac dicens: quidnam est hoc novum mysterium? iudex iudicatur et quietus est; invisibilis videtur neque erubescit, incomprehensibilis prehenditur neque indignatur; incommensurabilis mensuratur neque repugnat; impassibilis patitur neque ulciscitur; immortalis moritur neque respondet verbum*[EN19]. [177]

That God as God is able and willing and ready to condescend, to humble Himself in this way is the mystery of the "deity of Christ"—although frequently it is not recognised in this concreteness. This deity is not the deity of a divine being furnished with all kinds of supreme attributes. The understanding of this decisive christological statement has been made unnecessarily difficult (or easy), and the statement itself ineffective, by overlooking its concrete definition, by omitting to fill out the New Testament concept "deity" in definite connexion with the Old Testament, i.e., in relation to Jesus Christ Himself. The meaning of His deity—the only true deity in the New Testament sense— cannot be gathered from any notion of supreme, absolute, non-worldly being. It can be learned only from what took place in Christ. Otherwise its mystery would be an arbitrary mystery of our own imagining, a false mystery. It would not be the mystery given by the Word and revelation of God in its biblical attestation, the mystery which is alone relevant in Church dogmatics. Who the one true God is, and what He is, i.e., what is His being as God, and therefore His deity, His "divine nature," which is also the divine nature of Jesus Christ if He is very God—all this we have to discover from the fact that as such He is very man and a partaker of human nature, from His becoming man, from His incarnation and from what He has done and suffered in the flesh. For—to put it more pointedly, the mirror in which it can be known (and is known) that He is God, and of the divine nature, is His becoming flesh and His existence in the flesh.

[EN13] God appearing as a man
[EN14] God in the flesh
[EN15] our God
[EN16] blood of God
[EN17] passion of God
[EN18] the invisible was made visible, and the incomprehensible comprehensible, and the impassible passible
[EN19] Creation shudders and, astonished, says: 'How, pray, can this new mystery be? The judge is judged and has been put to rest; the invisible is seen and does not blush; the incomprehensible is comprehended and does not consider it improper; the immeasurable is measured and does not resist; the impassible suffers, and does not take revenge; the immortal dies and says no word in reply

We have seen that this includes in itself His obedience of suffering, i.e., (1) the obedience of the Son to the Father, shown (2) in His self-humiliation, His way into the far country, fulfilled in His death on the cross. It is in these two moments, and their combination, that there is enclosed the mystery that He is very God and of the divine nature. It is a mystery because true being as God and in the divine nature is His alone of all men and all creatures. It is enclosed and can be found only in Him. It is therefore completely and necessarily closed to any consideration or reflection which does not look at Him. It is a genuine mystery because it is disclosed, if at all, from within, as it is spoken as the Word of God and received by His Holy Spirit. From the point of view of the obedience of Jesus Christ as such, fulfilled in that astonishing form, it is a matter of the mystery of the inner being of God as the being of the Son in relation to the Father. From the point of view of that form, of the character of that obedience as an obedience of suffering, of the self-humiliation of Jesus Christ, of the way of the Son into the far country, it is a matter of the mystery of His deity in His work *ad extra*[EN20], in His presence in the world.

[178]　To light up these two moments and their relationship to one another it will be helpful to look at the remarkable sayings in Mt. 11$^{25-30}$, and their parallels in Lk. 10$^{21-24}$.

The passage speaks of a "time"—Matthew connects it with the sayings about the Baptist and the woes on Chorazin and Bethsaida, Luke with the sending out of the disciples—when Jesus addressed to the Father a joyful Yes (ἐξομολογοῦμαί σοι, πάτερ, κύριε τοῦ οὐρανοῦ καὶ τῆς γῆς[EN21])—Luke indeed says that He "rejoiced in the Holy Spirit" (ἠγαλλιάσατο τῷ πνεύματι τῷ ἁγίῳ). Why? In the first instance, strangely enough, because of an obvious defeat, a failure: "that thou hast hid these things from the wise and prudent". But then there follows, "and hast revealed them unto babes." The former were obviously those who had succeeded in this world, the far-sighted and clear-sighted spiritual leaders of the people of whom it might be hoped and expected that they would welcome the proclamation of the kingdom and recognise the Son of God. They have not done so. The Father has hidden it (ταῦτα[EN22]) from them. The others (νήπιοι[EN23]) are the innocent and naive and unimportant disciples of Jesus. They have followed Him. The Father, the Lord of heaven and earth has—strangely and disappointingly—revealed it (the kingdom which has come, the presence of the Son) to them. The continuation shows that the sequence is not accidental. It is for this puzzling and scandalising distribution of the divine hiding and revealing that Jesus as Son gives thanks to the Father. A. Schlatter (*Der Evangelist Mathäus*, 1929, 382) says quite rightly that "this saying makes a passion of the work of Jesus." "Even so, Father, for so it seemed good in thy sight," i.e., in this course of events, which is humanly and externally a failure, in which the first are last and the last first, in which the work of Jesus becomes a passion, in which His cross is plainly foreshadowed, the will of God is done to which He says Yes, to which He subjects Himself, willingly and with joy. There can be no doubt that Jesus is the unconditionally omnipotent executor of God upon earth.

"All things are delivered unto me of my Father." Again in accordance with the sense Schlatter underlines the fact "that πάντα[EN24] does not carry any limitations ... there are no

---

[EN20] outside of God
[EN21] I praise you, Father, Lord of heaven and earth
[EN22] these things
[EN23] babes
[EN24] all things

170

limits for the giver and therefore no limits for the recipient" (p. 384). Therefore the saying implies the deity of Jesus. But it is in complete hiddenness that He is who and what He is. "No man knoweth the Son, but the Father; neither knoweth any man the Father, save the Son, and he to whomsoever the Son will reveal him." But that means that who and what He is as the human bearer of that unlimited omnipotence, and who and what is the One who has given it to Him, what there is of divine majesty in the giving and receiving of it—this and the revelation of it is not something which can be laid down and judged and evaluated from without. It does not shine out clear and bright and sparkling in the world. It does not appear to men as such. Its form does not correspond to it but contradicts it, so that—although it is its form—it cannot be deduced from it, it is more likely not to be recognised in this form, and in the ordinary course of things it will not be recognised. This door to the majesty of Jesus can open only from within. And when it does open it is this door—the poor humanity of the divine being and activity, the strange form of the divine majesty, the humility in which God is God and the Son the Son, and to that extent the Father the Father, the alien life in which He is manifest only to Himself alone.

Both Evangelists now add other sayings which they obviously regard as characteristic forms of that revelation, as descriptions of the opening of that door from within. In Luke ($10^{23f.}$) there follows the blessing of the few and the lowly, the disciples, to whom at the coming of the last time it is given to see and to hear what many (here equivalent to all) prophets and kings desired to see and to hear but did not in fact see and hear. This revelation has therefore the character of a breaking out from the general and profoundest hiddenness, which indirectly is simply confirmed by it (as the darkness is when a light is kindled). As Ignatius of Antioch later wrote (*ad Magn.* 8, 2), it has the character of a breaking of the great silence in which God had previously and still for the most part conceals Himself.

[179]

Matthew ($11^{28f.}$) inserts at this point the so-called "call of the Saviour." To whom does it apply? To whom, therefore, does the self-revelation of the Son apply? Whom does He call to Himself? Not those who are religiously, morally, politically and socially vital and exalted and triumphant in this world, but the "weary and heavy-laden," those who are retiring in their relation to God and men, those who are at an end of their own resources in both respects, those who are at their wits' end in both respects. The affinity of Jesus is not with the former class, but the latter. Not the former but the latter are His people, in whom He can see Himself again and to whom He for His part can give Himself to be known as Saviour and prove Himself as such. It is to these that He promises rest, a fulfilment which the others can never enjoy, because they do not know of it, because it cannot mean anything to them, His own rest, the rest of His own being in the unity of the obedient Son with the will of the Father and with the Father Himself. It is these that He summons to come to Himself, to be with Him in this rest, to take His yoke upon them. His rest consists in the fact that He carries the yoke and burden of the obedience of the Son to the Father—an easy yoke, a light burden, as whose bearer He is really at rest, and can promise rest (ἀνάπαυσιν) to those whom He calls, as Joshua (1^{13}) promised possession of the land to the Israelites, and a dwelling in their former and latter homeland. Freely and willingly and in complete agreement with His commission He bears what He has to bear. But He does bear a yoke and a burden. He is at rest, but He is poor not rich, weak not strong, One who is subject not One who triumphs, like the weary and the heavy-laden, the man who finally will bear a cross and die on the cross. As this man He is the Saviour for those who are willing to be and are weary and heavy-laden with Him. He is πραΰς EN25 and ταπεινός EN26, and that not by any chance or fate but "from the

---

EN25 meek
EN26 humble

171

heart," not made from without but appointed from within, not forced by that which is inevitable, but of His own choice, in free obedience a bearer of the yoke and burden, and therefore at rest, and able to promise the same rest to others, that is, to call them to take His yoke upon them and to learn of Him, to follow Him, to be His disciples. That is the self-revelation of Jesus in His call as Saviour.

We will begin our attempt to understand this with a consideration of the second of those two moments of the mystery of the deity of Christ, and therefore with a consideration of the mystery of His being and work in the world, of the becoming man, the incarnation of the Son of God with all that it involved, of His way as a way into the far country.

The Christian theological tradition has always been in agreement that the statement "The Word was made flesh" is not to be thought of as describing an event which overtook Him, and therefore overtook God Himself, but rather a free divine activity, a sovereign act of divine lordship, an act of mercy which was necessary only by virtue of the will of God Himself. The statement cannot be reversed as though it indicated an appropriation and overpowering of the eternal Word by the flesh. God is always God even in His humiliation. The divine being does not suffer any change, any diminution, any transformation into something else, any admixture with something else, let alone any cessa-

[180]   tion. The deity of Christ is the one unaltered because unalterable deity of God. Any subtraction or weakening of it would at once throw doubt upon the atonement made in Him. He humbled Himself, but He did not do it by ceasing to be who He is. He went into a strange land, but even there, and especially there, He never became a stranger to Himself.

The word ἐκένωσεν [EN27] in Phil. 2⁷ certainly does not mean this. It says that "being in the form of God," enjoying it, freely disposing of it (ἐν μορφῇ θεοῦ ὑπάρχων [EN28]) He carried through a self-emptying, that is. He took the form of a servant (μορφὴν δούλου). The κένωσις [EN29] consists in a renunciation of His being in the form of God alone. The decisive commentary is given by the text itself. He did not treat His form in the likeness of God (τὸ εἶναι ἴσα θεῷ [EN30]) as a robber does his booty. He was not bound by it like someone bound by his possessions, a servant of unrighteous mammon. He did not treat it as His one and only and exclusive possibility, as though He stood or fell by it. It was not to Him an inalienable necessity to exist only in that form of God, only to be God, and therefore only to be different from the creature, from man, as the reality which is distinct from God, only to be the eternal Word and not flesh. He was not committed to any such "only." In addition to His form in the likeness of God He could also—and this involves at once a making poor, a humiliation, a condescension, and to that extent a κένωσις [EN31]—take the form of a servant. He could be like men. He could be found in fashion as a man. As God, therefore (without ceasing to be God) He could be known only to Himself, but unknown as such in the world and for the world. His divine majesty could be in this alien form. It could be a hidden majesty. He could, therefore, humble Himself in this form. He could be obedient in the determination corres-

---

[EN27] emptied
[EN28] being in the form of God
[EN29] emptying
[EN30] being like God
[EN31] an emptying

ponding to the being of this form, although contradicting point blank the actualisation of this form by other men. He could be obedient even to death, even to the death of the cross. He had this other possibility: the possibility of divine self-giving to the being and fate of man. He had the freedom for this condescension, for this concealment of His Godhead. He had it and He made use of it in the power and not with any loss, not with any diminution or alteration of His Godhead. That is His self-emptying. It does not consist in ceasing to be Himself as man, but in taking it upon Himself to be Himself in a way quite other than that which corresponds and belongs to His form as God, His being equal with God. He can also go into the far country and be there, with all that that involves. And so He does go into the far country, and is there. According to Phil. 2 this means His becoming man, the incarnation.

At the most decisive point, this was the exposition of Augustine: *Sic se inanivit: formam servi accipiens, non formam Dei amittens; forma servi accessit, non forma Dei discessit*[EN32] (*Sermo*, 183, 4 f.). *Occultavit quod erat*[EN33] (*Sermo*, 187, 4). Origen (*De princ. praef.* 4) thought that it is self-evidently established as a rule of faith that the Logos *homo factus mansit, quod erat*[EN34]. It was only to men, says Gregory of Nyssa (*or. cat.* 26), that the humanity of Christ concealed the glory of the Logos; the Godhead is in Christ ὑπὸ τῆς ἀνθρωπίνης φύσεως κεκαλυμένη[EN35].

It was the same basic thought which many years later Calvin was trying to express in his well-known statement: *Etsi in unam personam coaluit immensa Verbi essentia cum natura hominis, nullam tamen inclusionem fingimus*[EN36]. An absolute *inclusio*[EN37] of the Logos in the creature, the man Jesus, would mean a subordination of the Word to the flesh, a limitation and therefore an alteration of His divine nature, and therefore of God Himself. For that reason, according to Calvin, we ought to say side by side or rather together: *Mirabiliter de caelo descendit Filius Dei, ut caelum tamen non relinqueret. Mirabiliter in utero virginis gestari, in terris versari et in cruce pendere voluit, ut semper mundum impleret sicut ab initio*[EN38] (*Instit.* II, 13. 4). This is what was known as the *Extra Calvinisticum* of Lutheran polemics. The Lutherans [181] rejected it because they thought they could see in it a "Nestorian" separation of the divine and human natures, because on their doctrine of the communication of the attributes the fact that He "filled the whole world" had also to be said of the man Jesus as such on the basis of His union with the Logos. We may concede that there is something unsatisfactory about the theory, in that right up to our own day it has led to fatal speculation about the being and work of the λόγος ἄσαρκος[EN39], or a God whom we think we can know elsewhere, and whose divine being we can define from elsewhere than in and from the contemplation of His presence and activity as the Word made flesh. And it cannot be denied that Calvin himself (and with particularly serious consequences in his doctrine of predestination) does go a good way towards trying to reckon with this "other" god. It may also be noted, however, that the theory was not an innovation on the part of Calvin, nor was it a revival of the teaching

---

EN32 He emptied himself in this way: taking the form of a servant, he did not lose the form of God. The form of a servant came, but the form of God did not leave
EN33 He concealed what he was
EN34 having been made man, remained what he was
EN35 concealed by his human nature
EN36 Even though the immeasurable essence of the Word joins with the nature of man in one person, nevertheless, we are not fabricating any inclusion
EN37 inclusion
EN38 Wonderfully, the son of God descended from heaven, yet not such that he should leave heaven. Wonderfully, he was carried in the womb of the virgin, dwelt on earth, and willed to hang on the cross, in order that he might always fill the world as he did from the beginning
EN39 discarnate Word

condemned under the name of Nestorius. For in this matter Athanasius, Cyril of Alexandria and Hilary of Poitiers had all thought and taught as he did, as had indeed the whole early and mediaeval Church, so that it was the abstract Lutheran denial of a being of the Logos *extra carnem*[EN40] which was the real innovation (cf. F. Loofs, Art. *Kenosis P.R.E.³* 10, 246 f.). Nor for his part did Calvin any more than his predecessors try to maintain an abstract *Extra*, thus separating again, at any rate in part, the Son of God and the man Jesus. On the contrary, it was his aim in that theory to hold to the fact that the Son of God who is wholly this man (*totus intra carnem*[EN41] as it was formulated by a later Calvinist) is also wholly God and therefore omnipotent and omnipresent (and to that extent *extra carnem*[EN42], not bound or altered by its limitations). He is the Lord and Creator who because He becomes a creature and exists in that *forma servi*[EN43] does not cease to be Lord and Creator and therefore to exist in the *forma Dei*[EN44].

We can only mention in passing the great controversy about the *kenosis* which broke out at the beginning of the 17th century between the Lutheran theologians of Giessen and those of Tübingen. It was not a matter of the intactness of the Godhead of Christ in the state of His humiliation. Both parties were agreed in giving a positive answer to this question in line with earlier tradition. It was a problem which arose only on the specifically Lutheran presupposition of the divinisation of the man Jesus as such, but on this presupposition it was almost necessarily an acute problem: Whether the man Jesus exalted to unity with the Son of God and therefore divinised—according to the logic of the Lutherans—was even in the state of His humiliation secretly present to all His creatures, and ruled the world? The Giessen party denied this, the Tübingen group affirmed it. In what did the *kenosis* consist? Both sides agreed that it does not consist in the surrender or diminution of the possession (κτῆσις) of the divine glory imparted to the man Jesus. But adopting a statement of Martin Chemnitz the Giessen party taught a genuine κένωσις χρήσεως[EN45], an at any rate partial abstention by the man Jesus, in the *exinanitio*[EN46], from the use of the majesty imparted to Him. Jesus Christ *regnavit mundum*[EN47], but *non mediante carne*[EN48], only *qua* Logos, only in the power of His deity. But in Tübingen, following J. Brenz, there was taught a far more subtle κρύψις χρήσεως[EN49], an abstention by the man Jesus in the *exinanitio*[EN50] only from the visible use, a *retractatio*[EN51] and *occultatio*[EN52] of the revelation of His power, or positively, a majesty of the Son of God which is, in fact, exercised and operative and actual, but concealed. When the Saxon theologians were called in to decide the matter (*Decisio saxonica*, 1624), in the main issue they found in favour of Giessen. And in this they were followed by later Lutheran orthodoxy. That is surprising and noteworthy. The thesis of Giessen derived from a concern at the threatened Docetism of the Tübingen antithesis. But on Lutheran soil this concern had come too late. Already in the 16th century it had been expressed by the Reformed theologians against the Lutheran doctrine of the communication of the attributes, by

---

[EN40] outside of the flesh
[EN41] wholly within the flesh
[EN42] outside of the flesh
[EN43] form of a servant
[EN44] form of God
[EN45] emptying of usage
[EN46] emptying
[EN47] ruled over the world
[EN48] as he is mediator in the flesh
[EN49] concealment of usage
[EN50] emptying
[EN51] retention
[EN52] hiding

1. The Way of the Son of God into the Far Country

Zwingli against Luther. It is a fact that a bold Lutheran theologian does not need to fear the menace of Docetism unduly, but must accept the risk and suspicion involved. The intention of the basic view common to all Lutherans, that the man Jesus as such shares the totality of the divine attributes, undoubtedly points in the direction taken in Würtemberg with the mere κρύψις χρήσεως EN53. Ready to follow through their logic, they challenged their opponents on their own theory (and not unjustly from the Lutheran standpoint): *Hic Rhodus! Hoc est illud ipsum Extra Calvinisticum, cui se hactenus nostri opposuerunt*EN54. Granted the κένωσις χρήσεως EN55 maintained by them, there would be a time at least, the time of Christ's state in humility, *quo* λόγος *sic est in carne, ut etiam sit extra carnem*EN56. Among the Lutheran theologians of the period the great J. Gerhard expressly repudiated the *Decisio saxonica* which approved this. And on the specifically Lutheran presupposition we are forced to ask whether the Giessen idea of a merely potential and facultative divine majesty and glory only partly used and actualised is not logically and theologically an impossible one, an inner contradiction? That is how it was unashamedly described by a 19th century Lutheran, G. Thomasius (*Christi Person und Werk³*, vol. I, 1886—in which there is a detailed discussion of the whole controversy).

The victory of the impossible theory of Giessen anticipated a step which in the 19th century was taken first of all by Ernst Sartorius (*Lehre von der heiligen Liebe*, 1844), then by G. Thomasius, then by the more extreme W. F. Gess (*Das Dogma von Christi Person und Werk*, 1887) and others. Ostensibly (and in one respect perhaps not only so) this step was taken in fulfilment of the original Lutheran intention. But clearly it was not uninfluenced by the modern "historical" problem of the "life of Jesus." And it meant an open breach with the whole tradition of the Church. Alongside the theses of Giessen and Tübingen (and avoiding the threatened "Nestorianism" or Calvinism of the former and the even more dreaded Docetism of the latter), there was a third alternative rejected in the earlier controversy, but already visible from afar along the line of the Giessen teaching. This was the alternative of a partial or complete abstention not only on the part of the man Jesus as such but on the part of the Son of God, the Logos Himself, from the possession and therefore the power to dispose of His divine glory and majesty, a κένωσις κτήσεως EN57. This was the possibility seized by the so-called modern "kenotics" under the mounting modern pressure of the need to find a place for the historical form of Jesus in its human limitation—the idea of a self-limitation of God in the incarnation (or, to put it in the categories of the so-called doctrine of the attributes, the possibility of a *genus tapeinoticum*EN58). "The Son of God closes His all-embracing eye on earth, and gives Himself to human darkness, and then opens His eye again as the rising light of the world, until He causes it to shine in full glory at the right hand of the Father" (E. Sartorius, p. 21 f.). Or, according to the teaching of Thomasius, the *kenosis* consisted in the fact that in the incarnation the divine Logos renounced the attributes of majesty in relation to the world (omnipotence, omnipresence, etc.), in order that in the man Jesus, until His exaltation. He might be God only in His immanent qualities, His holiness and love and truth. In Gess (who used the rash heading, "The Degradation of the Logos," *op. cit.*, p. 344) we are told that "a change took place in the Son of God." In the incarnation He ceased to be actually God, in order to become conscious of Himself as God with the developing self-consciousness of Jesus, undergoing an "evolution" (p. 366 f.) in His

---

EN53 concealment of usage
EN54 Here is Rhodes! This is that very Extra Calvinisticum, to which our theologians have thus far opposed themselves!
EN55 emptying of usage
EN56 in which the Word is in the flesh just as he is also outside the flesh
EN57 emptying of possession
EN58 'category of humiliation'

[183]

identity with the man Jesus, and finally (p. 400 f.) being clothed again with the glory which He had had before in His exaltation. A. E. Biedermann called this doctrine "the complete *kenosis* of reason." But that is not its worst feature. The knot which the earlier Lutheran Christology had arbitrarily tied rather too tightly was certainly loosed. But it was loosed at too great a cost when it meant the open abandonment of the presupposition common to all earlier theology, including Calvinists and Lutherans, Giessen and Tübingen, that the God-head of the man Jesus remains intact and unaltered. It was this surrender which even among the Liberals of the 19th century and in the school of Ritschl earned for "modern kenotics" only the taunt that in trying to improve and complete orthodox Christology they had simply reduced it to absurdity. Their intention was good. They wanted to clear away the difficulties of the traditional teaching and make possible a "historical" consideration of the life of Jesus. But they succeeded only in calling in question the "God was in Christ" and in that way dam-aging the nerve of a Christology orientated by the Old and the New Testaments. There are many things we can try to say in understanding the christological mystery. But we cannot possibly understand or estimate it if we try to explain it by a self-limitation or de-divinisation of God in the uniting of the Son of God with the man Jesus. If in Christ—even in the humili-ated Christ born in a manger at Bethlehem and crucified on the cross of Golgotha—God is not unchanged and wholly God, then everything that we may say about the reconciliation of the world made by God in this humiliated One is left hanging in the air.

But it is not enough simply to follow the great line of theological tradition and to reject all thought of an alterability or alteration of God in His presence and action in the man Jesus. What depends on this rejection is clear. If God is not truly and altogether in Christ, what sense can there be in talking about the reconciliation of the world with God in Him? But it is something very bold and profoundly astonishing to presume to say without reservation or subtraction that God was truly and altogether in Christ, to speak of His identity with this true man, which means this man who was born like all of us in time, who lived and thought and spoke, who could be tempted and suffer and die and who was in fact tempted, and suffered and died. The statement of this identity cannot be merely a postulate. If with the witnesses of the New Testament we derive it from what took place in this man, if it only confirms that the reconciliation of the world with God has actually taken place in the existence of this man, if it can only indicate the mystery and the miracle of this event, we must still know what we are presuming to say in this statement. It aims very high. In calling this man the Son or the eternal Word of God, in ascribing to this man in His unity with God a divine being and nature, it is not speaking only or even primarily of Him but of God. It tells us that God for His part is God in His unity with this creature, this man, in His human and creaturely nature—and this without ceasing to be God, without any alteration or diminution of His divine nature. But this statement concerning God is so bold that we dare not make it unless we consider seriously in what sense we can do so. It must not contain any blas-phemy, however involuntary or well-meant, or however pious. That it does do this is to this very day the complaint of Judaism and Islam against the Christian confession of the deity of Christ. It cannot be taken lightly. It cannot be secured by a mere repetition of this confession. We must be able to answer for this confession and its statement about God with a good conscience and with good reason. We must be able to show that God is honoured and not dishon- [184] oured by this confession. And at this point the traditional theology of the Church gives rise to an ambiguity. One service which we cannot deny to earlier and more recent discussions of the *kenosis* is that they drew attention to this ambiguity. The ambiguity is one which needs to be removed.

Cur Deus homo?[EN59] is the question we shall have to deal with in the second part of this section—the question concerning the necessity of the incarnation of the Word. But it presupposes that we have already answered the question concerning its possibility from the standpoint of God: *Quo iure Deus homo*[EN60] And we must pause to consider this for a moment. At this point the following alternatives suggest themselves.

The incarnation of the Word, the human being of God, His condescension, His way into the far country, His existence in the *forma servi*[EN61], is something which we can understand—this is (or appears to be) the first alternative—by supposing that in it we have to do with a *novum mysterium*[EN62] (in the strict and literal sense of the expression of Melito of Sardis), with what is noetically and logically an absolute paradox, with what is ontically the fact of a cleft or rift or gulf in God Himself, between His being and essence in Himself and His activity and work as the Reconciler of the world created by Him. It therefore pleased Him in this latter, for the redemption of the world, not to alter Himself, but to deny the immutability of His being, His divine nature, to be in discontinuity with Himself, to be against Himself, to set Himself in self-contradiction. In Himself He was still the omnipresent, almighty, eternal and glorious One, the All-Holy and All-Righteous who could not be tempted. But at the same time among us and for us He was quite different, not omnipresent and eternal but limited in time and space, not almighty but impotent, not glorious but lowly, and open to radical and total attack in respect of His righteousness and holiness. His identity with Himself consisted strictly in His determination to be God, our God, the Reconciler of the world, in this inner and outer antithesis to Himself. The *quo iure*[EN63], the possibility of the incarnation, of His becoming man, consisted in this determination of God to be "God against God," in His free will to be this, in His fathomless mercy as the meaning and purpose of that will. On this view God in His incarnation would not merely give Himself, but give Himself away, give up being God. And if that was His will, who can question His right to make possible this impossibility? Is He not supremely right to exercise His mercy in this way?

Of course this view is seldom or never expressly stated in this pointed way. But it can and must be said that when there is no mention of the second alternative (as is usually the case in traditional theology) the matter has to be more or less clearly stated as though this first

---

EN59 Why did God become man?
EN60 How is it that God became man?
EN61 form of a servant
EN62 new mystery
EN63 'how'

alternative has been chosen, as though this "God against God" has to be accepted as the presupposition of the incarnation, of the existence of God in humility. Even the modern kenotics did not go so far as to express themselves in this way. And although in the *Christologie* of Heinrich Vogel (Vol. I, 1949) we may at first get the impression of a tendency in this direction, there are constant warnings against this deduction, and even some clear and positive statements which point in a completely different direction (cf. especially the twenty theses on the unity of the truth in the reconciliation of the contradiction, pp. 192–218). But what we need to show and to say clearly at this point is that we do not choose this alternative and why we do not choose it. We also need clearly to set against it its opposite as the only possible alternative.

We must not deceive ourselves. The incarnation, the taking of the *forma servi*[EN64], means not only God's becoming a creature, becoming a man—and how this is possible to God without an alteration of His being is not self-evident—but it means His giving Himself up to the contradiction of man against Him, His placing Himself under the judgment under which man has fallen in this contradiction, under the curse of death which rests upon Him. The meaning of the incarnation is plainly revealed in the question of Jesus on the cross: "My God, my God, why hast thou forsaken me?" (Mk. 15^{34}). The more seriously we take this, the stronger becomes the temptation to approximate to the view of a contradiction and conflict in God Himself. Have we not to accept this view if we are to do justice to what God did for man and what He took upon Himself when He was in Christ, if we are to bring out the mystery of His mercy in all its depth and greatness?

But at this point what is meant to be supreme praise of God can in fact become supreme blasphemy. God gives Himself, but He does not give Himself away. He does not give up being God in becoming a creature, in becoming man. He does not cease to be God. He does not come into conflict with Himself. He does not sin when in unity with the man Jesus He mingles with sinners and takes their place. And when He dies in His unity with this man, death does not gain any power over Him. He exists as God in the righteousness and the life, the obedience and the resurrection of this man. He makes His own the being of man in contradiction against Him, but He does not make common cause with it. He also makes His own the being of man under the curse of this contradiction, but in order to do away with it as He suffers it. He acts as Lord over this contradiction even as He subjects Himself to it. He frees the creature in becoming a creature. He overcomes the flesh in becoming flesh. He reconciles the world with Himself as He is in Christ. He is not untrue to Himself but true to Himself in this condescension, in this way into the far country. If it were otherwise, if in it He set Himself in contradiction with Himself, how could He reconcile the world with Himself? Of what value would His deity be to us if—instead of crossing in that deity the very real gulf between Himself and us—He left that deity behind Him in His coming to us, if it came to be outside of Him as He became ours? What would be the value to us of His way into the far

---

[EN64] form of a servant

country if in the course of it He lost Himself? In the folly of such a contra- [186]
diction to Himself He could obviously only confirm and strengthen us in the
antithesis to Him in which we find ourselves. A God who found Himself in this
contradiction can obviously only be the image of our own unreconciled
humanity projected into deity. We cannot, therefore, choose this alternative in
understanding the possibility of His becoming flesh. Nor can we leave it open
as a possibility with which we can seriously reckon and sometimes toy. We have
to reject it. But it can be positively rejected only as it is firmly replaced by the
other alternative (which is not really another, but the only possible one).

We begin with the insight that God is "not a God of confusion, but of peace"
(1 Cor. 14^{33}). In Him there is no paradox, no antinomy, no division, no inconsistency, not even the possibility of it. He is the Father of lights with whom
there is no variableness nor interplay of light and darkness (Jas. 1^{17}). What He
is and does He is and does in full unity with Himself. It is in full unity with
Himself that He is also—and especially and above all—in Christ, that He
becomes a creature, man, flesh, that He enters into our being in contradiction, that He takes upon Himself its consequences. If we think that this is
impossible it is because our concept of God is too narrow, too arbitrary, too
human—far too human. Who God is and what it is to be divine is something
we have to learn where God has revealed Himself and His nature, the essence
of the divine. And if He has revealed Himself in Jesus Christ as the God who
does this, it is not for us to be wiser than He and to say that it is in contradiction
with the divine essence. We have to be ready to be taught by Him that we have
been too small and perverted in our thinking about Him within the framework of a false idea of God. It is not for us to speak of a contradiction and rift in
the being of God, but to learn to correct our notions of the being of God, to
reconstitute them in the light of the fact that He does this. We may believe that
God can and must only be absolute in contrast to all that is relative, exalted in
contrast to all that is lowly, active in contrast to all suffering, inviolable in contrast to all temptation, transcendent in contrast to all immanence, and therefore divine in contrast to everything human, in short that He can and must be
only the "Wholly Other." But such beliefs are shown to be quite untenable, and
corrupt and pagan, by the fact that God does in fact be and do this in Jesus
Christ. We cannot make them the standard by which to measure what God can
or cannot do, or the basis of the judgment that in doing this He brings Himself
into self-contradiction. By doing this God proves to us that He can do it, that to
do it is within His nature. And He shows Himself to be more great and rich and
sovereign than we had ever imagined. And our ideas of His nature must be
guided by this, and not *vice versa*.

We have to think something after the following fashion. As God was in
Christ, far from being against Himself, or at disunity with Himself, He has put [187]
into effect the freedom of His divine love, the love in which He is divinely free.
He has therefore done and revealed that which corresponds to His divine
nature. His immutability does not stand in the way of this. It must not be

denied, but this possibility is included in His unalterable being. He is absolute, infinite, exalted, active, impassible, transcendent, but in all this He is the One who loves in freedom, the One who is free in His love, and therefore not His own prisoner. He is all this as the Lord, and in such a way that He embraces the opposites of these concepts even while He is superior to them. He is all this as the Creator, who has created the world as the reality distinct from Himself but willed and affirmed by Him and therefore as His world, as the world which belongs to Him, in relation to which He can be God and act as God in an absolute way and also a relative, in an infinite and also a finite, in an exalted and also a lowly, in an active and also a passive, in a transcendent and also an immanent, and finally, in a divine and also a human—indeed, in relation to which He Himself can become worldly, making His own both its form, the *forma servi*[EN65], and also its cause; and all without giving up His own form, the *forma Dei*[EN66], and His own glory, but adopting the form and cause of man into the most perfect communion with His own, accepting solidarity with the world. God can do this. And no limit is set to His ability to do it by the contradiction of the creature against Him. It does not escape Him by turning to that which is not and losing itself in it, for, although He is not the Creator of that which is not, He is its sovereign Lord. It corresponds to and is grounded in His divine nature that in free grace He should be faithful to the unfaithful creature who has not deserved it and who would inevitably perish without it, that in relation to it He should establish that communion between His own form and cause and that of the creature, that He should make His own its being in contradiction and under the consequences of that contradiction, that He should maintain His covenant in relation to sinful man (not surrendering His deity, for how could that help? but giving up and sacrificing Himself), and in that way supremely asserting Himself and His deity. His particular, and highly particularised, presence in grace, in which the eternal Word descended to the lowest parts of the earth (Eph. 4⁹) and tabernacled in the man Jesus (Jn. 1¹⁴), dwelling in this one man in the fulness of His Godhead (Col. 2⁹), is itself the demonstration and exercise of His omnipresence, i.e., of the perfection in which He has His own place which is superior to all the places created by Him, not excluding but including all other places. His omnipotence is that of a divine plenitude of power in the fact that (as opposed to any abstract omnipotence) it can assume the form of weakness and impotence and do so as omnipotence, triumphing in this form. The eternity in which He Himself is true time and the Creator of all time is revealed in the fact that, although our [188] time is that of sin and death, He can enter it and Himself be temporal in it, yet without ceasing to be eternal, able rather to be the Eternal in time. His wisdom does not deny itself, but proclaims itself in what necessarily appears folly to the world; His righteousness in ranging Himself with the unrighteous as One who

---

[EN65] form of a servant
[EN66] form of God

is accused with them, as the first, and properly the only One to come under accusation; His holiness in having mercy on man, in taking his misery to heart, in willing to share it with him in order to take it away from him. God does not have to dishonour Himself when He goes into the far country, and conceals His glory. For He is truly honoured in this concealment. This concealment, and therefore His condescension as such, is the image and reflection in which we see Him as He is. His glory is the freedom of the love which He exercises and reveals in all this. In this respect it differs from the unfree and loveless glory of all the gods imagined by man. Everything depends on our seeing it, and in it the true and majestic nature of God: not trying to construct it arbitrarily; but deducing it from its revelation in the divine nature of Jesus Christ. From this we learn that the *forma Dei*[EN67] consists in the grace in which God Himself assumes and makes His own the *forma servi*[EN68]. We have to hold fast to this without being disturbed or confused by any pictures of false gods. It is this that we have to see and honour and worship as the mystery of the deity of Christ—not an ontic and inward divine paradox, the postulate of which has its basis only in our own very real contradiction against God and the false ideas of God which correspond to it.

To establish this point from Scripture we must turn again to Phil. 2. We have already drawn attention to the twofold ἑαυτόν[EN69] used in relation to the emptying and humbling of the One who exists in the divine form of the divine likeness. Whatever He Himself does, even this, takes place in His freedom, and therefore in unity and not in contradiction with Himself, as a self-giving but not as a giving up, not at the cost of Himself, not as an entering into conflict with Himself. And having pictured this self-giving the passage continues: "Wherefore (not 'Nevertheless') God also hath highly exalted him, and given him a name which is above every name"—the name *Kyrios*[EN70] given (to the glory of God the Father) to the One who emptied and humbled Himself. And that means that not in spite of the fact that He emptied and humbled Himself, but because of it, because of the fact that in Him that self-giving and concealment of God (in and under the form of a servant) actually took place, there belongs to Him the name as the bearer of which He exercises the function in which He glorifies God with all creatures in heaven and earth and under the earth, in which He is the One in acknowledging whom all creation must give God the glory. We are again reminded of the call of the Saviour in Mt. 11[28f.], the imperative of which: Come unto me, Take my yoke upon you, Learn of me, has such an astonishing basis: For I am meek and lowly in heart. This basis is meaningful if the One who speaks the imperative is the Lord and has authority and can give a binding command for the very reason that He is meek and lowly in heart. But at this point we have to do with a far-reaching consideration in New Testament ethics.

The hymn on the humiliated and therefore the exalted Jesus Christ quoted by Paul in Phil. 2[6f.] is obviously set in the context of an exhortation to concord, in which the final lesson is that in lowliness of mind (τῇ ταπεινοφροσύνῃ) the readers should each esteem other

---

[EN67] form of God
[EN68] form of a servant
[EN69] 'himself'
[EN70] Lord

[189] better than themselves, not looking every man on his own things, but every man also on things of others. They are to have the mind (τοῦτο φρονεῖτε) in them (ἐν ὑμῖν) which was also in Christ Jesus (ἐν Χριστῷ Ἰησοῦ), who having the form of God. … As we have seen, the law of ταπεινοφροσύνη EN701 applies in the first instance to Christ Jesus. He entered under this law, and because He went His way under it He was exalted to be the Lord. They are to model themselves on His bowing beneath this law. In this way they are to live with one another and to be at peace. We have to do with the one binding law for both the Head and the members, for Jesus and His people, and because for Jesus therefore also for His people. Why is it this law? Why is it in ταπεινοφροσύνη EN72 that Christians are to unite themselves with Christ?

The same thought occurs elsewhere in Paul. With a remarkable similarity to this passage in Phil. 2 he says in 2 Cor. 11⁷: "I abase myself that ye might be exalted." According to 2 Cor. 10¹ he had been κατὰ πρόσωπον EN73 base among the Corinthians. According to 2 Cor. 7⁶ His God is the God "that comforteth them that are cast down." In Phil. 4¹² Paul boasts that he knows how to abase and how to abound. The exhortation in Rom. 12¹⁶ is to the same purport: "Mind not ὑψηλά EN74 but condescend to that which is lowly." Hence the summons in Gal. 6² to bear one another's burdens and so fulfil the law of Christ. Hence ὑποταγή EN75 as the basic concept in the Christian attitude to the civil powers (Rom. 13¹ᶠ·), but also in the attitude of wives to their husbands (Col. 3¹⁸), and also according to Eph. 5²⁰ in the attitude of all Christians one toward another. Hence the ὑπακοή EN76 of children to their parents (Col. 3²⁰) and servants to their masters (Col. 3²²). Hence the τιμή EN77, the respect in which, according to Rom. 12¹⁰, all Christians are to prefer one another, and which, according to 1 Pet. 2¹⁷, they all owe one another. Hence the description of ταπεινοφροσύνη EN78) in 1 Pet. 5⁵ as the "girdle" with which all Christians are to be girdled in their relationship one to another, setting themselves in the appropriate place. And to the same category there obviously belongs 1 Cor. 1²⁶ᶠ·, the well-known passage on the external aspect of the Christian community: "For ye see your calling, brethren, how that not many wise men after the flesh, not many mighty, not many noble are called; but God hath chosen the foolish things of the world to confound the wise; and God hath chosen the weak things of the world to confound the things which are mighty; and base things of the world, and things which are despised, hath God chosen, yea, and things which are not, to bring to nought things that are: that no flesh should glory in his presence." Why is this necessarily the case? Why is there this radical downward trend? Why do the authors of the First Epistle to Peter (5⁵) and the Epistle of James (4⁶) love that saying from the Proverbs (3³⁴): "God resisteth the proud, but giveth grace to the humble"? Why can Paul (necessarily) write in 1 Cor. 15³¹: "I die daily," and in 2 Cor. 12⁹ᶠ·: "Most gladly therefore will I rather glory in my weakness, that the power of Christ may rest upon me," and: "I take pleasure (εὐδοκῶ) in infirmities, in reproaches, in necessities (ἐν ἀνάγκαις), in persecutions, in distresses for Christ's sake: for when I am weak, then am I strong"? And what is the Word of the Lord addressed to him and heard by him: "My grace is sufficient for thee: for my strength is made perfect (τελεῖται) in weakness"? We see that it is a matter of fellowship with Christ, with His life and finally with His suffering: "Always bearing about in the body the dying (in Gal. 6¹⁷ the marks, στίγματα) of

---

EN71 lowliness of mind
EN72 lowliness of mind
EN73 outwardly
EN74 lofty things
EN75 submission
EN76 obedience
EN77 honour
EN78 lowliness of mind

the Lord Jesus ... always in our mortal flesh delivered unto death for Jesus' sake" (2 Cor. 4$^{10f.}$). The necessity to follow in His steps rests on a looking to Christ and His way as an example (ὑπογραμμός), just as in the First Epistle of Peter (2^{21} and *passim*) we are in the same context compellingly summoned to patience in suffering. Even in 1 Cor. 1$^{26f.}$ it is a matter of the connexion of the communion of the lowly with the crucified Jesus. But what is the authority and force of the law that necessarily leads into this community with Christ?

At this point we are taken beyond the indications which point in this direction in the New Testament Epistles to the (if possible) even more radical and comprehensive sayings of the Gospels. The kind of thing that we already find in Lk. 1^{51} in the Song of Mary even before the birth of Christ: "He hath put down the mighty from their seats, and exalted them of low degree." Why does it say this? Or the saying that we must humble ourselves like a child placed in the midst of adults if we are to be the greatest in the kingdom of heaven (Mt. 18^4). Or the saying in Lk. 14^{11}: "For whosoever exalteth himself shall be abased, and (the second part is remarkably like Phil. 2) he that humbleth himself shall be exalted." Or the similar inversion in Mk. 10^{31}: "But many that are first shall be last and the last first." Or even more sharply in Mk. 8^{35}, the saying about trying to save one's life and losing it, and saving it in losing it for the sake of Jesus and the Gospel. Or in Mk. 8^{34} the saying about the necessity to deny one's self and take up one's cross. Or at the beginning of the Sermon on the Mount (Mt. 5$^{3f.}$) the blessing of the poor in spirit—taken simply as praise of the poor in Luke's Gospel and the Epistle of James—of those that mourn, of the meek, of those that hunger and thirst after righteousness, of the merciful, of those who are persecuted and reviled and slandered for righteousness' sake. Or (in Mt. 5$^{39f.}$) the command not to resist evil, to allow oneself to be smitten on both cheeks, to give one's coat and one's cloak also, and above all, in Mt. 5$^{43f.}$ the injunction to love one's enemies and to pray for one's persecutors. Why is it that here too—and especially here—this is the tenor of New Testament exhortation?

The very strange and yet in some way remarkably illuminating content and the unconditional form of these demands have often been rather idly admired and valued as exemplary, while their manifest impracticability has been indolently affirmed and deplored. As against that, men like Francis of Assissi and Tolstoy and others have called us to take it all quite literally and to put it into practice, and that was obviously the original idea of monasticism in a Church which was being rapidly secularised. Again, it was this which so dreadfully affected the nerves of Nietzsche as the perverse philosophy of the small man triumphing at the time of the decadence of antiquity. Our simple question is: What underlies this conception of human life? What is it that gives to New Testament ethics this direction, this tendency, this dynamic, this pull which in experience has again and again been found to be dominant and exclusive and irresistible, setting aside all pretexts and excuses, the pull from the heights to the depths, from riches to poverty, from victory to defeat, from triumph to suffering, from life to death? This pull is obviously connected with the way and example of Jesus Christ. It is nothing other than the call accepted by the New Testament witnesses, the compulsion which they felt, to enter into and to remain in fellowship with the Crucified. This is clearly enough emphasised in many passages in the New Testament. Col. 1^{24} is a culminating statement with a genuine Pauline flavour. Here the apostle describes his sufferings as a filling up in the place of Christ, an ἀνταναπληροῦν τὰ ὑστερήματα^{EN79}, "of the afflictions of Christ for his body's sake, which is the church." To understand this properly, we must disperse any remaining appearance of chance or arbitrariness with which the whole phenomenon might be enshrouded.

As we have seen, in its ethics the New Testament is speaking in terms of necessity, not of chance or arbitrariness, if in all these sayings—as in those concerning the lowly existence of

---

^{EN79} vicarious filling up of sufferings

the man Jesus as the Son of God—we have to do with a reflection of the New Testament concept of God. If in fellowship with Christ Christians have to be μιμηταὶ θεοῦ [EN80] (Eph. 5¹), if the τελειότης [EN81], the fulfilment of the being and essence, of their heavenly Father is the measure and norm of their own τελειότης [EN82] (Mt. 5⁴⁸), then in its original and final authority and compulsion the demand addressed to them is necessarily this and no other. The περισσόν [EN83], the special thing which is commanded of and has to be done by them as distinct from the publicans and Gentiles, is that which marks them out as the children of the Father in heaven, the περισσόν [EN84] of God Himself which cannot be lacking in His children. God does not love only those who love Him, or greet only His brethren: "He maketh his sun to rise on the evil and on the good, and sendeth rain on the just and on the unjust" (Mt. 5⁴⁵). He obviously does not have to be exalted; He can also be lowly. He does not have to be alone or among friends; He can also be abroad among enemies. He does not have to judge only; He can also forgive. And in being lowly He is exalted. Among His enemies as their God He is supremely exalted. In forgiving He judges in righteousness. As this God, in this divine nature, as the "Father of mercies" (2 Cor. 1³), as the "God that comforteth those that are cast down" (2 Cor. 7⁶), He is the Father of Jesus Christ, the One who in Him reconciles the world to Himself. And as this God He is the Law-giver and Himself the law for those who know Him in Jesus Christ, who can rejoice in their own atonement made in Jesus Christ: those who can recognise themselves as the children of God in Jesus Christ (exalted in Him and by Him). From this point their way leads into the depths, and ταπεινοφροσύνη [EN85] is not to them something strange or remarkable, an ideal which is quite impracticable in its strict sense. It is necessarily that which is natural to them. From this point they cannot choose whether they will exalt or abase themselves, whether they will save their life or lose it and in that way save it, whether they will leave or take up their cross, whether they will be offended by the beatitudes or put themselves under the light of them, whether they will hate their enemies or love them, whether they will accept or not accept the exhortation to ὑποταγή [EN86], to ὑπακοή [EN87], to τιμή [EN88], to the bearing of the burdens of others, to suffering in the discipleship of Christ. This could and would be a matter of choice, and the choice would not be in accordance with the directions of the New Testament, if the God in whose name and authority it is demanded were like the scribes and Pharisees of whom it is said in Mt. 23⁴: "For they bind heavy burdens grievous to be borne, and lay them on men's shoulders; but they themselves will not move them with one of their fingers," or if He were like the doctors who take good care not to take the medicine they prescribe for others, if He had no part in the ταπεινοφροσύνη [EN89] He demands of others, if He were the wholly other God, absolute, high and exalted, far removed from any lowliness and quite alien to it. To achieve the obedience demanded in the New Testament no less than everything depends upon the fact that He is not this God. If He were, then that strange basic feature in New Testament ethics might be regarded as accidental and arbitrary, as facultative and non-obligatory. There would then be good reason to turn this ethics into a moral system, with high praise for its idealism or impatience at its unworldliness and unpractical nature, or perhaps in the form of doubtful

---

[EN80] imitators of God
[EN81] perfection
[EN82] perfection
[EN83] abundance
[EN84] abundance
[EN85] lowliness of mind
[EN86] submission
[EN87] obedience
[EN88] honour
[EN89] lowliness of mind

184

experiments, filling it out from the goodly store of practical wisdom and so reducing it *ad absurdum*[EN90]. According to the New Testament this obviously cannot happen because God does not stand in the far distance high above this ethics, but it is His divine nature to exist in the sense of this ethics, this ethics being only the reflection of His own being. It does not call man under a yoke that He must bear in the name of God because God wills it. It calls him into the freedom of the children of God, into a following of the freedom and the work in which God Himself is God.

Although it has seldom been appealed to in this way. New Testament ethics is an indirect and additional attestation of the true Godhead of Christ. True Godhead in the New Testament is being in the absolute freedom of love, and therefore the being of the Most High who is high and almighty and eternal and righteous and glorious not also but precisely in His lowliness. The direct New Testament attestation of this Godhead of Christ is the attestation of the man Jesus Himself as the Son of God become flesh and suffering and crucified and dying for us, the message of Christ crucified (1 Cor. 1^{23}, 2^2). It is clear that in the sense of the New Testament this and this alone is decisive and basic. There is no lowliness which is divine in itself and as such. There is therefore no general principle of the cross in which we have to do with God (in principle). The cross in the New Testament is not a kind of symbol of an outlook which is negatively orientated, which speculates *à la baisse*[EN91]. The limits of humanity are one thing, but God's visitation of us in the limits of humanity, in our creatureliness, in our humanness, in our sinfulness and mortality, in the incarnation of His Word and the crucifixion of His Son, that is quite another. Salvation is not in those limits, but in the concrete event of this visitation, in what took place in the man Jesus. And the Godhead revealed and active in this event is His Godhead. But the Godhead which the New Testament attests directly as His alone it attests indirectly in the form of the commandment under which it sees His people placed with Him, which it applies to the men of this people. The existential factor in the Christian claim which calls men from the heights to the depths, and therefore to suffering and dying with Christ, is not the first thing in the New Testament but the second, not the *a priori* of the *kerygma*[EN92] but the *a posteriori*. The content of the New Testament *kerygma*[EN93] is in substance the way of Jesus Christ and only in accident the way of the believer in Him. The second stands or falls with the first. First of all Jesus Christ is the Son of God and as such, in conformity with the divine nature, the Most High who humbles Himself and in that way is exalted and very high. Only then are Christians "in Christ," delivered by God "from the power of darkness, and translated into the kingdom of the Son of his love" (Col. 1^{13}). It is only because He is the Son of God in this sense that they are called and empowered in fellowship with Him to choose the ταπεινοφροσύνη[EN94] which is natural to the children of God. Always this second and existential aspect follows and confirms the first. That it should follow and confirm it is necessary, just as it is necessary that there should be this fellowship of man with the God who is in being and essence this God, just as it is necessary that this fellowship should be a fellowship with Christ in whom He has made His being and essence open and accessible to men, just as it is necessary that this fellowship grounded in Him should be lived out by men and put into effect in their existence. The true deity of Christ is to be known and understood and believed and confessed in both the first and the second, the direct and the indirect form, but in this irreversible order and sequence. It is the deity of the true God revealed in the humility of Christ which as such can and must find its

[192]

[EN90] to absurdity
[EN91] with pessimism
[EN92] proclamation
[EN93] proclamation
[EN94] lowliness of mind

confirmation in our own humiliation. But the confirmation is of something which so far as I know Gregory of Nyssa (*Or. Cat.* 24) was the only one of the Church fathers expressly to mention: that the descent to humility which took place in the incarnation of the Word is not only not excluded by the divine nature but signifies its greatest glory: περιουσία τίς ἐστιν τῆς δυνάμεως [EN95].

The way of the Son of God into the far country is the way of obedience. This is (*in re*) the first and inner moment of the mystery of the deity of Christ. Now that we have dealt with the second and outer moment, it is to this that we must turn.

We have seen already that if in faith in Jesus Christ we are ready to learn, to be told, what Godhead, or the divine nature, is, we are confronted with the revelation of what is and always will be to all other ways of looking and thinking a mystery, and indeed a mystery which offends. The mystery reveals to us that for God it is just as natural to be lowly as it is to be high, to be near as it is to be far, to be little as it is to be great, to be abroad as to be at home. Thus that when in the presence and action of Jesus Christ in the world created by Him and characterised *in malam partem* by the sin of man He chooses to go into the far

[193] country, to conceal His form of lordship in the form of this world and therefore in the form of a servant, He is not untrue to Himself but genuinely true to Himself, to the freedom which is that of His love. He does not have to choose and do this. He is free in relation to it. We are therefore dealing with the genuine article when He does choose and do this. Even in the form of a servant, which is the form of His presence and action in Jesus Christ, we have to do with God Himself in His true deity. The humility in which He dwells and acts in Jesus Christ is not alien to Him, but proper to Him. His humility is a *novum mysterium* [EN96] for us in whose favour He executes it when He makes use of His freedom for it, when He shows His love even to His enemies and His life even in death, thus revealing them in a way which is quite contrary to all our false ideas of God. But for Him this humility is no *novum mysterium* [EN97]. It is His sovereign grace that He wills to be and is amongst us in humility, our God, God for us. But He shows us this grace, He is amongst us in humility, our God, God for us, as that which He is in Himself, in the most inward depth of His Godhead. He does not become another God. In the condescension in which He gives Himself to us in Jesus Christ He exists and speaks and acts as the One He was from all eternity and will be to all eternity. The truth and actuality of our atonement depends on this being the case. The One who reconciles the world with God is necessarily the one God Himself in His true Godhead. Otherwise the world would not be reconciled with God. Otherwise it is still the world which is not reconciled with God.

But we must dig deeper if we are to understand the free love of God established in the event of atonement. If the humility of Christ is not simply an

---

[EN95] it is an abundance of power
[EN96] new mystery
[EN97] new mystery

186

attitude of the man Jesus of Nazareth, if it is the attitude of this man because, according to what takes place in the atonement made in this man (according to the revelation of God in Him), there is a humility grounded in the being of God, then something else is grounded in the being of God Himself. For, according to the New Testament, it is the case that the humility of this man is an act of obedience, not a capricious choice of lowliness, suffering and dying, not an autonomous decision this way, not an accidental swing of the pendulum in this direction, but a free choice made in recognition of an appointed order, in execution of a will which imposed itself authoritatively upon Him, which was intended to be obeyed. If, then, God is in Christ, if what the man Jesus does is God's own work, this aspect of the self-emptying and self-humbling of Jesus Christ as an act of obedience cannot be alien to God. But in this case we have to see here the other and inner side of the mystery of the divine nature of Christ and therefore of the nature of the one true God—that He Himself is also able and free to render obedience.

We remember again the prayer in Gethsemane, and also the fact that in Phil. 2^8 His $\tau\alpha\pi\epsilon\iota\nu o\phi\rho o\sigma\acute{\upsilon}\nu\eta$ [EN98] is explained in terms of a becoming obedient, and in Heb. 5^8 His suffering in terms of a learning of obedience. In Heb. 12^3 the fact that He suffered on the cross and despised the shame is described as a $\acute{\upsilon}\pi o\mu\acute{\epsilon}\nu\epsilon\iota\nu$ [EN99] and in Heb. 2^{18} as endurance in temptation. Rom. 5^{19} tells us unmistakably that through the obedience of one many shall be made righteous, and in 2 Cor. 10^5 Paul shows us that it is his aim to bring every thought captive to the $\acute{\upsilon}\pi\alpha\kappa o\grave{\eta}$ $\tau o\hat{\upsilon}$ $X\rho\iota\sigma\tau o\hat{\upsilon}$ [EN100], an expression which surely has to be understood as a *Gen. sub.* as well as a *Gen. obj.* To the same context belongs the fact that there is at least one stratum in the tradition, still maintained in the 2nd century, in which Jesus Christ (Mt. 12^{18}; Ac. $3^{13\ 26}$; $4^{27\ 30}$) is not called $\upsilon\acute{\iota}\acute{o}s$ [EN101], or rather this concept is given a particular nuance in reminiscence of David and the Servant of the Lord (Is. 53) and He is called the holy $\pi\alpha\hat{\iota}s$ $\theta\epsilon o\hat{\upsilon}$ [EN102]. We also remember the pitiless $\delta\epsilon\hat{\iota}$ [EN103] of the Synoptic prophecies of the passion. And it should again be emphasised that the same Gospel of John which leaves no possible doubt about the deity of Christ in His unity with the Father no less plainly—and with particular reference to His way of suffering and death—represents Him as the One who is sent, who has a commission and who has to execute it as such, as the Son who lives to do His Father's will, to speak His words, to accomplish His work and to seek His glory.

[194]

Why is it so important to see that when we say all these things about the man Jesus we say them about God? Obviously because the being of Jesus Christ in humility, His suffering and dying, and therefore the act of atonement made in Him, are marked off by their characterisation as an act of obedience from the accidental events of nature or destiny. Jesus cannot go any other way than this way into the depths, into the far country. And if it is the case that as the Son of God He is not alone on this way, if the Father is on this way with Him (Jn. 16^{32}),

---

EN 98 lowliness of mind
EN 99 perseverance
EN100 obedience of Christ
EN101 Son
EN102 child/servant of God
EN103 it is necessary

if therefore in going this way He acts in the freedom of God, making use of a possibility grounded in the being of God, then the fact that He does so in obedience makes it plain that there is no question of God Himself being controlled by caprice or chance. The freedom in which God can be lowly as well as exalted, abroad as well as at home, our God in the hidden form of One who is accused and judged as well as in Himself (and known only to Himself) the Lord of glory—this freedom of which God makes use in His action as the Reconciler of the world is not simply an arbitrary ability. It is not a mere capacity to be now in this way and now in some other way, now above and now below. It is not a disorderliness and carelessness in God. But if "the Father's Son, by nature God, A guest this world of ours He trod" (Luther), if God made use of His freedom in this sense, then the fact that the use of this freedom is an act of obedience characterises it as a holy and righteous freedom, in which God is not a victim driven to and fro by the dialectic of His divine nature, but is always His own master. He does not make just any use of the possibilities of His divine nature, but He makes one definite use which is necessary on the basis and in fulfilment of His own decision. If this really happens, if God (in virtue of the richness of His divine being) does make it a fact in our history, in the created world and as a temporal event, that He "dwells in the high and holy place, with him also that is of a contrite and humble spirit," if in virtue of His true divine

[195]   nature it is His own good-pleasure actually in this condescension "to revive the spirit of the humble, and to revive the heart of the contrite ones" (Is. 57^{15}), then this is quite in order, since it is His own will which is done, His own plan and decision which is executed. In this happening we have to do with a divine commission and its divine execution, with a divine order and divine obedience. What takes place is the divine fulfilment of a divine decree. It takes place in the freedom of God, but in the inner necessity of the freedom of God and not in the play of a sovereign *liberum arbitrium*[EN104]. There is no possibility of something quite different happening. When we are confronted with this event as the saving event which took place for us, which redeems us, which calls us to faith and penitence, we do not have to do with one of the throws in a game of chance which takes place in the divine being, but with the foundation-rock of a divine decision which is as we find it divinely fulfilled in this saving event and not otherwise. It is therefore worthy of unlimited confidence and only in unlimited confidence can it be appreciated. It can demand obedience because it is not itself an arbitrary decision but a decision of obedience. That is why it is so important to see that this is the character of the self-humiliation of God in Jesus Christ as the presupposition of our reconciliation.

But it is clear that once again, and this time in all seriousness, we are confronted with the mystery of the deity of Christ. Let us grant that this insight is right, that what the New Testament says about the obedience of Christ, on His way as a way of suffering, has its basis, even as a statement about the man Jesus,

---

[EN104] free will

188

in His divine nature and therefore in God Himself. Does this make the mystery of His deity even more difficult and perhaps impenetrable? Or do we have in this insight the real key to an understanding of it, to the knowledge of it as an open secret?

We cannot conceal the fact that it is a difficult and even an elusive thing to speak of obedience which takes place in God Himself. Obedience implies an above and a below, a *prius*[EN105] and a *posterius*[EN106], a superior and a junior and subordinate. Obedience as a possibility and actuality in God Himself seems at once to compromise the unity and then logically the equality of the divine being. Can the one God command and obey? Can the one God be above and below, the superior and the subordinate ? If we speak of an obedience which takes place in God, do we not have to speak necessarily of two divine beings, and then of two beings who are not equally divine, the first and commanding properly divine, the second and obeying only divine in an improper sense? But what is divinity in an improper sense? Even if this second being which is divine in an improper sense is supremely distinguished by the true and proper God both in quality and in orientation to Him, is he not still on the side of the world created by Him and therefore of the reality which is distinct from Him, and therefore not qualified to be the subject of the reconciliation of the world with God?

Subordinationism of every age and type has committed itself to this questionable path. It [196] has solved the mystery of the deity of Christ by dissolving it, by taking the statement about the deity of Christ only in an improper sense, by trying to understand it as the designation of a second divine being of lesser divinity—which, if we follow it through logically, necessarily means the hyperbolic description of a heavenly or earthly creature standing in supreme fellowship with God and to that extent itself supremely qualified. In favour of those who support this view we have to admit that they were obviously impressed by, and tried to take with full seriousness, the witness of the New Testament to the humiliation of Christ and therefore to His lowliness and obedience. But they regarded it as quite impossible to harmonise the assertion of His true deity with this witness. Obstinately preferring this witness, and in order to maintain it, they interpreted the assertion in such a way that its content was explained away and lost. They did not see that in doing this they destroyed the meaning and weight of the witness to the humiliation and the lowliness and the obedience of Christ. If the deity of Christ is interpreted in that way, this obedience acquires the character of an event in this world. But it was and is impossible to see how many can be made righteous by the obedience of a being which is not properly God, of a supremely qualified creature (Rom. 5^{19}). It was and is impossible to see what value or justification there can be for trying to bring every thought captive to the obedience of such a being.

A second alternative which presents itself is as follows. We must certainly accept and take seriously the whole sphere in which we have to speak of a divine obedience, in which, therefore, we have to reckon with an above and a

---

[EN105] before
[EN106] after

below, a *prius*[EN107] and a *posterius*[EN108], a superiority and a subordination in God. We must regard it as a definite sphere of God's revelation, of His speaking and activity and operation. But we must isolate this whole sphere by stating that in it we have to do only with a kind of forecourt of the divine being, with a divine dispensation (economy) in favour of, and with respect to, the particular nature of the world, not therefore with the true and proper and non-worldly being of God. There is, then, a commanding and an obeying divine being, but in a true equality, only as worldly forms or appearances of true Godhead, and therefore only in the sphere of the improper being of Godhead. But that is the weakness of this explanation. For obviously we have to ask what is this worldly, and purely economic, and therefore improper being of the true God. If His economy of revelation and salvation is distinguished from His proper being as worldly, does it bring us into touch with God Himself or not? Has He Himself really taken up the cause of the world or not? Has He really made Himself worldly for the world's sake or not? Obviously, according to this theory, He has not done so. In fact He has only acted as though He had done so. But if He has not, how can there be on this theory any reconciliation of the world with God?

[197]

We are referring to a solution—the direct opposite of Subordinationism—which has been attempted both in ancient and more modern times along the lines of Modalism. The main point of Modalism is to try to keep the true deity of the humiliated and lowly and obedient Christ, but to interpret the being of this Christ as a mere mode of appearance or revelation or activity of the one true Godhead, beside which there are the other modes of the ruling Father and also of the Holy Spirit. Sometimes, indeed, it is preferred, as it was originally, to identify God the Father with the true Godhead which does not appear in this world. On this view Christ is not deprived of true deity, but of any true and proper being. The drift is obvious. We must maintain the true deity of Christ as identical with the Godhead of the Father, but only in such a way that no hurt is done to His deity by His humiliation, lowliness and obedience. Hence the distinction between a proper and an improper being of God, an immanent and a purely economic. Hence the true deity of Christ only in this second sense, only in the forecourt of the divine being, only as a mode of appearance of the true Godhead which is untouched by this dualism of above and below. Unfortunately it was not noticed that in this way the meaning and relevance of the statement maintained against the Subordinationists were compromised, and it was no less emptied of force than on the opposite side where it was explained and ultimately explained away. For if in His proper being as God God can only be unworldly, if He can be the humiliated and lowly and obedient One only in a mode of appearance and not in His proper being, what is the value of the true deity of Christ, what is its value for us? It is as the humiliated and lowly and obedient One that He is the Reconciler. But can He reconcile if He has no proper being as the Reconciler, but only that of a form of appearance of the one true God, who has no part in the atonement?

These two attempts at a solution were often made in the 2nd and 3rd centuries in relatively harmless, because inconsistent and ambiguous, forms. We find both of them in acknowledged teachers of the Church: a kind of Subordinationism in Tertullian, for example, and a kind of Modalism in Irenaeus. Both were finally rejected as unsatisfactory by

---

[EN107] before
[EN108] after

the early Church. In their developed form (in the doctrine of Paul of Samosata, on the one hand, and that of Sabellius on the other) they were recognised to be heretical, being condemned as errors in which we cannot do justice to the mystery of the deity of Christ.

The questions raised by these two solutions are questions which we cannot evade. It will be wiser, then, not to try to circumvent the difficulty as these two solutions did, but to engage it in frontal assault.

Let us first review the three presuppositions which, at all costs, we must accept and affirm.

It is a matter (1) of determining the acting subject of the reconciliation of the world with God. According to the witness of the New Testament, when we have to do with Jesus Christ we are dealing with the author and finisher of this work, with the Mediator between God and man, with the One who makes peace between the two, with no other and no less than the One who has taken upon Himself and away from the world the enmity of the world against God and the curse which rests upon it, with the One who (we shall treat of this in the second part of the section) accomplishes the ineluctable judgment of the world in such a way that He Himself bears it in order to bear it away. We have to do with the One who has the competence and power for this work. In relation to the fact that He is the One who does this, the New Testament witness to His deity has to be understood and taken seriously as expressed in the different titles under which it speaks of Him. Everything depends upon our seeing and understanding as the New Testament does that He is the acting subject in this work. If we grant that we are at one with the New Testament in this, we must [198] also follow it in seeing the true God at work in Him. In matters of the atonement of the world with God the world itself cannot act—for it is the world which is at enmity with God, which stands in need of reconciliation with Him. It cannot act even in the form of a supreme and best being produced by it and belonging to it. Anyone other or less than the true God is not a legitimate subject competent to act in this matter. At this point the subordinationist interpretation is evasive. And it has to be rejected as unsatisfactory. When we have to do with Jesus Christ we have to do with God. What He does is a work which can only be God's own work, and not the work of another.

But (2) it is a matter of the subject of the atonement as an event which takes place not only to the world but in the world, which not only touches the world from without but affects it from within to convert it to God, which is itself an event in the world. According to the witness of the New Testament, the world is not abandoned and left to its own devices. God takes it to Himself, entering into the sphere of it as the true God, causing His kingdom to come on earth as in heaven, becoming Himself truly ours, man, flesh, in order to overcome sin where it has its dominion, in the flesh, to take away in His own person the ensuing curse where it is operative, in the creaturely world, in the reality which is distinct from Himself. It is in relation to the fact that what He does in the atonement He does in this way, in the power of His own presence and action, that we have to take seriously the New Testament witness to the being of the one true God in Jesus Christ; the realistic and not the nominalistic sense in which it accords these titles to Jesus Christ, whatever they are and however their formulation may be taken. Again everything depends on our accepting and following out in all its realism the New Testament presupposition "God was in Christ." If we grant this—as the *credo*[EN109] of Christian confession assumes—we have to follow the New Testament in understanding the presence and action of God in Jesus Christ as the most proper and direct and immediate presence and action of the one true God in the sphere of human and world-history. If this is not so, then as the subject of the act of atonement He can only touch the world from without, not affect it from within, not truly convert it to Himself. It would not, therefore, be a real reconciliation of the world with Him. At this point the modalistic interpretation of the deity of Christ is evasive. And for that reason it must be regarded as unsatisfactory and rejected. When we have to do with Jesus Christ we do have to do with an "economy" but not with the kind of economy in which His true and proper being remains behind an improper being, a being "as if." We have to do with an economy in which God is truly Himself and Himself acts and intervenes in the world. Otherwise the atonement made in this economy is not a true atonement.

[199]   It is a matter (3)—and this is the connecting point—of the one true God being Himself the subject of the act of atonement in such a way that His presence and action as the Reconciler of the world coincide and are indeed identical with the existence of the humiliated and lowly and obedient man Jesus of Nazareth. He acts as the Reconciler in that—as the true God identical with this man—He humbles Himself and becomes lowly and obedient. He becomes and is this without being in contradiction to His divine nature (He is not therefore exposed to the postulate that He can become and be this only as a creature), but in contradiction to all human ideas about the divine nature. He becomes and is this without encroaching on Himself (He is not subject to the postulate that He can become and be this only improperly, in an appearance which is alien to His own being), but as a saving approach to us, an encroachment upon us which is authoritative and demands our conversion. According to the New Testament witness we have the presence and action not only of the man Jesus, but in the existence of that man the action and presence which is supremely proper to God Himself as the Reconciler of the world. God chooses condescension. He chooses humiliation, lowliness and obedience. In this way He illuminates the darkness, opening up that which is closed. In this way He brings help where there is no other help. In this way He accepts solidarity with the creature, with man, in order to reconcile man and the world with Himself, in order to convert man and the world to Himself. The God of the New Testament witness is the God who makes this choice, who in agreement with Himself and His divine nature, but in what is for us the revelation of a *novum*

[EN109] 'I believe'

mysterium[EN110], humbles Himself and is lowly and obedient amongst us. In this respect, too, the New Testament witness has to be taken seriously. Everything depends on our accepting this presupposition, on our seeing and understanding what the New Testament witnesses obviously saw and understood, the proper being of the one true God in Jesus Christ the Crucified. Granted that we do see and understand this, we cannot refuse to accept the humiliation and lowliness and supremely the obedience of Christ as the dominating moment in our conception of God. Therefore we must determine to seek and find the key to the whole difficult and heavily freighted concept of the "divine nature" at the point where it appears to be quite impossible—except for those whose thinking is orientated on Him in this matter—the fact that Jesus Christ was obedient unto death, even the death of the cross. It is from this point, and this point alone, that the concept is legitimately possible.

We can now see the error which is common to the subordinationist and the modalist presentation and solution of the problem. Both suffer from the fact that they try to evade the cross of Jesus Christ, i.e., the truth of the humiliation, the lowliness and the obedience of the one true God Himself as it became an event amongst us in Jesus Christ as the subject of the reconciliation of the [200] world with God. They evade it because they start from the assumption that it cannot be accepted as true. And they then err in their different ways as they try to escape the dilemma which they themselves have created, interpreting the obedient Christ either as some heavenly or earthly being distinct from God, or as a mere mode of appearance of the one true God. Both damage and indeed destroy the nerve of the New Testament knowledge of Christ. Both solve the christological mystery by juggling it away, and for that reason both show themselves to be quite useless.

They were both rightly rejected by the early Church. We can add that in the first instance they could both be undertaken in good faith, because even serious and perspicacious theologians of both schools did not at first see that they were in fact taking offence where no offence must be taken, and that by trying to remove the offence they were compromising the very centre of all Christian knowledge. We can also add that the attempts had to be made because only then could their unsatisfactory character be exposed. If they had not been made, the possibility of evasion in one or other of these directions would have worked like an arrested fever in the thought of the Church. In the history of theology and dogma there have been many such blind alleys which had to be followed to the point where they proved to be such in order that they should no longer be confused with the right way, and in order to make necessary and to stir up a search for the right way. This is the relative necessity more than once ascribed to heresy by the fathers. In fact, Athanasius and Nicaea would not have been possible without the obscurities and errors of the 2nd and 3rd centuries.

It is another question to maintain, and to make again as we ought, the distinction between the right and the wrong path as it was made by Athanasius and at Nicaea. The blind alleys are always there, and have proved attractive again and again as they still do to-day. The warning signs set up at the entrance to them can easily be overlooked, and have often been overlooked. The right way found at that time can still be lost again, and has from time to time

---

[EN110] new mystery

been lost. Subordinationism and Modalism, the teachings of Paul of Samosata and Sabellius, are not dead, and by nature we all of us incline to one or the other or perhaps both in some form. We have continually to seek afresh for the right way in thankfulness for what has been known and stated. That is what we have tried to do here. We shall not serve the cause of the recognition which is necessary in the Church to-day simply by retreating or paraphrasing or commentating on the decision which brought the controversy to the 2nd and 3rd centuries to a victorious end. We are reminded by Nicaea in which direction we have to look. Our own conclusions, which are formally independent of the dogma proclaimed there, have inclined us to look in the same direction. We will now try to go further in this direction, not losing contact with the dogma but again following our own path.

Is it a fact that in relation to Jesus Christ we can speak of an obedience of the one true God Himself in His proper being? From the three inalienable presuppositions just expounded it is plain that we not only can do so but have to do so, that we cannot avoid doing so either on the one side or on the other. We have not only not to deny but actually to affirm and understand as essential to the being of God the offensive fact that there is in God Himself an above and a

[201] below, a *prius*[EN111] and a *posterius*[EN112], a superiority and a subordination. And our present concern is with what is apparently the most offensive fact of all, that there is a below, a *posterius*[EN113], a subordination, that it belongs to the inner life of God that there should take place within it obedience.

We have to reckon with such an event even in the being and life of God Himself. It cannot be explained away either as an event in some higher or supreme creaturely sphere or as a mere appearance of God. Therefore we have to state firmly that, far from preventing this possibility, His divine unity consists in the fact that in Himself He is both One who is obeyed and Another who obeys.

There is another thing outside of God, the world created by Him as the totality of the reality willed and posited by Him and distinct from Him. In this totality as His elect creature there is another person, His worldly counterpart κατ᾽ ἐξοχήν[EN114] man, who, according to Gen. 1^{27}, is in his twofoldness as man and woman the image of God, the image primarily of His co-existence as Creator with the creature, His will not to be alone as God, but to be together with His creature, the God of His creature—yet not merely the image of this relationship *ad extra*[EN115]. God did not need this otherness of the world and man. In order not to be alone, single, enclosed within Himself, God did not need co-existence with the creature. He does not will and posit the creature necessarily, but in freedom, as the basic act of His grace. His whole relationship to what is outside Himself—its basis and history from first to last—rests on this fact. For everything that the creature seems to offer Him—its otherness, its being in antithesis to Himself and therefore His own existence in

---

EN111 before
EN112 after
EN113 after
EN114 pre-eminently
EN115 outside of himself

co-existence—He has also in Himself as God, as the original and essential determination of His being and life as God. Without the creature He has all this originally in Himself, and it is His free grace, and not an urgent necessity to stand in a relationship of reciprocity to something other outside Himself, if He allows the creature to participate in it, if, as it were, in superfluity He allows its existence as another, as a counterpart to Himself, and His own co-existence with it. In superfluity—we have to say this because we are in fact dealing with an overflowing, not with a filling up of the perfection of God which needs no filling.

Primarily and originally and properly it is not the cosmos or man which is the other, the counterpart of God, that which co-exists with God. Primarily and originally and properly God is all this in Himself. He does not need on this account to divide into two gods of unequal divinity. That is how myth would have it, confusing the world and man with God, and carrying its own inner differentiation into the Godhead, speaking of the co-existence and reciprocity of a superior god in heaven and a subordinate goddess of earth. No, not in unequal but equal, not in divided but in the one deity, God is both One and also Another, His own counterpart, co-existent with Himself. We can say quite calmly: He exists as a first and as a second, above and below *a priori*[EN116] and *a posteriori*[EN117]. To grasp this we have to free ourselves from two unfortunate and very arbitrary ways of thinking. [202]

The first consists quite naturally in the idea that unity is necessarily equivalent with being in and for oneself, with being enclosed and imprisoned in one's own being, with singleness and solitariness. But the unity of God is not like this. It is, of course, exclusively His unity. No other being, no created being, is one with itself as God is. But what distinguishes His peculiar unity with Himself from all other unities or from what we think we know of such unities is the fact that—in a particularity which is exemplary and instructive for an understanding of these others—it is a unity which is open and free and active in itself—a unity in more than one mode of being, a unity of the One with Another, of a first with a second, an above with a below, an origin and its consequences. It is a dynamic and living unity, not a dead and static. Once we have seen this, we will be careful not to regard that mean and unprofitable concept of unity as the last word of wisdom and the measure of all things. And its application to God will be ruled out once and for all.

The second idea we have to abandon is that—even supposing we have corrected that unsatisfactory conception of unity—there is necessarily something unworthy of God and incompatible with His being as God in supposing that there is in God a first and a second, an above and a below, since this includes a gradation, a degradation and an inferiority in God, which if conceded

---

[EN116] before
[EN117] after

excludes the *homoousia*[EN118] of the different modes of divine being. That all sounds very illuminating. But is it not an all too human—and therefore not a genuinely human—way of thinking? For what is the measure by which it measures and judges? Has there really to be something mean in God for Him to be the second, below? Does subordination in God necessarily involve an inferiority, and therefore a deprivation, a lack? Why not rather a particular being in the glory of the one equal Godhead, in whose inner order there is also, in fact, this dimension, the direction downwards, which has its own dignity? Why should not our way of finding a lesser dignity and significance in what takes the second and subordinate place (the wife to her husband) need to be corrected in the light of the *homoousia*[EN119] of the modes of divine being?

As we look at Jesus Christ we cannot avoid the astounding conclusion of a divine obedience. Therefore we have to draw the no less astounding deduction that in equal Godhead the one God is, in fact, the One and also Another, that He is indeed a First and a Second, One who rules and commands in majesty and One who obeys in humility. The one God is both the one and the other. And, we continue, He is the one and the other without any cleft or differentiation but in perfect unity and equality because in the same perfect unity and equality He is also a Third, the One who affirms the one and equal

[203] Godhead through and by and in the two modes of being, the One who makes possible and maintains His fellowship with Himself as the one and the other. In virtue of this third mode of being He is in the other two without division or contradiction, the whole God in each. But again in virtue of this third mode of being He is in neither for itself and apart from the other, but in each in its relationship to the other, and therefore, in fact, in the totality, the connexion, the interplay, the history of these relationships. And because all division and contradiction is excluded, there is also excluded any striving to identify the two modes of being, or any possibility of the one being absorbed by the other, or both in their common deity. God is God in these two modes of being which cannot be separated, which cannot be autonomous, but which cannot cease to be different. He is God in their concrete relationships the one to the other, in the history which takes place between them. He is God only in these relationships and therefore not in a Godhead which does not take part in this history, in the relationships of its modes of being, which is neutral towards them. This neutral Godhead, this pure and empty Godhead, and its claim to be true divinity, is the illusion of an abstract "monotheism" which usually fools men most successfully at the high-water mark of the development of heathen religions and mythologies and philosophies. The true and living God is the One whose Godhead consists in this history, who is in these three modes of being the One God, the Eternal, the Almighty, the Holy, the Merciful, the One who loves in His freedom and is free in His love.

[EN118] consubstantiality
[EN119] consubstantiality

And His speaking and activity and work *ad extra*[EN120] consist in the fact that He gives to the world created by Him, to man, a part in the history in which He is God, that there is primarily in the work of creation a reflection, in the antithesis of Creator and creature an image and likeness, and in the twofoldness of the existence of man a reflection of this likeness of the inner life of God Himself. And then supremely and finally (at the goal and end of His whole activity as established at its beginning) they consist in the fact that God Himself becomes a man amongst men in His mode of being as the One who is obedient in humility. In the work of the reconciliation of the world with God the inward divine relationship between the One who rules and commands in majesty and the One who obeys in humility is identical with the very different relationship between God and one of His creatures, a man. God goes into the far country for this to happen. He becomes what He had not previously been. He takes into unity with His divine being a quite different, a creaturely and indeed a sinful being. To do this He empties Himself, He humbles Himself. But, as in His action as Creator, He does not do it apart from its basis in His own being, in His own inner life. He does not do it without any correspondence to, but as the strangely logical final continuation of, the history in which He is God. He does not need to deny, let alone abandon and leave behind or even diminish His Godhead to do this. He does not need to leave the work of the Reconciler [204] in the doubtful hands of a creature. He can enter in Himself, seeing He is in Himself not only the One who rules and commands in majesty, but also in His own divine person, although in a different mode of being, the One who is obedient in humility. It is the free grace of the atonement that He now not only reflects His inner being as God as He did in creation, that He not only represents it in a likeness as He did in the relationship of Creator and creature, but that He causes it to take outward form in itself and as such. In His mode of being as the One who is obedient in humility He wills to be not only the one God but this man, and this man as the one God. He does not owe this to the creaturely world. He does not owe it even to Himself. He owes it just as little and even less than He did the creation. Neither in the one case nor in the other—and even less in this case—can there be any question of the necessary working of an inward divine mechanism, or a mechanism which controls the relationship of God and the world. God gives Himself to the world in coming to the world as its Reconciler. But He can give Himself to it. He is His own master in such a way that He can go into the far country to do it. He does not need to cease to be radically and totally above, the first, in order to become radically and totally below, the second. Even below, as this second, He is one with Himself, equal with Himself as God. He does not change in giving Himself. He simply activates and reveals Himself *ad extra*[EN121], in the world. He is in and for the world what He is in and for Himself. He is in time what He is in

---

[EN120] outside of himself
[EN121] outside of himself

eternity (and what He can be also in time because of His eternal being). He is in our lowliness what He is in His majesty (and what He can be also in our lowliness because His majesty is also lowliness). He is as man, as the man who is obedient in humility, Jesus of Nazareth, what He is as God (and what He can be also as man because He is it as God in this mode of divine being). That is the true deity of Jesus Christ, obedient in humility, in its unity and equality, its *homoousia*[EN122], with the deity of the One who sent Him and to whom He is obedient.

Up to this point we have refrained from using the concepts which dominate the New Testament and ecclesiastical dogma. Our first task has been to show what is their place and purpose in our present context. We can now introduce them. Jesus Christ is the Son of God who became man, who as such is One with God the Father, equal to Him in deity, by the Holy Spirit, in whom the Father affirms and loves Him and He the Father, in a mutual fellowship.

> For the basis and development and explanation of the doctrine of the Trinity in its own context and in all its details, and for an understanding of its exegetical and historical implications, we must refer back to *C.D.* I, 1 § 8–12. We have here approached this first and final Christian truth from a special standpoint, and in this context we can speak of it only briefly, selectively, and in a limited way.

[205] By Father, Son and Spirit we do not mean what is commonly suggested to us by the word "persons." This designation was accepted —not without opposition—on linguistic presuppositions which no longer obtain to-day. It was never intended to imply—at any rate in the main stream of theological tradition—that there are in God three different personalities, three self-existent individuals with their own special self-consciousness, cognition, volition, activity, effects, revelation and name. The one name of the one God is the threefold name of Father, Son and Holy Spirit. The one "personality" of God, the one active and speaking divine Ego, is Father, Son and Holy Spirit. Otherwise we should obviously have to speak of three gods. And this is what the early Church not only would not do, but in the conception of the doctrine of the Trinity which ultimately prevailed tried expressly to exclude, just as it did any idea of a division or inequality between Father, Son and Holy Spirit. Christian faith and the Christian confession has one Subject, not three. But He is the one God in self-repetition, in the repetition of His own and equal divine being, and therefore in three different modes of being—which the term "person" was always explained to mean. He does not exist as such outside or behind or above these modes of being. He does not exist otherwise than as Father, Son and Holy Spirit. He exists in their mutual interconnexion and relationship. He exists in their difference, not in their identity: the Father in His mode as the Father of the Son; the Son in His as the Son of the Father; the Spirit in His as the Spirit of the Father and the Son. He is not threefold, but trine, triune, i.e., in three

---

[EN122] consubstantiality

different modes the one personal God, the one Lord, the one Creator, the one Reconciler, the one Perfecter and Redeemer. He is all this as He is Father, Son and Holy Spirit. He is it in the relationships to Himself thereby posited. His being as God is His being in His own history.

The terms for these modes of being in which God is God are human terms, the best possible, but inadequate approximations, attempts to describe what since the New Testament has always been found in God on the basis of the revelation which takes place in His action, which we cannot therefore pass over in silence, let alone deny, but are forced to confess. The Church has always known and constantly stated that it cannot in these terms reach or comprehend or exhaust the sense of what it knows in faith. It has always confessed the incomprehensibility of God. And it has always made this clear in its understanding of the triune being of God and especially of His three modes of being. It has been well aware that in these terms it can only aim at the real thing which is in question.

This is also true of that description of Jesus Christ as the Son of God which particularly concerns us. There can be no doubt that linguistically the New Testament took over this term from the Old, although there was, of course, a certain co-operation and stimulation from the Hellenistic environment, and some regard for the concepts more or less current within it. And it is no accident that of all the titles used of Jesus Christ in the New Testament sphere it [206] was that of Son which came to the forefront when it was desired to refer to His being as revealed in His activity from the standpoint of its origin; when it was intended to describe Him as the One who in a particular and unique way had come from God, who was revealing God, who belonged wholly and directly to God, who was united with God; when it was purposed to refer to the deity of the subject by which we are here confronted. Even in the creeds it is this title which takes precedence in the second article: Jesus Christ is the Son of God, and as such He is the Lord (as we are told in the enlarged and completed creed of 381). He is "of one substance with the Father, by Whom all things were made, who for us men and for our salvation came down from heaven, and was made man"—*et incarnatus est*[EN123]—who as such is the subject of all the events that follow, who as such is *conceptus de Spiritu Sancto, natus ex Maria virgine*[EN124], who as such is crucified, risen and seated at the right hand of the Father, who as such will come again to judge the quick and the dead. He is all this, and He does all this divine work, because He is the Son of God, the only Son, the only begotten Son of God, *Filius Dei unicus*, as was added from the very first (cf. Jn. 1$^{14-18}$) in order to distinguish Him from others who were given this title, in order to distinguish Him even from Christians who are called by this name as they are exalted to be His brethren, in order to bring out the singularity and the uniqueness of this subject and therefore of His work.

[EN123] and became flesh
[EN124] conceived of the Holy Spirit, born of the Virgin Mary

But what does it mean: the Son of God? We do not ask what the strange conjunction of these two words may or can mean in any reference, but what they do mean in reference to Jesus Christ, as a description of what He was and is and will be. What does the New Testament mean, and what did the early Church mean, when in an emphatic way and at a decisive point—as though it were the key to the whole—it gave Him this title? What can we try to mean and say when we accept the confession: Amen, yes, Jesus Christ is the only Son of God?

It certainly will not serve any useful purpose to burden the New Testament, or the Church which followed it, or ourselves, with the idea that Jesus Christ as the Son of God is begotten in time, in an event in which God does that which makes a man a father, and that He was born in consequence of this event as such. When we are dealing with Jesus Christ there is no question of a temporal event in which He began to be the Son of God, of an action on the part of God like that of a human father in which He began to be the Father of this Son, and therefore of a so-called "physical divine Sonship" of Jesus Christ in the fairly well-known sense of so many mythologies. The New Testament and the Church never understood His Sonship in this way. Even in the light of the Old Testament it was impossible to think along these lines. And what confronted [207] the New Testament witnesses and through them the Church, what laid the term "Son of God" on their lips as they looked at Jesus Christ, compelled them to exclude this idea and to think on quite different lines. There is therefore no reason to pursue this thought.

It would have to be imported into the passages in Mt. 1$^{18-25}$ and Lk. 1$^{26-38}$ and the credal statement about the Virgin birth in the creeds founded on these passages (cf. for what follows *C.D.* I, 2 § 15, 2). And careful exegesis and dogmatics have always safeguarded them against this importation. In the creeds the assertion of the Virgin Birth is plainly enough characterised as a first statement about the One who was and is and will be the Son of God. It is not a statement about how He became this, a statement concerning the basis and condition of His divine Sonship. It is a description of the way in which the Son of God became man. The New Testament and the early Church never understood the relationship between the Holy Spirit and the Virgin Mary in mythical fashion as a ἱερὸς γάμος EN125. The Holy Spirit has never been regarded or described by any serious Christian theologian as the divine Father even of the man Jesus. In the exposition of this dogma—and thoroughly in the sense of its New Testament presuppositions—it has been frequently and energetically explained that it might have pleased God to let His Son become man in some quite different way than in the event of the miracle attested as the Virgin birth. It did in fact please Him to let Him become man in this way, but this event is not the basis of the fact that the One who there became man was the Son of God. It is the sign which accompanies and indicates the mystery of the incarnation of the Son, marking it off as a mystery from all the beginnings of other human existences. It consists in a creative act of divine omnipotence, in which the will and work of man in the form of a human father is completely excluded from the basis and beginning of the human existence of the Son of God, being replaced by a divine act which is supremely unlike any human action which might arise in that connexion, and in that way

---

EN125 holy marriage

characterised as an inconceivable act of grace. "Conceived by the Holy Ghost" does not, therefore, mean "begotten by the Holy Ghost." It means that God Himself—acting directly in His own and not in human fashion—stands at the beginning of this human existence and is its direct author. It is He who gives to man in the person of Mary the capacity which man does not have of himself, which she does not have and which no man could give her. It is He who sanctifies and ordains her the human mother of His Son. It is He who makes His Son hers, and in that way shares with humanity in her person nothing less than His own existence. He gives to her what she could not procure for herself and no other creature could procure for her. This is the miracle of the Virgin birth as it indicates the mystery of the incarnation, the first attestation of the divine Sonship of the man Jesus of Nazareth, comparable with the miracle of the empty tomb at His exodus from temporal existence. The question is pertinent whether His divine Sonship and the mystery of His incarnation are known in any real seriousness and depth when these attestations of it are unrecognised or overlooked or denied or explained away. But in any case these attestations are based on His divine Sonship, not His divine Sonship on these attestations. They have a great deal to do with it noetically, but nothing at all ontically.

To answer our question concerning the sense in which Jesus Christ is called and is the Son of God, we have to look in another direction altogether. And why not in the direction in which we have constantly looked from the very first? So far we have tried to understand Jesus Christ as the One who humbles Himself, as the One who is obedient in humility, and therefore as the fulfilment of the Old Testament concept of a Son. In His being and activity, in His [208] suffering and dying as this obedient One, He is quite different from all other men. He is a man, but quite unlike all other men. He is among men, yet in contrast to all other men He is at the side of God. In His human person He is the kingdom of God come down from heaven to earth. This kingdom (the power of God exercised by Him as Lord, His glory as King) is incorporated and truly present and active in Him. It has truly and actually become flesh in Him. And it has done so because He is simply but totally its first and proper subject, because He realises perfectly the ὑπακοή EN126 and ὑποταγή EN127 and τιμή EN128 which correspond to the perfect lordship of God as its necessary complement. He sets up the lordship of God and reveals it in the quite free but quite necessary decision, in the determination which is native to Him and therefore utterly natural, to go the way of the servant of God, the way downwards, to lowliness and finally to the cross. He activates and reveals the unconditional royal power of God by living it out unconditionally as man; in its likeness, in its correspondence, as it must be lived out on earth and among us men if there is to be a reconciliation of the world with God. The image, the correspondence in which He has set it up and revealed it among us, for our salvation, for the reconciliation of the world with man, is, however, His obedience in humility. What the whole world lacks, what it cannot produce of itself—as a creature and especially as a sinful creature—is this complement,

---

EN126 obedience
EN127 submission
EN128 honour

this obedience which corresponds to the lordship of God and reflects it. Jesus Christ achieves it. He does so self-evidently, naturally, in His own freedom, and therefore perfectly. He knows and goes this way alone. He enters and treads it without ever missing the way, without ever making any mistakes, pursuing it to the very end. It is His whole being to be this obedient One. This is what distinguishes Him from all creatures either in heaven or earth. This is what proves Him to be the Mediator between God and man. This is what proves Him to be the Son of God. It is as the One who proves Himself to be the Son of God by entering this way that He is attested by the miracle of the Virgin birth; and by the miracle of the empty tomb He is attested as the One who has pursued this way to the bitter end.

But in this way He does show Himself to be the Son of God. In this way He is the Son of God made flesh. The fact that He shows Himself to be the Son of God in this way does not mean that He becomes the Son of God thereby, let alone by the miracle which attests Him as such. He shows Himself the One He is by the obedience which He renders as man. And His unconditional, self-evident, natural and wholly spontaneous being in obedience is just as little the affair of a man, or of a creature generally, as the unconditional lordship to which this being corresponds, and which He reflects in it, can ever be the affair of a man or of any creature. In rendering obedience as He does, He does [209] something which, as in the case of that lordship, only God can do. The One who in this obedience is the perfect image of the ruling God is Himself—as distinct from every human and creaturely kind—God by nature, God in His relationship to Himself, i.e., God in His mode of being as the Son in relation to God in His mode of being as the Father, One with the Father and of one essence. In His mode of being as the Son He fulfils the divine subordination, just as the Father in His mode of being as the Father fulfils the divine superiority. In humility as the Son who complies, He is the same as is the Father in majesty as the Father who disposes. He is the same in consequence (and obedience) as the Son as is the Father in origin. He is the same as the Son, i.e., as the self-posited God (the eternally begotten of the Father as the dogma has it) as is the Father as the self-positing God (the Father who eternally begets). Moreover in His humility and compliance as the Son He has a supreme part in the majesty and disposing of the Father. The Father as the origin is never apart from Him as the consequence, the obedient One. The self-positing God is never apart from Him as the One who is posited as God by God. The One who eternally begets is never apart from the One who is eternally begotten. Nor is the latter apart from the former. The Father is not the Father and the Son is not the Son without a mutual affirmation and love in the Holy Spirit. The Son is therefore the One who in His obedience, as a divine and not a human work, shows and affirms and activates and reveals Himself—shows Himself to be the One He is—not another, a second God, but the Son of God, the one God in His mode of being as the Son.

It is clear that this brings us to the final meaning and limit of the term "Son of God" as used in relation to Jesus Christ.

What we call "Son" points in the right direction, but does not reach the fulness of what is here in question and what the term is meant to convey here. What the term can convey is the natural determination of a son to subjection to a father, the self-evident presupposition that a son owes obedience to a father, the mutual relationship revealed in what a father can expect and demand of a son and also in the way in which a son has to respect the will of his father. And the unity of the will and aims of a father and a son rests on the fact that there is a close relationship between them, that the one cannot be the father without his son, nor the other the son without his father.

But the term cannot bring out the ontological necessity in which this Father has this Son, and this Son this Father, the perfection in which this Father and this Son are one, i.e., are the different modes of being of one and the same personal God, the eternity of the fatherly begetting and of the being begotten of the Son, which is the basis of their relationship, their free but also necessary fellowship and love in the activity of the Holy Spirit as the third divine mode of being of the same kind, the self-evident fulfilment of that determination of a son to his father, the actual rendering of a perfect obedience, the ceaseless [210] unity of the One who disposes and the One who complies, the actual oneness and agreement of that which they will and do. The history in which God is the living God in Himself can only be indicated but not conceived by our terms son and father and spirit.

The sense in which the New Testament speaks of men as the "children of the kingdom" (Mt. 8^{12}), the "children of the resurrection" (Lk. 20^{36}), the "children of promise" (Gal. 4^{28}), the "children of light" (Jn. 12^{36}; Eph. 5^9), or the "children of the day" (1 Thess. 5^5), or on the other side as the "children of unbelief" or the "children of wrath" (Eph. 2$^{2f.}$), or even the "children of the devil" (1 Jn. 3^{10}), does, of course, include within it something of the relationship, the dependence, the subordination, the good or evil love, the good or evil obedience, in which these men may find themselves to forces of a *quasi* fatherly character. But even formally it does not attain to what the New Testament means when it calls Jesus Christ the Son of God. Therefore it can be used as an analogy only with the greatest caution. The same is true of the description of Christians as the "children of your Father in heaven" (Mt. 5^{45}) or the "children of God," which presupposes the incomparable and in the last resort inconceivable divine sonship of the one Jesus Christ. We are called the sons of God, and in our own way are the sons of God, only because in His own way, for which there are ultimately no analogies, Jesus Christ is the Son of God.

As applied to Jesus Christ we can legitimately call the term "Son of God" a true but inadequate and an inadequate but true insight and statement. This means that on the one side we can be sure that the term as applied in this way does correspond to its object, that it does express it, that it is therefore true, that it tells us what Jesus Christ in fact is. We have no better term, and this one forces itself necessarily upon us. From the standpoint from which we have tried to understand Jesus Christ it is very suitable and indeed indispensable if we are to say what has to be said concerning His deity. It is quite right that it should have acquired its very particular importance and role in the New Testament and in the language of the later Church. It confesses the filial thing that we have to confess of Him, and therefore necessarily it takes the first place. But it confesses it in the way that we men can confess the mystery to which it points. As a true description of Jesus Christ it goes far beyond anything that it can say in any other application. As applied to this "Son" it is in a certain sense burst wide open, and can be thought through to the end only as we bring into it meanings which it cannot have in any other use which we can make of it. As applied in this way it deserves our every confidence because it is true, but it must be used with great reserve because of its inadequacy. And is it not fitting that the true deity of the One who is obedient in humility, of the Son who is in this way the only begotten Son of the Father, wills to be known and can be known only in this way—with every confidence but also with great modesty? For in this matter, as others, what can all our Christian statements be but a serious pointing away to the One who will Himself tell those who have ears to hear who He is?

[211]   2. THE JUDGE JUDGED IN OUR PLACE

When I formulated this title I first thought of *Qu.* 52 of the *Heidelberg Catechism*, in which the returning Christ is called the judge who "has represented me before the judgment of God, and has taken away all cursing from me," whom the Christian can therefore await "with uplifted head in every affliction and persecution." From the passage in *Melito of Sardis (fragm.* 13), which I quoted in another connexion (p. 176), and which sets at the head of a whole string of paradoxes the statement: *judex judicatur et quietus est*[EN129], I realised that we are dealing with a thought which was not unknown to the early Church. A well-versed patristic scholar who heard my lecture on this theme has pointed out to me that at the head of a similar string Eusebius of Emesa (ed. E. M. Buytaert, 1949, 72) also wrote: *judex noster judicatus est, vita morti tradita est, cibans universum fuit in fame*[EN130], and also that Athanasius (presupposing the genuineness of the tractate on "The Cunning of the Devil," edited by R. P. Casey, 1935) found the deepest point in the grace shown by God to man in the fact: ὁ τῶν ὅλων κοιτὴς ἐκοίθη διά σε, ἵνα σὺ ὑφωθῆς[EN131] (*op. cit.* p. 81 f.). I cannot vouch for the detailed thinking of the fathers in this connexion—if what they say is more than rhetorical, as it certainly seems to be in the passage from Athanasius.

The way of the Son of God into the far country, i.e., into the lowliness of creaturely being, of being as man, into unity and solidarity with sinful and

---

[EN129] judge is judged and has been put to rest
[EN130] our judge has been judged, life has been handed over to death, the one who nourishes the world has been in hunger
[EN131] the judge of all things has been judged through you, so that you might be exalted

therefore perishing humanity, the way of His incarnation is as such the activation, the demonstration, the revelation of His deity. His divine Sonship. That is the conclusion of our first section.

But now we enter a whole sphere of new considerations. For this way has an end, a scope, a meaning. It does not contradict His deity, His divine Sonship. It conforms supremely to it. By going this way Jesus Christ represents and discloses to us the mystery of the riches, the height and the depth of His deity which is the one true deity, and the particular mystery of His divine Sonship, Himself as the image of the ruling and commanding Father in the humility of His obedience, and therefore as the Son who is one with Him and equal with Him. That is the one side. And we had to begin with this side—the doctrine of the "person of Christ"—because it is the presupposition of everything that follows: not merely of the further development which is now necessary of the christological basis of this first part of the doctrine of reconciliation, but of all that we can think and say within this first part, under the first controlling aspect, in our attempt to understand the whole reconciliation of the world with God. We had to know who the servant is who is here actively at work as subject. We had to know that He is the Lord, the Lord of all lords, the one true God, the Son of God, to whom in Mt. 11^{27} and 28^{18} everything, all power in heaven and in earth is given. That is one thing. Quite another is the answer to the question: Why did He become a servant? why did the Son of God concretely render obedience in this way, concretely manifesting and disclosing Himself in this way as the One He is? why did He go this way in divinely free compliance with the freely disposing will of the Father? In other words: *Cur Deus homo?*[EN132] With what purpose and to what end does God will this and do this? [212]

Certainly we shall not be answering incorrectly, but indicating the background against which we have to understand everything else, if we begin by simply repeating that He wills this and does this in an outward activation and revelation of the whole inward riches of His deity in all its height and depth, that He wills it and does it especially that the world created by Him might have and see within it, in the Son as the image of the Father, its own original, that He wills it and does it for the sake of His own glory in the world, to confirm and proclaim His will not to be without the world, not to be God in isolation.

We must not be put off from thinking in this direction by the charge that it is mere speculation and far too good to be true. If we will not accept the fact that God is also and primarily *pro se*[EN133], we shall find it hard to understand what it means that in being *pro se*[EN134] He is also *pro nobis*[EN135], and therefore *pro me*[EN136]. It is no accident that in the song of the Christmas angels (Lk. 2^{14}) the "Glory to God in the Highest" comes first, and the "Peace on earth

---

[EN132] Why did God become man?
[EN133] for himself
[EN134] for himself
[EN135] for us
[EN136] for me

to the men of the (divine) good pleasure" only second. And a similar consideration seems to have guided the New Testament writer when (in Lk. 19³⁸) the words ἐν οὐρανῷ εἰρήνη καὶ δόξα ἐν ὑψίστοις EN137 are added to the ὡσαννὰ ἐν ὑψίστοις EN138 of Matthew and Mark in the disciples' song of praise on the entry into Jerusalem, thus giving to the event a clear significance for God Himself. Preceding everything that the event can mean for men, there is obviously something prior and higher at which we have to rejoice. And it seems to be not only good but true that quite apart from anything else, and before anything else, the act of atonement, and therefore the incarnation of the Word, includes within itself the fact that by His presence, action and self-proclamation in the world, as the King of Glory who comes in through its doors and gates (Ps. 24⁷ᶠ·), God vindicates Himself, and is therefore Himself the meaning and basis and end. Whatever else may be called the meaning and basis and end of the divine being and action in Jesus Christ can best be understood, can it not, if we understand this divine work as above all else purposeful in itself, and everything else within the realisation of this divine self-purpose?

But this answer is obviously not enough unless it is given with the more precise and concrete definition which the situation demands—that God reveals and increases His own glory in the world by this event, by hastening to the help of the world as its loyal Creator, by taking up its cause. In doing what He does for His own sake, He does it, in fact, *propter nos homines et propter nostram salutem*EN139. For Himself He did not need that He and His glory should be revealed and confessed in the world and by us. He might have been content with His own knowledge of Himself, just as He might have been content earlier with His being as God in glory, not needing the being of the creature and its co-existence with Him, not being under any necessity to be its Creator. But the world had radical need of His work as Creator, to which it owes no less than its very being. And, again, it has radical need that He should take up its cause in the work of atonement. Not by divine creation, but by the sin of man, it is the world which is thrown back on the faithfulness of God, a world which is lost apart from the fact that He Himself hastens to its help and takes up its cause. It has perverted the being which He lent it. It has fallen, i.e., it is rushing headlong into nothingness, into eternal death. Of itself it is not capable of any counter-movement to arrest this fall. In itself it has no power, no effective will, no sufficient basis, for any such counter-movement. On the contrary, of its own will and ability it makes only such movements as serve to repeat the origin of its fall, which is sin, and to accelerate its headlong course to the abyss. But God reveals and increases His own glory in the world in the incarnation of His Son by taking to Himself the radical neediness of the world, i.e., by undertaking to do Himself what the world cannot do, arresting and reversing its course to the abyss. He owes this neither to the world nor to Himself. Not to the world, because the sin of man as the origin of its fatal movement to eternal death is directed against Himself, is always presented and characterised as enmity against Himself. Not to the world because the world has no claim that

[213]

EN137 peace in heaven, and glory in the highest
EN138 Hosanna in the highest
EN139 for us men and for our salvation

He should exercise in its favour the omnipotence of His free love, and in the perfect form of Himself accepting unity and solidarity with sinful man. And not to Himself, because nothing would be lacking in His inward being as God in glory, as the Father, Son and Holy Spirit, as the One who loves in freedom, if He did not show Himself to the world, if He allowed it to complete its course to nothingness: just as nothing would be lacking to His glory if He had refrained from giving it being when He created it out of nothingness. That He does, in fact, will to reconcile it with Himself, and to save it, and therefore to magnify His glory in it and to it, is from every standpoint the sovereign will of His mercy. We cannot deduce it or count on it from any side. We cannot establish in principle from any side that it must be so, that God had to link the revelation and increase of His glory with the maintaining and carrying through to victory of our cause, that He had to cause it to take place as an event in which salvation is given to us. How can it be necessary in principle that He should take to Himself—and conjoin and unite with what He does to His own glory— the cause which we had so hopelessly lost, turning it in His own person to good, to the best of all? If we can speak of a necessity of any kind here, it can only be the necessity of the decision which God did in fact make and execute, the necessity of the fact that the being of God, the omnipotence of His free love, has this concrete determination and is effective and revealed in this determination and no other, that God wills to magnify and does in fact magnify His own glory in this way and not in any other, and therefore to the inclusion of the redemption and salvation of the world. This fact we have to recognise to be divinely necessary because it derives from and is posited by God. This fact we have to perceive and reverence and receive and glorify as the mystery of the atonement, the incarnation of the eternal Word. And we have to do it with a thankfulness which cannot be limited by any supposed necessity [214] of this free gift. *Cur Deus homo?*[EN140] Because the salvation of the world and of men, we ourselves and our salvation, are in fact included in the self-purposiveness of this divine action. Because the great and self-sufficient God wills to be also the Saviour of the world. Because what He does for Himself takes place with the intention and is complete in the fact that in its purpose and result we will not perish but have everlasting life. This, then, is why the Lord became a servant. This is why concretely the Son of God rendered that obedience, the obedience of self-humiliation. This is why in free compliance with the freely disposing will of the Father He entered on the strange way into the far country and followed it to the bitter end.

Here, then, we have our general answer to the question confronting us. We cannot deduce it from any principle, from any idea of God or of man and the world. We can read it only from the fact in which the omnipotent mercy of God is exercised and effective and revealed, in which His own glory and our salvation meet, in which that which God does for Himself is also done for us.

[EN140] Why did God become man?

Our answer can only be a repetition of the answer which God Himself has given in this fact, in which He Himself has pronounced concerning the end and scope and meaning of His activity. *Deus pro nobis*[EN141] is something which He did not have to be or become, but which, according to this fact, He was and is and will be—the God who acts as our God, who did not regard it as too mean a thing, but gave Himself fully and seriously to self-determination as the God of the needy and rebellious people of Israel, to be born a son of this people, to let its wickedness fall on Him, to be rejected by it, but in its place and for the forgiveness of its sins to let Himself be put to death by the Gentiles—and by virtue of the decisive co-operation of the Gentiles in His rejection and humiliation to let Himself be put to death in their place, too, and for the forgiveness of their sins. The end and scope and meaning of this downward way, the reconciliation of the world with Himself, is God Himself as the God of this mean and wicked people for the men of this people, and at the end of its history God Himself in the midst of this people and all peoples for the men of this people and all peoples, God in this direct relationship to men and man, God the one man for many. In all that follows we can only hear and intelligently repeat the answer which God Himself has already given to our question.

But we must now state rather more precisely the general meaning of this *Deus pro nobis*[EN142]. How is God for us? How has He taken up the cause of the world in revealing and magnifying His own glory? How has He met its radical need? How has He arrested and reversed its course to the abyss? How especially has He met the fact that the cause of its impending destruction is the sin of man, his enmity against God? How has He shown Himself to be its Saviour in face and in spite of this cause of its impending destruction?

[215]   In giving Himself in the Son to this alien life, in becoming concretely the God of Israel and an individual man of this people and as such a man amongst all men, He obviously did it first of all simply by taking upon Himself to share with it its place and status, its situation, by making it His own situation. The way of His humiliation is simply the way which leads Him to us, the way on which He draws near to us and becomes one of us. And this means first that the mortal peril in which man stands becomes and is His peril, the need of man His need. The Son of God exists with man and as man in this fallen and perishing state. We should be explaining the incarnation docetically and therefore explaining it away if we did not put it like this, if we tried to limit in any way the solidarity with the cosmos which God accepted in Jesus Christ. We have already said that in this event God allows the world and humanity to take part in the history of the inner life of His Godhead, in the movement in which from and to all eternity He is Father, Son and Holy Spirit, and therefore the one true God. But this participation of the world in the being of God implies necessarily His participating in the being of the world, and therefore that His being, His

---

[EN141] God for us
[EN142] God for us

history, is played out as world-history and therefore under the affliction and peril of all world-history. The self-humiliation of God in His Son would not really lead Him to us, the activity in which we see His true deity and the divine Sonship of Jesus Christ would not be genuine and actual, the humble obedience of Jesus Christ would not be rendered or the will of the Father fulfilled, the way into the far country would not be followed, if there were any reservation in respect of His solidarity with us, of His entry into world-history. But the self-humiliation of God in His Son is genuine and actual, and therefore there is no reservation in respect of His solidarity with us. He did become— and this is the presupposition of all that follows—the brother of man, threatened with man, harassed and assaulted with him, with him in the stream which hurries downwards to the abyss, hastening with him to death, to the cessation of being and nothingness. With him He cries—knowing far better than any other how much reason there is to cry: "My God, my God, why hast thou forsaken me?" (Mk. 15^{34}). *Deus pro nobis*[EN143] means simply that God has not abandoned the world and man in the unlimited need of his situation, but that He willed to bear this need as His own, that He took it upon Himself, and that He cries with man in this need.

But on the same lines we have to go further and say that in giving Himself up to this alien life in His Son God did not evade the cause of man's fall and destruction, but exposed Himself to and withstood the temptation which man suffers and in which he becomes a sinner and the enemy of God. We should again be explaining the incarnation docetically and therefore explaining it away, we should be closing our eyes to the plainest possible statements of the New Testament, concealing the central point which we have to grasp and consider, if we had any reservations in this respect. That the Word became "flesh" [216] means that the Son of God made His own the situation of man in the sense that with him He faced the impossible in all its power, that He faced the dreadful possibility of ingratitude, disobedience, unfaithfulness, pride, cowardice and deceit, that He knew it as well as He did Himself, that He came to closer grips with it than any other man. He had to achieve His freedom and obedience as a link in the chain of an enslaved and disobedient humanity, the new thing in a strict and, for Him and Him alone, hampering connexion with the old. He had to wrestle with that which assaulted Him as one man with others, which for the first time brought all its force to bear against Him as the Son of God in the flesh. He was not immune from sin. He did not commit it, but He was not immune from it. In this respect, too, He became the brother of man. He did not float over the human situation like a being of a completely different kind. He entered into it as a man with men. In this second and more incisive sense *Deus pro nobis*[EN144] means that God in Jesus Christ has taken our place when we become sinners, when we become His enemies, when we stand

---

[EN143] God for us
[EN144] God for us

as such under His accusation and curse, and bring upon ourselves our own destruction.

But now we have to face the question in all seriousness: Why did He come amongst us, why did He enter our situation, as our brother? What is it that takes place when the Son of God becomes flesh of our flesh?

We are not only at liberty, but it is right and relevant, to give first of all the great positive answer as we have it in a verse like 1 Jn. 4[14]: "The Father sent the Son to be the Saviour of the world." Therefore our salvation, the salvation of men and the world, takes place in Him, in His being and activity as one with us. "God became man on thy behalf, O man." He humbles Himself to our status in order to be our companion in that status, in order to share with us the assault and temptation, in order to be with us in the misery of that status with all the omnipotence of His divine mercy, in order to change that status from within, in order to turn it for good, for the very best, in order to take away the curse which rests upon us, in order to obviate the impending destruction. He comes, therefore, as a helper, as a redeemer, as the one who brings another and proper order, a life which is life indeed. He comes as the kingdom of God in person. He comes to reconcile the world with God, i.e., to convert it to God.

But we cannot pass on at once to the development of this positive answer. It is the answer of the grace of God and we must hear and understand it as such. But the grace of God is not a cheap grace. It cost God dear enough to give this answer, to send His Son as the Saviour of the world. Therefore if our answer is to correspond to His, if it is to have weight and meaning, it cannot be a cheap or over-hasty answer. We must pause for a moment to consider a statement [217] which plays no little part in the New Testament, that the coming into the world of the Son of God includes within itself the appearance and work of the Judge of the world and of every man. If He were not the Judge, He would not be the Saviour. He is the Saviour of the world in so far as in a very definite (and most astonishing) way He is also its Judge.

And it is to the point if we remember that the Judge is not simply or even primarily the One who pardons some (perhaps a few or perhaps none at all) and condemns the rest (perhaps many and perhaps all)—whose judgment therefore all have to fear. Basically and decisively—and this is something we must never forget when we speak of the divine Judge—He is the One whose concern is for order and peace, who must uphold the right and prevent the wrong, so that His existence and coming and work is not in itself and as such a matter for fear, but something which indicates a favour, the existence of One who brings salvation.

The so-called "Judges" of the Old Testament in the early period of the occupation of Canaan are described as men awakened by God and their main office is to be helpers and saviours in the recurrent sufferings of the people at the hand of neighbouring tribes. It was only in addition to this activity in "foreign affairs" that they engaged in judging in the narrower sense of the term. Similarly in the New Testament—a fact which was later forgotten— the coming of the Judge means basically the coming of the Redeemer and Saviour.

2. The Judge Judged in Our Place

But, of course, this involves judging in the more obvious sense of the word, and therefore pardoning and sentencing. Thus the solemn question arises: Who will stand when the Son of God—to create order and peace, but by setting some on His right hand and others on His left—comes into the world, when He calls the world and therefore all men (and every individual man) to render an account and to make answer for its condition? *Quid sum miser tunc dicturus, quem patronum rogaturus, cum vix justus sit securus?*[EN145] All other men will be measured by the One who is man as they are under the same presuppositions and conditions. In His light, into which they are *nolentes volentes*[EN146] betrayed by His being as a fellow-man, they will be shown for what they are and what they are not. With His existence there will fall upon them in all its concreteness the decision, the divine and ultimate decision. What will become of them? How shall they stand?

In this respect we must not overlook especially the message of John the Baptist. According to the Synoptic narrative he stands in the closest relationship with the appearance and work of Jesus. And he gives to it a character which, as we read on, we may easily overlook and forget because of its strangeness, but which we ought not to forget or overlook. In one place (Lk. 3^{18}) the function of the Baptist is itself called an εὐαγγελίζεσθαι[EN147]. And at the end of the quotation from Is. 40 (about the voice crying in the wilderness to prepare the way of the Lord), which the same Evangelist uses to show that the coming of the Baptist has to be understood as a fulfilment of Scripture, there stands the saying: "And all flesh shall see the salvation of God" (Lk. 3^5). But what we are told of his proclamation of the near coming of the kingdom (Mt. 3^2) has at first quite a different ring. According to Mt. 3^7 the scribes and [218] Pharisees who came to him by Jordan (and in Lk. 3^7 the ὄχλοι[EN148]) are welcomed with the words: "Ye generation of vipers, who hath warned you to flee from the wrath to come (μέλλουσα ὀργή)? The axe is already laid at the root of the tree, and every tree that bringeth forth not good fruit will be hewn down and cast into the fire (Mt. 3^{10}). This is what happens when the kingdom of God comes. And in express reference to the greater one who will then come after the Baptist: "He shall baptise you with the Holy Ghost, and with fire: Whose fan is in his hand, and he will throughly purge his floor, and gather his wheat into the garner; but he will burn up the chaff with unquenchable fire" (Mt. 3^{12}). No appeal: "We have Abraham to our father," will then be of any help (Mt. 3^9). No, to obtain forgiveness of sins and to escape the coming wrath on the day when this One comes, repentance is necessary to-day (Mk. 1^4), the confession of sins (Mk. 1^5), and fruits meet for repentance (Mt. 3^8). What this means is shown by some examples in Lk. $3^{10f.}$ The baptism of John is therefore the sign of penitent expectation of the Judge and His *dies irae*[EN149]. And it is to this baptism that Jesus of Nazareth submits, having come to Jordan from Galilee and accepting it with all the people. He does so as the Judge who has been proclaimed. This is surprising enough to the Baptist himself, who had need to be baptised of Him (Mt. 3^{14}); but he had to suffer it to be so, for "thus it becometh us to fulfil all righteousness" (Mt. 3^{15}). Here we see the limit of this strand.

[EN145] What then, wretched as I am, am I to say? Who can I call in my defence? For even the righteous are hardly safe

[EN146] – whether they like it or not –

[EN147] a preaching of the Gospel

[EN148] crowds

[EN149] day of wrath

§ 59. *The Obedience of the Son of God*

warding to note that the same strand appears again and again in the New Testa-
her one has built on the rock or on the sand is determined by whether one does
do the words of Jesus (Mt. $7^{24f.}$). "Why call ye me, Lord, Lord, and do not the
1 I say?" (Lk. 6^{46}). Those who confess Him before men. He will also confess, but
those who deny Him before men He will also deny before His Father in heaven (Mt. $10^{32f.}$).
He is not come to bring peace on the earth but a sword (Mt. 10^{34}), or, according to Lk. 12^{49},
"to send fire on the earth." Those who will not take up their cross and follow Him are not
worthy of Him (Mt. 10^{38}). Only those who will lose their lives for His sake will find them (Mt.
10^{39}). The Saviour of the Evangelists is also the One who pronounces those woes on
Chorazin, Bethsaida and Capernaum because they have seen His mighty works and not
repented (Mt. $11^{20f.}$). He is also the One who pronounced that almost intolerably severe woe
on the scribes and Pharisees which our clever modern exegetes have mildly reproved (Mt.
23^{13-36}). He always proclaims His last and manifest appearance to the whole world as the
event when He will make a distinction between those who have watched and those who have
fallen asleep, between those who have been found ready and loyal, and those who have not
been found ready and loyal, between those who have seen and supported Him in suffering
brethren and those who have failed to do so, between those who are merely called and those
who are chosen.

We find the same teaching again and again in the Gospel of St. John. Here the concept of
judgment is explicitly used, and there is a distinctive correlation of the judicial decision
which has yet to be revealed with the decision which is in fact already being made: "He that
believeth not the Son shall not see life; but the wrath of God abideth on him" (Jn. 3^{36}). "He
that rejecteth me, and receiveth not my words, hath one that judgeth him: the word that I
have spoken, the same shall judge him in the last day" (Jn. 12^{48}). Conversely, "He that
heareth my word, and believeth on him that sent me, hath everlasting life, and shall not
come into condemnation; but is passed from death unto life" (5^{14}). For to Him, the Son, the
Father "hath committed all judgment" "because he is the Son of man" ($5^{22\ 27}$). He judges,
and His judgment is just because He hears Him that sent Him and seeks His will (5^{30}). His
judgment is true, because He does not execute it alone, but in fellowship with Him that sent
Him (8^{16}). And according to the remarkable sayings in 9^{41} and $15^{22f.}$ it is only in confronta-
[219] tion with Him that there is any real sin: "If I had not done among them the works which
none other man did, they had not had sin: but now have they both seen and hated both me
and my Father" (15^{24}).

The Paul of Acts seems to see things in a similar light: "And the times of this ignorance
God winked at; but now commandeth all men every where to repent: Because he hath
appointed a day, in which he will judge the world in righteousness by that man whom he
hath ordained" (Ac. $17^{30f.}$). And 2 Cor. 5^{10} maintains: "We must all appear before the judgment seat of Christ; that every one may receive the things done in his body, according to that
he hath done, whether it be good or bad." Again, in Ac. 10^{42} and 2 Tim. 4^1 Jesus is called the
One who will judge the quick and the dead. In Rev. 1^{16}, too, He is described as the One out
of whose mouth there issues a sharp, two-edged sword. And in Heb. 12^{29} the exhortation to
thankfulness for the received "kingdom which cannot be moved" is based on the statement
that "our God is a consuming fire."

The *locus classicus*[EN150] for this significance and function of Jesus Christ as the Judge, and
therefore for the judicial work of the Gospel concerning Him, is the whole sequence from
Rom. 1^{18}–3^{20}. In the following sections, in which—in the light of Christology—we shall be
dealing for the first time with the doctrine of sin, we shall have to return expressly to this
context. The passages already adduced, which are not by any means complete, are sufficient

---

[EN150] principal passage

to bear out what we wished to maintain—that the "Saviour of the world" has also this character and commission and aspect. We cannot, therefore, overlook this fact or dismiss it from our mind. What follows can be understood only if we see that He has this aspect. He would not be who He is, nor would He do what, as the Son of God who has come to us, He does do for us, if He were not this Judge who pronounces against us.

Even more incisively, it is not just any judgment which He exercises and executes, but the judgment of God. And as we have already said, it is for this reason the ultimate judgment. It is the judgment against which there can be no appeal to a higher court. Nor is this merely because the world is in the power of this Judge and has no means to refuse or escape Him. It is decisively because this Judge is the measure of all righteousness, because any right which man might seek apart from Him or set up and assert side by side with Him could only be wrong, because conversely any right being or action on the part of man can consist only in His bowing before the judgment of this Judge and recognising and accepting His sentence as just whatever it may be.

This fact that God has here come amongst us in the person of His Son, and that as a man with us He exercises judgment, reveals the full seriousness of the human situation. In this judgment God obviously has something to say to man which apart from this direct confrontation with God he is unwilling to say to himself, and caught in this unwillingness he cannot say to himself. Man has obviously given himself quite a different account of himself than that which he is now given by God. It obviously was and is something strange to him that he, for his part, can be in the right and do right only in subjection to the judgment of God. Obviously the righteousness of God is something strange to him as the measure of all righteousness, and therefore God Himself is a stranger. Obviously he for his part is estranged from God; although as the creature, the human creature of God, he is appointed to know God, although he is as near, [220] no, nearer to God, than he is to himself, and therefore can and must be truly acquainted with Him. Obviously he does that which in the knowledge of God he could never do: he sets up his own right against God; he measures himself by this right; he thinks that measuring himself by this right he can pronounce himself free and righteous. He wants to be his own judge, and he makes himself his own judge. All sin has its being and origin in the fact that man wants to be his own judge. And in wanting to be that, and thinking and acting accordingly, he and his whole world is in conflict with God. It is an unreconciled world, and therefore a suffering world, a world given up to destruction.

It is for this reason—the fault and evil are evidently great and deep enough to make it necessary—it is for this reason that God Himself encounters man in the flesh and therefore face to face in the person of His Son, in order that He may pass on the one who feels and accepts himself as his own judge the real judgment which he has merited. This judgment sets him in the wrong as the one who maintains his own right against God instead of bowing to God's right. We will have to explain this when we come to speak of sin as such. For the moment it is enough to maintain that because it is a matter of the appearance and work of the true Judge amongst those who think they can and should judge and therefore exalt themselves, therefore the abasement of the Son to our status, the obedience which He rendered in humility as our Brother, is the divine accusation against every man and the divine condemnation of every man. The whole world finds its supreme unity and determination against God in looking for justification from itself and not from God. And as a world hostile to God it is distinguished by the fact that in this way it repeats the very sin of which it acquits itself. In this way that which is flesh is flesh. And for this reason the incarnation of the Word means the judgment, the judgment of rejection and condemnation, which is passed on all flesh. Not all men commit all sins, but all men commit this sin which is the essence and root of all other sins. There is not one who can boast that he does not commit it. And this is what is revealed and rejected and condemned as an act of wrong-doing by the coming of the Son of God. This is what makes His coming a coming to judgment, and His office as Saviour His office as our Judge.

But those who are judged and rejected and condemned by God as wrong-doers are lost and condemned to perish, indeed they are already perishing. They stand on the left hand of God, under the divine No, in the sphere of that which God does not will, but rejects, and therefore in the sphere of that which is not, in the darkness in which there is no light, in the affliction in which there is no help, in the need from which there is no redemption. The power of God still rules over them, but as the power which holds and imprisons them, the power of His condemnation. The love of God burns where they are, but as the [221] fire of His wrath which consumes and destroys them. God lives for them, but the life of God can only mean death for those who are His enemies. That is how the men exist who will be their own judges, who will acquit themselves, who in so doing commit all sins *in nuce*[EN151], and who are therefore judged and rejected and condemned by God as wrong-doers. And because all men are determinedly against God in this, this is how every man necessarily exists—in a lost state as one who is lost. God would not be God if there could be any altering the universality and logic and completeness of what is necessarily done here, if there could be any escaping this sequence of sin and destruction. It means eternal perdition to have God against us. But if we will what God does not will, we do have God against us, and therefore we hurry and run and stumble and fall into eternal perdition.

But again God would not be God if His reaction to wrong-doers could be compared to a mechanism which functions, as it were, independently of His free ruling and disposing. That is not how it is on His right hand, where He says Yes to the creature, where He frees his powers and blesses his love and gives him life which is life indeed. God is the Lord in all His rule, even in that of His wrath and the destruction and perdition which it brings. He Himself determines the course and direction and meaning of it: not some necessity

---

[EN151] in a nutshell

immanent to its occurrence; not a force to which man when he sins against God becomes subject absolutely, i.e., otherwise than in conformity to the sovereign will and disposing of God which obtains even in His rule on the left hand. How God will fulfil the sentence to which man has fallen inescapably victim is a matter for Him to decide. He can fulfil it—in all its strictness—in such a way that in fulfilling it there is attained that which man in his perversity tried and never could secure for himself—his pardon. Without relaxing or mitigating the sentence, let alone as a judge who is unjust by reason of his laxity, He can exercise grace even with His judgment and in execution of it. He can be so much in earnest against sinful man that He is for him. He can bring on him all that must come on him as a wrong-doer at the left hand of God and under His No, in order to set him at His right hand, in order finally to say Yes to him, in order to address and treat him as one who does right and not wrong. God is free to judge in this way. He is not obliged to do so. There is no inner compulsion forcing Him to exercise this strange judgment. Even less is there any right or claim on the part of man on the ground of which he can expect this strange judgment. Everything is against any such judgment being even conceivable: a serious judgment of God's enemies the result of which is grace, liberation, redemption proceeding out of captivity, love out of wrath, life out of death; a judgment which in the event makes the enemies of God His friends; a judgment in which this does not happen arbitrarily but in a fixed order, not in a wild divine inconsequence but with a clear purpose and according to a [222] firm plan; and therefore a judgment beside and after and beyond which there need be no further fear of judgment; a judgment which concludes once and for all with the redemption and salvation of the man who had been rightly accused and condemned and had fallen a helpless victim to destruction. Everything is against the possibility of a judgment like that. But we cannot encroach on the freedom of God. We cannot, therefore, say that it could not please God in His grace, out of sheer faithfulness and mercy to us men, to be our Judge in this strange fashion.

But in the last resort there is only one thing which tells us that this is in fact possible—that in Jesus Christ His Son our Lord He has acted in this and no other way as our Judge and the Judge of all men. We now return to our question: Why did the Son of God become man, one of us, our brother, our fellow in the human situation? The answer is: In order to judge the world. But in the light of what God has actually done we must add at once: In order to judge it in the exercise of His kingly freedom to show His grace in the execution of His judgment, to pronounce us free in passing sentence, to free us by imprisoning us, to ground our life on our death, to redeem and save us by our destruction. That is how God has actually judged in Jesus Christ. And that is why He humbled Himself. That is why He went into the far country as the obedient Son of the Father. That is why He did not abandon us, but came amongst us as our brother. That is why the Father sent Him. That was the eternal will of God and its fulfilment in time—the execution of this strange judgment. If this strange judgment had not taken place, there would be only a lost world and lost men. Since it has taken place, we can only recognise and believe and proclaim to the whole world and all men: Not lost. And since it did take place, what does it matter what may be said against the possibility of it?

But what did take place? At this point we can and must make the decisive statement: What took place is that the Son of God fulfilled the righteous judgment on us men by Himself taking our place as man and in our place undergoing the judgment under which we had passed. That is why He came and was amongst us. In this way, in this "for us," He was our Judge against us. That is what happened when the divine accusation was, as it were, embodied in His presence in the flesh. That is what happened when the divine condemnation had, as it were, visibly to fall on this our fellow-man. And that is what happened when by reason of our accusation and condemnation it had to come to the point of our perishing, our destruction, our fall into nothingness, our death. Everything happened to us exactly as it had to happen, but because God willed to execute His judgment on us in His Son it all happened in His person, as His accusation and condemnation and destruction. He judged, and it was the [223] Judge who was judged, who let Himself be judged. Because He was a man like us, He was able to be judged like us. Because He was the Son of God and Himself God, He had the competence and power to allow this to happen to Him. Because He was the divine Judge come amongst us. He had the authority in this way—by this giving up of Himself to judgment in our place—to exercise the divine justice of grace, to pronounce us righteous on the ground of what happened to Him, to free us therefore from the accusation and condemnation and punishment, to save us from the impending loss and destruction. And because in divine freedom He was on the way of obedience, He did not refuse to accept the will of the Father as His will in this self-giving. In His doing this for us, in His taking to Himself—to fulfil all righteousness—our accusation and condemnation and punishment, in His suffering in our place and for us, there came to pass our reconciliation with God. *Cur Deus homo?*[EN152] In order that God as man might do and accomplish and achieve and complete all this for us wrong-doers, in order that in this way there might be brought about by Him our reconciliation with Him and conversion to Him.

It came to pass, we have just said; as we do when we tell the story of something that happened in the world at a definite place and a definite point of time. To think the matter out further and to understand it in detail, all that remains actually for us to do is simply to recount it in the manner of a story which has come to pass (which it is), to bring it before ourselves as something which has objectively happened. There and then, in the existence of the man Jesus of Nazareth, who was the Son of God, this event came to pass in the kingly freedom of the God who is holy and righteous in His faithfulness and mercy. There and then there took place the strange judgment which meant

---

[EN152] Why did God become man?

216

the pardon and redemption of man the wrong-doer, the making possible of that which seemed to be contrary to every possibility. It was made possible as it was done. And it was done as God became man in Jesus Christ, in order to do that in our place and for us. It took place in Him, in the one man, and therefore there and then, *illic et tunc*[EN153], and in significance *hic et nunc*[EN154], for us in our modern here and now. To be known and explained and proclaimed with this significance it cannot and must not be ignored or dissolved in favour of its significance, so that it disappears in it. Before there is any consideration of its significance, it can and must be taken as that which is significant in its significance, and therefore in and for itself as the history of Jesus Christ as it took place there and then, and as it can be and is recounted: That is how it happened for us. For upon the fact that it happened for us there depends the further fact that it has a significance for us as something which happened for us. Upon the fact that it confronts us as something that happened there depends the further fact that it can be seen by us to have this significance. Where there is nothing significant, and seen to be significant, there can be no [224] significance or recognition of it. But the significant thing is what happened in Him, in Jesus Christ, in this one man. It is His history as such. It alone is the basis of faith. Its proclamation alone is the summons to faith—faith in this strange judgment, and the invitation and constraint to submit to it. Jesus Christ for us as a supremely objective happening is the word of reconciliation on the basis of which there is a ministry of reconciliation.

The New Testament distinguishes this happening in relation to its significance by an ἅπαξ[EN155] or ἐφάπαξ[EN156]. This marks it off as an event which has to be considered in its uniqueness and particularity, which cannot be dissolved, or merely commemorated *sotto voce*[EN157] for the sake of completeness. Jesus Christ died for sin once, is the highly compressed form in which it is stated in Rom. 6[10]. And it is from this that in v. 11 there is derived the necessity to reckon ourselves dead indeed unto sin. According to Rom. 5[6f.] it happened at a particular time (κατὰ καιρόν). It was indeed when we were still without strength, sinners (v. 8), even enemies (v. 10), that He died for us (ὑπὲρ ἡμῶν, v. 8), that we were reconciled to God by the death of His Son (v. 10). Christ died once for our sins, the just for the unjust, to bring us to God (1 Pet. 3[18]). And especially in the Epistle to the Hebrews: Not with a daily repetition like the High Priests of the Old Testament, but once only did Christ offer sacrifice with the offering of Himself (7[27]). Again in contradistinction to the sacrificial ministry of the Old Testament, He entered once into the holy place by His own blood and made (in that way) an eternal redemption (αἰωνία λύτρωσις) for us. Just as man dies once, so He is once revealed at the end of the age to take away sin by His sacrifice (9[26f.]) And all that has still to be done, according to this passage, is that He should finally appear in correspondence to the judgment which awaits man after death. In that He fulfilled the will of God we are sanctified once and for all by the sacrificial offering of His body (10[10,14]), again in contradistinction to

---

[EN153] there and then
[EN154] here and now
[EN155] once
[EN156] once for all
[EN157] quietly

the Old Testament order, within which there can be no question of a cleansing of man once and for all (10^2).

In order to see and grasp this event as such, and therefore in its uniqueness and distinction in relation to its significance, we must try to find some way of making the accustomed unaccustomed again, the well-known unknown and the old new: that is, the outline of the evangelical history with which we are so familiar and the stimulating singularity of which we may so easily overlook, especially in the form in which it is presented in the Synoptic Gospels. It is obvious that in these Gospels there is relatively little express mention of the significance of the Christ event which took place then and there. For that reason, up to our own day they have often been estimated less highly (even by Luther) in comparison with Paul and John as mere "history," although, of course, on the other hand, they have sometimes been given a no less dubious preference. But now let us consider this history carefully once more: how radically puzzling and therefore significant it is just as it stands, factually and without any great attempt to draw attention to it, in its simple character as history. What do we find in this history?

In a first and larger part we have a picture of the sayings and acts of Jesus Christ in His entry into and life in Galilee within the wider and narrower circle of His disciples, the multitudes, and the spiritual and (on the margin) the political leaders of the people. Jesus over against and in the midst of His disciples stands out in marked contrast to this whole world of men. He belongs to it, and He intensively addresses Himself to it, but He is a stranger within it. His indications of the kingdom of God coming on earth, both spoken and confirmed in signs and wonders; the imperatives spoken by Him as a summons to recognise and acknow-

[225]

ledge this kingdom: all these are seen again and again to be in practical and theoretical antithesis to the whole being and thinking and willing of these men. He brings, and in His whole existence He is, the evangel, good news for all of them. But what comes of it? What can and will the crowds finally make of it? What comes of it in the ears and hearts of the scribes and Pharisees? What does it mean for a Herod? We hear of the poor and sick and publicans and sinners who seem to receive it gladly and willingly, as Jesus believes they can and will. But where are they at the last? What has become of them and the Gospel they heard? When Jesus goes to Jerusalem, they remain anonymously in Galilee, and none of the Evangelists thinks it worth while even to mention them again. We hear of the disciples and women who followed Him, and that Jesus counted those blessed who did so. Among them is Peter, who was honoured (Mt. $16^{15f.}$) with that revelation of the Father concerning the Son, who became the first confessor and who was described by Jesus as the rock on which He would build His Church. But immediately after Peter is rebuked as Satan because he will not and cannot think as God but only as man. And later Peter will deny Him thrice. Among them, too, is Judas, who will betray Him. And finally all the disciples will forsake Him and flee, just flee. What has really happened? According to this presentation there has passed through the midst of all these men One who is absolutely superior to them, exalted above them, and fearfully alone. And He has finally gone from them after confirming and for the first time revealing their corruption, after showing and revealing them to be, in His light and confronted by Him, blind and deaf and lame, driven and controlled by all kinds of demons, even dead. The Lord has been among them. And in the course, and as the result of His being among them, in fulfilment of His proclamation and work, and as its consequence, the Lord has shown Himself their Judge, the One for whom not one of them was a match, on whom they were all broken to pieces, in face of whom they all showed themselves once more and this time finally to be sinful and lost Israel, sinful and lost humanity and—we have to see and say it—an inadequate and also a sinful and lost band of disciples.

Certainly from the very first the Evangelists do indicate one or two strands which point in another direction, which soften this hard picture of the contrast, the picture of the judgment that falls on all flesh with the coming of the kingdom, which plainly give us to understand that in this picture we have the first, but not the final, word. But these are either obvious reminiscences of sayings and acts which the disciples did not then understand on that first stage of the way of Jesus, prophecies the meaning of which they only perceived and introduced into their accounts in the light of their fulfilment—or else (and there are passages in which this is palpable) *vaticinia ex eventu*[EN158], an expression of the instruction which the community itself had later to undergo in face of the event in which that strange progress of the Lord through their midst came to its inconceivable climax. It is often difficult to decide whether we are dealing with the one group or the other when we come across these strands. But the main strand gives us the picture offered by the first main section of the evangelical records, and, impartially considered and estimated, it undoubtedly confirms the hard picture which John the Baptist had and drew of the One who was to come: the picture of the man with the fan in His hand, of the judgment of God which would fall in His existence, of the One at whose coming the Baptist saw the axe laid at the root of the trees. It has to be added that we go far beyond this picture, for at the end of this first part of the evangelical record there are no good trees left to stand. The formulation in which Paul gathered together the results of the first part of the Epistle to Romans is not too stringent to fit here: that every mouth will be stopped, and the whole world guilty before God. By the works of the Law—even the Gospel Law as proclaimed by Jesus of Nazareth—no flesh will be pronounced righteous before God (Rom. 3$^{19f.}$).

But now there comes the great surprise of the second part of the history. In the Synoptic tradition it overlaps a good deal with the first. The sections from the record of the entry into Jerusalem up to and including the Last Supper can be regarded as belonging to the first or the second part, or as the transition from the one to the other. But from the description of the scene in Gethsemane at any rate the second part forms a self-contained whole. It is essentially shorter than the first, but it obviously presents the—strange—end towards which the earlier narratives hasten. Yet it cannot fail to be noticed formally by the unity of its subject-matter, and by the unbroken sequence of the events reported in it (which are substantially the same in all the Evangelists). And in substance it stands out by reason of the fact that we have now very few sayings of Jesus and no actions at all, although more than once there seems to have been a temptation to act (the twelve legions of angels in Mt. 26^{53}, and that He should "come down from the cross" in Mt. 27^{42}). Jesus no longer seems to be the subject but the object of what happens. His speech is almost exclusively that of silence and His work that of suffering. [226]

What these chapters bring before us is an arrest, a hearing and prosecution in various courts, a torturing, and then an execution and burial. They are, of course, a logical consequence of the first part as seen in the light of the result of what it has to tell us and of the initial preaching of John the Baptist. It is only to be expected that Jesus of Nazareth will try the world which has so shamefully rejected Him, will try Israel and even the band of disciples. It is not difficult to postulate that there will now take place the destruction of Jerusalem and the temple, and that the presentation of it will form the continuation and a suitable complement to the first part. In the last larger collection of sayings before the transition to the second part, the Synoptic apocalypse, this later event already emerges in its main outlines. And Jesus has a saying about His destruction and re-erection of the temple which, whether it was understood or misunderstood, played a particular role in the hearing before the high priests in Mk. 14^{58}, and then again in the taunting of the Crucified in Mk. 15^{29}. To the same context belongs quite naturally the saying to the daughters of Jerusalem in Lk. 23^{28}, when He tells them not to weep for Him but for themselves and their children. But all

---

[EN158] prophecies after the event

that is still future. And—however obvious—it is not in the events of A.D. 70 that the Gospels and the rest of the New Testament find the decisive divine answer to Israel's rejection of its Christ. Even in the Synoptic apocalypse this forms only, as it were, the next horizon of the final events there depicted, with no autonomous significance in relation to the true centre. And although in the real second part of the Gospels we have the description of a judgment which falls on Israel, the surprising thing is that it is not a judgment which falls directly on the guilty—as formerly on Samaria and Jerusalem. The One who is prosecuted according to this story, the One whose passion is enacted in all its stages, is the only innocent One, the One who has indeed divine authority to accuse in the midst of sinful Israel, the "King of the Jews." There is, in fact, a complete reversal, an exchange of roles. Those who are to be judged are given space and freedom and power to judge. The Judge allows Himself to be judged. That is why He came to Jerusalem, entering it as a King. He is, in fact, judged. The content of the second part of the Gospel story gives us, therefore, a second and a difficult picture: difficult because of the oppression, anguish and execution of the one man who stands silent and suffering in the midst; difficult because the accusation, condemnation and punishment to which it refers all fall on the very One on whom they ought to fall least of all, and not at all on those on whom they ought to fall. The most forceful expression of this scandalous contrast is the Barabbas episode (Mk. 15$^{6-15}$) in which a murderer is in every respect acquitted instead of Jesus, and Jesus is condemned to be crucified in his place. It is only under compulsion that Simon of Cyrene (Lk. 23^{26}) carries His cross after Him. And those who are—unwillingly—crucified with Him are both robbers (Mk. 15$^{27f.}$) whose fellow-ship with Him shows that He is not dying a hero's death, but the death of a criminal—"He was numbered with the transgressors" (Is. 53^{12}), He, the King and the Judge of Israel. Those who taunted Him on the cross (Mk. 15^{29}) were quite right: instead of the destruction of the temple—this! the man who had seemed to threaten it hanging in shame and agony and helplessness on a Roman gallows. That is what we are told in the second part of the Gospel story.

[227]

It is content simply to tell the story—this is how it was, this is how it happened. There is interpretation only in the lightest and sometimes rather alien strokes, of which we have to say much the same as we did of what we called the softenings occasionally found in the first part. The real commentary on this first part and the whole is, of course, the Easter story, which we can describe as the third and shortest part of the Gospel history. This tells us that God acknowledged this Jesus of Nazareth, the strange Judge who allowed Himself to be judged, by raising Him from the dead. It tells us of the forty days in which this same One—whose history this was and had to be—was again in the midst of His disciples, differently, but still actually in time and space, talking with them, eating and drinking with them, beginning with them a new Gospel history, the time of His community, the time of the Gospel as the good news about the Judge who allowed Himself to be judged, the time of the proclamation of this event. He Himself was and is this event, the origin, the authority, the power, the object of the proclamation laid on the community. He Himself, He alone: He who was alone and superior and majestic in Galilee; He who was again alone but beaten and humiliated in Jerusalem, in the very midst of Israel. He, the Judge who allowed Himself to be judged, lives and rules and speaks and works. He is Himself the word which is to be proclaimed to all creatures as the Word of God. That is what the Easter narrative tells us. It gathers together the sum of all that has been told before. Or, rather, it tells us how the sum which God Himself had already gathered together in all that had gone before was revealed as such to the disciples—again by Jesus Himself. The Easter story is the Gospel story in its unity and completeness as the revealed story of redemption. The Easter story is the record of how it became what it was (in all its curious structure a history of redemption) for the disciples—not by their own discovery but by the act of God in the word and work of Jesus Himself. It tells us, therefore, that this history, Jesus Christ Himself as He exists in this history, is significant in and by itself. It tells us that all the significance which Jesus Christ as the subject and subject-matter of this history can acquire for individual men by means and as a result of proclamation (which has Him as its origin and object), has its basis and truth and practical and theoretical power in the fact that He is significant in and by Himself—even as He exists in this history. What is significant in itself has the power to become significant and will in fact become significant. But only that can become significant which is already significant, and in such a way that this being is the power of the corresponding becoming.

The Gospel story in its unity and completeness, Jesus Christ Himself who was the Judge and who allowed Himself to be judged in execution of His judgment, is the being which is the power of the corresponding becoming, the significant thing which can and will acquire significance for many individual men. It is of Him that we can and must speak, His story that we must recount, in Him as the One who existed in this story that we can and must believe. That this should happen is the meaning and purpose of the time of the community which begins with the Easter story. But He does not need first to be spoken of. Existing in that history, living and ruling and speaking and working as the One who exists in that history, He speaks for Himself whenever He is spoken of and His story is told and heard. It is not He that needs proclamation but proclamation that needs Him. He demands it. He makes it possible. He makes Himself its origin and object. He is its basis and truth and power. Our need of proclamation is another matter, but we need the proclamation which has its centre not in itself but outside itself in Him, in His history. Again, He does not need our faith, but our faith needs Him. He awakens and nourishes and maintains it by making Himself its origin and object, by allowing man to believe in Him. It is, of course, true that we need faith, but only the faith in which we look beyond ourselves, not to something that cannot be passed on to us, but to Him, considering and apprehending Him in the history in which He has His existence. Again, He does not need a fulfilment in our life, the life of believers. But if there is to be a fulfilment, if faith is not to be a mere acceptance of the truth of an old story, but the determination of our actual life in time, there is again a need of Him, of the fact that in virtue of the Easter story by which it happened, in the power of the sum which God has gathered in it, His history is itself not an old and past history, but a history which is the new history for every man, the presence and action of Jesus Christ Himself, true in the sense of being actuality for us, to be accepted as true because it proves itself to be actuality by its own power. We need this proof, this fulfilment in life—but only the proof and fulfilment which He gives, the actuality which does not need first to be brought about in us, but which is proper to Him, to His history and the telling of His history in itself, so that from Him and by Him it can become actuality for us. Jesus Christ as He exists in this history cannot, therefore, be merged into all the significances which do, in fact, come to Him, or disappear in them. He cannot, therefore, be identified with them or forgotten by reason of them or shame-facedly relegated to the sphere of a purely historical beginning and cause of the thing which really matters, proclamation, faith, fulfilment (and, if possible, the Church and sacraments). He Himself is the thing which really matters. He is always the Lord over and in everything that has its beginning and cause in Him. It all comes from Him, or better: He comes when it comes. It all lives by Him. It cannot be without Him. It looks back to Him. It also looks forward to the future as His future. It has to be guided by Him. It has to be interpreted by Him, and not *vice versa*EN159. He Himself and His history as it took place then and there is identical with the Word of God, not with that which may result from the Word of God in the way of proclamation and faith and fulfilment in and through and from us men who hear it.

[228]

EN159 the other way around

The relationship between the significant thing which He is in Himself and the significances which He may acquire for us is an irreversible relationship.

On this basis and in this sense we say and must say, as when we tell a story: It came to pass that Jesus Christ, the Son of God, as man, took our place in order to judge us in this place by allowing Himself to be judged for us. In saying this, and saying it in this way, we keep to the Easter story as the commentary on the Gospel story in the unity and completeness of its first two parts: to the affirmation made in the event of Easter that in and for itself, in and through the existence of the One who acts and suffers in it, and therefore objectively for us, this Gospel story is the story of redemption.

We now turn to the question of a right understanding of the decisive words "for us" in this formula of the Judge judged for us.

We must begin by making a basic delimitation. In this context "for us" cannot have merely the general and formal meaning that what took place in Jesus Christ stands in relation to us to the extent that it applies to us, that our own existence is intended and envisaged and affected in this happening, in the existence of Jesus Christ. This is true, of course, but it needs to be defined much more precisely.

We could say the same of the creation of God both as a whole and in detail. What creature of God is there in which we do not to some extent find ourselves [229] and our existence intended and envisaged and affected, so that in our own existence we have to come to some sort of reckoning with it? Jesus Christ is, of course, a fellow-creature, and only as He is with us as such can He be "for us." But He is not "for us" merely in the sense that He is with us in this sense. Every fellow-man impinges on us as such in a most penetrating way, so that we could not fulfil our own human existence if we refused to fulfil it as a fellow human existence in relation to, and in encounter with, those who are near to us and implicitly those who are far away from us. But it is only in a very remote sense that we can say of the men that are with us that because by the very nature of things they are with us they are also "for us." Even the strongest "with us" is not enough to describe what Jesus Christ is in relation to us. No one and nothing in the order of creation can be "for us" in the strict sense, in the way in which Jesus Christ is "for us" in the order of reconciliation.

But we must be careful that the strict "for us" that we have to do with here does not become a "with us" which unites our existence with that of Jesus Christ, in which He is simply the author and initiator of what has to be fulfilled in and through us on the same level, in His discipleship and in fellowship with Him, as though the redemptive happening which has to be proclaimed and believed under His name were something which embraces both Him and us. It is true that Jesus Christ is the fellow-man who goes before us as an example and shows us the way. It is true that there is a discipleship, a fellowship with Him, and therefore an existence of Christians. It is true that what took place in Him, the redemptive happening which has to be proclaimed and believed under His name, does embrace Christian existence and in a certain sense all human existence. But if we are to look and think and speak more precisely it is not a redemptive happening which embraces both Him and us, but the redemptive happening which embraces us in His existence, which takes us up into itself. He is the fellow-man who goes before us as an example and shows us the way because and in the power of the fact that He is "for us": in a "for us" which cannot be equated with any "with us," by which every conceivable "with us" is established—as it were from without, from which all discipleship must derive its meaning and its power. Discipleship, the being of the Christian with Him, rests on the presupposition and can be carried through only on the pre-supposition that Jesus Christ is in Himself "for us"—without our being with Him, without any fulfilment of our being either with or after Him—on the contrary (Rom. 5⁶ᶠ·), even when we were without strength, godless, and enemies. He does not become "for us" when there is some self-fulfilment either with or after Him, but He is for us in Himself, quite independently of how we answer the question which is put to us of our fulfilment with or after Him. The event of redemption took place then and there in Him, and there-fore "for us." In Him, as that which took place then and there, it embraces us, [230] it becomes the basis of fellowship, it calls us to discipleship, but not in such a way that it becomes an event of redemption only through our obedience to this call, or is not an event of redemption through our disobedience, but in such a way that as the event of redemption which took place for us in Him it always comes before the question of our obedience or disobedience, it is always in itself the event of redemption which took place for us, whatever may be our answer to that question.

"Jesus Christ for us" means that as this one true man Jesus Christ has taken the place of us men, of many, in all the authority and omnipotence and com-petence of the one true God, in order to act in our name and therefore validly and effectively for us in all matters of reconciliation with God and therefore of our redemption and salvation, representing us without any co-operation on our part. In the event of His, the Gospel history, there took place that which permits and commands us to understand our history as a history of redemp-tion and not of perdition. It has happened fully and exclusively in Him, excluding any need for completion. Whatever may happen in consequence of the fact that Jesus Christ is for us cannot add to it. It can only be the con-sequence of that which has taken place fully in Him and needs no completion. We can speak of it only as we look back to the fact that this One has acted as very man and very Son of God, that He has acted as our Representative and in our name, that His incarnation, His way of obedience has had and has fulfilled as its ultimate meaning and purpose the fact that He willed to do this and has done it: His activity as our Representative and Substitute.

In the New Testament the words ἀντί, ὑπέρ EN160 and περί EN161 are used to bring out the meaning of this activity of Jesus Christ. They cannot be understood if—quite apart from the

---

EN160 'in place of', 'on behalf of'
EN161 'for'

223

particular view of the atonement made in Him which dominates these passages—we do not see that in general these prepositions speak of a place which ought to be ours, that we ought to have taken this place, that we have been taken from it, that it is occupied by another, that this other acts in this place as only He can, in our cause and interest, that we cannot add to anything that He does there because the place where we might do so is occupied by Him, that anything further which might happen can result only from what is done by Him in our place and in our cause. If someone gives his life a λύτρον ἀντὶ πολλῶν[EN162] (Mk. 10⁴⁵), then he necessarily acts in the place and as the representative of πολλοί[EN163], paying on their account but without their co-operation what they cannot pay for themselves. If he sheds his blood περὶ πολλῶν[EN164] (Mt. 26²⁸), that again is an act which is to the advantage of πολλοί[EN165], but it is his blood which is shed and not a drop of theirs. Whoever it is, Peter who fled or one of the Roman soldiers, they none of them have a part in this blood-shedding. The Jesus who was condemned to be crucified in the place of Barabbas (Mk. 15⁶⁻¹⁵) stands on the one side, and Barabbas who was pardoned at the expense of Jesus stands on the other; for he was not crucified, nor did he really contribute to his own liber-ation which came about when sentence was pronounced on that other. The Lamb of God which takes away the sin of the world (Jn. 1²⁹) stands on the one side in this supremely active relationship to the world, and the world for which it is done stands on the other side, with nothing to add to this relationship. If the good shepherd of Jn. 10¹¹ ¹⁵ ¹⁷ gives His life ὑπὲρ τῶν προβάτων[EN166], He does so to save the life of the sheep, but without any co-operation on their part. If, according to the saying of the High Priest in Jn. 11⁵⁰, it was expedient that one man should die ὑπὲρ τοῦ λαοῦ[EN167], this expressly involves that the people should not die, but that he should die in place of the people to save the people. The same contrast is very clearly developed in the passage in Rom. 5⁶ᶠ· to which we have frequently alluded. Jesus Christ "maketh intercession for us" (ἐντυγχάνει ὑπὲρ ἡμῶν), we are told in Rom. 8³⁴ in a passage which shows the significance for believers to-day of an event of redemption which took place once and for all. And according to the Pauline eucharistic formula what Chris-tians continually receive at the Lord's Table is τὸ σῶμά μου τὸ ὑπὲρ ὑμῶν[EN168] (1 Cor. 11²⁴). He obviously pursues our interest in our place by "giving Himself for our sins, that he might deliver us from the present evil world" (Gal. 1⁴). But, again, there is no suggestion of our participating in this action. He is made a curse for us (Gal. 3¹³) to free us from the curse: for us, but without us—everything depends on this—without our having any longer to bear or partially to bear the curse. We are simply those who have been redeemed from the curse by Him. And when we consider the many New Testament passages which point to the mean-ing and purpose of the existence of Jesus Christ "for us," whether or not they use these prepositions, can we understand any one of them except in the light of this unbridgeable antithesis? Can they point us to any other activity than that which involves this consistent exchange? It is true that certain imperatives result from this exchange. But where is the meaning and purpose of the event made dependent on what we have to do or not to do on the basis of this event? Where especially is the decisive demand of faith as it is addressed to us related to anything but this in itself meaningful event, to the "for us" there and then accom-plished in Jesus Christ once and for all, and therefore valid before ever we even heard the demand of faith, let alone fulfilled it?

[231]

[EN162] ransom for many
[EN163] many
[EN164] for many
[EN165] many
[EN166] on behalf of the sheep
[EN167] on behalf of the people
[EN168] my body which is for you

2. *The Judge Judged in Our Place*

We will now try to expound and understand in detail the "for us" interpreted in this strict sense. In so doing it will be our concern (in contrast to certain one-sided elements in earlier dogmatic conceptions) to keep in view as far as possible the whole of the New Testament witness to this event, and especially, of course, the whole of the event itself.

1. Jesus Christ was and is "for us" in that He took our place as our Judge. We have seen that in its root and origin sin is the arrogance in which man wants to be his own and his neighbour's judge. According to Gen. 3^5 the temptation which involves man's disobedience to God's commandment is the evil desire to know what is good and evil. He ought to leave this knowledge to God, to see his freedom in his ability to adhere to God's decisions in his own decisions. He becomes a sinner in trying to be as God: himself a judge. To be a man—in the world which is hostile to God and unreconciled with Him—is to be the pseudo-sovereign creature which finds its dignity and pride in regarding it as its highest good and most sacred duty to have knowledge of good and evil and to inform itself about it (in relation to itself and others). To be a man means in practice to want to be a judge, to want to be able and competent to pronounce ourselves free and righteous and others more or less guilty. We enjoy ourselves in this craft and dignity. We find our consolation and refuge and strength in [232] exercising it. In our supposed right to do this we all have our safe stronghold, a trusty shield and weapon in relation to ourselves, our neighbours and God. The event of redemption in Jesus Christ not only compromises this position, not only attacks this safe stronghold, but destroys it. It is not merely a moral accusation against the pride of man. It is not merely an intellectual exposure of the error which has led him into it. It is the fact by which the position of man is taken away, by which it is made impossible and untenable, by which the safe stronghold is breached. Jesus Christ as very man and very God has taken the place of every man. He has penetrated to that place where every man is in his inner being supremely by and for himself. This sanctuary belongs to Him and not to man. He has to do what has to be done there. What is man in relation to Him? One who is dispossessed, expelled, a displaced person. He has no more say even in this home of his, this place where the flesh is most intensively and happily and seriously flesh. His knowledge of good and evil is no longer of any value. He is no longer judge. Jesus Christ is Judge. He is not only over us—a final court which we must finally remember and respect. He is radically and totally for us, in our place. He knows and judges and decides at the very point where we regard it as our business to do this. To do this is really His affair, not ours, and He sees to it. Certainly this knowing and judging and deciding, this judgment has necessarily to do with us. To be a man means to exist under the occurrence of this judgment. Yet not—this is the error of man reversed in Jesus Christ—in the occurrence of the judgment in which man himself is the judge, but in the occurrence of the judgment in which this function is that of God Himself. It is this function of God as Judge which has been re-established once and for all in Jesus Christ. What we want to do for ourselves has been

taken out of our hands in Him. Not by a prohibition, the renewal of the command not to eat of the tree of knowledge. We have transgressed this command, and how would its repetition help us? The fruit of this tree which was eaten with such relish is still rumbling in all of us. It is by an action that we are removed from the judge's seat, by the fact that Jesus Christ did for us what we wanted to do for ourselves. However radically we are transgressors of that command, however much that fruit may rumble in us, we are not what we wanted to be because He is for us, He—the man who knows and judges and decides for us. In His hand there lies this solemn and powerful and redemptive instrument. In ours there is only a copy, a foolish and dangerous but ultimately ineffective toy. That is how things are between Him and us.

[233]   The fact that Jesus Christ judges in our place can and must be understood from two different standpoints. It certainly means the abasement and jeopardising of every man. This happening puts an end to his supposed greatness, his dream of divine likeness. At the very place where he finds his own glory he must see another dispose and rule. Another man? It is not merely a matter of some harmless idea of God, the comfortable transcendence which we can know and which makes us exalt ourselves all the more self-consciously. No, it is a matter of the concrete form of a fellow-man occupying that place which we all think it our sacred right to occupy. It is a matter of the very man Jesus of Nazareth in whom God has crossed our path and by whom we find ourselves deposed. Abasement by an abstract "god" is a safe enough matter which we can turn to our own glory. But abasement by God in the flesh, in the person of this fellow-man, is a dangerous matter. It is a real and concrete abasement. If this man is my divine Judge, I myself cannot be judge any longer. I have forfeited the claim to be it and the enjoyment of being it. In the history of this man it came to pass that I was relegated from the sphere in which I wished to judge and placed in the sphere in which I can only see and hear and learn what the judgment really is by which I have to judge myself. And that means that I am jeopardised. For where does our own judgment always lead? To the place where we pronounce ourselves innocent, and where, on account of their venial or mortal sins, and with more or less indulgence and understanding or severity and inflexibility, we pronounce others guilty. That is how we live. And that is how we can no longer live in the humiliating power of what took place in Jesus Christ. We are threatened by it because there is a complete turning of the tables. He who has acted there as Judge will also judge me, and He and not I will judge others. What then? Do I not gather from His coming in my place and my deposition that I have been a bad judge, that all my judgments are annulled, and that my turn will now come in a way in which it could not do before? Before this Judge I obviously cannot stand, because all my previous being and activity was based on and determined by the fact that I wanted to be my own judge and acted as such. And will not others be justified, at least—and to my shame—in relation to the fine way in which I judged them, which was in fact so bad and incompetent a way? That is the one aspect.

2. The Judge Judged in Our Place

The other is that the fact that Jesus Christ judges in our place means an immeasurable liberation and hope. The loss which we always bewail and which we seem to suffer means in reality that a heavy and indeed oppressive burden is lifted from us when Jesus Christ becomes our Judge. It is a nuisance, and at bottom an intolerable nuisance, to have to be the man who gives sentence. It is a constraint always to have to be convincing ourselves that we are innocent, we are in the right. It is similarly an affliction always to have to make it clear to ourselves so that we can cling to it that others are in one way or another in the wrong, and to have to rack our brains how we can make it clear to them, and [234] either bring them to an amendment of their ways or give them up as hopeless, withdrawing from them or fighting against them as the enemies of all that is good and true and beautiful. It is a terrible thing to know good and evil if only in this ostensible and ineffective way, and to have to live with this doubtful knowledge. It agrees quite simply with what is written in Gen. 2^{17}, that if we eat of this tree we must die. We are all in process of dying from this office of judge which we have arrogated to ourselves. It is, therefore, a liberation that it has come to pass in Jesus Christ that we are deposed and dismissed from this office because He has come to exercise it in our place. What does that mean but that at one stroke the whole of the evil responsibility which man has arrogantly taken to himself is taken from him? It is no longer necessary that I should pronounce myself free and righteous. It is no longer necessary that even if only in my heart I should pronounce others guilty. Neither will help either me or them in the very least. Whatever may be the answer to the question of their life and mine, at any rate it no longer needs to be given by me. To find it and to pronounce it is no longer my office or in any way my concern. I am not the Judge. Jesus Christ is Judge. The matter is taken out of my hands. And that means liberation. A great anxiety is lifted, the greatest of all. I can turn to other more important and more happy and more fruitful activities. I have space and freedom for them in view of what has happened in Jesus Christ. And that also means hope. I have good cause to fear before the true Judge, who is not I. When I think of Him I may have fears for others. But not in the obscure or reluctant fear I might have before any judge and his rule if they are outside my control. In fear before the Son of God who became man for me, whose coming in my place as Judge—for all the hardship it involves for me—is a benefit, being made as part of God's turning to man and therefore to me, for the reconciliation of the world with God and therefore for my reconciliation with God. That means, therefore, in fear before the Judge on whose good and redemptive will I can already count, whose decision I can look forward to with trust whatever it may be, in whose hands I can know that my own case and that of others is at least safe. In a fear, therefore, which at bottom is hope. He who knows about myself and others as I never could or should do, will judge concerning me and them in a way which is again infinitely more just than I could ever do—and judge and decide in such a way that it will be well done. Indeed, in such a way that it *is* well done, this real Judge having already decided at the point when the Word became and was flesh. And whatever the decision may be, I have reason to look forward to its disclosure with terror, but with a terror-stricken joy.

This is the first concrete sense in which we have to see and understand the fact that Jesus Christ was and is for us.

[235]   That He is the Judge, and that He makes judgment impossible for us and takes it away from us, is the explanation of the terrible address to the scribes and Pharisees who let themselves be called rabbis, fathers and teachers (Mt. 23$^{1f.}$). It is the indicative which stands behind the evangelical command not to take the top seats but the lower (Lk. 14^8), not to exalt but to abase ourselves (Mt. 23^{12}), and especially: "Judge not, that ye be not judged. For with what judgment ye judge, ye shall be judged; and with what measure ye mete, it shall be measured to you again" (Mt. 7$^{1f.}$). The One who forbids men to judge, who restrains and dispenses them from it, is the One who has come as the real Judge. He makes clear what is true and actual in His existence among men as such: that the one who exalts himself as judge will be abased, that he can only fall into the judgment which will come upon himself. The evangelical prohibition frees us from the necessity of this movement in a vicious circle. Freed in this sense, Paul writes in triumph: "But with me it is a very small thing that I should be judged of you, or of man's judgment: yea, I judge not mine own self ... he that judgeth me is the Lord" (1 Cor. 4$^{3f.}$). And even more strongly in Rom. 8^{34}: "Who is he that condemneth? It is Christ that died, yea rather, that is risen again, who is even at the right hand of God." Hence the admonition that the brethren must not judge one another, for we must all appear before the judgment seat of God (the βῆμα τοῦ Χριστοῦ^{EN169} in 2 Cor. 5^{10}). "As I live, saith the Lord, every knee shall bow to me, and every tongue shall confess to God" (Rom. 14$^{11f.}$). No man can judge another man's servant (Rom. 14^4). This is the reflection of the first sense of the "for us" in the mirror of Christian ethics.

It is the basic sense for all that follows. We should have to suppress or obviously misinterpret the first great section of the Gospel story—Jesus in Galilee—if we tried to ignore the fact that as He judges for us it is decided who it is that lets Himself be judged for us in order to pronounce that divine word of power by which we are pardoned: the One who is justified and who overcomes for us. He is the subject and not the object of what happens—the subject even when He is object. He is the Lord as He fulfils the work which He has undertaken for us, the work of His own deepest humiliation. He has the omnipotence in the power of this work to bear our sins, to bear them away from us, to suffer the consequences of our sins, to be the just One for us sinners, to forgive us our sins. He has this because primarily He Himself is the Judge who overlooks and eliminates our liability to be judged. It is in this omnipotence that He confronts Israel, goes to Jerusalem, enters the city of the kings as a King, shows and promises and gives His body and blood to His disciples with the bread and wine of the Lord's Supper, allows Himself to be kissed by Judas and delivers Himself up into the hands of the soldiers. This is all a sovereign action. It is completed and its meaning is revealed in the passion of Christ, on the cross. Even on the cross it is a divine act. Rightly to understand the passion and cross of Christ, we must not abstract it from the sequence in which this is clear. We must understand the first part of the story as a commentary on the second, and *vice versa*^{EN170}. His passion and the cross are therefore to be understood as His action. It is as the One who carries His cross to Golgotha that He comes to judge the quick and the dead.

EN169 judgement seat of Christ
EN170 the other way around

2. Jesus Christ was and is for us in that He took the place of us. sinners. That sounds hard, and naturally it needs to be explained. But the fact itself is a hard one however we explain it. From what we have just said it is not for us to judge. It is our basic sin to take the place of the judge, to try to judge ourselves and others. All our other sins, both small and great, derive ultimately from this source. But if this is so, how can the Son of God take our place, which means in this context the strange place where we make the illegitimate and impossible attempt to leave the place which belongs to us and to occupy that which does not? How does He come to the place where we are caught in this sin and therefore in the outbreak of every sin; our place as wicked disputants and therefore evil-doers; our place as enemies against God? [236]

We must say at once that He does not come to this place to do there what we ourselves do. In taking our place as Judge He takes the place which belongs to Him, which is His own from all eternity. He does not, therefore, do anything illegitimate. And it is not like ours an unrighteous but a righteous judgment which He exercises in this place. He does in this place the very opposite of what we usually do. In this place He is pure and spotless and sinless. From the fact that He takes it there do not follow any of the transgressions which in our case follow from that first transgression.

But the great and inconceivable thing is that He acts as Judge in our place by taking upon Himself, by accepting responsibility for that which we do in this place. He "who knew no sin" (2 Cor. 5²¹)—who knew nothing of that illegitimate and impossible attempt and all the transgression that it inevitably brought with it, nothing of our disputing and evil-doing and enmity against God—gives Himself (like a *rara avis*ᴱᴺ¹⁷¹) to the fellowship of those who are guilty of all these things, and not only that, but He makes their evil case His own. He is above this fellowship and confronts it and judges it and condemns it in that He takes it upon Himself to be the bearer and Representative, to be responsible for this case, to expose Himself to the accusation and sentence which must inevitably come upon us in this case. He as One can represent all and make Himself responsible for the sins of all because He is very man, in our midst, one of us, but as one of us He is also very God and therefore He exercises and reveals amongst us the almighty righteousness of God. He can conduct the case of God against us in such a way that He takes from us our own evil case, taking our place and compromising and burdening Himself with it.

And as He does that, it ceases to be our sin. It is no longer our affair to prosecute and represent this case. The right and possibility of doing so has been denied and taken away from us. What He in divine omnipotence did amongst us as one of us prevents us from being our own judges, from even wanting to be, from making that senseless attempt on the divine prerogative, from sinning in that way and making ourselves guilty. In that He was and is for us that end is closed, and so is the evil way to that end. He is the man who

---

ᴱᴺ¹⁷¹ rare breed

entered that evil way, with the result that we are forced from it; it can be ours no longer.

[237]   But that means that it became His way: His the sin which we commit on it; His the accusation, the judgment and the curse which necessarily fall on us there. He is the unrighteous amongst those who can no longer be so because He was and is for them. He is the burdened amongst those who have been freed from their burden by Him. He is the condemned amongst those who are pardoned because the sentence which destroys them is directed against Him. He who is in the one person the electing God and the one elect man is as the rejecting God, the God who judges sin in the flesh, in His own person the one rejected man, the Lamb which bears the sin of the world that the world should no longer have to bear it or be able to bear it, that it should be radically and totally taken away from it.

This is undoubtedly the mystery of the divine mercy. God acted in this way because He grieved over His people, because He did not will to abandon the world in its unreconciled state and therefore on the way which leads to destruction, because He willed to show to it an unmerited faithfulness as the Creator, because in His own inconceivable way He loved it. But in this respect it is as well to be clear that the mystery of His mercy is also the mystery of His righteousness. He did not take the unreconciled state of the world lightly, but in all seriousness. He did not will to overcome and remove it from without, but from within. It was His concern to create order, to convert the world to Himself, and therefore genuinely to reconcile it. He did not, therefore, commit an act of arbitrary kindness—which would have been no help to the world. He did what we might call a neat and tidy job. He accepted the world in the state in which He found it, in its alienation from Himself, in the state of sinful men. To bring about this conversion He really took the place of this man. And He did not take the place of this man merely as God but as man: "to fulfil all righteousness," to do right at the very place where man had done wrong, and in that way to make peace with man, to the triumph of His faithfulness, to His own magnifying in creation and by the creature. The Word became flesh that there might be the judgment of sin in the flesh and the resurrection of the flesh.

We must be careful not to describe this event, the coming of Jesus Christ in place of us sinners, this exchange between the divine and our false human position, as an exchange only in appearance, as a kind of dressing up or masquerade, in view of the sinlessness of Jesus Christ. If anything is in bitter earnest it is the fact that God Himself in His eternal purity and holiness has in the sinless man Jesus Christ taken up our evil case in such a way that He willed to make it, and has in fact made it, His own. He did not, in fact, spare His only Son but delivered Him up for us all (Rom. 8^{32}). And the sinlessness, the obedience of this one man (we shall have to speak of it later), is that He did not refuse to be delivered up and therefore to take the place of us sinners.

2. The Judge Judged in Our Place

As such He is quite alone amongst us, the only One who is judged and con- demned and rejected, just as He is the only One who has come and acts amongst us as the Judge. He is quite alone as disputatious man, the transgressor, the enemy against God, which each of us must recognise in ourselves, but because He is there and we can look at Him, we no longer have to recognise in ourselves, being freed from the intolerable responsibility of it—not because it is no longer a fact, but because He has made it His own for us. It can only be the pride which will not bow to Him as the Judge acting in our place which in face of the fact that He has made Himself a sinner for us still clings to it as man's own case, still tries to ascribe it to man that he will and can and must answer for his own sin before God. Our sin is no longer our own. It is His sin, the sin of Jesus Christ. God—He Himself as the obedient Son of the Father— has made it His own. And in that way He has judged it and judged us as those who committed it.

Luther was not exaggerating when he put the alternative: *Oportet peccatum nostrum fieri Christi proprium peccatum, aut in aeternum peribimus*[EN172] (*On Gal.* 3[13], 1535. W.A. 40[1], 435, 17). When in fulfilment of the divine judgment it took place that He willed to make our sin His own, and did in fact make it His own, it was decided that in no other way could it cease to be our sin which as such would inevitably bring us to eternal perdition. And in substance Luther's drastic commentary on this exchange is quite right, that God the Father said to God the Son: *Tu sis Petrus ille negator, Paulus ille persecutor, blasphemus et violentus, David ille adulter, peccator ille qui comedit pomum in Paradiso, latro ille in cruce, in summa: Tu sis omnium hominum persona, qui feceris omnium hominum peccata, tu ergo cogita, ut solvas, et pro eis satisfacias*[EN173] (*ib.* 437, 23). And so Christ must and is willing to stand as *omnium maximus latro, homicida, adulter, fur, sacrilegus, blasphemus*, etc., *quo nullus maior unquam in mundo fuerit*[EN174] (*ib.* 433, 26). And it is the secret of what took place in Jesus Christ that in Him there met and clashed, *summum, maximum et solum peccatum*[EN175] and *summa, maxima et sola iustitia*[EN176], but in such a way that there could be no doubt as to the outcome: *In Christo vincitur, occiditur et sepelitur universum peccatum et manet victrix et regnatrix iustitia in aeternum*[EN177] (*ib.* 439, 13).

To verify this, to see the truth of it, we have only to look at the Gospel passion-narrative and especially the role of Jesus in it. We have already said that the divine subject of the judgment on man as which Jesus appears in the first part of the evangelical record becomes the object of this judgment from the time of the episode in Gethsemane onwards. If this judgment is fulfilled at all—and that is what the Evangelists seem to be trying to say in the second part of their account—then it is with this reversal. Jesus represents men at the place which is theirs according to the divine judgment, by putting Himself in the place which is

---

[EN172] Our sin must become Christ's own sin, or we shall perish in eternity

[EN173] You are to be Peter the denier, Paul the blasphemous and violent persecutor, David the adulterer, that sinner who ate the fruit in paradise, that robber on the cross. In sum: You are to be the one person of all men who has committed the sins of all men. So, consider, so that you might release them, and make satisfaction for them

[EN174] the greatest robber, murderer, adulterer, thief, defiler and blasphemer etc. of all, than whom no-one has ever in the world been greater

[EN175] highest, greatest, and only sin

[EN176] highest, greatest and only righteousness

[EN177] In Christ, the sin of all is conquered, put to death, and buried, and righteous remains the victor and ruler for eternity

theirs on the basis of and in accordance with their human unrighteousness. Jesus maintains the right by electing to let Himself be put in the wrong. He speaks for Himself by being silent. He conquers by suffering. Without ceasing to be action, as action in the strongest sense of the word, as the work of God on earth attaining its goal, His action becomes passion.

The Gospel records betray something of the great and well-grounded astonishment at the unheard of nature of this happening, this transition, this reversing of roles. The shrinking of Jesus in the prayer in Gethsemane is a strong trace of it. According to this record it is not self-evident that He should be given this cup to drink and that He should take it upon Himself to drink it (Mk. 14^{36}). This prayer is, as it were, a remarkable historical complement to the

[239] eternal decision taken in God Himself, one which was not taken easily but with great difficulty, one to which He won through, which He won from Himself. And, of course, the question of the Crucified: Had God forsaken Him? (Mk. 15^{34}), points even more strongly in the same direction. On a very different level we can think of the shrinking of the unrighteous judge Pilate as he made the human decision: its unusual and scandalous nature is not concealed from him. Similarly we may think of the darkness which we are told later came down at the hour of Jesus' death (Mk. 15^{33}), the rending of the veil of the temple (Mk. 15^{37}), the earthquake which shook the rocks and opened the graves (Mt. 27^{51}), as though—in anticipation of its own end—the cosmos had to register the strangeness of this event: the transformation of the accuser into the accused and the judge into the judged, the naming and handling of the Holy God as one who is godless. But it could not be prevented. It had to take place, and it did in fact take place. Not by the reign of chance, nor in consequence of a human nexus of guilt and destiny. The historical pragmatics which is necessary to bind together the two parts of the Gospel story, to explain the transition from action to passion, is as obscure as it possibly could be in the Gospels. In what happens to Jesus, the participants, both Jews and Gentiles, are described in the factual commentary of Acts (2^{23}, 4^{28}) as—for all the obvious and supreme guilt and reprehensibility of their action—only instruments in the hand of God, agents and executors of "the determinate counsel and foreknowledge of God." It does not excuse them—but it was necessary that Christ should "suffer these things" (Lk. 24^{26}). No, His God had not really forsaken Him. In that strange and scandalous reversal we have a necessary fulfilment of the divine purpose which the Son accepts in fear and trembling as the will of His Father, and which the participants in what is done to Jesus must serve *nolentes volentes*[EN178]. They thought to do Him evil, as once the brethren of Joseph had done (Gen. 50^{20}): "But God meant it unto good, to bring to pass, as it is this day, to save much people alive." Yet the divine benefit consists with merciless clarity in the hard thing that Jesus must and will allow Himself to be the one great sinner among all other men: *quo nullus maior unquam in mundo fuerit*[EN179]—to be declared to be such by the mouth of every man, and treated as such at the hand of every man, yet not apart from the will of God, not in abrogation of it, but according to its eternal and wise and righteous direction, in fulfilment of the divine judgment on all men. Jesus must and will allow Himself to take the place which is presumably not His but theirs for the sake of righteousness in the supreme sense. This allowing was determined and effected in divine necessity and freedom. It took place when Jesus was sought out and arrested as a malefactor, when He was accused as a blasphemer before the Sanhedrin and as an agitator against Caesar before Pilate, in both cases being prosecuted and found guilty. It took place when He refrained from saving Himself, from proving His innocence, from defending and justifying Himself, from making even the slightest move to evade this prosecution and verdict. It took place when by means of His great silence He

[EN178] whether they like it or not
[EN179] than whom no-one has ever in the world been greater

confessed eloquently enough that this had to happen, that He must and will allow it to do so. We might ask why—even if His life was forfeit—He set so little store by His honour as the One sent by God? We can explain this only if He saw the triumph of His honour as the One sent by God in what happened to Him, in what He had to suffer when He was set in antithesis to all other men as the one great sinner, because He fulfilled the will of God in so doing, because He did what had to be done for them and the world, taking upon Him their sin and in that way taking it away from them. If this action is the meaning of His passion, then it is meaningful as such. The Gospel story says this factually, It does not offer any theological explanation. It says hardly anything about the significance of the event. But in telling us what it has to tell, and in the way it does, it testifies that we are dealing with the event which at bottom cannot bear any other theological explanation than that which we have here tried to give it in actual agreement with every Church which is worthy of the name of Christian.   [240]

We now turn to a short discussion of the scope of this event. In view of the fact that Jesus Christ took the place of us sinners there are three directions at least in which we have to look.

If it is the case that Jesus Christ made His own our evil case, our sin, then in Him we obviously have to do with the reflection, the supremely objective source of knowledge of that case. That we are sinners, and what our sin is, is something we can never know by reflection about ourselves in the light of a standard of good and evil which we have freely chosen or discovered. This is made impossible by the fact that with His coming we are displaced from the office of judging. We cannot tell ourselves that we are accused, and what the accusation is against us. We have to be told it by that in which we fail. We have to learn it where God Himself has told it to us by taking so seriously the accusation against us and our corruption that He took it upon Himself in His Son, that He willed to encounter us as the man corrupted and accused. For what do we know of ourselves, so long as He does not tell us, so long as He does not tell us in such a way that in His own person He holds out to us and shows us what we are? He knows, and He gives us authentic information about ourselves, about our way as the disputants and wrong-doers and enemies of God that we are. He does it by coming amongst us in the character and form and role of a man like that, and therefore showing us by example what the being of every man is in His eyes and therefore in truth: How He knows us, and what we are before Him. In that He takes our place it is decided what our place is. In that He allows Himself to be sentenced as man, sentence is pronounced on us. The wrath of God against all ungodliness and unrighteousness of men, who hold the truth in unrighteousness, is revealed, and revealed concretely and finally from heaven (Rom. 1¹⁸), in the fact that God gives Himself not only to encounter the man against whom He must and does turn His wrath but to take His place. In Jesus Christ we see who we are by being seen as those we are—being seen as God in Him acknowledges what we are, accepting solidarity with our state and being, making Himself responsible for our sin. In respect of the knowledge of our evil way there is in face of Jesus Christ no escape. There are no excuses or explanations. There is no possibility of understanding evil in the light of some higher necessity. There can be no diminution of its essence as

233

that which is against God, or of our responsibility for it. In face of Jesus Christ we are forced to a simple recognition of the nature of evil as that which is against God, and of the fact that we do it. For in Him God has sought us out in our own state and being, accepting solidarity with us. He does not lie. In that God acknowledges us as sinners in Jesus Christ, His truth is the guarantee that we are such: that we are doers of that which is against Him. We would have to deny Him instead of acknowledging Him if we tried to deny that we are such, if we tried to deny that we are those in whose place Jesus Christ came to convert us to Himself. A confession of faith which in, with and under the confession of faith was not ready to be a confession of sin would not be a confession of faith.

[241]

From the same point we look at another dimension. If it is the case that Jesus Christ has made our sin His own, then He stands in our place as the Representative of our evil case and it is He who answers for it (as ours). It is then (as ours) the sin which is forgiven us in Him. If we are not to say something which is merely cheap and frivolous at this point we have to say most emphatically: as ours. The knowledge of what we are which is based on His coming for us must not be forgotten or obliterated in the other things this coming means for us. As the One who bears our sin, as the One who answers for it while it is taken away from us and forgiven, He does not stand in some far-off neutral state. He is not for us in such a way that we hardly see Him, that we can let His work be done for us as spectators of an alien work which is indeed done in our favour but which hardly affects us because it is done for us, that we do not have to let it take place to us in the true sense. It is true that we are crowded out of our own place by Him in that He made our sin His own. It is true that we can dwell only beside His being for us—His being as the who has made Himself responsible for our evil being. It is true that we can look on His work only as in fact an alien work. It is true that we cannot contribute anything at all to this His being and work for us. But it is also true that the place from which we find ourselves crowded out is always our place. It is also true—and if our consideration is not to be an idle and unprofitable gaping, if it is to be the active and fruitful contemplation of the redemption which has taken place for us in Him, the looking of faith, this is something we must remember as the old Passion-songs always do remember so impressively: *tua res agitur*[EN180]; it is our sin which He has made His own and which now rests on Him. Made sin for us, He stands in our place. He represents us in that which we truly are. That He represents us in it does not mean that we are not it, but that what we truly are, our being in sin, is taken over by Him, that He is responsible for it in divine power, that it is taken from us with divine authority, and forgiven. But although He takes it over, and is responsible for it and it is forgiven us, it is still our being in sin. To look in faith on the One who took our place means always to see ourselves in Him as the men we are, to recognise ourselves in Him as the men for whom He

---

[EN180] your business is dealt with

has taken responsibility, who are forgiven. It is on the fact that this first aspect remains and does not disappear, that in Him we again find ourselves and indeed for the first time see ourselves as we really are, that there rests the meaning and power of the further fact, that we know that He has taken over from us that which we are, that we are no longer responsible for it, that as our own sin it is forgiven us in Him. It is a matter of this liberation. Because our evil case otherwise meant our inevitable destruction, God willed to make it His own in Jesus Christ. What we are He Himself willed to become, in order to take and transform it from within, to make of it something new, the being of man reconciled with Himself. Our being in sin is now in His hands: as such in all its reality it is no longer in our own hands. It is no longer the object of our care and anxiety before Him as our Judge. But no more is it the object of all kinds of artifices by which we try to justify ourselves, to save ourselves from what we are. As such we can only effect and confirm once again what we really are, those who die at the judgment throne of God, and therefore sinners. If our being in sin in all its reality is now in the hands of God (and in Jesus Christ it has happened that God has put it in His hands), then as such it is, of course, the object of our knowledge—not of our knowledge of ourselves, but of our knowledge of God. But if it is the object of our knowledge of God, then in Jesus Christ we find that as our being in sin it has been taken over by God. He took it upon Himself as a matter of the care and anxiety and shame and anguish which He accepted in His Son when the Son took to Himself the accusation which was against us. Therefore it cannot be any more a matter of our care and anxiety and shame and anguish. In Him, not in ourselves but in Him, we see its removal, its taking away, its destruction as an object of our responsibility. We are now summoned—not in ourselves but in Him—to see and acknowledge that we are liberated, and that—again not in ourselves but in Him, by His coming for us, by His taking our place—our sin is cancelled and forgiven. We are summoned to accept our life on this presupposition, as those who are liberated, whose sin is cancelled and forgiven in Him: in the genuine confidence that our being in sin (as our own) belongs to God and not to us, that the responsibility which we owe Him in this matter has been borne by Him. We do not believe in Jesus Christ if this is not our fully assured confidence. The Son of God has sought and found His glory in accepting the dishonour of our state. We therefore do Him despite if we try to shake the fact that He has done it truly and effectively, so that the wrestling with our dishonour, our thought and imagination, has been taken once and for all out of our own hands.

[242]

This forces us to look in yet another direction. If Jesus Christ came and took our place as the Representative of our evil case, then there is nothing more that we can seek and do there even as evil-doers. Even at the place where we had and exercised our supposed glorious liberty to justify ourselves, to prove ourselves in the right, to make a sin of our freedom, He Himself now stands, accused and condemned and rejected for us, but in all His divine majesty. The way back is therefore cut off and barred to us. To look at Jesus Christ who is for

[243] us means to look at ourselves as those who are utterly guilty of sin but who are no longer pledged and committed to it, who have no other ground to do evil now that the ground has been cut from under our feet. It is only if we look past Jesus Christ, not in faith but in unbelief, that we can still think that we have that freedom. We will have something even more strong and radical to say about this later. For the moment it is enough to state that if we find in Jesus Christ the One who stands in our place as the one great sinner, if we find ourselves again in Jesus Christ, ourselves as sinners represented by this One, then we can never again ascribe to ourselves this freedom, nor can we see any further future for us in our sin, as we confess ourselves guilty of it. In the reflection of the existence of Jesus Christ who took our place, who made His own the disputing of which He Himself knew nothing, we find ourselves utterly accused and condemned and rejected for what we are, but in Him who took our place. The only possibility which is still open to us as we look at Him and at ourselves in Him is that of repentance, of turning away from the being and activity, from all that we have to see and acknowledge as guilty in Him, of readiness for this, of turning to what can be made of our evil case now that it is the case of Jesus Christ, now that He has undertaken to be responsible for it and to wrestle with it. As we look at Jesus Christ we can no more will and affirm and accept it than the responsibility of it can cause us care and anxiety. The two belong directly together: If we want to be careful and anxious about it, we are back again on the crooked way of inquiring concerning our own self-justification and therefore on the way of sin; and if we take this way again, our sin will inevitably cause us fresh care and anxiety. As we look at Jesus Christ and ourselves in Him, we are prevented from doing either and both. There is no "way back."

As we look back on the whole of our second point we are reminded that it has a clear complement in New Testament ethics.

Why is it so forcefully impressed upon the heart of a Christian that he must not only not regard persecution as a "strange thing" (1 Pet. 4^{12}), or fear it (Mt. 10^{26}, 1 Pet. 2^{14}), but that he must think of being persecuted and despised and slandered for righteousness sake as joy (Mt. 5^{12}, 1 Pet. 4^{13}), and blessedness (Mt. $5^{10f.}$, 1 Pet. 3^{14}) and acceptable with God (1 Pet. 2^{20})? What is the meaning of this self-sacrifice? Might it not be perhaps a kind of masochism, and therefore an introverted sadism, which can sometimes revert to its real self? Why are Christians not to avenge themselves (Rom. 12^{19}), not to resist evil (Mt. 5^{39}), not to give evil for evil or reviling for reviling (Rom. 12^{17}, 1 Pet. 3^9)? Why not? Does not this give an opening for all kinds of unrighteousness and folly and wickedness amongst men? How can this defencelessness not be dishonourable? Why are Christians even to love their enemies (Mt. $5^{43f.}$), to give them food and drink (Rom. 12^{20}), to pray for them (Mt. 5^{44}), as Stephen actually did (like Jesus Himself in Lk. 23^{34}), when in his final words he said: "Lord, lay not this sin to their charge" (Ac. 7^{60})? Is not this command of an exaggerated enthusiasm of love binding only on a few, without our being able to say in what way it can be binding even on them? And if not, in what sense and on what ground is it a clear commandment of God?

[244] It would be difficult if not impossible to answer these questions if we had not to take account of the fact that when we look at the Lord by whose work and Word the New Testament community was assembled and ordered we are looking at the One who did not come to

call the righteous but sinners (Mt. 9^{13}), who from the very first (Lk. 15^2) received sinners and ate with them and therefore held the most concrete fellowship with them, and in the end took the place of all other sinners as the one great sinner. If the disciples are persecuted and despised and slandered, then their existence is a faint but not obscure reflection of His. "The disciple is not above his master, nor the servant above his lord. It is enough for the disciple that he be as his master, and the servant as his lord. If they have called the master of the house Beelzebub, how much more shall they call them of his household?" (Mt. 10$^{24f.}$). For that reason—we have here a participation in the passion of Christ (1 Pet. 4^{13})—it is all joy and blessedness and grace to be persecuted, not something strange or to be feared. "For even hereunto were ye called: because Christ also suffered for us, leaving us an example, that ye should follow his steps" (1 Pet. 2^{21}). For that reason, under the compelling power of our consideration of the One who was and acted for us as One accused and condemned and rejected, we are given the admonition: "Who, when he was reviled, reviled not again; when he suffered, he threatened not; but committed himself to him that judgeth righteously; who his own self bare our sins in his own body on the tree, that we being dead to sins should live unto righteousness" (1 Pet. 2$^{22f.}$). From this we learn that we are not to oppose evil, as we are tempted, by repaying it with evil. Christians who know that He did this for them belong to Him. In their opposition to evil and evil men they have to comport themselves as these words demand. From this there follows quite naturally the supreme command to love our enemies. Jesus Christ fought His enemies, the enemies of God—as we all are (Rom. 5^{10}, Col. 1^{21})—no, He loved His enemies, by identifying Himself with them. Compared with that what is the bit of forbearance or patience or humour or readiness to help or even intercession that we are willing and ready to bring and offer in the way of loving our enemies? But obviously when we look at what Jesus Christ became and was for us, we cannot leave out some little love for our enemies as a sign of our recognition and understanding that this is how He treated us His enemies. It is indeed a very clear commandment of God which points us in this direction from the cross of shame.

3. Jesus Christ was and is for us in that He suffered and was crucified and died. Along the line that we are following, the witness to Christ in the New Testament moves towards this statement (in the Gospels) in order to proceed from it (in the Acts and Epistles). The work of the Lord who became a servant, the way of the Son of God into the far country, His appearance in the flesh, His humiliation, all aims at that of which this statement speaks. The work of His obedience rendered in humility is when it is completed in this happening. The Judge who judges Israel and the world by letting Himself be judged fulfils this strange judgment as the man who suffered under Pontius Pilate, was crucified, dead and buried. It is clear that we must give to this statement our very special attention.

On the basis of the presuppositions indicated in the two preceding discussions we now have to do with the true fulfilment of what God had to do for us in Jesus Christ—the passion of Jesus Christ. We must first emphasise generally that (1) in it as a passion we have to do with an action. That in it the subject of the Gospel story became an object does not alter this fact. For this took place [245] in the freedom of this subject. According to the common consent of the Gospels Jesus Christ not only knew but willed that this should happen. This distinguishes His passion from the series of other passions in world-history (which we might describe and understand as one long passion in view of the flood of blood and tears which it seems always to be). But it also makes it very puzzling. An offering which offers itself—and that without any obvious meaning or end! But it is with a free self-offering of this kind and therefore with an act and not a fate that we have to do in this passion. In explanation we must add (2) that we are dealing with an act which took place on earth, in time and space, and which is indissolubly linked with the name of a certain man. The history of religious and cultic speculation knows of other suffering and dying gods, and the similarity with these pictures forces itself upon our attention. But the Gospels do not speak of a passion which might just as well have been suffered in one place as another, at one time as another, or in a heavenly or some purely imaginary space and time. They indicate a very definite point in world-history which cannot be exchanged for any other. They point to its earthly theatre. They do not speak of a passing moment in the occurrence of a myth which is cyclic and timeless and therefore of all times. They speak of a unique occurrence for which there is no precedent and which cannot be repeated. They speak of it (3) as an act of God which is coincident with the free action and suffering of a man, but in such a way that this human action and suffering has to be represented and understood as the action and, therefore, the passion of God Himself, which in its historical singularity not only has a general significance for the men of all times and places, but by which their situation has objectively been decisively changed, whether they are aware of it or not. It is, of course, necessarily the case that the knowledge of it as the act of God and the knowledge of the change in the world situation brought about by it can come about individually only in the decision of faith, in which this act becomes to the individual a word, the Word of God accepted in obedience, in which the passion of Jesus Christ is attested as having happened for him, and therefore in very truth for the world.

Let us now try to understand it in general terms.

It cannot be ignored that many men have suffered grievously, most grievously, in the course of world-history. It might even be suggested that many men have perhaps suffered more grievously and longer and more bitterly than did this man in the limited events of a single day. Many who have suffered at the hands of men have been treated no less and perhaps more unjustly than this man. Many have been willing as He was to suffer in this way. Many in so doing have done something which, according to their intention and it may be in fact, [246] was significant for others, perhaps many others, making a redemptive change in their life. And in face of any human suffering do we not have to think ultimately of the obscure but gracious control of divine providence and therefore of the good will of God which becomes act and event in it? The suffering of man may be deserved or undeserved, voluntary or involuntary, heroic or not heroic, important for others or not important for others. But even if it is only the whimper of a sick child it has in it as such something which in its own way is infinitely outstanding and moving and in its human form and its more or less recognisable or even its hidden divine basis something which we can even describe as shattering. This is true of the passion of Jesus of Nazareth, but in so far as it is a human passion it is not true in a way which is basically different from that of any other human passion. If this is the scope of the Gospel story and the starting-point of Gospel proclamation, it was not the intention of the New Testament, nor was it seriously the intention of the Church as it understood itself in the light of the New Testament, that the fundamentally unique occurrence should be found in the human passion as such. If we single out this human passion above others, we may be able to see and to say something which is noteworthy as such, but we shall not be helped forward a single step towards an understanding of what this occurrence is all about. For this reason we have already had to look beyond the human story at every point.

The mystery of this passion, of the torture, crucifixion and death of this one Jew which took place at that place and time at the hands of the Romans, is to be found in the person and mission of the One who suffered there and was crucified and died. His person: it is the eternal God Himself who has given Himself in His Son to be man, and as man to take upon Himself this human passion. His mission: it is the Judge who in this passion takes the place of those who ought to be judged, who in this passion allows Himself to be judged in their place. It is not, therefore, merely that God rules in and over this human occurrence simply as Creator and Lord. He does this, but He does more. He gives Himself to be the humanly acting and suffering person in this occurrence. He Himself is the Subject who in His own freedom becomes in this event the object acting or acted upon in it. It is not simply the humiliation and dishonouring of a creature, of a noble and relatively innocent man that we find here. The problem posed is not that of a theodicy: How can God will this or permit this in the world which He has created good? It is a matter of the humiliation and dishonouring of God Himself, of the question which makes any question of a theodicy a complete anticlimax; the question whether in willing to let this happen to Him He has not renounced and lost Himself as God, whether in capitulating to the folly and wickedness of His creature He has not abdicated from His deity (as did the Japanese Emperor in 1945), whether He can really die and be dead? And it is a matter of the answer to this question: that in this humiliation God is supremely God, that in this death He [247] is supremely alive, that He has maintained and revealed His deity in the passion of this man as His eternal Son. Moreover, this human passion does not have just a significance and effect in its historical situation within humanity and the world. On the contrary, there is fulfilled in it the mission, the task, and the work of the Son of God: the reconciliation of the world with God. There takes place here the redemptive judgment of God on all men. To fulfil this judgment He took the place of all men, He took their place as sinners. In this passion there is legally re-established the covenant between God and man, broken by man but kept by God. On that one day of suffering of that One there took place the comprehensive turning in the history of all creation— with all that this involves.

Because it is a matter of this person and His mission, the suffering, crucifixion and death of this one man is a unique occurrence. His passion has a real dimension of depth which it alone can have in the whole series of human passions. In it—from God's standpoint as well as man's—we have to do not merely with something but with everything: not merely with one of the many hidden but gracious over-rulings of God, but in the fulness of its hiddenness with an action in which it is a matter of His own being or not being, and therefore of His own honour or dishonour in relation to His creation. We are not dealing merely with any suffering, but with the suffering of God and this man in face of the destruction which threatens all creation and every individual, thus compromising God as the Creator. We are dealing with the painful confrontation of God and this man not merely with any evil, not merely with death, but with eternal death, with the power of that which is not. Therefore we are not dealing merely with any sin, or with many sins, which might wound God again and again, and only especially perhaps at this point, and the consequences of which this man had only to suffer in part and freely willed to do so. We are dealing with sin itself and as such: the preoccupation, the orientation, the determination of man as he has left his place as a creature and broken his covenant with God; the corruption which God has made His own, for which He willed to take responsibility in this one man. Here in the passion in which as Judge He lets Himself be judged God has fulfilled this responsibility. In the place of all men He has Himself wrestled with that which separates them from Him. He has Himself borne the consequence of this separation to bear it away.

The New Testament has this in mind when in the Gospels it looks forward to the passion story of Jesus Christ and in the Epistles it looks forward from it to the future of the community and therefore to the future of the world and of every man. It is a matter of history. Everything depends upon the fact that this turning as it comes from God for us men is not simply imagined and presented [248] as a true teaching of pious and thoughtful people, but that it happened in this way, in the space and time which are those of all men. But it is a matter of this history. That it took place once at this time and place as this history is what distinguishes the passion, crucifixion and death of this one Jew from all the other occurrences in time and space with which the passion of Jesus Christ is otherwise similar in every respect. Distinguished in this way, it is the subject of Christian faith and proclamation.

But what do we have to believe? and proclaim? It is true enough to say that in this one passion at this time and place, the passion of this one man, we have to do with God's act for us. But the question of content still remains. And we must not turn it into a question concerning the significance of this act, i.e., the determination of the being of man which takes place when the passion is proclaimed to a man and believed by him. This question, too, is legitimate and necessary. But to answer it presupposes a definite message concerning the passion itself and as such. New Testament faith and proclamation do in fact imply

a definite experience by the being of the man who accepts in faith the proclamation concerning Jesus Christ. They imply the imperatives which come to
him in this acceptance, the questions before which and the decision in which
he is posited. But they do not exhaust themselves in these implicates. New
Testament faith does not curve in upon itself or centre on itself as *fides qua
creditur*[EN181]. The content of New Testament proclamation does not consist
only of the description and reception of this *fides qua creditur*[EN182]. Rather they
relate to and are based upon a primary message concerning Jesus Christ Himself, to which New Testament faith is open and has constantly to open itself,
which must always be the first word of New Testament proclamation not only
because in this message we have its historical starting-point, but because in it
we have its origin and primary theme, because without it there cannot be
those implicates, because this message is the thing which implies, without
which anything we might say here about the being of man would be left hanging in the air, like a subsidiary clause which has no principal clause. Our present question is primarily a question concerning this principal clause, the
message about the passion of Jesus Christ itself and as such. To answer it we
must keep to the original form of the question and not evade it.

If we are to keep to it, if we are not to turn the "What" into something else,
but answer it with a plain "This," then we must not be afraid to take the true
statement that in the passion of Jesus Christ we have to do with God's act for
us, and to put it in a slightly different form, that it is in the passion of Jesus
Christ that we have to do with the act of God for us. It then tells us—further
elucidation is, of course, necessary—something definite about this act of God
for us, something which has real content, something which is independent of   [249]
the particular experience of being envisaged and implied in faith in it and its
proclamation. It speaks to us of that which is the basis of this experience, of the
source of the imperatives which come to the men who receive the proclamation in faith, of the source of the questions before which, and of the decision
in which, they are posited. As an answer to this question of the "What," it will
then run as follows: Allowing for all the explanations, and for the legitimate
and necessary implications of this occurrence, it is the passion of Jesus Christ
itself and as such which has to be believed and proclaimed as the act of God
for us.

In the reversal of this declaration, in the question of the source, the independent basis of
the Christian experience of being, we are not dealing with a question of idly speculative
interest, and certainly not with an attempt to back up the certainty of faith and proclamation. On the contrary, it is a question of simple truth, or rather of a recognition of the
answer to the question of truth which is given and included in the act of God for us. Truth is
the disclosure and recognition of that which *is* as it appears to man. It is, therefore, the
disclosure and recognition of that without which man cannot live unless he consoles himself
with a mere and probably deceptive appearance, but which he cannot tell to himself because

---

[EN181] faith by which it is believed
[EN182] faith by which it is believed

by its very nature it is accessible only in appearance and not in essence, which he can only allow himself to be told and told concretely, which he has always concretely to learn afresh. When this happens in the encounter with that which is, we attain to truth, to that disclosure and recognition. To be of the truth is to "hear his voice" (Jn. 18³⁷). The act of God for us fulfils and includes the answering of the question of its own truth—and the same is true of faith in it and its proclamation—for in it we have to accept His voice as the voice which speaks of Him as that which is and which appears as such. Christian experience, as the manifestation of that which is, i.e., of Him who is, can be true and of the truth. But it is not so *in abstracto*EN183, in itself and as such. It is true to the extent that it proceeds from the truth, and therefore from that disclosure and recognition. It is true to the extent that it rests on something that is said concretely to man about Him and learned concretely about Him, to the extent that it lives entirely by Him and cannot curve in upon itself in self-sufficiency. It is true in and by its source, in and by Jesus Christ as its basis, upon which it is dependent but which is not dependent upon it. It is true in its openness to this location and source of its truth. For that reason we cannot be content to define the passion of Jesus Christ as the act of God for us, however true that may be, but we must go on to define the act of God for us as the passion of Jesus Christ. In this, and this alone, is it the act of God for us. With this there stands or falls the truth of Christian experience.

The most simple, and in its simplicity the most impressive, explanation of this definition has always consisted in its mere repetition. As, for instance, in the action and words at the giving of the bread in the Lord's Supper: This is my body (which is given for you). Its strength lies in the fact that it simply points to the event itself. It presupposes that the event speaks for itself, is self-explanatory. It only needs to be indicated. And faith only needs to confess that it has happened. It happened for us, but it happened without us, without our co-operating or contributing. Even the intellectual activity of our understand-
[250] ing and explaining cannot add to what happened and is and is effective. It cannot add to its authenticity, or to its open validity, or even to the physical force of its fulfilment. It does not receive all this from our insight into its inner coherence. It has this inner coherence, and we can and should perceive it. But its authenticity, its validity and its force are in itself. The *theologia crucis*EN184 can and should point to them, but all theology lives by the fact that the cross of Jesus Christ is itself the work and therefore the wholly sufficient Word of God: not a Word which is empty, but one which is filled and which can be heard in its fulness, God's own Word. Simply to co-relate without commentary *crux*EN185 and *unica spes*EN186 cannot and must not be the totality of what we have to say on this matter. But in its simplicity it is a basic and indispensable reminder of who is at work and who is speaking.

There are many New Testament passages from which we may gather that in the most primitive communities there was no need to do more than mention the death of Jesus Christ as God's accomplished act of redemption, because those who read or heard already knew of

---

EN183 in the abstract
EN184 theology of the cross
EN185 cross
EN186 single hope

whom or what they were reminded by it, because everything that was decisive was included in it. The event itself, testified as such by the apostles—"set forth before your eyes," as Paul says in Gal. 3^1—was through the thin veil of this human mediation its own proclamation awakening and sustaining faith. It could be and had to be explained what "the word of the cross" was (1 Cor. 1^{18}), that it was to preach Christ crucified (1 Cor. 1^{23}) or to "shew the Lord's death" (1 Cor. 11^{26}), but it was already perceived and known even before it was explained. God gave His Son "for us all" (Rom. 8^{32}). He gave Himself "for me" (Gal. 2^{20}). He "suffered for you" (1 Pet. 2^{21}). He died for us (1 Thess. 5^9). By the grace of God "he tasted death for every man" (Heb. 2^9). He gave His life "for his friends" (Jn. 15^{13}). As the Good Shepherd, He gave His life for the sheep (Jn. 10^{11}). In our brother we have to see the one "for whom Christ died" (Rom. 14^{15}). All these and similar sayings are expressions to indicate the passion of Christ, expressions which certainly could be and needed to be interpreted in the ears of New Testament Christians, but which certainly did not sound empty or obscure, but filled out and very clear; not by virtue of faith as the existential reaction of these men, but by virtue of the event itself as it happened in space and time and as it is simply indicated in these expressions.

We may well ask whether the preaching of Good Friday would not in many cases be better if it took the form, not of all kinds of inadequate theology, but of a simple repetition—*Spiritu sancto adiuvante*^{EN187}—of the evangelical passion-narrative; whether it would not be a more "existential" address as such.

All the same, the event and the recollection do call for further explanation, not to add to this event, but for joy at that which has happened in it, in consideration of it and thankfulness for it. Its very content demands an explanation in this sense, the *intellectus fidei*^{EN188}.

What actually took place in this suffering and dying? We are still speaking in more general terms when in relation to the statements of the New Testament and our own previous considerations we reply: In this suffering and dying of God Himself in His Son, there took place the reconciliation with God, the conversion to Him, of the world which is out of harmony with Him, contradicting and opposing Him. The world is not itself capable of this reconciliation. Man cannot convert Himself. He cannot make himself the friend of God instead of the enemy of God. He cannot save himself from the destruction which must inevitably follow His enmity against God. He cannot do anything to escape the wrath of God which threatens him in the position in which he has placed himself. He cannot alter the fact that this position is a place of shadows, and that from this place he enters irresistibly on a slope which leads to outer darkness.

[251]

It is not a pessimistic anthropology or an exaggerated doctrine of sin which makes us say this but the fact that, according to the decision of God made and revealed in power, it needed nothing less than God Himself to remedy the corruption of our being and ourselves, to restore order between Himself as Creator and the world as His creation, to set up and maintain again the covenant broken by man, to carry it through against man for the sake of man, and in

---

^{EN187} with the aid of the Holy Spirit
^{EN188} understanding of faith

that way to save man from destruction. Where the intervention of God in person is needed, everything is obviously lost without that intervention, and man can do nothing to help himself. That God has intervened in person is the good news of Good Friday. For in the suffering and dying of Jesus Christ He has done this in the event in which He, the Judge, delivers Himself up to be judged. He could do this only against us, opposing to our contradiction His own superior contradiction, to our opposition His own superior opposition. We are all on the other side. In ourselves, we are always on the other side. Therefore what He has done He has done without us, without the world, without the counsel or help of that which is flesh and lives in the flesh—except only for the flesh of Jesus Christ. He has done it entirely in this His Word which became flesh. Reconciliation is a comprehensive occurrence, embracing many in the One in whom it was made, and through the many embracing all. But it is not a repeated, let alone a general occurrence. There is no other reconciliation of the world with God for any other man than that which took place in this One, that which comes to the world and directly or indirectly to every man in Him. In Him the world is converted to God. In Him man is the friend of God and not His enemy. In Him the covenant which God has faithfully kept and man has broken is renewed and restored. Representing all others in Himself, He is the human partner of God in this new covenant—He in the authenticity, validity and force of His suffering and dying.

But He is this for us. In Him—as He fulfils His judgment on us all, but fulfils it in this way—God Himself is for us. In this divine judgment the atonement made in the passion of this One is ours. This is the origin and primary theme of faith and proclamation. And from this it follows that in faith we believe primarily in Jesus Christ, and in proclamation we primarily proclaim Jesus [252] Christ: Him in whom God will freely give us all things (Rom. 8^{32}). All things! But the relation between Him and the all things which He will give us cannot be reversed if we are not to come into conflict with the question of truth, or rather with the answering of the question of truth as we have it in God's act fulfilled in Him for us. He is the truth. He is the disclosure and knowledge of that which is. For He is. To be of the truth means to hear His voice in encounter and confrontation with Him: not to hear first the voice of that which God will give us in Him but to hear His voice. To be of the truth means first to believe in Him. And to proclaim the truth means first to proclaim Him, to proclaim this principal clause and only then the subsidiary clauses which derive from it.

In the accounts of the Last Supper in 1 Cor. 11^{25} and Lk. 22^{20} that which is actuality and truth in Jesus Christ, that which takes place in Him as event and revelation, is called "the new covenant in my blood," while in Mk. (14^{24}) and Mt. 26^{28} it is described conversely and more simply as "my blood of the covenant." In both cases the unity of outlook and concept is evident. In the shedding of Christ's blood, i.e., in the offering of His life to the powers of death we have the constancy, the maintenance or the restitution of the covenant between

God and man. "We have peace with God" and προσαγωγὴν εἰς τὴν χάριν[EN189] is how it is put in Rom. 5[1f.], and in Rom. 5[10] "we are reconciled by the death of his Son"—both agreeing with the chief passage in 2 Cor. 5[18f.]. The message of Col. 1[20] is obviously the same: God determined "by him to reconcile all things to himself, making peace διὰ τοῦ αἵματος τοῦ σταυροῦ αὐτοῦ[EN190], or as we have it in Col. 1[22] "in the body of his flesh through death." He Himself is "our peace" is what we are told in Eph. 2[14], He who in His own flesh removed the enmity between Jew and Gentile and their common enmity against God to reconcile both (2[16]) in one body (His own) with God by the cross, having ἐν αὐτῷ (in or by Himself) slain the enmity thereby. In substance 1 Pet. 3[18] says exactly the same: "He died, the just for the unjust, to bring us to God. And in Heb. 10[19f.] we are told that in the blood of Jesus Christ we have τὴν εἴσοδον τῶν ἁγίων[EN191] "by a new and living way which he hath consecrated for us, through the veil, that is to say, his flesh." Therefore if this covenant, this peace, this reconciliation with Him, this access to Him is the meaning and purpose of the act which He has accomplished for us, then it is the unanimous witness of these passages that this act took place in the blood, in the cross, in the death of Jesus Christ and not in any other place, at any other time or in any other way.

Our final question is why and in what sense it is in the suffering and dying of Jesus Christ that we have to do with the act of God which has taken place for us? In our answer (in which again we have regard to the very express statements of the New Testament and the course we have so far followed), we must pay particular attention to the concept and reality of human sin, to its relation to the reality of the atonement on the one side and to that of death on the other.

The sin and sins of man form the disruptive factor within creation which makes necessary the atonement, the new peace with God, the restoration of the covenant with a view to the glory of God and the redemption and salvation of man as the work of God's free mercy. Sin, therefore, is the obstacle which has to be removed and overcome in the reconciliation of the world with God as [253] its conversion to Him. But it is also the source, which has to be blocked in the atonement, of the destruction which threatens man, which already engulfs him and drags him down. Its wages is death (Rom. 6[23]). It is the sting of death (1 Cor. 15[56]). By it death came into the world (Rom. 5[12]). And the concept death in the New Testament means not only the dying of man but the destruction which qualifies or rather disqualifies it, eternal death, death as the invincibly threatening force of dissolution. It is to this place that man moves as a sinner.

The very heart of the atonement is the overcoming of sin: sin in its character as the rebellion of man against God, and in its character as the ground of man's hopeless destiny in death. It was to fulfil this judgment on sin that the Son of God as man took our place as sinners. He fulfils it—as man in our place—by completing our work in the omnipotence of the divine Son, by treading the way of sinners to its bitter end in death, in destruction, in the

---

[EN189] access to grace
[EN190] through his blood shed on the cross
[EN191] entry to the Holy Place

limitless anguish of separation from God, by delivering up sinful man and sin in His own person to the non-being which is properly theirs, the non-being, the nothingness to which man has fallen victim as a sinner and towards which he relentlessly hastens. We can say indeed that He fulfils this judgment by suffering the punishment which we have all brought on ourselves.

The concept of punishment has come into the answer given by Christian theology to this question from Is. 53. In the New Testament it does not occur in this connexion. But it cannot be completely rejected or evaded on this account. My turning from God is followed by God's annihilating turning from me. When it is resisted His love works itself out as death-dealing wrath. If Jesus Christ has followed our way as sinners to the end to which it leads, in outer darkness, then we can say with that passage from the Old Testament that He has suffered this punishment of ours. But we must not make this a main concept as in some of the older presentations of the doctrine of the atonement (especially those which follow Anselm of Canterbury), either in the sense that by His suffering our punishment we are spared from suffering it ourselves, or that in so doing He "satisfied" or offered satisfaction to the wrath of God. The latter thought is quite foreign to the New Testament. And of the possible idea that we are spared punishment by what Jesus Christ has done for us we have to notice that the main drift of the New Testament statements concerning the passion and death of Jesus Christ is not at all or only indirectly in this direction.

The decisive thing is not that He has suffered what we ought to have suffered so that we do not have to suffer it, the destruction to which we have fallen victim by our guilt, and therefore the punishment which we deserve. This is true, of course. But it is true only as it derives from the decisive thing that in the suffering and death of Jesus Christ it has come to pass that in His own person He has made an end of us as sinners and therefore of sin itself by going to death as the One who took our place as sinners. In His person He has delivered up us sinners and sin itself to destruction. He has removed us sinners and sin, negated us, cancelled us out: ourselves, our sin, and the accusation, [254] condemnation and perdition which had overtaken us. That is what we cannot do and are not willing to do. How can we be able and willing to remove ourselves as those who commit sin and therefore sin itself? That is what He could and willed to do and actually did for us in His right and authority and power as the Son of God when He took our place as man. The man of sin, the first Adam, the cosmos alienated from God, the "present evil world" (Gal. 1⁴), was taken and killed and buried in and with Him on the cross. On the one side, therefore, He has turned over a new leaf in the history of the covenant of God with man, making atonement, giving man a new peace with God, reopening the blocked road of man to God. That is what happened when Jesus Christ, who willed to make Himself the bearer and Representative of sin, caused sin to be taken and killed on the cross in His own person (as that of the one great sinner). And in that way, not by suffering our punishment as such, but in the deliverance of sinful man and sin itself to destruction, which He accomplished when He suffered our punishment, He has on the other side blocked the source of our destruction; He has seen to it that we do not have to suffer what we ought to suffer; He has removed the accusation and condemnation and perdition which had passed upon us; He has cancelled their relevance to us; He has saved us from destruction and rescued us from eternal death.

The passion of Jesus Christ is the judgment of God in which the Judge Himself was the judged. And as such it is at its heart and centre the victory which has been won for us, in our place, in the battle against sin. By this time it should be clear why it is so important to understand this passion as from the very first the divine action. As the passion of the Son of God who became man for us it is the radical divine action which attacks and destroys at its very root the primary evil in the world; the activity of the second Adam who took the place of the first, who reversed and overthrew the activity of the first in this place, and in so doing brought in a new man, founded a new world and inaugurated a new aeon—and all this in His passion. It is only as His passion that it can be this action; only as sin is, as it were, taken in the rear, only as it is destroyed by the destruction and eternal death which threatens the world, only as this worst becomes an instrument in the hand of the merciful and omnipotent God for the creation of the best. For the sake of this best, the worst had to happen to sinful man: not out of any desire for vengeance and retribution on the part of God, but because of the radical nature of the divine love, which could "satisfy" itself only in the outworking of its wrath against the man of sin, only by killing him, extinguishing him, removing him. Here is the place for the doubtful concept that in the passion of Jesus Christ, in the giving up of His Son to death, God has done that which is "satisfactory" or sufficient in the victorious fighting of sin to make this victory radical and total. He has done that which is sufficient to take away sin, to restore order between Himself as the [255] Creator and His creation, to bring in the new man reconciled and therefore at peace with Him, to redeem man from death. God has done this in the passion of Jesus Christ. For this reason the divine judgment in which the Judge was judged, and therefore the passion of Jesus Christ, is as such the divine action of atonement which has taken place for us.

From this we may readily understand that in the overwhelming majority of passages in the New Testament which touch on it directly or indirectly the death of Jesus Christ is explicitly set in some relationship to sin. The positive side is always in the background, as in Jn. 6[51]: "The bread that I will give is my flesh, which I will give for the life of the world," or Rom. 5[9]: "Being now justified by his blood," or 2 Cor. 5[15]: "He died for all, that they which live should not henceforth live unto themselves, but unto him which died for them, and rose again," and in this sense, Ac. 20[28]: "He has purchased the church with his own blood." But the direct end of the passion is a negative one—the overcoming of the rift which has come between God and man, of the enmity of man against God. Jesus Christ was delivered "for our offences" (Rom. 4[25]), or "for our sins" (Gal. 1[4]). He died "once for sins" (1 Pet. 3[18]), or "for our sins according to the Scriptures" (1 Cor. 15[3]) is how we have it in more general expressions which only indicate the problem. More concretely He is the "Lamb of God which (bears is not strong enough for $\alpha i\rho\omega\nu$) removes, takes away, overcomes the sin of the world" (Jn. 1[29], cf. 1 Jn. 3[5]). Again, in Heb. 9[28]: "He was once offered to bear the sins of many," or 1 Pet. 2[24]: "Who his own self bare our sins in his own body on the tree that we should be dead to sins." In substance again: "The blood of Jesus Christ his Son cleanseth us from all sin" (1

247

Jn. 1⁷); "Offering himself, he purges our conscience from dead works" (Heb. 9¹⁴); "He puri-
fies unto himself a peculiar people" (Tit. 2¹⁴). By His blood, the blood of the Lamb, the
clothes of His own people are washed and made white (Rev. 7¹⁴). Even more pointedly: "God
sent his own sin in the likeness of sinful flesh, and for sin, and condemned sin in the flesh"
(Rom. 8³). And very much to the point: "Through death he destroyed him that had the
power of death, that is, the devil" (Heb. 2¹⁴); "He slew the enmity in himself" (Eph. 2¹⁶); "He
died unto sin once" in such a way that Christians can and should reckon themselves dead
unto sin (Rom. 6¹⁰ᶠ·). It is the case that "if one died for all, then were all dead" (2 Cor. 5¹⁴).
And because all this took place (in Him for us), according to the remarkable verses in Col.
2¹⁴ᶠ·, God has blotted out the handwriting of ordinances that was against us, He has taken it
out of the way, nailed it to His cross, spoiled principalities and powers, made a show of them
openly (as prisoners), and triumphed over them—and all this in Him, in the circumcision of
Christ, in which there has taken place already that of His people, in His putting off of the
body of the flesh, in which they too have put it off (Col. 2¹¹).

It is in this sense that we have to understand the saying at the giving of the cup at the Last
Supper as recorded by Matthew (26²⁸), which speaks of the "blood of the covenant" which is
shed for many "for the forgiveness of sins." Elsewhere in the New Testament the latter concept is brought into surprisingly little direct relation to the death of Jesus Christ. The Word
of the Crucified Himself: "Father, forgive them; for they know not what they do" (Lk. 23³⁴),
can, of course, be mentioned in this connexion. In Eph. 1⁷ the ἀπολύτρωσις EN192 which
has taken place in His blood is obviously equated with the "forgiveness of sins." And in Col.
1¹⁴ we find the same equivalent in plain juxtaposition with a mention of our redemption
from the powers of darkness accomplished in Jesus Christ. Again in close proximity to a
mention of the event of the cross, it is said of God in Col. 2¹³: χαρισάμενος ἡμῖν πάντα τὰ
παραπτώματα EN193. And when we are told in Heb. 9²² that "without the shedding of blood
there is no remission," this obviously does not refer only to the Old Testament rites then
under discussion. Have we to assume that the direct relating of the concept of the forgiveness of sins, which is from the very first so important in the Gospels, with the death of Jesus
Christ is relatively so infrequent for the very reason that for those who heard and read the
New Testament writings it was self-evident that it could be meaningful only in this relationship? From what is said about the removing, the taking away, the judging, the destroying of
sin which takes place in the death of Christ, the purging of it accomplished in the blood of
Christ, it is clear that the forgiveness of sins, whether mentioned in connexion with this
death or otherwise, cannot mean anything less radical than that. ἄφεσις, ἀφιέναι,
χαρίζεσθαι EN194 is a releasing of man from a legal relationship fatal to him, from an intolerable commitment which he has accepted, from an imprisonment in which he finds himself.
And it is not something which comes accidentally or arbitrarily but in the strictest necessity,
not partially but totally, not conditionally but unconditionally, not provisionally but definitively. As the subject of sin, sins and transgressions man finds himself in this fatal relationship, under this intolerable commitment, in this imprisonment. He cannot release himself
from it. But at one stroke he is wholly and finally released from it when Jesus Christ takes his
place, takes from him his sin, sins and transgressions, deals with them Himself, removes
them, takes them away, judges and destroys them in His death, purges him from them. That
is how his reconciliation with God is effected and he himself is saved from destruction.
Because Jesus Christ is the power of this decisive happening of the forgiveness of sins, the sin
forgiven is now the old thing—the essence of all that is old, something which is past and

[256]

EN192 redemption
EN193 he forgave us all our sins
EN194 forgiveness, forgiving, being gracious

done with, which is only the past, which is not the present and has no future: παρῆλθεν EN195 (2 Cor. 5¹⁷). To that extent the forgiveness of sins is the central meaning of the divine action in the passion of Jesus Christ, and because it concerns the forgiveness of sins, this action must consist in a passion.

4. Jesus Christ was and is for us in that He has done this before God and has therefore done right. We must now return for a moment to the first three aspects. We have spoken of the Judge, the judged and the judgment, and in each of these we have spoken of Jesus Christ who took our place and acted for us. What we have still to do is to say that this aspect of the atonement made for us in Him only *seems* to be purely negative. In fact—to take up again our earlier concept—in the disclosure and knowledge of that which truly is as it takes place in this act of God, it is the case that this action which is negative in form is the great positive act of God within and against the world which is hostile to Him, which does not do Him honour and which therefore destroys itself. The Judge, the judged, the judgment—the one Jesus Christ who is all these things and in and by Himself does all these things—is the justice or righteousness of God in the biblical sense of the term: the omnipotence of God creating order, which is "now" (νυνὶ δέ EN196 Rom. 3²¹) revealed and effective as a turning from this present evil aeon (Gal. 1⁴) to the new one of a world reconciled with God in Him, this One. This righteousness cannot come from the world, from us. It cannot be done by us, fulfilled by us, or in any way completed or improved or maintained by us. It is the righteousness of God. And because *rebus sic stantibus* EN197 this "without us" necessarily means "against us" the action has to [257] take this negative form; Jesus Christ has to be the Judge, the judged and in His own person the fulfilment of the judgment; His decisive work and word has to be His suffering and dying. But that is only the negative form of the fulness of a positive divine righteousness, which itself and as such is identical with the free love of God effectively interposing between our enmity and Himself, the work and word of His grace. The suffering and death of Jesus Christ are the No of God in and with which He again takes up and asserts in man's space and time the Yes to man which He has determined and pronounced in eternity. Because Jesus Christ is the Yes of God spoken in world-history and itself become a part of world-history, therefore and to that extent God is in Jesus Christ *pro nobis.* EN198 *Cur Deus homo?* EN199 Because God, who became man in His Son, willed in this His Yes to do this work of His, but His human work, and therefore this work for the reconciliation of the world which is effective for us men.

Our task now is to understand the fact and extent to which this did take place for us in Jesus Christ in this negative form. And first of all we have to say comprehensively that in this action Jesus Christ was amongst us and lived and

---

EN195 it has passed away
EN196 but now
EN197 as things are
EN198 for us.
EN199 Why did God become man?

acted for us as the just or righteous man: "the just for the unjust" (1 Pet. 3^{18}).
The omnipotence of God in the world, without and against the world, and
therefore creating order for the world, is concretely identical with this righteous man, this second Adam who took the place of the first and put right what
he had perverted. As the Judge, as the judged, as the One who in His own
person has accomplished the judgment, He is the end of the old aeon and the
beginning of the new. He is the righteousness which dwells in the new heaven
and the new earth (2 Pet. 3^{13}). We wait for Him when, placed in Him and with
Him at this turning-point of the times, we wait for this new heaven and new
earth. He sits on the throne and says: "Behold, I make all things new," and
more than that: "It is done. I am Alpha and Omega, the beginning and the
end" (Rev. 21$^{5f.}$)—He, this righteous man.

But He is the righteous man in that—and here we take up again the title of
this whole section—as the Son of God obedient to the Father in fulfilment of
this action of God He lived and acted as the one man obedient to God. For the
righteousness which is upon earth, the righteousness of man, in and against
and for world-history, is the obedience of the creature—just as sin is unrighteousness (1 Jn. 3^4) because it is the disobedience of the creature (Rom. 5^{19}).
In obedience man lives and acts in freedom. He is true to his own nature as the
creature of God, the creature which is appointed in its own decisions to follow
and correspond to the decisions of God, to follow and correspond to the
decisions of God in its decisions which are its own. In sin, and therefore in
disobedience, man forfeits this freedom. He is therefore untrue not only to
[258] God but also to his own nature as the creature of God. This is his unrighteousness, the unrighteousness of the first Adam, of this present evil aeon. Every
man shares this unrighteousness and is therefore in the wrong before God.
The atonement is therefore positively the removal of this unrighteousness by
the existence of the one obedient and therefore free man. He is "the new
man." And in fulfilment of the divine action and therefore in His passion Jesus
Christ has acted for us as this new and obedient and therefore free man. As the
Son obedient to the Father—and therefore in the freedom which, like the
freedom of God Himself, has the character of obedience—He has brought in
the man who is the child of this God, this new and obedient and free man. As
this man He has revealed and made operative the righteousness of God on
earth.

But the righteousness of Jesus of Nazareth for us as the obedient Son of God
consists simply in His complete affirmation of this reversal, this execution of
judgment in the judging of the Judge. It consists in the fact that He delivered
Himself up to this. Our second point is decisive for a true understanding: Jesus
Christ was obedient in that He willed to take our place as sinners and did, in
fact, take our place. When we speak of the sinlessness of Jesus we must always
think concretely of this. It did not consist in an abstract and absolute purity,
goodness and virtue. It consisted in His actual freedom from sin itself, from
the basis of all sins. That is why He was not a transgressor and committed no

sins. That is why He could take on Himself and deliver up to death the sins of all other men. That is why He could forgive sins and transgressions. He came and occupied, as it were, an archimedian point from which He could move, and did in fact move, the earth. He did it by willing to take our place as sinners, and thus putting God in the right against Him. From the time of Adam it had been man's sin to want to become and be his own judge in place of God. The fall of man is that he would not keep to the limits appointed for him in relation to God as a human creature. And man's being in sin is that he will not accept that he is the rebel against God that he is, that he will not see and acknowledge his usurpation for what it is, that he will not confess it and therefore his own fall, that he wants to explain and excuse and justify himself, to be in the right against God. If he ceased to do this, He would acknowledge that God is in the right against him, thus returning to the place which is proper to him as a creature in relation to God, and reversing the fall which consists in his usurpation. His unwillingness to repent is the constant renewal of his sin. The sinlessness of Jesus Christ consists in the fact that He does not take part in this game. He was a man as we are. His condition was no different from ours. He took our flesh, the nature of man as he comes from the fall. In this nature He is exposed every moment to the temptation to a renewal of sin—the temptation of impenitent being and thinking and speaking and action. His sinlessness was [259] not therefore His condition. It was the act of His being in which He defeated temptation in His condition which is ours, in the flesh. Note that He who as the Son of God was like God did not count it His "prey" (a prize to be held fast) to be like God, to be God, but He emptied Himself, becoming as we are—and in so doing demonstrating and confirming the true deity of God—placing Himself in the series of men who rebelled against God in their delusion that they would be as God, not in order to try to refuse or conceal or deny this, but in the place of all other men—who refuse to do so—to confess it, to take upon Himself this guilt of all human beings in order in the name of all to put God in the right against Him. In so doing He acted justly in the place of all and for the sake of all. In their place and for their sake, instead of committing fresh sin, He returned to the place from which they had fallen into sin, the place which belongs to the creature in relation to God. In so doing, in His own person, He reversed the fall in their place and for their sake. He acted justly in that He did not refuse to do what they would not do. The one great sinner, with all the consequences that this involves, penitently acknowledges that He is the one lost sheep, the one lost coin, the lost son (Lk.15$^{3f.}$), and therefore that as the Judge He is the One who is judged. In this way He was obedient to God. For this reason He, Jesus of Nazareth—among the many who in Jordan received the baptism of John for the future forgiveness of sins—was the One in whom God was well pleased as His beloved Son, the One upon whom John saw the Spirit descend from heaven, Himself the One who, proclaimed by John, was to come as the bringer of forgiveness. In this way, in the free penitence of Jesus of Nazareth which began in Jordan when He entered on His way as Judge and was completed on the cross of Golgotha when He was judged—there took place the positive act concealed in His passion as the negative form of the divine action of reconciliation. In this penitence of His He "fulfilled all righteousness" (Mt. 3^{15}). It made His day—the day of the divine judgment—the great day of atonement, the day of the dawn of a new heaven and a new earth, the birthday of a new man.

That Jesus could be tempted—like all other men—is something upon which the Epistle to the Hebrews lays particular emphasis. Because "he that sanctifieth and they that are sanctified are all of one (Abraham? Adam?) he is not ashamed to call them brethren" (2^{11}). "Forasmuch then as the children are partakers of flesh and blood, he also himself likewise ($\pi\alpha\rho\alpha\pi\lambda\eta\sigma\iota\omega\varsigma$) took part of the same" (2^{14}). "Wherefore it behoved him in all things ($\kappa\alpha\tau\grave{\alpha}$ $\pi\acute{\alpha}\nu\tau\alpha$) to be made like unto his brethren, that he might be to them (in his likeness with them) a merciful and faithful high priest in things pertaining to God" (2^{17}). Like them, therefore, in being able to be tempted and in the fight against temptation. How else could He represent them except in a serious entering into their whole situation? Therefore: "In that be himself hath suffered being tempted, he is able ($\delta\acute{\upsilon}\nu\alpha\tau\alpha\iota$) to succour them that are tempted" (2^{18}). And again in 4^{15}: "For we have not an high priest which cannot be touched with the feeling of our infirmities ($\sigma\upsilon\mu\pi\alpha\theta\hat{\eta}\sigma\alpha\iota$ $\tau\alpha\hat{\iota}\varsigma$ $\grave{\alpha}\sigma\theta\epsilon\nu\epsilon\acute{\iota}\alpha\iota\varsigma$ $\grave{\eta}\mu\hat{\omega}\nu$—"sympathise" with [260] them is too weak a rendering and one that evokes false associations), but one that was in all points tempted like as we are, yet without sin." In His likeness He was also unlike in that He did not yield to temptation. That He learned obedience by the things which he suffered (5^8) means that He maintained it in freedom in a way which was not by any means self-evident. In His acts He was without sin. He was perfectly obedient. In the $\tau\epsilon\lambda\epsilon\iota\acute{o}\tau\eta\varsigma$ [EN200] of His decision, although His condition was like that of all other men. He broke the common rule of all their decisions. In this way He surpassed this likeness, and became "the author of eternal salvation unto all them that obey him" (5^9).

To what is this Epistle referring? Obviously in $5^{7f.}$ to the conflict of Jesus in Gethsemane as reported in the Synoptics (but not in John). But to understand this we must return to the story of His temptation in the wilderness, which again is not mentioned in John, is referred to only briefly by Mark, but is developed in threefold form in Mt. $4^{1f.}$ and Lk. $4^{1f.}$.

In Matthew and Mark it is significantly placed immediately after His baptism, and in Luke it is separated from it only by the genealogy. With the baptism it forms the supreme dialectical *anacrusis* to the first main part of the Gospel story. From it we can see in what way the Judge who has just come will finally fulfil the divine judgment. All three Evangelists agree that it was not chance or caprice but the Spirit—the same Spirit that the Baptist had seen descending on Him in Jordan—who led and indeed drove Jesus into the wilderness (Mk. 1^{12} $\grave{\epsilon}\kappa\beta\acute{\alpha}\lambda\lambda\epsilon\iota$ [EN201]).

Why? According to Matthew and Luke for a forty-day fast. To these forty days—and nights as stressed in Mt. 4^2; it was a total fast—at the beginning of the whole Gospel story there correspond the forty days after Easter at the end (Ac. 1^3). The fasting until He was an hungred, which forms the content of this period in contrast to the later one, points back to the penitence of Jesus and His fulfilling of all righteousness in the baptism of John, and it is obviously a continuation and emphasising of the same strand. Fasting expresses man's knowledge of his unworthiness to live, his readiness to suffer the death which he has merited for his sins, and therefore the radical nature of his repentance. There is no question of any glory in this achievement of Jesus as such.

EN200 perfection
EN201 'drove out'

2. *The Judge Judged in Our Place*

The Spirit does not drive Him into the wilderness—as many commentators have suggested with a view to edification—because of the stillness and solitude of the wilderness and the opportunity which it offers for concentration, contemplation and prayer. In another sense J. A. Bengel was quite right when he said: *in his diebus, in hoc secessu maximae res intercesserunt inter Deum et Mediatorem*[EN202]. But Mt. 4¹ tells us expressly: Jesus was brought here to be tempted (πειρασθῆναι). On the old view the wilderness was a place which, like the sea, had a close affinity with the underworld, a place which belonged in a particular sense to demons. It was to encounter these that He was led there and kept His fast there. For Him as the Son, the One in whom God was well pleased, this had to be the case. He will frequently encounter demons again. His way will never be at a safe distance from the kingdom of darkness but will always be along its frontier and finally within that kingdom. But already at the outset it brings Him into confrontation and encounter with it. Bengel is again right when he says that the story of the temptation to which particular prominence is here given is a *specimen totius exinanitionis Christi, omniumque tentationum … epitome, quas machinatus est diabolus ab initio*[EN203]. The Pharisees themselves tempted Him later (Mk. 8¹¹ᶠ·) when they asked of Him a sign from heaven. Their question about the tribute money (Mk. 12¹³ᶠ·) was recognised and rejected as a temptation. And Jesus is not simply proof against the temptation of this kingdom. He is a man, flesh and blood, as we are. He is the Son of God who has come into the far country, who has come to us and become one of us. He is therefore able to be tempted. But—and in this His way diverges from all other human ways—He is also willing to expose Himself to temptation. All other men can and ought and must refrain from seeking out temptation. But He cannot. He has to suffer it on the offensive and not on the defensive, just as later He goes with open eyes to the death of the cross, to Jerusalem. It is to this offensive that the Spirit drives Him.   [261]

And now temptation does in fact break over Him—the temptation which, as the Evangelists imply, has never broken over man before or since, the temptation with which He alone could be assailed. The great and definitive decision does not figure here, but it is authentically prefigured by what takes place here. Satan, the πειραζόμενος [EN204], the διάβολος [EN205], comes to Him (προσελθών, Mt. 4³); he speaks with Him; he takes Him with him (παραλαμβάνει, Mt. 4⁵ ⁸), he takes Him up into a high mountain (ἀναγαγών, Lk. 4⁵). In view of the One with whom the temptation has to do, this power—which is almost like that of the Spirit—is quite astonishing. But the Evangelists state that it has this power over Jesus. What was it all about? Mark does not say. But Matthew and Luke have given us a threefold exposition of the πειράζεσθαι [EN206] of Satan and the πειρασθῆναι [EN207] of Jesus. Are these three little stories the original sequence of the story in which they now appear (in a slightly different order) in these two accounts? They are a little disjointed and may go back to three sources which were originally different. But there is a thread which runs through them all and confirms their identity in substance. In none of the three temptations is there brought before us a devil who is obviously godless, or dangerous or even stupid. And in none of them is the temptation a temptation to what we might call a breaking or failure to keep the Law on the moral or judicial plane. In all three we have to do "only" with the counsel, the suggestion, that He should not be true to the way on which He entered in Jordan, that of a great sinner repenting; that He should take from now on a direction which will not need to have

---

[EN202] in these days, in this solitude, very great things passed between God and the mediator
[EN203] symbol of the complete emptying of Christ, and the high point of all the temptations which the devil has schemed from the beginning
[EN204] tempter
[EN205] devil
[EN206] test
[EN207] testing

the cross as its end and goal. But if Jesus had done this He would have done something far worse than any breaking or failure to keep the Law. He would have done that which is the essence of everything bad. For it would have meant that without His obedience the enmity of the world against God would have persisted, without His penitence the destruction of the cosmos could not have been arrested, and man would inevitably have perished. All the three stories assembled by Matthew and Luke speak in different ways of this temptation. The order and climax are different in the two Evangelists. At a first glance those of Matthew seem to be logically and pragmatically the more illuminating. But here we will follow that of Luke, for on a closer inspection it is the more instructive.

In both Evangelists the first Satanic suggestion is that after the forty days of hunger He should change the stones of the wilderness into bread in the power of His divine Sonship by His Word. What would it have meant if Jesus had yielded? He would have used the power of God which He undoubtedly had like a technical instrument placed at His disposal to save and maintain His own life. He would then have stepped out of the series of sinners in which He placed Himself in His baptism in Jordan. Of His own will He would have abandoned the role of the One who fasts and repents for sinners. He would have broken off His fasting and repentance in the fulness of divine power and with the help of God, but without consulting the will and commandment of God, because in the last resort His primary will was to live. He would have refused to give Himself unreservedly to be the one great sinner who allows that God is in the right, to set His hopes for the redemption and maintenance of His life only on the Word of God, in the establishment of which He was engaged in this self-offering. He would have refused to be willing to live only by this Word and promise of God, and therefore to continue to hunger. In so doing He would, of course, only have done what in His place and with His powers all other men would certainly have done. From the standpoint of all other men He would only have acted reasonably and rightly. "Rabbi, eat" is what His disciples later said to Him (Jn. 4^{31}) quite reasonably and in all innocence. But then He would not have made it His meat "to do the will of him that sent him, and to finish his work" (Jn. 4^{34}). Instead of acting for all other men and in their place. He would have left them in the lurch at the very moment when He had made their cause His own. Jesus withstood this temptation. He persisted in obedience, in penitence, in fasting. He hungered in confidence in the promise of manna with which the same God had once fed the fathers in the wilderness after He had allowed them to hunger (Deut. 8^3). He willed to live only by that which the Word of God creates, and therefore as one of the sinners who have no hope apart from God, as the Head and King of this people. His decision was, therefore, a different one from that which all other men would have taken in His place, and in that way it was the righteousness which He achieved in their stead.

[262]

According to Luke, the second Satanic suggestion is that Satan, to whom the world belongs, should give him lordship over it, at the price of His falling down and worshipping him. What would it have meant if Jesus had done this? Obviously He would have shown that He repented having received the baptism of John and that He did not intend to complete the penitence which He had begun. He would have ceased to recognise and confess the sin of the world as sin, to take it upon Himself as such, and in His own person to bring to an issue the conflict with it (as with man's contradiction against God and himself). He would have won through and been converted to a simpler and more practical and more realistic approach and way. He would have determined to drop the question of the overcoming and removing of evil, to accept the undeniable fact of the overlordship of evil in the world, and to do good, even the best, on this indisputable presupposition, on the ground and in the sphere of this overlordship. Why not set up a real kingdom of God on earth? an international order modelled on the insights of Christian humanitarianism, in which, of course, a liberal-orthodox, ecumenical, confessional Church might also find an appropriate place?

Note that to do this He was not asked to renounce God or to go over to atheism. He had only to lift His hat to the usurper. He had only to bow the knee discreetly and privately to the devil. He had only to make the quiet but solid and irreversible acknowledgment that in that world of splendour the devil should have the first and final word, that at bottom everything should remain as it had been. On this condition we can all succeed in the world, and Jesus most of all. In the divine and human kingdom set up on this condition there would have been no place for the cross. Or rather, in this world ostensibly ruled by Jesus but secretly by Satan, the cross would have been harmlessly turned into a fine and profound symbol: an ornament in the official philosophy and outlook; but also an adornment (e.g., an episcopal adornment) in the more usual sense of the word; a suitable recollection of that which Jesus avoided and which is not therefore necessary for anyone else. What other man in Jesus' place would not have been clever enough to close with this offer? But what He had to do and willed to do in place of all would not then have been done. He would again have left them in the lurch and betrayed them, in spite of all the fine and good things that the world-kingdom of Satan and Jesus might have meant for them. For of what advantage is even the greatest glory to a world which is still definitively unreconciled with God? Of what gain to man are all the conceivable advantages and advances of such a kingdom? But Jesus resisted this temptation too. He refused to be won over to this attractive realism. As the one great sinner in the name and place of all others, without any prospect of this glory, quite unsuccessfully, indeed with the certainty of failure, He willed to continue worshipping and serving God alone. He willed to persist in repentance and obedience. This was the righteousness which He achieved for us.

The third temptation, according to Luke's account, is the most astonishing of all. The dignity of the setting, the temple of God in the holy city of Jerusalem, is obviously incomparably greater than the still secular dignity of that high mountain from which Jesus was shown and offered all the kingdoms of the world. It is of a piece that Satan now appears as an obviously pious man who can even quote the Psalms of David, and he gains in the serious- [263] ness and weight of his approach. Above all, his suggestion—we can hardly describe it by the horrible word temptation—is quite different from everything that has preceded it. It now consists in the demand to commit an act of supreme, unconditional, blind, absolute, total confidence in God—as was obviously supremely fitting for the Son of God. We might almost say, an act in the sense of and in line with the answers which Jesus Himself had given to the first two temptations, to live only by the Word of God, to serve and worship Him alone. In the last decades we have become accustomed to think of the seeking and attaining of totalitarian dominion as the worst of all evils, as that which is specifically demonic. But if the climax in Luke is right, there is something even worse and just as demonic. It is not just a matter of a miraculous display to reveal the Messiahship of Jesus. It is often interpreted in this way, but by a reading into the text rather than out of it. The text itself makes no mention whatever of spectators. It is rather a question of the testing and proving, of the final assuring of His relationship to God *in foro conscientiae*[EN208], in the solitariness of man with God. Jesus is to risk this headlong plunge with the certainty, and to confirm the certainty, that God and His angels are with Him and will keep Him. Schlatter has rather mischievously said that what we have here is what is so glibly described "in contemporary theological literature" as the "leap" of faith. It certainly does seem to be something very like "existence in transcendence," or "the leap into the unknown," or in Reformation language "justification by faith alone," justification in the sense that (in face of death and the last judgment, and in the hope that in trust in God these can be overcome) man presumes to take it into his own hands, to carry it through as the work of his own robust faith, and in that way to have a part in it and to be

---

[EN208] in the sphere of his conscience

certain of it; just as Empedocles (we do not know exactly why, but seriously and with courage) finally flung himself into the smoking crater of Etna, which is supposed to have thrown out again only his sandals; just as on this very same rock of the temple, when it was stormed by the Romans in A.D. 70, the last of the high priests put themselves to death with their own hands, possibly in despair, possibly in the hope that there would be a supreme miracle at that last hour. What would it have meant if Jesus had taken this leap? Note the remarkable closeness of the temptation to the way which Jesus did in fact tread. In this respect the Lucan order, in which this is the last and supreme temptation, is most edifying. He will "dare the leap into the abyss, the way to the cross, when the will of God leads Him to it" (Schlatter). But what would have led Him to it here would have been His own will to make use of God in His own favour. He would have experimented with God for His own supreme pleasure and satisfaction instead of taking the purpose of God seriously and subjecting Himself to His good-pleasure and command. He would have tried triumphantly to maintain His lightness with God instead of persisting in penitence, instead of allowing God to be in the right against Him. In an act of supreme piety, in the work of a mystical enthusiasm. He would have betrayed the cause of God by making it His own cause, by using it to fulfil His own self-justification before God. If He had given way to this last and supreme temptation He would have committed the supreme sin of tempting God Himself, i.e., under the appearance of this most robust faith in Him demanding that He should accept this Jesus who believes so robustly instead of sinful man by Him and in His person. He would have demanded that He should be the most false of all false gods, the god of the religious man. And in so doing He would Himself have withdrawn from the society of sinful men as whose Representative and Head He was ordained to live and act. He would have left in the lurch the world unreconciled with God. "Farewell, O world, for I am weary of thee." But again we may ask, what other man, all things considered, would not actually have done this in His place? For Adamic man reaches his supreme form in religious self-sacrifice as the most perfect kind of self-glorification, in which God is in fact most completely impressed into the service of man, in which He is most completely denied under cover of the most complete acknowledgment of God and one's fellows. Jesus did not do this. He rejected the supreme ecstasy and satisfaction of religion as the supreme form of sin. And in so doing He remained faithful to the baptism of John. He remained the One in whom God is well pleased. He remained sinless. He remained in obedience. In our place He achieved the righteousness which had to be achieved in His person for the justification of us all and for the reconciliation of the world with God, the only righteousness that was necessary.

[264]

We cannot ignore the negative form in which the righteousness of God appears in the event handed down in these passages. This is unavoidable, because we have to do with it in the wilderness, in the kingdom of demons, in the world unreconciled with God, and in conflict with that world. It is unavoidable because what we have here is a prefiguring of the passion. But in the passion, and in this prefiguring of it, the No of God is only the hard shell of the divine Yes, which in both cases is spoken in the righteous act of this one man. That this is the case is revealed at the conclusion of the accounts in Mark and Matthew by the mention of the angels who, when Satan had left Him, came and ministered unto Him. The great and glorious complement to this at the conclusion of the passion is the story of the resurrection.

In Luke (4^{13}) the story of the temptation concludes with the statement of the narrator: "And when the devil had (unsuccessfully) ended all the temptation, he departed from him until the decisive moment" ($\overset{\text{'}}{\alpha}\chi\rho\iota\ \kappa\alpha\iota\rho o\hat{\upsilon}$). The last phrase cannot refer to any specific incident in the activity of Jesus in Galilee or to this activity as a whole. Jesus has to do constantly with the kingdom of darkness in this activity, and in many different forms. But neither in Luke nor in any of the other Gospels (apart from the saying to Peter in Mt. 16^{22}) do we hear explicitly of any special encounter with the διάβολος EN209 or of a renewal of the temptation in all its forms. If this reference to a coming καιρός EN210 is not an empty one, then obviously it must mean the night and day of the passion (as in Mt. 26¹⁸ and Jn. 7⁶ ⁸). We obviously have to think of His cry of dereliction on the cross (although this is not reported by Luke, cf. Mk. 15³⁴). We obviously have to think of all the events of Good Friday. We obviously have to think especially of the story of Gethsemane. In this story there is already compressed the whole happening of Good Friday to the extent that it already speaks of a passion of Jesus, but of a passion which has to do strictly with the establishment of His definitive willingness for the real passion which comes upon Him immediately after. In this respect the story forms the turning-point between the two parts of the whole Gospel record. It is now shown where the victory which Jesus won in the temptation in the wilderness leads, that the end will involve the death of the victor. The penitence and the fulfilment of righteousness which Jesus has undertaken is now approaching its climax. The reversal in which the Judge becomes the judged is now about to take place. The story closes with the present: "The hour is come; behold, the Son of man is betrayed (παραδίδοται) into the hands of sinners."

But it brings out once again the whole absolutely inconceivable difficulty of the matter: the Son of man come down from heaven, the King and Judge sent by God, in the hands of sinners, betrayed, delivered up, surrendered to them. "The hour is come," and in a moment there will appear, and with him the first of those ἁμαρτωλοί EN211, the little παραδιδούς EN212 Judas, a chosen apostle, who with his kiss sets the whole event in train. Does all this have to happen? In this solemn moment, quite naturally but unexpectedly and disruptively in view of all that has gone before, there is a pause. Jesus Himself—in prayer to God—raises the whole question afresh. He prays that "if it were possible, the hour might pass from him" (Mk. 14³⁵). This is repeated in direct speech: "Abba, Father, all things are possible unto thee; take away this cup from me" (Mk. 14³⁶). But had not His whole way from Jordan been a single march—which Satan could not arrest, not even in the form of Peter (Mt. 16²³)—to this very hour, a single and determined grasping of this cup of the divine wrath (Is. 51¹⁷)? But now there is a stumbling, although only for a—repeated—moment: a moment in which there is a pause and trembling not only on earth and in time, not only in the soul of Jesus which is "sorrowful even unto death" (Mt. 26³⁸), but in a sense in heaven, in the bosom of God Himself, in the relationship between the Father and the Son; a moment in which the question is raised of another possibility than that which will in fact be realised relentlessly and by divine necessity in view of all that has gone before. We may well be surprised that the Synoptics regarded it not only as not repellent but as important and right to record this moment, to incorporate this story so directly and emphatically into their witness to Jesus and His way. We are told of an ἐκθαμβεῖσθαι EN213 of Jesus (Mk. 14³³); of a horror which gripped Him in face of the frightful event which confronted Him; of an ἀδημονεῖν EN214; of a foreboding from which there was no escape, in which He could find no help or comfort, which was only foreboding; of an ἀγωνία EN215 (Lk. 22⁴⁴) in which His sweat fell to the earth like drops of blood; of a λυπεῖσθαι EN216, a sorrow, a heaviness, an oppression which was "even unto death" (Mt. 26³⁸)—*talis tristitia communem hominem potuisset ad sui necem adigere* EN217 is

[265]

EN209 devil
EN210 decisive moment
EN211 sinners
EN212 betrayers
EN213 deep distress
EN214 great troubling
EN215 agony
EN216 grief
EN217 such a sadness could have driven any man to his death

the comment of Bengel. The words of Heb. 5[7] are also relevant: "Who in the days of his flesh, when he had offered up prayers and supplications with strong crying and tears unto him that was able to save him from death." And the Gospel of John, if it is not more explicit, does not conceal His situation immediately before the actual onset of His passion: "Now is my soul troubled (τετάρακται); and what shall I say? Father, save me from this hour" (Jn. 12[27]). The question arises whether He has not taken up once again the suggestion of Peter (Mt. 16[22f.]) which He had rejected as all too human and even satanic: "Be it far from thee, Lord; this shall not be unto thee." Schlatter has rightly pointed out that there is completely lacking here that defiance with which we see the martyr receiving joyfully and boldly the baptism of blood, not to speak of the glad resignation with which Socrates is supposed to have drunk his cup.

There is a striking difference between the story of Gethsemane and that of the temptation in the wilderness. In the latter there is not even the remotest glimpse of any hesitation or questioning on the part of Jesus Himself. Self-evidently and with the greatest precision the tempter is at once resisted. But then it was only a matter of continuing without deviation on the way He had entered at Jordan. Now He had to face the reckoning. Now He was confronted with the final fruit and consequence of what He had begun. Why is His attitude so different? Especially, why is it so different from that displayed by many a Christian martyr, by a Socrates, by many Communists—as we can see from their letters—who were under sentence of death in the time of Hitler, even by the German general Jodl, executed as a war-criminal in Nuremberg? It is obviously not simply a matter of suffering and dying in itself and as such. But what then? What is the frightful thing which, according to these passages, He foresaw in His suffering and dying, which now forces Him to this terrified and shaken halt, to this question whether it really has to be, as had not been the case in the wilderness? We shall find the answer in a further comparison with that first and very different form of His conflict.

There is no mention now of suggestions on the part of Satan, or even of his presence. If this hour, as we must gather from Luke, is the second and final καιρός[EN218] of Satan, if he is in some way present and at work in this event as the other Evangelists seem to presuppose— if he will now (and obviously finally) be "rejected " according to Jn. 12[31], and "judged" according to Jn. 16[11]—then he is present in quite a different way and quite a different form from that of the earlier occasion. Jesus is quite ready to deal with him as a counsellor, to deal [266] with the temptation that he should leave the way of penitence and obedience which He had entered at Jordan, that he should be forced away from His mission as "the friend of publicans and sinners." Indeed, in spite of the seriousness of the temptation it is almost child's play for Him to deal with it. Perhaps the saying in Lk. 10[18] has something to say to us in this connexion: "I beheld Satan as lightning fall from heaven." But Satan has not yet done with Him. He has more than one form. He can do more than speak and entice. He can do more than "tempt" in the simple or rational or religious form. He can just act and work. His equipment includes not only "much cunning" but also in the last resort "great power." When He is resisted as the tempter he can return all the more powerfully as the avenger of this defeat. In place of other things he can speak for himself in the simple language of facts. It is of something like this that he boasts in Lk. 4[6]: that the power and glory of the kingdoms of this world belong to him. To the extent that the world is the world which is at enmity and unreconciled with God, this is so in the old aeon. *Per definitionem*[EN219] it is his sphere of influence, the world in which apart from the counter-operation of God it is his will which is not only revealed but everywhere done. As we are so clearly told in Eph. 2[2], he is the prince

---

[EN218] decisive moment
[EN219] By definition

of the power (ὁ ἄρχων τῆς ἐξουσίας) of the air, of the atmosphere, of the conditions of life in this aeon, or, to put it plainly: "the spirit that now worketh in the children of disobedience," the motor which drives them, the driver who without their knowing it determines and directs their activity. And because in this aeon all men are as such "children of disobedience," because they are ἁμαρτωλοί, sinners, those who fall into the hands of men fall into the hands of this prince, of this spirit, and therefore of Satan, who acquires his power—whether he knows it or not—under the pseudonym of human will and action, who acquires it as the highest secular power to fbeseen. So Jesus falls into the hands of men, of sinners. Note, into the hands io those in line with whom He had placed Himself and willed to be and to remain in His utter obedience. It now came to Him what that involved and carried with it, to what He had given Himself, the power of the unbreakable law to which these men are subject in their willing and doing, to which the world itself is subject, the overwhelming retribution which must come upon Him at the hand of these men because He has undertaken and dared to be unique amongst them, to resist temptation, to achieve righteousness in their place. He saw that in so doing He would not only be alone but would necessarily have them all against Him: those who had not resisted temptation, but constantly gave way to it; who all existed and acted as more or less useful instruments of the power of temptation and the tempter; who could act in relation to Jesus only in the service of the will and dominion of Satan. This was the world which in His own person He was to reconcile and willed to reconcile with God. He saw this world as it was. He saw what it was that dominated it and was fulfilled in it. He saw and felt the "great burden of the world." He saw what even the greatest of Christian and other martyrs did not see: that this burden is overwhelming, that in the last resort it can only overwhelm and crush Himself and other men. He saw this because He had contradicted and withstood the tempter, because He had chosen and done that which is right. But it was one thing to enter and continue on this way, it was another to tread it to the end, and in this world its necessarily bitter end. It was one thing to contradict and withstand the tempter, it was another to see him actually triumphant as he necessarily would be in this world, in the humanity ruled by him, to be refuted by him in the hard language of facts. From this we may gather something at least of the convulsion of that hour.

But the real meaning of the hour in Gethsemane was not this vision of the world and of that which rules in it. In the texts there is no mention at all of any coming of Satan. And the men who serve him appear and act only when the hour is over. It is not a matter of the riddle of the world and the riddle of evil as such. Nor can we really say that in the problem of the world and evil as forcefully presented in this way it was a question of God, or the problem of a theodicy, or reflection where God is in this triumph of humanity and the world as ruled by Satan, whether He is forced to retreat or to abdicate or to die in face of it. Considerations like this are quite foreign to the New Testament context. If we find them there they will have had to be imported. There is no question of considerations at all, whether about Satan and the world or about God. Above and in and through the event which is now disclosed and works itself out, God rules and does His work, the work which Jesus has to finish and is determined to finish. He is the living Lord even of the world which is in conflict with Him. As such He can never be idle. He can never grow weary, He can never resign. In this world Satan can have only the power which is given and allowed him as he is powerfully upheld by the left hand of God. This is the self-evident presupposition of everything that happens. Jesus does not think about this God, but speaks to Him. And we have to seek the problem of Gethsemane (1) in the content of what He says, (2) in the fact that He is quite alone in what He says, without companion or helper, and (3) in the fact that the answer of God will be given only in the language of facts. [267]

259

We will take the second point first. It is emphasised in the texts in a way that we cannot overlook. They tell us plainly that Jesus wished to pray this prayer a little ahead of His disciples but in their presence and with their participation. To do this He withdraws only a little (Mk. 14³⁵), only "about a stone's cast" from them (Lk. 22⁴¹). That His soul is sorrowful even unto death is something which He does not tell to God but to them (Mk. 14³⁴), and He asks that they should watch with Him (Mt. 26³⁸), and later expressly that they should pray with Him (Mk. 14³⁸); that is, that they should see what He sees, world-occurrence as it is, and God ruling over and in and through it, and that they should do what He does, call upon this God. It is not self-evident that He should be alone in this matter. He had called the disciples to be His apostles, the foundation of His community in the world. He had made His cause theirs. He had promised that where two or three of them were gathered in His name He Himself would be there in the midst (Mt. 18²⁰). It could and indeed necessarily was the case that where He was at any rate two or three of them would be gathered. And Jesus knew—here we see directly the connexion between Gethsemane and the temptation in the wilderness—that what was about to happen would again mean temptation, πειρασμός EN220, that with the event which was about to break in all its malice there might come the suggestion of an easier way for Himself and His disciples than that which He had entered. That is why He Himself watches and prays in this hour. That is why He calls to His disciples: "Watch and pray, lest ye enter into temptation." He knows that man is lost unless he is in some sense aware of it. He knows that for Himself and His disciples calling on God is the only way to meet and defeat it. For the spirit is willing, but the flesh is weak (Mk. 14³⁸). The flight of the disciples at the crucial moment (Mk. 14⁵⁰) and the denial of Peter (Mk. 14⁶⁶ᶠ·) will show how weak the flesh is, how quickly they will find and take the easier way, how necessary it was for them to obey His call to watch and pray. For His sake and for their own they ought not to have left Him alone when He went forward to pray. But they did leave Him quite alone. "Couldest not thou watch one hour?" He asks Peter (Mk. 14³⁷). No, he could not, and neither could the others. Again and again He was to find them sleeping: "For their eyes were heavy, and they wist not what to answer him" (Mk. 14⁴⁰). In other words, the apostolate, the community, Christendom, the Church (far from existing eschatologically) sleeps. It is present, but it has no part at all in that prayer to God. Jesus makes it alone. There is no one to bear the burden with Him. There is none to help. No Christian individual had the insight, and no Christian group put it into effect, that this was a matter for Christians and Christianity itself, that for their own sake Christians and Christianity had good reason to have a part in this prayer. to join with Jesus in crying to God. In doing this for Himself Jesus does it for them, and "for them" in the strictest sense, in their place. It is now true: "Simon, Simon, Satan hath desired to have you (as once he desired to have Job), that he may sift you as wheat; But I have prayed for thee, that thy faith fail not" (Lk. 22³¹ᶠ·). If Jesus had not prayed in their place (and in the same way acted in their place in His passion) the apostolate and the community would have fallen victim to the satanic determination of world occurrence like its other agents. The Fourth Evangelist regarded this aspect of the matter, this meaning of the final hour, as so decisively important that at the very place where we miss the report of Gethsemane (Jn. 17) he has reported the "high-priestly " prayer of Jesus which anticipates so remarkably the whole event of the passion: "And now I am no more in the world, but these are in the world" (v. 11). "I pray not that thou shouldest take them out of the world, but that thou shouldest keep them from the evil" (v. 15). "And for their sakes I sanctify myself, that they also might be sanctified through the truth" (v. 19). "Father, I will that they also, whom thou hast given me, be with me where I am" (v. 24), "that the love wherewith thou hast loved me may be in them and I in them" (v. 26). We must have this glorified picture before us to understand the

[268]

EN220 trial

account of the Synoptics. But properly to estimate Jn. 17 we must also have before us the hard picture of the Synoptics: the complete denial of Christianity and the Church in relation to Jesus; their notorious non-participation in His decisive action; the frightful loneliness in which they left Him, and in which quite alone—not with them but without them and therefore for them—He had to do and did what had to be done. If there is anything which brings out clearly this simple "for us" as the content of the Gospel, then it is this aspect of the event in Gethsemane, in which the act of God in Jesus Christ had absolutely nothing to correspond to it in the existence of those who believe in Him. They could not watch with Him even one hour. He alone watched and prayed in their place.

We must now take up the third point we mentioned. It is only with reservations that we can call the prayer in Gethsemane a "conversation" with God. In the texts there is no mention of any answer corresponding to and accepting the address of Jesus. We might think of the appearance of the angel to strengthen Him mentioned in Luke (22⁴³). And this naturally recalls the angels who, according to Mark and Matthew, came and ministered to Him in the wilderness. But this ἐνισχύων αὐτόν EN221 in the Lucan account does not form a conclusion, but is, as it were, refreshment by the way. It is only after the strengthening which comes to Jesus that we hear of His ἀγωνία EN222 (v. 44), of the sweat which fell to the earth like great drops of blood. It is not an ending of the necessary conflict brought about from heaven, but, according to the presentation in Luke, the battle in which He is engaged only becomes severe after this strengthening. Jesus does not, in fact, receive any answer, any sign from God. Or, rather, He has "the sign of the prophet Jonah" (Mt. 12³⁹ᶠ·) who was three days and three nights in the whale's belly. For Him, as for all this evil and adulterous generation, the only sign will be the actual event of His death: "So shall the Son of man be three days and three nights in the heart of the earth." God will give His answer to the prayer only in this inconceivable, this frightful event, and not otherwise. For the event of His resurrection lies beyond the answer. It is the disclosure of its meaning. The answer which Jesus receives is in itself this and no other, this answer which was no answer, to which His prayer itself alluded. Note that it came in the same language in which Satan now spoke with Him as the prince of this aeon, triumphantly avenging His contradiction and opposition in the wilderness. The will of God was done as the will of Satan was done. The answer of God was identical with the action of Satan. That was the frightful thing. The coincidence of the divine and the satanic will and work and word was the problem of this hour, the darkness in which Jesus addressed God in Gethsemane.

This brings us to the main question of the content and meaning of this address. For a [269] moment it holds out before the reader another possible form of the coming event: not in any clear outline, only vaguely—for Jesus is not proposing to God any alternative plan— defined only in a negative way; not this event, the frightful event which now impends. Jesus prays that this hour, this cup of wrath might pass from Him, might be spared Him. He prays, therefore, that the good will and the sacred work and the true word of God should not coincide with the evil will and the corrupt work and the deceitful word of the tempter and of the world controlled by him, the ἁμαρτωλοί EN223. He prays that God should not give Him up to the power the temptation of which He had resisted and willed to resist in all circumstances. He prays that God will so order things that the triumph of evil will be prevented, that the claim of Satan to world dominion will not be affirmed but given the lie, that a limit will be set to him, and with him to the evil course of the world and the evil movement of men. He prays that, directed by God's providence, the facts might speak a different language from

---

EN221 'strengthening him'
EN222 agony
EN223 sinners

261

that which they are about to speak, that in their end and consequence they should not be against Him, just as He had decided for God and not against Him in the wilderness. He prays that for the sake of God's own cause and glory the evil determination of world-occurrence should not finally rage against Himself, the sent One of God and the divine Son. Surely this is something which God cannot will and allow. Such is the prayer of Jesus as prayed once in Luke, twice in Mark and as many as three times in Matthew.

In the continuation of the prayer He set this content in opposition to the real will of God as His own will, which He was determined to surrender to the former. We must be careful to explain that the content of this petition, the passing of the cup, would have been the will of Jesus if it had corresponded to the real will of God. But it is not. Jesus clearly wished that it might have been so. But the texts do not tell us that He set His will in this direction, first resisting what was revealed to be the real will of God, and then abandoning it in favour of this will. They tell us that He would have set His will in this way, and quite legitimately, if it had corresponded to the real will of God. At the very beginning of the prayer there is interposed the proviso: "Abba, Father, all things are possible to thee" (Mk. 14³⁶), "if it be possible" (Mt. 26³⁹), or even more simply and clearly "if thou be willing" (Lk. 22⁴²), then let it be done otherwise. The prayer and the expressed wish of Jesus stand from the very first under this pre-condition. He did not think out and choose some other possibility. He did not reject the impending reality. He did not establish some other direction of His own will. He did not refuse that which forced itself upon Him in view of what lay ahead. He made His request to God only with a view to some other possibility which might be God's own will, and not with any particular bias in this or that direction.

This does not affect the urgency of His request, to which the texts refer in such a drastic way. Nor does it affect the extremity in which He prays. Nor does it affect the full seriousness with which He gives to His prayer this content. The riddle confronts Him with all the horror that it evokes: that of the impending unity between the will of God on the one hand, that will which He had hitherto obeyed, and which He willed to obey in all circumstances and whatever it was, that will which He was quite ready should be done—and, on the other hand, the power of evil which He had withstood, and which He willed to withstand in all circumstances and in whatever form He might encounter it, which He could not allow to be done. What shook Him was the coming concealment of the lordship of God under the lordship of evil and evil men. This was the terrible thing which He saw breaking on Himself and His disciples and all men, on His work as the Reconciler between God and man, and therefore on God's own work, destroying everything, mortally imperilling the fulfilment of His just and redemptive judgment. This was what He saw, and which His disciples, not to speak of other men, did not see. It was to avoid this dreadful thing that He prayed, He alone, while His disciples did not pray. It was to prevent this event that He cried alone to God—that some other possibility should be put into effect, that this future should not become the present.

But He only prays. He does not demand. He does not advance any claims. He does not lay upon God any conditions. He does not reserve His future obedience. He does not abandon His status as a penitent. He does not cease to allow that God is in the right, even against Himself. He does not try to anticipate His justification by Him in any form, or to determine it Himself. He does not think of trying to be judge in His own cause and in God's cause. He prays only as a child to the Father, knowing that He can and should pray, that His need is known to the Father, is on the heart of the Father, but knowing also that the Father disposes what is possible and will therefore be, and that what He allows to be will be the only thing that is possible and right.

If we understand the beginning of Jesus' prayer to God in this way—and how else can we understand it in view of what the texts say and in the context of the Gospels?—then the meaning of what follows is clear: "But (ἀλλά), or nevertheless (πλήν), not what (τί, or as, ὡς)

I will, but what (as) thou wilt" (Mk. 14³⁶, Mt. 26³⁹). Or more explicitly: "Nevertheless, not my will, but thine, be done" (Lk. 22⁴²). Or even more explicitly: "O my Father, if this cup may not pass away from me except I drink it, thy will be done" (Mt. 26⁴²). If our previous interpretation is correct, this is not a kind of return of willingness to obey, which was finally forced upon Jesus and fulfilled by Him in the last hour; it is rather a readiness for the act of obedience which He had never compromised in His prayer. The proviso "if it be possible" which was an integral part of the prayer now comes into force. The prayer reckoned on the possibility of quite a different answer. This is what had made it a genuine prayer to God. But now this possibility fades from view. Jesus does not change His mind when He says, "Thy will be done." After pausing with very good reason, He now proceeds all the more determinedly along the way which He had never left. But we must be careful how we praise the humility which Jesus displayed in the second form of His prayer. Naturally, it is the prayer of humility of the Son of God made man. But we must also see that in the "Thy will be done" He emerges from the serious and inevitable astonishment and oppression in which He had prayed that the cup should pass from Him. He stands upright in what we might almost call a supreme pride. He faces the reality the avoidance of which He had so earnestly desired. Because it is the reality of the will of God He grasps it as that which is better, which alone is good. He does not do so in sad resignation, therefore, but because He will and can affirm this reality and this alone. In the last analysis, therefore, we can describe what Jesus does as renunciation only if we explain it more closely. He does renounce the content of that wish which He had spread before God, and therefore the prospect of a different future from that which actually came to Him, and therefore the fixing of a different will to correspond to this different future. But what Jesus did is ill adapted to be used, as we love to use it, as an example of that renunciation of all kinds of hopes and fears which is demanded of man. For, according to the sense of the texts, we cannot speak of any intention which was opposed to that of God and which He then renounced. Above all, the emphasis of the prayer is not at all upon that which might not happen, as in all kinds of mysticism both new and old, both higher and lower. It is upon that which might happen. It is a positive prayer and not a negative. The statement—and in this it goes far beyond the answers of Jesus to the tempter in the wilderness—is at its open core a radiant Yes to the actual will of God. It is radiant because the decision which it expresses and fulfils ceases to regard any other divine possibilities which there might be and fixes itself on the one actual will of God—"what thou wilt"—and unreservedly accepts it. This is not a withdrawal on the part of Jesus, but a great and irresistible [271] advance. It is not a resignation before God. It is an expression of the supreme and only praise which God expects of man and which is rendered to Him only by this One man in place of all, the praise which comes from the knowledge that He does not make any mistakes, that His way, the way which He whose thoughts are higher than our thoughts actually treads Himself, is holy and just and gracious. But in all this we do not forget what it was all about, what Jesus was affirming and accepting and taking on Himself, with this "Thy will be done." It was not simply that He had to suffer and die, and that in contrast to others who have gone a similar way He accepted it rather painfully and tardily, as the moralists have easily been able to hold against Him. It was not a matter of His suffering and dying in itself and as such, but of the dreadful thing that He saw coming upon Him in and with His suffering and dying. He saw it clearly and correctly. It was the coming of the night "in which no man can work" (Jn. 9⁴), in which the good will of God will be indistinguishably one with the evil will of men and the world and Satan. It was a matter of the triumph of God being concealed under that of His adversary, of that which is not, of that which supremely is not. It was a matter of God Himself obviously making a tryst with death and about to keep it. It was a matter of the divine judgment being taken out of the hands of Jesus and placed in those of His supremely unrighteous judges and executed by them upon Him. It was a matter of the enemy who had been repulsed as the tempter having and exercising by divine permission and appointment the right, the irresistible right of might. It was a matter of the obedience and penitence in which Jesus had persisted coming to fruition in His own rejection and condemnation—not by chance, but according to the plan of God Himself, not superficially, but in serious earnest. That was what came upon Him in His suffering and dying, as God's answer to His appeal. Jesus saw this cup. He tasted its bitterness. He had not made any mistake. He had not been needlessly afraid. There was every reason to ask that it might pass from Him.

"Thy will be done" means that Jesus, like all this "evil and adulterous generation," is to receive only the sign of the prophet Jonah, but that as the one man, the only One in this generation. He willed on behalf of this generation to see in it the true sign of God. "Thy will be done" means that He put this cup to His lips, that He accepted this answer of God as true and holy and just and gracious, that He went forward to what was about to come, thus enabling it to happen. "Thy will be done" means not only that Jesus accepted as God's sentence this language of facts, this concealment of the lordship of God by the lordship of evil, this turning and decision against Him according to the determined counsel of providence, but that He was ready to pronounce this sentence Himself and therefore on Himself; indeed. He was ready to fulfil the sentence by accepting His suffering and dying at the hands of ἁμαρτωλοί[EN224]. That is what He did in His prayer when there was none to stand by Him, when there was none who could or would help Him, when He was not surrounded or sustained by any intercession, when He could only intercede for others, when He prayed for His disciples and therefore for the world that most necessary, most urgent and most decisive prayer, the high-priestly prayer.

But what happened when Jesus prayed in this way in Gethsemane? How was this prayer heard, which no other ever could pray or ever has prayed before or since, but which was in fact heard as no other prayer was heard when it received the answer which it requested?

One thing is clear. In the power of this prayer Jesus received, i.e., He renewed, confirmed and put into effect, His freedom to finish His work, to execute the divine judgment by undergoing it Himself, to punish the sin of the world by bearing it Himself, by taking it away from the world in His own person, in His death. The sin of the world was now laid upon Him. It was now true that in the series of many sinners He was the only One singled out by God to [272] be its bearer and Representative, the only One that it could really touch and oppress and terrify. That the deceiver of men is their destroyer, that his power is that of death, is something that had to be proved true in the One who was not deceived, in order that it might not be true for all those who were deceived, that their enmity against God might be taken away from them, that their curse might not rest upon them. This was the will of God in the dreadful thing which Jesus saw approaching—in that conjunction of the will and work and word of God with those of evil. The power of evil had to break on Jesus, its work of death had to be done on Him, so that being done on Him it might be done once and for all, for all men, for the liberation of all men. This is what happened when Jesus took the cup and drank it to the last bitter drops. "For this cause came I unto this hour" is what He says in Jn. 12²⁷ when He had just prayed on this occasion too: "Father, save me from this hour." If the Father was the Father of Jesus, and Jesus His Son, He could not save Him from this hour. That would have been not to hear His prayer. For Jesus had come to this hour in order that the will of God should be done in this hour as it actually was done.

And Satan, the evil one, and the world ruled by him, and the ἁμαρτωλοί[EN225] as his agents and instruments? Is it not clear that in the prayer prayed by Jesus in this hour the

---

EN224 sinners
EN225 sinners

"prince of this world" is judged (Jn. 16[11]), "cast out" (Jn. 12[31])? "He hath nothing in me." He does Him every possible injury, but He cannot injure that which He does when He allows this to happen. In relation to Him he makes his supreme and final effort. He has his supreme καιρός[EN226]. For the world must "know that I love the Father, and as the Father gave me commandment, even so I do" (Jn. 14[31]). He uses his power to overwhelm Jesus, and he succeeds, but his power loses its subjects, for the world and men escape him once and for all, and it ceases to be power over them, an impassable gulf being opened between him and the world ruled by him, between him and the ἁμαρτωλοί[EN227] deceived by him. He Himself is impressed into the service of the will of God as fulfilled in the suffering and death of Jesus. His act of violence on this one man can achieve only what God has determined to His own glory and the salvation of all. A limit is therefore set to his lordship and its end is already in sight. That is what happened to him when Jesus prayed that not His will but God's will should be done.

Moreover in this prayer it also takes place that the world, even the sinful men at whose hands Jesus will suffer and die—all of them from Judas to Pilate—will all actively take part in the event of His self-giving to death which takes place for the reconciliation of the world with God. Note that they will do so as His enemies, not in the decision of faith but in the decision of a supreme unbelief. But even as His enemies, His accusers, His judges and His executioners they will actively take part in it. They are no longer merely wicked men, but in their very wickedness they are involuntary instruments of God. In all their speaking and tumult, in all the evil and foolish activity with which they bring about Good Friday, they necessarily testify to themselves and to all men of all ages how much this happening affects them, and that it is their own cause which is prosecuted in it.

One last thing: in this prayer of Jesus there took place quite simply the completion of the penitence and obedience which He had begun to render at Jordan and which He had maintained in the wilderness. Had not His whole resistance in that temptation, the No which He had victoriously opposed to it, aimed at the different but no less victorious Yes which He said to the will of God in this hour? Was He not even then representing God and therefore the world and sinful men? In the light of it, what else does His "Thy will be done" mean but that this first word of His was and remained His final word? So, then, in this prayer we can see the essence of the positive content of the suffering and dying of Jesus—the act of righteousness (δικαίωμα) and obedience (ὑποταγή) of the one man, in the power of which the vindication of all men was accomplished as the promise of life (δικαίωσις εἰς ζωήν[EN228]), in which in the last judgment many will be presented righteous (δίκαιον) in the sight of God and His angels and the whole world (Rom. 5[18f.]).

[273]

We are now at the end of the important section dealing with the general question (closely linked with that of the previous section) which was asked by Anselm: *Cur Deus homo?*[EN229] and with the particular question what Jesus Christ was and did *pro nobis*[EN230], for us and for the world. To this question we have given four related answers. He took our place as Judge. He took our place as the judged. He was judged in our place. And He acted justly in our place. It is important to see that we cannot add anything to this—unless it is an Amen to

---

EN226 decisive moment
EN227 sinners
EN228 justification unto life
EN229 Why did God become man?
EN230 for us

indicate that what we say further has this fourfold but single answer as a pre-supposition. Whatever we say further depends upon the fact that in the sense we have noted He was the Judge judged in our place. All theology, both that which follows and indeed that which precedes the doctrine of reconciliation, depends upon this *theologia crucis*[EN231]. And it depends upon it under the particular aspect under which we have had to develop it in this first part of the doctrine of reconciliation as the doctrine of substitution. Everything depends upon the fact that the Lord who became a servant, the Son of God who went into the far country, and came to us, was and did all this for us; that He fulfilled, and fulfilled in this way, the divine judgment laid upon Him. There is no avoiding this strait gate. There is no other way but this narrow way. If the nail of this fourfold "for us" does not hold, everything else will be left hanging in the void as an anthropological or psychological or sociological myth, and sooner or later it will break and fall to the ground. If it is to be meaningful and true, and with it all those doctrines of man's plight and redemption, of his death and life, of his perdition and salvation, which seem to be so sure in themselves, then it must first be demythologised in the light of this "for us." For that reason this is the place for a full-stop. Many further statements may follow, but the stop indicates that this first statement is complete in itself, that it comprehends all that follows, and that it can stand alone.

To make this point, we will not proceed any further for the moment, but test the statement by asking whether it still holds good even in the variations forced upon us by the different ways in which the New Testament speaks of this *pro nobis*[EN232] and in which the Church too will always speak of it. If we fail to notice these variations, there will be a formal if not a substantial lacuna in our presentation, and we shall also miss certain definite insights. A long, retrospective note is therefore required.

When we spoke of Jesus Christ as Judge and judged, and of His judgment and justice, we were adopting a definite standpoint and terminology as the framework in which to present our view of the *pro nobis*[EN233]. In order to speak with dogmatic clarity and distinctness we had to decide on a framework of this kind. And the actual importance of this way of thinking and its particularly good basis in the Bible were a sufficient reason for choosing this one. But exegesis reminds us that in the New Testament there are other standpoints and termin-[274] ologies which might equally be considered as guiding principles for dogmatics The fact that in the New Testament more than one starting-point is proposed for our systematic reflection on the *pro nobis*[EN234] ought to be a salutary reminder that in dogmatics we cannot speak down from heaven in the language of God but only on earth as strictly and exactly as we can in a human language, as the New Testament writers themselves did—the variety of the standpoints and concepts which they adopted being the attestation. In all its contexts theology can speak only approximately. It is a matter of finding and keeping to those lines of approximation which are relatively the best, which correspond best to what we want to express. That is what we have tried to do in this matter of the *pro nobis*[EN235] with the selection and expos-

---

EN231 theology of the cross
EN232 for us
EN233 for us
EN234 for us
EN235 for us

ition of four concepts taken from the sphere of law. But we have to recognise that in the New Testament there are other similar spheres, and therefore that other lines of approximation are possible in principle.

For example, in addition to the forensic imagery which we have chosen there is also, strangely enough, a financial in which the being and activity and even the self-offering of Jesus Christ for us and in our place are described as the payment of a ransom ($\lambda\acute{v}\tau\rho\sigma\nu$, Mk. 10⁴⁵), and therefore as a $\lambda v\tau\rho\sigma\hat{v}\nu$EN236 (1 Pet. 1¹⁸, Tit. 2¹⁴), an $\mathring{a}\pi\sigma\lambda\acute{v}\tau\rho\omega\sigma\iota\varsigma$EN237 (Rom. 3²⁴), an $\mathring{\epsilon}\xi\alpha\gamma\rho\rho\acute{a}\zeta\epsilon\iota\nu$EN238 (Gal. 3¹³, 4⁵). In the majority of these passages, although not all, the important concept $\mathring{a}\pi\sigma\lambda\acute{v}\tau\rho\omega\sigma\iota\varsigma$EN239 does, of course, speak of an event which will take place only in and with the appearance of Jesus Christ. This strand is relatively slender. Not infrequently (as in Rom. 3²⁴) it crosses the one of which we have been particularly thinking. And it would be difficult and not very profitable to try to think out the whole event within the framework of this imagery. Fundamentally, no doubt, that is possible. But it is surely enough if we are ready to use the particular force of these categories in an occasional and subsidiary manner to clarify the matter to ourselves and others.

There is perhaps also a military view of the work of Jesus Christ behind passages like Mk. 3²⁷ (the invasion of the house of the strong man and his binding), or Col. 1¹³ (our snatching away from the power of darkness and removal to the kingdom of God's Son), or even the $\pi\alpha\nu\sigma\pi\lambda\acute{\iota}\alpha$ $\theta\epsilon\sigma\hat{v}$EN240 of Eph. 6¹¹ᶠ. The Eastern Church especially, but also Luther, loved to regard and describe this work as a victorious overcoming of the devil and death which took place on our behalf. But it may again be asked whether it is advisable to try to work out systematically our thinking in this direction. What is clear is that a place should be found for this group of images and the particular truth which it presents.

There is, however, one group of New Testament views and concepts and terms which stands apart both from those we have just mentioned, and from the forensic group we have preferred, with sufficient distinctness and importance to merit a special appraisal. We can give it the general title of cultic. One important New Testament writing, the Epistle to the Hebrews, is almost completely dominated by it. But it is obviously presupposed and expressly used in Paul and the Johannine writings. May it not be that the most primitive Christianity, because of its great nearness to the Old Testament, partly in agreement with it and partly in opposition to it, did in fact think and speak far more in the images and categories of this group than we can detect from the New Testament? It occurs again and again in unmistakable allusions. For example, the Jesus Christ who gives Himself for us is called the "Lamb of God," and the giving of His life is referred to as "His blood." When this happens, we are clearly using cultic language. Of course in the New Testament the different groups of terms cut across each other very frequently. It is therefore inevitable that we should have occasionally met expressions from this group in our previous discussion. And of itself it would be quite possible to put our whole presentation within the framework of this standpoint. The older Protestant dogmatics did in fact give to the doctrine of the work of Jesus Christ the title *munus Christi sacerdotale*EN241 when they treated it under the aspect of the *pro nobis*EN242 as we have done in this section. The only trouble was that their expositions under this title did at their heart slip into forensic notions (which were more or less foreign, or were applied in a way that was more or less foreign to the Bible itself). At any rate, they did not bring out the

[275]

EN236 ransoming
EN237 redemption
EN238 purchase
EN239 redemption
EN240 army of God
EN241 priestly office of Christ
EN242 for us

specific features in the cultic standpoint and terminology. If we ourselves have refrained from presenting the whole in this framework it is for two reasons. First, and quite simply, material which is already difficult would have been made even more difficult by trying to understand it in a form which is now rather remote from us. Second, and above all, we are able to see the matter better and more distinctly and more comprehensively under the four selected concepts taken from the forensic area of biblical thinking than would have been possible even at the very best if we had committed ourselves radically to a cultic view. But this need not prevent us from now trying briefly to see and test from this different standpoint, which is so very important in New Testament thinking, the knowledge which we have gained in the framework of this other outlook. In this respect we may remember Zinzendorf, whose theology of blood I have not really been trying to avoid. What we have tried to say in another way, if it is said correctly, cannot be anything other than that which could and can be said in the images and categories of cultic language. It would therefore bode ill for our results if we could not recognise them in the mirror of this other language in which it was so important to the men of the New Testament to think and speak. For the moment, then, we will not continue our thinking, but re-state and verify it in another direction.

1. Jesus Christ took our place as Judge. We can say the same thing in this way. He is the Priest who represented us. He represented a people oppressed by its sins, threatened because of them, and in need of propitiation, a people from which the will of *Yahweh* is concealed, which will not be instructed properly concerning His rights and law, which cannot really sacrifice or pray for itself. The priest is the mediator and representative who by virtue of his office (originally, perhaps, understood in charismatic terms) actually makes possible the access of the people to its god. We must not be vexed when we see that the close parallel between this image and the work of Jesus lies in the very characteristics of the concept of priest which make it quite impossible for us to use the term to describe any order of men in the Church. According to the definition of Thomas Aquinas (*S. th.* III, 22, 1) a priest is a *mediator inter Deum et populum in quantum scilicet divina populo tradit, unde dicitur sacerdos, quasi sacra dans*[EN243]. In relation to the work of Jesus Christ for us this is not only not too strong, but not strong enough. The exclusiveness with which the priest acts alone, not only in His function of imparting the *divina*[EN244] or *sacra*[EN245] to the people, but also in that of representing the people before God, is, of course, the *tertium comparationis*[EN246]. Jesus Christ is *the* Priest, between God and man, the one μεσίτης [EN247] (1 Tim. 2⁵). The image indicates the fact. But the fact is greater and more powerful than the image. It necessarily transcends it.

The exclusiveness of all other priests is limited by the fact that all other priests, even the high priests of the Old Testament in their representative capacity, need to do for themselves what they do for others. "He shall make atonement for himself, and for his household, and for all the congregation of Israel" (Lev. 16⁶, Heb. 9⁷). This reservation makes his position and function understandable and tolerable from the human standpoint but it also compromises it. He acts as a *primus inter pares*[EN248]. But only symbolically, or representatively, is he a *sacra dans*[EN249]. He himself must receive the *sacra*[EN250] no less than others. There is no

---

[EN243] mediator between God and the people, evidently inasmuch as he gives divine things to the people. Hence he is called sacerdos (priest), as he is a giver (dans) of holy things (sacra)

[EN244] divine things

[EN245] holy things

[EN246] basis of comparison

[EN247] mediator

[EN248] first among equals

[EN249] giver of holy things

[EN250] holy things

such reservation in the case of Jesus Christ. As the Son of God He acts exclusively on behalf of the people and not for Himself.

For this reason He is the true, and essential and original Priest, the "great high-priest" (Heb. 4^{14}), "not after the law of a carnal commandment, but after the power of an endless life" (Heb. 7^{16}), not "after the order of Aaron, for even as man He did not belong to the tribe of Levi, but to that of Judah" (Heb. $7^{11f.}$). but as Hebrews constantly repeats from Ps. 110^4 [276] "after the order of Melchisedec, King of Salem" (Gen. $14^{18f.}$), who met Abraham and blessed him, to whom Abraham (and in his loins Levi) paid tithes and therefore recognised his precedence, who was a king of righteousness and peace, "without father, without mother, without descent, having neither beginning of days, nor end of life; but made like unto the Son of God" (Heb. $7^{1f.}$). What the priest after the order of Aaron does must be authorised by the Law, which is before him and after him and therefore over him and those like him. And the dignity and force of his offering consists in the fact that it is brought according to this Law, that the bringing of it is a single case under this Law. That is why it has to be repeated. That is why—and this is the great limitation of all other priestly work—it is not the thing itself, the reconciliation of man with God, but only the "type and shadow" of it (Heb. 8^5), an indication only, a powerful symbolising and attesting of the atonement which will be made by God Himself. If in Jesus Christ we had to do with a high-priest of this kind, with another symbolical representation of the atonement, then we have to ask under what law He stands, what He represents, what general necessity there is for the "satisfaction" He makes, what higher truth is revealed in the reality of His cross. There is always a strong temptation to look for Him on this level and therefore to put questions like this. But He is a Priest after the order of Melchisedec. That is, He is an instance of priestly action for which there is no parallel, which cannot be deduced from anything else, which stands under no law but that established and revealed in the fact that there was this instance. And this is the instance of effectively priestly action because in it the action is complete. It is not the symbol for a general truth which lies above it. It is the instance in which satisfaction—that which suffices for the reconciliation of the world with God—has been made (*satis fecit*) and can be grasped only as something which has in fact happened, and not as something which had to happen by reason of some upper half of the event; not, then, in any theory of satisfaction, but only as we see and grasp the *satis-facere*[EN251] which has, in fact, been achieved.

From this it follows that in His ministry, unlike other priests and high priests. He cannot and need not be replaced by any other priestly person. He does not have and exercise this office within the framework of an institution, as one of its many representatives, but on the basis of an oath which God swore by Himself, and therefore as a Priest for ever (Heb. 7^{20-24}), not with daily or annual repetitions, but ἐφάπαξ[EN252] (Heb. 7^{27}, $9^{12\ 26}$, 10^{10}), in a single action accomplished and effective once and for all, by a θυσία[EN253], by a προσφορά[EN254] (Heb. $10^{12,\ 14}$) accomplished, not in the forecourt or the outer court, but with His entry into the innermost tabernacle, the Holiest of Holies of God Himself (Heb. $9^{1f.}$). In this way the work of Jesus Christ is at once the essence and fulfilment of all other priestly work but also that which replaces it and makes it superfluous. At the point to which the existence of the Old Testament priest, the human priest called by God, points and can only point, there now stands and acts Jesus Christ in a way which is different from that of every other human priest, even the priest and high priest of the Old Testament. And from this point He has now

---

EN251 satis-faction ('enough-doing')
EN252 once for all
EN253 sacrifice
EN254 offering

crowded out and replaced from the very outset every other human priest. He is the Mediator, the Representative of His people before God. He is that which every other priest can only signify in his work—and signifying it in this way can only do that which—as the Epistle to the Hebrews emphasises again and again—is completely insufficient: insufficient to create a genuine correspondence of man to God in the divine covenant; insufficient to make man capable of acting in relation to God; insufficient for the reconciliation of the world with God. In the work of Jesus Christ and in that work alone there takes place the real and sufficient priestly work, the *sacra dare*[EN255]. In Him we have the One we need as a Priest to act for us (Heb. 4^{14}, 8^1, 10^{21}): $\H{\epsilon}\chi o\mu\epsilon\nu$[EN256]. And by Him we obviously have that which we also have

[277] as those justified by Him as Judge (to revert to our earlier terminology), that is, peace with God, access to Him, and hope in Him (cf. Heb. 10$^{19f.}$ with Rom. 5$^{1f.}$).

In fact we can equally well describe the work of Jesus Christ as His high-priestly work as His judicial work, and we shall mean and say exactly the same thing. In both cases He takes the place of man, and takes from man an office which has to be filled but which man himself cannot fill. In both cases a new order comes into force to establish a new covenant, which is really the genuine fulfilment of the old. It does so in this very different man who in both cases as the Son of God made man takes the matter into His own hands to execute it according to its true meaning and purpose. In both cases this involves the deposing and therefore the serious discrediting and humiliating of man. And in both cases this and this alone means the liberation and hope of man.

2. We will combine the second and third points of our main discussion. Jesus Christ is the One who was accused, condemned and judged in the place of us sinners. But we can say the same thing in this way: He gave Himself to be offered up as a sacrifice to take away our sins. It is perfectly plain that whichever view we take or expression we use it is with reference to the same thing, the passion of Jesus Christ. We have not yet mentioned that which according to the Epistle to the Hebrews constitutes the decisive difference between Himself and all other priests and high priests. The supreme and distinctive function of the priest is to offer sacrifice. But this Priest—and here the image breaks down completely and the parallel with Melchisedec is abandoned—is not only the One who offers sacrifice but also the sacrifice which is offered; just as He is also the Judge and the judged. He does not offer anything else—not even the greatest thing—He simply offers Himself. He does not pour out the blood of others, of bulls and calves, to go into the Holiest with this offering (Heb. 9$^{12\ 25}$). It is a matter of His own blood, of the giving of His own life to death. "Through the eternal Spirit He offered himself without spot to God" (Heb. 9$^{14\ 23\ 26}$; cf. 7^{27}, 10$^{12\ 14}$)—Himself as $\pi\rho o\sigma\phi o\rho\grave{a}$ $\kappa a\grave{\iota}$ $\theta v\sigma\acute{\iota}a$[EN257] Eph. 5^2). He Himself is the Lamb of God which taketh away the sin of the world (Jn. 1^{29})—a lamb without spot or blemish, i.e., the lamb most suitable for this offering, as is emphasised in 1 Pet. 1^{19}. He Himself was offered as our Passover (1 Cor. 5^7). Similarly the expression "my blood of the covenant" in the saying at the giving of the cup at the Last Supper (Mk. 14^{24}) undoubtedly involves a similar comparison of His own self-giving with the blood of sacrifice which, according to Ex. 24^8, was sprinkled over the people on the conclusion of the covenant at Sinai. Or, again, His blood is for those who believe in Him that which the *kapporeth*[EN258] sprinkled with the blood of the animal sacrifice, the $\iota\lambda a\sigma\tau\acute{\eta}\rho\iota o\nu$[EN259] of the covenant, could only signify for the people of the old covenant: the demonstration, the revelation, the event, the $\H{\epsilon}\nu\delta\epsilon\iota\xi\iota\varsigma$ $\tau\hat{\eta}\varsigma$ $\delta\iota\kappa a\iota o\sigma\acute{v}\nu\eta\varsigma$ $\theta\epsilon o\hat{v}$[EN260] on earth (Rom. 3^{25}). Because

---

EN255 giving of holy things
EN256 we have
EN257 an offering and a sacrifice
EN258 mercy seat
EN259 mercy seat
EN260 demonstration of the righteousness of God

it is this Priest, the Son of God, who makes this offering, which is Himself, therefore in contrast to all others His sacrifice is effective and complete, making an "eternal" redemption (Heb. 9[12]). It is the one true sacrifice, just as He who makes it is the one true Priest: the fulfilment of what is meant by all sacrifices, and at the same time the end of all sacrifices, just as He who makes it fulfils the concept priest and at the same time makes the existence of any further priests superfluous and impossible.

For what does the term sacrifice mean? There is no doubt that like the term priest it stands in relation to that of sin, to that of the discord in which man finds himself with God and himself. Sacrifice is an attempt to deal with this discord. This is something which can perhaps be shown even from most or perhaps all the views of sacrifice that we find in non-biblical religions. But there is no doubt that in the system of sacrifice which was normative for the New Testament, that of the covenant with Israel in its completed form, its purpose is to order the encounter of a sinful people with God in the way which God Himself has instituted. It is the possibility and actuality of a communication and communion of Israel and the [278] individual Israelite with God which, if they do not do away with that gulf, do at least temporarily bridge it. The member of the covenant people still belongs to *Yahweh* even though he has a part in the rebellion and transgression in which this people is caught up. He cannot forget Him. He cannot escape his guilt and responsibility in relation to Him, his commitment to Him. He can and must make an offering (this is where the mediatorial ministry of the priest is so important). Offerings are substitutes for what he really ought to render to God, but never does do, and never will. They are gifts from the sphere of his most cherished possessions which represent or express his will to obey, which symbolise the life which has not in fact been offered to God. He can bring these gifts. He ought to do so. He acknowledges *Yahweh* and the fact that he belongs to Him by bringing them. He recognises his guilt and obligation. He confesses that he is a member of the people which, in spite of everything, is His elect people. It is not, therefore, a fact that in his sacrifices the man of the Old Testament merely gave proof of a longing for reconciliation, that he only expressed and tried to mitigate the unrest which filled him by reason of his situation in conflict with God and himself. The sacrifices of the Old Testament do belong to the human history of religion, but there is more to them than that. They are also a provisional and relative fulfilment of the will and commandment of God. They are a genuine element in the history of the covenant and the history of redemption. In sacrifice Israel—fallible, sinful and unfaithful Israel—is summoned to bow beneath the divine judgment, but also to hold fast to the divine grace. Of course, this living meaning of sacrifice can sometimes fade. It may become a mere religious observance. It may be understood as a *do ut des*[EN261]. It may become an attempt on the part of the people to acquire power over God, to assure oneself before Him, to hide one's sin instead of acknowledging it. Instead of a terror-stricken flight to God it may become a sinful flight from Him to a sacred work. When this happens, but only when this happens and as an attack upon it, the prophets (Amos 5[21f.], Is. 1[10f.], Jer. 7[21f.]) and many of the Psalms (like 40[7f.], 50[13f.], 51[18f.]) take up their well-known inflexible attitude against it.

The real problem of sacrifice is not the imminent misuse to which like any cult it can be put, but the fact that in face of the sin of man, while it can mean an impressive summons to repent and convert, a cheerful encouragement to do the best we can, and even a serious encouragement, and while its fulfilment does call us to remember the presence and will and commandment of the holy and merciful God, it does not in any way alter either sin itself or the situation of conflict and contradiction brought about by sin. As Paul has put it in Rom. 3[25], we have to do with a πάρεσις τῶν προγεγονότων ἁμαρτημάτων ἐν τῇ ἀνοχῇ τοῦ

EN261 I give so that you might give

θεοῦ[EN262] which has to be sought and attained again and again. Sacrifice in the Old Testament cannot bring to an end the state of things between God and His people, replacing it by a new state. It can only restore a temporary order (so far as this is possible without more savage penalties). It can only leave open and in the air the disturbed and broken relationship between the two, making a common existence at least bearable and possible. But the alteration which it brings about is only temporary and incidental. Things are made easier and better until the next time. There is promise, but no fulfilment. There is truth, but no actuality. That is why in the bitter terms of Heb. 10³ it is ultimately only an ἀνάμνησις ἁμαρτιῶν[EN263]. It does shed a certain light, but in so doing it can only make man all the more bitterly conscious of the dark background to his existence, which is still unchanged. It aims at atonement, but it only represents it; it only symbolises it, it does not make it. It is permitted. It is commanded. At its best, it is offered with obedience and thankfulness and a readiness to serve. But it is still only a substitute for what has to happen, for an offering which is made to God in true faithfulness. It is only a substitute for what has to happen when

[279] the people and individuals who are disobedient to God are set aside, in order to make way for the new individual and the new people. Sacrifice does not do this. An animal is brought and slain, and its blood is shed. But this animal is not the old man which has to be made to disappear. And the showing of it is not that ἔνδειξις τῆς δικαιοσύνης θεοῦ[EN264] (Rom. 3²⁵ ²⁶). It is not the establishment of that radical and effective and definitive new order in which a man who is righteous before God can encounter the righteous God. It does not accomplish any τελειῶσαι[EN265] of those who bring the animal. The offering of it is only a "shadow of things to come" (Heb. 10¹). *Significat?*[EN266] Yes. *Est?*[EN267] No. That is the limitation and problem of sacrifice in the Old Testament.

Of course alongside this we can and must set the fact that the history of Israel attested in the Old Testament is one great series of dark and heavy judgments on the part of God, and that Israel is a people which is constantly judged by God in the severity of His faithfulness. The forbearance of God revealed in His institution and acceptance of sacrifices is not without its limits. There are some sins of individuals which cannot be atoned by any sacrifices but when they are committed can be met only by the extirpation of the guilty from the community. Similarly, sacrifices do not exclude the punishments of God for the inconstancy and obstinacy of the people as a whole. The history of the dealings of God in and with this people is one which gives many proofs of His goodness and help, but it is also a history of the great and greatest retributions and excisions which come upon it. These, too, are full of the secret grace of God. They are signs of the election of this people. They are never without promise. But nowhere is it apparent that any one of them (not even the destruction of Jerusalem and the temple) could really or basically alter the perverted situation between God and this people, the disharmony in its existence as the unfaithful people of its faithful God. At his own time and place and in his own way, does not each of the prophets who have to announce these judgments have to begin at the beginning like his predecessors, as though nothing had happened? They all attest the judgment, the day of the Lord, which will be accompanied and followed by salvation. But the day itself remains obstinately on the horizon of the history of Israel. It is not any of the days in that history. None of the events in that history is this judgment. None of them brings in an Israel which has been really and finally judged by its God, that is, put finally in the right, effectively and definitively subjected to His will and

---

[EN262] passing over, in God's patience, of the sins committed beforehand
[EN263] remembering of sins
[EN264] demonstration of the righteousness of God
[EN265] perfecting
[EN266] Signifies?
[EN267] Is?

therefore well pleasing to Him. It is judged again and again, just as it must offer sacrifice again and again. But in all the frightful events of this history there is as little of the ἔνδειξις τῆς δικαιοσύνης θεοῦ[EN268] as in the offerings of its sacrifices. This people is always the same and fundamentally untrustworthy partner in relation to God. On its side the covenant of God with it is always the covenant which has not been kept but broken. The punishments which come upon it from God, like the sacrifices which are commanded by God and made according to His institution, can be described only as "shadows of things to come." Israel signifies man judged by God and judged therefore to his salvation, man brought to actual conversion by the judgment of God, man passing through death to life. But Israel is not that man.

This is where the one sacrifice of Jesus Christ intervenes: the real sacrifice for sin, the sacrifice which sets it aside, which effects and proclaims its effective and complete forgiveness, which brings before God the just man which Israel could signify in its sacrifices as well as in the judgments it had to undergo, but which it could only signify, which it could introduce only in substitute, in a kind of *quid pro quo*[EN269]. The sacrifice of Jesus Christ, the offering of which is taken out of the hands of all priests, is entirely His own affair, and it is no longer a shadow and figure, but a fulfilment of the reconciliation of man with God. That ἔνδειξις[EN270] of the righteousness of God is no longer an episode on the way, but the goal of the history of the covenant and redemption determined by God from all eternity and initiated with the election of Israel. To what extent? To the extent that in it we no longer have to do with a human and therefore a merely human, an improper and provisional fulfilment of the divine will. It is, of course, a human action—but in and with the human action it is also a divine action, in which there takes place that which all human offerings can only attest, in which the reservation under which all human offering takes place, and its character as merely representative, symbolical and significative are done away, in which the concept of sacrifice is fulfilled and the true and effective sacrifice is made. Our whole understanding depends upon our recognising that God's own activity and being, His presence and activity in the One who is His own Son, very and eternal God with the Father and the Holy Spirit, is the truth and power of that which takes place here as a history of human sacrificing and sacrifice.

[280]

God wills and demands—what? Further substitutes in a further ἀνοχή[EN271] for the purpose of further πάρεσις[EN272]? Further attestations of the covenant which He has established between Himself and man? Further temporary communications and communions of man with Himself? The further and more serious and perfect offerings of all kinds of *quid pro quo*[EN273]? A further and perhaps final history of priests and sacrifices? No: all the things which are temporary and on this level are done away and superseded. God Himself has intervened in His own person. His great day has come. He now wills and demands the fulfilment of the covenant, the new man who not only knows and recognises and actively gives it to be understood, but lives wholly and utterly by the fact that He belongs to God, that He is His man. He wills and demands not merely the bridging and lessening of the conflict between Himself and us, but its removal, not only light in darkness, but as on the first day of creation the dispersal of darkness by light. He wills and demands the sacrifice of the old man (who can never be this man, who can only die). He wills and demands the setting aside of this man, his giving up to death, which is not fulfilled merely by giving up this or that, even

---

[EN268] demonstration of the righteousness of God
[EN269] this for that
[EN270] demonstration
[EN271] patience
[EN272] passing over
[EN273] this for that

the best he has. God wills and demands the man himself, to make an end of him, so that the new man may have air and space for a new life. He wills and demands that he should go through death to life. He wills and demands that as the man of sin he should abandon his life, that his blood as this man should finally be shed and fall to the ground and be lost, that as this man he should go up in flames and smoke. That is the meaning and end of sacrifice. And that is the judgment which is not fulfilled in any other sacrifices. It is fulfilled in the sacrifice of Jesus Christ, in the shedding of His "precious blood" (1 Pet. 1¹⁹). It has the power of a real offering and taking away of the sinful man, the power to bring about his end and death as such, and therefore to create a new situation in which God no longer has to do with this man, in which His own faithfulness will meet a faithful people and a faithful man. In the sacrifice of Jesus Christ the will of God is fulfilled in this turning, in this radical conversion of man to Himself which posits an end and therefore a new beginning.

But it is fulfilled in this sacrifice because now it is God Himself who not only demands but makes the offering. He makes it in that He the Lord willed to become a servant, in that His Son willed to go into the far country, to become one with us and to take our place as sinners, to die for us the death of the old man which was necessary for the doing of the will of God, to shed our wicked blood in His own precious blood, to kill our sin in His own death. In Israel's sacrifices in obedience to the command of God this could only be intended and willed and attested and represented—because they were made within and under the presupposition of a constant rebellion against God, and in the sign of the constant provocation of His wrath. But now it has actually taken place—taken place because and to the extent that in Jesus Christ God Himself has acted in place of the human race, Himself making the real sacrifice which radically alters the situation between Himself and man. In Him God not only demands but He gives what He demands. In Him He does that which has to take place to set

[281]

aside sin and remove the conflict. He shows Himself to be pure and holy and sinless by not refusing in Him to become the greatest of all sinners, achieving the penitence and conversion which is demanded of sinners, undertaking the bitter reality of being the accused and condemned and judged and executed man of sin, in order that when He Himself has been this man no other man can or need be, in order that in place of this man another man who is pleasing to God, the man of obedience, may have space and air and be able to live. He who gives Himself up to this is the same eternal God who wills and demands it. Christ *certo respectu sibi ipsi satisfecit*EN274 (Hollaz, *Ex. Theol. acroam.*, 1707, III, 3, qu. 77). Both the demanding and the giving are a single related decision in God Himself. For that reason real satisfaction has been done, i.e., that which suffices has been done, that setting aside and repudiation has been utterly and basically accomplished.

3. We have seen that Jesus Christ was just in our place. In cultic terms this is equivalent to saying that in our place He has made a perfect sacrifice. He who as the perfect Priest took the place of all human priests, by offering Himself, has substituted a perfect sacrifice for all the sacrifices offered by men.

That He has made a perfect sacrifice means primarily and comprehensively and decisively that He has fulfilled the will of God the doing of which the action of all human priests and all the sacrifices made by men could only proclaim and attest. With His sacrifice He has left the sphere of that which is improper and provisional and done that which is proper and definitive. His offering was that which God affirmed, which was acceptable and pleasing to Him, which He accepted. His sacrifice meant the closing of the time of the divine ἀνοχή EN275, the time of the mere πάρεσις EN276 of human sins endlessly repeating themselves, the time of the

---

EN274 in a certain sense made satisfaction for his very self
EN275 patience
EN276 passing over

alternation of divine grace and divine judgment, in which human priests had their function and the offerings made by men had a meaning. His sacrifice means that the time of being has dawned in place of that of signifying—of the being of man as a faithful partner in covenant with God, and therefore of his being at peace with God and therefore of the being of the man reconciled with Him and converted to Him. We are told in Jn. 19^{28} concerning the crucified Jesus that He knew ὅτι ἤδη πάντα τετέλεσται[EN277]. And His last word when He died was τετέλεσται[EN278] (Jn. 19^{30}). Jesus knew what God knew in the taking place of His sacrifice. And Jesus said what God said: that what took place was not something provisional, but that which suffices to fulfil the divine will, that which is entire and perfect, that which cannot and need not be continued or repeated or added to or superseded, the new thing which was the end of the old but which will itself never become old, which can only be there and continue and shine out and have force and power as that which is new and eternal. Notice the exposition of Ps. 40^7 in Heb. $10^{8f.}$: "Above when he said, Sacrifice and offering and burnt offerings and offering for sin thou wouldest not, neither hadst pleasure therein; which are offered by the law; Then said he, Lo, I come to do thy will, O God. He taketh away the first, that he may establish the second. By the which will we are sanctified through the offering of the body of Christ once for all." In this respect we can and must think of the positive intention and meaning of the Old Testament opposition to the sacrifices which Israel misused and therefore God rejected, and even to the institution of sacrifice itself. For in and with this one perfect sacrifice it comes about that "judgment runs down as waters, and righteousness as a mighty stream" (Amos 5^{24}). The evil deeds of men are removed from the sight of God. The doing of evil ceases. It is now learned how to do good. Regard is now had for right. The violent are now restrained, the orphans are helped to their right and the cause of the widow is taken up (Is. $1^{16f.}$). Thanks is brought to God, and in this way vows are paid to the Most High. In the day of need He is now called upon, that He may redeem man and that man may praise Him (Ps. $50^{14f.}$). There is now offered to God the sacrifice which pleases Him and which He will not despise, that of a broken spirit and a contrite heart (Ps. 51^{19}). Ears are open to Him; there is a desire to do His will; His Law is in the hearts of men (Ps. $40^{7f.}$). All these things have now taken place: "by the which will (the taking place of the sacrificial action of Jesus Christ) we are sanctified." There has been brought about that radically altered human situation to which all human priests and all the offerings brought by men could only look forward, the reconciliation which lit up their whole activity only as a promise on the horizon, warning and comforting, but only as an indication, not as presence and actuality. Now that Jesus Christ has done sacrifice as a priest and sacrificed Himself, all these things have come, for in Him that which God demanded has taken place; it has been given and accomplished by God Himself. In the person of His Son there has taken place the event towards which the history of the old covenant was only moving, which it only indicated from afar—the rendering of obedience, humility and penitence, and in this way the conversion of man to God, and in this conversion the setting aside, the death, of the old rebellious man and the birth of a new man whose will is one with His. In Jesus Christ there has come the Priest who feels with the ignorant and errant, who is Himself compassed with infirmity (Heb. 5^2), who as a Son "learned obedience by the things which he suffered" (Heb. 5^8), and in this way proved Himself to be "holy, harmless, undefiled, separate from sinners" (Heb. 7^{26}), "in all points tempted like as we are, yet without sin" (Heb. 4^{15})—in fact, the only Priest who is qualified to act. And in that He has offered Himself there has been done by this Priest the acceptable work, indeed the work which was already accepted and approved by God even as it was performed, the work which was necessary on man's side for the making of atonement.

[282]

[EN277] all things were now finished
[EN278] 'It is finished'

In His sacrifice God has affirmed Himself and the man Jesus as His Son. This is, therefore, the true and perfect sacrifice.

We do not add to the completeness of this exposition, but simply describe it once more, when we say that this perfect sacrifice which fulfils the will of God took place in our stead and for us. For what other reason was there? God did not need to act as a priest and to suffer as a sacrifice in the person of His Son. But we need this Mediator and His mediation. The will of God towards us is the purpose of this sacrifice, and His good pleasure towards us is its end. In Him there takes place that which we need but which we cannot do or bring about for ourselves. It is a matter of our reconciliation, our peace with God, our access to Him, our freedom for Him, and therefore the basic alteration of our human situation, the taking away of that which separates us from Him and involves His separation from us, our death as sinful men and our living as obedient men. The perfection of the sacrifice of Jesus Christ, the whole divine height and depth of the turning made in Him, is therefore the perfection of the love with which God has loved us. In the making of this sacrifice He loved us in perfect love; He Himself and by Himself doing and bringing about all that is necessary for us; without any merit of ours, indeed against all our merits; without any assistance from us, indeed in face of our resistance. As we close it is as well to look at this perfection again in contrast with us whom it favours. There can be no question of a love with which we loved Him in the fact that this happened, that He sent His Son as ἱλασμός EN279 for our sins (1 Jn. 4¹⁰; cf. 2²). For who are we? We are defiant sinners, the obstinately godless, the open enemies of God, who cannot contribute anything to this happening, who if it were in our power would only interrupt and prevent it. The only good thing that can be reported of us is that this perfect sacrifice was made in our place and for us—a superior act of divine defiance meeting our defiance; that it is the perfect action of God in this turning to us (which we cannot interrupt or prevent). All that can be said of us is that without this perfect action of God we would be lost; that apart from it we can have no refuge or counsel or consolation or help. But of God we have to say that this perfect action which He Himself did not need has in His merciful good-pleasure taken place for us; that He willed to make it and did make it a need of His, a matter of His own glory, to do this for us, that is, to accept the perfect sacrifice, the righteousness of Jesus Christ as our righteousness, our sacrifice, and therefore as the finished work of our reconciliation. Not only as though we had brought this sacrifice, but as the sacrifice which we have brought. Not only as though the righteousness of Jesus Christ were ours, but as the righteousness which we have achieved. Not only as though the work of reconciliation finished in Him were our work, but really as the work which we have done. We remember that in the sacrifice of Jesus Christ we no longer have a substitute for that which we cannot do. It is no longer a question of a *quid pro quo* EN280, an "as if," beyond which we still need something more perfect, a real reconciliation which has still to come. In the doctrine of the justification of man, of the reach of that which has taken place in Jesus Christ, we have to see that we are saying far too little when we use a favourite expression of the Reformers and call it an imputation of the alien righteousness of Jesus Christ. It cannot in any sense be an improper justification of man which has its basis in this happening. Otherwise how could it be a perfect happening, and how could the love of God for man realised in it be a perfect love? Rather, the alien righteousness which has been effected not in and by us but in the sacrifice of Jesus Christ does become and is always ours, so that in Him we are no longer unrighteous but righteous before God, we are the children of God, we have the forgiveness of our sins, peace with God, access to Him and freedom for Him. That this is the case is the righteousness which Jesus Christ has accomplished for us, the perfection of His sacrifice

[283]

EN279 an atoning sacrifice
EN280 symbol

which cannot be added to by anyone or anything. He has sacrificed in our name with a validity which cannot be limited and a force which cannot be diminished. What He has done He has done in order that being done by Him it may be done by us; not only acceptable to God, but already accepted; our work which is pleasing to Him; our own being as those who are dead to sin and can live to righteousness. He alone has done this, but because He has done it, in a decision which cannot be reversed, with a truth which is absolute, He has done it for us.

3. THE VERDICT OF THE FATHER

In the first part of this section we dealt with the way of the Son of God into the far country—a part of what the older dogmatics used to call the doctrine of the person of Christ and especially the doctrine of His true deity. Then in the second we dealt with the Judge judged in our place—a part of the old doctrine of the work of Christ and especially His "high-priestly" work. We will have to proceed to an understanding of the sin of man (in this instance, pride) from the particular standpoint of this first part of the doctrine of reconciliation and in the light of the humiliation of the Lord as servant which has taken place in Jesus Christ. It will also be our task to understand the justification of man as the immediate consequence of that divine human action, the existence of the Christian community in its human and historical form as that which provisionally corresponds to it, and faith as that which grasps and apprehends it all. At every point we can only proceed along the way the beginning of which we have already learned to know. We can only build on the christological basis which has been exposed. We shall proceed and build in our own anthropological sphere. For it is in this sphere that the atonement made in Jesus Christ has taken place. It is here in the context of human history, at a certain point in this sphere, that it took place that this sphere was entered by God Himself in the person of His Son, that He, the Judge, was judged in our place and favour. It was this sphere which needed atonement with God, and it has a part in it. To what extent? With what effects and consequences? This is what we shall have to show under the concepts sin, justification, community and faith (which all belong to the anthropological sphere) and in the light of that event, in demonstration of the reach of that event. [284]

But before we enter on this series of further problems, and in order to do so with good protection and clear conscience, in the third part of this section we must engage in a kind of transitional discussion between the problems and answers we have just given and the further questions we will now have to add to them. What is the connexion between these new problems and our previous questions and answers? How are we going to proceed and build on this christological basis? Why do we think that this is even possible, that our anthropological sphere will prove to be one which is co-ordinated with and subordinated to the christological, which both needs that which has taken place in Jesus Christ and also has a part in it? Or, conversely, why do we think that there can be any demonstration of the relevance of that one event in and for this whole sphere? With what right can we speak of our sin, of our justification, of ourselves as a community and of our faith, in the light of what Jesus Christ is and has done for us? How does He come to us or we to Him?

It is true that He has already come to us and we are already with Him. For what is the meaning of the incarnation and the τετέλεσται EN281 of the Crucified if it does not tell us of His being with us and our being with Him? From the very first we have not thought of His being abstractly, but *per definitionem* EN282 as belonging to us and us to it. Again, from the very first we have thought of His activity *per definitionem* EN283 as His activity for us, *pro nobis* EN284. In the great turn which will now have to be executed by us it can only be a matter of explaining what we have to say *per definitionem* EN285 of His being and activity, His person and work, of explaining the form of His being and activity which is from the very first concrete and comprehensive. His being as it belongs to us (and ours as it belongs to Him), His activity *pro nobis* EN286, does not need any amplification. When we work out the bearing of the one event of His being and activity, the basis and climax will always have to be in specific statements about Himself and His person and work. And the basic transitional discussion on which we must now engage, the question of the legitimacy of the turn which we will have to execute as we work it out, does not in any way compromise but can only confirm the fact that it is He Himself in whom this turn has already been executed and is a fact.

[285]

It is a fact. I emphasise this in opposition to the conception represented by G. Thomasius in *Christi Person und Werk*, Vol. 3, 2, 1888, 206. Thomasius makes a distinction between the restoration of fellowship between God and man accomplished once and for all in Jesus Christ, and the "continual" mediation of it. He introduces his presentation of the latter with the words: "It is only with the objective reconciliation by which humanity has become the object of the grace of God that the actual possibility, i.e., the right and power to be reconciled with God, is won for the individual members of the race. But this possibility has to become actuality. That which Christ has worked out once and for all for the whole race, that which is available for everyone in Him, now has to come to every individual, so that there is a real fellowship of men with God. This is the purpose of the whole objective mediation of salvation, and with it it reaches its goal." A doubtful feature in this presentation is the distinction between an objective atonement and a subjective which is obviously quite different from it. So, too, is the distinction between that which has been worked out and is available in Christ and that which has still to come to me. So, too, and above all, is the description of the antithesis in categories of possibility and actuality, which later becomes the differentiation of a purpose which is only present in Jesus Christ and which attains its goal only in some other occurrence. To express ourselves in the language of Thomasius we should have to attempt the paradoxes of trying to understand the once and for all as that which is also continual and

---

EN281 'It is finished'
EN282 by definition
EN283 by definition
EN284 for us
EN285 by definition
EN286 for us

comes, the objective side as the essence of the required subjective, the so-called possibility as the true reality, the purpose achieved in Jesus Christ as the goal of all goals. There is no room for a cramping "only" in relation to the atonement made in Jesus Christ, unless we are going to open wide the door to historicisation, i.e., mythologising, and in this way to make the knowledge of its relevance ineffective from the very first. It is a remarkable fact in theological history that a very "positive" theologian like Thomasius could, and in fact did, do this in so unsuspecting a way. And what do we find in R. Bultmann in our own day (*Theol of the N.T.*, E.T., 1952, I, 252)? "By Christ there has been created nothing more than the possibility of ζωή EN287, which does, of course, become an assured actuality in those that believe." This is the very thing which will not do.

This does not make our question superfluous. In our christological basis, in Jesus Christ Himself, everything that can be said of the relevance of His being and activity in our sphere is already included and anticipated. That is one thing, the thing to which all our knowledge of this relevance must constantly be referred back. But there is another thing which is not so self-evident. This is that we are not merely in a position to hear and accept as an assertion (possibly in something like the form we have tried to give it in our own more detailed commentary) the *pro nobis*EN288 of the being and activity of Jesus Christ, and because *per definitionem*EN289 His being and activity is *pro nobis*EN290, the being and activity itself. We can also believe and accept it as true in the sense that we truly believe ourselves to be those for whom He is and has acted. Our christological basis includes within itself the fact (and with it quite simply ourselves, our participation in that event), that the turn from Jesus Christ to us has already been executed and is a fact in Him, that in and with Him we, too, are there as those for whom He is and has acted. This fact is the subject of a specific second step as we try to follow out the truth of it. Naturally the first step must precede. Jesus Christ must have come to us in that existence of His which embraces ours but is also proper to Himself and superior to ours. He must [286] have met us in that Word of His which is a new word and strange to us. He must have encountered us from afar, from outside. It has to be like this. We have to be told and have to let ourselves be told by Him that He is for us and has acted for us. But when we have made the first step we then have to make a specific second step when we realise, that is, when we can and will say to ourselves, that we are those to whom His *pro nobis*EN291 refers. This seems to follow very simply from the first one, with the simplicity with which in logic a minor and conclusion can be deduced from a given major. It is simple, so long as we hold fast by the major as such, the being and action of Jesus Christ for us. Why should we not be ready to hear this and to accept its relevance to ourselves? But this being and action takes place in our sphere. This major is spoken in all its completeness in our sphere. Our sphere is not as such qualified for this novelty. It is the

---

EN287 life
EN288 for us
EN289 by definition
EN290 for us
EN291 for us

sphere of the unreconciled world, of man contradicting and opposing God. There is a great gulf between "Jesus Christ for us" and ourselves as those who in this supremely perfect word are summoned to regard ourselves as those for whom He is and acts. How do we come to find ourselves in these, or these in us, as is really and actually the case in virtue of this major, in Jesus Christ? By what right or power dare I make the corresponding minor, or draw the simple conclusion, that I myself am one of those for whom Jesus Christ is and acts? thus recognising and confessing that He is for me: "I know that my Redeemer liveth"? By what right do we follow the invitation and summons of that major, applying that which He is and does to us who are not He? How can we dare to extend His being and activity so that we count it our own, speaking of our own sin (this, too, is a new thing that we cannot know of ourselves), of our own justification, of ourselves as His community, and of our own faith, in relation to Him? Who calls and authorises us to set up these standards in our own sphere? in short, to execute the turn which, according to the Word and message of Jesus Christ, has already been executed and completed in Him? How can that which is proper to Him be recognised as proper to us? No, this thing which is apparently simple, and which is in fact simple in Jesus Christ, cannot be simple for us, as we work it out for ourselves. Yet on every presupposition, even on the best conceivable, we do need to recognise its real simplicity. That is the transitional problem which must concern us in this section.

But before we can say anything positive about it we must try to define the problem rather more precisely. Why and to what extent is it not self-evident that we can proceed and build on Jesus Christ in our own sphere? Why is it that the turn which has been executed in the person and work of Jesus Christ, in a perfect way which needs no amplification, why is it that the "Jesus Christ for us," still needs this more detailed explanation?

[287]   According to the most recent view our problem is at bottom only a particular form of the problem of time. How can that which has happened once, even if it did happen for us, be recognised to-day as having happened for us, seeing it does not happen to-day? Or, to put it in another way, how can that which happened once have happened for us when we who live to-day were not there and could not experience it ourselves? Or, to put it in yet another way, how can we to-day exist as those for whom it happened when it happened once and not to-day? The only answer which it seems we can give is the profoundly ambiguous and unsettling one that it can do so only as we accept it from others, from the tradition of the Church and ultimately from the biblical witnesses; that it is, in fact, the case that "Jesus Christ for us" is valid to-day, and is relevant to us, only as we accept what is told to us as true in this sense. But how can we hold to be true what we have not seen and cannot attest to be true? especially a truth which is so decisive for ourselves as that of the then being and activity of Jesus Christ for us to-day and in our place?

Put in this way, the problem is identical with one which was widely treated in the first decade of this century—the problem of faith and history. It was posed with particular acuteness in the theology of W. Herrmann. In our own day the discussion has been renewed by R. Bultmann in the form of the problem of the relationship between the act of God which took place once and for all historically in Jesus of Nazareth and the existential actuality of the Christian faith referred to and based upon it. In substance it is identical with Lessing's question concerning the relationship between the contingent truths of history and the necessary truths of reason (*Der Beweis des Geistes und der Kraft*, 1777). "This, this is the gaping and wide chasm which I cannot cross, however often and seriously I have attempted the leap. If anyone can help me over, let him do so; I implore and entreat him. He deserves from me a divine reward."

It should be noted that for an older type of Christian thinking—and especially for Christian mysticism in every age—the problem was not so much one of time as of space, not that of the relationship of the then and now but of the there and here. That is how it was represented, e.g., by Calvin, who attacked strongly the idea of a *Christus otiosus*[EN292] existing *frigide extra nos, procul a nobis*[EN293], apparently separated from us and we from Him *eminus nobis*[EN294]—an idea which he described as an *obliquum cuniculum*[EN295] of Satan designed to undermine our assurance of salvation. As the basis of his whole exposition *De modo percipiendae Christi gratiae*[EN296] he opposed to it his peculiar doctrine of the *societas, coniunctio, communio*[EN297] created by the Holy Spirit between Christ and us, of a *coniugium*[EN298] between Him and us, of our *insitio in Christum*[EN299] (*Instit.* III, 1, 3 and 2, 24). And in a way which is more direct and less guarded theologically, but obviously in answer to the same question, in face of the same gaping and wide chasm, and in an attempt to leap it, Angelius Silesius (in the first book of his *Cherubinischer Wandersmann*, 61–63) wrote:

> Were Christ a thousand times to Bethlehem come,
> And yet not born in thee, 'twould spell thy doom.
> Golgotha's cross, it cannot save from sin.
> Except for thee that cross be raised within.
> I say, it helps thee not that Christ is risen.
> If thou thyself art still in death's dark prison.

The problem has indeed this temporal and spatial aspect. It has the form of [288] the problem of the historical distance between the being and activity of Jesus Christ in its own place and our being and activity in a different place. That there is this distance cannot be denied. "Jesus Christ for us," the incarnation and the crucifixion, do not exist or take place in an abstract always and everywhere in which our here and now are included, but in a concrete and singular then and there which cannot be taken away or exchanged—outside our here and now and opposed to it. In this respect the greatness of the historical remove does not greatly matter. It may exceed 1900 years or it may not. It is enough that it is there. It is enough that the connexion between the here and

---

[EN292] idle Christ
[EN293] coldly … outside of us, far from us
[EN294] aloof from us
[EN295] crooked device
[EN296] On the Means of Obtaining the Grace of Christ
[EN297] partnership, conjunction, communion
[EN298] marriage
[EN299] ingrafting into Christ

there, the now and then, can apparently take only the form of recollection, that it can apparently be only indirect or historical, mediated by the report and tradition and proclamation of others, bound up with their truthfulness and credibility, with whether we are able to trust them, to accept the truth of what they say, to make the connexion in this roundabout way as recollection. And if everything does finally hang by this thread, it is obviously a very disturbing fact. We can accept many things on the word of others and with full confidence in them, but can we accept the being and activity of Jesus Christ for us and in our place? Can a second-hand report of this—even one which is most certain and stimulates the greatest confidence—really serve as a basis for our faith in it? Can the connexion of which the message speaks really be a matter of mere recollection? If it is really to be received, can it come to us or be received by us in any but a direct way, removing the distance altogether, establishing between the one remembered and our recollection a contemporaneity which has to be explained but which is real, enabling that distant event to become and to be true to us directly and therefore incontrovertibly? But what is the mediation in which recollection becomes presence, indirect speech direct, history present-day event, the *Christus pro nobis tunc*[EN300] the *Christus pro nobis nunc*[EN301], the Christ who meets us, the Christ who is our Saviour not only as He is known and remembered historically, but as He Himself saves us to-day? The genuineness of this question cannot be disputed. The problem has this aspect, and has to be considered from this standpoint.

But we ought not to stand, as it were, rooted to this one spot, trying to find and remove the difficulty only in this spot. The well-known offence in the fact of atonement does not exhaust itself in this problem of distance. We ought to be warned against too great or exclusive a preoccupation with this aspect by the fact that this problem which has become so acute within more recent Protestantism has, all things considered, more the character of a technical difficulty in thinking than that of a spiritual or a genuine theological problem. In it it is only formally and not in substance, only incidentally and secondarily and [289] not primarily and centrally, that the question concerns God and ourselves, Jesus Christ and His cross and our reconciliation. It is a methodological question. There must have been innumerable serious-minded Christians—even theologians and even in the modern period—who have been disturbed and very radically disturbed by the point which is really and basically at issue, and yet who have not been touched at all, or only very slightly, by the concern which occupies us to-day.

For example, when Paul (in 1 Cor. 1[23]) writes that the crucified Christ is to the Jews a stumbling-block and to the Greeks foolishness, he can hardly have been thinking of the paradox of the relationship between faith and history, or of the relationship between the

---

[EN300] Christ for us then
[EN301] Christ for us now

historical singularity of His existence and cross and our contemporaneity with Him, or of the relationship between indirect and direct news concerning Him. And Calvin in the passage we have mentioned may perhaps have given us a faint outline of the problem of Lessing, but, according to the context and tenor of his remarks, he certainly did not have only this problem before him, nor was it of primary importance. He was dealing rather with its deeper presuppositions.

This does not prevent us from taking the problem of distance with the seriousness proper to it. What it does prevent us from doing is stopping at this discussion, as though it was there that we had to, and could, come to the decision which is necessary. What it does enjoin upon us is that we should consider the deeper presuppositions which we have to treat if we are to handle it rightly. When we solve this problem, our real difficulties are only just beginning. For is there really no difficulty more serious than that of the formal antithesis of the then and the now, the there and the here, with all the questions involved in this antithesis? Is there not a difficulty of which this antithesis is only representative and indicative? May it not be that the real scandal is grounded in the fact, in the Christ-occurrence, in the event of the atonement itself? May it not be that it consists simply in the strangeness and remoteness of this event as it has taken place in our anthropological sphere? Is it not the case that it is not primarily its historical distance and singularity but its own nature which makes this event a riddle, a kind of erratic block in our sphere and time and space? How can the Son of God be ours who as such went into the far country? How can this our Judge be judged for us? How can He be anything to us but a stranger, and His activity a new and peculiar activity to which access is not open but closed? Not in spite of the fact but just because it concerns us so much! What can His being and activity mean in our sphere? We have to remember the immeasurable alteration in our situation, in our whole existence, which has taken place in Him, which His being and activity inexorably brings with it. What are we going to make of that, or, rather, what are we going to make of ourselves in relation to it? How are we going to deal with that? How are we going to apprehend Jesus Christ, or, rather, how are we going to apprehend ourselves in relation to Him, ourselves as those for whom that has taken place [290] which has taken place in Him? What does it mean to live as His fellow? What does it mean to live as a man, as one for whom this took place in Him, as one whose conversion to God took place in His death?

The whole difficulty which really faces us here is gathered up in the saying of Peter in Lk. 5[8]: "Depart from me, for I am a sinful man, O Lord." Does not this mean: How is it that You have come into my presence, and what will become of me in Yours? How can You and I be together in the same time and space? But we can also think of the saying of Isaiah (6[5]), who, seeing *Yahweh* sitting on the throne high and lifted up, and His train filling the temple, and hearing the threefold *Sanctus*[EN302] of the seraphim, cries out: "Woe is me! for I am undone; because I am a man of unclean lips, and I dwell in the midst of a people of unclean lips."

EN302 'Holy'

These are the sayings of men who saw and heard, for whom there was no problem of distance in the form in which it occupies us, to whom the question of the possibility of accepting the testimony of others or of their credibility could not present any difficulty. Their difficulty was a problem of distance of quite another kind. We can and should think of the description of the attitude of the women when they were confronted by the empty tomb, at the end of the genuine St. Mark: "And they went out quickly, and fled from the sepulchre; for they trembled and were amazed: neither said they anything to any man, for they were afraid." And do we not read something similar in Lk 2⁹ concerning the shepherds of Bethlehem who were the first and direct hearers of the Christmas message? The directness of the encounter with the Lord, the absence of Lessing's "gaping and wide chasm," contemporaneity with the historical act of God, does not mean any easing of the relationship to that act, any lessening of the tension, but at the very point where there seems to be no room for it it attains its maximum, and the difficulty of the encounter with the God acting and speaking in history seems to become intolerable. "But who may abide the day of his coming? and who shall stand when he appeareth? (Mal. 3²). "Thou canst not see my face: for there shall no man see me, and live" (Ex. 33²⁰).

This is obviously the underlying form of our problem—the real distance in which the God appearing in the human sphere, and acting and speaking for us in this sphere, confronts us to whom He turns and for whom He acts. Note that on the one hand it is God for man, on the other man against God. There are two orders (or, rather, order and disorder), two opposite world-structures, two worlds opposing and apparently excluding one another. Note that it is He and we—and He and we in a direct encounter, we before Him—how can we live before Him and with Him?—we with the God who by Himself reconciles us with Himself, we in His presence, in the sequence of His work and Word. On the side of man the only possible word seems to be a deep-seated No, the No of the one who when God comes and acts for Him and tells him that He is doing so is forced to see that his day is over and that he can only perish.

[291] And now we have to ask whether our whole concern about our temporal distance from Jesus Christ, our indirect relationship to Him, is not a genuine problem only in the sense that it represents a genuine movement of flight from this encounter. Are we not putting up a technical difficulty, knowing all the time that it is not this difficulty which oppresses us, but rather the concern that this difficulty is not so great that it cannot be removed, that it has in fact been removed?

Supposing our contemporaneity with the Word of God made flesh, with the Judge judged in our place, is already an event? Supposing the *Christus pro nobis nunc*[EN303] is already *Christus pro nobis praesens nunc*[EN304], here and now, present with us? Supposing it is in fact incontrovertible, the most certain of all things, that He is present here and now for us in the full efficacy of what, according to the Gospel, He was and did then and there? Supposing that by Him and in Him our judgment has been accomplished? that in consequence we now and here are those for whom He went to His death? that in and with Him we are

---

[EN303] Christ for us now
[EN304] Christ present for us now

crucified and dead as the sinners that we are? that we can therefore have the space to live which is granted to us after this event (and to that extent *post Christum*) EN305? that we can exist only as those who have no more freedom to sin? Supposing this is so? Supposing we have to recognise that it is so? that this is the situation in which we find ourselves? Does not this mean that we have to see that it is all up with us, that our case has been taken out of our hands as an evil case, and ended and removed and done away? but that since we have no other case, our existence has lost its point, and we, too, are removed and done away and without any future? It is obvious that we do not want this, that we do not want to accept the fact that our evil case is done away and ourselves with it, that we do not therefore want to accept the coming of the Son of God in our place, His being and activity in contemporaneity with us, and our being in contemporaneity with Him. The assault this makes on us is too violent and incisive. If all this is true and actual, it is clear that we have good reason to close our eyes to it, to keep as far from us as we can the knowledge of this truth and actuality.

And if there is a technical difficulty in the matter—the difficulty of making the contemporaneity of Jesus Christ with us and of us with Him conceptually intelligible and perspicuous—do we not have good reason to occupy ourselves with it as much as possible, not to minimise but to magnify it as much as possible, to see to it that its force remains? As long as we are occupied with this difficulty, we do not really need to worry about what has taken place and been done to us with the incarnation of the Son of God, in His appearance in our place, in His effective action for us now as well as then and here as well as there. As long as we can question and discuss the presence of that once and for all event, as long as we can make it the most serious question how we can honestly accept as true to-day that which comes to us as the truth and actuality of something which happened then and which is maintained by others—so long we are obviously protected against the catastrophe which the knowledge of the content, the knowledge of the *Christus pro nobis praesens*EN306, would [292] mean for us. We do not then have to notice that we are in exactly the same position as Peter in the boat and the women at the empty tomb and the shepherds of Bethlehem, that we can only tremble as on the day of the Lord which has dawned for us, that we can only be afraid and terrified. We find ourselves in a relatively sheltered corner where we can dream that we are still in some way existing *ante Christum*EN307 since He is not there for us, where we can imagine that it is not yet all up with us; and all because we think that we are excused and safeguarded by the gaping and wide chasm of temporal distance; all because of the existence of Lessing's question. It is understandable that we have a supreme interest in trying to make out that our relationship to Jesus

---

EN305 after Christ
EN306 Christ present for us
EN307 before Christ

Christ is purely historical and therefore mediated and indirect, that it is a relationship of mere recollection. We need to be able to question and discuss this relationship. We need the consciousness of historical distance, the neutralising historical consideration, the remembrance of the 1900 years, the thought of the message and tradition and proclamation of others which binds but also separates the there and here, the question of authenticity and credibility, the feeling of the uncertainty of the mediation, the unsettlement which it involves for us. We need all this because it seems to create a delay. The genuineness of Lessing's question cannot be disputed in that it springs from a very genuine need: the need to hide ourselves (like Adam and Eve in the garden of Eden) from Jesus Christ as He makes Himself present and mediates Himself to us; the need to keep our eyes closed to that about which we ask with such solemn concern, taking ourselves and our "honesty" with such frightful seriousness; the need to safeguard ourselves as far as this movement of flight allows against the directness in which He does in fact confront us, against His presence, and the consequences which it threatens.

In any other sense than this the question of Lessing, the question of historical distance, is not a genuine problem. In a singular way it derives and has its real weight from the very fact that it is soluble and has actually been solved. Its seriousness is the seriousness of human concern that Jesus Christ is in fact yesterday and to-day. It is the product of this concern, and therefore of fear of the truth. This fear is well-founded. The being and activity of Jesus Christ for us bring us face to face with a vacuum, a place where we apparently have no place or future. What is to become of the sinner when his being as such is taken away from him and made over to death, when he cannot therefore be any more? What then? What can he be when he cannot be a sinner any longer, because God in Jesus Christ has put behind Him his being as a sinner, making it a thing only of the past, but when he cannot of himself be anything but a sinner? Here we come to the spiritual and the theologically relevant difficulty [293] of the relationship between Jesus Christ and us. And before this difficulty we have to pause. Put in this way its character is not simply technical or logical or methodological. To be or not to be is the question now, the question, be it noted, posed in acute and unavoidable form by the grace of God. Our task is to answer this question. It is in answering it that we make the decision we have to make in this context whether it is legitimate and practicable that Christology should break through and go forward in the anthropological sphere which is our sphere. In the answer we shall give it will become clear that, however great the difficulty is, it has been overcome. The fear of the truth which is well-founded when this difficulty is perceived is not ultimately well-founded. From the point of view of the whole truth it has no final validity and can therefore be dissipated. We ought not to fear, and we do not need to fear. The movement of flight into Lessing's problem is unnecessary. In and with the overcoming of the real and spiritual problem of the relationship between Jesus Christ and us, the technical problem of the relationship between the then and there and the now and here is also soluble and has in fact been solved.

To sum up: Granted the possibility of an actual contemporaneity of Jesus Christ with us, and therefore of the directness of our encounter and presence with Him, and of the overcoming of the temporal barrier between Him and us, we are forced to put the question with a final and true seriousness: how will it stand with us when we are alongside Jesus Christ and follow Him, when we are in His environment and time and space? can the reconciliation of the world with God accomplished in Him consist in anything but the dissolution of the world? can the transition from the christological to the anthropological sphere consist in anything but an assertion that the latter has been displaced altogether by the former? is it not impossible to proceed from Christ and to build on Him in this sphere because of the very perfection of that which Jesus Christ has done for us? Is this so? Or is this an imperfect understanding of the perfection of what has taken place in Christ? Has theology to content and limit itself, perhaps, to be nothing more than Christology? Or would this mean that in this totality and exclusiveness we neither do justice to the problem of Christology, nor are in actual agreement with the full witness to Christ in the New Testament? However that may be, it is here that we come face to face with the real problem of decision. It is here that we come to our point of departure, to the turning to us which has, as we have stated, actually taken place in Jesus Christ for us, to the question of what this turning to us as it has actually taken place in Jesus Christ can in fact mean for us. It is here that we have to do with the thing itself, not with its outward aspect as in the problem of time. That we have made this provisional presupposition in respect of the problem of time means simply that we have accepted the call back to Jesus Christ and the thing itself. In a new and full discussion of it, in which we take into account the whole of the New Testament witness, it will necessarily be seen whether we can [294] or cannot proceed any further from the understanding which we have gained so far. And in this new discussion it will be occasionally revealed what we have and have not to teach concerning the problem of its outward aspect, the temporal distance between Jesus Christ and us.

Undoubtedly the proper starting-point for a positive answer to the question as put in this way is that it is not at all self-evident that it should not be answered in the negative. There is indeed every reason to fear that the being and activity of Jesus Christ for us can be understood only as the ending of all other human being, the reconciliation of the world with God accomplished in Him only as the reversal of its creation, only as its end. In this case the question of a point of departure and a transition is a completely empty one, seeing that we do not exist at all, or that we do so only in the nothingness to which we are delivered by that which Jesus Christ has done in our place. We must not too easily dismiss such a possibility as absurd. It might have pleased God to execute His good and holy will with the world in this way. This did not have to include either the continuance of the world or a further being of man. His grace might have consisted in the fulfilment of a final judgment. The way of the Son of God into the far country might have been for the purpose of setting a term to this foreign being by simply removing its existence. The judgment executed on Him in the place of all might have meant the end of all things. We would do well to keep before us this possibility and the negative answer to our question which corresponds to it. For one thing, the reality of our atonement, which God has actually elected, is in direct contrast to this possibility. The positive answer to the question does confront this negative answer. There can thus be no understanding or appraisal of it without an honest consideration of this negative alternative. Again, although this negative alternative has been forcefully surpassed by what God has actually willed and done in Jesus Christ, it has not simply been excluded but maintained by it, so that it cannot be ignored in the positive answer which we have to give but must be seriously considered. If God in Jesus Christ has reconciled the world with Himself this also means that in Him He has made an end, a radical end, of the world which contradicts and opposes Him, that an old aeon, our world-time (the one we know and have of ourselves) with all that counts and is great in it, has been brought to an end. The humility in which God willed to make Himself like us, the obedience of Jesus Christ in which this self-humiliation of God and in it the demonstration of His divine majesty became a temporal event, does mean, in fact, that our hour has struck, our time has run its course, and it is all up with us. For the fact that God has given Himself in His Son to suffer the divine judgment on us men does not mean that it is not executed on us but that it is executed on us in full

[295]   earnest and in all its reality—really and definitively because He Himself took our place in it. That Jesus Christ died for us does not mean, therefore, that we do not have to die, but that we have died in and with Him, that as the people we were we have been done away and destroyed, that we are no longer there and have no more future.

"Old things are passed away" (2 Cor. 5^{17}). How? "Ye are dead" (Col. 3^3), for "if one died for all, then were all dead" (2 Cor. 5^{14}). "I am crucified with Christ, I live no more" (Gal. 2^{20}). "We are (Rom. 6^8), ye are (Col. 2^{20}) dead with Christ." σύμφυτοι γεγόναμεν τῷ ὁμοιώματι τοῦ θανάτου αὐτοῦ[EN308] (Rom. 6^5), which is then explained as follows: "Our old man is crucified with him, that the body of sin (our person as the victim of sin) might be destroyed" (Rom. 6^6). "In whom also ye are circumcised with the circumcision made without hands, in putting off the body of the sins of the flesh by the circumcision of Christ" (Col. 2^{11}). By the cross of our Lord Jesus Christ "the world is crucified unto me, and I unto the world" (Gal. 6^{14}). That is what took place unequivocally and definitively when "God commended his love toward us, in that, while we were yet sinners, Christ died for the ungodly" (Rom. 5^8). It took place once and for all on Golgotha. We were there, for there took place there the dying of the Son of God for us. It was, therefore, His dying for our sins (1 Cor. 15^3). In His death the wages of our sins were paid in our place (Rom. 6^{23}). In Him we are dead to sin (Rom. 6^2). For then and there, in the person of Christ taking our place, we were present, being crucified and dying with Him. We died. This has to be understood quite concretely

---

[EN308] We have become united in the likeness of his death

and literally. In His dying, the dying which awaits us in the near or distant future was already comprehended and completed, so that we can no longer die to ourselves (Rom. 14$^{2f.}$), in our own strength and at our own risk, but only in Him, enclosed in His death. We died: the totality of all sinful men, those living, those long dead, and those still to be born, Christians who necessarily know and proclaim it, but also Jews and heathen, whether they hear and receive the news or whether they tried and still try to escape it. His death was the death of all: quite independently of their attitude or response to this event, not only when the proclamation of it comes to them and is received and accepted by them, not only in virtue of the effect of certain ecclesiastical institutions and activities, not only in the dark process of their taking up the cross, certainly not only in certain sacramental or mystical or even existential repetitions or reflections or applications of the event of the cross, not only by the various channels through whose mediation it does finally become actual and significant for them. Not, then, as though on Golgotha it was simply a matter of the creation of a possibility, the setting up of a model and example, an extraordinary offer of dying, or quite simply the institution of a law: "Die and become," the reality of which will come only when it is followed. That is how Angelus Silesius viewed the matter, with many others, in the verses quoted above. But the New Testament views it quite differently. Certainly there are exhortations and imperatives which stand in very clear connexion to the happening at Golgotha: to "mortify the deeds of the body" (Rom. 8^{13}); to "put off the old man" (Col. 3^9); to "crucify the flesh with its affections and lusts" (Gal. 5^{24}). These are consequences of the dying of man which has already taken place. They are commands to attest this event which can be characterised only indicatively, in the form of a narrative, because it can be grasped only as we look back to Golgotha. These attestations of the affirmation and acknowledgment of what took place there are still lacking; they must be filled up, as we are told in the much quoted text, Col. 1^{24}, which does not really say anything about a perfection or completeness or efficacy lacking in the event itself. Similarly, in the demand for the "reasonable service" (Rom. 12^1) which must be offered with the self-offering of the Christian there can be no question of any repetition or representation of that event, or even of an actualisation which has still to be effected. It needs no completion or re-presentation. It would encroach on its perfection and glory if we were to place alongside it events which complete or represent or actualise it. The confession of Christians, their suffering, their repentance, their prayer, their humility, their works, baptism, too, and the Lord's Supper can and should attest this event but only attest it. The event itself, the event of the death of man, is that of the death of Jesus Christ on Golgotha: no other event, no earlier and no later, no event which simply prepares the way for it, no event which has to give to it the character of an actual event. This is the one *mysterium*^{EN309}, the one sacrament, and the one existential fact before and beside and after which there is no room for any other of the same rank.

[296]

And we must be clear that this event as such has the character of a catastrophe breaking on man, and that the grace of God effective and revealed in it has indeed the form of a judgment executed on man. Jesus Christ dies because of trespasses, but for man, for the man who is "dead in trespasses and sins" (Col. 2^{13}; Eph. 2^1), who has fallen a victim to death because of His transgressions. In His death He dies the death of man. Order is created, then, not by any setting aside of sins, but by that of the sinner himself, of the σῶμα τῆς ἁμαρτίας^{EN310} (Rom. 6^6), of the σῶμα τῆς σαρκός^{EN311} (Col. 2^{11}), of the subject of sin. Can we avoid the comparison that it is not by the giving of medicine, or by an operation, but by the killing of the patient that help is brought? No word of separating him from his sin, or

---

^{EN309} mystery
^{EN310} body of sin
^{EN311} body of the flesh

his sin from him. He stands or falls with it. If it disappears, he disappears. And that is what happened on Golgotha. The dying took place in the death of Jesus Christ for him, intervening powerfully and effectively for him and taking up his case. In His own person, in His giving up to death, He actually took away sinful man, causing him to disappear. This man as he was was of no use to the kingdom of God and as the covenant-partner of God. He could not be helped except by his extinction. If the faithfulness of God and the love of God towards him in Jesus Christ was to attain its goal, it had in fact to have the form of the consuming fire of His wrath, burning down to the very foundation, consuming and totally destroying the man himself who had become the enemy of God.

God sent His Son into the world in order that this might happen to it in His person. The reconciliation with Him which has taken place in Jesus Christ has also the aspect that it is the end of the world. The "for us" of His death on the cross includes and encloses this terrible "against us." Without this terrible "against us" it would not be the divine and holy and redemptive and effectively helpful "for us" in which the conversion of man and the world to God has become an event. This is something we have also to take into account. It is the decision and act of God which has taken place actually, irrevocably, and with sovereign power. It is a completed fact, to which nothing can be added by us in time or in eternity, and from which nothing can be taken away by us in time and in eternity. It is something that we have to see and read like an opened page which we have no power to turn, like a word which we cannot go beyond dialectically, making it equal with some other word, and thus depriving it of all its force. Judgment is judgment. Death is death. End is end. In the fulfilment of the self-humiliation of God, in the obedience of the Son, Jesus Christ has suffered judgment, death and end in our place, the Judge who Himself was judged, and who thereby has also judged. In His person, with Him, judgment, death and end have come to us ourselves once and for all. Is there something [297] beyond this coming to us, and above it? Is there a sure place and basis from which the judgment which has fallen upon us, the end in which we are posited, and the death which has overtaken us in that Jesus Christ died for us, can be seen in all their frightful seriousness and yet not accepted as final and absolute, but only in a certain relationship and connexion and subordination? Is there a point from which a positive aspect of the event of atonement is disclosed, and disclosed as the decisive and controlling aspect, the one which originally and exclusively determines the particularity of the event?

To be clear about this matter we must not weaken what we have just said, or take away anything from it. There can be no question of avoiding or overlooking what happens. And we must understand that this beyond cannot be a matter of a human postulate, or the content of a human assertion, or the result of a dialectical operation of the human mind, if it is to be a genuine beyond, if in it we are to find a sure place and basis in face of this catastrophic event. It cannot be had cheaply, but this is too dear a price. It will not be by such violent and serious exertion, in any supreme height or depth of our consideration and comprehension, that we shall be able to attain this beyond, and that it will be possible and legitimate for us to think in the light of it. What has come to us in the crucifixion of Jesus Christ would not be our judgment, end and death if we could (even theoretically) transcend it, if we could even hypothetically place ourselves on an upper level of this event, and view and penetrate and understand and interpret it from this level. If we have to do with such a beyond, then in no case or form can it be on the basis of an independent human judgment or an invention or intuition reached in this way.

If there is to be a genuine beyond of this kind, then it must positively fulfil at least five conditions.

1. It must be the beyond of an equally effective and sovereign and irrevocable act of the same God who judged man in Jesus Christ, and brought him to his end and delivered him up to death. Our recognition of this beyond must rest on, and refer to, the fact that the same God has turned another page after the first one, has spoken a new word after the first one. An act of the same one true God will necessarily enable and permit us to count on the actuality of this beyond. As His act this beyond will be actual and revealed (together with what has come to us in the crucifixion of Jesus Christ).

2. This beyond must be actual and revealed in a new act of God which is clearly marked off from the first. To be above the first, to stand to it in a definite relationship in which the first is co-ordinated with and subordinated to it, it must be in distinctive contrast to the first. It cannot simply be a predicate, or adjunct, or closer definition of the first. It cannot be a second event which simply consists in an extending or deepening or manifesting of the first: just as it cannot cancel or encroach upon the first, degrading it to the level of a mere appearance

3. This beyond must stand to that first event in a relationship which is mean- [298] ingful in substance. It must correspond to it in all its distinctiveness. It must have in it its presupposition, and it must affirm it. It must be a beginning where the first is an end, an answer and solution where the first is a riddle. In the sequence of these two acts of God—for all the autonomy, the utter freedom with which the second follows the first—there must actually be, and be revealed, the identity of the acting divine Subject, the unity of His will and way. Both events must be independent and complete, but both must stand to one another in a relationship which is concealed but which is none the less real and unbreakable.

4. The beyond of that first event (if it is to be no less actual and revealed and to be taken no less seriously as the act of God) must have no less than the first the character of an event which has taken place in human history, in the time and space of man; of an event which is perhaps peculiar and even unique ontically as well as noetically; but of a definite event, of a concrete, specific, once and for all, contingent fact of history, and not merely of a horizon which embraces all occurrence yesterday, to-day and to-morrow, here, there and everywhere, and which itself can be equally well apprehended always and anywhere and nowhere and never, a horizon of the kind of transcendence which

per definitionem[EN312] is immanent to human existence. This event must stand in a sequence of time and space. However different it may be in other respects, as history it must be like all other history in regard to its historicity.

5. The beyond which is this new historical act of God must above all form a unity with the event which precedes and is opposed to it by being together with the first an event in the existence of the same historical Subject, a moment in the history of Jesus Christ and therefore in the history of all other men. The actuality and revelation of this event cannot, therefore, be a matter of another divine intervention which is foreign to the divine action in Jesus Christ and in competition with it. There is, of course, a general activity and operation of God in the course of the over-ruling of His providence and world-government. But even this is not independent of His work as Lord of the covenant, as the Reconciler of the world and the human race as they have fallen away from Him (cf. *C.D.*, III, 3, § 49, 3). And in the course of this general divine over-ruling there is no Word or work of God which does not directly or indirectly have its subject and object in His Son. The new act of God in which He introduced the genuine beyond of the judgment, end and death which comes on man in Jesus Christ must, like this event, be an event which takes place by and in and to Jesus Christ.

We have not spun these five conditions out of the void. We do not need merely to postulate or to affirm in this matter. No dialectical skill is required to

[299] demonstrate this beyond. The New Testament witness to Christ knows and names an event which corresponds to and satisfies all the five conditions of the actuality of such a beyond. We have, in fact, taken the conditions from the event. We have to speak of this event if we are to see the positive aspect of the reconciliation of the world with God which took place in Jesus Christ, and in that way to give a positive answer to the transitional question of this third section. This event is the awakening or resurrection from the dead of the crucified and dead Jesus Christ (the Jesus Christ who was really and truly dead according to the emphasised fact of His burial). The beyond which, according to the New Testament witness, is introduced in this event is really above. In this event there is taken a decision on the whole meaning and character of the whole Christ-occurrence attested by it. This event is undoubtedly the sure ground and basis from which the New Testament witnesses could look back to the crucifixion and death of Jesus Christ, but also to the way which led and had to lead to this goal, to what this way and goal implied for themselves and all men, to the happening which broke catastrophically upon us all in and with Jesus Christ. We can say confidently, and we have to say, that the whole New Testament thinks and speaks in the light of this event, and to understand it we must be prepared to think with it in the light of this event.

The New Testament proclaims the death of the Lord (1 Cor. 11[26]), the crucified Christ (1

[EN312] by definition

Cor. 1^{23}), the One who is dead ἀποθανών—μᾶλλον δὲ ἐγερθείς EN313 (Rom. 8^{34}). But it proclaims this One who is crucified and dead (in and with whom the death of Christians and all men has taken place) as the One whom God has raised from the dead, as the One who is alive, as πάντοτε ζῶν εἰς τὸ ἐντυγχάνειν ὑπὲρ αὐτῶν EN314 (Heb. 7^{25}). It proclaims His death (and in and with it the death of Christians and of all men, the judgment, the end of the world which has come upon us), but as the death of the One who has been called ἐκ τῶν νεκρῶν EN315, from the ranks of the dead, the first of the dead to escape death (1 Cor. 15^{20}, Col. 1^{18}), the raising of whom is to the men of the New Testament the guarantee of their own future resurrection and that of all men, in whose resurrection they have the basis of a life in this world which is assured of a future resurrection, which hastens towards it, which antici-pates in hope their own future life out of death. It is to Him, the Resurrected, that their μνημονεύειν EN316 (2 Tim. 2^8) and witness (Ac. 1^{22}, 4^{33}) refer. Their proclamation and the faith which it evokes are not "empty" or "vain" (κενὸν τὸ κήρυγμα ἡμῶν, κενὴ—ματαία—ἡ πίστις ὑμῶν EN317); they are not still in their sins; those who have fallen asleep in and with Him are not lost, because the One who died on the cross has been raised again from the dead (1 Cor. 15$^{14\ 17f.}$). To know Him is identical with knowing the power of His resurrection (Phil. 3^{10}). The confession that He is the Lord is based on the faith that God has raised Him from the dead (Rom. 10^9). Even the Christian's faith in God is itself and as such faith in the One who raised Him from the dead (1 Pet. 1^{21}). It is because according to the Scriptures this took place on the "third day" that we can and must positively and thankfully confess what took place on the "first" day, the day of His cross: He died for our sins "according to the scriptures" (1 Cor. 15$^{3f.}$). He, the risen One, opened up the Scriptures to them and opened their eyes to the Scriptures (Lk. 24$^{25f.}$).

For a more precise understanding it will be best, for the sake of comprehen-siveness, to follow the way which we have already indicated. We begin there-fore (1) by stating basically that the raising of Jesus Christ (with all that it implies for us and for all men) is in the New Testament comprehended and understood as an act of God with the same seriousness as the preceding event of the cross with its implication for us and for all men. The judgment of the grace of God fulfilled there was the work of God which could be fulfilled and was fulfilled only by Him. So, too, it is with the emergence here of the grace of this judgment, the grace which as such does not cancel or encroach upon this judgment but leaves it behind as its presupposition, its first work. [300]

With the same seriousness, but in a way which is characteristically marked off and distinguished from the first, it can be fulfilled and was, in fact, fulfilled by God alone. The death of Jesus Christ was, of course, wholly and altogether the work of God to the extent that it is the judgment of death fulfilled on the Representative of all other men appointed by God. The way to the cross and death in which this judgment took place is indeed the work of the Son of God obedient in humility. But it is also as such the work of the obedient man Jesus of Nazareth in His identity with the Son of God, just as His condemnation and

---

EN313 who died, much more – was raised
EN314 the one who is always alive to intercede for them
EN315 from the dead
EN316 remembrance
EN317 if our preaching is futile, then your faith is futile and vain

execution, although it was determined and willed by God, was also the work of the sinful men who put into effect the decision and will of God, the Jews and Gentiles into whose hands Jesus was delivered, or delivered Himself. As the judgment of God, the event of Golgotha is exclusively the work of God. Its fulfilment is ordained by God even in detail. But all the same it has a component of human action—both obedient and good on the one hand and disobedient and evil on the other. In the light of this part we can say of the event of the cross that it has a "historical" character, that it can be understood and interpreted in the pragmatic context of human decisions and actions, although, of course, in this case it will be misinterpreted and misunderstood, and its real meaning will not be perceived.

The happening on the third day which followed that of Golgotha is the act of God with the same seriousness, but it is unequivocally marked off from the first happening by the fact that it does not have in the very least this component of human willing and activity. Not merely in purpose and ordination, but in its fulfilment, too, it is exclusively the act of God. It takes place quite outside the pragmatic context of human decisions and actions. It takes place in such a way that it cannot possibly be understood and interpreted, i.e., misinterpreted and misunderstood, in the light of this context. It takes place, but it obviously does so without our being able to see it in this context, to ascribe to it a "historical" character in this sense. Like creation, it takes place as a sovereign act of God, and only in this way.

[301]   We do not come to this conclusion merely because of its specific content, the coming to life of a man who was actually and in truth dead and buried.

> It is, of course, true that even in this respect it breaks through this context; it is not the kind of event which can be the result of human will and activity or can be made clear or intelligible as such. An event which continues the being of man after death cannot be the result of the will and activity either of the man himself or of other men. To be dead means not to be. Those who are not, cannot will and do, nor can they possibly be objects of the willing and doing of others. ἀνάστασις ἐκ νεκρῶν[EN318] is not one possibility of this kind with others. Where it takes place, God and God alone is at work. To raise (ἐγείρειν) the dead, to give life (ζωοποιεῖν) to the dead, is, like the creative summoning into being of non-being, a matter wholly and exclusively for God alone, quite outside the sphere of any possible co-operating factors (Heb. 11^{19}; 2 Cor. 1^9; Rom. 4^{17}). And this is primarily and particularly the case in the resurrection of Jesus Christ.

The coming alive and living of a dead man would be a *contradictio in adiecto*[EN319] as a human work. This consideration is a true one. Yet when we say that the raising of Jesus Christ, His coming alive and living after death, his resurrection from the tomb, is God's act, and as opposed to His death on the cross only God's act, we are not saying something which can be arrived at only by way of this consideration—for to talk of that which is impossible to man is not by a long way to speak of God—but something which can be taken only

---

EN318 Resurrection from the dead
EN319 contradiction in terms

from the divine revelation which has taken place in this event. What it was for the New Testament witnesses of this event was not a miracle accrediting Jesus Christ, but the revelation of God in Him. It was not, therefore, something merely formal and noetic. It was also the true, original, typical form of the revelation of God in Him and therefore of revelation generally, the revelation which lights up for the first time all God's revealing and being revealed (in Him and generally). For the first community founded by this event, the event of Easter Day and the resurrection appearances during the forty days were the mediation, the infallible mediation as unequivocally disclosed in a new act of God, of the perception that God was in Christ (2 Cor. 5^{19}), that is, that in the man Jesus, God Himself was at work, speaking and acting and suffering and going to His death, and that He acted as, and proved Himself, the one high and true God, not in spite of this end, but on this very way into the far country which He went to the bitter end, in this His most profound humiliation, at the place where an utter end was made of this man.

To the community this event was the mediation of a perception hitherto closed and inaccessible to them. It had not been given them by the fact that the Son of God was amongst them as man, in the flesh and to that extent to be known by them after the flesh (2 Cor. 5^{16}). It had not been given them by the fact that the whole occurrence of the living, speaking, acting, suffering and dying of Jesus had been played out before their very eyes and ears. An anticipatory exception like the confession of Peter at Caesarea Philippi can in this respect only prove the general rule. In a strange way this perception was [302] unattainable by the disciples as long as they had the opportunity for it, as long as it seemed to be attainable, as long as the happening still had that component of human willing and action, and could to that extent be accepted and understood by them. In this form the character of the happening as the act of God was not revealed to them. In other words, it was not revealed to them at the very point where we might have thought that it could and should be revealed to them. They were in fact witnesses of this act of God. It took place before their very eyes and ears—but before eyes that were blind and ears that were deaf. According to Lk. 24^{25}, in spite of the witness of Moses and the prophets speaking to them, they were, like the rest of Israel, "fools and slow of heart" in relation to it. The perception was mediated, their eyes and ears and hearts were opened, not in and with this event, but in the event which presupposed the closing of this event. The glory of the Word made flesh (Jn. 1^{14}), the kingdom of God which had drawn near to them in bodily form, the obedience of the Son of God, His death in our place and for our redemption, for the restoration of our peace with God—all this as the mystery of the way of the man Jesus, and of the end of that way on the cross of Golgotha, was first revealed to them and perceived by them when the event was already past, when the man Jesus was dead and buried and had been taken from them and was no longer there, when all the bridges between Himself and them which had previously been available and possible had been broken.

The perception was mediated to them when on the third day, Easter Day, He came amongst them again in such a way that His presence as the man He had been (had been!) was and could be exclusively and therefore unequivocally the act of God without any component of human will and action; that it was and could be understood by them only and exclusively as such, exclusively and therefore unequivocally as the self-attestation of God in this man without any co-operation of a human attestation serving it. The perception was therefore mediated. God in Christ became conceivable to them in the inconceivable form of the unmediated presence and action of its origin and subject-matter without any other mediation at all—in such a self-attestation of the Lord that in face of it the disciple can only fall at His feet as dead, until He lays His right hand upon Him and allows and commands him not to fear: "I was dead, and behold, I am alive for evermore" (Rev. 1$^{18f.}$). This was the formal side of the resurrection of Christ which made it the true and original and typical form of the revelation of God made in Him. This was what gave it as an act of God its special and distinctive character for the first community, deciding and underlying their whole knowledge of Jesus Christ. This was what gave it its peculiarly indisputable certainty. This was what made the forty days for them the sure and higher place from which they looked back to the life and death of Jesus Christ with an enlightened perception of the act of God which took place in this life and death, and from which they then looked forward to the determination of their own existence, and that of the whole world, given by this life and death.

[303]

This is underlined in Gal. 1^1 and Rom. 6^4 by the fact that the Subject of the resurrection is not simply θεός[EN320], according to the regular usage, but θεός πατήρ[EN321]. Obviously there can be no question of any co-operation of God with the man Jesus, or even with the will and activity of other men (for He is now dead and buried). And we must also be careful how we handle the thought (which is correct not merely in the sense of later trinitarian theology) that Jesus Christ as the Son of God was associated with the Father as the Subject of His own resurrection. The New Testament does not put it in this way. The saying "I am the resurrection and the life" (Jn. 11^{25}) could, of course, be turned in this direction, but on the analogy of similar Johannine statements it means only that in and with me that becomes event and actuality which even outside the Christian community is proclaimed as ἀνάστασις[EN322] and ζωή[EN323]. The one whole Jesus Christ, very man and very God, was dead and buried. It is true that as such He had the power to give His life and to take it again (Jn. 10^{18}): that is, as the Son of the Father to receive and take again what the Father willed to give back to Him. The passage tells us that as opposed to all other creatures the dead and buried Jesus Christ as the Word made flesh is worthy of this (in the sense of the doxology of Rev. 5^{12}). We have to compare it with Jn. 5^{26}, where we are told that the Father has given it to the Son to have life in Himself even as He, the Father, has life in Himself; and with Rom. 1^4, where we are told that in His resurrection from the dead by the power of the Holy Spirit He was characterised, designated, declared to be the Son of God (as opposed to all others who are dead and

---

EN320 God
EN321 God the father
EN322 resurrection
EN323 life

296

buried): ὁρισθείς EN324—not that He made and proved Himself to be such. Above all, we have to note Phil. 2. In v. 7 we are, of course, told that "He emptied himself, and took the form of a servant," and in v. 8 that "he humbled himself, even unto death." But in v. 9 it says: "Wherefore God also hath highly exalted him, and given (ἐχαρίσατο) him a name which is above every name." It is one thing that He "rises again" and shows Himself (ἐφανερώθη) to His disciples as the One raised again from the dead (Jn. 21¹⁴). Quite another thing is the act of this resurrection. He shows Himself alive to His disciples (Ac. 1³), but He lives, after He (ἐξ ἀσθενείας EN325) was crucified, ἐκ δυνάμεως θεοῦ EN326 (2 Cor. 13⁴). "The God of peace has brought him again from the dead" (Heb. 13²⁰). The resurrection, the being alive of One who was dead and buried, His new presence and action, are not simple equivalents for His raising from the dead, with He Himself the acting Subject in the one case and God (the Father) in the other. This is how the matter has recently been stated by H. Vogel (*Gott in Christo*, 1951, 739 f.). But we have to remember that on this view we are enmeshed in the particular difficulty of having to speak of a mere "impotence" of the One dead and buried from which He recovered on His own initiative and in His own strength. If this does not amount to the theory of a mere appearance of death once put forward by Schleiermacher and others, it approximates to a suspiciously docetic view of what is meant by death. But the facts themselves tell us decisively that the event of Easter has to be understood primarily as the raising which happens to Jesus Christ, and only secondarily and (actively) on that basis as His resurrection. For in the New Testament it is everywhere described as an act of divine grace which follows the crucifixion but which is quite free. Phil. 2⁹ tells us expressly that the name which is above every name is given to Him, and Heb. 5¹⁰ that He is greeted and addressed (προσαγορευθείς) by God as a High Priest "after the order of Melchisedec." Certainly it is said of His raising by God no less than of His putting to death by men that it had to [304] happen (ἔδει EN327, Lk. 24²⁶, Acts 17³; δεῖ, Jn. 20⁹), that it was "according to the scriptures" (1 Cor. 15⁴), that is, according to the continuity of the divine will and plan as especially attested in the transition in Is. 53⁹⁻¹⁰ᶠ or in Ps. 16⁸⁻¹¹ as quoted in Ac. 2²⁵ᶠ. But this "had to" does not mean that in this event God was acting any the less freely than in the giving of His Son or in the divine act of the obedience of the Son even to the death of the cross. His resurrection did not follow from His death, but sovereignly on His death. It was not the result of His death. Its only logical connexion with it was that of the sovereign and unmerited faithfulness, the sovereign and free and constantly renewed mercy of God. Certainly in the resurrection of Jesus Christ we have to do with a movement and action which took place not merely in human history but first and foremost in God Himself, a movement and action in which Jesus Christ as the Son of God had no less part than in His humiliation to the death of the cross, yet only as a pure object and recipient of the grace of God. We must not be afraid of the apparently difficult thought that as in God Himself (as we have seen), in the relationship of the Son to the Father (the model of all that is demanded from man by God), there is a pure obedience, subordination and subjection, so too in the relationship of the Father to the Son (the model of all that is given to man by God) there is a free and pure grace which as such can only be received, and the historical fulfilment of which is the resurrection of Jesus Christ. We obscure and weaken the character of the resurrection as a free pure act of divine grace (in contrast to the character of His death on the cross suffered in obedience), if appealing to His divine sonship we describe it as His own action and work. No, not simply as man, but even as the Son of God Jesus Christ is here simply the One who takes and receives,

---

EN324 declared
EN325 out of weakness
EN326 from the power of God
EN327 it was necessary

the recipient of a gift, just as in His death on the cross it is not only as man but as the Son of God that He is wholly and only the obedient servant. The fact that as very God and very man He is worthy of the divine gift of new life from the dead does not alter in the slightest the fact that He did not take this new life but that it was given to Him. We may also ask, and must ask, why Jesus Christ can be called the "first-begotten from the dead" (Col. 1[18]) if the case is otherwise, if His resurrection is also something that the resurrection of others can never be—His own work. In what sense can it then be—as we shall see it is—the pledge and indeed the actual beginning of the resurrection of us all? The comprehensive relevance of the resurrection, its redemptive significance for us, depends upon its being what it is described in the New Testament, God's free act of grace.

2. We have to emphasise that in relation to the happening of the cross it is an autonomous, new act of God. It is not, therefore, the noetic converse of it; nor is it merely the revelation and declaration of its positive significance and relevance. It is this, as we have seen. And obviously it is in fact related to that first event. But in spite of this it is distinguished from it as an event of a particular character. It is not enclosed in it, but follows on it as a different happening. On the other hand, it is not a light which makes that first happening a meaningless shadow. The *theologia resurrectionis*[EN328] does not absorb the *theologia crucis*[EN329], nor *vice versa*[EN330]. The event of Easter in its indissoluble connexion with the event of the cross is an event which has its own content and form. We have already said one important thing in relation to this statement when we have laid down that the event of Easter must be understood as the true and original and typical act of revelation, and therefore as an act of God *sui*

[305]   *generis*[EN331]—a free act of grace, free even in its innermost divine basis, according to the New Testament evidence. But we now have to add the fresh consideration that as the act of God's grace the resurrection of Jesus Christ from the dead confronted His being in death, that is, His non-being as the One who was crucified, dead, buried, and destroyed, as the One who had been and had ceased to be. It was to His being in death that He had gone as the end of His way into the far country, in fulfilment of His obedience in our place, in His self-offering as the Judge who is judged and as the Priest who is sacrificed. He was "delivered up for our trespasses" (Rom. 4[25]). He had delivered Himself up (Gal. 2[20]). His resurrection from the dead did not cancel this. It had its unaltered *terminus a quo*[EN332] in His death in our place. The One who was raised was the One who was crucified, dead and, to prove it, buried. The One who was exalted was the One who was abased.

The Gospel of St. John (20[25f.]) thought it worth reporting that the risen Christ bore the wounds of the Crucified. Life was given to the One who had been slain. The One who belonged hopelessly to the past was present. The Humiliated was exalted, being given the name of *Kyrios* (Phil. 2[9]), being declared the Son of God (Rom. 1[4])—to be seen and heard

---

[EN328] theology of the resurrection
[EN329] theology of the cross
[EN330] the other way around
[EN331] in a category of its own
[EN332] starting point

and handled (1 Jn. 1¹) as such by His disciples for forty days, to eat and drink with them as such (Ac. 10⁴¹), and as such to die no more (Rom. 6⁹).

His raising, His resurrection, His new life, confirmed His death. It was God's answer to it, and to that extent its revelation and declaration. But as God's answer to it, it was distinct from it. It was God's acknowledgment of Jesus Christ, of His life and death. As a free act of divine grace, it had formally the character of an act of justice on the part of God the Father in His relation to Jesus Christ as His Son, just as the obedience of the Son even to the death of the cross, as a free act of love, had formally the character of an act of justice of the Son in His relation to God the Father. It came in the midst of His real death and delivered Him from death. To that extent it was the expression and fulfilment of the sentence of the Father on the way which He had gone—His judicial sentence that the action and passion of Jesus Christ were not apart from or against Him, but according to His good and holy will, and especially that His dying in our place was not futile but effective, that it was not to our destruction but to our salvation. It was a second act of justice after the first to the extent that it was the divine approval and acknowledgment of the obedience given by Jesus Christ, the acceptance of His sacrifice, the proclamation and bringing into force of the consequences, the saving consequences, of His action and passion in our place.

In the concepts answer, confession and sentence, we gather together the distinctive thing which the New Testament sees in the resurrection of Jesus Christ as opposed to the event of His death. It is all summarised in the remarkable phrase used to describe the resurrection in the hymn quoted in 1 Tim. 3¹⁶: ἐδικαιώθη ἐν πνεύματι EN333. He Himself, Jesus Christ, the Son of God made man, was justified by God in His resurrection from the dead. He was justified as man, and in Him as the Representative of all men all were justified. Hence the continuation of the statement in Rom. 4²⁵: ἠγέρθη διὰ τὴν δικαίωσιν ἡμῶν EN334. [306]

But what gives to the justification which took place there its true and decisive power is that in the unity of God with this man (and in and with Him in His fellowship with us all), in the resurrection of Jesus Christ, God Himself, His will and act in the death of Jesus Christ, was justified by God, by Himself and therefore definitively. Was this necessary? Certainly not in the sense that at Golgotha everything had not taken place which had to take place for the reconciliation of the world with God, that the representation and sacrifice of Jesus Christ in His death were not wholly sufficient, that they were therefore referred back to some completion and continuation. Anything pointing in this direction, any limitations of the τετέλεσται EN335 are quite alien to the New Testament. But the direct continuation of the τετέλεσται EN336 in Jn. 19³⁰ is: καὶ κλίνας τὴν κεφαλὴν παρέδωκεν τὸ πνεῦμα EN337. And the occurrence of Golgotha which is complete in itself consists ultimately in the fact that Jesus "bowed his head." What does this mean? In obedience to the will of God? Before God as Father? His obedience consists in the fact that He commends or offers up His spirit, that

---

EN333 it was justified in the Spirit
EN334 he was raised for our justification
EN335 'it is finished'
EN336 'it is finished'
EN337 He bowed his head and gave up his Spirit

is, Himself—He delivers up Himself. To whom? To God His Father, to His decree and disposing ? Naturally, and this is emphasised in the saying handed down in Lk. 23⁴⁶: "Father, into thy hands I commend my spirit," myself. But there, too, there is the continuation: τοῦτο δέ εἰπὼν ἐξέπνευσεν EN338. It is therefore to death that He bows His head and commits Himself. In and with the fulfilment there of the will of God it is nothingness which can triumph over Him—and in and with Him over the whole of the human race represented by Him. According to the disposition and in the service of God death and nothingness are brought in and used for the reconciliation of the world with God, as instruments in His conflict with the corruption of the world and the sin of man—but death and nothingness in all their evil and destructive power. It is also to the wrath of God which permits this force and judges evil by evil that Jesus commits Himself and in and with Himself the world and the individual sinner. The reconciliation of the world with God which took place in Jesus Christ had therefore the meaning that a radical end was made of Him and therefore of the world.

And that might have exhausted its meaning. The saying: "My God, my God, why hast thou forsaken me?" (Mk. 15³⁴) shows how close was this frightful possibility. It might have been that God turned away His face finally from us. It might have been that by the same eternal Word by which as Creator He gave being to man and the world He now willed to take away that being from them, to let them perish with all their corruption and sin. The relationship between Himself and His creation might have been regularised by depriving it of its perverted actuality. He might have repented of having created it (Gen. 6⁷), and carried this repentance to its logical conclusion. Ruling as the Judge, He might have given death and nothingness the last word in relation to the creature. He would still have been in the right.

But He would have been in the right only in complete concealment, within Himself, and only by granting to death and nothingness as the instruments of His judgment a final right in relation to the creature. He would then have surrendered to them His own right in relation to the creature. He would then have renounced His own right, His own creature. And in so doing He would have recognised the power of death and nothingness over the creature, de facto EN339 if not de iure EN340. He would not have confirmed His original choice between heaven and earth on the one hand and chaos on the other. His decision for light and His rejection of darkness (Gen. 1³), Himself therefore as the Creator of the world and humanity which He made and found to be good. In short, He would not have justified Himself. But this is to say that He would have been in the right only in and for Himself. In His wrath He [307] would have been content to maintain His right against the world, in its destruction. He would not have sustained or demonstrated or revealed His right to the world and in the world.

Did He need to do this? Certainly not. On what ground can we postulate that He had to do it? What reason is there to blame Him if He willed not to do so? He did not owe it to anyone to justify Himself. It could only be His grace which bade Him do it. But in His grace He was, in fact, free to do it; and therefore not to go back on His choice between chaos and the world which He created good, even in view of its corruption and in His righteous anger; not to resign as Creator and Lord of the creature, but to act and confirm Himself as such; to call in and use death and nothingness in His service, to fulfil His judgment on sinful man and a perverted world, but in grace not to surrender His own right, and His creature; and therefore to be in the right without giving chaos the last word and supreme power over the creature; to throw aside and trample underfoot these instruments when they have served their purpose; to act and demonstrate and reveal Himself as God and Lord of the world after the

---

EN338 saying this, he breathed his last
EN339 as a matter of fact
EN340 as a matter of right

fulfilment of His judgment on the world; in relation to it not to be in the right in and for Himself in His wrath, but beyond that to maintain His right to it in an inconceivable love, which is again, to justify Himself; and in so doing, when judgment has taken its course, when that which is worthy of death and nothingness has fallen a prey to death and nothingness, when that which is dust has returned to dust, to justify the creature, to justify man, to acknowledge Himself the Creator once again and this time in fulness, to create him afresh with a new: "Let there be light," to beget him and to cause him to be born again from the dead, freed from his sin and guilt, freed from the claim and power which death and nothingness and chaos necessarily had over him in his former corrupted state, freed for life for Him and with Him, and therefore for life everlasting. God was free to do this. He did not have to do it, but He was free to do it.

And this is what in His grace He actually has done in raising Jesus Christ from the dead when He had been delivered up to death for our trespasses, as our Representative, in fulfilment of the judgment which ought to have fallen on us. In so doing He answered the question which in Mark and Matthew forms the last words of the Crucified. But we can and must say that in so doing He has shown that as recorded in St. Luke's account Jesus commended His spirit into His hands, and that only in so doing did He subject Himself to death, that He bowed His head before Him, and only because He bowed before Him did He also bow before the claim and power of nothingness, that He was obedient even unto death only in this way and in this order (and to that extent as already the secret Lord of the death to which He subjected Himself). God abandoned Him to chaos, as had to happen because of our transgressions, only in order to save Him from it—the One whom chaos could only serve, in order to do despite to it and to make a show of it: "Death is swallowed up in victory. O death, where is thy victory? O death, where is thy sting" (1 Cor. $15^{54f.}$). He made Him the victor over death by letting death conquer Him, as He had to do in fulfilment of the judgment laid upon Him. He recognised and proclaimed not merely the innocence but the supreme righteousness and holiness, the incomparable and unsurpassable goodness, of the work of Him who gave Himself up to death in pure obedience—who was not a sinner in the very fact that He took upon Himself the sin of the world. According to the rendering of Ps. 16^{10} in Ac. 2^{27}, He did not suffer His Holy One to see corruption. And in that He did not suffer it, in that He reopened the doors of death which had necessarily closed behind Him, in that He caused Him to rise from the grave to life unto Himself (Rom. 6^{10}), and therefore to eternal life, He confirmed the verdict which, according to Mk. 1^{11}, He had already pronounced at Jordan when He entered on the way which led Him to Golgotha: "Thou art my beloved Son, in whom I am well pleased." In raising Him from the dead, He justified Him (1 Tim. 3^{16}).

And in and with Him He justified us (Rom. 4^{25})—we shall be returning to this. But primar- [308] ily He justified Himself. He did this first in the revelation of His faithfulness as the Creator and Lord of heaven and earth and all men, to whom in the person of this their Representative, after their destruction in their old and corrupted form of life, He has spoken a second Yes which creates and gives them new life: a Yes which He did not owe them, but which He willed to speak, and which was the gracious confirmation of His own original will to create and His act of creation. But then, and at an even higher level, He did it in the revelation of His faithfulness as the Father of this Son, in the revelation of the love with which He loved Him from all eternity and all along His way into the far country, at Jordan and in the wilderness and in Gethsemane, and never more than when the Son asked Him on the cross (Mk. 15^{34}) whether He had forsaken Him, and when He then cried with a loud voice and gave up the ghost. His whole eternal love would still have been His even if He had acquiesced in His death as the Judge who was judged, if His mission had concluded at that ninth hour of Good Friday, if it had been completed with His fulfilling and suffering in His own person the No of the divine wrath on the world. But then, like His right as Creator and Lord of the world, it would have been, and remained, a completely hidden love: without witnesses, without participants, because without proclamation, without outward confirmation and form, concealed in the mystery of the inner life and being of the Godhead. It pleased God, however, to justify Himself, that is, to reveal and give force and effect to His faithfulness and love in this supreme sense, by an $\dot{o}\rho i\zeta\epsilon\iota\nu$[EN341] (Rom. 1⁴) of His Son which the disciples of Jesus could see and hear and grasp, and which was ordained to be publicly proclaimed. He willed to give to His eternity with Him and therefore to Himself an earthly form. He willed to give to the inner and secret radiance of His glory an outward radiance in the sphere of creation and its history. He willed to give to His eternal life space and time. And that is what He did when He called Jesus Christ to life from the dead.

This helps us to understand an important characteristic in the New Testament view of the resurrection of Jesus Christ, that as a free work demonstrating and revealing the grace of the Father it took place by the Holy Spirit: $\dot{\epsilon}\delta\iota\kappa\alpha\iota\dot{\omega}\theta\eta\ \dot{\epsilon}\nu\ \pi\nu\epsilon\dot{\nu}\mu\alpha\tau\iota$[EN342] is how we have it in 1 Tim. 3¹⁶, and in Rom. 1⁴: $\dot{\epsilon}\nu\ \delta\upsilon\nu\dot{\alpha}\mu\epsilon\iota\ \kappa\alpha\tau\dot{\alpha}\ \pi\nu\epsilon\hat{\upsilon}\mu\alpha\ \dot{\alpha}\gamma\iota\omega\sigma\dot{\upsilon}\nu\eta\varsigma$. Similarly in 1 Pet. 3¹⁸: $\zeta\omega\omega\pi\omega\iota\eta\theta\epsilon\dot{\iota}\varsigma\ \pi\nu\epsilon\dot{\upsilon}\mu\alpha\tau\iota$[EN343]. And surely this is the sense of Rom. 6⁴: $\dot{\eta}\gamma\dot{\epsilon}\rho\theta\eta\ ...\ \delta\iota\dot{\alpha}\ \tau\hat{\eta}\varsigma\ \delta\dot{o}\xi\eta\varsigma\ \tau\omega\hat{\upsilon}\ \pi\alpha\tau\rho\dot{o}\varsigma$[EN344], of 2 Cor. 13⁴: $\zeta\hat{\eta}\ \dot{\epsilon}\kappa\ \delta\upsilon\nu\dot{\alpha}\mu\epsilon\omega\varsigma\ \theta\epsilon\omega\hat{\upsilon}$[EN345], and Col. 2¹²: $\delta\iota\dot{\alpha}\ \tau\hat{\eta}\varsigma\ \pi\dot{\iota}\sigma\tau\epsilon\omega\varsigma\ \tau\hat{\eta}\varsigma\ \dot{\epsilon}\nu\epsilon\rho\gamma\epsilon\dot{\iota}\alpha\varsigma\ \tau\omega\hat{\upsilon}\ \theta\epsilon\omega\hat{\upsilon}$[EN346], as it clearly is of Rom. 8¹¹, which speaks of the Spirit indwelling the Christian as Him who raised Christ Jesus from the dead.

The Holy Spirit—who is also the $\kappa\dot{\upsilon}\rho\iota\omega\varsigma$[EN347] according to 2 Cor. 3¹⁷—is within the Trinity: God Himself maintaining His unity as Father and Son, God in the love which unites Him as Father with the Son, and as Son with the Father; and outside the Trinity, in His work as Creator and Reconciler of the world: God Himself as the One who creates life in freedom, who gives life from the dead, thus making His glory active in the world: $\tau\dot{o}\ \pi\nu\epsilon\hat{\upsilon}\mu\dot{\alpha}\ \dot{\epsilon}\sigma\tau\iota\nu\ \tau\dot{o}\ \zeta\omega\omega\pi\omega\iota\omega\hat{\upsilon}\nu$[EN348], according to the definition of Jn. 6⁶³; $\tau\dot{o}\ \pi\nu\epsilon\hat{\upsilon}\mu\alpha\ \zeta\omega\omega\pi\omega\iota\epsilon\hat{\iota}$[EN349] (2 Cor. 3⁶)—and revealing it in this its characteristic activity: as $\pi\nu\epsilon\hat{\upsilon}\mu\alpha\ \tau\hat{\eta}\varsigma\ \dot{\alpha}\lambda\eta\theta\epsilon\dot{\iota}\alpha\varsigma$[EN350] (Jn. 14¹⁷, 15²⁶, 16¹³; 1 Jn. 4⁶), as the Spirit by whom God discloses Himself to man in all His profundity (1 Cor. 2¹⁰, Eph. 3⁵), who helps our infirmities (Rom. 8²⁶), who bears witness with our spirit with a divine incontrovertibility (Rom. 8¹⁶), by whom the love of God is shed abroad in our hearts (Rom. 5⁵).

In this context it is important that at least one group in the New Testament tradition understood the human existence of the Son of God, that is, the justification and sanctification of human nature in the person of the Virgin Mary which was indispensable to union with the Son of God, as the work of the Holy Spirit (Mt. 1¹⁸ ²⁰, Lk. 1³⁵). It is also important that another series of passages—not 2 Cor. 3¹⁷, but 1 Cor. 15⁴⁵ ("the second Adam was made a $\pi\nu\epsilon\hat{\upsilon}\mu\alpha\ \zeta\omega\omega\pi\omega\iota\omega\hat{\upsilon}\nu$[EN351]"), Jn. 3⁶ ("That which is born of the Spirit, is spirit") and especially the accounts of His baptism in Jordan—understands His whole being as $\pi\nu\epsilon\hat{\upsilon}\mu\alpha$[EN352], that is, as filled and controlled by the Spirit, so that in Heb. 9¹⁴ it can already be said of His way to death that $\delta\iota\dot{\alpha}\ \pi\nu\epsilon\dot{\upsilon}\mu\alpha\tau\omega\varsigma\ \alpha\dot{\iota}\omega\nu\dot{\iota}\omega\upsilon$[EN353] He offered Himself without spot to God. If

[309]

[EN341] a declaration
[EN342] he was justified in the Spirit
[EN343] he was made alive by the Spirit
[EN344] he was raised ... through the glory of the Father
[EN345] he lives by the power of God
[EN346] through faith in the power of God
[EN347] Lord
[EN348] the Spirit is the life-giver
[EN349] the Spirit gives life
[EN350] Spirit of truth
[EN351] life-giving Spirit
[EN352] Spirit
[EN353] through the eternal Spirit

we were to try to speak of a necessity of His resurrection, then it is along these lines that we could and would have to do so, applying the question of Gal. 3³ whether that which has begun and is continued in the Spirit can be made perfect in the flesh—which is here the destruction of the flesh. But it is better not to follow this track, remembering Jn. 3⁸: "The Spirit bloweth where it listeth, and thou hearest the sound thereof, but canst not tell whence it cometh, or whither it goeth," and also 2 Cor. 3¹⁷: "Where the Spirit of the Lord is, there is liberty;" remembering, therefore, that when we speak of the Spirit, *per definitionem*[EN354] we do not speak of a necessary but of a free being and activity of God. The fact that Jesus Christ was raised from the dead by the Holy Spirit and therefore justified confirms that it has pleased God to reveal and express Himself to the crucified and dead and buried Jesus Christ in the unity of the Father with the Son and therefore in the glory of the free love which is His essence: a revelation and expression which as such—and where the Spirit of God blows, where the Holy Spirit is at work, this does take place necessarily—must consist in the merciful work of creating the καινότης ζωῆς[EN355] (Rom. 6⁴) of this One who is dead, in His presentation and exhibition as the One who is alive for evermore.

To sum up, the resurrection of Jesus Christ is the great verdict of God, the fulfilment and proclamation of God's decision concerning the event of the cross. It is its acceptance as the act of the Son of God appointed our Representative, an act which fulfilled the divine wrath but did so in the service of the divine grace. It is its acceptance as the act of His obedience which judges the world, but judges it with the aim of saving it. It is its acceptance as the act of His Son whom He has always loved (and us in Him), whom of His sheer goodness He has not rejected but drawn to Himself (and us in Him) (Jer. 31³). In this the resurrection is the justification of God Himself, of God the Father, Creator of heaven and earth, who has willed and planned and ordered this event. It is the justification of Jesus Christ, His Son, who willed to suffer this event, and suffered it to the very last. And in His person it is the justification of all sinful men, whose death was decided in this event, for whose life there is therefore no more place. In the resurrection of Jesus Christ His life and with it their life has in fact become an event beyond death: "Because I live, ye shall live also" (Jn. 14¹⁹).

We come to the point which is decisive for our investigation when we ask (3) what is the positive connexion between the death of Jesus Christ and His resurrection. The comprehensive answer to this question with which the whole investigation must terminate can only be this. They belong together in that in these two events of God with and after one another there is effective and expressed the Yes of the reconciling will of God—the Yes fulfilled and proclaimed by the one Jesus Christ, first in His act of obedience in our place, then—again in our place—as the first recipient of the grace of God the Father. But before we come to this final answer we have to say concerning the question [310] of this relationship that which is implied in it, that the positive connexion between the death and resurrection of Jesus Christ consists in the fact that

---

EN354 by definition
EN355 newness of life

these two acts of God with and after one another are the two basic events of the one history of God with a sinful and corrupt world, His history with us as perverted and lost creatures. The one concerns our trespasses, the other our justification (Rom. 4^{25}). In a comprehensive sense Jesus Christ "died and rose again for us" (2 Cor. 5^{15}). It is our case which is undertaken, our conversion to God which is brought about, both in the one and in the other, on the way from the one to the other, in the sequence and correspondence of the two. The relationship of the two events is that of the alteration in our situation and status and being which took place in them. To the making of this alteration and therefore to the reconciliation of the world with God there belong both the free obedience of the Son in His death and also the grace of God the Father in His resurrection: the event of Golgotha and the event in the garden of Joseph of Arimathea.

The fact that the alteration of our situation is made in both events does not mean that their sequence and correspondence is that of repetition, or that their relationship is that of the unity of two equal factors, of which either the one or the other might appear to be superfluous or simply a closer definition. On the contrary, it is a genuine sequence and correspondence in a differentiated relationship in which both factors have their proper form and function. In all this alteration we have to do with the conversion of man to God and therefore with his reconciliation and that of the world with God. It is, therefore, clear that we have to distinguish a *terminus a quo*[EN356] and a *terminus ad quem*[EN357]: first, a negative event (with a positive intention), a turning away (for the purpose of turning to), a removing (in the sense of a positing), a putting off (with a view to a putting on, 2 Cor. 5^2, Eph. 4^{22-24}), a freeing from something (with a view to freeing for something else); then a positive event (with a negative presupposition), a turning to (made possible by a definite turning from), a putting on (after a previous putting off), a freeing for something (based upon a freeing from something else). According to the resurrection the death of Jesus Christ as the negative act of God took place with a positive intention. It had as its aim the turning of man to Himself, his positing afresh, his putting on of a new life, his freeing for the future. And, according to the prior death of Jesus Christ, the resurrection has this negative presupposition in a radical turning of man from his old existence, in a total removing of man in his earlier form, in his absolute putting off, in his complete freeing from the past. It is in this correspondence that we see their difference but also their relationship—which is, of course, necessarily a differentiated relationship.

We will try to put it in another way, reversing the sequence. The justification which took place in the resurrection of Jesus Christ confirmed and revealed in

---

[EN356] starting point
[EN357] end point

what sense God was in the right in His death—not surrendering but asserting [311]
His right against sinful men who, as such, were judged in the death of their
Representative, being destroyed and necessarily crucified and dying with Him;
but also not surrendering His right over these men as His creatures, and therefore not surrendering the right of these creatures of His, but with a view to
re-establishing and maintaining it. The death of Jesus Christ preceded His resurrection. God established and maintained His own right against man and
over man, and the right of man Himself. This makes it clear in what sense in
the resurrection of Jesus Christ He willed to justify both Jesus and Himself, and
has in fact done so, proclaiming His own twofold right and the right of man as
His creature as they were there established and maintained to be the basis and
the beginning of a new world, putting them into force and effect, making it
plain that the history of the humiliation of His Son, the history of His way into
the far country, is redemption history within universal history; against man,
and therefore for him.

This is the sequence and correspondence of the death of Jesus Christ and
His resurrection. This is how they are with and after one another the basic
events of the alteration of the human situation in which there took place the
reconciliation of the world with God. This, then, is the differentiated relationship between the two events.

We read of this whole alteration in the remarkably central verse 2 Cor. 5^{17}: "If any man be
in Christ, he is a new creation: old things are passed away; behold, all things are become
new." Alongside this we have to place Rom. 8^{10}: "And if Christ be in you, the body (you
yourself in virtue of what has taken place for you in the death of Jesus Christ) is dead because
of sin (judged there in His body as your Representative); but the Spirit (you yourself in
virtue of what is promised and has already taken place for you in the resurrection of this your
Representative) is life because of righteousness (proclaimed and put into effect there)."
Alongside it, too, we must put Rev. 21$^{4f.}$: "And God shall wipe away all tears from their eyes;
and there shall be no more death, neither sorrow, nor crying, neither shall there be any
more pain: for the former things are passed away. And he that sat upon the throne said,
Behold, I make all things new." All these can and should be read (according to the meaning
of the New Testament writers) as a commentary on Is. 43$^{18f.}$: "Remember ye not the former
things, neither consider the things of old. Behold, I will do a new thing; shall ye not know it?
I will even make a way in the wilderness, and rivers in the desert." Or on Is. 65$^{17f.}$: "For,
behold, I create new heavens, and a new earth: and the former shall not be remembered,
nor come into mind. But be ye glad and rejoice for ever in that which I create: for, behold, I
create Jerusalem a rejoicing, and her people a joy." The New Testament community knows
what is meant by this. It stands at the heart of the event which is proclaimed here, face to face
with the Jerusalem which comes. Again, the prophetic word is for it a commentary on that
which confronts it as its basic text. It is the witness of it. The old, the former thing, has passed
away: the new has come, has grown, has been created. It is "in Christ"—the Crucified and
Risen—and Christ is in it. In His death its own death and that of the world is, in fact, already
past, and in His life its own life and that of the future world is before it. It has turned away
from the one, it has turned to the other. It has put off the one, it has put on the other. Its
existence looks back to the Crucified and forward to the Risen. It is an existence in the

[312]   presence of the One who was and will be. He is its *terminus a quo*EN358 and its *terminus ad quem*EN359. It is an existence in that alteration, that is, in that differentiated relationship between the death and the resurrection of Christ. When a man is in Christ, there is a new creation. The old has passed, everything has become new. This means that the event of the end of the world which took place once and for all in Jesus Christ is the presupposition of an old man, and the event of the beginning of the new world which took place once and for all in Jesus Christ is the goal of a new man, and because the goal, therefore the truth and power of the sequence of human existence as it moves towards this goal. The world and every man exist in this alteration.

Note that it is not dependent upon whether it is proclaimed well or badly or even at all. It is not dependent upon the way in which it is regarded, upon whether it is realised and fulfilled in faith or unbelief. The coming of the kingdom of God has its truth in itself, not in that which does or does not correspond to it on earth.

By way of illustration, let us suppose that the kingdom of heaven is like a king whom it has pleased to confer on someone an order. Now normally the man will be in the happy position of being able to receive the distinction. But there may be the abnormal case when because of pressing or tragic circumstances, or because he is hindered by outside forces, he is not in a position to do this. Is it not clear that in both cases the will and act of the king form a complete action, and all is well and good for the recipient even in the second and abnormal case? Has he failed to receive the order because he could not do so in person?

The men of the New Testament are the normal case, those who not only receive that which has taken place in Jesus Christ, but do so in person, those who with open eyes and ears and hearts, in faith and in the knowledge of faith, hold to the fact that they can and must, not only exist, but walk (περιπατεῖν, στοιχεῖν, πολιτεύεσθαι) from this presupposition to this goal and in this sequence, who are therefore summoned and empowered and enabled to proclaim this alteration and therefore the death and resurrection of Jesus Christ, or rather the crucified and risen Jesus Christ Himself. The divine verdict pronounced in the resurrection of Jesus Christ has been heard by them. The "blowing" (Jn. 3⁸) of the Holy Spirit which creates life and leads into all truth is received by them. They are "baptised" (Mk. 1⁸) by Jesus Christ Himself, or they have "drunk" of Him (1 Cor. 12¹³). As they pray for Him, He is to them the One who is "given" by their Father in heaven (Lk. 11¹³). He "dwells" in them (Rom. 8¹¹). They are "led" by Him (Gal. 4⁶, 5¹⁸; Rom. 8¹⁴). They walk in conformity with Him (κατὰ πνεῦμα EN360, Rom. 8⁴) or in Him (πνεύματι EN361, Gal. 5¹⁶, 2 Cor. 12¹⁸), not as blind and deaf participants in this alteration of the human situation, but as those who see and hear.

But what is said in the New Testament concerning the alteration of the human situation which has its basis in the death and resurrection of Jesus Christ compels us to make a further distinction in our understanding of this relationship. It is a matter of the character of the two events which underlie this alteration as temporal events, their relation as they are with and after one another in time. In respect of their distinctness in this regard the third of the points in our investigation which now occupy us is the decisive one—decisive, that is, in the answering of our main question whether and to what extent we can and must proceed from the obedience which Jesus Christ rendered for us

EN358 starting point
EN359 end point
EN360 according to the Spirit
EN361 in the Spirit

to the thought of its relevance for us. We have seen that the resurrection of Jesus Christ from the dead, as a second and new divine act, was the revelation of the meaning and purpose of the obedience demanded from and achieved [313] by Jesus Christ, and therefore of His death, the answer of the grace of God the Father to the self-humiliation of the Son, His confession of Him, the validation of His act as the establishment and maintaining of His right against and for us, the justification of God Himself as the Father and our Creator, and therefore the justification of Jesus Christ and our justification as His creatures, the verdict of God. So far we have tried to understand these two acts of God, these two basic events in the alteration of the human situation, as they took place through and to Jesus Christ, in their differentiated togetherness in content.

To appreciate the matter further, we must now start from the fact that there is also a togetherness in time.

The resurrection of Jesus Christ tells us—and it is decided in this second divine act, the act of God fulfilled in His verdict—that as the Crucified "He lives and reigns to all eternity" (Luther), that as the One who was, having been buried, He is not of the past, He did not continue to be enclosed in the limits of the time between His birth and death, but as the One who was in this time He became and is the Lord of all time, eternal as God Himself is eternal, and therefore present in all time. But the fact that He is risen to die no more, to be taken from the dominion of death (Rom. 6⁹), carries with it the fact that His then living and speaking and acting, His being on the way from Jordan to Golgotha, His being as the One who suffered and died, became and is as such His eternal being and therefore His present-day being every day of our time. That which took place on the third day after His death lifted up the whole of what took place before in all its particularity (not in spite of but because of its particularity) into something that took place once and for all. It is in the power of the event of the third day that the event of the first day—as something that happened there and then—is not something which belongs to the past, which can be present only by recollection, tradition and proclamation, but is as such a present event, the event which fills and determines the whole present.

In virtue of His resurrection from the dead Jesus Christ—"the man Christ Jesus, who gave himself a ransom for all"—is (in the same way as the One God) the one Mediator between God and man (1 Tim. 2⁵). He was this in the event of Good Friday to be it for ever—this is what the event of Easter Day revealed and confirmed and brought into effect. He not only did represent us, He does represent us. He not only did bear the sin of the world, He does bear it. He not only has reconciled the world with God, but as the One who has done this, He is its eternal Reconciler, active and at work once and for all. He not only went the way from Jordan to Golgotha, but He still goes it, again and again. His history did not become dead history. It was history in His time to become as such eternal history—the history of God with the men of all times, and therefore taking place here and now as it did then. He is the living Saviour. This [314] would be a fantastic and not very helpful statement if it simply meant that He is something like this for certain men of His own age, and that He can be something of the same for certain men of other ages by their recollection of Him, by the tradition and proclamation concerning Him, by a sympathetic experience of His person, or by some form of imitation of His work. He would then be alive only in virtue of the life breathed into Him as a historical and therefore a dead figure by the men of other ages. But the fact that He is the living Saviour is true and helpful because He is risen from the dead and therefore—the Father of whom the same can be said has given it to Him—He has life in Himself (Jn. 5²⁶), and in His own omnipotence, on His own initiative, and by His own act, He is the same here and now as He was there and then: the Mediator between God and us men.

Therefore He not only did but does stand before God for us—not in a different form but in exactly the same form as He stood before Him for us "in the days of His flesh" as the Judge judged and the priest sacrificed. Ἐντυγχάνει ὑπὲρ ἡμῶν EN362: He who died, yea rather, who is risen, is at the right hand of God. Therefore, on this basis and in relation to this fact, it can and must be asked triumphantly: "Who will condemn?", and further: "Who will separate us from the love of Christ?" (Rom. 8³⁴ᶠ·). Similarly in 1 Jn. 2¹ᶠ: "If any man sin, we have an advocate (παράκλητον EN363) with the Father, Jesus Christ the righteous: and he is the propitiation for our sins: and not for ours only, but also for the sins of the whole world." Similarly in Heb. 7²⁵: "He is the One that ever (πάντοτε) liveth to make intercession for us." His sacrifice has power for ever (εἰς τὸ διηνεκές, Heb. 10¹⁴). By His blood He has entered in once into the Holiest of Holies, gaining an eternal redemption (Heb. 9¹²). He is a "high-priest for ever" (Heb. 5⁶, 6²⁰, 7¹⁷). His is an unchangeable priesthood (Heb. 7²⁴). He appears now for us in the presence of God (Heb. 9²⁴). It is not that we had but have Him as a High Priest (Heb. 4¹⁴ᶠ·, 8¹, 10¹⁹). He is "the same yesterday, today, and for ever" (Heb. 13⁸). It is no accident that the Epistle to the Hebrews which emphasises this so strongly brings out the To-day so sharply in the call to faith, repentance and obedience (3⁷ ¹⁵, 4⁷). These are just a few of the explicit statements of the New Testament about the eternal unity, or the temporal togetherness, of the humiliated and the exalted, the crucified and the risen Jesus Christ, the obedience of the Son and the grace of the Father. It might also be shown that quite a number of verses in the so-called "high-priestly" prayer (Jn. 17) ought to be regarded even in the sense of the Evangelist himself as prayers of the exalted Christ for His own and for His work in the world. This unity and togetherness are—if we look back to the event of Easter—among the self-evident presuppositions of the whole of the New Testament.

It was in this connexion that in the doctrine of the *munus sacerdotale*EN364 the older dogmatics had a second section on the *intercessio Christi*EN365 side by side with the idea of the *satisfactio vicaria: victimae Christi in terra oblatae et mactatae in coelo repraesentatio et nova velut oblatio*EN366 (J. H. Heidegger, *Med. Theol. chr.*, 1696, XIX, 59). In fact it had to do with the same problem as now concerns us—that of the transition from the understanding of the person and work of Christ to soteriology proper, to the question of the *applicatio salutis*EN367: How does the atonement made then and there come to us and become our atonement? And

---

EN362 He intercedes for us
EN363 Paraclete
EN364 priestly office
EN365 intercession of Christ
EN366 vicarious satisfaction: the representation, and likewise new offering, of Christ, the victim offered on earth, and sacrificed in heaven
EN367 application of salvation

at this supreme point the question is answered by the recognition that Jesus Christ as the Son who was once obedient to the Father and offered Himself and reconciled the world and us with God is in eternity and therefore to-day now, at this very hour, our active and effective Representative and Advocate before God, and therefore the real basis of our justification and hope. If only this recognition had been maintained, then for all its apparent inflexibility the alternative of contingent facts of history and necessary truths of reason would necessarily have been thought through in the 18th century and rejected and overcome. The moment of this particular "contingent fact of history" was the moment of all moments. There is no moment in which Jesus Christ is not Judge and High Priest and accomplishes all these things. There is no moment in which this perfect tense is not a present. There is no moment in which He does not stand before God as our Representative who there suffered and died for us and therefore speaks for us. There is no moment in which we are viewed and treated by God except in the light of this *repraesentatio*[EN368] and *oblatio*[EN369] of His Son. All honour to the human and historical pragmatism of recollection, tradition and proclamation. But in relation to the divine history of this *repraesentatio*[EN370] and *oblatio*[EN371] it can be considered only as an epiphenomenon, with a significance which is only secondary, and indirect, that of an instrument and witness. The eternal action of Jesus Christ grounded in His resurrection is itself the true and direct bridge from once to always, from Himself in His time to us in our time. Because as crucified and dead He is risen and lives, the fact of His death on the cross can never be past, it can never cease to be His action, the decision which God makes *hic et nunc*[EN372] to His own glory and in our favour, summoning us on our part to responsibility, as is brought out so impressively and in a way to stir the conscience in Heb. 10^{19-29}. "Let us draw near with a true heart in full assurance of faith, having our hearts sprinkled from an evil conscience, and our bodies washed with pure water. Let us hold fast the profession of our hope without wavering, for he is faithful that promised" (Heb. 10^{22-23}). Jesus Christ Himself lives, His obedience pleading for our disobedience. His blood shed in obedience speaks against us and for us to-day as it did on the day of Golgotha. He receives for us to-day as on Easter Day the grace of God which we have not deserved. For this reason the judgment fulfilled by Him, the sacrifice offered by Him, is effective for us. Not therefore in some answer of ours to our questions: What are we going to make of it? How can we bring home this matter to ourselves and other men? Or how can we bring ourselves and other men to this matter? Where and how do we experience and prove its efficacy? There is a relative place for these questions and answers, but only in the light and in strict explanation of the one question and answer which God Himself has put and given in Jesus Christ, which indeed He does put in eternity and therefore to-day, and which He answers in the antithesis of the obedient Son and the gracious Father. Our answer and our question have to be sought (Col. 3^1) "above, where Christ is seated at the right hand of God." But this means in prayer, prayer in the name of Jesus, prayer which we expect to be heard only—but without doubt or hesitation—because God has loved and loves and will love the one who offers it as a lost sinner in Jesus Christ, because, therefore, Jesus Christ has come between this one and God, and is there between to-day and every day.

To this we have to add that this living being of Jesus Christ the Mediator is the immovable barrier opposed to all who have tried to make to themselves another saviour than the Saviour of sinners crucified between and with the thieves; to all who are too proud to pray

[EN368] representation
[EN369] offering
[EN370] representation
[EN371] offering
[EN372] here and now

with the publican: "God be merciful, to me a sinner;" to all who try to believe that they can treat and act on their own account in relation to God. They must be clear that even in Christian history and the Christian Church, in spite of the *kerygma*[EN373], with or without the sacraments, in spite of their faith and discipleship, they would necessarily be lost and damned were it not that as their Representative between themselves and His and their Father there stands "above" the crucified Son of God, the Saviour of sinners who was crucified between and with the thieves as the One who gave Himself up for our trespasses. "If we say that we have no sin, we deceive ourselves. and the truth is not in us. If we confess our sins, he is faithful and just to forgive us our sins, and to cleanse us from all unrighteousness" (1 Jn. 1[8f.]). In this sense the *intercessio Christi*[EN374] is not simply the origin and the lasting basis of our righteousness and hope, but its continual turning-point, the way which is always open to God and the sharp corner around which it leads us. And in this twofold sense it is the eternal act of the crucified and risen One for us, the one truly contemporaneous divine act to us, the To-day, To-day! of atonement against which we must not harden our hearts.

[316]

He who was crucified is risen, and as such He lives unto God (Rom. 6[10]). He is the same yesterday, to-day and for ever. This temporal togetherness of the Jesus Christ of Good Friday and the Jesus Christ of Easter Day as created by the divine verdict is the basis of life for men of all ages. And as such it is the basis of the alteration of their situation. The event of Easter Day is the removing of the barrier between His life in His time and their life in their times, the initiation of His lordship as the Lord of all time. What He has done in His time He has done as the Representative of all other men, as the elect man, for them. In His resurrection it is fixed that what He did in His time He did in their time for and to them. The fact that in His death God maintained and asserted His right against and to them and therefore their right as His creatures is their justification. And God's verdict when he raised Him to life beyond death was His verdict on them. This answer of grace to His obedience was the answer to the question of their being in disobedience, the revelation of the judgment which came on them in Jesus Christ, of the death which they died in Him, of the end to which they were brought in Him. God's gracious answer in the resurrection of Jesus Christ from the dead was this. In their quite different time with its quite different content (in and with what Jesus Christ was and did in His time, in and with this Son who became man and died as man and was raised again as man), as those who are elected with Him, as the brothers of this His Son, He has called them His children and received them as such. This was said to them, no, is said to them, by the Word of God made flesh, in the glory in which it was spoken and heard on Easter Day, and in which from that day it will be spoken and can be heard as the living Word, as the redemptive history which takes place to-day within universal history.

Thus the death and resurrection of Jesus Christ are together—His death in the power and effectiveness and truth and lasting newness given to it by His

---

[EN373] proclamation
[EN374] intercession of Christ

resurrection—the basis of the alteration of the situation of the men of all times. In virtue of the divine right established in the death of Jesus Christ, in virtue of the justification which has come to them in His resurrection, they are no longer what they were but they are already what they are to be. They are no longer the enemies of God but His friends, His children. They are no longer turned away from Him, but away from their own being in the past, and turned to Him. They are no longer sinners, but righteous. They are no longer lost, but saved. And all this as He belongs to them and they to Him, He who was in His [317] time to them in their time, and they in their time to Him in His time. All this as He is and does the same for them to-day as He was and did yesterday, the Lord of every time and its content. The resurrection of Jesus Christ affirms that which is actual in His death, the conversion of all men to God which has taken place in Him. For it is the pure and acceptable word which is spoken in every age, that all men are in Him the One, and that He the One is in them, He the One in the midst of them.

Not all hear this word. Not all are obedient to Him. But it comes to all, it is relevant to all, it is said for all and to all, it is said clearly and acceptably enough for all. And the situation of all is the situation which is altered by this word. It is not one which is first altered in and by them. They can and must recognise and acknowledge that they are altered in and by it, drawing out the consequences of this alteration, bowing before the divine verdict, repenting in face of the judgment of God which has come upon them and does come upon them. They can and must believe only the justification which has come and still comes to them, accepting that they are the children of God, accepting that which is old as old, and that which is new as new. What makes the community the community and Christians Christians is that the alteration of the human situation is manifest to them (and not in vain), that they cannot therefore evade or arrest the consequences of it, that they can make use of the freedom which is granted to them by it, that they cannot refrain from attesting it to others in the world as it has been attested to them. But this alteration is not made and being made by them, or in the consequences which they can and must deduce from it. This word does not become pure and acceptable only as they hear it with their ears and believe it in their hearts and confess it with their mouths. Rather they hear and believe and confess it as a word which, whether they hear and believe and confess it or not, is clear and acceptable in and for itself, as the word of the crucified and risen Lord, speaking in truth about reality, and significant and right for their own as for every age, for them-selves and for all men. In Jesus Christ the alteration of the human situation did take place, and does take place to-day, the situation of Christians and of all men, the reconciliation of the world with God in Him who is the living Medi-ator between God and man in the power of His resurrection. What remains for them is high and appropriate and joyful and stringent enough—to welcome the divine verdict, to take it seriously with full responsibility, not to keep their knowledge of it to themselves, but by the witness of their existence and proclamation to make known to the world which is still blind and deaf to this verdict the alteration which has in fact taken place by it. Their existence in the world depends upon the fact that this alone is their particular gift and task. They have not to assist or add to the being and work of their living Saviour who is the Lord of the world, let alone to replace it by their own work. The community is not a prolongation of His incarnation, His death and resurrection, the acts of God and their revelation. It has not to do these things. It has to witness to them. It is its consolation that it can do this. Its marching-orders are to do it.

[318]

But we must now turn our attention to another aspect or form of the relationship between the two events. According to the report and message of the New Testament they are separated by the gulf between the first and the third days. They stand to one another, therefore, in a relationship of temporal sequence. On the one side there is the time of the way of Jesus Christ moving towards and fulfilling itself in His death. On the other there is that of His new life limited in the first instance to the forty days. He is the living Saviour in these two times, the one after the other, on the two sides of His death, now humiliated, now exalted, the One who lives and rules eternally, in all ages, as the Lord of time. But the fact that the two times followed one another means that the forty days too, being a temporal event, have their beginning and end like the first form of the life of Jesus. What took place in these days was the divine acceptance, putting into effect, and revelation of what had taken place before, something complete in itself, sufficiently clear as a living word for the men of all times, sufficiently true as the divine verdict on the whole world, sufficiently high and deep to alter its situation, a sufficient missionary impulse for the disciples and basis of the community which receives and proclaims that verdict. The resurrection of Jesus Christ, His living presence, His *parousia* in the direct form of the events of Easter was, however, a happening in time with a definite beginning and end like other happenings. Its end was marked by the ascension as a sign of His exaltation to the right hand of God, to eternal life and rule; of His transition to a presence which is eternal and therefore embraces all times. But it did end with the ascension, just as it had begun with the sign of the empty tomb. With the end of the time of this particular event there began the time of another form of His *parousia*, His living present—no less complete and sufficient in itself, but quite different. There began a time in which He was no longer, or not yet again, directly revealed and visible and audible and perceptible (as He had been) either to the disciples, the community, or the world: directly, of course, in the divine verdict pronounced in that event and received by them, but not without the mediation of recollection, tradition and proclamation; the living Word of God, but not without the ministry of the attesting word of man which is proclaimed and heard. There began a time in which He was and continues to be and ever again will be directly present and revealed and active in the community by His Spirit, the power of His accomplished resurrection (although not, of course, without that mediating ministry); but in which the alteration of the human situation which has taken place in Him can be, and apart from the community is in fact, hidden from the [319] world. There began a time in which the community, Christians, are aware, and will and must always be aware, that they themselves, the hearers of the Word, those who are justified by it, the children of God, believers, the witnesses to the Crucified and Risen, are still in the world, and are still like it in the sphere of human perception, so that to themselves and one another they are not visible or audible or perceptible as those who are dead and resurrected to new life, they cannot be known outwardly or inwardly as such, they are still hidden, they can recognize in themselves as in others an altered world only in relation to Jesus Christ, only according to the verdict of the Holy Spirit, only by faith and not by sight. There began a time in which the light of the One who in His own time was crucified and raised again did in fact give light to all that were in the house, but to them all—believers and unbelievers—only as the isolated light of the event of that time, of the resurrection. This light is shed abroad, of course, over the events of all times, and to that extent it is the indication of the com- prehensive alteration of the human situation which has already taken place. It is not yet, however, the light of the altered world itself which we can expect on the ground of this alteration. It is not yet the revelation of the altered creation, of the children of God as they are transformed by what has taken place for them and to them in Jesus Christ. It is not yet the time of the resurrection of all the dead. Obviously, therefore, it is not yet the time of the fulfilment of the resurrection which has come to them in Jesus Christ. To that extent it is not yet the fulfilment of His *parousia* and presence and salvation in the world recon- ciled by Him.

This time, which begins with the end of the forty days and therefore with the resurrection of Jesus Christ, is the time of the community in the world, its grounding on the foundation of the apostles and prophets (Eph. 2^{20}), its appearance and tribulation and activity in the world, its internal and external history right up to the present day. The development of the New Testament belongs to this time. And everywhere it has its characteristics. It looks back both to the life and death of Jesus and also to the happening of the forty days. It looks forward in the light of the consequences of these two related events, first to its own time and then to all the times that follow. It understands and attests the life and death of Jesus Christ in the light of His presence and revela- tion in the forty days. It understands and attests the Crucified, therefore, as the Resurrected, the One who for us took His place for ever at the right hand of the Father, who therefore lives and reigns in every age, who from there speaks and acts and works on earth, in human history, by His Spirit, in the power of His resurrection as it is disclosed and given to His disciples and enlightens and guides them. It understands and reveals Him, therefore, on the clear presup- position that He is no longer present and revealed to its own time as He once [320] was in the forty days, but in a way which does not correspond to that type and form and appearance. We have to say at once, therefore, that the New Testament not only relates its own time and the ensuing time of the community in the world to the time of the new present of the Crucified, but also clearly differentiates them from it.

It does relate them to it to the extent that it sees them in the light of the time which began on Easter morning and ended with the ascension, to the extent, therefore, that it looks and holds to the fact that Jesus Christ risen and alive, as He appeared to and encountered His disciples, is the Lord of all times and that (even here and now, in its own time, the time of the community in the world) He lives and reigns and acts and is at work in the power of His resurrection, the force and authority of the verdict of the Holy Spirit.

The early Church knew what it was doing when it remembered the accounts of His sayings and acts before His death, collecting them, finally putting them together in different ways—although always under the name and title of $\epsilon\dot{\nu}\alpha\gamma\gamma\dot{\epsilon}\lambda\iota o\nu$ EN375—and repeating and hearing and reading them, and all this with an understanding of what had not previously been understood, and not merely for the sake of writing and maintaining and repeating the history of it or occupying themselves with it as such. The much quoted verse in 2 Cor. 5^{16} is relevant here: "Though we have known $X\rho\iota\sigma\tau\dot{o}\varsigma$ $\kappa\alpha\tau\dot{\alpha}$ $\sigma\dot{\alpha}\rho\kappa\alpha$ EN376, yet now henceforth know we him no more." There is no question of appealing to His remembered form as it had necessarily appeared to His disciples before the verdict of the Holy Spirit was pronounced on His life and death, abstracted from the verdict of the Holy Spirit. In the editing and composition of the Evangelical narratives the interest and art and rules of the historian do not matter. What matters is His living existence in the community and therefore in the world. What matters is His history as it has indeed happened but as it is present and not past. What matters is His speaking and acting and suffering and dying to-day as well as yesterday. What matters is the "good news" of His history as it speaks and rings out *hic et nunc* EN377. It is not a question of digging out and preserving Himself and His history in order to have them before us and study them. It is a matter of living with Him the living One, and therefore of participating in His history as the history of the salvation of the world and our own salvation, to hear Himself speak to the men of our own age in the *logia* EN378 which have been handed down, to see Him act among the men of our own day in the records of His miracles, in the story of His passion to stand to-day before the fact that in His death everything—the gracious judgment, the redemptive sacrifice for the sins of all men—is accomplished, the old has passed away, and all things have become new; in the astonishing accounts of His resurrection on the third day to see here and now, with those who were the witnesses of His appearing, that He lives, He who there and then went that way, He who there and then was crucified and died for us. It is a matter of discovering and receiving as the life of all men and our own life, and of letting it take root and grow, that life of His which is the life of the Son of God in the place of all men and as the Mediator between all men and God. It is quite right that the voice and form of Jesus cannot in practice be distinguished with any finality in the Gospels from the community founded by Him and sharing His life. The historian may find this disconcerting and suspicious (or even provocatively interesting). It is further evidence

---

EN375 'Gospel'
EN376 Christ according to the flesh
EN377 here and now
EN378 words

of that submission to the divine verdict without which the Gospels could never have taken shape as Gospels.

In the New Testament this relating of the time of the community to the time of the living and dying of Jesus in the light of His presence and revelation in the forty days corresponds to a very definite view of the alteration of the human situation which took place in the first time and determines the second as a living event. In other words, from this standpoint the men of this second time are to address themselves not merely to the redemptive judgment, death and end which came to them with the death of their Representative Jesus Christ, not merely to the right established and asserted against them and for them in the happening of Golgotha, but to its validity and proclamation for them as it took place in the resurrection of this Representative, to the fulfilment of their own justification, to the beginning of their own new life in and with Jesus Christ. The saying about the καινὴ κτίσις EN379 (2 Cor. 5¹⁷, cf. Gal. 6¹⁵) which there is when any man is in Christ must surely be taken to mean that this man is a new creature already. "Reckon ye also yourselves to be dead indeed unto sin, but alive unto God through Jesus Christ our Lord" (Rom. 6¹¹). "Whether we live, we live unto the Lord" (Rom. 14⁸). "For to this end Christ both died, and rose, and revived, that he might be Lord both of the dead and the living" (Rom. 14⁹). "I live, yet not I, but Christ liveth in me" (Gal. 2²⁰). To Paul, to live is Christ (Phil. 1²¹). "For we are his workmanship, created (κτισθέντες) in Christ Jesus unto good works" (Eph. 2¹⁰). "He hath delivered us from the power of darkness, and hath translated us into the kingdom of his dear Son" (Col. 1¹³). Which means, "ye are risen with him" (συνηγέρθητε, Col. 2¹², cf. 3¹). God has made us who were dead alive (συνεζωοποίησεν) in Christ. He has raised us up (συνήγειρεν) with Him. Indeed, in and with Him He has already set us (συνεκάθισεν, Eph. 2⁵ᶠ·) in the heavenly world. We can, of course, say that these latter formulations are peculiar to Ephesians and Colossians, but we cannot deny that they are the necessary consequence or rather presupposition of the earlier formulations. How can there be ascribed to them a life from the dead here and now in their own time, which is the time after the forty days, if the meaning is not the same as in the case of their death after the death of Christ on Golgotha, that as their own death took place there, so in the resurrection of Jesus Christ their own raising from the dead has already been initiated?—so that it can be said to them personally; "Ye have put on Christ" (Gal. 3²⁷); "Ye are washed, ye are sanctified, ye are justified in the name of the Lord Jesus and by the Spirit of our God" (1 Cor. 6¹¹); "Ye are all the children of God by faith in Christ Jesus" (Gal. 3²⁶); or: "The Spirit beareth witness … that we are the children of God" (Rom. 8¹⁶); we "are called" and are the children of God (1 Jn. 3¹). These are the indicatives which describe the human situation as altered by that first time present in the second.

But the imperatives, too, derive from the human situation as it is altered in this dimension: "Walk worthy of the gospel of Christ" (Phil. 1²⁷); "Awake, thou that sleepest, and arise from the dead" (Eph. 5¹⁴); "Like as Christ was raised up from the dead by the glory of the Father, even so we also should walk in newness of life" (Rom. 6⁴). As the living people they are, Christians should offer to God themselves and their members as "instruments" in the service of the justification which has come to them in and with Jesus Christ (Rom. 6¹³ ¹⁹). They are dead to the Law in the death of Christ in order to live to another, Him who has been raised from the dead, and to bring forth fruit unto God (Rom. 7⁴). "If we live in the Spirit, let us also walk in the Spirit" (Gal. 5²⁵). "If ye then be risen with Christ, seek those things which are above" (Col. 3¹). It is a matter of putting on the new man, which "after God is created in righteousness and true holiness" (Eph. 4²⁴). "Ye are all children of light, and the children of the day: we are not of the night, nor of darkness. Therefore let us not sleep, as do others, but let us watch and be sober. For they that sleep sleep in the night; and they that be drunken are

EN379 new creation

drunken in the night. But let us, who are of the day, be sober, putting on the breastplate of faith and love; and for an helmet the hope of salvation. For God hath not appointed us to wrath, but to obtain salvation by our Lord Jesus Christ, who died for us, that, whether we wake or sleep, we should live together with him" (1 Thess. 5[5f]). It is clear that these are not demands to give ourselves a new life and resurrection and glory by the fulfilment of a new law. Those who are dead in Christ (Col. 2[20]) and therefore liberated (Gal. 5[1]), are expressly warned against such dangerous and futile undertakings. It is equally clear that these are consequences which we have necessarily to draw from the alteration of our situation. If we come from this point and stand in this place, this is again the acknowledgment and affirmation which has become inevitable, the grateful praise of God for what He has done for us and to us. Walking worthy of the Gospel does not work the work of God. God Himself does that and only God, the God who calls Himself our Father and us His children in Jesus Christ. Nor does our walk guarantee the work of God. The Holy Spirit alone does that, dwelling in us and constraining us as such. But where the work of the Father who alone can do it is done, where it is guaranteed by the only One who can guarantee it, His Holy Spirit, it is inevitable that it should be honoured and attested by the walk of Christians. This is the intention and the demand of the imperatives addressed to them.

That is one side of the matter. But the other is equally and even more insistent, that the New Testament clearly differentiates its own time, the time of the community in the world, from the time of the new present of the Crucified and Risen, not merely looking back to His appearance and action to understand it again and again as a present event, yet looking forward to it, knowing and presupposing that He has come, but awaiting and expecting the coming of the Lord in His new Easter form, understanding Him in that way too as the One who is already present, who knocks at the door to-day and here.

The differentiation of the times does not, of course, affect as such the action and revelation of the Crucified as He was made eternal and therefore always present in His resurrection and for every age from the days of His resurrection. It does not, therefore, alter the fact of the relation of the time of the community in the world with that time, the reality of the life from the dead which is here and now an event in the community and therefore in the world in virtue of that time, the actuality of the alteration of the human situation which has taken place in the death of Jesus Christ in virtue of His resurrection from the dead. It does not in any way limit this or call it in question. In the New Testament there is no minimising of what it clearly says along these lines, of what it had to say in view of the actual death and resurrection of Jesus Christ from which it derived and to which it bore witness, of what it had to say in view of the fact that His death was absolutely present in the power of the verdict of the Holy Spirit spoken in the resurrection of the Crucified.

But the differentiation of the times does affect the manner of the making present of the Crucified and His living word and effective action, the form of the relation of His time with that of the community in the world which followed it, the form of its life out of and with the life of the Resurrected, the appearance of the alteration of the human situation as it took place there and

then. The New Testament understands the being of Jesus Christ as the One [323]
who rose from the dead not only as the being of the One who was and is as
such, but of the One who comes and is as such. Therefore it understands its
own time, in the present of the One who was there and then, as the time of the
expectation of and hope in, the One who is also future as the One that He was
and is.

The men of the New Testament, therefore, have not ceased to look forward
to Him with the men of the Old. On the contrary, those to whom He has come,
those who could know Him as the One who has come, who did not do so, but
then did do so in truth, were the first to learn to read and understand the Old
Testament as the book of those who looked forward to Him, the record of
prophecy. They were the first to know that their Old Testament predecessors
could and had to look forward to Him, and the reason why they could and had
to do so. Knowing the event for which these others had looked, and as it had
now taken place and was present, knowing the present of that event, they are
the first to know what is meant by future and expectation and hope.

From the present of the Crucified in which they stand, trusting and obeying
the divine verdict, they reach forward to a new and different and complete
and definitive form of His presence. From the relation of His time with theirs
they stretch out to a new form of this relation. From their life from and with
the life of the Resurrected they stretch out to a new form of life with Him.
From the alteration of the human situation which He has brought about and
in which they stand, they stretch out to its definitive manifestation.

As they do this, they no longer see the two times together (that of Jesus
Christ and their own), but they come to distinguish them. The time of Jesus
Christ is marked off from their own as not merely present but future, the time
which has still to come but is expected and hoped for. And their own time (in
and with its retrospective unity with the time of Jesus Christ) becomes to them
a time between the times. It is the time between the times of the crucified and
risen Jesus Christ, between a first and present form of His presence and a form
which is still to come but will come, between the present form of life with Him
and a future form, between the present manifestation of the alteration of the
human situation and a future manifestation.

Strangely enough the position of the men of the New Testament has on this
so-called eschatological aspect an unmistakable similarity with the being of
Jesus Christ Himself between His death and resurrection, with His being in the
tomb, where the rendering of the obedience demanded of Him as the Son, in
the fulfilment and suffering of the divine judgment, of the offering of the
sacrifice which redeems the world, is already as completely behind Him as the
grace of God the Father in His reawakening is before Him. The time of the
community and the world after the first time of Jesus, and before the second
time which has now come into view, has a similarity with the three days which [324]
in the New Testament record and testimony form a puzzling interval between
the two great acts of God by and in Jesus Christ.

In this respect we have to note that Christians recognise and confess their position between the times. They are those who believe in the Jesus Christ crucified for them and hope in the Jesus Christ raised again for them. Paul describes them in fact as those who—in their baptism—are buried with Christ: συνετάφημεν αὐτῷ[EN380] (Rom. 6⁴), συνταφέντες αὐτῷ[EN381] (Col. 2¹²). And we have to ask very seriously what it means for the Pauline understanding of baptism, and the understanding of baptism generally, that Christians are called, not those who are dead or raised again with Christ in their baptism, but those who in it are buried with Him.

We must now try to give some account of the basis, the meaning, the *ratio*[EN382], of this differentiation of the times. How is it that the risen One is future, that we look, therefore, for a new and different form of His *parousia*, His living presence? We must be careful not to formulate the answer in a way which would give to this final coming and consummation any other necessity than that of the free grace of God. The New Testament does not do this. It confesses the One who was and is as the One who comes, who will come at the end of this time and all times, at the last day. But it does not deduce this statement from any general insight or truth. The resurrection of Jesus Christ gives us the insight that He is the Lord of time. And from this we might argue that He who was and is cannot be without being the One who comes. But the well-known text in Revelation which describes Him in this threefold way is a three-fold witness to Him as the Lord of time, not an analysis of the concept of time. As the One who lives eternally He does in fact demand this threefold witness. The verdict of God pronounced in His resurrection tells us that He not only was and is but also will be, not only at the end of time, but as Himself the end of time. He is not, therefore, just one future of men and the world behind and after which there might be others. He is the absolute and final future. The verdict of God forbids the men of the New Testament to be satisfied with Jesus Christ as the One who was, as the One who is in the time of the community in the world which follows, as the One who will continue to be in that time. It forbids them to "hope in Christ only in this life" (1 Cor. 15¹⁹), that is, to hope only for continuations of His present in the mode in which He now is the One He was. The verdict of God commands that they should look afresh to Himself beyond the whole future of their present being in and with Him, beyond the whole present manifestation of the alteration of the human situation as accomplished in and by Him, beyond all the deduction which they themselves can now draw from it. It commands that they should look afresh to Himself as the final future of the world and man, their own ultimate and definitive future.

[325] The verdict of God wills this from them. Jesus Christ Himself, empowered by the Father and operative by His Holy Spirit, attests and proves Himself to them not only as the First but also as the Last (Rev. 1¹⁷, 2⁸), and therefore as the One who comes (Rev. 1⁴ ⁸). By the free grace of God He is this Last, the One who

---

[EN380] we have been buried with him
[EN381] having been buried with him
[EN382] ground

comes. That and that alone is the necessity of expectation, and therefore of the differentiation of the times attested in the New Testament.

We have to emphasise this strongly because there is a temptation to base and deduce the New Testament hope of the final presence of Jesus Christ not from Himself but pragmatically from a state of things in the time after the end of the forty days, the time of the community in this world, a state which points forward to and demands a consummation. There is a temptation to deduce it from the imperfection of the form of present of the Crucified in this our own time, from the incompleteness of the form of its relation with the time of Jesus Christ, from a deficiency in the present form of life by and with the life of the Resurrected, from the insufficiency of the present manifestation of the alteration of the human situation which has come about with His death, in short, from a limitation of the presence and action and revelation of the living Jesus Christ as we have it in this our time.

That in this our time of the community in the world there is this limitation of His being with us and ours with Him cannot be denied. We have already mentioned some of the aspects in which it may be stated. There is the indispensability of an indirect and historical connexion with Him in the service or as a garment of the true and direct connexion which He Himself institutes and continues between Himself and us from the right hand of the Father. Again, there is the isolation of the community which confesses Him in faith and serves Him in love in a world in which He appears to be and to remain a stranger. Again, there is the hiddenness of the calling and sanctification and justification and divine sonship even of Christians. Again, there is the focussing of the light of His resurrection on a sphere which, apart from the forty days, seems afterwards as well as before to be very like that of the dead bones of Ezekiel. All these things speak plainly of the existence of this limitation. And we might go on to ask: Where is the alteration of the human situation, the peace and joy of man converted to God? Where are the tears wiped away, and no more death, the pain removed, the sorrow stilled, the hurt healed, not to speak of the silencing of the groaning of non-human creation? Where is then the new heaven and the new earth, the old passed away and all things become new? In a word, where is the kingdom of Jesus Christ as it has come on earth in virtue of His resurrection? Again, where is the right there established? Where is life in the power of the justification there accomplished? At bottom, and in the last resort, it may not be wise to ask these questions in this time of ours. But we certainly *can* ask them in this time of ours. And who can dispute that the presence and action and revelation of the living Lord in this our time, the time [326] of the community in the world, have in fact this limitation?

And now the temptation arises to find the basis for His eternal future and the Christian hope directed towards it simply in these statements and questions, to regard it as the answer which we necessarily have to give to these questions, the necessary making good of these very obvious deficiencies, the necessary removing of this undeniable limitation. But it cannot be grounded in this way, and it ought not to be regarded in this way.

The New Testament was well enough aware of the limitation of its own time and all that is in it. There are no illusions about the presence or actuality of this limitation. It does not describe the world or the community or even the existence of individual Christians in optimistic terms, but very soberly, with an awareness of the presence of this limitation, and therefore with an incisiveness of judgment on the actual state of affairs which has always been to the detriment of an optimistic outlook, and which has prevented quite a number from thinking that they can accept the good news which it nevertheless proclaims.

But it was definitely not with the presence of this limitation that the men of the New Testament began when they hoped for the coming of the Lord and prayed: "Even so, come, Lord Jesus." In the last resort they did not simply cry to heaven out of the depth of human imperfection, corruption and need, out of the depth of the visible and palpable contradiction of the world, out of the depth of the sorrow of creation also crying to heaven. They did not attempt a rash assault on heaven: "O Saviour, rend the heavens in twain, And from the heavens descend again." They did not picture and in some sense posit a God who would reveal Himself and help them, or Jesus Christ as such, as some kind of *Deus ex machina*, eagerly and with expectation hoping for Him and looking to Him. They certainly expected the removal of that limitation at His return. But they did not postulate and prove His return because they wanted that limitation removed, because their confinement by it seemed intolerable. They lived with a burning longing for the sight denied them in this time, for the liberation and redemption which are still to come, for an immediacy of contact with the Lord without the help or the distraction of mediation, for the breaking down of the wall of partition between the Christian community and a world which is a-Christian or non-Christian or anti-Christian, for the manifestation of the Judge, for the revelation of their own divine sonship, for the general resurrection of the dead. But they had this burning longing because they looked for Jesus Christ Himself. And they looked for Him because He Himself in His present as the Crucified and Resurrected as He encountered them in this time showed Himself to them as the One He once was, as the One [327] who was with them and indeed in them, but also as the One who stood before them as eternally future. They looked for Him because as they came from Him, as He went with them and they had to go with Him, they were necessarily aware that He comes to us and we must go forward to Him. He "encloses us before and behind" (Ps 139⁵), and therefore altogether and in eternity. That we are in Him is true unreservedly and without any loophole for escape.

They knew only too well their human and Christian poverty and need, as we see from the apostle Paul (Rom. 7). But it was not this which compelled them to look in this dimension, to look forward to a final and eternal future quite different from any temporal future. It was the fulness of Jesus Christ Himself, "the breadth and the length and the height and the depth" (Eph. 3¹⁸), the

3. *The Verdict of the Father*

fulness of the love and power of God active in Him and speaking through Him, the fulness of the revelation and knowledge given to them in His present in spite of and in that limitation, which invited and indeed summoned them to this forward looking. It was not, therefore, that Jesus Christ was too small for them within this limitation, that the salvation and life given them in Him were too little and mean and deficient. Even within this limitation they knew and believed and loved Him as the One who lives eternally, and they found that they themselves, and indirectly the whole world which God loved in Him, were granted eternal life and true and heavenly benefits. Was there not present in Him everything that was still lacking even to the new heaven and the new earth? The triumph-songs into which Paul burst at the end of 1 Cor. 15 and Rom. 8, the majestic assurances in the introduction to Ephesians, the well-known words in John about the eternal life which those who believe already have, all refer to that being of man accepted by Christians now, on this side of the coming of Jesus Christ envisaged in the New Testament, on this side of all that is hoped from and with that coming. And when we read passages like this we might well ask where is the deficiency or limitation—what is still lacking—in His present action and revelation.

Indeed, His final coming is not something which is still lacking in His present action and revelation, but positively, the finality proper to it which opens up to Christians as it takes place in the mode of their present time. The eschatological perspective in which Christians see the Crucified and Resurrected and the alteration of their own situation in Him is not the minus-sign of an anxious "Not yet," which has to be removed, but the plus-sign of an "Already," in virtue of which the living Christ becomes greater to them and altogether great, in virtue of which they here and now recognise in Him who is the first word the final word, in Him who is the subject and object of the basic act of God the subject and object of the consummating act of God which reveals that basis, so that believing in Him and loving Him they can also hope in Him; in Him—and because in Him in the removal of that limitation in which He is now present and revealed and within which they here and now [328] find themselves with Him; in Him, and because in Him the setting aside of that fatal "still" which also characterises their Here and Now. That in this their time, the time of the community in the world, they can only look forward to the removal of the barrier, does not mean that their present being in and with Him is in any way minimised, but that it is augmented, that it is immeasurably deepened and enriched in its extent. For all that it is provisional, this time between is made for them a time of joy, in which every moment and every hour means not simply the continuation of that which has been received, not simply an advance in the consequences which can be drawn from it, but also the approach of the making absolute of that which has been received, of its new and definitive form: not in virtue of their human faithfulness and effort, but in virtue of the new and conclusive act of the Giver Himself proclaimed to them (in and with what they have received), in virtue of His grace and the fact that

He is alive for evermore. Between the New Testament relating of the times, to which we referred earlier, and the differentiating, between the fact that the men of the New Testament come from the Crucified and Resurrected and the fact that they move towards Him, there is therefore no contradiction. How could they come from Him if they did not move towards Him? How could He Himself have come, how could He have been truly delivered up for our offences and raised again for our justification, if He were not also the One who comes as the eternal future of man and the world? Conversely, how could He come as such if He had not already come, if He had not done all that had to be done for the reconciliation of the world with God, for its conversion to Him, if He had not done all that was necessary in the way of additional revelation for its consummation?

It is, therefore, clear that between that view of the human situation which comes from a relating and that which comes from a differentiating of the times there cannot be more than a formal antithesis. From both standpoints it is the situation which has been radically and irrevocably altered in the crucifixion of Jesus Christ. It is only the manifestation of the alteration that is different in the time which moves from the sign of the ascension to its end. It is only a provisional manifestation which will yield to the final in the time of that coming and revelation of the Resurrected which we still await. The one crucified and risen Jesus Christ is the object of New Testament faith and the content of New Testament hope. There can, therefore, be no question of understanding the alteration as more real and complete in its final form and less real and complete in its provisional. As we are told in 2 Cor. 3^{18}, in His image we are "changed from glory to glory" ("from one distinctness to another": Luther). Yet it is also the case that the great alteration in the provisional form in which [329] we know it in this interim is directed and looks forward to its final manifestation. It is directed and looks forward to it. We know it now in its first and earthly and temporal manifestation, not in its second and heavenly and eternal. In the New Testament as such there can be no disputing that the alteration of the human situation has taken place, just as there can be no disputing that the death and resurrection of Jesus Christ have taken place. In the power of the divine verdict they are a present event in this time between. But with a frequency which borders on regularity a distinction is made—corresponding to that between the first and the second times of Jesus Christ Himself—between the form and manifestation of the alteration which is known to us and the future and definitive manifestation which is not yet known to us but has still to come.

For reasons which we can well understand this distinction is very prominent in the New Testament. We cannot do more than indicate it by recalling the various passages. In formal contradistinction to the statements concerning our resurrection as it has already taken place in Jesus Christ, we know "that he which raised up the Lord Jesus shall raise up us also with Jesus" (2 Cor. 4^{14}, cf. 1 Cor. 6^{14}). "As in Adam all died, even so in Christ shall all be made alive" (1 Cor. 15^{22}). "If we be dead with Christ, we believe that we shall also live with him"

(Rom. 6⁸). "He that raised up Christ from the dead shall also quicken your mortal bodies by his Spirit that dwelleth in you" (Rom. 8¹¹). "He that soweth to the Spirit shall of the spirit reap life everlasting" (Gal. 6⁸). Our Lord Jesus Christ died for us, that "we should live with him" (1 Thess. 5¹⁰). "We always bear about in our body the dying of the Lord Jesus, that the life also of Jesus might be manifest in our body. For we which live are always delivered unto death for Jesus' sake, that the life also of Jesus might be made manifest in our mortal flesh" (2 Cor. 4¹⁰ᶠ·). To the same category there belongs perhaps the saying in 2 Cor. 1¹⁰ about the God "who delivered us from so great a death, and doth deliver: in whom we trust that he will yet deliver us." If these are all statements which also describe the event which has already taken place and the standing of Christians as determined by it, and if for the most part they also bring out the ethical imperative, it is unmistakable that in the second instance they have to be understood temporally, speaking of something future which is the goal and purpose of that which has already happened and is now happening.

To look in this dimension too belongs inseparably to the glory of the present standing of man as grounded in the death and resurrection of Jesus Christ. It is impossible to hope in Christ only in this life (1 Cor. 15¹⁹). The doctrine of a certain Hymenaeus and Philetus that the resurrection (i.e., the general resurrection of the dead) is already past ($\check{\eta}\delta\eta$ $\gamma\epsilon\gamma o\nu\acute{\epsilon}\nu\alpha\iota$)—something similar seems to have been taught by those who denied the resurrection in 1 Cor. 15—is for that reason sharply rejected in 2 Tim. 2¹⁸ as a deviation from the truth. Being made conformable ($\sigma\upsilon\mu\mu o\rho\phi\iota\zeta\acute{o}\mu\epsilon\nu o\varsigma$) to the death of Christ, that event being already behind him, or present in the power of His resurrection, Paul is only pressing on to his resurrection from the dead: "Not as though I had already attained, either were already perfect: but I follow after, if that I may apprehend that for which I am apprehended of Christ Jesus ... forgetting those things which are behind, I reach forth unto those things which are before, and press toward the mark for the prize of the high calling of God in Christ Jesus" (Phil. 3¹⁰ᶠ·). And in Col. 3³ᶠ·, "Ye are dead, and your life is hid with Christ in God ($\kappa\acute{\epsilon}\kappa\rho\upsilon\pi\tau\alpha\iota$ᴱᴺ³⁸³: we can hardly help thinking here of an *analogatum*ᴱᴺ³⁸⁴ of the great *analogans*ᴱᴺ³⁸⁵ of the being of Christ in the tomb, on which there is in fact a play some verses later). When Christ, who is our life, shall appear, then shall ye also appear with him in glory.". "We through the Spirit wait for the (fulfilment of the) hope of righteousness by faith" (Gal. 5⁵). "We wait for the adoption"($\upsilon\acute{\iota}o\theta\epsilon\sigma\acute{\iota}\alpha$ᴱᴺ³⁸⁶) in so far as this is "the redemption of our body" (Rom. 8²³). "Now are we the sons of God, and it doth not yet appear what we shall be: but we know that, when he shall appear, we shall be like him, for we shall see him as he is" (1 Jn. 3²). "Blessed be the God and Father of our Lord Jesus Christ, which according to his abundant mercy hath begotten us again unto a lively hope by the resurrection of Jesus Christ from the dead"—the hope of" an inheritance incorruptible, and undefiled, and that fadeth not away, reserved in heaven for you, who are kept by the power of God through faith unto salvation ready to be revealed in the last time" (1 Pet. 1³ᶠ·). If by the resurrection of Jesus Christ from the dead we have been born again to a life which we now live in hope, then already we are the children of God, already *per definitionem*ᴱᴺ³⁸⁷ we have been rightly instituted as heirs (Gal. 4⁷, Rom. 8¹⁷)—joint-heirs with Christ, those who await that inheritance, those who have the certain promise of it (Gal. 3²⁹, Heb. 9¹⁵). The kingdom of God in its final and definitive form is the inheritance promised to His children (Gal. 5²¹). Already, in Jesus Christ, as brothers of the Son of God, we have a legal right to this inheritance. But, of course,

[330]

ᴱᴺ³⁸³ has been hidden
ᴱᴺ³⁸⁴ analogy drawn
ᴱᴺ³⁸⁵ basis of analogy
ᴱᴺ³⁸⁶ adoption
ᴱᴺ³⁸⁷ by definition

we have not yet entered into it. It has not yet been divided and handed over. We still wait and hope for it in this time between. This will be the revelation of our hidden sonship. Already in what we are and have here and now, in the being and work of the Spirit in us, we have an instalment (ἀρραβών EN388, 2 Cor. 1²², 5⁵; Eph. 1¹⁴) of this future possession, or a first-fruits, or a gift from the income (ἀπαρχή EN389, Rom. 8²³) on the capital of this future inheritance as it is laid up for us and appointed and assured to us as the brothers of Jesus Christ and the children of God. We possess it in a way which corresponds to the manner of this possession, eternal life. We possess it as the gift of God's grace of which we ourselves cannot dispose (Rom. 8²³). We do possess it as such. Our hands are not altogether empty. But we only have an instalment, a first-fruits, not the capital, not the kingdom of God which is promised. Even in this possession we cannot cease to pray: "Thy kingdom come."

It is all provisional: not our new creation and regeneration as accomplished in the cross and resurrection of Jesus Christ, but its present manifestation; not our justification, but its present form; not the being of Jesus Christ in us and our being in Him, but the form in which we are now with Him, raised and quickened and resurrected with Him. This is the reference of the New Testament differentiation of the times and the corresponding depiction of the situation. According to 2 Cor. 5¹ᶠ· we now live in a tent which has to be dissolved, knowing that "we have a building of God, an house not made with hands, eternal in the heavens." Therefore we sigh and groan, not to be unclothed and found naked, but to be clothed upon with this eternal οἰκητήριον EN390, or negatively, for mortality to be swallowed up by life, according to 1 Cor. 15⁵⁴, and death in victory. According to 1 Cor. 15⁴²ᶠ·, it will be sown in corruption, raised in incorruption, sown in dishonour, raised in glory, sown in weakness, raised in power, sown a natural body and raised a spiritual body. According to 1 Cor. 15⁵³, this "corruptible must put on incorruption, and this mortal must put on immortality." Even in the sowing, the passing, the dying and the burying of our temporal life we are a new creation, born again, the children of God, justified, partakers of the Holy Spirit. But this whole reality of our being in and with Christ is not visible in this sowing. What is visible is the temporal, the sowing as such, but the eternal which is to be raised up is invisible (2 Cor. 4¹⁸). What is visible is the destruction of the outward man which perishes day by day, but the renewal of the inward man which forbids us to be discouraged is invisible (2 Cor. 4¹⁶). What is visible is the present θλῖψις EN391 which causes us to sigh, but that this will quickly pass and is light, that "it worketh for us a far more exceeding and eternal weight of glory" (2 Cor. 4¹⁷), that the sufferings of this present time are not worthy to be compared with the glory which [331] shall be revealed in us" (Rom. 8¹⁸), that the earnest expectation of the rest of creation does not wait in vain for the revelation of us the children of God (Rom. 8¹⁹ᶠ·), that love will not perish when prophecy and tongues and knowledge are done away with every else that is transitory (1 Cor. 13⁸ᶠ·): all this is invisible. It is something which can be seen when we look not at that which is seen but at that which is not seen (2 Cor. 4¹⁷). σκοπεῖν τὰ μὴ βλεπόμενα EN392: according to the explanation in Rom. 8²⁴ᶠ·, which almost amounts to a definition, it is the nature of hope to wait patiently (δὶ ὑπομονῆς ἀπεκδέχεσθαι EN393) for the coming, at that day, of the revelation of this invisible.

Hence the antithesis in 1 Cor. 13¹²: "For now we see through a glass darkly; but then face to face: now I know in part; but then shall I know even as also I am known." And the even

---

EN388 down-payment
EN389 first-fruits
EN390 dwelling
EN391 suffering
EN392 seeing what is not seen
EN393 we wait for it with patience

simpler antithesis in 2 Cor. 5[7]: "We walk διὰ πίστεως EN394 and not διὰ εἴδους EN395. The two manifestations or forms of the alteration of the human situation, which has taken place in Jesus Christ and is now in train, differ comprehensively in this way: in the one it is invisible, or only indirectly visible, in the other it is visible in the true and direct sense; in the one it is hidden, in the other it is revealed. The faith of the community in the world is, therefore, essentially bound up with hope, with the confidence that the reality which is now believed will be seen. ἐσώθημεν EN396 is the in itself complete and unassailable statement of New Testament faith as far as concerns the human situation, but τῇ ἐλπίδι ἐσώθημεν EN397 (Rom. 8[24]), in a state of hope in a revelation of this redemption which has still to come—for hope which is seen is not hope—which is still awaited with the new and definitive coming of the crucified and risen Jesus Christ.

Perhaps the strongest New Testament account of this New Testament faith, which is not only bound up with hope but ultimately identical with it, is the eleventh chapter of the Epistle to the Hebrews. It is not for nothing that this is the New Testament passage in which the human situation *post Christum natum*EN398 is most strongly related to the Advent situation of the men of the Old Testament (or *vice versa*). It begins with that statement which has the force of a definition: "Faith is an assurance of things hoped for, a conviction of things not seen (ἐλπιζομένων ὑπόστασις ἔλεγχος οὐ βλεπομένων—it may be asked seriously whether the Vulgate for all its obscurity: *sperandarum substantia rerum, argumentum non apparentium*EN399, does not come closer to what is meant than the customary modern translation in German, French and English). The statement is then made in v. 2 that in the faith which they had in God as defined in this way the elders (πρεσβύτεροι) obtained confirmatory witness. This is illustrated with variations by the examples of Abel, Enoch, Noah, Abraham, Isaac, Jacob, Moses, and the harlot Rahab, with references to the Judges Gideon, Barak, Samson and Jephtha, to David and Samuel, and to the prophets. Yet in their day they were never granted to see that which was promised (v. 39), the πράγματα ἐλπιζόμενα EN400, the οὐ βλεπόμενα EN401. They will not therefore (v. 40) be made perfect without us, but with us, for whom God has laid up a new and better promise. And in the continuation in Heb. 12[1f.] this is shown to mean that formally we have the same faith as this "cloud of witnesses." On a better presupposition we, too, are in Advent. We look forward in hope. We are on the way to the fulfilment, τελείωσις. In v. 8 it is said of Abraham that "by faith, when he was called to go out into a place which he should after receive for an inheritance, he obeyed; and he went out, not knowing whither he went"; and again, that dwelling in tents—we are irresistibly reminded of 2 Cor. 5[1f.]—"he looked for a city which hath foundations, whose builder and maker is God." Similarly it is said of Moses in v. 27: "By faith, he endured, as seeing him who is invisible." And of all those so far mentioned it is said in vv. 13–16: "These all died in faith, not having received the promises, but having seen them afar off, and were persuaded of them and embraced them, and confessed that they were strangers and pilgrims on earth. For they that say such things declare plainly that they seek a country. And truly, if they had been mindful of that country from whence they came out, they might have had opportunity to have returned. But now they desire a better country, that is, an heavenly: wherefore God is not ashamed to be called their God: for he hath prepared for them a city."

[332]

EN394 by faith
EN395 by sight
EN396 we have been saved
EN397 we have been saved in hope
EN398 after the birth of Christ
EN399 the substance of what is to be hoped for, the proof of what is not apparent
EN400 things hoped for
EN401 things not seen

It is relevant to recall at this point what Calvin said concerning the relationship of *fides*[EN402] and *spes*[EN403] at the end of the great chapter *Inst.* III, 2 and with reference to Heb. 11. Like the other Reformers, he was not always at his best when dealing with eschatology. But this exposition can claim to be a genuine interpretation of the twofold view of things that we find in the New Testament. Preferring the Vulgate rendering, Calvin paraphrases (*ad loc.* 41) the definition of Heb. 11[1] in this way: that the *substantia*[EN404], the object and content of the promise, is the true basis of faith, the *fulcrum, cui pia mens innititur et incumbit*[EN405]. On this basis faith, as a grasping of the content and object of the promise, is a *certa quaedam et secura possessio eorum quae nobis a Deo promissa sunt*[EN406]. But we must be clear that until the last day, when (according to Dan. 7[10]) the books will be opened, this that is promised us by God is too high to be apprehended by our reason or seen with our eyes or grasped by our hands. We have to remember that we cannot possess it except as we go beyond all the capacities of our own spirit, looking beyond everything that is in the world, in a *superar* (transcending) of ourselves. To help us to do this Heb. 11[1] adds that in this *securitas possidendi*[EN407] we have to do with things that stand in hope and are therefore invisible. The expression ἔλεγχος οὐ βλεπομένων[EN408] (which Calvin renders *index non apparentium*[EN409]) gives us the unavoidable paradox that faith is the *evidentia non apparentium rerum*[EN410], the *visio eorum, quae non videntur*[EN411], the *perspicuitas obscurarum*[EN412], the *praesentia absentium*[EN413], the *demonstratio occultarum*[EN414], in short, the seeing and apprehending of that mystery of God, which in itself cannot be seen or apprehended, by the Word of God which speaks for itself and is in itself certain. Where there is a living faith in the Word of God, Calvin continues (*ad loc.* 42), it cannot be otherwise than that that faith should have hope as its inseparable companion, or rather, that it should beget and create it. If we have no hope, we can be sure that we have no faith. Those who believe, those who apprehend the truth of God with the certainty which corresponds to it, which is demanded and imparted by it, expect that God will fulfil the promises which He has spoken in truth. At bottom hope is simply the expectation of what faith believes as that which God has truly promised. *Ita fides Deum veracem credit: spes expectat, ut in temporis occasione veritatem suam exhibeat; fides credit, nobis esse patrem: spes expectat, ut se talem erga nos semper gerat; fides datam nobis vitam aeternam credit: spes expectat, ut aliquando reveletur; fides fundamentum est, cui spes incumbit: spes fidem alit ac sustinet*[EN415]. Waiting quietly for the Lord, hope restrains faith, preventing it from rushing forward in too great a hurry. It confirms it so that it does not waver in its trust in God's promises or begin to doubt. It revives it so that it does not grow weary. It keeps it fixed on its final goal so that it

---

[EN402] faith

[EN403] hope

[EN404] substance

[EN405] pivot, on which the godly mind rests and leans

[EN406] sure and certain possession of those things which have been promised to us by God

[EN407] security of possessing

[EN408] 'conviction of things not seen'

[EN409] indication of what is not apparent

[EN410] evidence of things not apparent

[EN411] seeing of those things which are not seen

[EN412] perspicuity of obscurities

[EN413] presence of absences

[EN414] revelations of secrets

[EN415] Thus faith believes God to be true; hope expects that he will show his truth at a point in time. Faith believes that he is our Father; hope expects that he will always act as such a one towards us. Faith believes that eternal life has been given to us; hope expects that it will at some time be revealed to us. Faith is the basis on which hope rests. Hope nourishes and sustains faith

does not give up half-way or when it is in captivity. It continually renews and re-establishes it, thus seeing to it that it continually rises up in more vital forms and perseveres to the end.

We have now made three statements with regard to the resurrection of the crucified Lord Jesus Christ. The first was that it has to be understood wholly and exclusively as an act of God. The second was that in relation to the crucifixion it is a new and independent act of God in which the former is acknowledged and proclaimed as the act of obedience of the Son of God which has taken place for the redemption and salvation of all men. The third was the decisive one which we have just considered and to which we had to give the greatest attention, that the resurrection of Jesus Christ is connected with His death in two ways: in the first *parousia* of the risen Crucified which began on   [333] Easter Day, and in virtue of which He is the same then and now, yesterday and to-day, the One who lives, who has come, who is present; and in His final *parousia*, in which (as the risen Crucified who lives and is present then and now, yesterday and to-day) He is the One who will be revealed and come at the end and as the end of all time and history. Here in particular there is disclosed the possibility and necessity of understanding the death of Jesus Christ, not as a conclusion, but as a beginning, and therefore of considering the existence of man in the light of the decisive word of Christology, of turning to the problem of the sin and justification of man, the problem of the community and the faith of the community. This possibility is disclosed, this necessity created, by the resurrection of Jesus Christ, or more exactly, by the being of the crucified Jesus Christ raised from the dead in His twofold form as the One who has come and is present and the One who is present and has still to come, by the verdict of the Father which has been passed and which is in force in this being of the Resurrected. The interval between the first and the final *parousia* of Jesus Christ is that of the existence of man, and therefore of the secondary problems of the doctrine of reconciliation. But before we come to this conclusion and therefore to the answer to the question raised in this third part of the section, we must make two shorter and concluding statements in relation to the resurrection of Jesus Christ itself. On the resurrection of Jesus Christ there depends the permission and command to proceed from Him, from His person and from the work which He completed in His death. Does it give us this permission, this command? Is it, as we said at the outset, the other side of the end which came upon man and the world in His death? Can we, must we think forward past this happening, this end, because by it—revealed and demonstrated in the being of Jesus Christ as the Resurrected—man and the world are again disclosed, or rather disclosed for the first time in their true reality? What we have said in our first three statements about the resurrection of Jesus Christ still needs formal but important amplification in two ways.

4. The resurrection of Jesus Christ from the dead, with which His first *parousia* begins to be completed in the second, has in fact happened. It has happened in the same sense as His crucifixion and His death, in the human

sphere and human time, as an actual event within the world with an objective content. The same will be true of His return to the extent that as the last moment of time and history it will still belong to time and history. But we need not deal with this question here, because we are not looking backward from His return but forward from His resurrection. To do this as the New Testament does, it is possible and necessary only because it happened in time, as a particular history in history generally, with a concrete factuality. In the course of

[334]

this particular history Jesus Christ appears to His disciples, revealing Himself to them as the One who has risen again from the dead, who is no longer under the threat of death, but under God (Rom. 6^{10}), and therefore as the One who lives to-day as yesterday. That He appeared to them, with all that this implies, that this history took place, is the content of the apostolic *kerygma*[EN416], the theme of the faith of the community which it awakened (1 Cor. 15^{14}). The *kerygma*[EN417] tells us, and faith lives by the fact, that God has ratified and proclaimed that which took place for us, for redemption, for our salvation, for the alteration of the whole human situation, as it will finally be directly and everywhere revealed. That this history has happened crowns and reveals the obedience rendered by the Son, and the grace and mercy of the Father shown with Him and in Him to all men. That it has happened is our justification as it follows the divine and human right established and maintained there. It is itself the verdict of God radically altering the human situation. It is the indication and the actual initiation of the direct and definitive revelation of this justification and alteration as it will be consummated in the second coming of Jesus Christ. In the light of it the community understands itself and its time in the world, and looks forward to its end and goal in the second coming of Jesus Christ. Because the resurrection has taken place just as surely as the crucifixion, the cross of Jesus Christ is to us light and not darkness, and it does not have to be changed from a "bare cross" into something better by the fact that we take up our cross.

We must not miss the differences between the two events. They differ in substance as God's right and God's justification, as end and new beginning, as work and revelation. They also differ as the act of the obedient Son and the act of the gracious Father. They also differ formally in the way in which they take place in the human sphere and human time, and therefore in the way in which they have to be understood as history.

We cannot read the Gospels without getting the strong impression that as we pass from the story of the passion to the story of Easter we are led into a historical sphere of a different kind. It is striking that, as at the beginning of the evangelical narratives, mention is made of the appearance and words of angels. Again there is a full account of how Jesus suffered and was crucified and died, but there is no real account of His resurrection. It is simply indicated by a reference to the sign of the empty tomb. Then it is quietly presupposed in the form of attestations of appearances of the Resurrected. This is all the more striking because the

---

[EN416] proclamation
[EN417] proclamation

Gospels did fully narrate and describe other resurrections, that of Jairus' daughter (Mt. 9^{18-25}), that of the young man at Nain (Lk. 7^{11-16}, and that of Lazarus (Jn. 11)—the latter in a direct and almost plastic way. But here it is not possible to speak of someone superior to Jesus Christ who took Him by the hand and by his word called Him to life from the dead. Here we can think only of the act of God which cannot be described and therefore cannot be narrated, and then of the actual fact that Jesus Himself stood in the midst (Lk. 24^{36}). Whether we take the accounts of the resurrection appearances in detail or put them together, they do not give us a concrete and coherent picture, a history of the forty days. [335] Rather we are confronted by obscurities and irreconcilable contradictions, so that we are surprised that in the formation of the canon no one seems to have taken offence at them or tried to assimilate the various accounts of this happening which is so basically important for the New Testament message. There is the further difficulty that Paul not only presupposes and gives in 1 Cor. 15^{4-7} another account of what happened, which is different again from the Gospels, but that in 1 Cor. 15^8 (cf. Gal. 1^{16}) he connects the appearance to himself (obviously the Damascus experience as presented several times in Acts) with the events of those days, although it took place long after the forty days, and the *schema* of the forty days is thus strangely broken. From this side, too, there is the final point that the reported appearances according to all the New Testament accounts came only to those who by them were quickened to faith in the crucified Jesus Christ. The appearances cannot, in fact, be separated from the formation and development of the community (or of the original form of the community as the narrower and wider circle of the apostles). It was in them that this formation and development took place. None of them is represented as having occurred outside this context.

It is beyond question that the New Testament itself did not know how to conceal, and obviously did not wish to conceal, the peculiar character of this history, which bursts through all general ideas of history as it takes place and as it may be said to take place in space and time. There is no proof, and there obviously cannot and ought not to be any proof, for the fact that this history did take place (proof, that is, according to the terminology of modern historical scholarship).

Even 1 Cor. 15^{4-8} cannot be claimed as an attempt at such a proof, and therefore as an attempt at an external objective assurance that the history did, in fact, take place. For the witnesses to whom Paul appeals with such solemnity are not the outside impartial witnesses which such an attempt would demand. They are the tradition which underlies the community, which calls for a decision of faith, not for the acceptance of a well-attested historical report. They are those who have themselves made this decision of faith, Cephas, the Twelve, five hundred brethren, James, then all the apostles, then finally, and in the same breath, Paul himself. In these well-known verses there is an appeal to faith, not on the basis of Paul's knowledge, but in recollection of the faith which constitutes the community.

No such proof is adduced or even intended in the New Testament. Therefore we ought not to try to deduce such a proof from it. If in modern scholarship "historical ground" means the outline of an event as it can be seen in its "How" independently of the standpoint of the onlooker, as it can be presented in this way, as it can be proved in itself and in its general and more specific context and in relation to the analogies of other events, as it can be established as having certainly taken place, then the New Testament itself does not enable us to state that we are on "historical ground" in relation to the event here recorded. There is no reason to deplore this. After all that we have seen of the nature and character and function of the resurrection of Jesus Christ as the basis, and in the context, of the New Testament message, it is inevitable that this should not be the place for the "historicist" concept of history. There is

[336] also no reason to protest if in common with the creation story and many others, indeed the decisive elements in biblical history, the history of the resurrection has to be regarded and described—in the thought-forms and terminology of modern scholarship—as "saga" or "legend." The death of Jesus Christ can certainly be thought of as history in the modern sense, but not the resurrection.

On the other hand, we should be guilty of a fundamental misunderstanding of the whole New Testament message if, because the history of the resurrection is not history in this sense, we tried to interpret it as though it had never happened at all, or not happened in time and space in the same way as the death of Jesus Christ, or finally had happened only in faith or in the form of the formation and development of faith. Even the use of the terms "saga" and "legend" does not force us to interpret it in this way. If we want to understand what the New Testament says, we must not allow ourselves to be forced into it by the use of these terms—perhaps through confusing them with the term "myth" which does not apply in this context. Even accounts which by the standards of modern scholarship have to be accounted saga or legend and not history—because their content cannot be grasped historically—may still speak of a happening which, though it cannot be grasped historically, is still actual and objective in time and space. When we have to do with the kind of event presented in such accounts, the event which has actually happened although it cannot be grasped historically, it would be better to speak of a "pre-historical" happening. But whatever terms we select to describe the New Testament records of the resurrection and their content, it is quite certain that we do not interpret them, i.e., we do not let them say what they are trying to say, if we explain away the history which they recount, a history which did take place in time and space, and that not merely in the development of a conception of the disciples, but in the objective event which underlay the development.

The problem narrows itself down to this final point. It is certainly a unique thing which the New Testament records in so singular a manner at this decisive point in its message. But that it has necessarily to do with an event is something which cannot be disputed on any exegesis which is in any way sound or permissible. And we can widen the circumference of agreement which can be presupposed: the New Testament is speaking of an event in time and space. It must not be overlooked that in this event we have to do on the one hand with the *telos*[EN418], the culminating point of the previously recorded concrete history of the life and suffering and death of Jesus Christ which attained its end with His

---

[EN418] goal

330

resurrection, and on the other hand with the beginning of the equally concrete history of faith in Him, of the existence of the community which receives and proclaims His Word, Himself as the living Word of God. Since the presupposition and the consequence of the Easter message of the New Testament are [337] of this nature, it would be senseless to deny that this message (between the two) does at least treat of an event in time and space. It would be senseless to suppose that it is really trying to speak of the non-spatial and timeless being of certain general truths, orders and relationships, clothing what it really wanted to say in the poetical form of a narrative.

If the latter is the case, what is really intended and expressed in these texts is a veiled cosmology, anthropology, theology or mysticism—a partial consideration of the system of that which is always and everywhere, but which has never taken place as such and never can or will take place. The veil, the poetic form, of the accounts is then this consideration in the form of the report of something that has happened in time and space, a report given with a twitching of the eyelids *ad usum*[EN419] of the esoterics. In these Easter narratives we are dealing with a myth only if we ascribe to their authors, i.e., the original community which formed and handed down the accounts, the intention to speak at this point—and because at this decisive point at many other points as well—of a non-spatial and timeless being (the being of God or the world or man or the religious man) instead of an event which took place in time and space. We are dealing with a myth only if we are challenged by the accounts to separate their true content from their poetic form as narratives, bringing out that content by an idealised, symbolical and allegorical interpretation of the form. Among Christian gnostics and mystics both ancient and modern there have never been lacking exegetes who have been bold to see here the true intention of the New Testament passages and the hermeneutical key to their exposition.

A. E. Biedermann seems to come near to this view of the relationship of content and form in these passages when in his *Dogmatik* (1869) he gives classical form to the distinction between the Christian as the supreme religious "principle" on the one hand, and on the other the personality of Jesus as presented in the Bible and ecclesiastical doctrine and mythologically identified with this principle. He sums up his discussion of the resurrection of Jesus Christ in the words that "when we get back to the real factuality of the story, it was an actualisation in the symbolical form of world-history of that truth which is the heart of the dogma, that to the absolute spirit even the natural finitude of the human spirit necessarily serves as a medium for historical revelation and self-demonstration" (§ 828). But he only appears to be of this view, for he can still speak of the factuality of a story, of the actualisation of that truth in the symbolical form of world-history. He can still describe the resurrection as "a real event in the history of Jesus" which, as such, formed "the foundation of apostolic preaching." The heart of the dogma of the resurrection of Christ is still the impressing into service of the finite spirit of man to reveal the absolute. As he sees it, dogma and history come together in "one point" in the "historical fact" of the resurrection of Christ. The dogma can be deduced from the history because in the latter there has taken place that revelation of the absolute spirit in the finite and human as its "positive medium." "The point of departure of the dogma is an historical event" (§ 588).

We therefore presuppose agreement that a sound exegesis cannot idealise, symbolise or allegorise, but has to reckon with the fact that the New Testament

---

EN419 for the purposes

was here speaking of an event which really happened, as it did when it spoke earlier of the life and death of Jesus Christ which preceded it and later of the formation of the community which followed it. And in relation to modern discussion we can extend the scope of this agreement. Agreement also extends to the fact that we can do justice to the Easter narratives of the New Testament only if we accept their presupposition that in the story which they recount we have to do with an "act of God," the act of God in which it was revealed to the disciples that the happening of the cross was the redemptive happening promised to them, on which therefore the community and its message were founded.

But now we come to our first real decision. In what did this story consist? What was it that God did in this happening?

We might start by saying that the result of it was the awakening and establishing of the faith of the disciples in the living presence and action of Jesus Christ, and by the creation of this Easter faith the laying of the foundation of the community, "the foundation of the apostolic message."

But this statement needs closer definition. According to the New Testament account, it was not in the events of the forty days directly and as such that there took place the beginning of the existence of the community and the going out of the apostles to the people of Jerusalem, let alone to the nations. In the events of the forty days the disciples were ordained and commissioned for this task. But in the strict sense these events are only the presupposition of this happening which began with the story of Pentecost. It is only in and with the outpouring of the Holy Spirit that the faith of the disciples is revealed as such and becomes a historical factor. It is only there that they become what they are here ordained and commissioned to be—those who bear the *kerygma*[EN420]. It is only there that the community develops from its original form as the company of disciples believing in the living Jesus Christ into the Church which grows and expands in the world. It is only there that there is laid the indispensable foundation for this building which does inevitably follow the Easter happening. We can say that this foundation was the faith of the disciples in the living Jesus Christ, and therefore that what took place in the forty days was the laying of this foundation. We have to distinguish between the act of laying a foundation, the creation of a presupposition, and the result of this act or action. In the strict sense the Easter narratives do not speak so much of the result as of the act as such. It may be asked whether an exegesis of the passages will suffice which simply equates the happening described in them and attested as the act of God with the awakening and development of the faith of the disciples, treating everything that does not seem to merge into this—rather after the manner of the exposition which scraps the history altogether—merely as a narrative and mythologising form, which is in the last resort irrelevant for an understanding of the texts and has therefore to be isolated. But the texts are rela-

---

[EN420] proclamation

tively very scanty, or, at any rate, very reserved in the information which, according to this exegesis, is their essential and ultimately their only affirm-   [339] ation, the Easter faith of the disciples.

In this respect ought we not to take warning from the lexicographical observation that the word πίστις EN421 does not occur at all in the Easter narratives and the word πιστεύειν EN422 only in Jn. 20?

What interests these narratives is who and what brought and impelled and drove the disciples to this faith, but not, or not primarily the fact and the manner of their coming to it, of its development in them. They do not tell us anything at all about a tangible form of this faith, unless we are to describe as the form which their faith took at this stage of its formation that confusion and astonishment in face of an incontrovertible fact which is described as the attitude of the disciples. The decisive element in the texts is surely that the disciples did find themselves faced with an incontrovertible fact, a fact which led to the awakening and development of their faith. Are we really giving a true interpretation if we take an aspect which at very best forms only the content of a secondary affirmation and describe it as the true and primary message, that which the texts regarded as the act of God?

Let us accept—as indeed we must—that they were really speaking of the laying of this foundation, the creation of the presupposition of the whole history which followed. Do we explain their particular account of the history which lays this foundation by simply repeating that the real subject of this history is the formation of the faith of the disciples, that this, and at bottom only this, was the real Easter happening? We have seen what this happening is supposed to be. The Easter happening now described in this way is understood as a special act of God. It is certainly understood as a special act of God in the texts. But if it is restricted to the development of the faith of the disciples, what can this mean? A kind of parthenogenesis of faith without any external cause; without any cause in an external event which begets it? A faith which is in the true and proper sense other-worldly? A Nevertheless which reached out defiantly, Prometheus-like, into the void and posits and maintains itself there? A faith which of itself—without any given reason—can explain the figure of the Crucified and recognise in the Crucified the living Lord? A faith which of itself (before the outpouring of the Holy Spirit) is able to reveal and make effective the happening of the cross as a redemptive happening? Is not this a concept of faith of which only God Himself could really be the Subject? Well, nothing is impossible with God. Even according to the texts it was God, and God alone, who created the faith of the disciples—or the original form of faith which is here in question. And certainly God might have created this faith in the form of a *creatio ex nihilo*EN423. But then we should have to reckon with the fact that,

EN421 faith
EN422 to have faith
EN423 creation out of nothing

333

[340]   under the name of faith in the resurrection of Jesus Christ and in Jesus Christ
as the Resurrected, the Church and the New Testament were really believing
in the development of this Easter faith of the disciples as a *creatio ex nihilo*[EN424].
And we should then have to admit that the riddle which replaces the riddle
posed in the texts as they are is not an easier but a much more difficult one.
This interpretation will no doubt please those who think that the truth is most
likely to be found where the paradox is most severe. If only we had one
example in the Bible of God creating a faith out of nothing in this way! If only
the texts gave us some slight indication that in the happening reported by
them they were at bottom treating of such a *creatio ex nihilo*[EN425]! If only they
demanded that we should look in this direction! But most definitely they do
not demand it. Like the rest of the Bible, they speak of a foundation of faith
which comes to those who have it, of a faith which is described in terms of its
object. And it is this foundation, an act of God fashioned as this object, a series
of appearances and sayings of Jesus Christ risen from the dead and raised from
the tomb, which is plainly the theme of their affirmation and the content of
their narrative. That they speak of this (and only in the light of it of the rise of
that original form of the faith of the disciples) is the presupposition of the rest
of the New Testament. Whatever attitude we take up, an exegesis of these texts
has to grapple with the fact that this is the theme of their affirmation and the
content of their narrative.

We have to ask seriously whether the older criticism of the Easter narratives (in the 18th
and 19th centuries) was not in advance of more recent criticism in that it did face squarely
and try to do justice to the problem of the objective foundation of the Easter faith as it is
posed by the meaning and wording of the texts.

Certainly the older criticism took some strange paths. It even supposed—the great
Schleiermacher took this view—that Jesus may have come round from an apparent death.
There were rationalists who did not shrink from explaining the empty tomb by a return to
the hypothesis suggested in Mt. 27[62f.], that the disciples fraudulently removed the body. It is
astonishing that even in our own day no less a figure than R. Seeberg (*Chr. Dog.*, 1925, II,
205) expresses the view that the removal of the body of Jesus might be explained by its being
covered over, and the rolling away of the stone at the entrance to the tomb by tremors
caused by an earthquake. Above all, to explain the appearances of Jesus recourse has been
had to the term "vision." Some have tried to think of them only in terms of the purely
subjective visions of the disciples. Others have had to correct them and go further, speaking
of objective visions, visions which have an objective basis in the corresponding activity of
God or in the continuing power of the personality of Jesus. A. E. Biedermann, for example,
was thinking of this kind of objective vision when (§ 588) he spoke of the resurrection of
Jesus as a "historical event." To-day we rightly turn up our nose at this, because (quite apart
from the many inconsistencies in detail) it all smacks too strongly of an apologetic to explain
away the mystery and miracle attested in the texts. And this is something that cannot be said
of the identification of the Easter event with the rise of the Easter faith, which does not seem
to make the paradox any less but greater. But in favour of these explanations which have now

---

[EN424] creation out of nothing
[EN425] creation out of nothing

gone out of currency we can at least say this, that they did in different ways try to stick to the   [341] question of the concrete derivation of the Easter faith. They did at least keep closer to the texts by not only maintaining but trying to show that the disciples did not come to this faith of themselves, but were brought to it by some factor concretely at work in the world—however perversely this factor might be represented.

This is where the decision must be made. The texts do not speak primarily of the formation of the Easter faith as such but of its foundation by Jesus Christ Himself, who met and talked with His disciples after His death as One who is alive (not outside the world but within it), who by this act of life convinced them incontrovertibly of the fact that He is alive and therefore of the fact that His death was the redemptive happening willed by God. According to the texts, this event of the forty days, and the act of God in this event, was the concrete factor—the concrete factor in its externality, its objectivity, not taking place in their faith but in conflict with their lack of faith, overcoming and removing their lack of faith and creating their faith.

The "legend" of the finding of the empty tomb is not of itself and as such the attestation of Jesus Christ as He showed Himself alive after His death. It is ancillary to this attestation. The one can be as little verified "historically" as the other. Certainly the empty tomb cannot serve as a "historical" proof. It cannot be proclaimed and believed for itself but only in the context of the attestation. But it is, in fact, an indispensable accompaniment of the attestation. It safeguards its content from misunderstanding in terms of a being of the Resurrected which is purely beyond or inward. It distinguishes the confession that Jesus Christ lives from a mere manner of speaking on the part of believers. It is the negative presupposition of the concrete objectivity of His being. Let those who would reject it be careful—as in the case of the Virgin birth—that they do not fall into Docetism. The older criticism of the Gospels already referred to did at least take it seriously—however well or badly it understood and treated it. We would do well to-day not to rush too hastily past it.

According to the texts, and in spite of the obscurities and contradictions with which they speak of it, in spite of their legendary, their non-historical or pre-historical manner of statement, the Easter event is quite plainly one of an encounter, an encounter with God, an act of God to the disciples in which, as before and for the first time, truly—revealed to them and recognised by them as such—God Himself confronted them and spoke with them in the person of Jesus Christ. They beheld the glory of the Word made flesh (Jn. 1^{14}); they heard and handled it (1 Jn. 1^1). In this seeing and hearing and handling, in this encounter, they were brought to faith and they for their part came to faith. We are not required to try to know and to be able to say more of this encounter, of the How of it, than the accounts themselves tell us. We are not required to translate into express terms the inexpressible thing which they attest (as was earlier attempted with theories about the new corporeality of the One who met them or the way in which He was seen and heard and handled). Any such translation can only obscure and efface the decisive thing which is told us.   [342] What we are required to do is to let ourselves be told what the texts do tell us, and whatever our attitude may be—affirmation, rejection or doubt—to stick to that which is told us, not trying to replace it by something that is not told us on the pretext that it needs to be interpreted. And what is told us is that Jesus Christ risen from the dead appeared to His disciples prior to their faith in Him, that He existed as the living One in clear distinction from their own existence as determined not by faith in Him but by lack of faith. What is told us is His action and Word as the object which underlies their faith. They tell us that this happened to the disciples after His death and prior to their faith, and that on this presupposition, taught by this event, knowing Jesus Christ as He gave Himself to be known by them, they later received from Him the Holy Spirit. They did not have Him themselves. They were able only to receive Him from Jesus Christ, in that confrontation in which He had disclosed Himself to them in the Easter period. In this sense the rest of the New Testament looked back to that which is attested in the Easter texts as the beginning of the *parousia* of the Lord in glory, the history which underlies and impels and legitimatises and authorises the *kerygma*[EN426], the history which follows the history of the life and death of Jesus Christ and precedes that of the community in the world, itself a real history within the history of the world.

5. The second amplification that we have to make is again with reference to the connexion between the death and resurrection of Jesus Christ, meaning by His resurrection (as we worked it out under 3.) the whole of His *parousia* as it began with the Easter events and will be completed as the end of all time, but equally His living present in which in the time between the Once and the One Day He is now concealed in God for us, being present and active in the work of the Holy Spirit, but also on earth, in history, in our very midst.

We have so far spoken of two different acts of God and therefore only of the "relationship" between them. But the time has now come when we must use a stronger term. For these are not two acts of God, but one. The two have to be considered not merely in their relationship but in their unity. It is the one God who is at work on the basis of His one election and decision by and to the one Jesus Christ with the one goal of the reconciliation of the world with Himself, the conversion of men to Him.

We have thought of the resurrection as the other side of His death, of the judgment which fell upon Him as our Representative, which therefore passed conclusively and irrevocably upon all men and every individual man in Him. But it is wholly and utterly the other side of "this side." It is the justification of Jesus Christ and our justification and therefore God's own justification in virtue of which life has actually come from this death—the life of Jesus Christ, and our life in Him. We have thought of the resurrection of Jesus Christ as the [343] work of grace of God the Father. But this work of grace is wholly and utterly the answer to the work of obedience of the Son fulfilled in His self-offering to death. This work of grace and this work of obedience as the act of God the Father, Son and Holy Spirit are one work. We have thought of the resurrection of Jesus Christ as God's proclamation and revelation. But what can it proclaim

---

[EN426] proclamation

and reveal, what can it disclose, but the act of reconciliation and redemption once and for all accomplished in His death, in the judgment fulfilled in Him and suffered by Him, the divine Yes already concealed under the No? It brings to light the grace, it puts into effect the mercy, which was God's purpose and goal in the dark event of Golgotha. And if the death of Jesus Christ on the cross is confronted by His life as the Resurrected in all its fulness—in the Easter period, at the right hand of the Father, and among us by the Holy Spirit, until He comes again in glory—yet in all the forms of His life this living One is none other than the One who once was crucified at Golgotha, who there took our place, who in His person allowed our judgment to be visited on Himself, who in that way accomplished our reconciliation with God, our conversion to Him. He lives as the One who has done this for us, and in Him as such we have the promise of our life; in Him our life has already begun. In this unity the death and resurrection of Jesus Christ are together the history of Jesus Christ, and as such the redemptive history to which everything earlier that we might call redemptive history in the wider sense moved and pointed, and from which everything later that we might call redemptive history in the wider sense derives and witnesses. Here in the unity of this death and this resurrection from death that history takes place *in nuce*[EN427]. It is an inseparable unity. We can and must explain each of these two moments by the other. We do not speak rightly of the death of Jesus Christ unless we have clearly and plainly before us His resurrection, His being as the Resurrected. We also do not speak rightly of His resurrection and His being as the Resurrected if we conceal and efface the fact that this living One was crucified and died for us.

But there is something else we have to say concerning this unity. It is the unity of a sequence. It is rather like a one-way street. It cannot be reversed. The crucifixion and death of Jesus Christ took place once. As this happening once it stands eternally before God and it is the basis and truth of the alteration of the human situation willed and brought about by God: from sin to righteousness, from captivity to freedom, from lying to truth, from death to life, our conversion to Him. For that reason the crucifixion and death of Jesus Christ does not ever take place again. But the life of the Resurrected as the life of the Crucified, as it began in that Easter period, and needs no new beginning, is an eternal life, a life which is also continuous in time. And that means that God, and we too, have to do with the Crucified only as the Resurrected, with the one [344] event of His death only as it has the continuing form of His life. There is no Crucified *in abstracto*. There is no preaching of the cross or faith in the cross *in abstracto*. For that reason there are serious objections to all representations of the crucified Christ as such. There is no going back behind Easter morning. To the extent that they may contain or express such a going back, all theologies or pieties or exercises or aesthetics which centre on the cross—however grimly in earnest they may be—must be repudiated at once. "He is not

---

[EN427] in a nutshell

here. He is risen." We must understand clearly what such a going back involves. It involves going back to the night of Golgotha as not yet lit up by the light of Easter Day. It involves going back and into the event of judgment not yet proclaimed and revealed as that of salvation. It involves going back into the sphere where the divine Yes to man which He Himself alone can reveal is still inaccessibly concealed under His No. It involves going back into the death in which all flesh is hopelessly put to death in and with the Son of God. As though we could find Jesus Christ in any other place, as though we could expect to be with Him in any other way, than in the wholeness of His history as it took place according to the witness of the New Testament! As though we had to begin again at the place where He made an end for us and of us! As though He had not done this once and for all for us all! As though—irrespective of the fact that we are not allowed to do this—there were still some place from which we ourselves have to take just one further step! As though it were something other than an act of desperation, or a radically culpable toying, to try to repeat for ourselves that which cannot be repeated because it has been accomplished by God! As though it were something other than the setting up of a new and most frightful law, or an idle fancy, where there is a practical or a theoretical or a cultic attempt to go back in this way, where we have not yet escaped from it and cannot escape from it! The community is not called upon to repeat this act of God, let alone to expect and demand that the world should be ready to do so. In every age, *post Christum*[EN428] means *post Christum crucifixum et resuscitatum*[EN429]. The two are one. The first is included in the second, the death of Jesus Christ in His life, the judgment of God in the grace of God. "Death is swallowed up in victory" (1 Cor. 15⁵⁴). The relationship can never be reversed. The second is no longer closed up and concealed and kept from us in the first, the life of Jesus Christ in His death, the grace of God in His judgment, His Yes in His No. Things can appear in this light only to unbelief, ingratitude, disobedience, and the uncertainty which results from it. It is only where these are present that a blind effort is made to begin with the first, the "bare cross," judgment, the divine No, the Law fulfilled for us in Jesus Christ, the wrath of God which He has suffered once and for all for us. The One who [345] has done this, who in and with Himself has delivered us up to death, reigns and lives to all eternity and dies no more. And in and with Him we have life before us and not death. The way of God the Father, Son and Holy Spirit, the way of the true God, is not a cycle, a way of eternal recurrence, in which the end is a constant beginning. It is the way of myth which is cyclic, an eternal recurrence, summoning man to endless repetitions, to that eternal oscillation between Yes and No, grace and judgment, life and death. We must not mythologise the Gospel of the way of the true God (not even in the name of Kierkegaard or Luther himself). We must not interpret it in terms of a cycle. We must

---

[EN428] after Christ
[EN429] after Christ crucified and raised to life

not make the Christian life and theological thinking and the Church's preaching and instruction and pastoral care like the ox which is bound to a stake and, driven by the owner's whip, has to trot round and round turning the wheel. We must not violently make of Christianity a movement of reaction and think that we can force it on the world in this form. God has rejected from all eternity. He has condemned and judged and put to death in time. He has put all to death in a Son who obediently willed to suffer death in the place of all. And He never comes back to this point. He never begins here. And in faith, in gratitude, in obedience, in the knowledge of His way, we ourselves can only be prevented from beginning here. Rather we are invited, indeed required, to accept this as something that has happened for us and to us, in order that we may go forward with this decision already behind us. God in His own action has Himself gone further along this road, and He summons us to go further. It was for the sake of His electing that from all eternity He rejected. It was in His love that in time He was wroth and condemned. It was to save that He judged. It was to make alive that He put to death. And now He has indeed elected and loved and saved and made alive. And the *telos*EN430 of the way which He has gone in the person and work, in the history of Jesus Christ, is our beginning—His electing, therefore, His love, His saving, His making alive.

Jesus lives—as the One who was crucified for us, as the One who has made an end for us and of us, as the One who once and for all in His resurrection—preventing any going back or looking back—has made a new beginning with us. Jesus lives—as the Lord, not as an indolent, easy-going Lord who invites us to be easy-going, but as a stern Lord. But He is stern in that He prevents us from going back or looking back, demanding that we should take up our little cross—our cross, not His—and follow Him, but follow Him where He Himself has long since carried His own, by way of Golgotha to the throne of God, to lay it down there with all the sin and guilt of the whole world, with our death, and to receive in our name as the obedient Son of the Father the grace of everlasting life. Jesus lives—relieved of the anguish and pain and distress of what He did for us as the Judge judged and the priest sacrificed for us. What we have to do is simply to take this consequence as our starting-point, to enjoy this Sabbath rest with Him as those who hear the message of Easter Day and are obedient to the verdict of the Holy Spirit pronounced there, praying that it may daily be disclosed afresh to us, looking forward in hope to the consummation of His *parousia* and therefore to our redemption, which is grounded in our reconciliation with God as it has already taken place on His cross, which has already begun in His resurrection, in which the disciples beheld His glory. [346]

This is the unity of the act of God in the death and resurrection of Jesus Christ, or, rather, the unity of the act of God in the person and work of His Son, who was put to death for our transgressions, but who now lives for our justification as the guarantor and giver of our life, having been raised from the

---

EN430 goal

339

dead in our mortal flesh. It is a unity which is securely grounded. It is the unity of an irreversible sequence. It is a unity which is established teleologically. Jesus Christ as attested in Holy Scripture is the One who exists in this unity.

In conclusion, we may add that as the One who exists in this unity He is the one Word of God that we must hear, that we must trust and obey, both in life and in death. If the crucified Jesus Christ is alive, if His community is the company of those among whom this is seen and taken seriously, as the axiom of all axioms, then the community cannot take account of any other word that God might have spoken before or after or side by side with or outside this word, and that He willed to have proclaimed by it. It accepts and proclaims this one Jesus Christ as the one Word, the first and final Word, of the true God. In it it hears the Word of all God's comfort, commandment and power. It is altogether bound to this Word, and in it it is altogether free. It interprets creation and the course of the world and the nature of man, his greatness and his plight, wholly in the light of this Word and not *vice versa*. It does not need to accept as normative any other voice than this voice, for the authority of any other voice depends upon the extent to which it is or is not an echo of this voice. As it seeks to know this voice, it is certainly allowed and commanded to hear other voices freely and without anxiety: as an echo of this voice they may share its authority. But it will always come back to the point of wanting to hear first and chiefly this true and original voice, and wanting to give itself to the service of this voice. And because He lives it will always be able to hear this voice which is His voice, and to give itself effectively to the service of this voice. In this respect we can say with Zwingli (and against any supposedly "natural" theology): "The holy Christian Church, whose one Head is Jesus Christ, is born of the word of God. It remains in the same, and it hears not the voice of a stranger."

[347] The living Jesus Christ, who is this one Word of God, is the Crucified, the One who was delivered up to death, and who in His death delivered up to death the world of sin and the flesh and death. But because He is risen and lives we have to add at once: the One who was crucified for us, for the sake of the burning fire of the love of God, for our redemption; who in His death delivered up the world to death in order that reconciled with God it might be a new world; not therefore for the death of the sinner, but that he should be converted and live; not therefore to his destruction but to his salvation. In this light, as the Word of the cross understood in the light of the resurrection of the Crucified, the one Word of God is certainly the word of judgment on all the arrogant pretension with which man would judge and justify himself. It is the disclosing and punishing of the sin which at its root consists in this obstinate ignoring of the truth that we do not need to help ourselves because God is for us and our cause is His cause. The community which hears the one Word of God in virtue of the life of the crucified Jesus Christ is that place in the world where man subjects Himself to this judgment, where he is willing to let it come upon him and to accept its consequences. And the community will not be afraid of the offence and hostility and hatred which come in the world when it

proclaims the message of this judgment which has been passed on all men. It can spare neither itself nor the world in its witness to that which has taken place for its salvation.

But because the risen and living Jesus Christ is the one Word of God, this Word—as the community hears and proclaims it—is the one Word of the divine will and act of reconciliation. It is God's Yes to man and the world, even in the No of the cross which it includes. God says No in order to say Yes. His Word is the Word of that teleologically established unity of the death and resurrection of Christ. It is the Word of the cross as the promise of life, not as the threat of death; as the Gospel, not as the Law; or as the Law only as it judges and directs as Gospel, demanding unconditional trust and total obedience. That is how the community hears this one Word. And it serves it as this one Word. It does not come before the world, therefore, as an accuser, as a prosecutor, as a judge, as an executioner. It comes before it as the herald of this Yes which God has spoken to it. It will be careful not to present God as a jealous competitor, a malevolent opponent or a dangerous enemy. It will not try to conceal the fact that as the Creator God has loved it from all eternity, and that He has put this love into action in the death of Jesus Christ. The community lives by the fact that the first and final Word of God is this Yes. It lives by the freedom in which when it hears this Word it is pledged in advance of the world but also to the world. It lives by the fact that Jesus lives, and therefore for the task of telling this good news to all people, to a people which is troubled because it has not yet been told to it, or not told in such a way that it has brought about its liberation.

We are now in a position to take up again the question we put at the begin- [348] ning of the section, and therefore to conclude the great transitional discussion which was necessary at this point.

The question was as follows: How can we arrive at the perception (grounded in the being of Jesus Christ as the Lord who became a servant, and in His action as the Judge judged for us) that Jesus Christ belongs to us and we belong to Him, that His cause is our cause and our cause is His? How can there be a doctrine of the atonement in a form which is not exclusively christological, a doctrine of the atonement which is a doctrine of the determinations of our own human destiny on a christological basis? We have already seen how this question arises and why it is so acute. Not in the fact of a temporal gulf between Jesus Christ and us, and the need to bridge it. This is one aspect of it, the aspect in Lessing's question. But on this aspect the difficulty is purely conceptual and can be overcome. We have seen that a concern for this difficulty is a movement of flight in an attempt to evade the real kernel of the question which arises in this context. The kernel of the question is simply the incompatibility of the existence of Jesus Christ with us and us with Him, the impossibility of the co-existence of His divine-human actuality and action and our sinfully human being and activity, the direct collision between supreme order and supreme disorder which we perceive when we start with the fact that our contemporaneity with Him has been made possible in the most radical form—and not merely by the device of a concept of time which enables us to accept it. For what will become of us if the real presence of Jesus Christ is going to be a fact in our time and therefore in the sphere of our existence? In face of this contrast and antithesis between Him and us—a contrast which is weighted absolutely in His favour as the Son of God—how can we ever arrive at the perception which is so well grounded in His person and work that He does belong to us and we to Him? How are we to understand that we are His fellows, i.e., those who are represented before God in Him? How dare we ever count on the fact that we are His, and therefore move on from Christology to an anthropology which is embraced by Christology, and in which we have to understand ourselves, us men, as His? In His work, His death on the cross, as the death of our Representative and substitute, it came to pass that, as the sinners and enemies of God we are, we were delivered up to death, and an end was made of us, and we came to an end with this whole world of sin and the flesh and death. Where are we then? And what is there to say of us? Is there something beyond this death, this conclusion, this end of man, in the light of which we can look back on all this and forward from it, to the men we are as those who have a place with Jesus Christ, who do in fact belong to Him because He belongs to them, who are not only there, but as the men they are can be there as His, concerning whose being as His there is therefore something that we dare to say? Is there something beyond this death, this conclusion, this end, in the light of which Christology is not exclusive but inclusive, in the light of which it is false if it is exclusive, in the light of which it can and must compre-hend within itself as yet another element in the doctrine of reconciliation a perception of our sin first, but then of our justification, of the community as the people of justified sinners, of what makes men members of this commun-ity, our faith? Is there something beyond in the light of which we can look forward in this way?

[349]

This was the question, and we have seen what the answer is as it is given by the same New Testament witness which forced us to put the question in this way. The answer is the resurrection of Jesus Christ from the dead, His life as the Resurrected from the dead, the verdict of God the Father on the obedi-ence of His Son as it was pronounced in this event and as it is in force in His being from this event. We must now explain to what extent this event and this being are the answer to our question.

We will develop the answer by running through once more the results or the main points we have just reached under our five heads, but this time in the reverse order, placing them alongside our original question in the expectation that in them—both in detail and as a whole—we shall find that something beyond for which we have been asking.

We begin at once with the result of our fifth and final insight, that the cruci-fied but also the risen and living Jesus Christ is God's Yes to man, which includes God's No, but in such a way that it is a mistake to try to hear the No independently, as a final word, with a validity which is absolute. "Death is swallowed up in victory."

It is death—how can we know what death is if it is not present and revealed to us in the death of Jesus Christ? According to the witness of Scripture our dying took place in the person of the Son of God who died in our flesh as the bearer of our sin and of that of the whole world. Here there came upon us that which had to come upon us as sinners and enemies of God. Here judgment fell upon the world as the only possible form in which God could and would reconcile it with Himself, convert it to Himself. Here—in exact correspondence with what He did as Creator when He separated light from darkness and elected the creature to being and rejected the possibility of chaos as nothingness—He pronounced His relentless and irrevocable No to disordered man. Here, in and with this No, He made an end of that man once and for all. That is why the Lord became a servant, why the Son of God went into the far country in obedience to the Father. That is why He took His way among us as the Judge judged and the Priest sacrificed. As the One who went this way He will be the end of all time. As the world in which and for which He went this way He will in His own person lay it at the feet of the Father (1 Cor. 15^{28}). The judgment on us fulfilled in Him will then be revealed as such.

But if it is true that this Jesus Christ who was crucified and delivered up to death for us is risen and alive, then it is also true that we who are crucified and dead in Him have a future and hope in the light of the judgment and end which has come upon us in Him. For all the strictness of its force, the negative aspect of that "for us," the No which fell upon us in the death of Jesus Christ, has no autonomous or definitive or absolute significance. With His death our death, the death which every man must some day suffer, the death of all flesh, is in fact "swallowed up in victory." But this means that it is revealed and put into effect that the judgment which came on the whole world, on all flesh, in Jesus Christ, is for all its strictness the form in which God willed, and in this judgment effected, the reconciliation of the world with Himself, converting it to Himself, not in its destruction but to its salvation. The No pronounced in the cross of Jesus Christ can and should be heard and accepted only as the necessary and in the true sense redemptive form of His Yes. The subjection of man to this No, to which he is relentlessly compelled, is then revealed as the exaltation which has already come to him by the Yes which is the purpose of the No, under which he is placed, under which he will be placed again and again by Jesus Christ risen again from the dead. It is not that he has first to acknowledge himself rejected by God, then to break through if possible to a discovery and appropriation of his election, calling and redemption. He is rejected, not in his own person, but in that of the one beloved and obedient Son of God. His suffering is only a pale reflection of the great and only true suffering of this One. And if this One who alone is truly rejected, and truly suffers, is revealed in His resurrection from the dead as the One He is,

[350]

343

revealed and confirmed as the beloved and obedient Son of God and therefore as His Elect from all eternity, then in the true rejection and suffering
which He has borne as our substitute and Representative we stand before our
own election, calling and redemption. That which came upon Him—and in
His person us—in His death, under the relentless and irrevocable No of God,
is our reconciliation with God as it took place not at our charge but at His, not
to our disadvantage but to our advantage. It is, then, our conversion to Him,
which cannot be understood only, or even at all in its end and consequence, as
an abdication, a surrender, a destruction, but has to be understood positively
as our setting in fellowship and peace with God, as our adoption as His children and to the inheritance of His children, and therefore as men who have a
future and hope. We are not oppressed and extinguished in the death of Jesus
Christ, but liberated and refashioned. In virtue of the death of Jesus Christ we
are allowed to be. Christology cannot, therefore, be exclusive but inclusive. We
cannot and we must not be afraid of Jesus Christ, or ask Him to depart from us
as Peter did because we are sinful men. We are this. But as the Son of the
[351]   Father He posited Himself for us—really for us and for our salvation—to suffer
in our place the divine rejection, the divine No, the divine judgment, and
faithful to His election to fulfil the divine Yes, the divine grace. As the One who
has done this He was raised again from the dead by the life-giving Spirit. As the
One who has done this He lives as the first-begotten from the dead, and therefore as the word of the divine assent, as God's permission and command that
as the sinners we are we should be there with Him. "I shall not die, but live; and
declare the works of the Lord" (Ps. 118^{17}). Because Jesus Christ the Crucified
is risen again and lives there is room for us and therefore—this is what we
wanted to know—for the problems of the doctrine of reconciliation in our
own anthropological sphere. This is what we gather from our fifth and final
consideration.

Our fourth consideration concerned the historical character of the content
of the Easter stories. Why was it so important to emphasise and underline the
concrete objectivity of the history there attested as against their evaporation
into a history of the development of the Easter faith of the disciples? Certainly
not in order to explain the resurrection of Jesus Christ as a historically indisputable fact. Certainly not to create for faith in the Resurrected a ground in
terms of this world which we can demonstrate and therefore control. Certainly
not to destroy its character as faith, to transform it into an optional knowledge,
which is not moved by any astonishment, which does not demand any contradiction, which does not require any hazard of trust and obedience. This is
opposed, as we have seen, by the decisive content and therefore by the form of
the stories. But the concrete objectivity of the Easter event cannot be interpreted out of the Easter stories. And on the objectivity of that event as the
beginning of the *parousia* of the living Jesus Christ there depends the otherness of His existence, His concrete otherness, the unequivocal way in which we
are placed over against Him, to hear in Him the Yes which has been spoken in

and with and under the No of His death and ours, to find ourselves addressed in Him as those who are liberated from judgment and death, as those who are set in fellowship and peace with God, as those who are adopted as the children of God. This address, He Himself as the One who addresses us in this way, is the basis of our faith. We do not, therefore, only believe that we are called and are the children—on the basis of a parthenogenesis or *creatio ex nihilo*[EN431] of our faith regarded as an act of God. We are the children of God because we who could not say this of ourselves, however strong our faith, are addressed as such by the Son of God who was made flesh and raised again in the flesh—we who in the death of Jesus Christ as it happened concretely and objectively (according to the narratives which precede the Easter story) are judged and put to death and brought hopelessly to our end. If Jesus Christ is not risen— bodily, visibly, audibly, perceptibly, in the same concrete sense in which He died, as the texts themselves have it—if He is not also risen, then our preach- [352] ing and our faith are vain and futile; we are still in our sins. And the apostles are found "false witnesses," because they have "testified of God that he raised up Christ, whom he raised not up" (1 Cor. 15[14f.]). If they were true witnesses of His resurrection, they were witnesses of an event which was like that of the cross in its concrete objectivity. The message that Jesus the Crucified lives, and that in Him there is given us a future and hope and room to be, has force and weight, the force and weight to summon to faith and to awaken faith, only in view of this content of their witness, and most definitely not in view of the fact that in the form of this mythological content they attested only the evocation and development of their own faith. The apostles witnessed that Jesus Christ risen from the dead had encountered them, not in the way in which we might say this (metaphorically) of a supposed or actual immanence of the existence, presence and action of the transcendent God, not in an abstract but in a con- crete otherness, in the mystery and glory of the Son of God in the flesh. He encountered them formally (eating and drinking with them) in the same way as He had encountered them before, and as they for their part encountered Him, as living men in the flesh (eating and drinking with Him)—in a real encounter, themselves on the one side, alive but moving forward to death, and He on the other, alive from the dead, alive no more to die, alive eternally even now in time. We can therefore say quite calmly—for this is the truth of the matter—that they attested the fact that He made known to them this side of His (and their) death wholly in the light of the other side, and therefore that He made known to them the other side, His (and their) life beyond, wholly in terms of this side, even as spoken in His resurrection from the dead, as the Yes of God to Him (and therefore to them and to all men) concealed first under the No of His (and their) death. As the One who really encountered them in this sense He constituted Himself the basis of their faith and the theme and content of their witness. And in the faith which had this basis they made their

---

[EN431] creation from nothing

witness, as filled out in this way, the witness of His self-attestation as the living One: confident that the power and truth of the same divine verdict in the power of which He encountered them as the living One would prove effective to those to whom they made this witness, and confident that this witness would summon them to faith and awaken faith; confident that the self-attestation of Jesus Christ as the living One would repeat itself in the making of their human witness to it. He Himself as the One raised from the dead is the other side which has invaded this side, and by which life is promised and given as life in and with Him to those who are put to death in and with Him. The possibility of witness to Him as this other side, and the possibility of faith in Him as the One who is this other side, are, as human actions, possibilities within this world and on this side (even though their theme and basis is the other side). As such they depend on the fact that Jesus Christ has attested and still attests Himself as the other side within this world and therefore on this side (and, because on this side, in a real confrontation of all other men). They depend upon the objectivity with which He has done this according to the Easter narratives (taken in their true sense). Because He has done this, it can be proclaimed and believed by men, it can be recognised by men, that with and after His death (and that of all men) there is freedom for human life (participant in His life), and a place for the problems of it (as they are posed and as they will be solved by Him). This is what we gather from our fourth consideration in answer to our question.

[353]

The third consideration, which was also the longest, culminated in the question of the meaning of the interval in the *parousia* of Jesus Christ as it began in the event of Easter and will be completed in His final revelation. We found its meaning in the existence of the community as the reality of the people of God in world-history, the company of those who are not only His but can know and confess themselves as His, and therefore Him as theirs, their Head. Where this community lives by the Holy Spirit, Jesus Christ Himself lives on earth, in the world and in history. It is immediately apparent that here we have the most tangible answer to our question. In the existence of the community in the world we have immediately before our eyes the fact that even after the event of the cross revealed in that of Easter, God still allowed and had time and space for human existence and history and problems. Man can and must come into view in all seriousness as such even *post Christum crucifixum et resuscitatum*[EN432]—not as perfect man as He will be presented in and with the final revelation of Jesus Christ, to live as such eternally with God, having passed through judgment, and not as perverted and sinful and lost man, but as man who in his perversion, sin and lostness has been visited by the reconciliation of the world with God as accomplished in Jesus Christ, and altered at the very root of his being. He is the man who, whether he knows it or not—the community knows it—stands in the light of the resurrection of Jesus Christ. He is

---

[EN432] after Christ crucified and raised to life

the man who, whether he fulfils it or not—the community is what it is by fulfill-ing it—stands under the determination to give the answer of his little human Yes, his modest praise of God and his actions, to the great Yes which God has spoken to him. God is not too great to expect this Yes from man and to accept it. God gives him the opportunity and summons him to utter it. That is the meaning and purpose of the interval between the first *parousia* of Jesus Christ and the second. And in the answer to this particular question we obviously have the direct answer to our main question of the legitimacy and possibility of dealing not only with Jesus Christ Himself but, because with Him, therefore also with us as those who are visited by the reconciliation of the world with God accomplished in His death. In virtue of the resurrection of Jesus Christ, and [354] with the same historical actuality within the world with which this took place, there now exists the community of Jesus Christ in the world, as the first-begotten of all God's creatures, as a lasting and living and concrete indication of the fact that all creation stands in this light, that the condescension of God is so great that He expects praise from all men and every man, that every man finds himself in the circle of which Jesus Christ is the centre. We should have to overlook this special dimension of the condescension of God revealed in the existence of the community if we tried to ignore the fact that our question is in fact answered by the resurrection of Jesus Christ from the dead, that the will of God, as it is in force and revealed in the calling and existence of the commun-ity, has decided that Christ would not be Christ without His own people (in the narrower and wider senses of the term), that there cannot, therefore, be an exclusive but only an inclusive Christology which embraces the existence of men both negatively and positively, that the doctrine of reconciliation cannot stop at that of the person and work of Jesus Christ. So much for the result of our third consideration.

Our second inquiry culminated in the term which we have adopted as a title for the whole of this transitional discussion. The resurrection is marked off from the death of Jesus Christ as a new and specific act of God by the fact that in it there is pronounced the verdict of God the Father on the obedience of the Son: His gracious and almighty approval of the Son's representing of the human race; His acceptance of His suffering and death as it took place for the race; the justification of the will of the Father who sent the Son into the world for this purpose, of the Son who willed to submit to this will, and of the totality of sinful men as brought to an end in the death of this their Representative. We can now say that as this creative and revelatory divine verdict, as this div-inely effective approval, acceptance and justification, the resurrection of Jesus Christ from the dead is the answer to our question concerning the partici-pation of the whole race in the person and work of the one man Jesus Christ as the Son of God, our question concerning the significance of His being and activity as it embraces us, as it embraces the anthropological sphere. In so far as this divine verdict has been passed and is in force in the resurrection of Jesus Christ, Jesus Christ lives and acts and speaks for all ages and in eternity, and in such a way that we are promised a future and hope, a being before God in reality and in truth. In this connexion we remember once more the words of Jn. 14[19]: "I live and ye shall live also." This is the comprehensive form of the divine verdict pronounced in the resurrection of Jesus Christ from the dead. But where in faith in the raised and living Jesus Christ this verdict is heard and accepted and understood as already passed and effective, there is a recognition of the divinely active approval, acceptance and justification, and therefore a recognition of the being which God has promised us in reality and in truth. This verdict is therefore both the ontic and also the noetic—first the ontic and then the noetic—basis of our being—not outside but in Jesus Christ as the elected Head of the whole race—but of our own being and to that extent of our being with Him and side by side with Him. In this verdict God willed to justify Himself and His Son after the death of His Son on the cross and in relation to it. But we all fell victim to death in that death, and therefore in relation to it He has also justified us; He has declared and addressed and accepted us as the brothers of the Son who was justified there, and children of the Father who was justified there. We have, therefore, the right and we are directed to understand the reconciliation which took place in the death of Jesus Christ as signifying for us not only an end but also a beginning, as giving to us something beyond this death. We are summoned by that verdict of God which has been passed and is in force to take seriously ourselves and the problems of our situation as it has been altered by His death. The hearing and receiving and understanding of this verdict, faith in the risen and living Jesus Christ, is the presupposition that we do this, that we make this recognition of our being in Him. Over this presupposition we have no power. Being as it is a matter of the Holy Spirit, of the faith which leads into all the truth in the power and enlightenment of the Holy Spirit, it is only given and will continually be given to us. Without prayer for it this presupposition cannot be had; we cannot possibly count on it or on its consequences; the recognition that we are and have a place in Jesus Christ, and therefore together with and side by side with Him, cannot be anything but imaginary and illusory; thought about our being can only be irrelevant and our speaking about it mere talk. This is something we must continually keep before us in our whole development of the doctrine of reconciliation. But in real prayer for it, the prayer which is confident that it will be heard, this presupposition, the hearing and receiving and understanding of the verdict pronounced by God, is quite possible, for as His verdict it has already been passed and is valid and divinely effective. Calling on the fact that Jesus lives—for this is the real prayer which is confident from the very first that it will be answered—can never be in vain. It lays hold of the promise: Ye shall live, and therefore the answer to the question which here concerns us. So much we learn from our second discussion.

We now go back to the beginning, and recall the result of our first consideration. We started by understanding the resurrection as an act of God. We had to be more precise: in its character as an event which is objective in this world,

[355]

it was exclusively an act of God, without any components of human will and activity. In this it differed from the suffering and death of Jesus Christ. It was a concrete revelation of God, and pure in its concreteness. It was God's self-attestation (the attestation of His glory in the flesh of His Word) without any co-operation on the part of a human witness serving it. As we say, it was the very model of a gracious act of God, the Son of God as such being active only as the recipient, God the Father alone being the One who acts, and God the Holy Spirit alone the One who mediates His action and revelation. This made the resurrection of Jesus Christ from the very first the sure and unequivocally transcendent place, the true other side here on this side, from which we can look back with enlightened and indisputable assurance on the first act of God which took place in His death, and forward to the determination which is there newly given to the being of man. [356]

From the place which we describe in this way we had and have to look forward to the being of humanity as it has come to its end in the death of Jesus Christ, but also to its salvation, with the disclosure of a future and hope, with the promise of life which has there been newly attained for it. The resurrection of Jesus Christ from the dead was the exclusive act of God, a pure divine revelation, a free act of divine grace. It is of this that we speak when we say: "Jesus lives," and when we deduce and continue: "and I with Him." The statement has this deduction and continuation. For Jesus lives as the One who was put to death for me, as the One in whom I am put to death, so that necessarily His life is the promise of my life. But with His life, my life too, the life of man who is not himself Jesus Christ but only His younger brother, is an exclusive act of God, a pure divine revelation, a free act of divine grace. Let us leave it now to emphasise that as such it is "hid with Christ in God" (Col. 3^3) in a way that we cannot comprehend or control. We were recalling the same thing when we understood it as the work of the divine verdict which is valid in Jesus Christ. More important for us is the positive side that as such, as that which is created and revealed in that divine act of sovereignty, our life, the life of man in and with Jesus Christ, is promised from the place whose sureness and unequivocal transcendence gives to the promise a clarity and certainty which are beyond comparison or compromise. It is a matter only of the act of God, the self-revelation of God, the free grace of God. The free act and self-revelation of God cannot be called in question. They are there. And that gives an unsurpassable clarity and an axiomatic certainty. The Yes of God, which cannot be disputed by any conceivable No, has been pronounced and has to be received. It was and is His Yes to the Son whom He elected and loved from all eternity. It was and is the Yes of His faithfulness to Himself. But as such it was and is His Yes to the human people whom from all eternity He has also elected and loved in His Son. He has spoken and speaks and will speak it in His Son; and on earth with the same sovereignty in which He is God in heaven. To that extent it is also spoken to us, without involving or leaving the way open for any possible objec- [357]
tions or doubts or questions. "Peace on earth to men of good-will." In the

Word of God spoken with this sovereignty we are the men of this good-will. We do not simply think or believe that we are. We believe that we are because we are. That is why we can go on to think of the existence of man as determined by the saving event of the death of Jesus Christ.

INDEX OF SCRIPTURE REFERENCES

INDEX OF SUBJECTS

Marxism   51
mercy
  grace and   61–2
  mystery of   230
  salvation and   10
Modalism   192–4
mutuality   21–2
mystery religions   159
mysticism   281, 331
myth   331, 338

natural theology   41
New Testament
  covenant of   29
  descriptions of human beings in   203
  dogmatics and standpoints of   266
  exegesis and standpoints of   266
  as witness to Jesus Christ   155–6, 287
Noachic covenant   23–4, 30–1, 60

obedience   157, 170, 187, 189, 194, 196, 198,
  202, 203, 205, 207, 250, 265, 288, 309
offering   271
Old Testament, covenant in   19–21, 25,
  28–31

pardon   215, 217
passion of Jesus Christ
  action of   237–8
  as act of God   238
  atonement in   244
  faith and   240–1
  human mediation of   243
  Jesus Christ as Priest and   270
  judgement of God and   247
  location in space and time of   238
  mystery of   239
  offering in   238
  proclamation and   244
  sin and   239
  Word of God and   238
peace with God   79
penitence   265
persecution   236–7
physical divine Sonship   200
Pietism   145
Pietists   51
predestination   60
Priest
  Jesus Christ as   268–70
  as mediator   268

problem of faith and history   281
problem of time   279
proclamation   244
promise of God   107–8, 110
psychologism   54
punishment   246

reconciliation
  acting subject of   191
  act of God and   80, 124
  anthropological sphere and   287
  as beginning   106
  christological basis of   134
  covenant fulfilled in   1, 19, 64, 67, 86,
    118
  defining   19, 72
  doctrine of   76
  faith and   74
  forms of   122, 124–49
  God's intervention and   71–2, 124,
    243–4
  Hegelian dialectic and   77
  Holy Spirit and   144
  humiliation and   188
  inward divine relationship in   197
  Jesus Christ and   70–1, 88–9, 112, 132,
    217, 290, 300, 313
  Jesus Christ mediating   118–24
  justification and   140–1
  ministry of   217
  permanent v. continual   278
  resurrection and   305
  sin and   137, 140–2, 342
  word of   75
redemption   217, 220–1
redemption-history school   51
redemptive grace   7
redemptive will   9–11, 25
Reformation   104, 142
Reformed Church   50, 51, 59
Reformed Evangelical Church   51
Reformed theology   55, 57, 128, 174
  justification in   105–6
  sanctification in   105–6
religious valuation   154
resurrection   292–350
  as act of God   332, 347–9
  anthropological sphere and   327–8
  criticism of narratives of   334–5
  death of Jesus Christ and   303–4, 336–7
  exegesis of   330–4

INDEX OF NAMES